Criminal Litigation Handbook

putyourknowledgeintopractice

with vocational law titles from Oxford University Press

LPC HANDBOOKS

➤ **CIVIL LITIGATION HANDBOOK**
Cunningham-Hill and Elder

➤ **CRIMINAL LITIGATION HANDBOOK**
Hannibal and Mountford

➤ **PROPERTY LAW HANDBOOK**
Abbey and Richards

➤ **FAMILY LAW HANDBOOK**
Sendall

LPC MANUALS

➤ **BUSINESS LAW**
Slorach and Ellis

➤ **EMPLOYMENT LAW**
Holland and Burnett

➤ **FOUNDATIONS FOR THE LPC**
Miles et al

➤ **LAWYERS' SKILLS**
Webb et al

A PRACTICAL APPROACH

➤ **A PRACTICAL APPROACH TO CIVIL PROCEDURE**
Sime

➤ **A PRACTICAL APPROACH TO CONVEYANCING**
Abbey and Richards

➤ **A PRACTICAL APPROACH TO ADR**
Blake et al

➤ **WRITING AND DRAFTING IN LEGAL PRACTICE**
Rylance

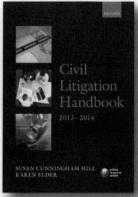
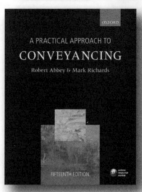

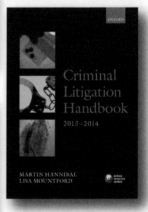

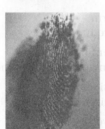

Criminal
Litigation
Handbook

MARTIN HANNIBAL

LISA MOUNTFORD

OXFORD
UNIVERSITY PRESS

OXFORD
UNIVERSITY PRESS

Great Clarendon Street, Oxford, OX2 6DP,
United Kingdom

Oxford University Press is a department of the University of Oxford.
It furthers the University's objective of excellence in research, scholarship,
and education by publishing worldwide. Oxford is a registered trade mark of
Oxford University Press in the UK and in certain other countries

Sixth edition copyright 2010
Seventh edition copyright 2011
Eighth edition copyright 2012

Impression: 1

Published in the United States of America by Oxford University Press
198 Madison Avenue, New York, NY 10016, United States of America

British Library Cataloguing in Publication Data

Data available

ISBN 978-0-19-967648-4

Printed in Great Britain by
Ashford Colour Press Ltd, Gosport, Hampshire

CONTENTS

ONLINE RESOURCE CENTRE CONTENTS

STUDENT RESOURCES

◔ Bad character case compendium

An account of a number of cases on bad character.

◔ Case study documentation

Documentation in support of three of the fictional court scenario video case studies:

> Case study 1: *Regina v Lenny Wise*
> Case study 2: *Regina v William Hardy*
> Case study 3: *Regina v Roger Martin*

◔ Police station checklist

To accompany Web Chapter 1 – Advising at the Police Station.

◔ Web Chapter 1: Advising at the Police Station—Practical steps

Offers practical guidance on the legal representative called upon to advise a suspect at the police station.

◔ Web Chapter 2: White Collar Crime—Regulatory offences

An additional chapter covering regulatory crime.

◔ Web Chapter 3: Sentencing in Road Traffic Cases

Leading on from the explanations of general sentencing practice in Chapters 21 and 22, this chapter examines the special sentencing considerations that apply to road traffic cases.

◔ Criminal litigation express train timeline

An interactive timeline to help students put criminal litigation in context.

◔ Answers to self-test questions

Freely accessible and printable answers to the self-test questions included in the book.

◔ Updates

Updates to cases and legislation since book publication.

◔ Web links

Direct links to some useful websites relating to criminal litigation.

LECTURER RESOURCES

◔ Video case studies:

> Case study 1: *Regina v Lenny Wise*
> Case study 2: *Regina v William Hardy*
> Case study 3: *Regina v Roger Martin*
> Case study 4: *Peter West role play*
> Case study 5: *Regina v Nicholas Jones*

FOREWORD TO THE FIRST EDITION

Few criminal firms can afford the luxury of taking a law graduate through a training contract in the way in which it was intended to be structured. Instead, the modern graduate is expected to be productive from day one and have a detailed understanding of their employer's work. For the graduate this did in the past present a dilemma in that it was outside the remit of traditional academic texts to fill this knowledge gap, and the practitioner texts assumed a higher level of knowledge than could be expected of the graduate. To this day practitioner texts do little to explain how professional work is *actually* carried out. This book fills that gap, and does so with distinction. Any graduate attending for interview and who is questioned on any aspect of criminal litigation will only have himself to blame if he does not answer with distinction, as it will simply mean that he has not studied the *Criminal Litigation Handbook*.

For the last few years conversation with aspiring legal aid lawyers has had a rather negative tone, with many practitioners actively urging graduates to choose another discipline that is better paid or more highly regarded. That type of guidance ought to be deprecated. Sure, the rewards are not great in comparison with other areas of law, but so what? If international shipping law excites you then go and do it, and if you ever get out of the office then enjoy spending the significant rewards. If, however, you want to be touched by every aspect of human behaviour, see glimpses of a world where there are the mad, bad, sad and downright silly, then criminal law is for you. It is hard work and it is as intellectually demanding as any other area of law, yet you will wake up every morning never quite knowing what you will experience next. It is more likely to be a shoplifting case than a murder, but you just never know! It can be a rollercoaster of emotion, but I can guarantee that it will never be dull.

This book covers every aspect of criminal litigation from investigation right through to appeal covering all important aspects of funding, practice, evidence and procedure. The text is littered with practical examples that will assist in understanding the principles being explained—in many ways this is one of the most unique features of the book, and it works very well indeed. The added bonus of an online resource further illustrates the sheer value for money offered—once word gets out I expect many lawyers will opt for this book in place of the more traditional offerings.

There has been a slight lull in legislation, but we can say with some degree of certainty that this will soon pass and the authors will need to get busy on the next edition; that day may be sooner than they perhaps would wish for given the mammoth task that they have set for themselves in producing such a comprehensive handbook.

Andrew Keogh

PREFACE

Our aim when we first conceived the *Criminal Litigation Handbook* was to deliver a concise yet comprehensive text on all areas of criminal practice whilst at the same time providing a highly practical, innovative and contextual learning resource for students studying the compulsory Criminal Litigation element on the Legal Practice Course and/or an elective in Advanced Criminal Litigation. The text is now in its ninth edition *and has proven to be* an ideal source of reference for trainee and newly qualified solicitors, BPTC students, CPS prosecutors, associate prosecutors and caseworkers, legal executives, paralegals and for other criminal justice professionals.

The extremely positive feedback we have received from students, lecturers and practitioners about the earlier editions of the *Handbook* have been very encouraging. We always welcome constructive comments from our readers about how the text or the extensive learning resources can be improved. Revisions are made with each published edition of the *Handbook* based on our readers' feedback. Your comments can be sent to us directly or through OUP.

An important part of the innovative approach the *Handbook* adopts as a learning resource is the extensive Online Resource Centre which includes specialist chapters on the practical aspects of advising a client at the police station and regulatory crime and fraud. A unique aspect of the Online Resource Centre is the video clips of selected parts of the case studies that form the basis of ongoing exercises throughout the text. The video clips include a bad character application and sentencing hearing in the Crown Court, the practice of police station representation, a contested bail hearing and a sentencing hearing in a road traffic case. We hope that you find all the video clips a useful tool in adding to your knowledge and understanding of criminal litigation.

The *Handbook* is divided into six sections:

Part I is an introduction to criminal litigation.

Part II considers the process of investigation up to the decision to charge, including relevant rules of criminal evidence.

Part III considers post-charge procedures up to and including trial.

Part IV considers the remaining rules of criminal evidence.

Part V considers the post-conviction matters of sentencing and appeals against conviction and/or sentence.

Part VI considers youth justice issues.

The pace of legislative change affecting the criminal justice system has been relentless in recent years. For practitioners, students and lecturers keeping up to date and in some instances ahead of the changes has been difficult! The new developments we cover in this edition include the reforms to criminal legal aid, bail, sentencing, and pre-court orders in youth justice cases introduced by the Legal Aid, Sentencing and Punishment of Offenders Act 2012. We also consider further the effect of the abolition of committal proceedings for either way offences to be tried on indictment and the full national implementation of the mode of trial/allocation procedure which requires those either way offences which are to be tried on indictment to be sent immediately to the Crown Court under s. 51 Crime and Disorder Act 1998 from the mode of trial/allocation hearing.

Please be aware that as the rules of criminal litigation and evidence are always at the forefront of political controversy, public concern and legislative reform, any significant developments during the currency of this edition of the *Handbook* will be explained in the update section of the Online Resource Centre.

The writing of the *Handbook* and the production of the video case studies and Online Resource Centre could not have been achieved without the co-operation and assistance of many friends and colleagues.

In relation to the video case studies of Lenny Wise/William Hardy and Roger Martin we say a special thank you to the following:

His Honour Paul Glenn
Milena Srdanovic (CPS lawyer)
Shaun Spencer (CPS lawyer)
Hayley Keegan (Defence lawyer)
Simon Leech (Defence lawyer)
Celia Laing (Defence lawyer)
Brian Baig (Staffordshire LPC student 2009–2010)
Francis Chattie (Staffordshire LPC student 2009–2010)
Alison Bailey (Legal adviser)
Sarah Murphy (Legal adviser)
Vicky Priestly (Legal adviser)
John Peel (CPS Associate prosecutor)
Jason Jamil (Staffordshire LPC student 2003–4)
Carol Hawthorne (Magistrate)
Dr Mike Carter (Magistrate)
Rev Christopher Dalton (Magistrate)
Prakash Samani (Magistrate)

For their contribution to the production of the Peter West Police Station Scenario, we would thank the following:

DC Keith Pagett (Staffordshire Police)
DS Angus Parker (Staffordshire Police)
Sgt Ian Cantrill (Staffordshire Police)
Lisa O'Shea (Accredited Police Station Representative with the Public Defender Service)
Peter Goold (Staffordshire LPC student 2004–5) who gave an outstanding and entirely convincing performance as Peter West, the suspect!
Each of these individuals very kindly gave up their time and volunteered their services for free thereby allowing us to bring our case studies to life.

Special thanks go to the camera crews involved in the filming of our various videos:

Ray Johnson (Professor of Film Heritage and Documentary, Staffordshire University)
Darren Teale (Final year media student 2004)
Richard Edwards (Final year media student 2004)
Gary Robinson (Final year media student 2004)
Peter Robinson (formerly Senior Technician Staffordshire Law School)

We are indebted to Professor Ray Johnson for his tremendous help in directing the early films and undertaking the voice-over analysis. Special thanks also go to Darren Teale who undertook the filming and editing of *R v Lenny Wise* and *R v Roger Martin*. We are grateful to our dear friend and former colleague Peter Robinson (Staffordshire Law School's Senior IT Technician) for helping us to film our Police Station Scenario and for his very patient editing of the material. Peter has also directed and edited the revised William Hardy scenario and the Nick Jones bad character application.

Thanks are also due to the Chief Constable's Office of Staffordshire Police for allowing us to take over Uttoxeter Police Station in rural Staffordshire and for allowing us to use real police offices!

We would like to thank Dr N. J. F. Smalldridge BA (Oxon), BM, MRC Psych for the time and effort he undertook in devising and writing a psychiatric report on behalf of our fictional defendant Lenny Wise.

We would like to single out Mike Benson for his immensely valuable comments and observations and Sarah Murphy for her assistance. Thanks also to Robin Lichfield, partner and defence solicitor with Lichfield Reynolds Solicitors, North Staffordshire and Andrew Keogh, partner at Keogh Solicitors, Wigan and creator of the superb CrimeLine (www.crime-line.info/) and Claire Pickard, Legal Development Manager with the CPS, for answering all our questions!

We thank the entire team at OUP past and present and specifically for this edition our assistant commissioning editor Claire Mullen. Special thanks must also go to Sarah Brett, Julia Whippy and their predecessor Kate Hilton (OUP's IT specialists) for their fantastic work in building and maintaining the Online Resource Centre. Most of all we thank our families (Merryn, Matt, Nick and Charlie Hannibal, Geoff and Joyce Hannibal, and Nick and Alexandra Mason) for their enduring patience!

This edition is dedicated to all those extremely committed and hard-working criminal defence practitioners who continue to uphold access to justice in the face of adversity. Acknowledgement is also due to our enthusiastic and hardworking students and colleagues on the Staffordshire Law School Legal Practice Course.

Any errors or omissions are entirely ours.

The law is stated as at 1 May 2013.

Lisa Mountford
Martin Hannibal
Staffordshire Law School

ACKNOWLEDGEMENTS

In Chapter 1, extracts from the SRA Handbook are © The Law Society and reproduced with permission.

The Crown Prosecution Service Press Releases and the Crown Prosecution Service logo are reproduced with the kind permission of the Crown Prosecution Service.

Criminal Procedure Rules forms are Crown Copyright and are reproduced by kind permission of the Ministry of Justice and the National Archives under the Open Government Licence (http://www.nationalarchives.gov.uk/doc/open-government-licence/).

The sentencing guidelines are Crown Copyright and are reproduced by kind permission of the Sentencing Council for England and Wales under the Open Government Licence. The guidelines are available online at http://sentencingcouncil.judiciary.gov.uk/guidelines/guidelines-to-download.htm.

Forms CDS14 and CDS1 are copyright of the Legal Services Commission and are reproduced by kind permission of the Legal Services Commission. Please note that the forms are current as at May 2012 but may be updated from time to time. The Legal Service Commission's website at www.legalservices.gov.uk holds the most up-to-date versions of all forms.

GUIDED TOUR OF THE BOOK

The Criminal Litigation Handbook by Hannibal and Mountford is a pedagogically rich text which has been designed to facilitate your learning and understanding of criminal litigation. This 'Guided Tour of the Book' will explain how to make the most of the text by illustrating each of the features used by the authors to explain the practical aspects of the criminal litigation process.

WITHIN EACH CHAPTER

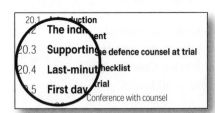

CHAPTER CONTENTS

A detailed contents list at the start of each chapter enables you to anticipate what will be covered and identify what the main topics of the chapter will be. Use this feature to also gain an understanding of how the topics fit together in the wider subject area.

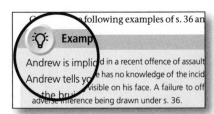

EXAMPLES

Look for the example icon to find relevant, practical examples of how the law has been or could be applied in common situations. These examples bring the subject to life and allow you to examine how principles, rules and statutes work in practice.

'LOOKING AHEAD' BOXES

These boxes are used to highlight areas where the law may change. Potential reforms are considered, ensuring that once you go into practice, you're already aware of the changes on the horizon.

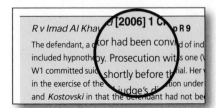

CASE OUTLINES

These case outlines give you an awareness of relevant case law in the subject area. Use these explanations to point you towards the most relevant case reports in your law library or to better inform your knowledge of how the law has been applied in court.

CASE STUDIES

Throughout the book, the authors refer to fictional case studies, which provide a practical focus on the law and procedures described in the text. The documentation for these case studies appears on the Online Resource Centre. See the 'Guided tour of the Online Resource Centre' at p. xx for more information.

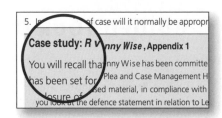

ONLINE RESOURCE CENTRE ICON

Wherever this icon appears in the margin, more information is available on the Online Resource Centre which accompanies this text. This may be video footage, case study documentation or links to other useful websites or guidance. See the 'Guided tour of the Online Resource Centre' at p. xx for more information.

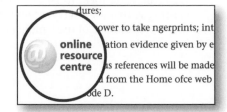

END OF CHAPTER FEATURES

KEY POINTS SUMMARY

The key points covered are summarised in a user-friendly list at the end of each chapter. Look to these summaries to help you consolidate your learning or to check your knowledge at revision time.

SELF-TEST QUESTIONS

These questions allow you to test yourself on particular areas of the law in preparation for your exams or to assess your learning throughout the duration of the course. Use these questions to highlight areas where you might need to improve your understanding by re-reading the text or asking your lecturer. You will find the answers provided as a printable document on the Online Resource Centre.

FIGURES

Flowcharts, shaded boxes or example forms provide a visual representation of what has been described within the chapter.

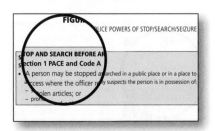

GUIDED TOUR OF THE ONLINE RESOURCE CENTRE

Online Resource Centres are developed to provide students and lecturers with ready-to-use teaching and learning resources. They are free of charge, designed to complement the text and offer additional materials which are well suited to electronic delivery.

All these resources can be downloaded and are fully customisable allowing them to be incorporated into your institution's existing virtual learning environment. Turn to page xii for a full list of the contents of the Online Resource Centre to accompany this book.

STUDENT RESOURCES

All the resources in this area of the site are freely accessible to all, with no password required. Simply visit the site at: http://www.oxfordtextbooks.co.uk/orc/crimhandbook13_14/.

UPDATES

Updates are posted on the website when the law changes or when an important case passes through the courts, allowing you to keep fully informed of developments. The updates are freely accessible to all and offer an easy way to keep abreast of changes in this rapidly changing subject area.

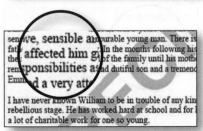

CASE STUDY DOCUMENTATION

The fictional case studies in the book are accompanied by all of the documentation you would expect to see in reality. This allows you to see what a solicitor's file might typically contain and prepares you for what to expect when you go into practice.

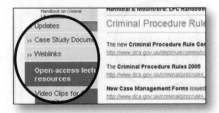

LINKS TO LEGISLATION, RULES, AND OTHER DOCUMENTATION

This part of the website provides links to useful information which is freely accessible elsewhere on the internet. Use this resource to find relevant guidelines, statutes, codes of practice, and other documentation quickly and easily.

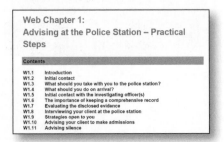

WEB CHAPTER 1: ADVISING AT THE POLICE STATION – PRACTICAL STEPS

For students who are interested in pursuing police station accreditation as a qualification, we have included an additional online chapter which explores the practice and dynamics of police station practice. To reflect the increasing importance of bad character evidence, we include a comprehensive case law compendium on bad character.

WEB CHAPTER 2: WHITE COLLAR CRIME – REGULATORY OFFENCES

For students whose course has a City focus, corporate crime will be an important topic. An online chapter on regulatory crime written by two leading barristers in this area, Nicholas Yeo and Sarah Le Fevre, enables you to get to grips with an aspect of criminal law which is key for City lawyers.

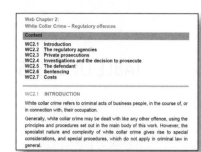

WEB CHAPTER 3: SENTENCING IN ROAD TRAFFIC CASES

For students with an interest in the particular sentencing considerations that apply to road traffic cases, this specialised chapter further develops the general sentencing practices explored in Chapters 21 and 22, in consideration of an area that occupies a considerable amount of time in magistrates' courts.

INTERACTIVE CRIMINAL LITIGATION TRAIN

You will find an interactive timeline which will help you to see how the whole criminal litigation process fits together and the issues that you need to keep in mind at particular points. The timeline distinguishes between the three classifications of offences (summary-only, either-way and indictable-only).

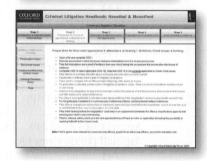

ANSWERS TO SELF-TEST QUESTIONS

Chapter-by-chapter answers to the self-test questions found in the book are provided online as a downloadable and printable pdf.

LECTURER RESOURCES

These resources are available solely to lecturers who are adopting the text. To obtain a username and password, complete the registration form at: http://www.oxfordtextbooks.co.uk/orc/crimhandbook13_14/. All of the resources on the site can be downloaded into your institution's virtual learning environment (VLE).

VIDEO CLIPS

High resolution video footage showing fictional criminal proceedings allows you to emphasise the practical application of what you describe in your teaching. Included on the site is video footage of:

*   the case studies featured in the book;
*   our 'free-standing' police station video scenario; and
*   our 'free-standing' bad character applications.

(Selected, low resolution video clips of the *R v Lenny* Wise case study are available to lecturers without a password.)

LINKS TO GUIDELINES AND CODES OF PRACTICE

Use this resource to easily find documents important for criminal litigators. Collected together in one place, this resource provides you with all the important documents to which you may want to refer your students.

TABLE OF CASES

TABLE OF STATUTES

The European Convention on Human Rights is tabled under Schedule 1 of the Human Rights Act

TABLE OF STATUTORY INSTRUMENTS

TABLE OF CODES OF PRACTICE AND PROFESSIONAL CONDUCT RULES

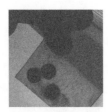

Part I

INTRODUCTION TO CRIMINAL LITIGATION

Part I equips the reader with important background information that will inform the substantive areas covered in later chapters.

Chapter 1 explains the aims of the *Criminal Litigation Handbook* and its unique features. It introduces the key personnel and organisations in the criminal justice system and explains the importance of classifying criminal offences. It also addresses human rights and the rules of professional conduct in criminal cases.

Chapter 2 provides an introduction to criminal evidence and advocacy.

INTRODUCTION

1.1 INTRODUCTION

CPS Press release 16 February 2009

Lorry driver guilty of causing deaths of family of six

A lorry driver's inattention caused an horrific accident which wiped out an entire family including four children, said CPS Cheshire Chief Crown Prosecutor Ian Rushton.

A jury at Chester Crown Court found Paulo Da Silva guilty of six counts of causing death by careless driving.

Mr Rushton said: 'This is a tragic case where Michelle and David Statham died in a terrible car accident with their four children, Reece, Jay, Mason and Ellouise.

The prosecution had to prove that not only did Mr Da Silva's driving fall below the required standard, but as a direct result he killed the whole family in their car on the M6.'

Evidence that Cheshire Police gathered showed that the Stathams' car was crushed between a large lorry, which had been queuing in a long tailback due to an earlier accident, and Paulo Da Silva's lorry.

The jury heard both the prosecution and defence case and decided that Paulo Da Silva's driving was careless. They therefore acquitted him of six counts of causing death by dangerous driving, which is the more serious offence.

Mr Rushton said: 'Da Silva admitted in court that he had seen the electronic signs warning that the M6 was closed ahead and that queues were likely. He said that he reduced his speed but could not explain how the collision happened.

The prosecution said that it was clear that for a period of approximately one minute, Paulo Da Silva was not paying proper attention to the road and fatally hit the Stathams' van with his 40-tonne lorry.

We would like to thank the work of Cheshire Police who carried out a thorough investigation and all the witnesses who gave evidence in that case. Our thoughts are with the family and friends of Mrs and Mr Statham and their children.'

This tragic case provides a dramatic snapshot of the work of those involved in the criminal justice system. The case took only four months to come to trial, but required many hours of investigation by the police as well as painstaking file preparation and evaluation of the evidence by the Crown Prosecution Service (CPS). Mr Da Silva's lawyers also spent many hours preparing his case for trial. As the trial date approached, a number of ancillary criminal justice organisations became involved, including victim support, witness care and Her Majesty's Court Service. At the defendant's trial, the prosecution and defence advocates presented their parties' interpretation of the law to the facts of the case to the judge and jury. The judge summed the case up to the jury and Mr Da Silva's guilt or innocence was decided by the jury, which was made up of ordinary members of the public from wide and diverse backgrounds. At the conclusion of the case Mr Da Silva faced years of imprisonment, away from family and friends. For the foreseeable future his life is in tatters. The loss is even greater for the victims' family and friends, who are deprived forever of their loved ones and left with only memories.

For those studying to be criminal lawyers and for those already in practice, the purpose of the *Handbook* is to explain the legal, procedural and evidential rules governing how cases like Mr Da Silva's and thousands of others each year are dealt with by the criminal justice system.

The *Handbook* covers all the key aspects of the criminal litigation process. Whether you are studying criminal litigation as part of your LPC or BPTC or already work as a CPS lawyer, private practice solicitor, legal executive or paralegal, or have another professional involvement in the criminal justice system, we hope that you find the book an invaluable source of reference.

In this introductory chapter, we aim to:

• explain the philosophy of the *Handbook* and its unique features;

• introduce the key personnel and organisations within the criminal justice system;

- introduce the Criminal Procedure Rules;
- explain the classification of offences according to their trial venue;
- provide a summary of the jurisdiction of the criminal courts;
- stress the importance of the pervasive issue of human rights; and
- highlight professional conduct considerations in the context of criminal litigation.

1.2 PHILOSOPHY OF THE *CRIMINAL LITIGATION HANDBOOK*

The *Criminal Litigation Handbook* provides an innovative approach to the study of criminal litigation and evidence and gives students and practitioners a highly practical and comprehensive explanation of the key substantive, procedural and evidential issues that are encountered by both prosecution and defence lawyers in a criminal case. For those who wish to further their knowledge and understanding, there are also extensive learning resources that illustrate, through practice-based examples, diagrams, self-test exercises and case studies, the operation of the law in a very practical context.

1.2.1 TAKING AN INTEGRATED AND PRACTICAL APPROACH

Working as a criminal lawyer requires the practitioner to take an integrated and practical approach to their work. This approach is adopted in the *Handbook*. The integrated approach is reflected in our belief that students and practitioners should be aware that the rules of criminal procedure, criminal evidence, professional conduct and legal skills are not discrete elements, but are part of the integrated picture that is involved in representing a client in a criminal case.

The treatment of the rules of criminal evidence highlights this integrated approach. Both prosecutors and defence lawyers must understand that key evidential issues are relevant at all stages of a case including from when the CPS lawyer advises the police about the appropriate charge to the defence lawyer's earliest representation of a client at the police station or during the first interview in the office. Chapter 2 entitled: 'An Introduction to the Law of Criminal Evidence and Advocacy' provides an overview of criminal evidence and is designed to encourage you to think about evidence at the very outset, before aspects of criminal procedure and the substantive rules of evidence are covered in more detail later in the *Handbook*.

The practical approach is achieved in different ways. We have attempted to explain the law and procedure in an accessible and reader-friendly style. The substantive content of each chapter is supplemented by practical examples and diagrams as well as self-test questions and answers. The *Handbook* integrates three case studies throughout the book which are an essential part of our practical approach. The integrated case studies are:

Case study 1:   *R v Lenny Wise*

Case study 2:   *R v Roger Martin*

Case study 3:   *R v William Hardy*

A selection of documentation supporting case study 1 is included in Appendix 1. The complete documentation to *R v Lenny Wise* and the other two case studies can be found in the case study section of the Online Resource Centre. The case studies form the basis of ongoing exercises throughout the *Handbook* which are designed to give you the opportunity to apply your knowledge of criminal procedure and evidence in the context of a 'real' case. Those using the *Handbook* for study should consider some of the documentation in support of the three integrated case studies at the conclusion of this introductory chapter. Keep the case studies in mind as you work through each stage of the criminal litigation process. Treat these fictional characters as your clients!

online
resource
centre

Key areas of practice and procedure in all our case studies have been filmed. The 'cases' were heard before a Bench of serving lay magistrates (and in the matter of *R v William Hardy* before a Crown Court judge). All the participants in the video clips gave up their valuable time to assist us in making the films. The clips (all of which are held on the Online Resource Centre) are learning aids that illustrate, in a practical way, aspects of criminal practice. The videos are not necessarily a depiction of how cases always proceed and they should not be regarded as definitive examples of how advocacy is conducted before a criminal court. Commentary is included on the clips. Transcripts of the principal submissions made by the advocates are included in the case study documentation.

1.2.2   DO I NEED TO READ ALL THE CHAPTERS?

LPC criminal litigation courses vary in length and substantive content. Whether you are a student embarking upon the vocational stage of your legal career or you work in criminal practice, the *Handbook* aims to provide a practical and comprehensive explanation of the key principles of criminal procedure and evidence. In addition, the *Handbook* includes several supplementary online chapters which, if you are an LPC student, you are more likely to need in an advanced criminal litigation elective. It may therefore be unnecessary for you to read every chapter. Your course tutor will tell you which learning outcomes you need to achieve for this area of legal practice and so concentrate on those chapters and online materials that are relevant to your specific needs.

1.3   **ONLINE RESOURCE CENTRE**

Our Online Resource Centre can be accessed at http://www.oxfordtextbooks.co.uk/orc/ crimhandbook13_14.

Features included on the website are fully explained in the 'Guided tour of the Online Resource Centre' at page xx but it is helpful to introduce the resource here also. The website is divided into useful sections to help the individual reader and includes the following resources:

Section 1: Password protected lecturer resources: High-quality video clips bring to life the key procedural stages of the *Handbook's* case studies and are formatted for download through broadband, suitable for viewing on a computer or intranet. Alternatively this resource is available as a higher resolution file on CD in order to project the clips on to a large screen in lectures. The clips include accompanying selective transcripts broadly based on the principal submissions made by the advocates. For those using the *Handbook* as a core text on the LPC or BPTC there are also two further role-play scenarios available in the lecturer resource section.

Case study 4:   *Peter West: Police Station Scenario.*

Case study 5:   *R v Nicholas Jones: Bad character applications before a Crown Court judge.*

Case study 4 was filmed at an operational, rural police station.

Full instructions on the use that you might make of these two learning resources are included.

Section 2: Open access lecturer resources: The video clips of the case scenarios are available for online browsing intended for lecturers to review the material available.

Section 3: Student and practitioner resources: These are freely available resources and include answers to the self-test questions which can be found at the conclusion of most of the chapters; updates to cover recent developments in criminal litigation and criminal evidence; complete documentation supporting case studies 1, 2 and 3; and a comprehensive web-links section which will take you directly to resources such as the PACE Codes of Practice and the Magistrates' Court Sentencing Guidelines. It also includes an interactive timeline which will help you to see how the whole criminal litigation process fits together and the issues that you need to keep in mind at particular points. The timeline distinguishes between the three classifications of offences of summary-only, either-way and indictable-only.

Wherever you see this symbol there is a link to our Online Resource Centre. In order to derive maximum benefit from the *Handbook* you should make full use of the learning and information resources on our Online Resource Centre.

1.4 LOOKING AHEAD—REFORM

These are challenging times for criminal lawyers. In recent years there has been a raft of new legislation, including most notably the Criminal Justice Act 2003, which have reformed many of the well-established rules of criminal procedure and evidence. At the time of writing, the Legal Aid, Sentencing and Punishment of Offenders Act 2012 has received Royal Assent making reforms to legal aid, sentencing, and bail. It is also expected that the long-awaited abolition of committal proceedings and revisions to the mode of trial enquiry in relation to either-way offences will be fully implemented during 2013. The update section of our Online Resource Centre will highlight any significant changes during 2013–14 and also consider the way in which the changes are being applied in practice. Any reforms likely to be brought into force in the next 12 months are highlighted in the text by the heading 'Looking Ahead'.

Students should be aware of these legislative changes, not only for learning and assessment purposes, but also because questions about recent legal developments are commonly asked at job interviews.

1.5 RESEARCH SOURCES

Legal research is a vital part of the work of a student and practitioner. While our Online Resource Centre provides invaluable links to related websites from which you can access further useful information, we include here a summary of useful practitioner texts and practitioner journals.

1.5.1 PRACTITIONER WORKS

Blackstone's Criminal Practice
Also published by Oxford University Press, *Blackstone's Criminal Practice* is a leading work of reference for criminal practitioners. Annually updated and written in an accessible and user-friendly way, *Blackstone's* provides a detailed explanation of the main substantive criminal offences, the key stages of criminal procedure and the rules of criminal evidence. *Blackstone's* is also available on CD-ROM.

Archbold Criminal Pleading and Practice
This well-established authoritative practitioner text is specifically directed to the practice and procedure of trials on indictment. *Archbold* now publishes a companion volume for proceedings in the magistrates' court.

Stone's Justices Manual
This is the most authoritative text for proceedings in the magistrates' court. *Stone's* is an indispensable source of reference for all criminal practitioners.

1.5.2 TEXTS

Defending Suspects at the Police Station **(Ed Cape; published by the Legal Action Group)**
This book offers a clear explanation covering all aspects of representing a client at the police station, including a detailed exposition of police powers and invaluable advice about the strategies to be adopted by the legal adviser.

Active Defence **(Ede and Shepherd; Law Society Publications)**
This is an excellent, informative guide to representing a client at the police station.

The Golden Rules of Advocacy **(Keith Evans; Oxford University Press)**
An informative, short and entertaining book on developing or refining your advocacy skills.

Disclosure in Criminal Proceedings **(David Corker and Stephen Parkinson; Oxford University Press)**
This very practical book comprehensively explains all aspects of disclosure, from investigation, through to trial and beyond.

1.5.3 JOURNALS

Journal articles can also provide information on current issues and recent developments in criminal procedure and evidence. The journals that might be of interest include the *Criminal Law Review*, *Criminal Law and Justice Weekly*, and the *Legal Action Group Magazine*.

1.5.4 ELECTRONIC RESEARCH SOURCES

Electronic research sources from the key criminal justice organisations and an extensive set of web links can be accessed via the web-links section from our Online Resource Centre.

1.6 CLASSIFYING CRIMINAL OFFENCES

Whilst criminal offences can be classified in several ways, the most significant classification for criminal litigators determines whether the case will ultimately be dealt with in the magistrates' court or the Crown Court. An offence will either be:

- summary-only;
- triable either way; or
- indictable-only.

Always check the classification of an offence if you are not sure, whether in an assessment or in practice. The classification of all criminal offences can be researched in a practitioner work, such as *Blackstone's Criminal Practice*. The correct identification of the classification of an offence helps you accurately to explain the procedural course that a case will follow.

1.6.1 SUMMARY-ONLY OFFENCES

The least serious offences are known as summary-only offences and are dealt with summarily in the magistrates' court, whether or not the defendant pleads guilty or not guilty. Common assault (s. 39 Criminal Justice Act 1988) is a summary-only offence, as are a number of less serious motoring offences.

1.6.2 OFFENCES TRIABLE EITHER WAY

Either-way offences are middle-ranking offences in terms of seriousness and can be tried either summarily before a magistrates' court or on indictment before a judge and jury in the Crown Court. Theft (s. 1 Theft Act 1968) is an either-way offence. It is the defendant's indication of plea which determines where an either-way offence will be heard. If a defendant indicates a guilty plea, the case will remain in the magistrates' court and the court will proceed to sentence. The magistrates' court has the power to commit the defendant to be sentenced before the Crown Court upon conviction for an either-way offence where it considers its limited powers of sentence are insufficient.

If a defendant indicates a not guilty plea to an either-way offence, the magistrates' court will conduct a mode of trial enquiry or allocation hearing to decide whether to keep jurisdiction and try the case summarily or to decline jurisdiction and send the case to the Crown Court to be tried on indictment. If the magistrates' court declines jurisdiction, the accused has no choice and the case will be committed to the Crown Court through a committal hearing conducted before the magistrates' court. (Please note that committal hearings are to be phased out during the currency of this edition of the *Handbook*. Either-way offences that are destined for the Crown Court will, in the near future, be sent to the Crown Court under s. 51 Crime and Disorder Act 1998 following the mode of trial/allocation enquiry.) If the magistrates' court accepts jurisdiction to try the either-way offence summarily, the accused has a choice: consent to summary trial, or elect trial by jury on indictment before the Crown Court.

1.6.3 INDICTABLE-ONLY OFFENCES

The most serious crimes are known as indictable-only offences, which will be tried at the Crown Court before a judge and jury. The common law offence of murder and the statutory offence of robbery (s. 8 Theft Act 1968) are indictable-only offences. Whilst the defendant's case will be heard at the Crown Court, the prosecution of an indictable-only offence will commence in the magistrates' court. Following the defendant's initial appearance before a magistrates' court, the case is immediately sent to the Crown Court for trial under s. 51 Crime and Disorder Act 1998.

Where a defendant is charged with more than one offence with different trial venue classifications, the general rule is that the most serious offence will dictate the procedural course of the cases.

Figures 1.1, 1.2 and 1.3 at the end of this chapter illustrate the stages of a summary-only, either-way and indictable-only offence. Figure 1.4 provides an overview of the criminal litigation process.

1.7 PERSONNEL AND ORGANISATIONS WITHIN THE CRIMINAL JUSTICE SYSTEM

1.7.1 INVESTIGATING AND PROSECUTING ORGANISATIONS

The responsibility for investigating and prosecuting a criminal offence is shared between several organisations.

The investigation of most criminal offences is undertaken by the police. At the completion of the investigation, the matter is passed to the CPS which decides whether there is sufficient evidence to charge the suspect. The CPS is divided into 42 areas, which are aligned to the number of police forces in England and Wales.

The conduct of most day-to-day prosecutions in the magistrates' court or the Crown Court will be dealt with either by a Senior Crown Prosecutor, Crown Prosecutor or an Associate Prosecutor. The former are legally qualified solicitors or barristers; the latter are not. An Associate Prosecutor's right to conduct a contested trial is restricted to non-imprisonable summary-only offences upon completion of designated training.

The CPS employs a number of administrative staff known as caseworkers. A caseworker will assist CPS lawyers and Associate Prosecutors by preparing cases, attending court with counsel, liaising with witnesses and other criminal justice agencies as well as post-trial administration. Whilst the CPS clearly plays a dominant role in the prosecution of criminal offences, other public bodies also investigate and prosecute criminal offences in their specific areas of responsibility:

* the Serious Fraud Office investigates and prosecutes serious or complex fraud (http://www. sfo.gov.uk/);
* the Serious Organised Crime Agency investigates serious organised crime;
* the Health and Safety Executive (HSE) investigates and prosecutes criminal offences arising out of accidents in the workplace under the Health and Safety at Work Act 1974 (the Enforcement section of the HSE's website contains a lot of useful information: http://www.hse.gov.uk/enforce/enforcementguide/index.htm);
* local authorities investigate and prosecute offences under the Trade Descriptions Act 1968, Education Act 1996, environmental law cases and prosecutions relating to food and hygiene;
* the Environment Agency investigates and prosecutes environmental crime (http://www. environment-agency.gov.uk/business/regulation/31851.aspx);
* the RSPCA brings private prosecutions for offences relating to the welfare of animals (http://www.rspca.org.uk).

1.7.2 THE LEGAL SERVICES COMMISSION AND THE CRIMINAL DEFENCE SERVICE

A detailed examination of public funding of criminal defence services is considered in Chapter 9. The provision of public funding for legal services in England and Wales is supervised by the Legal Services Commission. The day-to-day administration of public funding for criminal defence services is undertaken by the Criminal Defence Service (CDS). There are over 2,000 solicitors' firms having contracts with the Legal Services Commission to provide public funded criminal defence services. Public spending on criminal legal aid regularly exceeds £1 billion every year.

1.7.3 THE PUBLIC DEFENDER SERVICE

The Public Defender Service (PDS) provides a limited alternative to a criminal client seeking advice and representation from a solicitor in private practice. Through the LSC, the PDS employs solicitors, legal executives and paralegals to provide advice, assistance and representation to clients. Currently there are PDS offices located in Darlington, Swansea, Pontypridd and Cheltenham.

1.8 THE CRIMINAL COURTS AND PERSONNEL

It is likely that you studied the hierarchy of the criminal courts during your academic studies. This section is intended to briefly remind you of the jurisdiction of each criminal court.

1.8.1 MAGISTRATES' COURT

Prosecutors and defence lawyers spend most of their time preparing for and appearing in cases listed in the magistrates' court. It is the workhorse of the criminal justice system. Virtually all criminal prosecutions commence in the magistrates' court. Over 95% of all criminal cases are dealt with in the magistrates' court, with the remaining cases heard in the Crown Court. According to the Judicial and Court Statistics published by the Ministry for Justice, in 2011 an estimated 1.62 million defendants were proceeded against in the magistrates' court with 166,808 trials recorded. The practice and procedure in the magistrates' court is governed by the Magistrates' Courts Act 1980 (MCA 1980) and the Criminal Procedure Rules (2012).

The magistrates' court undertakes the following:

- deals with preliminary matters during the early stages of all prosecutions including:

  — application for an adjournment;
  — the defendant's bail status;

- tries summary offences (this includes an either-way offence which is to remain in the magistrates' court) and sentences defendants convicted of these offences;
- determines the mode of trial/allocation of an either-way offence for which the defendant has indicated a not guilty plea;
- commits a defendant convicted of an either-way offence to the Crown Court for sentence where the magistrates consider their maximum sentencing powers to be insufficient;
- commits/sends an either-way offence to the Crown Court which the magistrates' court has decided should be tried at the Crown Court or because the defendant has elected trial at the Crown Court;
- sends indictable-only offences to the Crown Court for trial under s. 51 Crime and Disorder Act 1998.

A magistrates' court can also issue warrants for arrest, removal to a place of safety, search of premises and seizure of property. If the police wish to detain a person for questioning beyond 36 hours they must get an order from the magistrates' court authorising this further period of detention without charge. The court also deals with fine enforcement and adjudicates on a number of civil law applications, including applications for anti-social behaviour orders and football banning orders.

1.8.2 **MAGISTRATES**

A magistrate is either a justice of the peace or a District Judge. Lay magistrates are unpaid, and whilst they are not required to hold any formal legal qualifications all magistrates undergo a period of induction and training. They are required to 'sit' for a prescribed number of days each year. There are approximately 30,000 active lay magistrates in England and Wales who normally try cases sitting as part of a Bench of three.

Salaried District Judges and Deputy District Judges are appointed from solicitors and barristers who have been qualified for at least seven years. A District Judge hears a case sitting alone and can exercise all the powers of a Bench of lay magistrates. A District Judge may also exercise some of the powers of recorders who sit as judges in the Crown Court in certain cases (s. 65 Courts Act 2003).

1.8.3 **THE LEGAL ADVISER**

When conducting a summary trial, lay magistrates will be assisted by a legal adviser who is usually a solicitor or a barrister. The law maintains a strict division of responsibilities between the magistrates and their legal adviser. The magistrates are the sole arbiters of law and fact. The *Practice Direction (Criminal Proceedings: Consolidation)* [2000] 1 WLR 2870 provides that the legal adviser will sit with lay magistrates to advise the Bench on matters of law, evidence, human rights points and procedure. The legal adviser will also put the charge to the accused, take a note of the evidence in the case and help an unrepresented defendant present his case.

When the justices retire to consider their verdict, the legal adviser must only advise them on points of law and evidence and not on issues of fact *(Stafford Justices, ex p. Ross* [1962] 1 WLR 456).

1.8.4 **YOUTH COURT**

Generally, defendants who are under 18 should be dealt with in the youth court. All magistrates' courts have a youth court panel of specially trained magistrates who have been appointed because of their suitability for dealing with youth cases. The practice and procedure is more informal and less intimidating than in the adult court. A District Judge (who has undertaken the required training) may also sit alone in the youth court. The youth court is regarded as a specialist jurisdiction. For this reason, youth justice is dealt with separately in Chapters 24 to 26.

1.8.5 **THE CROWN COURT**

The Crown Court, which sits at 77 different locations in England and Wales, deals with cases to be tried on indictment before a judge and jury. The practice and procedure in the Crown Court is now governed by the Senior Courts Act 1981 and the Criminal Procedure Rules (2011). In 2011, 91,910 defendants were committed or sent for trial to the Crown Court, of whom approximately 70% pleaded guilty. The Crown Court exercises the following jurisdiction:

* tries either-way offences committed/sent for trial at the Crown Court;
* tries indictable-only offences and any related offences;
* sentences offenders convicted before it and those who are committed for sentence by the magistrates' courts;
* hears an appeal against conviction and/or sentence arising out of a decision made by a magistrates' court or youth court.

Section 66 Courts Act 2003 enables a Crown Court judge to exercise the powers of a District Judge (magistrates' court).

The following types of judge preside over sittings of the Crown Court:

* High Court judges;
* circuit judges; and
* recorders and assistant recorders who are part-time judicial officers.

1.8.6 **THE DIVISIONAL COURT**

The Divisional Court has a limited jurisdiction in criminal matters. An action in judicial review can be commenced in the Divisional Court against a public body such as a court, the police or the CPS for exceeding or misusing their legal powers or for not following the correct procedures.

The Divisional Court hears appeals by way of case stated under s. 111 MCA 1980 arising from decisions taken in a magistrates' court. Both the prosecution and defence can appeal by way of case stated to the Divisional Court. This method of appeal is appropriate where it is submitted that the magistrates' court or its legal adviser has misinterpreted a point of law or evidence.

1.8.7 **THE COURT OF APPEAL (CRIMINAL DIVISION)**

The Court of Appeal (Criminal Division) hears appeals against conviction and/or sentence from cases tried in the Crown Court. It also hears appeals or 'points of reference' from the Attorney-General (A-G) on points of law and sentences that are considered too lenient. The work of the Court of Appeal is presided over by the Lord Chief Justice. Cases are normally heard by the Lord Chief Justice sitting with two puisne judges or a Lord Justice of Appeal sitting with two ordinary judges.

The Court of Appeal additionally gives guidance on the procedures and practices of the criminal courts by issuing sentencing guidelines and practice directions.

1.8.8 THE SUPREME COURT

The judicial work of the Supreme Court (formerly the House of Lords) is presided over by the President of the Supreme Court. It is the final and the highest court in the criminal jurisdiction and hears appeals from the Court of Appeal (and occasionally from the Divisional Court) on points of law of public and constitutional importance. Leave to appeal is required.

1.9 THE EUROPEAN CONVENTION ON HUMAN RIGHTS 1950 (ECHR 1950)

The Human Rights Act 1998 (HRA 1998) provides the legal framework for using the ECHR 1950 in UK domestic law. Section 1 HRA 1998 formally incorporates ECHR law into UK domestic law which means that ECHR law can be cited in the criminal courts in support of the defendant's case.

1.9.1 HOW ARE THE RIGHTS GUARANTEED UNDER THE CONVENTION ENFORCED IN DOMESTIC LAW?

Section 3 HRA 1998 places an obligation on the criminal courts to interpret all legislation 'as far as possible' to comply with ECHR law. This is known as the interpretive obligation. In discharging the interpretive obligation to ensure compliance between Convention law and domestic law, s. 2 HRA 1998 requires courts to have regard to Convention law and to the decisions of the European Court of Human Rights (ECtHR). Therefore when citing a relevant ECHR point in support of your legal argument you should research any ECtHR decisions on the point and any relevant domestic case law. Where it is not possible to give effect to the ECHR law in a case under the interpretive obligation, s. 4 HRA 1998 requires the superior courts (Court of Appeal and the Supreme Court) to make a declaration of incompatibility. It is then a matter for Parliament whether to amend the offending legislation.

In addition, s. 6 HRA 1998 places a duty on a public authority such as the police, the CPS and the courts, to discharge its legal duties in compliance with the ECHR 1950. Section 6(1) provides:

'It is unlawful for a public authority to act in a way which is incompatible with Convention rights.'

A range of remedies in the civil courts apply where a public authority acts in breach of its duties under s. 6 HRA 1998, including actions in tort and/or judicial review. Section 8 HRA 1998 requires that where a court finds that a public authority has acted unlawfully, it must grant a remedy that is 'just and appropriate'.

1.9.2 CRIMINAL LITIGATION—THE RELEVANT CONVENTION ARTICLES

Article 3—the prohibition of torture

'No one shall be subjected to torture or inhuman or degrading treatment or punishment.'

Thankfully this provision is unlikely to be invoked on a frequent basis, although it might be relevant when challenging the admissibility of a defendant's confession on the ground that it had been obtained by 'oppression' under s. 76(2)(a) Police and Criminal Evidence Act 1984. Article 3 will be relevant when arguing that the manner in which the police interrogated your client (for example by shouting or making threats to the suspect) breached Convention law.

Article 3 is an absolute right from which no derogation is permitted.

Article 5—the right to liberty and security

'1. Everyone has the right to liberty and security of person. No one shall be deprived of liberty save in the following cases and in accordance with a procedure prescribed by law:

(a) the lawful detention of a person after conviction by a competent court;

(b) the lawful arrest or detention of a person for non-compliance with the lawful order of a court . . .;

> (c) the lawful arrest and detention of a person except for the purpose of bringing him before a court of competent legal authority on reasonable suspicion of having committed an offence or fleeing after having done so; . . .
>
> 2. Everyone who is arrested shall be informed promptly, in a language which he understands, of the reasons for his arrest and of any charge against him.
>
> 3. Everyone arrested or detained in accordance with paragraph 1c shall be entitled to trial within a reasonable time or to release pending trial. Release may be conditioned by guarantees to appear for trial.
>
> 4. Everyone who is deprived of his liberty by arrest or detention shall be entitled to take proceedings by which the lawfulness of his detention shall be decided speedily by a court.
>
> 5. Everyone who has been the victim of arrest or detention in contravention of the provisions of this article shall have an enforceable right to compensation.'

Article 5 is a qualified right allowing the state to derogate from it in defined circumstances.

Article 5 may be invoked where your client has been unlawfully arrested or otherwise detained by the police and may be relevant when challenging the decision of the police or the court to deny your client bail.

Article 6—the right to a fair trial

> '1. In the determination of his civil rights and obligations, or of any criminal charge against him everyone is entitled to a fair and public hearing within a reasonable time by an independent and impartial tribunal established by law. Judgment shall be pronounced publicly but the press or public may be excluded in the interests of morals, public order or national security in a democratic society, where the interests of juveniles or the protection of private life of the parties so require, or to the extent strictly necessary in the opinion of the court in special circumstances where publicity would prejudice the interests of justice.
>
> 2. Everyone charged with a criminal offence shall be presumed innocent until proved guilty according to the law.
>
> 3. Everyone charged with a criminal offence has the following minimum rights:
>
>   (a) to be informed promptly, in a language which he understands and in detail of the nature and cause of the accusation against him;
>
>   (b) to have adequate time and facilities for the preparation of his defence;
>
>   (c) to defend himself in person or through legal assistance of his own choosing or, if he has not sufficient means to pay for legal assistance, to be given it free when the interests of justice so require;
>
>   (d) to examine or have examined witnesses against him and to obtain the attendance and examination of witnesses on his behalf under the same conditions as witnesses against him;
>
>   (e) to have the free assistance of an interpreter if he cannot understand or speak the language used in court.'

Article 6 is the most significant Convention right for criminal litigators and is relevant at all stages of a criminal case including:

- the defendant's right to have legal representation at the police station and at trial;
- the procedural and evidential rules adopted by the court at trial; and
- the principles applied when passing sentence.

The right to a fair trial in Article 6(1) is drafted in absolute terms. What constitutes a fair trial, however, is not defined. The presumption of innocence in Article 6(2) and the provisions of Article 6(3) are specified minimum general components of a fair trial. The jurisprudence of the ECtHR has implied a number of rights into Article 6, including the privilege against self-incrimination. In deciding the fair trial provisions under Article 6, it should be stressed that the ECtHR is not concerned with the guilt or innocence of the accused but rather whether the whole trial process was in accordance with Article 6.

It is open to a defence advocate to argue that the admissibility of a particular piece of evidence in a case will violate the defendant's right to a fair trial in accordance with Article 6.

Article 8—the right to respect for private and family life

'1. Everyone has the right to respect for his private and family life, his home and his correspondence.

2. There shall be no interference by public authority with the exercise of this right except such as is in accordance with the law and is necessary in a democratic society in the interests of national security, public safety or the economic well-being of the country, for the prevention of disorder or crime etc . . .'

Article 8 seeks to protect the individual from arbitrary interference by the state. It is, however, a qualified right and permits interference for the reasons stated above. Any interference, however, must be authorised in accordance with the law and must be proportional. Article 8 may be cited by defendants to challenge the admissibility of evidence obtained in breach of the defendant's right to a fair trial under Article 6 (see Chapter 6).

1.9.3 THE ECHR 1950 AND THE RULES OF CRIMINAL PROCEDURE AND EVIDENCE

Whilst generally the practice and procedure of the English criminal trial satisfies the obligations laid down by the Convention, since the implementation of the HRA 1998 a number of important decisions have been made by the courts where Article 5 or Article 6 have been directly invoked. These decisions include:

- *R (on the application of the DPP) v Havering Magistrates' Court* [2001] 2 Cr App R 2 confirmed that proceedings under the Bail Act 1976 were governed by Article 5;

- *T and V v United Kingdom* (2000) 30 EHRR 121 decided that the boys tried for the killing of James Bulger had not had a fair trial in the Crown Court under Article 6 because of their young age and the formality of the Crown Court procedures had prevented them from effective participation in the trial process;

- *R (Anderson) v Secretary of State for the Home Department* [2003] 1 Cr App R 32, the House of Lords decided that to comply with Article 6, where a prisoner was sentenced to life imprisonment, the decision as to how long the prisoner should serve in prison (known as the tariff) should be taken by a judge and not by the Home Secretary;

- *Murray v United Kingdom* [1996] 22 EHHR 29, the ECtHR held that adverse inferences could not be drawn from a suspect's silence at the police station where he had not been offered legal advice. United Kingdom domestic law was found to be in breach of Article 6(3) of the ECHR 1950. Section 34 Criminal Justice and Public Order Act 1994 had to be amended as a consequence.

These and other important decisions influenced by the ECHR 1950 are considered in more detail at appropriate places in the text. The recognition of a defendant's rights under Article 6 is specifically identified in Part 1 of the Criminal Procedure Rules as a component of the overriding objective of dealing with criminal cases justly.

1.10 CRIMINAL PROCEDURE RULES (CRIM PR)

The Criminal Procedure Rules (Crim PR) first came into effect on 4 April 2005. The rules, which were most recently revised in October 2012, provide a comprehensive criminal procedure code that governs the conduct of all criminal cases and should be read in conjunction with the Consolidated Criminal Practice Direction (CCPD). Both the rules and the CCPD can be accessed via the Criminal Procedure Rule Committee's website (http://www. justice.gov.uk/criminal/procrules_fin/rulesmenu.htm). The web-links section of our Online Resource Centre (Guidelines section) will take you there. You will see references to the application of the Criminal Procedure Rules throughout this work.

online resource centre

The overriding objective of the Crim PR is stated in Part 1. It requires that all criminal cases must be dealt with justly. Part 1.1 defines this to include:

'(a) acquitting the innocent and convicting the guilty;

(b) dealing with the prosecution and the defence fairly;

(c) recognising the rights of a defendant, particularly those under Article 6 of the European Convention on Human Rights;

(d) respecting the interest of witnesses, victims and jurors and keeping them informed of the progress of the case;

(e) dealing with the case efficiently and expeditiously;

(f) ensuring that appropriate information is available to the court when bail and sentence are considered; and

(g) dealing with the case in ways that take into account:

(i) the gravity of the offence alleged,

(ii) the complexity of what is in issue,

(iii) the severity of the consequences for the defendant and others affected, and

(iv) the needs of other cases.'

Everyone involved in the criminal justice process must prepare and conduct cases in accordance with the overriding objective (Crim PR Part 1.2).

To ensure that the overriding objective is achieved, courts are required to engage in robust and active management of cases (Part 3). Active case management is defined in Part 3.2 to include:

'(a) the early identification of the real issues;

(b) the early identification of the needs of witnesses;

(c) achieving certainty as to what must be done, by whom, and when, in particular by the early setting of a timetable for the progress of the case;

(d) monitoring the progress of the case and compliance with directions;

(e) ensuring that evidence, whether disputed or not, is presented in the shortest and clearest way;

(f) discouraging delay, dealing with as many aspects of the case as possible on the same occasion and avoiding unnecessary hearings;

(g) encouraging the participants to co-operate in the progression of the case; and

(h) making use of technology.'

Active case management involves courts giving directions to the parties that are appropriate to the needs of the case and are consistent with the overriding objective.

Crim PR, Part 3.3 imposes a duty on all parties to actively assist the court in fulfilling its duty under Part 3.2. A court can impose sanctions on parties for failing to comply with a rule or direction of the court (Part 3.5(6)). These might include a wasted costs order, the exclusion of evidence, or the refusal of a request for an adjournment. In *DPP v Hammerton* [2009] EWHC 921, the High Court upheld a decision of a magistrates' court (taken in accordance with the overriding objective) to refuse to allow the CPS to substitute at a late stage and for no good reason, a less serious charge in place of the original charge.

The extent to which the defence solicitor's duties under Part 3 conflict with duties owed to a client in the conduct of a criminal case are considered at para. 1.11.7.

The case management responsibilities under Crim PR Part 3 must now be read in conjunction with the principles enshrined in Stop Delaying Justice (SDJ) which applies to all cases that can be tried in the magistrates' court. SDJ is an initiative from the senior judiciary which came into effect in all magistrates' courts on 1 January 2012. It aims to ensure that all contested trials in the magistrates' court are fully managed from the first hearing and disposed of at the second hearing. SDJ builds upon the improvements to the more efficient disposal of summary cases begun by the Criminal Justice—Simple, Speedy and Summary (CJ-SSS).

The practical effect of both initiatives on the conduct and management of summary cases is fully explained in Chapter 9.

The Criminal Procedure Rules are revised from time to time. Any significant developments will be brought to you via the updating section of our Online Resource Centre.

online
resource
centre

1.11 PROFESSIONAL CONDUCT—AN INTRODUCTION

The rules of professional conduct are an important pervasive area of legal practice that governs the solicitors' profession. A new regulatory framework governing legal practice in England and Wales came into force in October 2011. The 2011 Code of Conduct moves away from the detailed and prescriptive rule-based approach adopted by the previous Code (published in 2007) to a more flexible, proportionate 'outcomes-focused' regulatory framework. All solicitors, legal executives and paralegals are required to uphold the spirit and letter of the 2011 Code.

A copy of the 2011 Code can be accessed at: http://www.sra.org.uk/handbook/. What follows is an early interpretation of the obligations imposed on practitioners by the 2011 Code when acting for a client in a criminal case. A failure to abide by the Solicitors Regulation Authority (SRA) Code of Conduct may result in disciplinary proceedings being brought against the individual concerned as well as the firm or organisation they work for. If a solicitor is found to have broken the Code he or she can be disciplined or even struck off the Roll.

The new regulatory framework published in the SRA Handbook identifies ten mandatory, all-pervasive *Principles*. The *Principles*, which are listed below, define the fundamental ethical and professional standards that are expected of all firms when providing legal services and should be used by firms as a starting point when faced with an ethical dilemma. The SRA *Principles* are:

You must:

'1. Uphold the rule of law and the proper administration of justice;

2. Act with integrity;

3. Not allow your independence to be compromised;

4. Act in the best interests of each client;

5. Provide a proper standard of service to your clients;

6. Behave in a way that maintains the trust the public places in you and in the provision of legal services;

7. Comply with your legal and regulatory obligations and deal with your regulators and ombudsmen in an open, timely and co-operative manner;

8. Run your business or carry out your role in the business effectively and in accordance with proper governance and sound financial and risk management principles;

9. Run your business or carry out your role in the business in a way that encourages equality of opportunity and respect for diversity;

10. Protect client money and assets.'

The 2011 Code of Conduct is divided into five sections. Each section in turn contains chapters dealing with particular regulatory matters. For example, in the first section of the Code (entitled 'You and your client') there are chapters on 'Conflicts of interest', 'Confidentiality and Disclosure' and 'Your Client and the Court'. Each chapter explains how the *Principles* apply in a particular context through mandatory and non-mandatory provisions. Each chapter identifies mandatory 'Outcomes' which individuals and firms are expected to achieve in order to comply with the relevant *Principles*. The 'Outcomes' provide a non-exhaustive list of the application of the *Principles*. They are supplemented by (non-mandatory) 'indicative behaviours' and 'notes'. The indicative behaviours specify, but do not constitute, an exhaustive list of the kind of behaviour which may establish compliance with, or contravention of the *Principles*.

1.11.1 **THE 2011 CODE AND ITS APPLICATION TO CRIMINAL LITIGATION**

Criminal cases are conducted in an adversarial system of enquiry where the aim of each side is to win. *Principle 4* requires a defence solicitor to act in the best interests of her client. In an effort to win, the solicitor will need to be a partisan advocate for and on behalf of her client. However, as an officer of the court, a solicitor also serves the wider public interest in upholding the highest standards in relation to the administration of justice (*Principle 1*). Serving the best interests of a client can sometimes bring a solicitor into conflict with her duty to the proper administration of justice. Where it does so, Note 2 of the *Principles* states:

'Where two or more *Principles* come into conflict the one which takes precedence is the one which best serves the public interest in the particular circumstances, especially the public interest in the proper administration of justice.'

The purpose of this final section is to provide an overview of your professional conduct duties, with specific emphasis on criminal practice.

Professional conduct issues in relation to criminal clients are most likely to arise in the following contexts:

- duties to the client;
- duties to the court;
- confidentiality;
- conflict of interest;
- interviewing witnesses;
- specific duties on advocates.

Nearly all of these are covered in the first section of the 2011 Code under the heading: *You and Your Client*.

1.11.2 **CHAPTER 1: CLIENT CARE**

Note: (O) denotes an Outcome; (IB) denotes Indicative Behaviours
The Outcomes identified in Chapter 1 of the code include, amongst others:

O (1.1) you treat your clients fairly;

O (1.2) you provide services to your clients in a manner which protects their interests in their matter, subject to the proper administration of justice;

O (1.3) when deciding whether to act, or terminate your instructions, you comply with the law and the Code;

O (1.4) you have the resources, skills and procedures to carry out your clients' instructions;

Indicative Behaviours include:

IB (1.1) agreeing an appropriate level of service with your client, for example the type and frequency of communications;

IB (1.2) explaining your responsibilities and those of the client;

IB (1.3) ensuring that the client is told, in writing, the name and status of the person(s) dealing with the matter and the name and status of the person responsible for its overall supervision;

IB (1.6) in taking instructions and during the course of the retainer, having proper regard to your client's mental capacity or other vulnerability, such as incapacity or duress;

IB (1.7) considering whether you should decline to act or cease to act because you cannot act in the client's best interests;

IB (1.9) refusing to act where your client proposes to make a gift of significant value to you or a member of your family, or a member of your firm or their family, unless the client takes independent legal advice;

IB (1.10) if you have to cease acting for a client, explaining to the client their possible options for pursuing their matter;

IB (1.14) clearly explaining your fees and if and when they are likely to change;

IB (1.15) warning about any other payments for which the client may be responsible;

IB (1.16) discussing how the client will pay, including whether public funding may be available, whether the client has insurance that might cover the fees, and whether the fees may be paid by someone else such as a trade union;

IB (1.18) where you are acting for a publicly funded client, explaining how their publicly funded status affects the costs;

IB (1.19) providing the information in a clear and accessible form which is appropriate to the needs and circumstances of the client;

Acting in the following way(s) may tend to show that you have not achieved these outcomes and therefore not complied with the *Principles:*

IB (1.28) acting for a client when there are reasonable grounds for believing that the instructions are affected by duress or undue influence without satisfying yourself that they represent the client's wishes.

Chapter 1 outcomes apply to all aspects of legal practice and are certainly not unique to the criminal litigator. A number of the indicative behaviours outlined above will be explained in the client care letter sent to the client upon acceptance of instructions to act. Of relevance to the criminal litigator is Outcome (1.4) which requires you to consider whether the nature or complexity of the case is beyond your experience and ability. As public funding is widely available for the conduct of criminal proceedings (see Chapter 9), you should discuss this funding option with your client. It falls within *Principle 4* acting in the best interests of your client. Similarly, it should be explained to a client charged with a criminal offence that if he is convicted, he could be made to pay some or all of the prosecution's costs. Whilst no client should be advised to plead guilty if the prosecution case against him is not strong, a defence solicitor (when purporting to act in the best interests of his client) ought to explain the advantages of a timely guilty plea in terms of sentence (see Chapter 21).

It is also important to be aware that when dealing with clients, staff, other lawyers and third parties, a solicitor must have regard to equality and diversity issues detailed in Chapter 2 of the new Code.

1.11.3 **CHAPTER 3: CONFLICTS OF INTEREST**

All legal firms are required to have in place a system that enables conflicts of interests to be identified. *Principle 4*, which requires you to act in the best interests of your client, also requires you to observe your duty of confidentiality (see later) and your obligations with regard to conflict of interests. The two sometimes overlap.

Chapter 3 of the code defines a conflict to include 'own interest conflict', which is a conflict between you and your client, and 'client conflict', which is a conflict arising between one or more current clients. An 'own interest conflict' could arise because of a financial interest; personal or employment relationship you may have; or because you or a member of your firm or family have been appointed to public office. Outcome (3.4) provides you must not act if there is an 'own interest conflict' or a significant risk of an 'own interest conflict'. Outcome (3.5) provides that you must not act if there is a 'client conflict' or a significant risk of a 'client conflict'. There are exceptions outlined in Outcomes (3.6) and (3.7) which include a situation where two or more clients have a substantially common interest. It is difficult to envisage a situation in a criminal litigation context where these exceptions would apply.

When considering instructions from more than one client, the solicitor needs to ask: Is there a conflict of interest between them or might a conflict arise at some point in the future? A conflict of interest can commonly arise when the solicitor is called upon to represent two or more suspects at the police station who are being investigated for the same offence. A conflict may subsequently arise in a case where both clients plead not guilty but one of them later pleads guilty. The solicitor should be aware that even when two clients indicate that they will plead guilty, a conflict of interest could still arise when the solicitor comes to mitigate on their individual behalf.

Further very useful guidance on the practical application of the conflict rule is available in the Law Society Practice Note 'Conflicts of interest in criminal cases' which was published on 19 December 2011. The Practice Note can be accessed at: http://www.lawsociety.org.uk/productsandservices/practicenotes/criminalconflicts/5048.article.

The Practice Note suggests that a conflict of interest can arise where it is in the best interests of client A:

(a) to give evidence against client B;

(b) to make a statement incriminating client B;

(c) to implicate client B in a police interview;

(d) to provide prejudicial information regarding client B to an investigator;

(e) to cross-examine client B in such a manner as to call into question his or her credibility;

(f) to rely upon confidential information given by client B without his or her consent; or

(g) to adopt tactics in the course of the retainer which potentially or actually harm client B.

The Practice Note cautions that if these obligations actually come into conflict when acting for two or more clients, the lawyer will have to cease to act for one and often both.

The obligation as regards conflict can arise at a very early stage (i.e. at the police station). The Practice Note advises that in order to assess whether you can act for both clients it is important that you do not interview the clients together and that you get instructions which are as full as possible from the first client before any substantial contact with the second client. You should not allow the police to deter you from seeing the second client because they think there is a conflict—that decision must be yours.

Obvious indicators of a conflict would include clients having differing accounts of the important relevant circumstances of the alleged crime, or where one seems likely to change his or her plea. Less obvious indicators which may give rise to a significant risk of future conflict include situations where there is clear inequality between the co-defendants which might, for example, suggest that one client is acting under the influence of the other rather than on his or her own initiative. If you act for both, it may be difficult to raise and discuss these issues equally with them. By helping one, you might undermine the other. If you believe you are unable to do your best for one without prejudicing the other, you should only accept instructions from one. Should two or more clients decide to plead guilty, you need to consider at the outset whether you would be able to mitigate fully and freely on behalf of one client without harming the interests of the other. If one client is more criminally sophisticated than the other, it may be that the other client was led astray or pressurised into committing the crime and would want you to emphasise this in mitigation. If there is a significant risk of this happening you should not accept instructions from either.

Where a conflict has arisen and you must decide whether you can continue to act for one client but not another, the Practice Note advises that you need to consider whether in the changed circumstances your duty to disclose all relevant information to the retained client will place you in breach of your duty of confidentiality to the other client. In practice you must decide whether you hold confidential information about the former client which is now relevant to the retained client. If you have this information then you cannot act for either client.

From a public funding perspective it is cheaper for the same solicitor to represent two clients than having different firms represent each client. However, the Practice Note clearly states that you should resist such pressure from whatever source (court or police station) if it would be unprofessional for you to act or to continue to act for both clients. If asked by the court why you cannot act for both defendants, you must not give information which would breach your duty of confidentiality to your client(s). This will normally mean that you can say no more than that it would be unprofessional for you to continue to act.

1.11.4 CHAPTER 4: CONFIDENTIALITY AND DISCLOSURE

Chapter 4 of the code states that protection of confidential information is a fundamental feature of your relationship with clients and that the duty continues after the end of the retainer and even after the death of the client. You therefore have a strict duty to keep your client's affairs confidential (Outcome (4.1)), which of course will be particularly important to a client under suspicion of a criminal offence. This duty continues for all time unless the client agrees to waive confidentiality. There are exceptional situations when the duty of confidentiality can be overridden. These include requirements under the money-laundering reporting regulations, and issues involving child protection and disclosure to the Legal Services Commission in the case of a publicly funded client.

Communications between a solicitor and her client are additionally protected from disclosure even to the court by legal professional privilege. The privilege extends in criminal cases to communications passing between a solicitor and a third party, such as a barrister or expert witness, provided the communication was made in connection with actual or contemplated litigation. Legal professional privilege does not extend where a solicitor has been used in furtherance of a crime. In such a case the police can seize documents relevant to the investigation. The rules relating to legal professional privilege are considered further in Chapter 20.

Issues of confidentiality are likely to arise in criminal cases where professional embarrassment (see the solicitor's overriding duty to the court later) forces the solicitor to withdraw from a case. Solicitors cannot in these circumstances explain to a court why they are no longer acting.

The issue of confidentiality may also arise at the police station. When advising a suspect to remain silent, the legal adviser may be called upon to explain the reasons for this advice if s. 34 Criminal Justice and Public Order Act 1994 is invoked at trial. The legal adviser can only do this if the client consents to waive his legal professional privilege. The matter is considered further in Chapter 5.

You are under a duty when advising a client to make the client aware of all information material to the client's retainer (Outcome (4.2)). The confidentiality and disclosure rule often overlaps with the conflict rule (see earlier, Chapter 3 of the 2011 Code). A solicitor cannot continue to act for A and B where a conflict of interest arises between them. Can the solicitor continue to act for A but not B? The answer is yes, but only where the solicitor's duty of confidentiality to B is not put at risk. Outcome (4.3) provides that where your duty of confidentiality to one client conflicts with your duty of disclosure to another client, your duty of confidentiality takes precedence. You cannot therefore continue to act for A in these circumstances.

1.11.5 CHAPTER 5: YOUR CLIENT AND THE COURT

Principle 1 requires you to uphold the rule of law and the proper administration of justice. The Outcomes identified in Chapter 5 of the code are:

O (5.1) you do not attempt to deceive or knowingly or recklessly mislead, the court;

O (5.2) you are not complicit in another person deceiving or misleading the court;

O (5.3) you comply with court orders which place obligations on you;

O (5.4) you do not place yourself in contempt of court;

O (5.5) where relevant, clients are informed of the circumstances in which your duties to the court outweigh your obligations to your client;

O (5.6) you comply with your duties to the court;

O (5.7)   you ensure that evidence relating to sensitive issues is not misused;

O (5.8)   you do not make or offer to make payments to witnesses dependent upon their evidence or the outcome of the case.

The outcomes apply to both litigation and advocacy, whilst some of the indicative behaviours outlined here may be relevant only when you are acting as an advocate.

Acting in the following way(s) may tend to show that you have achieved these outcomes and therefore complied with the *Principles:*

IB (5.1)   advising your clients to comply with court orders made against them, and advising them of the consequences of failing to comply;

IB (5.2)   drawing the court's attention to relevant cases and statutory provisions, and any material procedural irregularity;

IB (5.3)   ensuring child witness evidence is kept securely and not released to clients or third parties;

IB (5.4)   immediately informing the court, with your client's consent, if during the course of proceedings you become aware that you have inadvertently misled the court, or ceasing to act if the client does not consent to you informing the court;

IB (5.5)   refusing to continue acting for a client if you become aware they have committed perjury or misled the court, or attempted to mislead the court, in any material matter unless the client agrees to disclose the truth to the court;

IB (5.6)   not appearing as an advocate, or acting in litigation, if it is clear that you, or anyone within your firm, will be called as a witness in the matter unless you are satisfied that this will not prejudice your independence as an advocate, or litigator, or the interests of your clients or the interests of justice.

Acting in the following way(s) may tend to show that you have not achieved these outcomes and therefore not complied with the *Principles*:

IB (5.7)   constructing facts supporting your client's case or drafting any documents relating to any proceedings containing:

- any contention which you do not consider to be properly arguable; or
- any allegation of fraud, unless you are instructed to do so and you have material which you reasonably believe shows, on the face of it, a case of fraud;

IB (5.8)   suggesting that any person is guilty of a crime, fraud or misconduct unless such allegations:

- go to a matter in issue which is material to your own client's case, and
- appear to you to be supported by reasonable grounds;

IB (5.9)   calling a witness whose evidence you know is untrue;

IB (5.10) attempting to influence a witness, when taking a statement from that witness, with regard to the contents of their statement;

IB (5.11) tampering with evidence or seeking to persuade a witness to change their evidence;

IB (5.12) when acting as an advocate, naming in open court any third party whose character would thereby be called into question, unless it is necessary for the proper conduct of the case;

IB (5.13) when acting as an advocate, calling into question the character of a witness you have cross-examined unless the witness has had the opportunity to answer the allegations during cross-examination.

Chapter 5 of the Code makes it abundantly clear that a solicitor must not attempt to deceive or knowingly or recklessly mislead the court (O (5.1)).

It is common for clients charged with criminal offences to lie or be economical with the truth. What should a solicitor do if she becomes aware that her client intends to lie to the police or to the court or has lied? What if the prosecution gives information to the court which the defence solicitor knows is incorrect?

A solicitor must not be complicit in another person deceiving or misleading the court (O (5.2)). This could arise where a solicitor is satisfied that her client is adopting false particulars (name or address or date of birth) with the intention of deceiving a court by failing to disclose previous convictions to achieve a more favourable sentence or bail outcome. In such circumstances, the solicitor would need to explain to her client that she cannot allow such a course to be pursued and that unless her client is willing to correct the details or is willing to change his mind, the solicitor will have to withdraw from the case (IB (5.5)).

In accordance with *Principle 1* and Chapter 5, you should not:

(a) submit inaccurate information or allow another person to do so;

(b) indicate agreement with information that another person puts forward which you know to be false;

(c) call a witness whose evidence you know is untrue;

(d) attempt to influence a witness when taking a statement from that witness, with regard to the contents of their statement; or

(e) tamper with evidence or seek to persuade a witness to change their evidence.

IB (5.4) acknowledges that a solicitor may inadvertently mislead the court. If the solicitor becomes aware of this during the proceedings, the solicitor must, with the client's consent, immediately inform the court. If the client does not consent, the solicitor must cease to act. A solicitor may believe that the client is being untruthful. However, suspicion is not the same as knowledge. If a client was to admit to his solicitor, during ongoing proceedings, that he had misled the court or committed perjury, the solicitor must not act further unless the client agrees to disclose the truth (IB (5.4)).

Is a solicitor under a duty to correct an omission or mistake by the prosecution?

What if the prosecution gives information to the court which the solicitor knows is incorrect? For example, if on checking a client's list of previous convictions, the defence solicitor realises that it is incomplete by failing to show the client's most recent conviction. When the prosecutor hands in a copy of the defendant's previous convictions, is the solicitor under a duty to advise the court about the omission? The guidance to Rule 11 (Note 15) of the 2007 Code covered this dilemma. It provided that a solicitor acting for the defence is not under an obligation to correct information given to the court by the prosecution or any other party which the solicitor knows may allow the court to make an incorrect assumption provided the solicitor does not indicate agreement with that information. The position would of course be different if the defence solicitor was asked to confirm the list of previous convictions as being correct. Guidance Note 15 is not reproduced in the 2011 code. The incorrect assumption made by the court may well assist the client; however, it could also be said that you would not be upholding the proper administration of justice (*Principle 1*) or acting with integrity (*Principle 2*). The sensible course to take would be to discuss the prosecution's omission with your client and gain his consent to correct the omission.

Where there has been a procedural irregularity in the case or a failure by the prosecution to draw the court's attention to relevant case law or to a statutory provision then to comply with *Principle 1*, you should bring it to the court's attention (IB (5.2)). Apart from this, there is no wider obligation upon the defence to disclose to the court or the prosecution facts or witnesses that may be of assistance to the other side. Such disclosure would not be acting in the best interests of your client (*Principle 4*) and would be a breach of confidentiality in any event (Chapter 4 of the code).

Duties on the prosecutor

The prosecutor has a duty to act as a minister of justice and must never attempt to secure a conviction at all costs. The role of the CPS is considered in Chapter 8. The chapter explains in detail the onerous nature of the prosecutor's duty to make pre-trial disclosure of relevant material that undermines the case for the prosecution or assists the defence which is fundamental to a defendant's right to a fair trial under Article 6.

What action should a solicitor take where her client changes his version of events?

A commonly encountered professional conduct issue occurs where a client keeps changing his version of the facts in the case. There is no general duty upon a solicitor to enquire in every case whether the client is telling the truth. If a client makes inconsistent statements, this is not a ground for refusing to act. However, the solicitor would need to be wary and must cease to act where it is clear that the client is attempting to put forward false evidence as this will conflict with the solicitor's duty as an officer of the court (O (5.1) and (5.2) and IB (5.5)). A solicitor should never suggest a defence to the client to fit the facts, nor must the solicitor fabricate a defence. This extends to taking witness statements (IB (5.10)). A solicitor must never put words into a witness's mouth (IB (5.10)).

What is the position where a client admits guilt but wants to plead not guilty?

This situation can arise at the police station as well as at court. Can the solicitor continue to act? An earlier version of the code of conduct contained the following statement:

> 'A solicitor who appears in court for the defence in a criminal case is under a duty to say on behalf of the client what the client should properly say for himself or herself if the client possessed the requisite skill and knowledge. The solicitor has a concurrent duty to ensure that the prosecution discharges the onus placed upon it to prove the guilt of the accused.'

The statement was not reproduced in the 2007 Code and is not reproduced in the 2011 Code. In answer to the question posed above, a solicitor can continue to represent the client on a not guilty plea, as it is the solicitor's professional duty to require the prosecution to prove its case beyond reasonable doubt.

However, the solicitor must not do anything to positively assert his client's innocence. If at the close of the prosecution's case, the client gave evidence on oath or called witnesses to testify about the client's innocence (i.e. which expressly or by implication suggests someone other than the client committed the crime), the solicitor would be knowingly misleading the court. If the client persisted in this course of action, the solicitor would be required to withdraw from the case (O (5.1)) and IB (5. 5)).

In those cases where a solicitor ceases to act, the solicitor's duty of confidentiality owed to the client (Chapter 4 of the code) precludes the solicitor from informing the court of the reason for the decision to withdraw.

What if a client has a defence but wishes to plead guilty?

A client may not wish to stand trial even though he has a defence to the allegation. It is the duty of the defence solicitor to point out such a defence. If the client insists on pleading guilty because it is more convenient to do so, the solicitor can continue to act for the client but the client should be warned when the solicitor is delivering a plea in mitigation on his behalf, that the solicitor will not be able to rely on any facts that would constitute a defence. A solicitor should keep a file note of advice given and ask the client to sign a written statement confirming his wishes notwithstanding the advice given.

1.11.6 INTERVIEWING AN OPPONENT'S WITNESS

You will frequently encounter the phrase 'there is no property in a witness'. In a criminal case, this means that the defence solicitor may interview a prosecution witness and the prosecution may interview a defence witness. This is not something which a defence solicitor would routinely do because if the witness provides a statement which is inconsistent with the statement originally given to the police, there is a danger that the defence solicitor could be accused of attempting to influence the witness or persuading the witness to change his evidence which would be contrary to *Principle 1* and Chapter 5 (IB (5.10) and

(5.11)). The 2007 Code provided guidance on how to deal with this situation: 'To avoid such allegations it would be wise, when seeking to interview a witness for the other side, to offer to interview them in the presence of the other side's representative.' The guidance remains valid in our view. Consequently, if a defence solicitor takes the unusual step of wishing to interview a prosecution witness, it is good professional practice to contact the prosecution, in order to ascertain whether a member of the prosecution team wishes to be present at the interview.

1.11.7 SPECIFIC PROFESSIONAL CONDUCT OBLIGATIONS ON ADVOCATES

There are further indicative behaviours which apply specifically to the solicitor acting as an advocate. They are detailed in IB (5.6), (5.7), (5.8), (5.12) and (5.13). They cover the situation where an advocate or a member of the advocate's firm could be called as a witness at trial. You should not appear as an advocate if it is clear that you, or anyone within your firm, will be called as a witness in the matter unless you are satisfied that this will not prejudice your independence as an advocate, or litigator, or the interests of your clients or the interests of justice (IB (5.6)). They also govern the way in which an advocate should treat a witness whilst giving evidence.

Outcome (5.8) states quite simply that a solicitor must not make, or offer to make, payments to a witness dependent upon the outcome of the case or the nature of the evidence the witness should give. It is, however, permissible to pay reasonable witness expenses.

Can an advocate refuse to act on the grounds that the nature of the case is objectionable to her? Under the 2007 Code, rule 11.04 provided that a solicitor could not refuse to act as an advocate for any person on the grounds that the nature of the case was objectionable to them or to any section of the public or that the conduct, opinions or beliefs of the prospective client were unacceptable to the solicitor or to any section of the public. The 2011 Code makes no reference to this situation.

1.11.8 PROFESSIONAL CONDUCT AND THE CRIMINAL PROCEDURE RULES

A defence solicitor must always act in the best interests of her client (*Principle 4*). In a case where a solicitor is instructed by the client to plead not guilty, it is the duty of the defence solicitor to put the prosecution to proof of its case. In an attempt to frustrate the prosecution, the defence solicitor may feel that the client's best interests are served by playing a tactical game, perhaps by withholding certain information from the prosecution and the court. Such a tactical game could frustrate the obligation of the court to actively manage cases in accordance with Crim PR, Parts 1 and 3 (see para. 1.10 earlier). The effect of the case management powers given to the court under Crim PR Part 3 and initiatives like CJ-SSS and SDJ (see Chapter 9) have significantly increased the pressures on all those involved in the conduct of criminal cases as they are now much more accountable to the court for a failure to actively progress a case. In a situation where a solicitor perceives a conflict between his duty to act in the best interests of the client and the duty to promote the administration of justice by actively assisting the court's management of cases (*Principle 1*), which takes precedence?

In *R v Gleeson* [2004] 1 Cr App R 29, defence advocates were reminded that:

> 'A criminal trial is not a game under which a guilty defendant should be provided with a sporting chance. It is a search for truth in accordance with twin principles that the prosecution must prove its case and that a defendant is not obliged to inculpate himself, the object being to convict the guilty and acquit the innocent. Requiring a defendant to indicate in advance what he disputes about the prosecution case offends neither of those principles.'

In response to the challenges posed by Crim PR, Part 3, the Law Society has issued an important Practice Note (February 2012), entitled 'Criminal Procedure Rules 2011'. It can be accessed at: http://www.lawsociety.org.uk/productsandservices/practicenotes/criminalprocedure/5055.article.

The Practice Note makes it clear that defence solicitors must assist a court to conduct cases justly and expeditiously and be aware of the consequences of failing to do so. However, a court cannot, in the exercise of its case management powers, compel a defence solicitor to breach a professional conduct obligation owed to a client. Thus, for example, a court cannot compel a defence solicitor to represent two clients where the solicitor concludes there is a significant risk of conflict between them, even though single representation might be more expeditious. Neither can a court require the defence solicitor to disclose privileged communications with her client (*R (on the application of Kelly) v Warley Magistrates Court (the Law Society intervening)* [2008] 1 Cr App R 14).

The Practice Note echoes the 2011 Code. Outcome (5.3) makes it clear that you must comply with court orders. Outcome (5.4) states you must not place yourself in contempt of court. Outcome (5.6) states you must comply with your duties to the court. The new code therefore takes account of the overriding objective under the Criminal Procedure Rules. Outcome (5.5) specifically provides that where relevant, clients must be informed of the circumstances in which your duties to the court outweigh your obligations to your client. It is submitted that Outcome (5.5) adopts the position under the Practice Note outlined previously.

1.11.9 **YOUR CLIENT AND INTRODUCTIONS TO THIRD PARTIES**

It is not unusual for a criminal practitioner to refer a client to a third party such as another lawyer or to suggest that the client ought to obtain an expert's report. Outcome (6.1) provides that whenever you recommend that a client uses a particular person or business, your recommendation is in the best interests of the client (*Principle 4*) and that it does not compromise your independence (*Principle 3*). Outcome (6.2) requires that clients are fully informed of any financial or other interest which you have in referring the client to another person or business.

KEY POINT SUMMARY

- Understand that criminal offences are classified as either summary-only, either-way or indictable-only and that the classification enables you to chart the procedural course of the case.
- Always research the classifications of the offence/s you are dealing with: never guess.
- Know the jurisdiction of the criminal courts.
- Arguments based on Article 6 ECHR 1950 can arise in many situations in criminal procedure and evidence.
- The right to a fair trial in Article 6 comprises many rights, some of which are specifically defined in Article 6 while others are implied.
- Domestic courts must as far as possible interpret domestic law in accordance with Convention rights.
- In determining rights under the Convention, regard must be had to the jurisprudence of the European Court of Human Rights.
- Human rights issues and professional conduct are pervasive—they can arise at any time.
- Have a thorough working knowledge of the rules of professional conduct and know the typical instances where professional conduct dilemmas are likely to arise in the context of criminal litigation.

SELF-TEST QUESTIONS

1. We would like you to begin to familiarise yourself with our fictional clients, Lenny Wise, Roger Martin and William Hardy and the nature of the accusations that have been made against each of them. Documentation pertaining to the first case study can be found in Appendix 1 of this *Handbook*. **The complete version of the documentation supporting *R v Lenny Wise* and the entire documentation supporting *R v Roger Martin* and *R v William Hardy* can be accessed from**

the student resource section of the Online Resource Centre. Analysis of all self-test questions can be found on the Online Resource Centre.

(a) Case study 1: *R v Lenny Wise*

Consider Document 6 (Lenny Wise's (proof of evidence) and Documents 26(A)–(J) which comprise the nature of the prosecution's evidence against Lenny. What offence is Lenny charged with? What is the classification of this offence?

(b) Case study 2: *R v Roger Martin*

Consider Document 1 (Roger Martin's initial statement given to his solicitor) and Documents 9(A)–(F) which comprise the nature of the prosecution's evidence against Roger. What offences is Roger Martin charged with? What is the classification of the offences he faces?

(c) Case study 3: *R v William Hardy*

Consider Document 1 (William Hardy's initial statement given to his solicitor) and Documents 10(A)–(E) which comprise the nature of the prosecution's evidence against William. What offence is William Hardy charged with? What is the classification of the offence William is charged with?

2. How are the following offences classified according to place of trial? (You may have to do some legal research to discover the answer to some of the questions. A good place to start is *Blackstone's Criminal Practice*.)

   (i) Criminal damage where the value of the damaged property is less than £5,000, s. 1 Criminal Damage Act 1971.

   (ii) Criminal damage where the value of the damaged property is more than £5,000.

   (iii) Possession of a controlled drug, s. 5 Misuse of Drugs Act 1971.

   (iv) Careless driving, s. 3 Road Traffic Act 1988.

   (v) Burglary, contrary to s. 9 Theft Act 1986.

   (vi) Affray, contrary to s. 3 Public Order Act 1986.

3. Explain what is meant by a summary-only offence.

4. Explain what is meant by an indictable-only offence.

5. In what circumstances would an allocation hearing be held?

6. Identify the overriding objective of the Criminal Procedure Rules.

7. Explain how Convention rights are incorporated into domestic law and how a defence solicitor might make use of such Convention rights.

8. What are the potential consequences of failing to spot and comply with an aspect of the Solicitors' Code of Conduct?

FIGURE 1.1 SUMMARY-ONLY OFFENCE

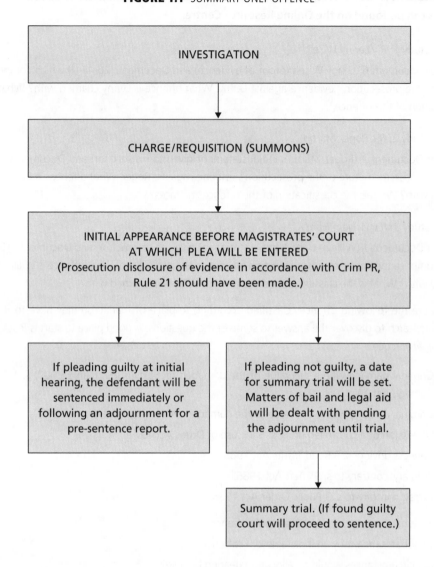

FIGURE 1.2 EITHER-WAY OFFENCE

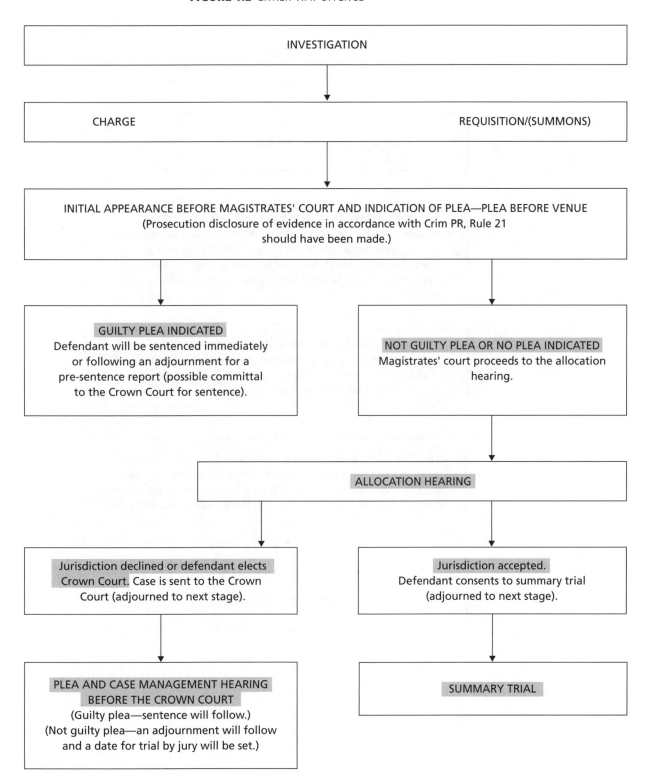

FIGURE 1.3 INDICTABLE-ONLY OFFENCE

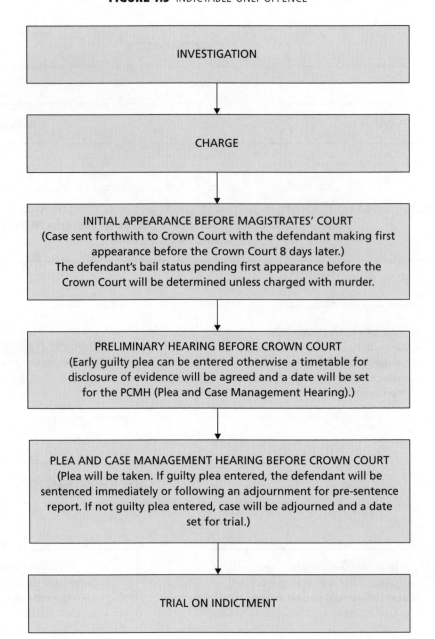

FIGURE 1.4 A FLOWCHART OF CRIMINAL PROCEDURE IN ENGLAND AND WALES

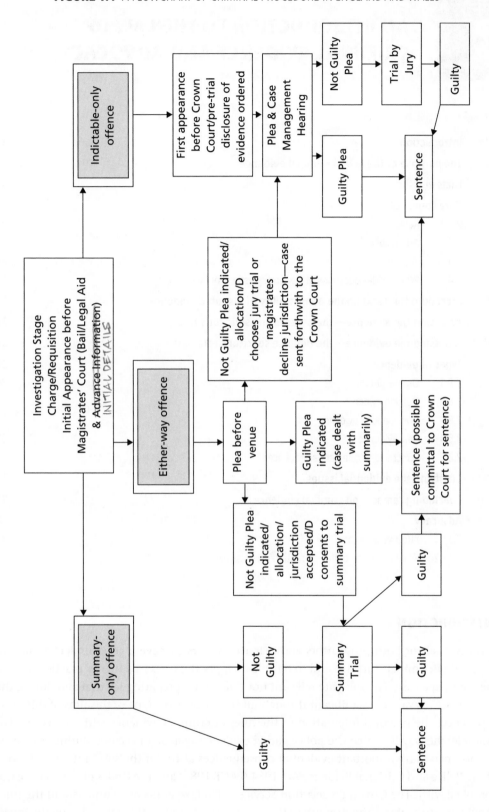

2 AN INTRODUCTION TO THE LAW OF CRIMINAL EVIDENCE AND ADVOCACY

2.1 INTRODUCTION

It is essential for both prosecutors and defence lawyers to have a good understanding of the rules of criminal evidence and to be able to apply the rules in a highly practical way to the issues in a case. The rules are relevant not only when preparing for trial and during the trial but are pervasively significant throughout the whole case. One of the aims of this book is to reflect the practical integration of the rules of criminal evidence with procedure. For example, the way in which the police gather evidence against an accused during the investigation may have important evidential consequences at trial if the substantive provisions of the Police and Criminal Evidence Act 1984 (PACE 1984) and the Codes of Practice are not complied with. The Crown Prosecution Service (CPS) lawyer needs to understand the rules of evidence to evaluate the strength of the evidence gathered by the police during the investigation to advise on the appropriate charge.

In preparing a client for the police interview the defence lawyer will need to apply his knowledge of the evidential rules to assess the strength of the prosecution evidence against his client to decide whether to advise silence.

Those of you in practice will already understand the importance of the rules of evidence to the work of a criminal lawyer. The challenge for law students is to recognise and apply the evidential rules in the practical context of real-life cases.

For those who require it this chapter provides a brief introduction to the main evidential rules which are considered further in later chapters. In particular, it addresses the following:

- the purpose of rules of evidence;
- the core concepts of relevance, admissibility and weight;
- the different types of evidence.

Later chapters will explain the rules of evidence in more detail.

2.2 THE PURPOSE OF THE LAW OF CRIMINAL EVIDENCE

The law of evidence is the body of rules which prescribe the ways in which evidence can be presented in a criminal trial. The rules regulate how the prosecution proves its case to the court and, in exceptional situations, how the defendant might prove his innocence. Most importantly, the rules of evidence seek to ensure that the accused receives a fair trial—a right guaranteed under Article 6 European Convention on Human Rights 1950. The right to a fair trial may require a court to exercise its judicial discretion to exclude or prevent the admission of a piece of evidence where it may have been obtained illegally or unfairly.

2.3 FACTS IN ISSUE

Where the defendant pleads not guilty, the facts in issue identify what has to be proven by the prosecution for the defendant to be found guilty, or exceptionally what the defendant has to prove in order to establish his or her innocence. The facts in issue are determined by reference to the *actus reus* and the *mens rea* of the offence with which the defendant is charged. Your knowledge of substantive criminal law is assumed. The burden of proving the defendant's guilt beyond reasonable doubt rests, for the most part, on the prosecution. In discharging the burden of proof, both the defence and the prosecution will have researched the elements of the offence(s) charged as these will identify what needs to be proved in a case. In a charge of theft under s. 1 Theft Act 1968 the facts in issue are:

Actus reus	*Mens rea*
Appropriates	Dishonestly
Property	Intention to permanently deprive
Belonging to another	

The prosecution must prove each element of the *actus reus* and the *mens rea* of the offence for the defendant to be found guilty. This may include disproving any defence relied on by the accused. This is known as discharging the legal burden of proof. The prosecution will discharge the legal burden of proof by putting evidence before the court in support of each fact in issue. Legal and evidential burdens of proof are considered in greater detail in Chapter 15.

2.4 CORE CONCEPTS

Criminal evidence has three core concepts: relevance, admissibility and weight.

2.4.1 RELEVANCE

For evidence to be put before the court, it must be relevant or probative of a fact in issue or to a collateral fact in a case such as the competency of a particular witness. Evidence assumes logical relevance if it has a bearing on the facts in issue in a particular case or to collateral facts that are relevant to the facts in issue. For evidence to be relevant, there must be a logical relationship between the evidence tendered and the fact to be proved.

All that is necessary for a piece of evidence to be admitted at trial is that it should increase or diminish the probability of the existence of a fact in issue. There are no special rules to decide the question of relevance—it is a matter of common sense. For example, on a charge of the theft of a bottle of wine from a supermarket, it is not relevant for the prosecution to put forward evidence that the defendant drove to the supermarket in a car with defective lights, or that the defendant has recently been divorced. It is relevant, however, for a prosecution witness to tell the court that he saw the accused put a bottle of wine under her coat and walk out of the supermarket without paying.

The relevance of evidence sometimes arises when admitting a defendant's bad character. For example, X is pleading not guilty to a sexual assault alleged to have been committed on an 11-year-old boy. Would it be relevant for the jury to know that X had pleaded guilty to an offence of downloading indecent images of children from the internet five years ago? What is relevant evidence when it comes to proving an intention to supply a controlled drug? On the general assumption that drug dealers prefer to deal in cash, is evidence of a quantity of cash found in the defendant's home, coupled with a lavish lifestyle, relevant to proving the defendant is currently dealing in drugs?

2.4.2 ADMISSIBILITY

For the court to receive evidence it not only has to be relevant to a fact in issue it must also be admissible. Admissible evidence is evidence which, as a matter of law, can be received by the court. Evidence will be admissible unless it is excluded either under a mandatory rule of exclusion or in the exercise of the court's discretion to ensure the defendant enjoys a fair trial. There are few categories of evidence which are mandatorily excluded apart from the opinion evidence of a lay witness and the unlawful disclosure of evidence protected by legal professional privilege. Most evidence is excluded at a criminal trial under the exercise of judicial discretion to ensure a defendant's right to a fair trial.

The right to a fair trial embraces many facets. Sometimes the right will require the exclusion of evidence which the prosecution seeks to admit as part of its case because of the manner in which the evidence was obtained by the police. This could apply to confession evidence or identification evidence obtained in breach of the defendant's rights under the substantive provisions of PACE 1984 and/or the Codes of Practice. Prosecution evidence may also be excluded if its admission would prejudice a fair trial. By prejudice we mean the damaging effect the admission of a particular piece of evidence might have on the minds of the jury or magistrates. Relevance and admissibility are closely connected. Would a jury or magistrates attach too much significance to a particular piece of evidence compared to other evidence in a case which might raise a reasonable doubt about the defendant's guilt? Consider the prejudice that could be caused by the admission of the defendant's previous conviction for downloading indecent images of children at X's trial for sexual assault in the earlier example. The discretion to exclude prosecution evidence is contained in s. 78 PACE 1984 (unfairness) whilst a general exclusionary discretion is available under s. 82(3) PACE 1984 (probative value outweighed by prejudicial effect).

Where the admissibility of evidence is disputed, the decision to admit or exclude evidence rests with the judge in the Crown Court and with the magistrates or District Judge in the magistrates' court. A decision to admit disputed evidence which results in a conviction may provide grounds for an appeal against conviction. Equally, a decision to exclude a particular piece of evidence may have profound implications for the prosecution's ability to discharge its legal burden of proof beyond reasonable doubt.

2.4.3 WEIGHT

Even where evidence is relevant and admissible, this does not mean that the jury or magistrates will find the evidence convincing or persuasive. In many cases an assessment of the weight of evidence is made on the basis of a wide range of factors. For example, when assessing the cogency of a witness giving oral testimony to the court, the following factors will be significant:

- the magistrate's or juror's intuition based on his or her life experiences;
- the age, demeanour, credibility of the witness; and
- the witness's involvement in the events about which he is testifying.

Less weight is likely to be attached to the evidence of a biased witness than to the testimony of a witness who is perceived to be 'independent'. Similarly, jurors or magistrates may be sceptical about believing a witness who has previous convictions for dishonesty and may therefore not attribute as much weight to that witness's evidence as to a witness with good character. Due to its exceptionally high reliability DNA evidence by contrast, is capable of carrying significant weight.

The weight to be attached to a particular piece of evidence is a matter for the jury in the Crown Court and the magistrates in summary proceedings. Advocates on either side may make representations about the weight to be attached to particular evidence in the case.

2.4.4 WHO DECIDES QUESTIONS OF LAW AND QUESTIONS OF FACT?

Questions arising in a trial will either be questions of law or questions of fact. In jury trials a strict division of responsibilities is applied between judge and jury: the trial judge determines all questions of law whilst the jury decides all questions of fact. Questions of law can include:

- issues of substantive criminal law;
- a witness's competence to give evidence;
- whether particular evidence should be admitted or excluded;
- whether to withdraw the case from the jury and direct an acquittal;
- the trial judge's directions when summing up to the jury.

An important part of the trial judge's role is summing up the case for the jury and directing the jury as to the relevant law. Judges are greatly assisted in this task by the Crown Court Bench Book (http://www.judiciary.gov.uk/publications-and-reports/judicial-college/Pre+2011/crown-court-bench-book-directing-the-jury) which contains explanations on all aspects of criminal law and evidence and examples of possible directions to the jury.

Questions of fact for the jury to decide include such matters as:

- the credibility of a witness;
- the weight to be accorded to a piece of evidence;
- whether the prosecution has discharged its legal burden of proof and proved the defendant's guilt beyond reasonable doubt.

In the magistrates' court, the magistrates are the ultimate arbiters of both fact and law. Advice on the law is provided by the magistrates' legal adviser.

2.5 PROCEDURE FOR DECIDING THE ADMISSIBILITY OF DISPUTED EVIDENCE

Often a dispute about the admissibility of evidence is resolved at a pre-trial hearing. A binding ruling on a point of law may be given at this hearing based purely on legal argument. Sometimes, however, it is necessary for evidence to be adduced and for findings of fact to be made before the admissibility of a particular piece of evidence can be decided. Where this is necessary a *voir dire,* or trial within a trial will need to be held during the course of the trial. The *voir dire* procedure works more effectively in the Crown Court because of the separation of functions between the judge and the jury as previously highlighted. If, after hearing the evidence and legal arguments the trial judge decides that the disputed evidence must be excluded, the jury will never know about the existence of the disputed evidence.

2.6 ASSESSING THE EVIDENCE—THE PROSECUTING SOLICITOR'S ROLE

In deciding whether a prosecution should be commenced, the Code for Crown Prosecutors (see Chapter 8) requires the CPS lawyer to determine whether there is sufficient evidence to secure a conviction. In making this assessment, the CPS lawyer will be mindful of the rules of evidence. The CPS lawyer has no active investigative role and therefore must assess the evidence gathered by the police by considering the witness statements and items of real evidence which may have been subject to forensic analysis. The prosecutor now has direct access to witnesses but this is not routinely exercised. Based on the assessment of the evidence, the CPS lawyer might suggest to the police that further investigation is needed or will be satisfied that there is sufficient evidence to charge the suspect.

2.7 ASSESSING THE EVIDENCE—THE DEFENCE SOLICITOR'S ROLE

Irrespective of whether the defendant is to be tried summarily or on indictment, the rules relating to pre-trial disclosure of evidence mean the defence solicitor will know the evidence against his client before trial. In assessing the strength of the disclosed prosecution evidence, the defence advocate should apply the core concepts of relevance, admissibility and weight to make an initial assessment of whether the prosecution has a case against the defendant; to identify any prosecution evidence that might be challenged; and to advise the client about plea. The defence lawyer should not advise a guilty plea unless the evidence against his client is relevant, admissible and persuasive.

2.8 TYPES OF EVIDENCE

Where evidence is relevant and admissible, it will be presented to the court in one of the following forms.

2.8.1 ORAL TESTIMONY

This is evidence given orally by a witness in court on factual matters within the witness's personal knowledge and experience. An example of a witness giving factual evidence would include the witness stating that: 'I saw the defendant break the car window and drive the car away at speed.' In a criminal trial, direct oral testimony is the preferred way for evidence to be put before the court and is likely to be the type of evidence that the court will find the most persuasive.

2.8.2 OPINION EVIDENCE

A witness is called at a trial to give factual evidence based on the witness's personal knowledge and experience. The witness should not offer an opinion on what they saw or heard. The general rule is that where a witness gives opinion evidence, it will be inadmissible. It would not be possible for a witness to state: 'It's obvious that the defendant killed him.'

There are two exceptions to this general rule: First, an expert may give opinion evidence on a matter that goes beyond the ordinary competence of the court. A common form of expert evidence adduced at a criminal trial is the evidence of a forensic scientist or medical expert. Expert evidence is considered in more detail in Chapter 17. Second, a lay person may state his or her opinion on a matter not requiring expertise as a way of conveying facts that they have personally perceived. A witness will be allowed to say that when she saw the accused 'he appeared to be drunk', or 'the car was speeding immediately before it hit the pedestrian'.

2.8.3 DOCUMENTARY EVIDENCE

Relevant and admissible evidence may be contained in a document. A witness statement is an example of documentary evidence. Other types of documentary evidence include:

- photographs;
- maps;
- plans;
- computer print-outs;
- business documents;
- expert reports.

2.8.4 REAL EVIDENCE

Real evidence comprises objects produced in court so the court may draw inferences from the condition and existence of the object. In a murder trial, a knife produced as the murder weapon, or the defendant's bloodstained clothing, would be examples of real evidence. In a public order offence, CCTV or mobile telephone footage of the incident would constitute real evidence.

2.8.5 DIRECT AND CIRCUMSTANTIAL EVIDENCE

In whatever form evidence is admitted, it will have either direct or circumstantial relevance. Direct evidence requires nothing more of the jury or magistrates than an acceptance or rejection of the evidence that has been given. If X testifies that he saw Y walk up to Z, take out a knife and stab Z, this is direct evidence of the *actus reus* of murder. At his trial for murder, however, Y calls a witness who states she was with Y at the time of the alleged murder 30 miles away. If accepted, this constitutes direct evidence of alibi. Circumstantial evidence requires the court not only to accept the witness's account but also to draw an inference from the evidence. If X testifies that he saw Y running away from Z and that he observed Y had bloodstains on his clothing, this would constitute circumstantial evidence linking Y to the murder of Z. Expert forensic evidence may suggest that the blood on Y's clothing matches that of the victim Z. Again, if the evidence is accepted by the court, it provides circumstantial evidence that Y was in close contact with the victim of the crime at the relevant time. A criminal case may be based entirely on circumstantial evidence. The trial of Ian Huntley (2003) for the murders of Holly Wells and Jessica Chapman and the trial of Steve Wright (2008) for the murders of five prostitutes in Ipswich are examples of two high-profile convictions based on circumstantial evidence.

2.9 CLARIFYING THE EVIDENTIAL ISSUES

In any contested criminal case there will be a number of evidential issues. It is important, however, not to lose sight of the 'big picture'. Advocates on each side need to make sense of the evidence and to develop a theory of the case which is supported by the evidence. In this way a coherent and focused case can be put before the jury or magistrates. The core issues in a case need to be distilled from the mass of detail and if the case is to be contested, a defence theory needs to be developed.

The defence theory is a clear and concise explanation of why the case should be resolved in the defendant's favour. In devising a plausible defence theory, the evidence that needs to be challenged and marshalled will become clear. On a charge of theft, for example, if the defendant denies a dishonest intent, the defence advocate will need to marshall the evidence and develop an argument with this central issue in mind. Perhaps the defendant will challenge the prosecution's suggestion that he or she was responsible for the crime, on the basis of mistaken identification. If this is the defence theory of the case, the defence advocate should concentrate on challenging the prosecution's evidence of identification and present any evidence which supports the theory advanced by the defendant such as evidence of alibi. The development of a theory of the case helps both the prosecution and defence advocates decide the questions to be asked of a witness in both examination-in-chief and in cross-examination. This is why, in a contested case, it is important for both the prosecution and the defence to crystallise the facts in issue.

2.10 CONCLUDING REMARKS ON CRIMINAL EVIDENCE

This chapter has introduced some of the core concepts that apply in the context of criminal evidence. Later chapters will examine the evidential considerations that arise in the context of:

- a confession made to the police;
- obtaining evidence of eye-witness identification;
- a defendant exercising a right to silence at the police station;
- admitting hearsay evidence;
- admitting evidence of a defendant's bad character;
- the admissibility of opinion evidence;
- evidence of corroboration;
- the evidence of a child or mentally handicapped witness;
- the admissibility of illegally/unfairly obtained prosecution evidence.

The rules are significant at all stages of a criminal case, and a good understanding of the law and the ability to apply the principles in a practical way to the facts of the case are important for the successful criminal litigator. The rules of criminal evidence cannot be ignored—so in a determined and purposeful way, after carefully reading this introductory chapter, move on to the other chapters which deal with the evidential rules in practice.

2.11 ADVOCACY

Advocacy is the legal skill most often associated with criminal litigation. Put simply, advocacy is the art of communication. Having come this far you will hopefully have begun to develop your oral communication skills and an ability to put forward structured and coherent arguments. Those skills now need to be harnessed and applied in a different context.

The most common situations where a criminal advocate's oral presentation skills can be highly significant are at contested bail hearings, pleas in mitigation of sentence and, of course, in conducting trials. Unless you are already qualified, it will be some time before you undertake any of these independently, although non-legally qualified staff do have rights of audience before Crown Court judges in chambers and may therefore represent a defendant on a bail application following a magistrates' court refusal to grant bail. In this short section on advocacy we identify some of the key components of the art of persuasion.

2.11.1 EFFECTIVE ADVOCACY

Whether appearing for the prosecution or the defence, effective advocacy depends on:

- good preparation; and
- persuasive oral communication skills.

Good preparation presupposes a thorough knowledge of both the facts in the case and the relevant law. For example, when making or opposing a bail application, you would be expected to have a good working knowledge of the Bail Act 1976 and to apply the facts of the case to the law. The submission of a plea in mitigation presupposes a thorough knowledge of sentencing principles and practice.

Similarly, if you were to make an application to have evidence excluded at trial, your preparation would have alerted you to the relevant legal basis of your submission and the facts that you would need to prove in order to substantiate your submission.

Whilst knowledge and understanding of the relevant law and facts are important, you must also be able to present your legal argument in a structured, coherent and persuasive way.

2.11.2 WHAT MAKES AN ORAL PRESENTATION PERSUASIVE?

The following checklist is based on our experience of developing and assessing advocacy skills in various contexts. Whatever the context of your presentation, an awareness of what may be termed 'credibility factors' may help.

Eye contact

Eye contact greatly enhances an oral presentation. It shows you are confident enough to move away from a prepared script and enables you to assess and gauge the reaction your submission is having on your listener. If you want to get your message across you must engage your listener. Maintaining eye contact is an obvious way of helping to achieve this.

Posture

Do not slouch. Stand up straight with your head slightly elevated. Posture affects the resonance of your voice. Your posture should make you appear relaxed and confident.

Voice

Accents are not a problem, providing you are clear in your enunciation of words. The acoustics vary from courtroom to courtroom so you may need to explore your voice audibility levels. Avoid being too loud and aggressive, or too softly spoken. The latter does not inspire confidence. Deep breathing (from the diaphragm) can help your voice to resonate more, thereby making you more audible. If you think you have a monotone delivery, try to get some vocal variety into your voice. Try reading a children's story to a young relative: you will soon find out ways to make your delivery more interesting.

Pace

It is very important to correctly pace your submission. True advocacy is not about reading from a prepared script, as this will make it more likely that you will read too quickly and consequently your audience will be unable to follow your argument. Too slow a delivery can have a stultifying effect upon your audience. Experiment, and choose a pace that is suitable.

Pause

The pause is a simple but very effective persuasive device. Use it for dramatic effect. If you have a particularly telling point to advance, make the point and then . . . pause momentarily. Allow the point to be considered by your listener. Used in combination with voice inflection, the effect should resonate with your audience.

Distracting mannerisms

We all have them. You will be the best judge of your own distracting mannerisms. If you have the opportunity, why not record yourself making an oral submission. When you review your performance, ask yourself: does my body language detract from the message I am putting across? Are you fiddling with the loose change in your pocket or juggling a pen in your hands? Do you sway from side to side? Are you constantly touching your face or your hair? Look at the expression on your face. Is it the face of someone who feels relaxed and confident in the submission they are making? Do you look up and smile occasionally or are you frowning/perplexed/refusing to make eye contact? All of these mannerisms distract from the message you are trying to put across.

Structure

A persuasive argument will be delivered in a structured fashion. Devising a structure should help you to avoid unnecessary repetition. The simplest and most effective structure for any submission is for it to have a beginning, middle and end. Break up your submission into listener-friendly portions, e.g.:

> 'Ma'am, I have three points I would like to make this morning: My first point is this . . . . my second point is this . . . . my third and final point is this. . . . . In summary, Ma'am . . . . '

Sometimes the nature of your submission will determine its structure. When preparing and delivering a submission on bail, for example, the Bail Act 1976 provides a logical structure within which to work.

Keep your submission concise. Cut down on the verbiage. Try to avoid reading out sections from statute and case law. Copy and highlight the relevant sections/passages and then hand them in for the Bench/judge to read.

Brevity

You will soon come to realise that a court's time is very precious. With this in mind, always try to make your submission succinct. Developing a logical structure to your submission will assist. Try to avoid unnecessary repetition.

Persona

It is important when appearing as an advocate that you look confident—even if you do not feel confident! Dressing suitably and smartly helps an advocate to step into the role. It also helps to inspire confidence in you and conveys the correct impression to the court, your client and the public. First impressions really do count. Without being dramatic, your opening address needs to capture the court's attention. Consider carefully what sort of individual engages you on an intellectual level? The more open and interesting the advocate's personality, the more likely the audience will be attentive. Behavioural psychology has much to teach the aspiring advocate!

Be prepared to make appropriate concessions. Avoid being arrogant or patronising. Organise yourself and your notes so that your composure and professionalism come across.

Etiquette

You must be familiar with the etiquette of the court you are appearing before. This includes dressing appropriately and properly addressing the court and your opponent.

A trainee defence solicitor does not have a right of audience before a magistrates' court or the Crown Court but can appear in a closed hearing before a Crown Court judge in chambers in connection with a bail application. Solicitors (and, subject to certain restrictions, Associate Prosecutors) have a right of audience before a magistrates' court. A solicitor has a limited right of audience before the Crown Court on an appeal against conviction and/or sentence where the solicitor represented the defendant in the magistrates' court. Some solicitors have a Higher Right of Audience qualification which enables them to exercise full rights of audience before the Crown Court. When appearing as a solicitor-advocate before a Crown Court, a solicitor must be appropriately robed in a black stuffed gown and winged collar.

The correct form of address before a judge of the Crown Court (which would include a circuit judge or recorder) is 'Your Honour . . . ' You should always defer to the court and be extremely courteous. With this in mind you will often hear the phrase: 'May it please Your Honour, I appear on behalf of the defendant in this matter.' 'Has Your Honour had the time to consider the pre-sentence report that has been prepared in connection with this matter? I am grateful for that indication.'

The correct form of address before a district or deputy District Judge sitting in a magistrates' court is 'Sir' or 'Madam'.

When addressing a Bench of lay magistrates, the correct term of address is 'Your worships, or Sir/Madam and your colleagues . . . '.

Solicitors refer to a fellow solicitor as 'my friend for the prosecution' or 'my friend for the defence'. A barrister or counsel is referred to as being 'my learned friend'. It is customary to refer to the court's legal adviser as 'your learned legal adviser . . .'.

As an officer of the court, a solicitor should always be appropriately attired when appearing before a court. Where this does not require the solicitor to be duly robed, suitable attire will normally be a sombre-coloured suit.

Language

Persuasion is as much about your choice of language as anything else. Words can be very powerful tools with which to convey a message. Think carefully about your choice of words. Can you find a more powerful adjective to advance the point you are making? Try to use language which includes your audience. For example, you might say: 'Let's examine together the circumstances in which the defendant's confession was obtained. . . .'. Personalise the situation: 'Ma'am, I invite you to consider what you would have done in the same situation as my client. . . .'.

Some people are natural advocates. They have charm and exude confidence. If they combine their natural ability with knowledge and application of the law, they are capable of making a persuasive submission even in the most hopeless of cases. Other individuals might initially be less comfortable in the spotlight which the art of advocacy demands. Advocacy skills can be developed with practice and reflection.

online
resource
centre

If you are accessing our Online Resource Centre you will be able to see some examples of advocacy in our filmed case studies. *R v Lenny Wise* contains a fully contested application for bail. *R v Hardy* and *R v Martin* both comprise pleas in mitigation. The specifics of each of these submissions are considered in the chapter on bail and the chapters on sentencing. **The clips should be viewed as learning aids that illustrate, in a practical way, aspects of criminal practice. They should not be regarded as definitive examples of how advocacy might be conducted before a criminal court.**

KEY POINT SUMMARY

- Generally the prosecution bears the legal burden of proving a defendant's guilt beyond reasonable doubt. The elements of the offence charged determine what the prosecution needs to prove if it is to secure a conviction.

- To be admissible, evidence must be relevant to the facts in issue but not all relevant evidence is admissible.

- Evidence can be excluded under the mandatory rules of exclusion and/or through the exercise of judicial discretion in the interests of ensuring a fair trial.

- In the Crown Court, matters of relevance and admissibility of evidence are determined by the judge in the absence of the jury. Matters of fact are determined by the jury. There is no separation of function in the magistrates' court and so magistrates determine matters of fact and law.

- An accused is entitled to pre-trial disclosure of the evidence to be used against him, enabling his advocate to evaluate the strengths and weaknesses of the prosecution case.

- Where an accused chooses to plead guilty, the evidence against him is not tested in open court.

SELF-TEST QUESTIONS

Case study: *R v Lenny Wise*

Consider documents 6 and 26(A–Q) in Appendix 1. Given that we have yet to cover the rules of criminal evidence in detail, simply describe in very general terms the nature of the evidence that is said to link

Lenny Wise to the burglary allegation. In doing so, can you identify any issues of evidence this scenario is likely to give rise to? In simplistic terms at this stage, consider how Lenny will challenge the nature of the evidence against him and in doing so, start to formulate a theory of the defence case.

online
resource
centre

An analysis of all self-test questions can be found on the Online Resource Centre.

FIGURE 2.1 AN OVERVIEW OF CRIMINAL EVIDENCE

PURPOSES OF THE LAW OF EVIDENCE

- The law of evidence regulates how the prosecution or the defence proves its case to the court.

- The rules determine what evidence may be received and what evidential use can be made of that evidence, and in so doing they seek to ensure the defendant receives a fair trial.

- In the Crown Court, the judge determines the admissibility of disputed evidence in the absence of the jury.

- In a summary trial, issues relating to the admissibility of disputed evidence are resolved by the magistrates with legal advice provided by their legal adviser.

FACTS IN ISSUE

- The primary facts in issue are the *actus reus* and the *mens rea* of the offence charged and any defence raised by the accused.

- It is for the prosecution (or exceptionally the defence) to prove the facts that are in issue at a trial.

- The facts in issue can also include secondary facts which are relevant to the facts in issue such as the admissibility of a piece of evidence.

BASIC EVIDENTIAL RULES

- To be heard at trial, evidence must be:

  - **relevant** to a fact in issue; and be

  - **admissible** (i.e. as a matter of law, the evidence can be put before the court).

- The **weight** to be afforded to a particular piece of evidence is a question of fact for the jury/magistrates.

TYPES OF ADMISSIBLE EVIDENCE

- Relevant and admissible evidence will be presented at trial as one of the following types:

  - oral testimony;

  - documentary evidence;

  - real evidence.

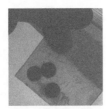

Part II

INVESTIGATION AND THE DECISION TO CHARGE

Part II deals with the investigation of criminal offences and the decision to charge.

In Chapter 3 we explain general and specific police powers of investigation and in Chapter 4 the process of detention and questioning. In Chapter 5 we explore the evidential rules and practical issues concerning the position of a suspect in the police interview. The rules of evidence for challenging 'tainted' prosecution evidence are considered in Chapter 6, and the admissibility of identification evidence in Chapter 7. Finally, the decision to charge a suspect or to offer alternatives to prosecution are considered in Chapter 8, which also examines the role of the Crown Prosecution Service (CPS) and its duties of pre-trial disclosure of evidence.

Part II is supplemented by a further chapter available online **online resource centre** through the Online Resource Centre which focuses on the practical steps that a legal adviser might take at the police station and explains the process of police station accreditation.

3 THE POWERS TO STOP, SEARCH AND ARREST

3.1 INTRODUCTION

The police have extensive statutory powers to stop and search and to arrest a person in connection with the investigation of a criminal offence. Under the Police and Criminal Evidence Act 1984 (PACE 1984), the power to stop and search and arrest are general powers, to be used in a wide range of situations. The police also have a vast array of specific powers to stop, search and arrest under various statutes, including the Terrorism Act 2000, the Misuse of Drugs Act 1971 and the Serious Organised Crime and Police Act 2005.

In this chapter we examine:

* powers of stop and search before arrest;
* powers of arrest under PACE 1984;

- powers to search a person and his property after arrest;
- the power to grant street bail; and
- the right to liberty under Article 5 European Convention on Human Rights (ECHR 1950).

Reference will be made throughout this chapter to PACE 1984 Code of Practice A, which deals with police powers to stop and search, and Code B, which governs the search and seizure of property. Both Codes can be accessed online from the Home Office. Our Online Resource Centre includes a link to the PACE 1984 Codes of Practice.

**online
resource
centre**

3.2 STOP AND SEARCH BEFORE ARREST

The primary purpose of stop and search is to enable an officer to allay or confirm his suspicion about a person being in possession of stolen or prohibited articles or drugs without arresting him. Stop and search is one of the most controversial aspects of police powers and consequently the law provides detailed guidance about the officer's conduct when questioning or searching a person in a public place before arrest.

3.3 STOP AND SEARCH AT COMMON LAW

At common law, an officer cannot stop or detain a person unless the person volunteers to co-operate with the officer (*Rice v Connelly* [1966] 2 All ER 64). Code A, Notes for Guidance para. 1, recognises that an officer may speak to a person in the normal course of his duties without detaining him or exercising any compulsion over the person. The person being questioned has a civic but not a legal duty to assist the officer.

Unless the officer exercises a statutory power to stop and search or arrest, the person cannot be compelled to remain with the officer.

3.4 STATUTORY POWERS TO STOP AND SEARCH IN A PUBLIC PLACE BEFORE ARREST

The police have wide statutory powers to stop and search a person or his motor vehicle, which can be exercised either under a general power or under a specific stop and search power.

3.4.1 THE GENERAL POWER TO STOP AND SEARCH—S. 1 PACE 1984

Section 1 PACE 1984 (as supplemented by Code A) gives the police the general power to stop and search a person and/or his vehicle before arrest in a public place or a place to which the public have access, where the officer has reasonable grounds for suspecting the person is in possession of stolen or prohibited articles.

Paragraph 1.1 Code A, requires that stop and search must be used 'fairly, responsibly, with respect for those being searched and without unlawful discrimination'.

To be a lawful search under s. 1 PACE 1984, the following factors must be present:

(1) The stop and search must be in connection with stolen or prohibited articles
Stop and search under s. 1 PACE 1984 may be exercised to discover:

- stolen articles; or
- prohibited articles; or
- an article to be used for an offence under s. 139 Criminal Justice Act 1988 (possession of a bladed instrument); or
- a prohibited firework.

What are stolen articles?

'Stolen' articles have the same meaning as in the Theft Act 1968 and includes items arising from an offence of theft, burglary, robbery or criminal deception.

What are prohibited articles?

'Prohibited' articles include offensive weapons or articles made or adapted for use or intended use in an offence under the Theft Act 1968 and under s. 1 Criminal Damage Act 1971. The Theft Act 1968 offences include theft (s. 1), burglary (s. 9), taking a motor vehicle without consent (s. 12) or fraud (s. 1 Fraud Act 2006) and includes items such as a crow-bar, car keys, a credit card or any relevant item provided the user has the necessary intent to commit an offence under the 1968 Act.

An offensive weapon, similar to s. 1 Prevention of Crime Act 1953, is an article made or adapted for use for causing injury to a person or intended for such use and includes articles that are offensive weapons in themselves such as knives and guns and everyday articles that have been made or adapted for use as an offensive weapon including, for example, a bottle that has been deliberately broken.

(2) The requirement for reasonable suspicion

Under s. 1 PACE 1984, reasonable suspicion will be present where:

- the officer has actual suspicion that the person is in possession of stolen or prohibited articles (the subjective test); and
- there are reasonable grounds for that suspicion (the objective test).

Detailed guidance on the meaning of reasonable suspicion is found in Code A paras. 2.2–2.11. Code A stipulates that reasonable suspicion:

- is determined on the facts of each case, including the time and the place the power was exercised and the suspect's behaviour, for example, where the suspect is seen by the officer on the street late at night and appears to be hiding something;
- can never be determined on the basis of personal factors such as the person's race, ethnic background, religion, appearance or previous convictions;
- should normally be based on good, reliable and recent police intelligence.

For judicial guidance on the reasonable suspicion test, see *O'Hara v Chief Constable, RUC* [1997] AC 286, at para. 3.7.6.

(3) Where can the stop and search take place?

The officer may only stop and search in a 'public place or a place to which the public has access', s. 1(1) PACE 1984. This includes the street or in a park or in a cinema, which are places to which the public has access. The power under s. 1 PACE cannot be exercised inside the suspect's home or in any other dwelling without the occupier's consent but may be exercised in a garden or yard attached to a house where the officer reasonably believes that the suspect does not live at that address and is not on the land with the express or implied permission of the occupier.

(4) Additional rights under s. 1 PACE 1984 and Code A

- In accordance with Code A para. 3.8, the officer must explain that the person is being detained for the purpose of a search. In addition, the officer must tell the person his name (unless the officer thinks this will place him in danger in which case a warrant or identification number must be given) and the police station at which he is based; the legal search power that is being used; the object of the proposed search; and the person's entitlement to a copy of the record of the search if they ask within three months of the date of the search. Code A requires a police officer in plain clothes who wishes to stop and search to produce a warrant card before exercising the power. A failure to do so will result in the search being unlawful as the officer would not be acting in the execution of his or her duty (see *B v DPP* [2008] EWHC 1655 (Admin)).

- The search must be conducted at or near the place where the suspect was first detained. Reasonable force may be used as a last resort.

- Generally, only the suspect's outer clothing should be searched—where the search requires the removal of more than the outer clothing it should be conducted in private (for example in a police van or nearby police station).

- The officer must make a record of the search at the time unless there are exceptional circumstances which would make this wholly impracticable. A copy of the record must be given immediately to the person. Alternatively, the person can be given an electronic receipt of the stop and search. The officer must explain how a full copy of the record can be obtained. The required contents of the written record are set out in Code A para. 4.3.

 Example

Consider the following illustration of a search conducted under s. 1 PACE 1984.

WPC Atherton is on uniform night patrol when she sees Danny walking through the town centre carrying a tool bag. There have been several burglaries in the locality in recent months. When the officer stops and questions Danny, she is exercising her powers under s. 1 PACE 1984. The officer will be acting lawfully if the following conditions are present:

- Danny has been stopped in a public place or a place to which the public has access;
- the officer had reasonable suspicion based on the recognised tests;
- the purpose of the stop and search was to discover whether Danny was in possession of stolen or prohibited articles or articles to be used in connection with an offence of criminal damage;
- the procedural requirements of Code A were complied with.

3.5 SPECIFIC POWERS TO STOP AND SEARCH BEFORE ARREST

There are statutory stop and search powers available to the police to use in specific situations. A summary of the main stop and search powers is contained in Annex A of Code A and includes the power to search for drugs (Misuse of Drugs Act 1971). In addition to the general power of stop and search under s. 1 PACE 1984, there is a further power to stop and search under s. 60 Criminal Justice and Public Order Act 1994 upon the authorisation of an inspector who reasonably believes that incidents involving serious violence may take place in the local area and it is expedient to give an authorisation to prevent their occurrence, or that dangerous or offensive weapons are being carried or have been used in the local area. An officer can stop and search under this statutory provision without any reasonable grounds. Code A similarly regulates the exercise of this power.

3.6 THE CONSEQUENCES OF AN UNLAWFUL STOP AND SEARCH

If a suspect has been unlawfully stopped and searched, for example, if the police officer cannot prove he or she had reasonable grounds to support the decision to stop and search, the admissibility of any resulting evidence may be challenged at trial by the defence under s. 78 PACE 1984 on the basis that the admission of the evidence would have 'an adverse effect on the fairness of the proceedings'. This provision is considered more fully in Chapter 6. An unlawful stop and search would provide a defence for a person suspected of obstructing/resisting or assaulting a police constable in the execution of his or her duty. In *R v Bristol* [2007] EWCA Crim 3214, B's conviction for obstructing a police constable in the execution of his duty was quashed as the officer, who was exercising a power to stop and search under the Misuse of Drugs Act 1971, had failed to give his name and police station when applying force to B's jaw in an attempt to get him to spit out a suspected ingestion of drugs.

3.7 POWERS OF ARREST

An arrest will occur during a criminal investigation where the police have the legal and factual grounds to justify depriving the suspect's liberty. The usual reason for arrest is to question the suspect about possible involvement in, or knowledge of, a criminal offence.

3.7.1 WHAT IS AN ARREST?

While there is no legal definition of 'arrest', *Christie v Leachinsky* [1947] AC 573 suggested that an arrest was 'the beginning of imprisonment'. On a factual basis, a person will be under arrest where the person is deprived of his or her liberty, usually, though not exclusively, by physical restraint, so that the person is not free to go where he or she pleases.

Common law and statutory powers of arrest exist in the following situations:

- at common law an officer can arrest the suspect for a breach of the peace;
- the execution of an arrest warrant obtained from a magistrate—s. 1 Magistrates' Courts Act 1980;
- arrest without a warrant by a police constable in connection with a criminal offence where the legal grounds under s. 24(1), (2) or (3) and s. 24(4) PACE 1984 apply;
- arrest without a warrant by a citizen in connection with an indictable offence where the legal grounds under s. 24A PACE 1984 apply;
- preserved powers of arrest in a limited range of offences listed in Sch. 2 PACE 1984.

3.7.2 ARREST AT COMMON LAW

The common law power of arrest applies in connection with an anticipated or an actual breach of the peace. The arrest may be made by a police officer or member of the public.

3.7.3 ARREST WITH A WARRANT—S. 1 MAGISTRATES' COURTS ACT 1980

Arrest under a warrant is now a less common method of detaining a suspect. Section 1 Magistrates' Courts Act 1980 states that a justice of the peace may issue an arrest warrant on the basis of written information substantiated on oath that a person has or is suspected of having committed an offence, and:

- the suspect is over the age of 18;
- the offence alleged is indictable or punishable with imprisonment; or
- the suspect's address cannot be sufficiently established for the service of a written charge/ summons.

3.7.4 STATUTORY POWER OF ARREST—S. 24 PACE 1984 AND CODE G

There is a single, generic power of arrest for all offences contained in s. 24 PACE 1984, as amended. Code G, para. 1.3 provides that the use of the statutory power of arrest must be fully justified and officers exercising the power should consider if the necessary objectives can be met by other, less intrusive means. It goes on to provide that the absence of justification for exercising the power of arrest may lead to challenges should the case proceed to court and could also lead to civil claims against police for unlawful arrest and false imprisonment.

3.7.5 ARREST WITHOUT A WARRANT BY A CONSTABLE

The main power of arrest without a warrant under s. 24(1)–(3) PACE 1984 is exercisable by a police officer in connection with any criminal offence. For there to be a lawful arrest, two key elements must be present:

- a person's involvement in or suspected involvement in or attempted involvement in the commission of an offence; and
- reasonable grounds for believing that the person's arrest is necessary.

Under s. 24(1) PACE 1984, an officer may arrest without a warrant:

'(a) anyone who is about to commit an offence; or

(b) anyone who is in the act of committing an offence; or

(c) anyone whom he has reasonable grounds for suspecting to be about to commit an offence; or

(d) anyone whom he has reasonable grounds for suspecting to be committing an offence.

(2) If a constable has reasonable grounds for suspecting that an offence has been committed, he may arrest without a warrant anyone whom he has reasonable grounds to suspect being guilty of it.

(3) If an offence has been committed a constable may arrest without a warrant—

(a) anyone who is guilty of the offence;

(b) anyone whom he has reasonable grounds for suspecting to be guilty of it.'

For the arrest to be lawful not only must one of the grounds in s. 24(1)–(3) PACE 1984 be made out, the officer must additionally prove that he or she had reasonable grounds for believing that an arrest was *necessary* (s. 24(4)) for one or more of the reasons listed in s. 24(5) PACE 1984.

The '*necessity*' conditions which are set out in s. **24(5)** PACE and which are further defined in Code G include:

(a) *to enable the person's name to be ascertained where the constable does not know and cannot readily ascertain the person's name or has reasonable grounds for doubting the name given by the person is the person's real name* – (this includes the situation where the person's name cannot be readily ascertained or the officer has grounds for doubting whether the name given by the person is, in fact, his real name);

(b) *to enable the person's address to be ascertained* – (an officer might decide that a person's address cannot be readily ascertained if they fail or refuse to give it when asked, particularly after being warned that such a failure or refusal is likely to make their arrest necessary);

(c) *to prevent the person in question:*

(i) causing physical injury to himself or another;

(ii) suffering physical injury;

(iii) causing loss or damage to property;

(iv) committing an offence against public decency;

(v) causing unlawful obstruction of the highway;

(This might apply where the suspect has already used or threatened violence against others and it is thought likely that he may assault others if he is not arrested or where the suspect's behaviour and actions are believed likely to provoke, or have provoked, others to want to assault him unless he is arrested for his own protection.);

(d) *to protect a child or vulnerable person from the person;*

(e) *to allow the prompt and effective investigation of the offence or, of the conduct of the person* – (This is the widest necessity ground and is the one that has given rise to a number of recent judicial review decisions. The prompt investigation of an offence can include the need to interview the suspect when the person's voluntary attendance is not considered to be a practicable alternative to arrest because it is thought that the suspect is unlikely to attend voluntarily for interview; or arrest would enable the special warning to be given under ss. 36 and 37 CJPOA 1994 (see Chapter 5); or it is thought likely that they will steal or destroy evidence or threaten potential witnesses; or because there is a need to exercise a power of search under s. 18 PACE 1984; or when considering arrest in connection with an offence to which the statutory Class A drug testing requirements in Code C apply, to enable testing when it is thought that drug misuse might have caused or contributed to the offence. See Chapter 4.);

(f) *to prevent the prosecution for the offence being hindered by the disappearance of the person in question* – (This may be used where there are grounds for believing that if the person is not arrested he will not attend court.).

The arrest conditions give police officers operational discretion to decide whether an arrest is necessary by requiring the officer to examine and justify the reason(s) why a person should be taken to the police station for the custody officer to decide whether the person should be detained (see Code G para. 2.6). In deciding whether to make an arrest, the officer will consider the particular circumstances of the case including the victim's situation; the nature of the offence; the circumstances of the offender; and the needs of the investigation (Code G para. 2.8). Instead of arresting an individual, a police officer could charge by post, grant street bail (see later) or issue a fixed penalty notice.

The requirement for an arrest to be necessary has given rise to an ever-increasing body of case law, particularly in relation to s. 24(5)(e) PACE (above). If a police officer cannot establish that it is necessary for him to arrest the individual concerned, the arrest and any continued detention is unlawful. No individual should be arrested simply because the power of arrest is available. Revisions to PACE Code G, para. 1.2 make it clear that the exercise of the power of arrest has 'an obvious and significant interference with the right to liberty and security under Art 5 ECHR'. It warns police officers that the absence of justification for exercising a power of arrest may lead to challenges in court and claims against police for unlawful arrest and false imprisonment. In *Re Alexander* [2009] NIQB 20, it was held that an officer who does not apply his mind to alternatives short of arrest (such as inviting the suspect to attend the police station for interview on a voluntary basis) is open to challenge. Further detailed guidance on the necessity test and its practical application by police officers is provided in Code G.

3.7.6 THE REQUIREMENTS FOR A LAWFUL ARREST UNDER S. 24 PACE 1984

An arrest will only be lawful under s. 24 PACE 1984 where:

(i)   the officer has reasonable grounds to suspect the person has been involved in a criminal offence; and

(ii) an arrest is necessary; and

(iii) the person is told the reason for his arrest and properly cautioned; and

(iv) the person is taken to a designated police station as soon as reasonably practicable.

The reasonable grounds requirement is applied in accordance with the two-part test from the House of Lords' case of *O'Hara v Chief Constable, RUC* [1997] AC 286.

• First, there must be actual suspicion on the part of the officer that an offence was at some stage of commission; and

• second, there must be reasonable grounds for that suspicion.

Code G, para. 2.3A provides that:

'Before making a decision to arrest, a constable should therefore make all efforts that it is reasonably practicable to make in the circumstances to identify facts and information which point to the person's innocence as well as their guilt.'

(1) The first requirement involves a subjective assessment by the police officer, whilst the second requirement is assessed objectively. Whilst the threshold to satisfy the reasonable grounds test is low, it will not be satisfied where the arresting officer has been instructed by a superior officer to make an arrest or where the arresting officer believes that a superior officer probably did have information to justify an arrest but which the superior officer had not conveyed to the arresting officer (see *Raissi v Metropolitan Police Commissioner* [2008] EWCA Civ 1237).

(2) The arresting officer must also have reasonable grounds for believing that an arrest is necessary in accordance with s. 24(5) PACE 1984; (see 3.7.5).

(3) The officer must inform the suspect of the grounds and reasons for the arrest (i.e. why an arrest is necessary—Code G para. 2.2) and must caution the suspect, in accordance with Code G paras. 3.1–3.7, in the following terms:

'You do not have to say anything. But it may harm your defence if you do not mention when questioned something which you later rely on in court. Anything you do say may be given in evidence.'

(4) The suspect must then be taken to a designated police station as soon as is reasonably practicable (s. 30 PACE 1984), unless the suspect is granted street bail (see later).

 Example

Consider the following scenario. Do you feel the arrest by PC Taylor was justified?

John is 30 but looks considerably younger. He drives an expensive Porsche. On 5 November at 18:30 hours, his car is pulled over by the road traffic police. John asks the police officer why he has been pulled over. The officer, PC Taylor, informs him that he wishes to check whether John is insured to drive such a powerful car. John assures PC Taylor that he is insured and that he does not wish to be delayed any further. John waits whilst the officer conducts a mobile check on his insurance details. The officer confirms there is no problem with the insurance. PC Taylor then asks John to get out of the car. When John asks why, PC Taylor replies that his colleague says he saw John using his mobile telephone whilst driving. John is incredulous and offers to show PC Taylor that his mobile telephone is in his jacket which is in the boot of his car. John informs PC Taylor that he is not prepared to be detained any longer and asks for PC Taylor's collar number. At this point, PC Taylor informs John that he is under arrest for driving whilst using a mobile telephone contrary to s. 41D Road Traffic Act 1988. In reply to being cautioned, John is recorded as having said: 'I have nothing to say. This has to be some kind of wind-up right?' John is granted police bail to attend the police station in seven days' time.

The arrest by PC Taylor is questionable on two grounds. The evidence suggests that John was pulled over because there were doubts about whether he was an insured driver. It is only when this is resolved in John's favour that it is suggested that John was driving whilst using a mobile telephone. This is denied by John. No attempt was made by PC Taylor to ascertain whether John was telling the truth about his mobile telephone being in his jacket pocket in the boot of his car (this is contrary to the requirements of Code G para. 2.3A). In the circumstances it is difficult to see how PC Taylor could have had reasonable grounds for suspecting that John has committed an offence. Even if PC Taylor had reasonable grounds, in what sense could the officer form the view that it was necessary to arrest John having regard to the offence and the needs of the investigation (s. 25(5) PACE and Code G para. 2.8)? PC Taylor had John's name and address. Having regard to the judgment in *R v Alexander* [2009] and to Code G para. 1.3, the actions of the police on this occasion appear to be wholly disproportionate. John might seek a judicial review of the actions of the police in this situation.

3.7.7 THE USE OF REASONABLE FORCE

Section 3(1) Criminal Law Act 1967 allows reasonable force to be used when making an arrest or when preventing a criminal offence. The 'reasonable force' test is decided by the magistrates or by the judge on the specific facts of each case.

3.7.8 CITIZEN'S POWER OF ARREST—S. 24A PACE 1984

Section 24A PACE 1984 permits a citizen to arrest a person in connection with an indictable offence (including an either-way offence).

Section 24A(1) PACE 1984 provides:

'A person other than a constable may arrest without a warrant—

(a) anyone who is in the act of committing an indictable offence; or

(b) anyone whom he has reasonable grounds for suspecting to be committing an indictable offence.'

Section 24A(2) PACE 1984 further provides that:

'Where an indictable offence has been committed a person other than a constable may arrest without a warrant—

(a) anyone who is guilty of the offence or

(b) anyone whom he has reasonable grounds for suspecting to be guilty of it.'

Section 24A(3)(a) PACE 1984 requires that *in addition* to satisfying one of the grounds mentioned, in s. 24A(1)–(2) PACE 1984, the arrest will only be lawful if the citizen has reasonable grounds for believing that an arrest is necessary for one or more of the reasons listed in s. 24A(4) PACE 1984 *and* it appears to the person making the arrest that it is not reasonably practicable for a constable to make the arrest instead.

Section 24A(4) PACE 1984 defines the grounds to include:

(a) causing injury to himself or any other person;

(b) suffering physical injury;

(c) causing loss or damage to property;

(d) making off before a constable can assume responsibility for him.

3.7.9 PRESERVED POWERS OF ARREST

The following statutory powers of arrest are preserved:

- in connection with the taking of fingerprints at a police station (s. 27 PACE 1984);
- for taking samples in specified circumstances at a police station (s. 63A PACE 1984);
- for failing to surrender to police bail (s. 46A PACE 1984);
- where a person has broken or is likely to break a condition of bail (s. 7 Bail Act 1976).

3.7.10 TAKING ACTION AGAINST AN 'UNLAWFUL' ARREST

A failure to comply with the correct procedure renders the arrest unlawful—although an unlawful arrest can be remedied after the proper formalities have been complied with (*Lewis v Chief Constable of South Wales* [1991] 1 All ER 206). Where the police have made an unlawful arrest, the defence may challenge the admissibility of prosecution evidence obtained as a result of it. The defence could submit that admitting the prosecution evidence would have an 'adverse effect on the fairness of the proceeding'; s. 78 PACE 1984 (see Chapter 6 for consideration of the principles that apply to the exclusion of unlawfully obtained evidence).

Where a suspect has not been properly cautioned, an application can be made by the defence at trial to have any resulting evidence excluded. An unlawful arrest may be subject to judicial review and a claim for damages for false imprisonment.

3.8 STREET BAIL

The traditional position has been that PACE 1984 has required an arrested person to be taken to a designated police station as soon as possible. It was then a matter for the custody officer to decide whether to charge the suspect, or to detain the suspect without charge, or to release the suspect on police bail.

Section 30A PACE 1984 now provides that where a suspect is arrested at the scene of the offence, he may be given 'street bail' without being taken to the police station. The suspect will be required to attend the police station to answer to bail at a later date unless he is informed otherwise. He must be given a written notice stating the offence for which he was arrested and the time and date at which he is required to attend the police station (s. 30B PACE 1984). Conditions can be attached to the grant of 'street bail' for the purposes of securing surrender, preventing further offences, preventing interference with witnesses or obstruction of the administration of justice, or for the person's own protection. Common conditions that can be imposed include residence; exclusion from a particular place or non-contact with a particular individual. Police officers are prohibited from imposing the following conditions on a suspect released on street bail:

- surety;
- security;
- residence at a bail hostel.

The written notice issued to the suspect under s. 30B PACE 1984, must state clearly any conditions that are to be attached to the grant of police bail and give details about how the conditions can be varied. An application to vary conditions may be made to the custody officer at the police station at which the person is required to attend (s. 30CA PACE 1984) or a magistrates' court (s. 30CB PACE 1984). There is a power of arrest for failing to attend at a police station and for breaking any conditions imposed.

The grant of police bail is considered further in Chapter 4.

3.9 SEARCHING THE SUSPECT'S PERSON AND/OR PROPERTY UPON ARREST

Where the suspect has been arrested, the police have a wide range of legal powers to search any property or premises owned or occupied by the suspect for evidence relating to the offence(s) under investigation. The power of the custody officer under s. 54 PACE 1984, to search the suspect on arrival at the police station and to seize and retain property is addressed in Chapter 4 where the process of detention and questioning of suspects is considered. The power to take intimate and non-intimate samples is considered in Chapter 7.

PACE 1984 Code B deals with police powers to search premises and to seize and retain property found on premises and persons.

3.9.1 SEARCHING WITH THE SUSPECT'S PERMISSION

The detained person may agree to his home or business premises being searched. Where consent is not given, however, the police have a wide range of legal powers to carry out a lawful search.

3.9.2   **SEARCH OF AN ARRESTED PERSON AWAY FROM THE POLICE STATION—S. 32(1) PACE 1984**

Where the suspect has been arrested away from the police station, s. 32(1) PACE 1984 permits a constable to search an arrested person if the constable has reasonable grounds for believing that:

- the arrested person may present a danger to himself or others; or
- may have concealed on him anything which he might use to assist the arrested person in escape from lawful custody; or
- may have concealed on him anything which might be evidence relating to an offence.

Section 32(1) gives the police wide discretion in the way in which the power to search is exercised. It means that a police officer may search an arrested person for 'anything' on that person. In practice this means that the officer can search an arrested person for items which might be wholly unrelated to the reason why the initial arrest was made as the words 'relating to an offence' do not necessarily relate to the offence for which the arrest is made. These wide powers are limited to some extent as the officer must have reasonable grounds for believing that a search is necessary. Simply making a search at the time of arrest would be unlawful unless the officer could prove the necessary 'reasonable grounds' for this belief. A power to seize and retain items found is included.

A police officer may not require a person to remove any clothing in public other than an outer coat, jacket or gloves, although the search can include the search of a person's mouth (s. 32(4) PACE 1984).

3.9.3   **SEARCH AT PREMISES WHERE THE SUSPECT HAS BEEN ARRESTED—S. 32 PACE 1984**

Section 32(2)(b) PACE 1984 confers on a police officer the power to enter and search any premises where the suspect was at the time of his arrest or immediately before his arrest, for evidence relating to the offence for which the suspect is under arrest provided the offence is an indictable offence (which includes all offences triable either way) and the officer has reasonable grounds for believing that there is evidence relating to the offence for which the suspect has been arrested.

In every case where entry is made under s. 32 PACE 1984, it is a question of fact whether the officer considered that reasonable grounds existed for the officer's belief that evidence might be found as a result of the search.

Where the reasonableness of the officer's belief and/or the admissibility of any evidence discovered as a result of the search is disputed by the defence, the issue will be decided prior to trial or in a *voir dire* (trial within a trial). Evidence obtained as a result of an unlawful search remains admissible subject to the court's exclusionary discretion under s. 78 PACE 1984 (see Chapter 6).

3.9.4   **THE POWER TO ENTER AND SEARCH—S. 17 PACE 1984**

Section 17 PACE 1984 allows a police officer to enter and search any premises for the purposes of:

(a) executing a warrant of arrest;

(b) arresting a person for an indictable offence;

(c) arresting a person for a specified non-indictable offence;

(d) recapturing any person who is unlawfully at large; or

(e) saving life or limb or preventing serious damage to property.

The power under s. 17 PACE 1984 can only be exercised (with the exception of (e)) if the police officer has reasonable grounds for believing that the person being sought is on the premises.

3.9.5 **SEARCH OF AN ARRESTED PERSON'S PREMISES—S. 18 PACE 1984**

Section 18 PACE 1984 deals with searching any premises *occupied or controlled* by a person who is under arrest for an indictable offence (which includes all offences triable either way). A search is permitted if there are reasonable grounds for suspecting that there is evidence on the premises (other than items subject to legal privilege) that relate either to the indictable offence or some other connected or similar indictable offence and the written authority of an inspector is obtained.) Prior authorisation is not required where the conditions under s. 18(5) PACE 1984 are met in that before the arrested person is taken to the police station, that person's presence at a place (other than a police station) is necessary for the effective investigation of the offence. Section 18(2) confers the power to seize and retain any item for which a police officer is authorised to search.

3.9.6 **THE POWER OF SEIZURE—S. 19 PACE 1984**

Section 19 provides that a constable who is lawfully on any premises has power to seize anything which is on the premises if the constable has reasonable grounds to believe that it has been obtained in consequence of the commission of an offence, or that it is evidence in relation to an offence, and that it is necessary to seize it in order to prevent it from being concealed, lost, altered or destroyed.

The power of seizure does not extend to items that the constable has reasonable grounds to suspect are subject to legal privilege (see para. 3.9.9). An additional power of seizure has been granted to the police under ss. 50 and 51 Criminal Justice and Police Act 2001, which enables the police to remove material which cannot be practicably examined on the premises with a view to determining whether it contains evidence capable of being seized or whether the material may be subject to excluded categories of material (see para. 3.9.9). The most obvious example of this would be a personal computer containing material that might disclose evidence of the commission of an offence or contain evidence relevant to an offence.

 Example

Police powers to search an arrested person and/or property under ss. 18 and 32 PACE 1984 can be confusing. Depending on the facts of the case in some situations either s. 18 or s. 32 can be used. In other situations only one of the statutory provisions may apply. Consider the following examples which illustrate the position.

Janice, who is a managing director of a small double-glazing firm, is arrested at work on suspicion of having committed fraud.

As Janice has been arrested, the police may search her office under s. 32 PACE 1984 because she has been arrested in connection with an indictable offence provided the officers have reasonable grounds for believing that there is evidence in Janice's office connecting her to the fraud offences.

The appropriate power of search is s. 32 PACE 1984 which permits the police to search premises where the arrested person was immediately before or at the time of his or her arrest.

The term 'where the suspect was at the time of arrest or immediately before arrest' is given a restrictive meaning as s. 32 could not be used if the police searched Janice's office six hours after her arrest. To be lawful under s. 32 PACE 1984, the search must be almost contemporaneous with the arrest.

Janice may also be the subject of a personal search under s. 32 PACE 1984 if the officer reasonably believes that Janice has concealed on her person anything which may present a danger to herself or others; or anything which she might use to assist her to escape or anything which might be evidence relating to an offence.

The police would have entered Janice's office under s. 17(1)(b) PACE 1984 to arrest her for an indictable offence.

> The police may use s. 18 PACE 1984 to search Janice's home and a lock-up garage that she rents close to home. Section 18 applies in this situation provided the police have reasonable grounds for believing there is evidence on the properties that relates to an indictable offence or to other similar or connected offences and the search is authorised by an officer of at least the rank of inspector. The house and lock-up garage satisfy the requirement that the properties are occupied or controlled by Janice. Section 32 PACE does not apply here because Janice was not at home or in the garage at or immediately before the time of her arrest.
>
> If Janice had been arrested at home, the police could have searched under s. 18 or s. 32 PACE 1984.

3.9.7 PRESERVED POWERS OF ENTRY

A number of statutes provide police officers with a power to search a suspect's premises to obtain evidence in relation to the investigation of a specific offence. Section 23(3) Misuse of Drugs Act 1971 allows the police to enter and search premises in connection with an investigation under the 1971 Act. A warrant to enter the premises must be obtained from a magistrate.

3.9.8 SEARCH WARRANTS—S. 8 PACE 1984 (CODE B)

The powers of search discussed so far give the police the power to search premises owned by the arrested person or to search the premises where the person was arrested. What can the police do where it is not possible or practicable to contact the person who could allow the police to enter premises to search for evidence in connection with an offence? In these circumstances, an officer of the rank of inspector or above can make a written application to a magistrate under s. 8 PACE 1984 for a warrant authorising a police officer to enter and search the premises specified in the application. Several other enactments permit an application for a search warrant for a wide range of different offences.

To be granted a search warrant under s. 8 PACE 1984, the officer must satisfy the magistrate that there are reasonable grounds for believing that:

- an indictable offence has been committed (this includes an indictable-only offence and an offence triable either way); and
- there is material on the premises which is likely to be of substantial value to the investigation of the offence; and
- the material is likely to be relevant evidence; and
- the evidence does not include items subject to legal professional privilege, excluded material, or special procedure material; and
- it is not practicable to communicate with any person entitled to grant entry, or, if it was, it is likely that the purpose of the search will be frustrated or seriously prejudiced.

Two types of warrant may be issued. First, a specific premises warrant authorises the police to search the address specified on the warrant. Alternatively, s. 8(2)–(4) SOCPA 2005 provides for an all-premises warrant which covers all premises owned or occupied by the person named in the application but where it is not reasonably practicable to specify each of the premises at the time of the application. The warrant gives the police access to all premises occupied or controlled by the person whether they are specified on the application or not. The warrant can authorise the police making multiple visits on multiple occasions to the premises specified in the warrant—subject to the requirement that any second and subsequent visits must be authorised by an officer of at least the rank of inspector. The entry and search under the warrant must be completed within three months of issue.

Sections 15 and 16 PACE 1984 provide further safeguards against potential misuse of the warrant by the police under s. 8 PACE 1984. Any non-compliance with the statutory safeguards renders a search and entry of premises unlawful, see *Harry and Sandra Rednapp v Commissioner of the City of London Police and the City of London Magistrates' Court* [2008] EWHC 1177. In *R (on the application of Waqar Bhatti) v Secretary of State for the Home Department*, Lawtel 3/2/2010, the Divisional Court held that the practice of officers inserting by hand the address of the property to be searched on the copy of an all-premises warrant at the point of execution was unlawful and in breach of the procedural requirements. As the search was unlawful the items seized had to be returned.

3.9.9 MATERIAL THAT MAY NOT BE SEIZED

It is important to note that certain categories of 'material' cannot be seized by the police. These are items subject to legal professional privilege, 'excluded material' and 'special procedure material'.

(1) Items subject to legal professional privilege
These are defined by s. 10(1)(a) PACE 1984 and include any communication containing legal advice. The doctrine of legal professional privilege requires that any written and/or oral legal advice passing between a lawyer and client in connection with a case is privileged and cannot be divulged to a third party without the client's consent.

(2) 'Excluded' material
'Excluded material' is defined by s. 11 PACE 1984 and consists of personal records held in confidence by the person who created them. Personal records are defined as medical records, records of spiritual healing and files kept by social workers and probation officers about their clients.

(3) 'Special procedure material'
Section 14 PACE 1984 defines 'special procedure material' as material which has been acquired by a person in the course of his or her trade, business or profession or other occupation or office, who holds it subject to an express or implied undertaking to keep it confidential. It also extends to journalistic material unless it has been acquired in confidence, in which case it will be regarded as excluded material under s. 11 PACE 1984.

3.10 THE EUROPEAN CONVENTION ON HUMAN RIGHTS 1950

A person who has been stopped and searched and/or arrested is entitled to the protections under the Convention. The Articles that are most relevant to this area are Article 5 (the right to liberty and security of the person including the right not to be detained by the police without lawful authority), Article 8 (the right to privacy), Article 10 (freedom of expression) and Article 11 (freedom of assembly and association).

When exercising stop and search powers, the police will be required to show that:

- the power to stop and search was prescribed by law; and
- the power was exercised in pursuance of a legitimate aim; and
- the exercise of the power was proportionate to the aim to be achieved.

In deciding the lawfulness of a stop and search the court will often balance the competing interests of a suspect's right to be free to go about his lawful business against the wider obligations on the police to prevent crime of which the powers under s. 1 PACE 1984 are considered to be a highly effective provision. This balancing exercise is well-illustrated by the decision in *Howarth v Commissioner of Police for the Metropolis* [2011] EWHC 2818 where the High Court decided that the power to stop and search the applicant was reasonable and proportionate for the legitimate purpose that existed on the facts of the case.

An arrest will satisfy the requirements of Article 5 ECHR 1950 where the person is brought before a competent legal authority such as a court either on reasonable suspicion of having committed an offence or to prevent that person from committing an offence or from escaping after having committed an offence (*Fox, Campbell and Hartley v UK* [1990] 13 EHHR 157).

The lawfulness of an arrest may also be judged according to whether:

- the legal authority for the arrest is precise and accessible; and
- is procedurally fair and not arbitrary; and
- proportionate to the aim of depriving a person of his or her liberty.

The test of reasonable suspicion will satisfy Article 5 provided that an objective observer would be satisfied that the suspect may have committed an offence (*Fox, Campbell and Hartley v UK* [1990] 13 EHHR 157).

KEY POINT SUMMARY

- Know the legal grounds that permit a person to be stopped and searched before arrest (s.1 PACE 1984).
- Know the legal grounds under which a person can be arrested (ss. 24 and 24A PACE 1984).
- Have a good working knowledge of the law governing the powers to search the suspect and/or the suspect's property after arrest.
- If you represent the defendant, where appropriate, be prepared to challenge the legality of an arrest and/or search and any evidence obtained as a result. The challenge may be made to the police, the CPS or to the court at the defendant's trial.
- Be aware of the pervasive influence of the ECHR 1950 in relation to stop and search and arrest and cite ECHR case law to support your submissions.

SELF-TEST QUESTIONS

1. Where can you find guidance on the reasonable suspicion or belief test?
2. Which caution should be given to the suspect on arrest?
3. Where are the police powers to search a person and his property after arrest contained?
4. In what circumstances will the police apply to a magistrate for a warrant to be issued under s. 8 PACE 1984?
5. Police are called to a public order disturbance in town. By the time they arrive, the incident appears to be over. CCTV operators have provided a description of a male wearing a football top who appears to have been the instigator of the trouble and was waving some kind of bottle or weapon in his hand. One of the police officers notices a male wearing similar clothing walking towards a taxi-rank. On approaching the male (Antonio), he runs off. He is apprehended within a matter of minutes. What powers do the police have in relation to Antonio?
6. A short, factual scenario based on the exercise of police powers appears at the end of Chapter 6 (scenario 1); although the focus of the question is based on the admissibility of unlawfully obtained evidence, you may wish to consider what aspects of police procedure relating to stop and search and arrest might be considered unlawful.

Analysis of all self-test questions can be found on our Online Resource Centre.

 online resource centre

FIGURE 3.1 POLICE POWERS OF STOP/SEARCH/SEIZURE AND ARREST

STOP AND SEARCH BEFORE ARREST
Section 1 PACE and Code A
- A person may be stopped and/or searched in a public place or in a place to which the public has access where the officer reasonably suspects the person is in possession of:
  - stolen articles; or
  - prohibited articles.

SEARCHING THE SUSPECT AFTER ARREST
- with the suspect's consent; or
- under s. 32 PACE where the officer:
  - has reasonable grounds for believing the suspect may present a danger to himself or others; or
  - has concealed anything on him he might use to escape from custody; or
  - has concealed on him evidence which might be related to an offence.

SEARCH OF PREMISES AFTER ARREST
- search with the suspect's consent;
- search of premises at which the suspect is arrested, s. 32 PACE 1984 (applies to an indictable offence);
- search of premises owned/controlled by the suspect, s. 18 PACE 1984 (applies to an indictable offence and inspector's authorisation needed);
- preserved powers of entry and search, e.g. s. 23 Misuse of Drugs Act 1971.

POLICE OFFICER ARREST WITHOUT A WARRANT
- s. 24 PACE 1984 where a police officer has reasonable grounds for suspecting that the person:
  - is about to commit an offence; or
  - is committing an offence; or
  - has committed an offence; AND
  - it is necessary to arrest the individual for any of the following reasons (s. 24(5)):
    - to enable the person's name to be ascertained where the constable does not know and cannot readily ascertain the person's name or has reasonable grounds for doubting the name given by the person is his real name; or
    - to enable the person's address to be ascertained;
    - to prevent the person in question:
    - causing physical injury to himself or another;
    - suffering physical injury;
    - causing loss or damage to property;
    - committing an offence against public decency; or
    - causing unlawful obstruction of the highway;
  - to protect a child or vulnerable person from the person; or
  - to allow the prompt and effective investigation of the offence or of the conduct of the person;
  - to prevent the prosecution for the offence from being hindered by the disappearance of the person in question.

CHECKLIST FOR A LAWFUL ARREST—S. 28 PACE 1984
- There must be a legal ground for the arrest, e.g. s. 24 PACE 1984.
- There must be the factual grounds for the arrest, e.g. reasonable grounds for believing that an offence has been committed.
- The person must be cautioned as follows:
  - 'You do not have to say anything. But it may harm your defence if you do not mention when questioned something which you later rely on in court. Anything you do say may be given in evidence.'
- The person must be informed of the reason for his arrest.
- The person should be taken to a designated police station as soon as is reasonably practicable.

4 DETENTION AND INTERROGATION

4.1 **INTRODUCTION**

Following arrest (unless granted street bail), the suspect should be brought to a designated police station as soon as is reasonably practicable. The suspect is now the centre of the police investigation and the police will want to question the suspect and may undertake certain investigatory procedures including:

- taking fingerprints;
- taking an intimate or a non-intimate sample;
- taking photographs;
- requiring the suspect to participate in a formal identification procedure.

In this chapter, we consider the process of detention, questioning and charge. The procedures for obtaining identification evidence (including biometric samples) are considered in Chapter 7.

A detailed legal framework for the treatment of suspects at the police station is provided by the substantive provisions of Police and Criminal Evidence Act 1984 (PACE 1984) and the Codes of Practice, particularly Code C. The provisions define the power(s) the police may exercise over a suspect but also provide a number of safeguards. A copy of Code C is freely accessible from the Home Office website—our Online Resource Centre includes a link taking you to the most recent version of the Codes of Practice. The safeguards contained in PACE 1984 and its accompanying Codes of Practice exist to ensure the suspect enjoys fair treatment while in detention and also to promote investigative integrity by the police, ensuring the quality and reliability of evidence obtained at the police station. Evidence obtained at the police station in breach of PACE 1984 and Code C is vulnerable to challenge, and a defence lawyer might seek to exclude any resulting evidence under s. 78 PACE 1984 and under s. 76 PACE 1984, in the case of a confession (see Chapter 6). Section 67(11) PACE 1984 allows the Codes of Practice to be admissible in evidence if relevant to a matter to be decided by a court.

It is the legal adviser's duty at the police station to advance and protect his client's rights. To do this, the legal adviser needs a detailed knowledge of PACE 1984 and the Codes of Practice to challenge the police if they breach the letter and/or the spirit of the suspect's legal rights.

Be aware that there are more extensive powers governing the detention and interrogation of persons suspected of involvement in terrorist activities. These provisions which are found in the Terrorism Act 2000 and Code H are outside the scope of this work. More details can be found in *Blackstone's Criminal Practice*.

In the password-protected lecturer resources section on our Online Resource Centre, we offer a 'stand alone' video case study/role play, entitled the 'Peter West Police Station Scenario', with supporting documentation. The video is divided into different sections covering the investigation of an offence of rape. It explores all aspects of a suspect's detention at the police station, including the legal adviser's role and illustrates many of the points covered in this chapter. (**In the freely available resource section, you will find an additional online chapter entitled 'Advising at the Police Station—Practical Steps' which comprehensively explores the practical nature of the defence solicitor's role at the police station,**

taking into account everything that is covered in this chapter and in the succeeding chapters which address some of the important rules of evidence that can arise out of the process of investigation.)

In this chapter, we explain the process of detention and charge including the following:

- the custody officer's role;
- the importance of the custody record;
- the circumstances in which a suspect can be detained without charge;
- the length of time a suspect can be kept in custody;
- the obligation to review the suspect's detention;
- the suspect's right to have someone informed of his arrest;

- the suspect's right to legal advice;
- the suspect's basic rights in custody;
- specific safeguards in relation to vulnerable suspects;
- the conduct of an interview; and
- the decision to charge and withhold bail.

We begin by mentioning those who voluntarily attend at the police station.

4.2 THE RIGHTS OF A VOLUNTEER AT THE POLICE STATION

It is often reported in the media that a person is 'helping the police with their enquiries'. During the high-profile murder investigation into the deaths of Holly Wells and Jessica Chapman in 2002, Ian Huntley and Maxine Carr 'assisted the police with their enquiries' before their arrests and eventual convictions. This expression means that a member of the public is voluntarily assisting the police in the criminal investigation without having been arrested. A volunteer is entitled to leave police custody at any time (Code C para. 3.21).

If the police wish to detain the volunteer, the volunteer must be arrested, at which point his legal status changes to a suspect.

4.2.1 QUESTIONING A VOLUNTEER

If the police wish to question a volunteer to obtain evidence which may be put before a court, the volunteer must be:

- cautioned before replying;
- told that he is not under arrest;
- told that he is free to leave if he wishes; and
- told that he may obtain free and independent legal advice (Code C para. 3.21).

4.3 ACTION IMMEDIATELY FOLLOWING ARREST

Unless 'street bail' is granted under s. 30A PACE 1984 (see para. 3.8), s. 30 PACE 1984 requires an arrested person to be taken to a designated police station as soon as practicable after arrest. A designated police station is equipped with the appropriate facilities for dealing with a suspect in detention. The rules permit the arrested person's arrival at a police station or release on 'street bail' to be delayed if the suspect's presence is required elsewhere to assist the police with their investigation. This might include a search of the arrested person under s. 32 PACE 1984 and/or entry and search of premises under s. 32 or s. 18 PACE 1984.

After arriving at the police station, the suspect will be taken to the custody suite for 'booking-in'. This will be carried out by the custody officer on duty.

4.4 THE ROLE OF THE CUSTODY OFFICER

The custody officer plays an essential role in ensuring that the suspect's legal rights at the police station are complied with (s. 39 PACE 1984). The officer should always remain independent and impartial of the criminal investigation and should not question the suspect about his involvement in the alleged offence. The custody officer is responsible for taking important decisions in relation to the suspect, including whether the suspect should be detained or released and, in conjunction with the CPS, whether the suspect should be charged.

4.4.1 THE CUSTODY RECORD

The custody officer is also responsible for compiling the suspect's custody record. A custody record must be opened as soon as is reasonably practicable for each person brought to a police station (Code C para. 2.1). The suspect's legal adviser and/or appropriate adult have a right of access to the custody record 'at any time while the person is detained' (Code C para. 2.4). When a detained person leaves the police station, he is entitled to a copy of the custody record upon request (Code C para. 2.4A).

The custody record has important evidential value to both the prosecution and defence by providing a detailed record of all aspects of the suspect's detention. (We have included extracts from the custody record in relation to our case study *R v Lenny Wise* in Appendix 1. The complete documentation, including the full custody record can be accessed on our Online Resource Centre.)

The custody record will include details of:

- the suspect's arrest;
- the reason for the suspect's detention;
- authorisation of search procedures or continued detention;
- requests for legal advice/medical advice;
- reviews of the suspect's detention;
- details of meals and refreshments; and
- any complaints made by the suspect.

The custody record should be carefully considered by the legal adviser to ensure that the suspect's rights have been complied with by the police.

Where questions about the admissibility of evidence obtained during the investigation arise, the custody record may be put in evidence at trial. For this reason, the legal adviser should ensure that any representations that he makes regarding his client's detention are recorded in the custody record.

4.4.2 INFORMING SUSPECTS OF THEIR RIGHTS

On arrival at the police station, the custody officer should explain to the suspect, in accordance with Code C para. 3.1, that the suspect has the following rights which may be exercised at any stage:

- the right to have someone informed of his arrest;
- the right to consult in private with a solicitor, such advice being free and independent;
- the right to consult the Codes of Practice.

The custody officer is also required, under Code C paras. 3.5–3.10, to undertake a risk assessment to consider the specific needs of each detainee. This will include asking the suspect on arrival at the police station whether he:

- wants legal advice;
- wants to inform someone of his arrest;
- might be in need of medical treatment;
- requires the presence of an appropriate adult;
- requires an interpreter.

4.4.3 SEARCH ON ARRIVAL AT THE POLICE STATION—S. 54 PACE 1984

The custody officer must record a suspect's property when brought into custody (s. 54 PACE 1984). Property and clothing may be seized and retained if they could cause injury or damage to persons or property or could be used to assist an escape from lawful custody. Strip searches and intimate searches require special justification (see Code C Annex A). A strip search involves the removal of more than outer clothing which includes socks and shoes (Code C, Annex A (B 9)). A strip search will not be routinely carried out and may only be undertaken in two situations. First, where the custody officer thinks it is necessary to remove an article which the detained person is not allowed to keep whilst in detention and the officer reasonably considers the detainee might have concealed such an article, or, secondly for the purposes of a search under s. 54A PACE 1984. Under s. 54A PACE 1984 a search or examination may be authorised by an officer of the rank of inspector or above for the purpose of ascertaining whether a detained person has any mark (such as a tattoo) that would tend to identify him as a person involved in the commission of an offence. Authorisation may only be given if the detained person refuses to consent to the examination/search or it is not reasonably practicable to seek the person's consent where the officer has reasonable grounds for suspecting that the detained person is not the person he claims to be or he refuses to confirm his identity. Any identifying marks may be photographed with or without consent.

An intimate search can only be carried out in accordance with the requirements set out in s. 55 PACE 1984 and Code C, Annex A.

4.4.4 IS THERE SUFFICIENT EVIDENCE TO CHARGE?

Following the suspect's arrival at the police station and having completed the formalities, the custody officer has a duty to decide whether there is sufficient evidence to charge the suspect with the offence for which the suspect has been arrested (s. 37(1) PACE 1984).

If the custody officer concludes that there is sufficient evidence to charge, s. 37(7) PACE 1984 requires that the suspect must either be:

- released without charge and on bail (with or without conditions) or kept in police detention for the purpose of enabling the CPS to make a charging decision under s. 37B (s. 37(7)(a));

- released without charge and on bail (with or without conditions) to allow for enquiries to continue, s. 37(7)(b);

- released without charge and without bail (s. 37(7)(c)); or

- charged (s. 37(7)(d)).

Police bail and the decision to charge are further considered at 4.14.

4.5 DETENTION WITHOUT CHARGE

Under s. 37 (2) PACE 1984, if the custody officer determines that there is insufficient evidence to charge, the suspect shall be released either on bail (conditional or otherwise) or without bail, unless the custody officer has reasonable grounds for believing that the suspect's detention without charge is necessary:

- to secure or preserve evidence relating to an offence for which the suspect is under arrest; or

- to obtain such evidence by questioning the suspect.

The reasons for continuing to detain the suspect without charge must be noted in the custody record. The grounds are easily made out in a case where the investigating officer needs to interview witnesses or the suspect, or to undertake personal searches. Where the custody officer becomes aware that the detention grounds have ceased to exist, there is an obligation on the custody officer to release the suspect immediately and unconditionally (s. 34(2) PACE 1984), unless it appears that there is a need for further investigation in which case release can be on bail (s. 34(5) PACE 1984). Currently, no conditions can be attached to the grant of bail under s. 34 (5) PACE 1984.

4.5.1   **HOW LONG CAN A SUSPECT BE DETAINED WITHOUT CHARGE?**

There are strict time limits on how long a suspect can be detained at a police station without charge. Unauthorised detention beyond the requisite time is unlawful. Detention time limits generally begin to run from the time of the suspect's arrival at the police station, which must be noted in the custody record. Since PACE 1984 came into force in 1986 it had been assumed by police officers, defence lawyers and the judiciary that the custody detention clock stopped ticking when a suspect was released on police bail during an investigation or pending a charging decision and resumed ticking when the suspect later attended the police station to answer to police bail. This universally accepted interpretation of the statutory pre-charge custody time limits was challenged by a decision of a District Judge sitting at Salford Magistrates' Court when, in April 2011, he refused to grant a police application for a warrant of further detention to be made against an arrested suspect. The suspect in question, Paul Hookaway, had been arrested on suspicion of murder and had previously been granted police bail during the investigation on three separate occasions. The District Judge ruled that the time Hookaway had already spent on police bail counted towards the maximum 96-hour custody time limit which had now expired. The District Judge's decision was upheld by an oral ruling of the High Court following an application for judicial review by the Greater Manchester Police and reported at *R (Chief Constable of Greater Manchester Police) v Salford Magistrates' Court and Paul Hookaway* [2011] EWHC 1578.

The significance of this decision for the police, CPS and defence lawyers, as well as the 80,000 suspects who at the time had been released on pre-charge bail, was immense. To avoid the potential draconian effect of the judgment, the Police (Detention and Bail) Act 2011 came into retrospective effect on 12 July 2012 through Parliament's fast-track legislative procedure. Section 1 reverses the decision in the *Hookaway* case by amending s. 47(6) PACE 1984 to explicitly provide that when calculating a statutory custody time limit or a period of pre-charge detention any period(s) a suspect spends on police bail shall be disregarded from the calculation.

4.5.2   **INITIAL DETENTION PERIOD OF 24 HOURS**

The general position is that the suspect can be detained at the police station without charge for 24 hours (s. 41 PACE 1984) providing the detention grounds in s. 37(2) PACE 1984 are met.

At the end of the 24-hour period the suspect must either be charged, or released unconditionally or on bail.

4.5.3   **DETENTION BEYOND 24 HOURS?**

The basic 24 hours of detention without charge can be extended up to 36 hours for an indictable offence (which includes either-way offences) where the provisions of s. 42(1) PACE 1984 apply. These are that:

- a senior officer of at least the rank of superintendent authorises the suspect's continued detention; and
- the officer has reasonable grounds for believing that it is necessary to detain the suspect without charge to secure or preserve evidence or to obtain evidence by questioning the suspect; and
- the investigation is being conducted diligently and expeditiously.

Where these conditions apply, the suspect can be detained for an additional period of up to 12 hours, making a total of 36 hours from the time of arrival at the police station. The reasons for extending the suspect's detention must be noted on the custody record. Continued detention is easily justified where investigating officers wish to interview or reinterview a suspect or to undertake an intimate search or to arrange an identification procedure. At the end of the 36-hour period the suspect must either be charged, or released unconditionally or on bail unless detention without charge is further extended (s. 42(10) PACE 1984).

4.5.4 DETENTION BEYOND 36 HOURS—WARRANT OF FURTHER DETENTION

Where the police wish to detain the suspect without charge beyond 36 hours, an application under s. 43 PACE 1984 must be made to the magistrates' court for a warrant of further detention. A court will grant a warrant if satisfied that there are reasonable grounds for believing that further detention is justified as per detention beyond 24 hours. An application for continued detention beyond 36 hours can only be made in relation to an indictable offence (which includes either-way offences). The police must make an application on oath supported by their reasons for seeking the warrant. In so doing, the police will need to explain the circumstances of the suspect's arrest, what investigatory steps have been undertaken so far and what further enquiries are needed.

The suspect has the right to be present at the hearing and to be legally represented. In practice, the application for a warrant of further detention is invariably granted by the magistrates.

Where the police persuade the court that the suspect should be detained for a further period without charge, the court may authorise detention for a further period of up to 36 hours making a total of 72 hours from his arrival at the designated police station.

At the end of 72 hours, where the police wish to continue holding the suspect without charge, a further application for an extension of the warrant of further detention must be made to the magistrates' court. Provided the court is again satisfied that there are reasonable grounds for believing that the further detention is justified, it can extend detention for a further 24 hours, making a total of 96 hours from the time of the suspect's arrival at the police station.

At the end of 96 hours, the suspect must either be charged, or released unconditionally or on police bail (s. 44 PACE 1984).

4.6 REVIEWING A SUSPECT'S DETENTION

Section 40 PACE 1984 requires the police to carry out periodic reviews of the suspect's detention, the details of which must be recorded in the custody record. The review is to ensure the suspect's continued detention is lawful.

Where the suspect has not been charged, the review of the suspect's detention must be carried out by an officer of at least the rank of inspector who has not been directly involved in the investigation. This officer is known as the 'review officer'. Under s. 40 PACE 1984 and Code C paras. 15.9–15.11, the review can be by telephone or by a video-link and the suspect has the right to make representations about his continued detention.

Where the suspect has been arrested and charged, the review can be carried out by the custody officer.

4.6.1 WHEN MUST THE REVIEWS BE CONDUCTED?

The first review of detention must be made no later than six hours after the detention was first authorised by the custody officer and thereafter every nine hours to ensure that the reasons for detaining the suspect's detention continue to apply.

The legal adviser should ensure the suspect's detention is lawful at all times. The custody record should help to determine this. If the detention ground under s. 37(2) PACE 1984 no longer exists or never existed or if a detention review was not carried out, the suspect's continued detention is unlawful.

BRIEF SUMMARY OF DETENTION TIME LIMITS		
Time	**Relevant officer**	**Requirements/Reasons**
10am: Suspect arrives at police station (detention clock begins to tick)	Custody officer	Custody record opened
10.15am: Detention without charge authorised (review clock begins to tick)	Custody officer	Reasonable grounds for believing that detention is necessary to secure or preserve evidence or to obtain evidence by questioning (s. 37(2) PACE 1984)
4.15pm: First review deadline	Inspector not involved in the case	First review of detention no later than six hours after detention first authorised (s. 40 PACE 1984). Thereafter, at nine-hourly intervals
1.15am: Second review deadline	Inspector not involved in the case	Second review of continued detention
10am: 24 hours (maximum duration for a summary-only offence)	Superintendent	Continued detention beyond 24 hours (s. 42 PACE 1984) for an indictable offence if there are reasonable grounds for believing that detention is necessary to secure or preserve evidence or to obtain evidence by questioning
10.15am: Third review deadline	Inspector not involved in the case	Reviews of continued detention will continue at nine-hourly intervals
10pm: 36 hours	Magistrates' court	(s. 43 PACE 1984) Warrant of further detention must be sought to continue to detain beyond 36 hours—same conditions must be present when further detention was authorised after 24 hours
72 hours	Magistrates' court	Extension of warrant of further detention must be sought
96 hours	Custody officer	(s. 44 PACE 1984) Charge or release as maximum period in detention has been reached
NB: At any time during the detention process, the suspect can be released on bail (with or without conditions) to attend the police station at a later date. The detention clock freezes at this point and resumes ticking once police bail is answered.		

4.6.2 **GRANTING POLICE BAIL PENDING FURTHER INVESTIGATION**

As outlined at para. 4.5, where the custody officer becomes aware that the detention grounds have ceased to exist, there is an obligation on the custody officer to release the suspect immediately and unconditionally (s. 34(2) PACE 1984), unless it appears that there is a need for further investigation in which case release can be on bail (s. 34(5) PACE 1984). As no conditions can currently be attached to the grant of police bail under s. 5.34(5) PACE 1984, the custody officer is more likely to release the suspect under s. 37(2) PACE 1984 which enables conditions to be attached to police bail where there is not sufficient evidence to charge but the grounds for continued detention are not met: *R (Torres v Commissioner of Police of the Metropolis* [2007] EWHC 3212 (Admin).

4.7 THE SUSPECT'S RIGHT TO INTIMATION AND/OR LEGAL ADVICE

The importance of a suspect's rights at the police station cannot be overstated. Where incriminating admissions or inferences from silence have been obtained in breach of these rights, exclusion of this evidence can be sought under ss. 76/78 PACE 1984 (see Chapter 6).

4.7.1 **THE RIGHT TO INFORM SOMEONE OF THE ARREST—S. 56 PACE 1984**

Section 56(1) PACE 1984 provides that where a person has been arrested and held in custody, that person is entitled, as soon as is reasonably practicable, to have a friend, relative or some other person who is likely to be interested in that person's welfare informed of the arrest. For some suspects, especially those inexperienced at dealing with the police, the right of intimation under s. 56 PACE 1984 is important.

Guidance on the right is contained in Code C para. 5 supplemented by Annex B.

Contact can extend to the suspect speaking on the telephone to a specified individual (although this is unlikely to be a private call) and writing to the person concerned (although this correspondence is likely to be read). At the custody officer's discretion, the suspect can be visited at the police station by the specified individual.

4.7.2 **DELAYING THE RIGHT TO HAVE SOMEONE INFORMED OF THE ARREST**

The suspect's general right to inform someone of his arrest may be delayed where the grounds in s. 56(2)–(5) PACE 1984 Code C Annex B are made out.

Section 56 provides that:

- the suspect must have been arrested in connection with an indictable offence (this includes an either-way offence); and
- an officer of at least the rank of inspector authorises the delay on the basis that the officer has reasonable grounds for believing that telling the suspect's relative, friend or other person likely to take an interest in the suspect's welfare of the arrest will:
  — lead to interference with or harm to evidence connected with an indictable offence; or
  — lead to interference with or physical injury to other persons; or
  — lead to the alerting of other persons suspected of having committed such an offence but not yet arrested for it; or
  — hinder the recovery of any property obtained as a result of such an offence.

The authorisation for the delay may be given to the suspect orally or in writing. The reason for the delay must be noted in the custody record and if justified, may not exceed 36 hours from the time the suspect arrives at the designated police station.

4.7.3 THE SUSPECT'S RIGHT TO LEGAL ADVICE—S. 58 PACE 1984

The general right to legal advice under s. 58 PACE 1984 (supplemented by Code C para. 6 (Annex B)) is one of the most important protections against the abuse of the suspect's legal rights by the police. Section 58(1) PACE 1984 provides that a person arrested and held in custody in a police station or other premises shall be entitled, if he so requests, to consult a solicitor privately at any time. The importance of ensuring a suspect has access to legal advice while in police detention has been repeatedly emphasised by the European Court of Human Rights: *Murray v UK* (1996) 22 EHRR 29 and *Condron v UK* (2001) 31 EHRR 1. Indeed, the right to a fair trial under Art. 6 ECHR 1950 normally requires that a suspect has access to a lawyer at the initial stages of a police investigation (*Salduz v Turkey* 49 EHRR 19, applied in *Cadder v HM Advocate* [2010] UKSC 43).

online resource centre

Legal advice at the police station may be provided by a solicitor or by a legal executive/ trainee/paralegal/clerk who is either accredited by the Solicitors Regulation Authority under the Police Station Representatives Accreditation Scheme (PSRAS) or is registered as a probationary police station representative whilst undertaking the process of accreditation in accordance with the PSRAS. The scheme is explained in more detail in our online chapter: 'Advising at the Police Station—Practical Steps' which comprehensively addresses the role of the legal adviser at the police station taking into account everything covered in Part II of the *Handbook*.

4.7.4 WHO PAYS FOR LEGAL ADVICE GIVEN AT THE POLICE STATION?

The Police Station Advice and Assistance Scheme administered by the Legal Aid Agency entitles a suspect to free legal advice. A suspect may request the services of a solicitor or legal adviser of his choice if he intends to pay privately for representation. Otherwise publicly funded legal advice is accessed by telephoning the Defence Solicitor Call Centre which determines whether legal advice should be limited to telephone advice or whether a solicitor should attend in person. Legal advice will be restricted to telephone advice if the suspect is:

- detained for a non-imprisonable offence;
- arrested on a bench warrant for failing to appear in court and is being held for production before a court;
- arrested on suspicion of driving with excess alcohol; failure to provide a specimen; driving while unfit;
- detained in relation to breach of police or court bail conditions.

Attendance in connection with these cases may be justified if an interview or identification procedure is going to take place; the client requires an appropriate adult or interpreter; is unable to communicate over the telephone; or is complaining of serious maltreatment.

4.7.5 PROVIDING ACCESS TO LEGAL ADVICE

Code C places strict obligations on the police to ensure access to legal advice including:

- All detainees must be informed of the right to consult and communicate with a solicitor in private and at any time, free of charge (Code C para. 6.1).
- Nothing must be said or done by the police with the intention of dissuading a detainee from obtaining legal advice (Code C para. 6.4).
- Any request for legal advice must be noted in the custody record.
- If the detainee declines to speak to a solicitor in person, it should be explained to the detainee that he has a right to speak with that person on the telephone and if the detainee continues to waive this right, the custody officer should ask the detainee why and the reasons should be recorded on to the custody record (Code C para. 6.5).

- When a solicitor arrives at the police station to see the suspect, the suspect must be informed of the solicitor's arrival and asked if he would like to see the solicitor—even where legal advice was earlier declined (Code C para. 6.15).

- A detainee who wants legal advice may not be interviewed until the detainee receives advice unless the circumstances listed in Code C para. 6.6 apply.

- Where the suspect has access to legal advice, the suspect must be allowed to have his solicitor present for the interview.

- If the solicitor is travelling to the police station an interview should not normally start until the solicitor arrives (note 6A).

- Where the suspect requests legal advice during an interview, there should be no further questioning until the suspect has spoken to the legal adviser (Code C para. 6.6).

The police are also required to remind the suspect about the right to legal advice at the following stages of detention:

- immediately before the commencement or recommencement of any interview at the police station (Code C para. 11.2);

- before a review of detention takes place (Code C para. 15.4);

- after the suspect has been charged, if a police officer wishes to draw the suspect's attention to any written or oral statements made by any other person (Code C para. 16.4);

- after the suspect has been charged, if further questions are to be put to the suspect about the offence (Code C para. 16.5);

- prior to an identification parade, group identification or video identification being held (Code D para. 3.17);

- prior to the taking of an intimate body sample (Code D para. 6.3).

4.7.6   **DELAYING THE RIGHT TO LEGAL ADVICE**

The suspect's general right to legal advice may be delayed where the grounds under s. 58(8) PACE 1984 (supplemented by Annex B, Code C) are made out. The decision to delay the right to legal advice in an individual case is a serious step and must be justified by the police, as it can have significant implications for the admissibility of evidence obtained from a suspect (*Salduz v Turkey* 49 EHRR 19, applied in *Cadder v HM Advocate* [2010] UKSC 43). The evidential rules that deal with the admissibility of confession evidence are covered in Chapter 6. The grounds for delaying the right to legal advice under s. 58(8) PACE 1984 and Annex B, Code C are as follows:

- the suspect has been arrested in connection with an indictable offence; and

- an officer of at least the rank of superintendent authorises the delay on the ground that the officer has reasonable grounds for believing that if the suspect was permitted to exercise his right to receive legal advice it will:

  — lead to interference with or harm to evidence connected with an indictable offence or interference with or physical injury to other persons; or

  — lead to the alerting of other persons suspected of having committed such an offence but not yet arrested for it; or

  — hinder the recovery of any property obtained as a result of such an offence.

The reason for the delay must be noted in the custody record and, if justified, may not exceed 36 hours from the time the suspect arrived at the designated police station. The suspect must be informed of the reason for the delay (s. 58(9) PACE 1984). If the grounds for delaying access to legal advice cease to apply, the suspect must be asked whether he wants to see his legal adviser (Code C Annex B, A.6).

The police may not delay access to a particular solicitor on the grounds that the solicitor may advise the suspect not to answer questions or that the solicitor was initially asked to attend the station by someone else (Code C Annex B, A.4).

If the authorising officer concludes that any of the risks identified here apply to the solicitor requested, the detainee must be allowed to choose another legal adviser (Code C Annex B, A.3). Where access to legal advice is delayed, inferences from a suspect's decision to remain silent cannot be drawn (see para. 4.11).

4.8 OTHER RIGHTS AND SAFEGUARDS ENJOYED BY THE SUSPECT WHILST IN DETENTION

Code C paras. 8–9 and 12 recognise that a suspect is entitled to certain fundamental rights while detained at the police station. They include:

- A right to an adequately heated, cleaned and ventilated cell; access to toilet facilities.

- At least two light meals and one main meal in any 24-hour period, taking account of special dietary requirements, and regular refreshments.

- A requirement that a detainee receives appropriate clinical attention as soon as reasonably practicable if the person appears to be suffering from physical illness, is injured, appears to need clinical attention or appears to be suffering from a mental disorder. If a detainee requests medical attention, a health-care professional must be called. If a detainee needs to take prescribed medication, an appropriate health-care professional must be called, and in some instances, may be the only person who can administer the medication.

- The requirement that in any 24-hour period, the suspect must be allowed at least eight hours' continuous rest, preferably at night and free from questioning (Code C para. 12.2).

- Breaks during the interview should occur at normal meal times, and short breaks should be held approximately every two hours (Code C para. 12.8).

- A right to an interpreter if the suspect is deaf or has speech difficulties or does not understand English (Code C para. 13).

4.9 THE TREATMENT OF VULNERABLE SUSPECTS

Code C makes specific provision for the identification and treatment of vulnerable suspects. Annex E provides a detailed summary of the important provisions in relation to detainees under 17, the mentally disordered or mentally vulnerable suspect. The risk assessment which the custody officer must undertake at the beginning of the suspect's detention in relation to all detainees should identify those detainees who might be 'vulnerable'. Aspects of criminal procedure specifically relevant to young people (those under the age of 18) are considered in Chapters 24 to 26.

A key right in protecting the vulnerable suspect is access to an appropriate adult. The custody officer must inform an appropriate adult as soon as possible about the detention and request the appropriate adult to attend the police station as soon as practicable (Code C para. 3.15). The appropriate adult is likely to be the vulnerable person's parent or guardian, a social worker or another responsible adult. The appropriate adult's role is to protect the vulnerable person's interests and to ensure that his legal rights are respected by the police. The right of access to an appropriate adult is additional to the right to legal advice. Code C para. 11.5 provides that in the case of a young person or mentally vulnerable person, no interview should be undertaken in the absence of the appropriate adult. For a more detailed explanation of the role of the appropriate adult, see Chapter 24.

4.10 INTERVIEWING THE SUSPECT

The police investigation will involve questioning the suspect and interviewing other witnesses to gather sufficient evidence to charge the suspect or to exclude the suspect from the investigation. Interviewing a person suspected of committing the crime is the centrepiece of most police investigations. Even for those experienced at dealing with the police, the police interview can be very intimidating. The intimidating environment may lead some suspects to admitting to crimes they have not committed, or being susceptible to a particular line of police questioning, bullying or inducements. For these reasons, the substantive provisions of PACE 1984 and Codes C and E closely regulate the conduct of police interviews.

A suspect's legal rights whilst in custody under the substantive provisions of PACE 1984 and the Codes of Practice exist to ensure the reliability and fairness of evidence resulting from the suspect's detention. The admissibility of evidence obtained in the police interview, particularly confession evidence, is vulnerable to challenge under s. 76(2)(a) or (b) and s. 78 PACE where it has been obtained in breach (accidental or otherwise) of PACE 1984 and the Codes of Practice (see Chapter 6).

4.10.1 WHAT CONSTITUTES AN INTERVIEW?

Code C para. 11.1A defines an interview as:

> 'the questioning of a person regarding his involvement in a criminal offence where there are grounds to suspect him of such an offence or offences which, by virtue of paragraph 10.1 of Code C must be carried out under caution.'

All interviews must be carried out at a police station except in the limited circumstances in Code C para. 11.1 where delay in conducting an interview would:

- lead to interference with or harm to evidence connected with an offence, or
- interference with or physical harm to other persons, or
- serious loss of or damage to property.

In this situation, contemporaneous written notes must be kept.

The effect of Code C para. 11.1A is to permit an informal conversation between an investigating officer and a suspect, provided it does not relate to the offence under investigation. This covers such matters as verifying someone's identity, but would not cover a prolonged conversation to encourage the suspect to make admissions to be used in evidence (see *R v Williams (Michael)* [2012] EWCA Crim 264).

4.10.2 FITNESS TO BE INTERVIEWED

Before any interview the custody officer must assess whether the detainee is fit to be interviewed (Code C para. 12.3). This is particularly appropriate to a detainee who is drunk or under the influence of an illicit substance. In some instances, the custody officer will need to consult an appropriate health-care professional to determine the suspect's fitness to be interviewed. As previously indicated, vulnerable suspects have the right to have an appropriate adult present during the interview (Code C para. 11.15).

4.10.3 WHEN MUST AN INTERVIEW CEASE?

Code C para. 11.6 provides that an interview should cease when the officer in charge of the investigation:

- is satisfied all the questions considered relevant to obtaining accurate and reliable information about the offence have been put to the suspect, including allowing the suspect an opportunity to give an innocent explanation and asking questions to test this;
- has taken account of any other available evidence; and
- the officer in charge of the investigation, or in the case of a detained person, the custody officer, reasonably believes that there is sufficient evidence to provide a realistic prospect of conviction.

4.11 THE REQUIREMENT TO CAUTION

At the beginning of the interview the suspect must be cautioned. Where the interview recommences after a break, the investigating officer must remind the suspect that he remains under caution and, where the officer considers it to be appropriate, the caution should be read to the suspect again.

The suspect can be cautioned in one of two ways depending whether an adverse inference may be drawn from the suspect's silence under ss. 34, 36 and 37 Criminal Justice and Public Order Act 1994 (see Chapter 5).

Where an adverse inference may be drawn at trial from the suspect's silence at the police station, the caution should be given as follows:

'You do not have to say anything. But it may harm your defence if you do not mention when questioned something which you later rely on in court. Anything you do say may be given in evidence.'

This caution will be appropriate where the suspect has been offered and/or received legal advice.

Under Code C the police are required to administer an alternative caution where:

- a person's right to legal advice has been delayed under s. 58(8) PACE 1984; or
- a superintendent authorises an interview to proceed under Code C para. 6.6(b) before the suspect has been given an opportunity to receive legal advice; or
- the suspect is to be interviewed after charge.

The alternative caution reads:

'You do not have to say anything. But anything you do say may be given in evidence.'

The alternative caution was introduced to comply with the European Court of Human Rights decision in *Murray v UK* (1996) 22 EHHR 29 and is given statutory effect in s. 58 Youth Justice and Criminal Evidence Act 1999.

4.12 WHAT CONSTITUTES A FAIR INTERVIEW?

4.12.1 OPPRESSIVE INTERVIEWS

It is an essential requirement of fairness that when interviewing a suspect about his involvement in an offence, the police do not abuse their position of trust by conducting the interview in an 'oppressive' manner. This requirement is recognised by Code C para. 11.3, which provides:

'No police officer may try to obtain answers to questions or to elicit a statement by the use of oppression.'

'Oppression' is not defined in Code C, but is partially defined by s. 76(8) PACE 1984, to mean torture, inhuman or degrading treatment and the use or threat of violence. Section 76(2)(a) PACE 1984 requires the court to exclude a confession that has been obtained through oppression and is considered further in Chapter 6.

4.12.2 INDUCEMENTS TO CONFESS

Code C para. 11.5 makes it clear that no interviewer shall indicate, except to answer a direct question, what action will be taken by the police if the person being questioned answers questions, makes a statement or refuses to do either.

4.12.3 PHYSICAL CONDITIONS OF THE INTERVIEW

An interview should take place in a room which is properly heated, lighted and ventilated (Code C para. 12.4). There is no limit to the number of officers who may be present during the interview, but the officer in charge must identify them to the suspect and should be aware of the possibility that the presence of too many officers might be seen as oppressive.

4.12.4 THE LEGAL ADVISER'S ROLE DURING THE INTERVIEW

Apart from a restricted number of exceptions, a suspect who has requested legal advice may not be interviewed or continue to be interviewed until the suspect has met with his legal adviser (Code C para. 6.6).

Code C Notes for Guidance para. 6D acknowledges the nature of the legal adviser's role in the interview:

'A detained person has a right to free legal advice and to be represented by a solicitor. The solicitor's only role in the police station is to protect and advance the legal rights of his client. On occasions this may require the solicitor to give advice which has the effect of his client avoiding giving evidence which strengthens a prosecution case. The solicitor may intervene in order to seek clarification or to challenge an improper question to his client or the manner in which it is put, or to advise his client not to reply to particular questions or if he wishes to give his client further legal advice.'

The practical aspects of the legal adviser's role at the police station are considered in a separate online chapter entitled 'Advising at the Police Station—Practical Steps'.

online resource centre

4.13 HOW SHOULD AN INTERVIEW BE RECORDED?

An explanation of the recording requirements for interviews is provided in Chapter 6, para. 6.4.1.

4.14 CHARGING A SUSPECT

The Criminal Justice Act 2003 (CJA 2003) made significant changes to the charging procedure at the police station. Charging decisions are divided between the CPS and the police under the statutory charging scheme. As an alternative to charging, the custody officer or CPS lawyer may decide to divert an individual from prosecution by offering a caution instead. A caution is an alternative to a prosecution and Code C Notes for Guidance 16A requires the custody officer to take account of alternatives to prosecution. The charging process and the availability of diversionary schemes are considered more fully in Chapter 8.

As we have already seen at para. 4.4.4, as soon as there is sufficient evidence to charge a suspect, s. 37(7) PACE 1984 requires the custody officer to charge or release the suspect. The decision to charge will be made either by the custody officer or by the CPS, in accordance with the statutory charging regime under the CJA 2003 and the *DPPs Guidance on Charging* (see Chapter 8).

4.14.1 PRE-CHARGE POLICE BAIL IN A CASE WHERE THERE IS SUFFICIENT EVIDENCE TO CHARGE

Where the custody officer has determined that there is sufficient evidence to charge but the final decision to charge is to be taken by the CPS, the suspect can either be detained in custody or released on unconditional or conditional bail under s. 37(7)(a) PACE 1984, pending a decision to charge or pending further investigation (s. 37(7)(b) PACE 1984). The suspect is under a duty to surrender to police bail at the appointed time unless notified in writing by the custody officer that his attendance is not required. Section 46A(1) PACE 1984 confers a power of arrest for failure to surrender to pre-charge police bail. A power of arrest exercised in these circumstances can result in a hastening of a decision to charge with the original offence for which pre-charge bail was granted (s. 37(C) PACE 1984) and would not assist a defendant's application for bail to a court.

Conditions can be attached to the grant of pre-charge bail under s. 37 PACE 1984 if it is necessary to prevent that person from failing to surrender to custody, or committing an offence while on bail, or interfering with witnesses or otherwise obstructing the course of justice, and/or for his own welfare (s. 3A Bail Act 1976). Any condition may be imposed that could be imposed by the court when granting court bail under the Bail Act 1976 other than a condition that the person resides at a bail hostel. (Court bail is explained in Chapter 10.)

Section 46A (1A) PACE 1984 gives a constable the power of arrest where there are reasonable grounds to believe that the person has broken pre-charge bail conditions. A person who has been made subject to bail conditions may apply to the same or another custody officer serving at the same police station for the conditions to be varied. The person may alternatively or in addition apply to a magistrates' court for variation (s. 47(1)(E) PACE 1984 and see Crim PR, r. 19.1 (1)). In *R (Carson) v Ealing Magistrates Court* [2012] EWHC 1456 (Admin), the imposition of pre-charge bail conditions were successfully challenged by judicial review. C was subject to pre-charge bail conditions, one of which was not to reside at her home address following an allegation of racially aggravated harassment by C against her neighbours. Carson unsuccessfully applied to the magistrates' court to have the bail restriction removed. The Divisional Court concluded that the condition forbidding the claimant to reside at her home address was disproportionate.

4.14.2 QUESTIONING AFTER CHARGE

On charging or informing the suspect that he might be prosecuted for an offence, no further questions may be asked of the suspect except in the circumstances provided for in Code C para. 16.5. They include where an interview is necessary:

- to prevent harm or loss to some other person, or the public; or
- to clear up an ambiguity in a previous answer or statement; or
- in the interests of justice for the officer to ask the question(s) and for the suspect to comment on, information concerning the offence which has come to light since the suspect was charged, or informed that he might be prosecuted.

Before an interview starts, detainees must be cautioned that they do not have to say anything, but that anything they do say may be given in evidence. The adverse inference provision under s. 34 CJPOA 1994 (see Chapter 5) has no application in this situation.

4.14.3 POLICE BAIL AFTER CHARGE

Once the defendant has been charged the decision whether to remand or release him pending his first appearance before a magistrates' court is made by the custody officer. Section 38 PACE 1984 requires the custody officer to have regard to the same considerations as those which a court is required to consider when taking a decision under the Bail Act 1976. Bail as a substantive topic in its own right is considered in detail in Chapter 10. A custody officer can refuse bail if one or more of the grounds under s. 38(1) PACE 1984 apply. They include:

- The suspect's name or address cannot be ascertained, or the custody officer has reasonable grounds for doubting whether a name or address furnished by the suspect is that person's real name or address.
- The custody officer has reasonable grounds for believing that the person arrested will fail to attend court to answer bail.
- In the case of a person arrested for an imprisonable offence, the custody officer has reasonable grounds for believing that the detention of the person arrested is necessary to prevent that person from committing an offence.
- In the case of a person arrested for a non-imprisonable offence, the custody officer has reasonable grounds for believing that the detention of the person arrested is necessary to prevent physical injury to any other person or causing loss or damage to property.

- The custody officer has reasonable grounds for believing that the detention of the person arrested is necessary to prevent that person from interfering with the administration of justice or with the investigation of offences or a particular offence.

- The custody officer has reasonable grounds for believing that the detention of the person arrested is necessary for that person's own protection.

These grounds are the same as those applied by a court under Sch. 1 Part 1 para. 2 Bail Act 1976 (see Chapter 10). In determining whether the accused is likely to abscond, commit further offences or interfere with the course of justice, the custody officer will have regard to the factors set out in para. 9, Sch. 1, Part 1 Bail Act 1976, including:

- the defendant's bail record;

- the nature of the offence;

- the defendant's community ties;

- the defendant's criminal record.

A person charged with murder cannot be granted bail by the custody officer (s. 38(1)(c) PACE 1984).

Where bail has been denied to a defendant in custody under s. 38(1) PACE 1984, he must appear before a magistrates' court as soon as is practicable (s. 46(1) PACE 1984). In practice, the defendant will be produced before the remand court the next day unless the next day is a Sunday or is Christmas Day or Good Friday.

Post-charge release on police bail

Instead of remanding a defendant into custody pending his first appearance before a court, the custody officer may release the defendant on unconditional or conditional bail pending his first appearance before a magistrates' court. A failure to answer police bail without reasonable excuse in these circumstances is an offence under the Bail Act 1976 and carries a power of arrest.

Under s. 47(1A) PACE 1984 the custody officer may impose conditions to post-charge police bail in much the same way as a court. These include conditions of residence, reporting to a police station, the imposition of a curfew, prohibiting contact with a particular individual or access to a particular place. A custody officer may not, however, impose a condition requiring the defendant to reside in a bail hostel. Conditions may only be imposed where the custody officer considers them to be necessary to ensure the defendant surrenders to custody, does not commit an offence while on bail, or interfere with witnesses or obstruct the course of justice. Conditions may also be imposed for the defendant's own protection or welfare. A failure by an accused to abide by the conditions of post-charge police bail will result in the accused being arrested and brought before a magistrates' court (s. 7(3) Bail Act 1976). A proven failure to abide by such conditions would be a significant factor in determining whether the accused should be remanded into custody throughout the rest of the proceedings. The accused may apply to the same or another custody officer serving at the same police station or a magistrates' court to vary post-charge bail conditions (see para. 4.14.1.).

The legal adviser at the police station may make representations to the custody officer where it is proposed to remand the defendant in custody pending his first appearance before a magistrates' court, or as to the appropriateness of bail conditions whether they be imposed post-or pre-charge.

4.14.4   DRUG TESTING AT THE POLICE STATION (CODE C PARA. 17)

Section 63B PACE 1984, as amended by s. 7 Drugs Act 2005, gives the police the power to demand a urine sample or non-intimate sample (saliva) from a suspect aged 18 and over upon arrest or after charge (this power extends to individuals over the age of 14 in order to test for the presence of a Class A drug at police stations where arrangements are in place).

The power to take a sample arises in relation to certain 'trigger offences' or for any offence where an inspector, or above, has reasonable grounds to suspect that misuse of a Class A drug caused or contributed to the offence. Additionally, s. 9 Drugs Act 2005 gives the police the power to require a person who has tested positive to undergo an initial assessment to see if the person has a propensity to misuse Class A drugs and would be suitable for treatment. A failure to give a sample or to consent to undergo an initial assessment or follow-up treatment results in the commission of an offence. Where the test shows the presence of a Class A drug and the person concerned refuses to consent to an initial assessment or to follow-up treatment, the information will be passed on to a court which must take it into account when making a bail decision under the Bail Act 1976 (see Chapter 10, para. 10.4.2). The testing procedure is currently operational in several police force areas.

4.15 CONCLUDING REMARKS

This and the preceding chapter have explained the procedures relevant to arrest, search, detention and processing of the suspect. Knowledge and understanding of the procedures is vital to those who prosecute and defend. In reviewing the evidence, for the purposes of deciding whether to charge the suspect or proving the case at trial, prosecutors will want to be sure that the police have gathered the evidence lawfully. In evaluating the evidence that has been disclosed by the prosecution and prior to advising on plea, the defence practitioner will know that the prosecution's case is weaker if the admissibility of evidence can be challenged on the basis that it was obtained unlawfully.

KEY POINT SUMMARY

- Be aware of the custody officer's extensive duties and responsibilities.
- Understand the suspect's right to legal advice and to have someone informed of his or his arrest at the police station and the circumstances in which the exercise of these rights can justifiably be delayed.
- Understand that the safeguards contained in PACE 1984 and in Code C not only seek to protect the suspect while in custody but that they also seek to promote the integrity of the investigative process so as to ensure the reliability of evidence obtained in consequence.
- Understand the importance of the custody record in evidential terms as it contains everything relevant to a suspect's detention at the police station, including the justifications for the decisions taken.
- Be aware of custody detention time limits and the obligation to charge or release when there is sufficient evidence etc.
- Know the definition of a vulnerable suspect and the additional rights that such a suspect enjoys.
- Know which caution should be administered in which situation.
- Understand that evidence obtained as part of the investigation into a criminal offence in breach of PACE/Code C is vulnerable to challenge under s. 78 PACE 1984 and/or s. 76 PACE 1984. Under s. 78 PACE 1984 such evidence can be excluded in the exercise of the court's discretion to ensure the defendant enjoys a right to a fair trial.
- Know the circumstances in which conditions can be imposed on the granting of police bail, both pre-charge and post-charge.
- Know the grounds upon which a custody officer can refuse police bail post-charge (s. 38 PACE 1984).

SELF-TEST QUESTIONS

The self-test questions that support this chapter are located at the conclusion of Chapter 6, which considers the admissibility of confession evidence. Chapter 6 also includes analysis of the admissibility of the confession in our case study, *R v Lenny Wise*.

FIGURE 4.1 MAXIMUM PERIODS OF DETENTION WITHOUT CHARGE AT THE POLICE STATION

Summary-only offence: 24 hours maximum, after which defendant must be released (unconditionally or on police bail) or charged, s. 41 PACE 1984.

Indictable offence (which includes an either-way offence): 24 hours unless a superintendent or above authorises detention for further 12 hours (24 + 12 = 36 hours) where the officer has reasonable grounds for believing that:

- the detention is necessary to secure or preserve evidence; or
- to obtain such evidence by questioning the suspect; and
- the investigation is being conducted diligently and expeditiously, s. 42 PACE 1984.

Detention beyond 36 hours

- Section 43 PACE 1984 permits detention without charge beyond 36 hours.
- Police must apply to a magistrates' court for a warrant of further detention where:
    - the detention is necessary to secure or preserve evidence; or to obtain such evidence by questioning the suspect; and
    - the offence is an indictable offence; and
    - the investigation is being conducted diligently and expeditiously.

A warrant may authorise detention for a further 36 hours (24 + 12 + 36 = 72 hours).
The police may apply for a further warrant of detention for 24 hours (24 + 12 + 36 + 24 = 96 hours).
At the end of 96 hours, the suspect must either be released on police bail or unconditionally, or charged (s. 44 PACE).

SUMMARY OF RIGHTS WHILE IN CUSTODY

- right to legal advice in private (s. 58 PACE 1984);
- right to have someone informed of your arrest (s. 56 PACE 1984);
- continual review of detention (s. 40 PACE 1984);
- right to an appropriate adult if you are vulnerable (Code C);
- right to medical advice (Code C);
- right to basic human rights (food/sleep/refreshments) (Code C).

THE RIGHT TO SILENCE
AT THE POLICE STATION

5.1   INTRODUCTION

An important part of the defence solicitor's role at the police station is to advise the suspect about what he should do in the police interview. The interview is a crucial stage in the police investigation of a criminal offence and will often result in evidence being obtained against the suspect which can be used by the prosecution at any later trial. Evidence obtained in the police interview commonly comprises lies or inconsistencies told by the suspect about his involvement in the offence. Alternatively the suspect may admit his involvement in the offence(s), or may refuse to answer police questions but at trial put forward a defence, and adverse inferences may be drawn against his silence at the police station. Whilst a suspect enjoys the right to silence at the police station and cannot be compelled to answer police questions or otherwise respond to the allegations that have been made against him, under the Criminal Justice and Public Order Act (CJPOA) 1994, the suspect no longer enjoys a completely unfettered right to silence at the police station. Adverse inference arising from silence can be drawn under the following sections:

* s. 34 CJPOA 1994 (failure to mention facts in interview or upon being charged which are subsequently relied on by the defendant in his defence at trial);
* s. 36 (failure to account for an object, substance or mark at the time of arrest);
* s. 37 (failure to account for presence at a particular place upon arrest).

In preparing a suspect to be interviewed by the police, the defence representative may advise her client to:

* admit guilt; or
* answer questions and perhaps advance a defence to the allegations made; or
* exercise the right to remain silent (which may include putting forward a prepared statement).

When advising silence, the legal adviser will always be aware that this can have evidential repercussions if the client is subsequently charged. A legal adviser must therefore fully understand the law relating to the right to silence, if silence is to be advised. **(For a detailed exploration of the defence solicitor's role at the police station please refer to our online chapter entitled 'Advising at the Police Station—Practical Steps'.)**

The purpose of this chapter is to explain the substantive law governing a defendant's silence at the police station under ss. 34, 36 and 37 CJPOA 1994.

The evidential implications of a defendant exercising his right to silence at trial under s. 35 CJPOA 1994, by choosing not to testify on oath, is explained in Chapter 19.

5.2 WHAT ARE THE RISKS ASSOCIATED WITH S. 34 CJPOA 1994?

Section 34 provides:

'(1) Where, in any proceedings against a person for an offence, evidence is given that the accused—

(a) at any time before he was charged with the offence, on being questioned under caution by a constable trying to discover whether or by whom the offence had been committed, failed to mention any fact relied on in his defence in those proceedings; or

(b) on being charged with the offence or officially informed that he might be prosecuted for it, failed to mention any such fact, being a fact which in the circumstances existing at the time the accused could reasonably have been expected to mention when so questioned, charged or informed, as the case may be . . .

(2) . . .

(c) the court, in determining whether there is a case to answer; and

(d) the court or jury, in determining whether the accused is guilty of the offence charged,

may draw such inferences from the failure as appear proper.'

Section 34 encourages an accused who has a defence to the allegation made against him to disclose that defence at the first, reasonable opportunity—in the police interview or on being informed that he is to be charged or when charged. If the accused remains silent but at trial chooses to rely on a fact in his defence, adverse inferences may be drawn against the accused's silence if the jury or magistrates consider that the accused could reasonably have mentioned the fact at the police station. The evidential effect of s. 34 is to undermine the accused's defence at trial.

A defendant does not need to remain completely silent in interview for s. 34 to be triggered. It is the defendant's failure to mention *any fact* which he subsequently relies on in his defence that may trigger s. 34. If a defendant puts forward facts or an explanation at the police station but then departs from that version at trial or advances new facts, the defendant is still at risk of an adverse inference.

5.2.1 THE CONDITIONS FOR DRAWING ADVERSE INFERENCES UNDER S. 34 CJPOA 1994

Adverse inferences may only be drawn from 'silence' where the following conditions are satisfied:

(1) the defendant was offered access to a legal adviser at the police station under s. 58 Police and Criminal Evidence Act 1984 (PACE 1984); and

(2) whilst being interviewed under caution or on being informed that he was to be charged or on being charged, the defendant failed to mention a fact which he later relied on for his defence; and

(3) the court concludes that the defendant 'could reasonably have been expected to mention' the fact that he later relies on for his defence.

If all these conditions are satisfied, the court may draw such inferences as appear proper. We will now consider each of these conditions in more detail.

(1) The police must have offered the defendant access to a legal adviser under s. 58 PACE 1984

Under s. 34(2A) CJPOA 1994 adverse inferences cannot be drawn where access to a legal adviser has been delayed, see *Murray v United Kingdom* (1996) 22 EHRR 29 at para. 5.2.6. Where the right to legal advice has been delayed (see Chapter 4, para. 4.7.6) and adverse inferences cannot be drawn, the defendant should be cautioned (see Chapter 4, para. 4.11) at the outset of the interview in this way: 'You do not have to say anything, but anything you do say may be given in evidence' (Code C Annex C).

(2) Whilst being interviewed under caution or on being informed that he is to be charged or on being charged the defendant failed to mention a fact which he later relies on for his defence

For adverse inferences to be drawn whilst being interviewed, the failure to mention facts must occur during questioning by the police to discover whether an offence has been committed and the identity of the person who committed it. The defendant must have been cautioned in this way: 'You do not have to say anything. But it may harm your defence if you do not mention when questioned something you later rely on in court. Anything you do say may be given in evidence.'

(3) The jury or magistrates conclude that the defendant 'could reasonably have been expected to mention' the fact that he later relies on for his defence

'Reasonableness' is a question of fact for the jury or magistrates to decide, see *R v Condron* [1997] 1 WLR 827; *R v Argent* [1997] 2 Cr App R 27. At trial, to prevent adverse inferences from being drawn, the defendant may well have to explain his reasons for remaining silent from the witness box and, if necessary, call the legal adviser who advised him at the police station to give evidence to explain the reasons for advising silence. This will almost certainly require an accused to waive legal professional privilege (see para. 5.2.5). It will then be a matter for the jury or magistrates to decide whether it was reasonable in the circumstances for the defendant to have remained silent.

What amounts to 'reasonable' will depend on the particular circumstances of each case.

In *R v Argent* [1997] 2 Cr App R 27, the Court of Appeal identified the following non-exhaustive factors to decide the reasonableness test including:

- the time of day;
- the defendant's age and state of mind;
- the defendant's experience of dealing with the police;
- the extent of the disclosure by the police of the evidence against the defendant.

The court or jury must consider these factors subjectively from the defendant's perspective at the time of detention at the police station. If the court or jury concludes that 'in all the circumstances existing at the time' at the police station, it was not reasonable for the defendant to have remained silent for the reason(s) given, adverse inferences may be drawn.

5.2.2 WHAT IS MEANT BY AN ADVERSE INFERENCE?

The jury or magistrates do not have to draw an adverse inference if they consider that it is not 'proper' to do so. If they choose to draw adverse inferences, they may conclude that the defendant remained silent because:

- the defendant had no answer to the allegations being made against him; or
- none of the defendant's answers would have stood up to critical examination by the police; or
- the defendant has subsequently made up a defence to fit the facts as disclosed by the prosecution.

5.2.3 REMAINING SILENT ON LEGAL ADVICE

Can adverse inferences be drawn where the accused remained silent on legal advice? The short answer is yes. A defendant is not insulated from having an adverse inference drawn against him because he remained silent on legal advice.

For adverse inferences not to be drawn, the court must be persuaded that the defendant's reliance on legal advice to remain silent was 'reasonable' and 'genuine'. This point has been made clear in numerous Court of Appeal decisions including: *R v Howell* [2005] 1 Cr App R; *R v Hoare* [2005] 1 Cr App R 1; *R v Knight* [2004] 1 Cr App R 9; and *R v Beckles* [2005] 1 Cr App R 22. In *Howell*, Lord Justice Laws observed:

'We do not consider . . . that once it is shown that the advice (of whatever quality) has genuinely been relied on as the reason for the suspect's remaining silent, adverse comment is thereby disallowed. The premise of such a position is that in such circumstances it is in principle not reasonable to expect the suspect to mention the facts in question. We do not believe that is so. What is reasonable depends on all the circumstances.'

In *Hoare,* Lord Justice Auld observed:

'. . . even where a solicitor has in good faith advised silence and a defendant has genuinely relied on it in the sense that he accepted it and believed that he was entitled to follow it, a jury may still draw an adverse inference if it is sure that the true reason for his silence is that he had no or no satisfactory explanation consistent with innocence to give . . . Legal entitlement is one thing. An accused's reason for exercising it is another . . . The question in the end, which is for the jury, is whether regardless of advice, genuinely given and genuinely accepted, an accused has remained silent not because of that advice but because he had no or no satisfactory explanation to give.'

It is instructive to consider the facts in *R v Howell*.

R v Howell [2005] 1 Cr App R 1

Howell was suspected of involvement in a serious assault on his flatmate. He told his solicitor, as he would later tell the jury, that he had acted in self-defence when he stabbed his flatmate. His solicitor asked the investigating officers if the victim of the attack had made a written statement. The victim had not made a written statement but had given the investigating officers a detailed verbal account, including the specific allegation that the defendant had attacked him with a knife. The defendant had indicated to his solicitor that the victim might withdraw his allegation. Consequently the solicitor advised him to make no comment in interview. No evidence was forthcoming from the solicitor as to the reasons for his advice. The defendant was asked in cross-examination, why, if he was an innocent man, he had not taken the opportunity of putting forward his version of events at the police station. The defendant gave as his reason for not answering questions the fact that he had simply followed his solicitor's advice. In his summing-up the trial judge instructed the jury to consider whether the defendant had been right to act upon the advice of his solicitor.

On the facts of *Howell*, the Court of Appeal concluded that the absence of a written complaint from the victim, especially as adequate oral disclosure had been given, and the belief that the complainant might not pursue a prosecution were not 'good reasons' for remaining silent. This was not a case where it would have been difficult for the defendant to recall events. The defendant had been there in the flat. He must have known whether he acted in self-defence or not. In the circumstances it had been permissible for the jury to draw an adverse inference on the basis that it had been reasonable to expect the defendant to mention such facts, notwithstanding the advice of his solicitor.

5.2.4 REMAINING SILENT ON LEGAL ADVICE AFTER *R v HOWELL*

In *Howell*, the Court of Appeal talked of the important responsibility defence solicitors have when giving advice at police stations:

'there must always be soundly based objective reasons for silence, sufficiently cogent and telling to weigh in the balance against the clear public interest in an account being given to the suspect by the police. Solicitors bearing the important responsibility of giving advice to suspects at police stations must always bear that in mind.'

The Court of Appeal further observed that:

'The kind of circumstance which may most likely justify silence will be such matters as the suspect's condition (ill-health, in particular mental disability; confusion; intoxication; shock, and so forth—of course we are not laying down an authoritative list), or his inability genuinely to recollect events without reference to documents which are not to hand, or communication with other persons who may be able to assist his recollection.'

Howell and the other cases cited have to be considered by the legal adviser when giving advice to remain silent at the police station, especially in an investigation where the suspect is indicating that he may have a defence to put forward or an explanation to offer. Notwithstanding the fact that legal advice might be genuinely given and received, it will be for the jury or magistrates to determine whether it was reasonable in all the circumstances for the defendant to have mentioned the fact he now seeks to rely on. This may well require the legal adviser to explain the basis for her advice. If the advice was based purely on tactical considerations, the defendant clearly risks having an adverse inference drawn against him.

5.2.5 ADVISING SILENCE AND LEGAL PROFESSIONAL PRIVILEGE

Communications between solicitor and client are protected from disclosure by legal professional privilege. The privilege belongs to the client and, as such, only the client may choose to waive it. In *R v Condron* [1997] 1 WLR 827, the Court of Appeal observed that for the defendant to simply assert in the witness box, 'I chose not to answer questions on the advice of my solicitor', would be unlikely to impress the jury. If sufficient weight is to be given to the defendant's reasons for not mentioning relevant facts, more explanation would almost certainly have to be given. In order to achieve this, the defendant may need to waive legal professional privilege in order to explain the basis on which his solicitor's advice was given. Having waived privilege, the defendant can be cross-examined on how much he told his solicitor at the relevant time. If the legal adviser is also called, the legal adviser can be asked whether there were any other reasons for the advice, in order to explore whether the advice may have been given for tactical reasons.

5.2.6 SILENCE AND THE RIGHT TO A FAIR TRIAL

The right to silence is an implied right under Article 6. Its importance was acknowledged in *Murray v United Kingdom* (1996) 22 EHRR 29:

'Although not specifically mentioned in Article 6 of the Convention, there can be no doubt that the right to remain silent under police questioning and the privilege against self-incrimination are generally recognised international standards which lie at the heart of the notion of a fair procedure under Article 6. By providing the accused with protection against improper compulsion by the authorities, these immunities contribute to avoiding miscarriages of justice and to securing the aims of Article 6.'

Is the decision to draw adverse inference compatible with Article 6 of the European Convention on Human Rights 1950? The short answer is yes—provided a number of safeguards contained in the Judicial Studies Board (JSB) specimen direction on s. 34 are met. These include:

(1) Under s. 38 CJPOA 1994, adverse inferences cannot be the sole reason for finding a defendant guilty. This is supported by *Murray v United Kingdom* (1996) 22 EHRR 29, in which the European Court of Human Rights (ECtHR) held that to base a conviction solely or mainly on a defendant's silence would contravene Article 6.

(2) Adverse inferences may not be drawn where the police have delayed a detainee's access to a solicitor under s. 58 PACE 1984 and Code C para. 6.6. This amendment to the CJPOA 1994 was enacted to take account of decisions of the ECtHR in *Murray v United Kingdom* (1996)

22 EHRR 29; *Condron v United Kingdom* (2001) 31 EHRR 1 and *Averill v United Kingdom* (2001) 31 EHRR 36 which have consistently stressed the fundamental importance of access to a solicitor at the police station.

(3) An adverse inference may only be drawn when, having listened to any explanation put forward by the defendant for his failure to mention facts and being satisfied that a sufficiently strong case against the defendant is made out, the jury or magistrates conclude that the only sensible explanation for his silence is that the defendant had no answer to the prosecution's case at the time or none that would stand up to scrutiny.

(4) The jury or magistrates should regard an adverse inference as providing additional support only in a situation where the prosecution's case, apart from the defendant's silence, is so strong, as to call for an answer from the accused.

5.2.7 SUBMITTING A PREPARED STATEMENT TO THE POLICE

An alternative to advising silence in interview is to put forward an accused's denial and/or his defence to the allegations against him in a written statement, which will then be read by the legal adviser to the police during the interview. This approach prevents a s. 34 CJPOA 1994 inference being drawn against a defendant at a subsequent trial, provided the facts disclosed in the written statement are consistent with the defence case at trial.

The prepared statement must be carefully drafted, as omitting a fact that is later relied on at trial or any departure from the statement at trial would leave the defendant vulnerable to an adverse inference under s. 34 CJPOA 1994. In *R v Knight* [2004] 1 Cr App R 9, the Court of Appeal held that, provided the defendant mentioned in his prepared statement all the facts he later relied on in court, adverse inferences would not be drawn, as this practice satisfied the purpose of s. 34, i.e. the early disclosure of the suspect's account.

5.3 DRAWING INFERENCES FROM A FAILURE TO ACCOUNT UNDER SS. 36 AND 37 CJPOA 1994

While most judicial attention has been focused on the application of s. 34 Criminal Justice and Public Order Act 1994, the potential for adverse inferences being drawn from the defendant's silence under ss. 36 and/or 37 should not be forgotten.

Adverse inferences may also be drawn where a suspect fails to account for an object, substance or mark found on the suspect's person (s. 36 CJPOA 1994) and/or from the suspect's failure to account for his presence at a particular place (s. 37 CJPOA 1994).

As with s. 34, a competent criminal defence lawyer will have a good understanding of the ambit of ss. 36 and 37 and be prepared to apply this knowledge in support of her client's case. Consider each section below.

Section 36

'(1) Where—

    (a) a person is arrested by a constable, and there is—

        (i) on his person; or

        (ii) in or on his clothing or footwear; or

        (iii) otherwise in his possession; or

        (iv) in any place in which he is at the time of his arrest,

        any object, substance or mark, or there is any mark on any such object; and

    (b) that or another constable investigating the case reasonably believes that the presence of the object, substance or mark may be attributable to the participation of the person arrested in the commission of an offence specified by the constable; and

(c) the constable informs the person arrested that he so believes, and requests him to account for the presence of the object, substance or mark; and

(d) the person fails or refuses to do so, then . . .

(2) . . .

(c) the court, in determining whether there is a case to answer; and

(d) the court and the jury, in determining whether the accused is guilty of the offence charged,

may draw such inferences from the failure or refusal as appear proper.

(3) Subsections (1) and (2) above apply to the condition of clothing or footwear as they apply to a substance or mark thereon.

(4) Subsections (1) and (2) above do not apply unless the accused was told in ordinary language by the constable when making the request mentioned in subsection (1)(c) above what the effect of this section would be if he failed or refused to comply with the request.'

Section 37

'(1) Where—

(a) a person arrested by a constable was found by him at a place at or about the time the offence for which he was arrested is alleged to have been committed; and

(b) that or another constable investigating the offence reasonably believes that the presence of the person at that place and at that time may be attributable to his participation in the commission of the offence; and

(c) the constable informs the person that he so believes, and requests him to account for that presence; and

(d) the person fails or refuses to do so, then if, in any proceedings against the person for the offence, evidence of those matters is given . . .

(2) . . .

(c) the court, in determining whether there is a case to answer; and

(d) the court or the jury, in determining whether the accused is guilty of the offence charged,

may draw such inferences from the failure or refusal as appear proper.

(3) Subsections (1) and (2) do not apply unless the accused was told in ordinary language by the constable when making the request mentioned in subsection (1)(c) above what the effect of this section would be if he failed or refused to comply with the request.'

5.3.1 WHAT IS THE EVIDENTIAL EFFECT OF SS. 36 AND 37 CJPOA 1994?

An adverse inference may only be drawn under s. 36 or s. 37 in accordance with the precise wording in the sections. Most importantly the suspect must be properly cautioned. A failure to properly caution the suspect about the evidential consequences of not providing an account under either s. 36 or s. 37 means that an adverse inference cannot be drawn, and the defendant's replies should be edited out of the transcript of the interview that is put before the court.

The evidential effect of an inference drawn under either section is to strengthen the prosecution's case, irrespective of any defence subsequently advanced by the defendant in court. The safeguard under s. 38(3) CJPOA 1994 applies, in that no one will have a case to answer, or be convicted of an offence, based solely on an inference drawn from a failure or refusal as prescribed in s. 36(2) and s. 37(2). Also, in accordance with s. 58 Youth Justice and Criminal Evidence Act 1999, an adverse inference under s. 36(4A) and s. 37(3A) CJPOA 1994 cannot be drawn where access to a solicitor has been delayed under s. 58 PACE 1984.

Unlike s. 34, very few cases have gone to appeal on ss. 36 and 37, although for further reference see *R v Compton* [2002] EWCA Crim 2835 in which the Court of Appeal considered the operation of s. 36 CJPOA 1994.

Consider the following examples of ss. 36 and 37.

Example 1

Andrew is implicated in a recent offence of assault. On his arrest, he has visible bruising on his face. Andrew tells you he has no knowledge of the incident alleged. Andrew will be asked to account in interview for the bruising visible on his face. A failure under caution to offer some explanation for the bruising may lead to an adverse inference being drawn under s. 36.

 Example 2

The police are investigating an attempted arson offence at a school. Tracey is arrested on the school play-ing fields shortly after the alarm was raised. Tracey denies any involvement in the matter. In interview, Tracey is bound to be asked to account for her presence on the school fields. A failure under caution to offer an explanation may result in an adverse inference being drawn under s. 37. If it later transpires that Tracey's jeans disclose traces of petrol, she can expect to be asked in interview to account for its presence in accordance with s. 36.

5.4 THE PRACTICAL ASPECTS ASSOCIATED WITH REMAINING SILENT

It will be apparent from all that has been said that the practical operation and effect of s. 34 CJPOA 1994 is complex. The law under ss. 36 and 37 CJPOA 1994 is much clearer. The practical issues associated with advising silence is a matter for the defence. For the prosecution the issue of adverse inferences will arise at the defendant's trial. In the case preparation, a prosecutor will have identified the possibility of adverse inferences being drawn where a defendant 'unreasonably' fails to mention a fact he is now relying on at trial or fails to account for objects etc. found on his person or fails to account for his presence at a particular place.

For the defence, the issue of adverse inferences potentially arises at the police station and at trial. The challenges for effective police station representation should not be overestimated. Advising clients at the police station makes demands on the police station advisers' powers of analysis, negotiation and advocacy as well as their legal knowledge and nerve!

A key question for the legal adviser at the police station is whether to advise a client to answer questions or to put forward a written statement or to remain silent. Relevant considerations in this regard include the strength or otherwise of the evidence the police claim to have; the client's instructions to the legal adviser and the client's ability to deal with the intense psychological pressure of the police interview. Do not forget that where silence is advised there should be a sound, objective, reason for the advice (*R v Howell*).

Anticipating questions likely to form the basis of an inference under s. 36 or s. 37 must also be considered. Good practice requires that the custody record should be carefully checked to see what has been seized from the suspect or his property and what searches have been undertaken and whether final or preliminary results are available. The defence lawyer may need to ask the client some searching questions about the state of the evidence against him and prepare him for the sort of questioning that could form the basis of an adverse inference.

A more detailed explanation of the practical issues involved in representing a client at the police station can be found in our online chapter section entitled 'Advising at the Police Station—Practical Steps'. This chapter is written exclusively from the defence perspective.

As with the prosecution, good case preparation will alert the defence to the possibility of adverse inferences being drawn at trial. The advocate will know the conditions that need to be satisfied under ss. 34, 36 and 37 CJPOA 1994 and will be prepared to argue against adverse inferences being drawn. For a summary of the precise conditions that a jury or magistrates must find before an adverse inference can safely be drawn, consider the JSB's specimen directions on s. 34 CJPOA 1994 which are reproduced in the Crown Court Bench Book. The specimen directions seek to ensure that all Crown Court judges adopt a consistent approach to the application of the rules relating to criminal law, evidence and procedure when summing up to the jury. The complete version of the JSB's specimen direction on drawing adverse inferences from a defendant's silence embodied in the *Crown Court Bench Book* can be accessed from the web-links section on our Online Resource Centre and at: http://www.judiciary. gov.uk/NR/rdonlyres/BE25EBB6-AAD2-4ACD-8115-28D3BF613164/0/benchbook_ criminal_2010.pdf.

KEY POINT SUMMARY

- If a defendant advances facts in support of his defence at trial which he failed to mention in interview, the defendant may have an adverse inference drawn against him if the court considers it was reasonable, at the time, for the defendant to have advanced the particular facts.

- The reasonableness of a defendant's decision depends upon a number of factors (some of them are canvassed in *R v Argent*).

- Adverse inferences may still be drawn where the defendant's decision to remain silent was based on legal advice given at the time—it is still a matter for the jury/magistrates.

- An inference can only be drawn by a jury/magistrates if, having worked through the specified safe-guards in the JSB's specimen directions, the jury/magistrates conclude the defendant remained silent because the defendant had no answer to the allegations, or none that he was prepared to have sub-jected to critical scrutiny.

- A conviction cannot be based solely upon an adverse inference.

- An adverse inference may not be drawn where the court concludes the accused genuinely and reason-ably relied on legal advice.

- Defence legal advisers must consider whether there are sound objective reasons for advising silence.

- Where a defendant relies on legal advice as the reason for seeking to avoid an adverse inference, the defendant must expect to waive legal professional privilege.

- Where an adverse inference is drawn, it is a contributing evidential component of the prosecution's case and a conviction cannot be based wholly or mainly on the fact of silence.

SELF-TEST QUESTIONS

Consider the following short scenarios and decide whether ss. 34 or 36 or 37 are engaged.

Scenario 1

Karl is being questioned on suspicion of manslaughter. He refuses to answer questions put by the police. At his trial Karl gives evidence to the effect that he acted in self-defence.

Scenario 2

Shania is arrested on suspicion of murder. During her interview she puts forward a defence of loss of self-control. At trial she gives evidence consistent both with loss of self-control and self-defence.

Scenario 3

Jason is arrested on suspicion of attempted rape. The victim of the attack retaliated, scratching her assailant's face. In interview Jason is cautioned and asked to account for scratch marks that can be seen on his face. Jason chooses not to reply. In fact, he remains silent throughout the interview. Giving evi-dence at his trial, Jason states he has been mistakenly identified in that he has an alibi.

Scenario 4

Following a burglary, Rio is arrested a few hours later. It is clear that the burglar exited the property along a muddy track and over a wall topped with metal spikes. In interview Rio advances a defence of alibi. In the course of the interview he is cautioned and asked to account for a tear on the sleeve of his jacket and mud on his shoes. Rio is unable to offer any explanation for either.

Scenario 5

Jane is arrested on a Sunday evening on suspicion of criminal damage. She is found by a police officer near to a field where genetically modified maize is under cultivation. Several crops have been uprooted. When questioned under caution about the alleged offence, Jane is asked to account for her presence near to the field. Jane refuses to reply. She also refuses to give evidence at her trial.

Scenario 6

Carley is arrested on suspicion of being in possession of a controlled drug with intent to supply. She admits to being in possession, but denies intent to supply. Her solicitor believes that she is unfit to be interviewed by the police due to drug withdrawal symptoms. The police doctor disagrees. Carley takes the advice of her solicitor and chooses not to answer questions during the interview. She is charged with possession with intent to supply. At trial she will give evidence denying intent to supply. Does she have anything to fear from her failure to answer questions at the police station?

online resource centre

An analysis of all self-test questions can be found on our Online Resource Centre in the Answers to the Self-Test Questions.

FIGURE 5.1 DRAWING ADVERSE INFERENCES FROM SILENCE

ADVERSE INFERENCES: S. 34 CJPOA 1994

- Section 34 CJPOA 1994 does not abolish the right to silence.

- Section 34 CJPOA 1994 applies where a defendant:
    - is questioned under caution; or on being charged;
    - fails to mention a fact that he later relies on in his defence.

- An adverse inference may only be drawn where:
    - the defendant has been offered legal advice, s. 34(2A) CJPOA 1994; and
    - the court considers it would have been reasonable for the defendant to have mentioned the fact; see *R v Condron*; *R v Argent*.

- The reasonableness test includes the defendant's:
    - age and experience of dealing with the police;
    - mental capacity;
    - state of health; and whether legal advice was given.

- It is a matter for the jury/magistrates as to whether an adverse inference should be drawn having regard to any reason advanced by the defendant in evidence.

- In a jury trial, the judge must direct the jury in accordance with the JSB's specimen direction on s. 34, which includes a host of safeguards, including:
    - conviction cannot be based wholly or mainly on a failure to mention;
    - the court must consider the reason for the defendant remaining silent;
    - an adverse inference may only be drawn if the jury concludes that the real reason for the defendant's failure was that he had no answer to the allegation, or none that would withstand critical scrutiny.

- A court may not draw an adverse inference where the defendant reasonably and genuinely relied on legal advice; see *R v Howell*.

- A solicitor advising silence at the police station must make his client fully aware of the risks.

- A prepared statement containing all the defence facts may prevent adverse inferences from being drawn; see *R v Knight*.

ADVERSE INFERENCES: S. 36 CJPOA 1994

- Adverse inferences may be drawn where, after arrest, the defendant refuses to account for any object, substance or mark on his person; or in his clothing; or otherwise in his possession; and

- the officer has a reasonable belief that the object etc may be attributable to his participation in the offence; and

- the possible effect of his failure or refusal to account for the object was explained to the defendant, Code C para. 10.11.

ADVERSE INFERENCES: S. 37 CJPOA 1994

- Adverse inferences may be drawn where, after arrest, the defendant refuses to account for his presence at a particular place; and

- the officer has a reasonable belief that his presence may be attributable to his participation in the offence; and

- the possible effect of his failure or refusal to account for his presence was explained to the defendant, Code C para. 10.11.

CHALLENGING UNLAWFULLY AND UNFAIRLY OBTAINED EVIDENCE

6.1 INTRODUCTION

The purpose of the police investigation into a criminal offence is to secure sufficient evidence to charge a person(s) suspected of committing the offence(s) and to take the matter to trial. It should be remembered that for both prosecution and defence, whilst the rules of evidence are applied primarily at trial, they also underpin the construction of the whole case. The manner in which the police obtain evidence during the investigation may have implications for the admissibility of evidence at any later trial. Therefore, working in partnership with the Crown Prosecution Service (CPS), the police will be aware that the chances of a conviction will be greatly enhanced by presenting admissible evidence to the court which has been obtained in a lawful, fair and reliable way. On the other hand, the defence will carefully scrutinise the prosecution case and should challenge the admissibility of any evidence obtained in breach of the substantive provisions of the Police and Criminal Evidence Act 1984 (PACE 1984), the Codes of Practice and other investigatory powers. Challenges to prosecution evidence by the defence can be made at a pre-trial hearing or at the trial itself.

With this in mind, both prosecution and defence will be aware that a defendant enjoys the right to a fair trial both in domestic law and under Article 6 European Convention on Human Rights 1950 (ECHR 1950). You should remember however, that Article 6 has broad application and is not solely concerned with unlawfully obtained evidence, as Article 6 applies to the 'fairness' of the trial process as a whole. To ensure the defendant's right to a fair trial is not prejudiced by being convicted on unlawfully or unfairly obtained evidence, the courts have powers to exclude any prosecution evidence where the admission of the evidence would prejudice a fair trial.

This chapter examines the court's powers to exclude unlawfully or unfairly obtained prosecution evidence by examining the position in relation to:

- confession evidence:
  — excluded under ss. 76 and 78 PACE 1984;
- other prosecution evidence excluded at:
  — common law; and
  — under s. 78 PACE 1984; and
  — as an abuse of process.

Challenging the admissibility of identification evidence is considered in Chapter 7.

First, however, how may the police obtain evidence against an accused in an unlawful or unfair way?

6.2 WHAT IS UNLAWFULLY OR UNFAIRLY OBTAINED EVIDENCE?

Unlawfully or unfairly obtained evidence can be described as any prosecution evidence which has been obtained in a 'questionable' manner and includes:

- a confession obtained in breach of the safeguards under PACE 1984 and the Codes of Practice;
- evidence obtained as a result of an unlawful search of a person or his or her property;
- evidence obtained by entrapment;
- identification evidence obtained in breach of Code D PACE Codes of Practice;
- evidence obtained by an unlawful search or by unlawful surveillance;
- evidence (including confession evidence) obtained by deception or trickery;
- evidence obtained in violation of legal professional privilege (unless specifically authorised by statute).

Whilst 'underhand' investigation methods can yield highly relevant evidence of a suspect's guilt, it poses a dilemma for the court because to exclude such evidence may mean a guilty defendant walking free, but to admit the evidence would be to condone unlawful activities by the police as well as potentially prejudicing the defendant's right to a fair trial. Unlawfully obtained evidence remains admissible subject to the exercise of judicial discretion to exclude it. How do the courts apply these exclusionary powers? We will first consider this question in the context of confession evidence.

6.3 WHAT IS A CONFESSION?

A confession is defined by s. 82(1) PACE 1984 as:

'Any statement wholly or partly adverse to the person who made it, whether made to a person in authority or not and whether made in words or otherwise.'

The definition of a confession is extremely wide and covers any statement made by the accused on which the prosecution relies in support of its case. In some situations, a suspect may fully admit his involvement in an offence by stating 'OK officer. It was me. I robbed the old lady in the High Street.' In other situations, the suspect's response may be more ambiguous by admitting to only a partial involvement in a crime.

To be admissible against the defendant, a confession does not have to be made to a person in authority, e.g. a police officer. It is also possible to secure a conviction on confession evidence alone. A well-known example is Michael Stone's conviction for the double fatal hammer attack on Lin and Megan Russell in 1996 which was based on a confession he was alleged to have made in earshot of a convicted, serving prisoner while on remand awaiting trial.

The prosecution is fully aware of the high probative value that attaches to a confession and therefore the police are well versed in the psychology of interrogation techniques as the entire interview process is geared to persuading the suspect to talk. By talking, the suspect is more likely to say something of a revealing, incriminating or contradictory nature, especially over the course of several interviews.

Conversely legal advisers at the police station must always be vigilant about how they advise clients to answer questions in the police interview to avoid their clients making incriminating statements.

6.4   A SUSPECT'S RIGHTS AT THE POLICE STATION

Crucially relevant to the admissibility of confession evidence are the safeguards contained in PACE 1984 and the Codes of Practice, including ss. 56 and 58 PACE 1984 Codes C and E. Many of these safeguards were considered in Chapter 4. Whilst a breach of PACE 1984 and/ or the Codes will not automatically persuade the court to exclude the defendant's confession, substantial breaches of a suspect's legal rights by the police provides evidence for the defence advocate to argue the confession should be excluded under ss. 76 and/or 78 PACE 1984. A causal link must always be established between the alleged breach and the resulting confession. In challenging the confession's admissibility, the custody officer's role and the evidential significance of the custody record will be highly relevant.

6.4.1   RECORDING REQUIREMENTS FOR INTERVIEWS

The recording requirements for interviews are of practical importance in providing an accurate account of what took place and assist the police and the suspect as they protect the police from accusations that they have 'verballed' the suspect (i.e. they have attributed comments to the suspect which the suspect denies making). Any departure from normal practice in recording the interview immediately compromises the integrity of the investigating officers and may form the basis of a challenge to exclude disputed evidence of incriminating admissions.

An interview in relation to an indictable and either-way offences must be tape-recorded (Code E para. 3.1). It is also common practice to tape-record interviews in connection with most summary-only offences. Interviews should be recorded with the full knowledge of the person being interviewed and are recorded on two tapes. One is a working copy, with the other being sealed at the completion of the interview. A transcript of the interview is produced from the working tape and must be a 'balanced' version of the interview. The tape and the transcript must record where the interview took place, the identity of the people present, the time the interview commenced, the time of any breaks and the time the interview finished. The transcripts of interviews in our case studies (*R v Lenny Wise*; *R v Roger Martin*; and *R v William Hardy*) can be located in the case studies section of our Online Resource Centre. Appendix 1 includes the transcript of interview in relation to *R v Lenny Wise*.

 online resource centre

A written summary of the tape-recorded interview will be sent to the defence as part of the prosecution's obligation to provide initial details of the prosecution case under Crim PR, Part 21 (See Chapter 8). The defence has the right to have a copy of the tape to check the accuracy of the summary prepared by the prosecution. If the defence agree that the summary served by the prosecution is accurate, the written summary will be part of the evidence in the case. If the defence does not agree with the summary, the tape will be transcribed in full for use at the trial. If necessary, the tape will be played in full at the trial (Consolidated Criminal Practice Direction IV 43).

A new PACE Code F provides for the video recording of interviews with the suspect. This practice is the subject of pilot projects in a number of police force areas prior to expected national implementation.

6.4.2 'OFF THE RECORD' COMMENTS

It is not unusual for a suspect to make unsolicited comments off the record outside the formal interview which may be relevant to the police investigation. Code C para. 11.13 requires the police to keep a written record of any unsolicited comments, which should be signed and dated. The suspect should be given the opportunity to read the record and to sign it as being an accurate record of what was said.

6.5 CHALLENGING THE ADMISSIBILITY OF A CONFESSION UNDER SS. 76 AND 78 PACE 1984

Section 76(2) provides two grounds under which a confession can be excluded—oppression and unreliability:

> 'If, in any proceedings where the prosecution proposes to give in evidence a confession made by an accused person, it is represented to the court that the confession was or may have been obtained—
>
> (a) by oppression of the person who made it; or
>
> (b) in consequence of anything said or done which was likely, in the circumstances existing at the time, to render unreliable any confession which might be made by him in consequence thereof,
>
> the court shall not allow the confession to be given in evidence against him except in so far as the prosecution proves to the court beyond reasonable doubt that the confession (notwithstanding that it may be true) was not obtained as aforesaid.'

Where the defence (or the court) raise the issue of the confession's admissibility the prosecution has the legal burden of proving that the confession was not obtained through oppression (s. 76(2)(a)) and/or is not unreliable (s. 76(2)(b) PACE 1984). If the prosecution cannot prove beyond reasonable doubt that the confession has not been obtained by oppression or is not unreliable, it must be excluded notwithstanding that it may be true.

Each provision will now be considered in turn.

6.5.1 OPPRESSION—S. 76(2)(A) PACE 1984

Oppression is partially defined in s. 76(8) to include torture, inhuman or degrading treatment, and the use or threat of violence (whether or not amounting to torture).

In the leading case of *R v Fulling* [1987] QB 426, the Court of Appeal stated that oppression should be defined by its dictionary definition as being 'the exercise of authority or power in a burdensome, harsh or wrongful manner; unjust or cruel treatment of subjects, inferiors, etc; the imposition of unreasonable or unjust burdens'.

Fulling establishes that for conduct to amount to oppression within the meaning of s. 76(8) there must be deliberate misconduct by the police. Oppression is a question of degree. What is oppressive to one suspect may not be oppressive to another. Therefore the accused's personal characteristics including his mental strengths and weaknesses are relevant.

'Oppressive' conduct was found to have occurred in *R v Paris, Abdullah and Miller* [1993] 97 Cr App R 99, in which the defendants appealed against their conviction for murder. During the investigation, M was interviewed a total of 13 hours over five days. A solicitor was not present during the first two interviews and M consistently denied his involvement in the crime during the first seven interviews. During interviews eight and nine, M accepted that he was present at the crime scene. He was then pressed to say who had stabbed the victim. M finally confessed that he had. Having denied his involvement over 300 times on tape, he later agreed with the officer's suggestion that he may have been under the influence of drugs and stabbed the victim without knowing what he was doing. He finally admitted: 'I just stabbed, not stabbed her . . . just thumped her in the face I mean.'

6.5.2 UNRELIABILITY—S. 76(2)(B) PACE 1984

The key issue under s. 76(2)(b) is whether the confession was obtained in circumstances that renders it unreliable. The 'unreliability' ground is much wider than the 'oppression' ground.

In applying the 'unreliability' test, s. 76(2)(b) requires the court to consider 'anything said or done to the accused . . . in the circumstances existing at the time'. Therefore the court must examine all the relevant circumstances of the accused's detention and interrogation and take account of what was said or done to the accused.

As well as the suspect's subjective characteristics, breaches of PACE 1984 and the Codes of Practice will be relevant to excluding a confession on the ground of unreliability. Although a breach will not render a confession automatically inadmissible, the safeguards under PACE 1984 and the Codes exist to ensure the reliability of a confession by protecting the suspect's basic rights.

Bad faith by the police is largely irrelevant to a s. 76(2)(b) submission. What is important is the effect any breach had on the particular suspect at the time. A failure by the police to identify a particular vulnerability due to a medical condition or substance abuse and to make an appropriate provision may provide grounds for the court to exclude a confession under this section. Inducements from the police to encourage the suspect to confess, such as the promise of bail or a lesser charge, are also relevant considerations. For s. 76(2)(b) PACE 1984 to apply, there must be a proven causal link between what was said and done at the police station and the resulting confession.

The following illustrate the case-by-case approach to assessing admissibility under s. 76(2)(b).

R v Delaney [1988] 86 Cr App R 18: failure to secure legal representation for a vulnerable suspect

The defendant was convicted of the indecent assault of a three-year-old girl. The only evidence against him was his confession. He had been interviewed at length, having declined the services of a solicitor. Although he was 17 he had an IQ of only 80 and was educationally subnormal. There was evidence from an educational psychologist, which, if accepted, established the defendant as a vulnerable suspect. The interview had been conducted on a sympathetic basis with the officers being at pains to minimise the seriousness of the defendant's position. On several occasions during the interview, reference was made to the defendant's need for treatment rather than punishment. Given the nature of the questioning on such a vulnerable suspect, who was not legally represented, the risk of it producing a false confession was too high and the confession was excluded.

R v Howden-Simpson [1991] Crim LR 49: inducement to confess

The appellant was an organist and choirmaster. His duties included paying junior choir members for their services at weddings. He failed to pay the money to the choristers and was charged with theft. His confession was excluded under s. 76(2) PACE 1984 because of an inducement to confess. The investigating officers had indicated that they would proceed on two non-payment charges only if he admitted the theft. If he did not admit the two charges they would interview every chorister not paid and make a separate charge for each. In the circumstances the Court of Appeal decided the confession should have been excluded under s. 76(2)(b) PACE 1984. The position the appellant was placed in by the officers rendered his confession unreliable.

A confession will not be excluded where the suspect's conduct created the unreliable circumstances (a so-called self-induced confession). In *R v Goldenberg* [1988] 88 Cr App R 285, it was held that s. 76(2)(b) does not apply where what was said or done was induced by the accused where he admitted the offence out of a desperate desire to obtain bail, as he was suffering from drug withdrawal. It was not possible in these circumstances to establish a causal link between anything said or done to the accused and the resulting confession.

6.5.3 'UNFAIRNESS'—S. 78 PACE 1984

The wider application of s. 78 PACE 1984 will also be considered later in the chapter in relation to unlawfully obtained prosecution evidence other than confessions. The judicial discretion under s. 78 provides:

> 'In any proceedings the court may refuse to allow evidence on which the prosecution proposes to rely to be given if it appears to the court that, having regard to all the circumstances, including the circumstances in which the evidence was obtained, the admission of the evidence would have such an adverse effect on the fairness of the proceedings that the court ought not to admit it.'

Section 78 PACE 1984 might be applied to incriminating admissions that have been obtained as a result of unfair conduct by the police, including:

- failing to secure access to a solicitor;
- failing to properly record an interview;
- failing to provide safeguards in relation to a vulnerable suspect;
- deceiving a suspect into making a confession or offering inducements;
- acting in deliberate breach of Code C.

An illustration of the application of s. 78 PACE 1984 is provided by *R v Mason* [1988] 1 WLR 139. The defendant (M) was in custody on suspicion of having petrol-bombed the car of his ex-girlfriend's father. M and his solicitor were told (untruthfully) by two police officers that M's fingerprints had been found on pieces of glass from the petrol bombs that had shattered near the car. As a result of this deception, and perceiving his position to be hopeless, M confessed, which led to his conviction for arson which the Court of Appeal later quashed. It appears from the judgment that the deception practised on the solicitor (an officer of the court) was particularly objectionable, and that the trial judge ought to have exercised his discretion to exclude the confession, as its admission had had an adverse effect on the fairness of the proceedings.

There is an overlap between the type of factors justifying exclusion under s. 76(2)(b) and under s. 78 PACE 1984 including any breaches of PACE 1984 and the Codes of Practice, although a breach of Code C does not guarantee that the confession will be automatically excluded under s. 78 PACE 1984. There must also be a causal connection between the breach of the suspect's legal rights and the resulting confession otherwise there is no unfairness (*R v Alladice* [1988] 87 Cr App R 380).

The importance that the Court of Appeal attaches to a suspect's access to a solicitor at the police station under s. 58 PACE 1984 has been underlined in a number of cases including *R v Samuel* [1988] QB 615 and *R v Walsh* (1990) 91 Cr App R 161. In *Walsh* access to a solicitor had been wrongfully denied and the interview was not contemporaneously recorded. W confessed to robbery. The judge admitted the confession into evidence. The Court of Appeal quashed the conviction concluding that if there had been: 'significant and substantial breaches of section 58, then prima facie the standards of fairness set by Parliament have not been met'.

Another helpful illustration of the application of s. 78 PACE 1984 to a confession is provided by *R v Aspinall* [1999] Crim LR 741. A, a schizophrenic, was convicted on drug charges. At the police station two police surgeons had pronounced him fit for interview.

When asked by the officers whether he wanted to see a solicitor, A had replied: 'No I want to get home to my missus and kids.' A was interviewed without a solicitor or an appropriate adult. The trial judge rejected a s. 78 submission, concluding that A had been lucid at the time of interview.

In allowing his appeal and quashing the conviction, the Court of Appeal held that A had been unable to assess what was in his best interests. According to A's consultant psychiatrist A had been tired and stressed whilst at the police station which resulted in him lacking assertiveness when dealing with the police. The absence of an appropriate adult (a specific requirement under Code C for a vulnerable person) rendered the confession unfair. The Court of Appeal concluded there had been a breach of Article 6 caused by the delay in access to legal advice as the duty solicitor had been otherwise engaged at the relevant time.

6.6 THE PROCEDURE FOR DETERMINING THE ADMISSIBILITY OF A CONFESSION

The procedure to challenge the admissibility of a confession is through a trial within a trial, otherwise known as a voir dire. Where the confession's admissibility is raised at trial, the issue will be resolved in the absence of the jury. A voir dire can, however, be conducted at a pre-trial hearing at which a binding ruling can be made. Section 45 (Sch. 3) Courts Act 2003 permits binding rulings to be made at a pre-trial hearing in summary proceedings.

A voir dire need only be held where it is represented that the confession was obtained by oppression or is unreliable. This will normally involve a mixed question of law and fact. If an accused denies making a confession, i.e. maintains his signature has been forged or denies words attributed to him, then this becomes a factual matter only and should be dealt with by the jury/magistrates (*R v Flemming* (1988) 86 Cr App R 32).

At either the pre-trial stage or at trial, the judge when conducting a voir dire will hear evidence about how the confession was obtained and will hear legal argument from both sides.

In discharging its legal burden to prove the confession's admissibility, the prosecution will usually call the interviewing officers and custody officer(s) to give evidence and will submit the custody record into evidence. The prosecution evidence will be cross-examined by the defence. The defendant may testify at the hearing and expert evidence may be heard. The judge will consider the evidence, apply the law and decide whether the confession should be admitted in evidence. If it is excluded, the jury will never know about the confession. If ruled admissible, the accused is still entitled to repeat his allegations about how the confession was obtained in an attempt to persuade the jury that the confession carries little evidential weight.

6.7 EDITING A CONFESSION

If a confession contains other inadmissible evidence, e.g. hearsay, or discloses the accused's previous convictions, the defence should seek to have the offending material edited out before it is put before the court. The rules regarding the evidence of tape-recorded interviews are contained in the Consolidated Practice Direction Part IV 43. The defence is required to notify the prosecution of whether the transcript of the tape-recorded interview is acceptable. If not, the rules require both parties to try to resolve any disputed issues as it will save valuable time at trial if an edited transcript can be agreed.

6.8 EVIDENCE OBTAINED IN CONSEQUENCE OF AN INADMISSIBLE CONFESSION

If a confession is ruled inadmissible, it does not mean that evidence obtained as a result of the confession must also be excluded. Sections 76(4) and 76(5) PACE 1984 permit other incriminating evidence discovered as a result of an inadmissible confession to be introduced provided no reference is made to the confession. Where the incriminating evidence cannot be adduced without referring to the inadmissible confession, neither the confession nor the facts discovered will be admissible.

6.9 CHALLENGING THE ADMISSIBILITY OF OTHER NON-CONFESSION PROSECUTION EVIDENCE

Where the defence or the court submit that 'other' prosecution evidence was obtained in an unfair or unlawful way, the evidence may be excluded by the court under the common law discretion or on the ground of unfairness or as an abuse of process.

6.10 COMMON LAW DISCRETION

The criminal courts have always retained the common law power to exclude evidence capable of prejudicing a fair trial. This discretion is specifically preserved by s. 82(3) PACE 1984. If the prejudicial effect of the evidence sought to be adduced by the prosecution exceeds its probative value, the evidence must be excluded. This requires a careful balancing exercise to be undertaken by the trial judge or magistrates.

Prosecuting lawyers have long relied on the narrow approach adopted by the common law to exclude illegally or unlawfully obtained evidence. Provided the evidence is relevant and reliable, its admission is not generally regarded as prejudicing the defendant's right to a fair trial. The discretion will certainly not be used to discipline the police about the way in which prosecution evidence was obtained. The limited application of the common law is illustrated by Lord Diplock in the leading case of *R v Sang* [1980] AC 402 (a case where the defendant argued he had been entrapped by prosecution authorities):

> '(1) A trial judge in a criminal trial has always a discretion to refuse to admit evidence if in his opinion its prejudicial effect outweighs its probative value. (2) Save with regard to admissions and confessions and generally with regard to evidence obtained from the accused after commission of the offence, he has no discretion to refuse to admit relevant admissible evidence on the ground that it was obtained by improper or unfair means. The court is not concerned with how it was obtained.'

Whilst the absence of significant case law under s. 82(3) PACE 1984 confirms that it is not commonly invoked, defence lawyers should always be prepared to cite the section when challenging the manner in which the police obtained evidence against the accused. It is common to base the defence argument not only under s. 82(3) PACE 1984 but also under the apparently wider discretion in s. 78 PACE 1984.

6.11 DISCRETION UNDER S. 78 PACE 1984

As previously explained, s. 78 PACE 1984 gives the court discretion to exclude any prosecution evidence where the admission of the evidence would have an adverse effect on the fairness of the proceedings. Although the fairness of the proceedings is not defined, the court is invited by the wording in the section to have regard to all the circumstances in which the evidence was obtained.

Consider the following examples illustrating the practical application of s. 78.

6.11.1 USE OF TRICKERY OR DECEPTION BY THE POLICE

Prosecution evidence (including incriminating admissions obtained outside a formal police interview) may be excluded under s. 78 PACE 1984 where the police obtained the evidence through trickery or deception. As *R v Bailey and Smith* illustrates, when exercising its discretion under s. 78 PACE 1984, the court is less concerned with the nature of the police conduct in breaching a defendant's legal rights than the reliability of the evidence that was obtained as a result of the trickery or deception.

R v Bailey and Smith [1993] 3 All ER 365

The accused were arrested in connection with an armed robbery. Both were legally represented and remained silent. They were charged and brought before a magistrates' court where they were remanded into police custody for the purposes of attending an identification parade. Although the questioning of suspects after charge is prohibited under Code C, the investigating officers put the defendants in the same cell, in an attempt to obtain further useful evidence by falsely telling the defendants that they must share a cell because of an unco-operative custody officer. The cell was bugged. The defendants believed the police even though their solicitor had warned them that the bugging of police cells was not uncommon. While together in the cell, they made incriminating admissions which were used in evidence against them. The Court of Appeal held the trial judge had rightly admitted the evidence.

6.11.2   UNAUTHORISED SURVEILLANCE METHODS

The increasing sophistication of surveillance technology allows the police to obtain evidence in many covert ways. Such surveillance operations must be authorised under the Regulation of Investigatory Powers Act 2000 (RIPA 2000). Where such surveillance methods are unauthorised or where the police act in breach of the criminal and/or the civil law, should the evidence be admitted? Consider the case of *R v Khan* which pre-dates the RIPA 2000.

R v Khan [1996] 3 All ER 298

Khan was suspected of drug smuggling. To obtain evidence against him, investigating officers attached a listening device to a property visited by Khan, of which neither Khan or the flat's owner had any knowledge. Whilst Home Office Guidelines existed regarding the use of covert surveillance, there was no statutory authorisation for the use of such devices at the time, although the officers had sought and obtained permission of the Chief Constable. As a result of the operation, the police obtained a tape recording that proved Khan was involved in importing heroin.

At Khan's trial the prosecution sought to admit the tape recording in evidence whilst accepting that there was no statutory authority for using the device and that placing it on the property without the owner's permission constituted a civil trespass. Khan conceded that the tape was authentic and that it was his voice which could be heard. On appeal it was argued on Khan's behalf that the evidence had been obtained in violation of Article 8, guaranteeing a right of privacy, and that the trial judge should have excluded the tape-recorded conversations in the exercise of his discretion either at common law or under s. 78 PACE 1984.

Notwithstanding there may have been a violation of Article 8, the House of Lords concluded that the evidence was rightly admitted at common law and under s. 78. The evidence was especially relevant and could not be said to have adversely affected the fairness of the proceedings.

Khan subsequently took his case to the European Court of Human Rights (ECtHR), in *Khan v United Kingdom* (2001) 31 EHRR 45. Whilst finding the UK to be in violation of Article 8, the ECtHR determined that the evidence against the applicant was reliable and had not been obtained by inducements. There had been no violation of Article 6 as the applicant had enjoyed a fair trial because s. 78 PACE 1984 had afforded Khan the opportunity to challenge the admissibility of the prosecution evidence in court.

As a result of this decision the use of covert/intrusive surveillance for investigatory purposes was placed on a statutory footing with the enactment of RIPA 2000 and its accompanying Code of Practice. Consideration of the provisions under RIPA fall outside the scope of this text.

6.11.3   **ENTRAPMENT**

Entrapment is conduct by a law enforcement agent inducing a person to commit an offence that the person would otherwise have been unlikely to commit.

Entrapment often involves an *agent* provocateur, such as an undercover police officer. Evidence obtained in this way can be challenged at common law or under s. 78 PACE 1984 or as an abuse of process subject to the proviso that entrapment is not a defence in English criminal law.

The law governing the admissibility of evidence obtained by entrapment has steadily evolved. A definitive statement of the principles which takes account of Convention law on the issue (see *Teixeira de Castro v Portugal* (1998) 28 EHRR 242) was provided by the House of Lords in the following case which combined two appeals.

R v Loosely; Attorney-General's Reference (No. 3 of 2000) [2001] 1 WLR 2060

In Loosely's case, an undercover officer posed as a prospective buyer of drugs. His actions were part of an authorised surveillance in the Guildford area, which had seen a rise in the supply of heroin. The focus of suspicion fell on a particular public house in which the undercover officer had been given the defendant's contact number as a possible source of supply. On contacting the defendant, the officer asked if he could 'sort us a couple of bags'. The defendant responded willingly to the request and immediately arranged to take the undercover officer to a place where he was able to obtain the drugs.

In the *Attorney-General's Reference*, undercover officers offered the defendant contraband cigarettes. After a lengthy conversation about the cigarettes, one of the officers asked the defendant if he could 'sort him some brown'. It was only after numerous conversations, much persuasion and the offer of further contraband cigarettes, that the defendant eventually obtained a quantity of heroin for the officers. On handing the drug over to the undercover officers, the defendant was recorded as saying: 'I am not really into heroin myself.' In interview he maintained he had nothing to do with heroin and had only supplied the officers because of their requests and as a favour for the contraband cigarettes.

The House of Lords concluded that in entrapment cases, the application to have the evidence excluded is in practice an application to stay the proceedings for an abuse of process since the evidence obtained through the use of entrapment usually forms the entire basis of the prosecution's case. If the evidence of entrapment was to be excluded the prosecution case would collapse. For this reason, an abuse of process application was the appropriate remedy. Accordingly, the relevant test to be applied in English law was that set out in *R v Latif and Shazard* [1996] 1 WLR 104: namely, where the conduct of the prosecuting authorities had been so shameful and unworthy as to constitute an affront to the public conscience the case should be stopped as an abuse of process. It is conduct so seriously improper as to bring the administration of justice into disrepute.

On the facts, the House of Lords concluded that Loosely's appeal should be dismissed. His arrest had come about as a result of legitimate concern in the rising supply of hard drugs in the Guildford area and from one public house in particular. As Loosely expressed himself keen to arrange a supply, the undercover officer had not needed to undertake any persuasion, and therefore his actions clearly fell within the bounds of acceptable conduct. In relation to the *Attorney-General's Reference*, the House of Lords concluded it would not interfere with the trial judge's exercise of discretion. The defendant in that case had come under considerable and sustained pressure by officers to supply them with a Class A drug and could be said to have been induced to commit the offence based on the continued supply of contraband cigarettes to him.

6.12   **ABUSE OF PROCESS**

In addition to the discretion to exclude evidence at common law and under s. 78 PACE 1984, the criminal courts have an inherent jurisdiction to stay proceedings for abuse of process. This would be a very serious step for a court to take as its effect is to bring the trial to an end. Where a stay is ordered the court believes that either the defendant cannot enjoy a fair trial or as a result of the actions of the prosecuting authorities, it is not fair to try the accused.

An abuse of process submission would be appropriate in the following circumstances where:

- there has been considerable delay by the prosecution in bringing charges; or
- adverse pre-trial publicity makes a fair trial impossible;
- there is a later prosecution where a previous trial was halted;
- it is decided to commence a prosecution in circumstances where the prosecution agreed an alternative course of action, i.e. to caution (see *R v Dobson* [2000] EWCA 1606);
- the prosecution has lost or failed to secure evidence relevant to the crime which might have assisted the defendant;
- the prosecution has withheld relevant evidence; or
- where evidence has been obtained by entrapment (see *R v Loosely* already mentioned).

Where proceedings are stayed because of the unlawful activities of the prosecuting authorities, the court is effectively stating that such activities will not be tolerated and cannot be condoned. The exercise of discretion under abuse of process is therefore wider than the discretion exercised under s. 78 PACE 1984. However, the type of misconduct involved for an abuse of process application to succeed must be such that it would be an affront to public conscience for the proceedings to continue or for the conviction to stand (*R v Latif* [1996] 1 WLR 104).

6.13 ILLEGALLY/UNFAIRLY OBTAINED EVIDENCE—PRACTICAL CONSIDERATIONS

Prosecutors and defence lawyers are aware from the case law that the courts appear to adopt a more proactive approach to excluding confession and identification evidence than to other 'tainted' prosecution evidence. This dual approach will be taken into account by both sides when preparing their case for trial.

6.13.1 ILLEGALLY/UNFAIRLY OBTAINED EVIDENCE FROM THE PROSECUTION PERSPECTIVE

For both prosecution and defence, the most important part of successful representation in court is case preparation. For cases to be tried in the Crown Court, the prosecutor is alerted from the defence statement, disclosed under the pre-trial disclosure of evidence rules (see Chapter 13), of any potential defence challenges to the admissibility of prosecution evidence. In summary cases where a defence statement is not mandatory, the defence is required, by Crim PR, Part 3, to assist the court in identifying the issues that are in dispute in a contested case. In anticipating any challenges the prosecutor will be prepared through diligent research of the relevant case law to argue against excluding any evidence either at pre-trial hearing or in the *voir dire* at trial.

6.13.2 ILLEGALLY/UNFAIRLY OBTAINED EVIDENCE FROM THE DEFENCE PERSPECTIVE

Under the pre-trial disclosure of evidence rules in both summary and indictable proceedings the prosecution will have made full disclosure of the case against the accused. The disclosed evidence should be looked at critically by the defence team and whilst the courts tend to adopt a relatively restrictive approach to their exclusionary powers, the defence advocate should argue against admitting 'tainted' evidence. Therefore the current law in relation to the exercise of judicial discretion under s. 76 and s. 78 in relation to confessions, and s. 78 and/or s. 82(3) PACE 1984 in relation to other prosecution evidence, should not inhibit a defence advocate from making an application to have unlawfully obtained evidence excluded. Defence advocates should also be aware of the potential for making an abuse of process application where appropriate and the pervasive influence of Article 6 ECHR 1950.

For a practical exercise to challenge the admissibility of prosecution evidence, consider the following self-test exercises.

KEY POINT SUMMARY

- A confession is widely defined and covers any incriminating admissions made by an accused.
- Breaches of PACE 1984 and the Codes of Practice are important in determining the admissibility of confession evidence where such evidence is disputed—although a breach will not automatically lead to a confession being excluded.
- 'Oppression' (s. 76(2)(a)) is narrowly defined and will invariably involve some deliberate misconduct on the part of the police.
- 'Unreliability' (s. 76(2)(b)) has a much wider application. It does not require bad faith on the part of the police and the defendant's mental state will be a relevant consideration.
- If a confession is admissible under s. 76 PACE 1984, it may still be excluded under s. 78 PACE 1984 if its admission would have an adverse affect on the fairness of the case.
- Every accused enjoys the right to a fair trial including the right to challenge any evidence that might be said to have been obtained unlawfully or in a dubious manner.
- The power to exclude evidence in the interests of securing a fair trial exists at common law and under s. 78 PACE 1984—both are exercised on a discretionary basis.
- Section 78 PACE 1984 has largely superseded the common law which is now found in s. 82(3) PACE 1984.
- Section 78 PACE 1984 applies to all types of prosecution evidence, including prosecution evidence that has been obtained unlawfully.

SELF-TEST QUESTIONS

A reminder of Code C safeguards

Exercise 1

In order to refresh your memory in this regard, see if you can answer the following short questions.

1. At what stages does the suspect have to be cautioned? Would a confession that has been obtained following a failure to properly caution an individual be admissible?

2. On arrival at the police station what rights should be explained to the suspect by the custody officer?

3. What initial assessment must the custody officer undertake in relation to each suspect and who might be said to constitute a vulnerable suspect?

4. The right of access to a solicitor is governed by the all-important s. 58 PACE 1984. In what circumstances may access to a solicitor be delayed? If access was delayed and a confession was obtained, would the confession be admissible?

5. Can the investigating officers begin to question a suspect when the suspect has requested a solicitor?

6. What are the maximum periods of detention and at what intervals should detention be reviewed? (It goes without saying that the longer an individual is detained in custody the more he or she may be tempted to confess in order to relieve the pressure of the situation.)

7. What basic human rights are suspects entitled to while in custody, including rest periods?

8. What actually constitutes an interview under Code C?

9. What is the procedure if the suspect appears to be unfit to be interviewed?

10. What safeguards apply as regards the conduct of an interview in relation to non-vulnerable and vulnerable suspects?

Exercise 2: *R v Lenny Wise*

Consider the Lenny Wise scenario.

We have begun the process of evaluating the evidence against Lenny Wise. You will see from Document 26E (included in Appendix 1) that Lenny makes a confession. What he states in his interview satisfies the statutory definition of a confession under s. 82(1) PACE. His interview is tape-recorded in accordance with the requirements of Code E para. 3.1. Having regard to Lenny's proof of evidence (Document 6) and the custody record (Document 9) consider the following questions:

- Do you feel you have grounds for challenging the admissibility of Lenny's confession in due course? If so, what will be the legal basis for your submissions?
- What arguments will you put forward in support of your submissions?
- Consider the manner in which the confession was obtained. Can you point to any specific breaches of Code C?
- How will the admissibility of Lenny's confession be resolved and what evidence will need to be adduced and challenged in this regard?

Exercise 3

Ranjit Singh will state as follows:

> 'Shortly before midnight last night I was driving home in my mother's Ford Escort Cabriolet, registration number R457 KYE. I had just parked the car and was removing my sports bag from the boot. It contained my squash equipment. I was wearing my black tracksuit trousers and hooded sweatshirt. I was searching for my mobile phone in the back of the car when two men approached me. One reached into the car and grabbed me by the arm. It was dark. I could not see what they were wearing. Fearing a racial attack, I just lashed out and hit one of them. I extricated myself and started to run. One of them shouted: "Stop we're police officers." I was grabbed in a matter of seconds. The other man began to search my bag and then me. The other searched my car. Finally, I heard one of them say, "Let's teach him a lesson." With that I was handcuffed. They emptied my pockets and removed my trousers, socks and shoes. They found a small quantity of cocaine tucked inside my sock. I was then arrested and subsequently charged with (a) possession of a controlled drug and (b) assaulting a police officer in the execution of his duty.'

Do you feel you can challenge the admissibility of the evidence in the case? If so, upon what grounds?

Guidance on all the above questions can be found on our Online Resource Centre.

 online resource centre

FIGURE 6.1 UNLAWFULLY AND UNFAIRLY OBTAINED EVIDENCE

WHAT CONSTITUTES UNLAWFULLY OBTAINED EVIDENCE?

- Any evidence obtained unlawfully or in an underhand manner, which can include:
  - evidence obtained in breach of Codes of Practice under PACE;
  - evidence obtained through the use of an *agent provocateur*;
  - evidence obtained in breach of rights under PACE—unlawful arrest search/seizure;
  - evidence obtained in violation of Article 8—the right to privacy;
  - evidence obtained in violation of the privilege against self-incrimination.

COMMON LAW PRESERVED BY S. 82(3) PACE

- illustrated in *R v Sang* and *R v Khan*;

- restrictive in its application;

- save for evidence of a self-incriminating nature obtained by means of trickery/deception after commission of offence, evidence obtained unlawfully or unfairly remains admissible if it is relevant and reliable;

- if the prejudicial effect of the evidence exceeds its probative value, the evidence will be excluded.

SECTION 78 PACE 1984

- gives courts discretion to exclude **any** prosecution evidence, the admission of which would have an adverse effect on the fairness of the proceedings;

- application of s. 78 is pervasive and is not confined to unlawfully obtained evidence;

- used most successfully to exclude confession evidence obtained in breach of safeguards of PACE and Code C (*R v Aspinall*; *R v Walsh*; *R v Samuel*);

- also used to exclude identification evidence obtained in breach of safeguards under Code D (*R v Finley*) - see Chapter 7;

- less successfully used in relation to other types of evidence, i.e. unlawful arrest/search/seizure, unauthorised surveillance/underhand tactics where the evidence yielded is relevant, reliable and authentic (*R v Khan*);

- on the use of an *agent provocateur* see *R v Loosely* and the application of abuse of process;

- case law suggests that unless the reliability of the evidence is tainted by the illegality or unfairness, making it more difficult for the defendant to challenge the evidence, it is likely to be admitted.

FIGURE 6.2 CONFESSION EVIDENCE

- A confession is any statement wholly or partly adverse whether made to a person in authority or not: s. 82(1) PACE 1984.
- Procedure for challenging the admissibility of confession evidence is a *voir dire* (trial within a trial).
- The admissibility of a confession may be challenged on the basis of:

OPPRESSION

- the exercise of power in a burdensome, harsh or wrongful manner;
- s. 76(2)(a) PACE 1984: requires deliberate and serious misconduct on the part of the police;
- see *R v Fulling* for definition of oppression.

UNRELIABILITY

s. 76(2)(b) PACE 1984: in consequence of anything said or done which, at the time, was likely to render unreliable any confession made by the suspect:

- breaches of Code C safeguards highly relevant to this ground;
- can include failure to secure access to legal advice in breach of s. 58 PACE 1984;
- offering a suspect inducements to confess;
- errors or omissions on the part of the police need not be deliberate;
- burden of proving the absence of unreliability on prosecution.

UNFAIRNESS

s. 78 PACE 1984: the admission of the confession would have an adverse effect on the fairness of the proceedings:

- significant and substantial breaches of Code C highly relevant to this ground;
- failure to spot and deal with a vulnerable suspect;
- taking advantage of a vulnerable suspect;
- failing to properly record an interview;
- factors relevant to this ground overlap with s.76(2)(b).

OBTAINING IDENTIFICATION EVIDENCE

7.1 INTRODUCTION

Proof of the defendant's presence at the crime scene through identification evidence can be presented at trial in a number of ways, including:

- visual identification of a suspect by an eye-witness;
- real evidence: CCTV surveillance has led to the increasing use of video tape and photographic stills at trials. This type of real evidence can give the court a direct view of the incident enabling the jury or the magistrates to decide whether the defendant is the person seen participating in the criminal activity captured on film;

- forensic evidence: identification may also be proved by the opinion of a forensic scientist establishing a connection between the defendant and the crime scene based on the scientific comparison of forensic samples, e.g. fingerprints or DNA discovered at the crime scene compared with evidence found on the defendant or otherwise in his possession.

In this chapter, we consider:

- the dangers of eye-witness identification;
- how identification evidence is obtained by the police during the police investigation;
- the pre-trial safeguards contained in the identification procedures under Code D;
- the admissibility of eye-witness evidence obtained in breach of Code D;
- obtaining fingerprints, intimate and non-intimate samples at the police station;
- identification evidence given by expert witnesses.

Numerous references will be made in this chapter to Code D which can be freely accessed from the Home Office website—our Online Resource Centre provides a link to the full text of Code D. online resource centre

7.2 THE DANGERS OF EYE-WITNESS IDENTIFICATION

Eye-witness identification has been proven to be inherently unreliable by psychological experiments and by miscarriages of justice. Identification is often made in difficult circumstances where, for example, a crime-related incident is over in a matter of seconds or minutes or in circumstances of heightened awareness where the witness is in fear. Safeguards are required to ensure identification evidence is gathered in a scrupulously fair manner and is treated with caution at trial. The principal safeguards are provided pre-trial by the Police and Criminal Evidence Act 1984 (PACE 1984) Code D and at trial by the Turnbull guidelines (*R v Turnbull* [1977] QB 224). The application of the Turnbull guidelines are considered in Chapter 17.

7.3 HOW IS EYE-WITNESS IDENTIFICATION OBTAINED?

Eye-witness identification may come about in many different ways. A witness to a crime will typically give an initial statement to the police including a description of the person or persons the witness believes were involved. Code D para. 3.1 requires the police to make a record of the suspect's description as first given by a potential witness and for the suspect or his legal adviser to be given a copy of the record.

On the basis of the information provided, the police may compile a photofit of a suspect they wish to speak to and circulate it to the media. In some instances, witnesses may be taken on a tour of the area in the immediate aftermath of a crime to see if they are able to spot the person(s) they think they saw involved in the offence. The police may show witnesses 'mug shots' of convicted offenders, or CCTV footage or photographic stills, to see if they can identify the culprit.

7.4 DISTINGUISHING BETWEEN KNOWN AND UNKNOWN SUSPECTS

For the purposes of identification procedures, Code D distinguishes between a known and an unknown suspect. The distinction is of considerable practical importance.

7.4.1 WHAT IS A KNOWN SUSPECT?

Code D para. 3.4 provides guidance about when a suspect is 'known' and 'available'. A suspect is known where there is sufficient information known to the police to justify the arrest of a particular person for suspected involvement in an offence. A suspect is available if he is immediately available or will be available within a reasonably short period of time and is willing to take part in an identification procedure.

7.4.2 WHERE THE SUSPECT IS UNKNOWN

Where the suspect is unknown, the police may take a witness to a particular neighbourhood or place to see if the witness can identify the suspect. Code D para. 3.2 stipulates the safeguards the police need to consider when taking a witness around an area. A detailed record of all the circumstances must be kept and the police must not direct the witness's attention to a particular individual.

7.4.3 SHOWING PHOTOGRAPHS TO A WITNESS

If the suspect's identity is not known, the witness may be shown photographs subject to safeguards contained in Annex E of Code D including:

- a requirement that the witness should be shown 12 photographs at a time which should be of a similar type;
- a witness must not be prompted or guided in his choice in any way;
- if a witness makes a positive identification from a set of photographs no other witness can be shown the set and each of the witnesses should be asked to attend a parade.

Once the police have a known suspect in mind they should proceed to an arrest and convene a formal identification procedure if required.

Code D para. 3.3 prevents a witness from being shown photographs if the suspect's identity is known to the police and the suspect is available to participate in an identification procedure. Showing photographs in advance of a formal identification procedure seriously compromises the integrity of the procedure and effectively renders the procedure irrelevant.

7.4.4 WHERE THE SUSPECT IS KNOWN AND AVAILABLE

Once a suspect is known and is available the police should proceed to a formal identification procedure where the circumstances prescribed by Code D para. 3.4 apply.

7.5 WHEN MUST AN IDENTIFICATION PROCEDURE BE HELD?

Where an eye-witness purports to identify a suspect at the crime scene and the suspect denies being the person the witness is alleged to have seen, Code D imposes a virtually mandatory requirement on the police to convene an identification procedure to confirm or disprove the witness's identification.

Code D para. 3.12 provides:

'Whenever:

(i) a witness has identified a suspect or purported to have identified them prior to any identification procedure set out in paragraphs 3.5 to 3.10 having been held; or

(ii) there is a witness available, who expresses an ability to identify the suspect, or where there is a reasonable chance of the witness being able to do so, and they have not been given an opportunity to identify the suspect in any procedures set out in paragraphs 3.5 to 3.10, and the suspect disputes being the person the witness claims to have seen, an identification procedure shall be held unless it is not practicable or it would serve no useful purpose in proving or disproving whether the suspect was involved in committing the offence. For example the useful purpose test may be satisfied when it is not disputed that the suspect is already well known to the witness who claims to have seen him commit the crime.'

7.5.1 **TYPES OF IDENTIFICATION PROCEDURES**

In order to test the witness's ability to identify a suspect and to safeguard against mistaken identity, the police use a number of formal identification procedures, which are governed by Code D and its Annexes A–D.

The Annexes to Code D provide the following procedures:

- Annex A: video identification.
- Annex B: identification parades.
- Annex C: group identification.
- Annex D: confrontation by a witness.

In the hierarchy of identification procedures, the video identification is the preferred choice. It is easier to organise and is less intimidating for witnesses. Where an identification procedure must be held in accordance with Code D para. 3.12, para. 3.14 provides the suspect must initially be offered a video identification unless:

- this is not practicable; or
- an identification parade is more practicable and suitable; or
- the officer in charge of the investigation considers that a group identification is more suitable than the other forms of identification and the identification officer believes it is practicable to arrange.

The decision to adopt a particular procedure is taken by the officer in charge of identification procedures in consultation with the investigating officer. A suspect must be allowed to make representations about the procedure to be adopted, and before an option is offered, the suspect must be reminded of his entitlement to free legal advice (Code D para. 3.14).

The conduct of the identification procedure is the sole responsibility of an officer of at least the rank of inspector who is independent of the investigation.

7.5.2 **THE SUSPECT'S RIGHTS AT AN IDENTIFICATION PROCEDURE**

Some important rights must be explained to the suspect by the police before convening an identification procedure. They are set out in Code D para. 3.17 and include:

- the suspect's right to free legal advice and their right to have a solicitor or friend present;
- an explanation that the suspect does not have to consent or co-operate in a video identification, identification parade or group identification but that if the suspect does not consent, his refusal can be given in evidence against him in any subsequent trial and the police may proceed covertly without the suspect's consent or make other arrangements to test whether a witness can identify him;
- that if the suspect has significantly altered his appearance between being offered an identification procedure and the convening of the procedure, the identification officer may consider other forms of identification and the fact that the suspect significantly changed his appearance may be given in evidence to the court if the case comes to trial;
- whether, before the suspect's identity became known, the police showed the witness photographs and/or a computerised or artist's composite image.

The formal identification procedures regarded as the fairest to the suspect are the video parade and the identification parade because they provide the suspect with the best chance of not being selected, as he has some control in their composition.

A suspect who refuses to co-operate in a video procedure can be treated as being unavailable (Code D para. 3.21). In these circumstances, the identification officer may make arrangements for the suspect's image to be captured covertly or for photographs to be used in the compilation of the video identification procedure. The confrontation procedure is a procedure of last resort and may not be used unless all other options are impracticable (Code D para. 3.23).

7.6 **IS A FORMAL IDENTIFICATION PROCEDURE A MANDATORY REQUIREMENT?**

The issue of whether the police must convene an identification procedure has been heard in a number of appeals culminating in the House of Lords decision in *R v Forbes* [2001] 1 AC 473, which concerned an earlier version of Code D.

In *Forbes*, the victim was attacked and almost robbed at a cash-dispensing machine. The victim managed to get away and called the police. He was taken on a tour of the area and was able to point out his assailant. The appellant was arrested. He vigorously protested his innocence. No parade was convened as the police believed it would have been futile as a firm street identification had been made. The House of Lords held that a parade was a mandatory requirement save in exceptional cases where the eye-witness insists that he cannot identify the person responsible, or in a case of pure recognition of someone well known to the eye-witness.

Statutory effect has been given to the decision in *R v Forbes* in the current edition of Code D. However, the question of whether an identification procedure is mandatory in all cases remains uncertain. The requirement to convene an identification procedure under Code D para. 3.12 is rebutted where, in all the circumstances, it would serve no useful purpose in proving or disproving whether the suspect was involved in the offence, including, for example, where the suspect is well known to the witness making the identification.

It will be apparent that Code D gives the police discretion to decide whether a suspect is well known to the witness and whether an identification procedure would therefore serve any useful purpose. A decision by the police not to convene an identification procedure should always be critically scrutinised by the defence lawyer as it provides a potential ground to seek the exclusion of the identification evidence on the ground of 'unfairness' under s. 78 PACE 1984. The failure to hold a formal procedure also means that the reliability of the identification was never tested before trial.

The issue of the mandatory requirement to convene a parade was central to the two cases mentioned here which concern earlier versions of Code D, although the decisions remain relevant to the current version of Code D.

R (on the application of H) v DPP **[2003] EWHC 133**

The victim (V) was 15. It was alleged that she had been assaulted by the defendant (D), a 16-year-old. The assault lasted several minutes. V had been assaulted on a previous occasion by D and had reported the matter to the police. D denied the assault and denied being present when the attack took place. No identification parade was held. At her summary trial, D's defence solicitor submitted there had been a breach of Code D para. 2.3 (under the previous Code D), and that consequently there was no evidence of identification.

V had known D for about 18 months and had been a credible witness. Finding D guilty, the magistrates concluded that the police were entitled to refuse to hold an identification parade as it would have been futile. Applying the dicta in *Forbes* (highlighted previously), the Divisional Court concurred with the magistrates' decision. The defendant had indicated she knew V and it was not suggested by the defendant or her legal representative at any time during her police interview that the question of recognition was an issue for her. In these circumstances this was a case of recognition and an identification parade would have served no useful purpose as V was bound to have identified D.

R v Harris **[2003] EWCA 174**

Two victims (A and B) were robbed of their mobile phones in the street by a group of youths. Both A and B claimed to recognise the appellant (C). They had previously been at school with C and knew him by his first name of Tristan. C had been in the year above them. A and B claimed to recognise C even though he was wearing a hooded top. (A) had recognised the boy's voice when he came over to him. It was accepted by A and B that they had not known C well at school and that they had not seen him since he had left. C denied any involvement and put forward an alibi. There was no other evidence to link him to the crime. Evidence was given from the school's headmaster, who confirmed that A and B would have been in attendance from 1998 until 2000 when C had left. There would have been 500 pupils in the school at the time and only one pupil at that time and since had the name of Tristan. No identification parade had been held and the defence submitted at trial that the identification evidence should have been excluded under s. 78 PACE 1984.

Although the defendant had not requested a parade, he had made it clear to the police that he denied involvement and that he did not know A or B. Was C well known to A and B, within the meaning of Code D? The Court of Appeal concluded he was not: neither A nor B had seen C for the past two years; C would have been 14 at the time; neither A, B or C had been in the same class; there had not been any direct contact between them. The Court of Appeal concluded that there was at least: 'a live possibility that one or both witnesses might not have picked out the appellant on an identification parade. In that event, the defence would have been able to rely at trial on such non-identification as adding weight to the defence of alibi.'

In quashing C's conviction, the Court of Appeal held that the trial judge's failure to properly direct the jury about the purpose of Code D and the effect of a breach, meant the defendant had not received a fair trial.

7.7 THE FORMAL IDENTIFICATION PROCEDURES

Whichever identification procedure the police use, the specific safeguards associated with each procedure are contained in the annexes supplementing Code D. We include here a summary of the main provisions.

7.7.1 VIDEO IDENTIFICATION (ANNEX A)

* A set of video images including the suspect and at least eight others is shown to the witness;
* where there are two suspects of similar appearance, at least 12 images should be shown to the witness;
* the eight other people should resemble the suspect in age, height, general appearance and position in life and should show the suspect and the other people in the same position or carrying out the same sequence of movements;
* steps must be taken to conceal any distinguishing features the suspect may have;
* the suspect's solicitor must be offered the opportunity to attend the identification suite when the video parade is compiled and when the compilation is subsequently shown to the eye-witness;
* witnesses must not be allowed to communicate with each other.
* the suspect or the suspect's solicitor/appropriate adult must be given the opportunity to see the complete set of images before it is shown to any witnesses. If the suspect has reasonable objections to the set of images or any of the participants, steps shall, if practicable, be taken to remove the grounds for objection;
* the witness sees all the images at least twice and be told that the person they saw on the earlier occasion may or may not appear in the images shown;
* the witness is asked whether the suspect is the person seen on a previous occasion;
* a record must be made of procedures and those involved and, in the absence of the suspect's solicitor, the viewing of the parade by a witness shall be video recorded.

7.7.2   **IDENTIFICATION PARADE (ANNEX B)**

- The parade should consist of at least eight people in addition to the suspect who as far as possible should resemble the suspect in terms of appearance, age, etc.;
- the suspect must be told that he may object to the arrangements or to a participant and that he may obtain legal advice;
- witnesses attending the parade must not be allowed to communicate with each other about the case or overhear a witness who has already made an identification;
- witnesses must not be allowed to see any participant in advance of the parade or see or be reminded of any photographs or description of the suspect or be given any indication as to the suspect's identity;
- the suspect may choose his own position in the line;
- each witness should be brought into the identification suite one at a time and be told that the person they saw on an earlier occasion may or may not be present and if they cannot make a positive identification, they should say so;
- video recording or colour photograph shall normally be made of the parade;
- where the identification officer is satisfied that the witness has properly looked at each member of the parade, the officer will ask the witness whether the person the witness saw on the earlier relevant occasion is on the identification parade and, if so, indicate the number of the person concerned;
- if the witness wishes to hear any identification parade member speak or adopt any specified posture or move, the witness will first be asked whether the witness can identify on the basis of appearance alone and will be reminded that the participants in the parade have been chosen on the basis of their appearance alone.

7.7.3   **GROUP IDENTIFICATION (ANNEX C)**

- May be held with or without the suspect's consent;
- the witness sees the suspect amongst a group of other people, e.g. shopping centre, railway station;
- the chosen location should take into account the number of people present, general appearance of people;
- a colour photo or video should be taken at the scene immediately after identification;
- the suspect's solicitor or friend can be present.

7.7.4   **CONFRONTATION BY A WITNESS (ANNEX D)**

- Before the confrontation takes place, the witness must be told that the person they saw at the crime scene may, or may not, be the person they are about to confront and that if the witness is unsure about the person's identity, the witness should say so;
- the confrontation must take place in the presence of the suspect's solicitor and/or interpreter and/or friend unless this would cause unreasonable delay;
- the witness is asked: 'Is this the person you saw on the earlier occasion?';
- force may not be used to make the suspect's face visible to the witness;
- the confrontation may either be through a one-way screen or face-to-face with the suspect;
- the confrontation will usually be held at the police station in a normal room or one equipped with a screen permitting a witness to see the suspect without being seen.

7.8 THE CONSEQUENCES OF FAILING TO COMPLY WITH CODE D

The safeguards provided by Code D are important. If the police obtain identification evidence in breach of the safeguards, the defence advocate can apply to have the evidence excluded under s. 78 PACE 1984. The court's discretion to exclude illegally or unfairly obtained evidence is considered in Chapter 6.

Breach of Code D does not inevitably lead to identification evidence being excluded. It is for the court to decide whether the admission of the evidence in these circumstances would have such an adverse effect on the fairness of the trial, that it ought to be excluded. Decisions on identification evidence turn largely on their own facts. The more blatant the breach, the better the prospects are for exclusion.

7.8.1 DIRECTING THE JURY WHERE THERE HAS BEEN A BREACH OF CODE D

The Court of Appeal in *R v Allen* [1995] Crim LR 643 makes it clear that a trial judge must explain to the jury why identification evidence is being admitted in breach of Code D. Guidance has also been provided by the House of Lords in *R v Forbes* [2001] 1 AC 473. Where there has been a breach of the requirement for the police to convene an identification parade or video parade, a trial judge must explain to the jury that the purpose of the parade is to enable a suspect to test the reliability of a witness's identification. In cases where an identification/video parade has not been held contrary to Code D, the suspect loses the benefit of the safeguard a parade gives him. The jury must be directed to take account of this when assessing the case against the defendant. Additionally, even where an informal identification is followed up by a properly conducted parade from which the defendant is chosen, a warning should still be given to the jury. The judge must explain that although the prosecution case is strengthened by the identification, the jury should be aware of the possible risk that the witness might have identified, not the culprit who committed the crime, but the suspect identified by the witness on the earlier occasion.

7.9 RECOGNITION BY POLICE OFFICERS FROM PHOTOGRAPHIC AND CCTV IMAGES

An increasingly common type of identification evidence is derived from either moving or still images captured on CCTV. Police officers are frequently asked to view CCTV records in the hope that they might pick out someone they know or recognise from past experience. In *R v Smith* [2008] EWCA 1342, the Court of Appeal held that Code D did not apply to this situation as the police officer reviewing CCTV footage is not in the same position as a witness asked to identify someone committing a crime. Whilst according to *R v Smith*, Code D had no formal application to this type of identification, safeguards should still be applied to ensure fairness to the defendant, including an independent, contemporaneous record of the police officer's reactions to the CCTV recording which enables a court to assess the reliability of the police officer's assertion.

A revised Code D now provides for the situation described in *R v Smith*. A new Part B has been inserted which applies to police officers asked to review CCTV and other visual media to see if they recognise anyone in the images. Code D paras. 3.34–3.37 identify several key safeguards that should be deployed in this situation, including the requirement that films, photographs and other images must be shown to officers on an individual basis to avoid any possibility of collusion. The showing of photographs or images shall as far as possible follow the principles for video identification if the suspect is known (Annex A), or identification by photographs if the suspect is not known (Annex E). A record must also be kept of the precise circumstances of the viewing, including what was communicated to the officer beforehand about the possible identity of a person(s) in the visual media and the confidence with which an identification is made (see Code D para. 3.36 (a)–(k)).

7.10 **VOICE IDENTIFICATION**

Code D does not apply to voice identification. Voice identification is fraught with more dangers than visual identification, and requires special caution. For two cases in which the defendant was identified by voice identification, see *R v Roberts* [2000] Crim LR 183 and *R v Flynn* [2008] 2 Cr App R 20. Home Office guidance on the use of voice identification is available.

7.11 **DOCK IDENTIFICATIONS**

Dock identifications occur where the victim or another witness testify on oath that the accused standing in the dock is the person they saw at the crime scene. Dock identifications are rare because they have little probative value as the identification of the accused in these circumstances is virtually inevitable and therefore highly prejudicial. Exceptionally a dock identification might be used where the defendant has resisted all other pre-trial identification methods. Even where this occurs, to ensure fairness, the defendant should be asked to take a seat in the courtroom as opposed to standing alone in the dock to be formally identified. The principles governing the use of dock identifications were restated in *Barnes v Chief Constable of Durham* [1997] 2 Cr App R 505 and *Karia v DPP* (2002) 166 JP 753.

7.12 **FORENSIC IDENTIFICATION PROCEDURES**

7.12.1 **FORENSIC EVIDENCE**

Forensic evidence found at the crime scene may provide compelling circumstantial evidence linking the defendant to the offence. Forensic evidence can be available in several forms. The defendant may have left fingerprints, a sample of handwriting, footprints, ear prints, a dental impression or DNA. DNA can be extracted from blood, semen stains, saliva, sweat or body hairs found at or near the crime scene or on the victim. Alternatively, specimens from the crime scene, such as fragments of glass, pollen or foliage, may be present on the suspect's clothing or footwear.

The forensic science service plays an important role in collecting and analysing forensic evidence. DNA is extracted from the crime scene sample and a profile is obtained. The profile is forensically compared to DNA profiles kept on the national database or to a suspect's known sample and an opinion is reached about the DNA's probable source. If the expert's opinion is accepted by the court it can provide very strong circumstantial evidence of the defendant's presence at the scene and his consequent involvement in the crime.

The police are able to assist the forensic investigation by exercising powers under PACE 1984 to obtain intimate and non-intimate body samples from suspects to enable forensic comparison with samples found at the crime scene.

The suspect is a very important source of evidence and as part of the criminal investigation, the police may wish to obtain a set of fingerprints or sample from a suspect for forensic comparison with evidence linked with the commission of the crime.

7.12.2 **FINGERPRINTS AND FOOTWEAR IMPRESSIONS**

The power to obtain fingerprints and footwear impressions is contained in s. 61 PACE 1984 (as amended) and s. 61A PACE 1984 respectively and can be exercised by a constable. The power to take fingerprints can be exercised in the following circumstances:

• Section 61(2) PACE 1984—with the suspect's written consent at the police station;

• Section 61(3) PACE 1984—without the suspect's consent where—

— the suspect has been arrested and detained in connection with a recordable offence; and

— the suspect has not had his fingerprints taken in the course of the investigation taken or if he has, a complete set was not taken or some or all of the fingerprints taken have proved unsuitable or insufficient.

Note s. 2 Crime and Security Act 2010 (C&SA 2010)) has extended this power to cover a suspect who has been arrested but released on bail:

- Section 61(4) PACE 1984—without consent where—

  — the detained person has been charged with or informed that he will be prosecuted for a recordable offence; and

  — he has not had his fingerprints taken in the course of the investigation; or

  — if he has, a complete set was not taken or some or all of the fingerprints taken have proved unsuitable or insufficient.

Note that s. 3 C&SA 2010 has extended this power to cover a suspect who has been charged but released from police detention:

- Section 61(6) PACE 1984—from a person who has been convicted, cautioned, warned or reprimanded for a recordable offence if—

  — since their conviction, caution, warning or reprimand their fingerprints have not been taken; or

  — their fingerprints which have been taken since then do not constitute a complete set; or

  — some, or all, of the fingerprints are not of sufficient quality to allow satisfactory analysis, comparison or matching; and

  — in either case, an officer of inspector rank or above is satisfied that taking the fingerprints is necessary to assist in the prevention or detection of crime and authorises the taking.

Section 61(6A) PACE 1984, allows an officer to take a person's fingerprints without consent prior to an arrest and away from the police station where:

- the officer reasonably suspects that the person is committing or attempting to commit an offence or has committed or has attempted to commit an offence; and

- the name of the person is unknown and cannot be readily ascertained by the officer; or

- the officer has reasonable grounds for doubting whether a name furnished by the person is that person's real name.

The power to take fingerprints other than at a police station using s. 61(6A) PACE 1984 is tied to the development and use of mobile digital fingerprint readers connected to the National Automated Fingerprint Identification System (NAFIS) by mobile communications technology means the police can verify a person's identity at the crime scene in accordance with s. 61(6A) PACE 1984. Section 61(6A) came into force on 7 March 2011.

As with intimate and non-intimate samples (considered later), fingerprint and footwear impressions may be used for a speculative search against forensic databases and the suspect should be warned of this fact.

7.12.3 NON-INTIMATE SAMPLE

A non-intimate sample is defined in s. 65 PACE 1984 to include a sample of hair other than pubic hair, a scraping from under a nail, a swab taken from the mouth, a footprint or bodily impression. Non-intimate samples may be taken with consent under s. 63 (2) PACE 1984. Where consent is withheld, s. 63 PACE 1984 (recently amended by the Crime and Security Act 2010 (C&SA 2010)) permits a non-intimate sample to be taken in the following circumstances:

- Section 63(2A) PACE 1984—where the suspect has been arrested and detained in connection with a recordable offence and no such sample has yet been taken or if it has, it has proved unsuitable or insufficient (note that s. 2 C&SA 2010 has extended this power to cover a suspect who has been arrested but released on bail);

- Section 63(3A) PACE 1984—where the suspect has been charged with a recordable offence (whether in police custody or not) and no such sample has yet been taken or if it has, it has proved unsuitable or insufficient;

• Section 63(3B) PACE 1984—following a conviction, caution, reprimand or warning if, since their conviction, caution, warning or reprimand, a non-intimate sample has not been taken from them or a sample which has been taken since then has proved to be unsuitable or insufficient and in either case, an officer of inspector rank or above is satisfied that taking the fingerprints is necessary to assist in the prevention or detection of crime and authorises the taking.

7.12.4 INTIMATE SAMPLE

An intimate sample (also defined in s. 65 PACE 1984) includes a dental impression or a sample of blood, tissue fluid, urine, pubic hair or swabs taken from a person's genitals or body orifice other than the mouth.

Two important conditions apply before an intimate sample may be lawfully taken. First, the sample may only be taken when authorised by a police officer of at least the rank of inspector who has reasonable grounds for suspecting the person to be involved in a recordable offence and that the sample would confirm or disprove the suspect's involvement. Second, under s. 62 PACE 1984, the suspect's written consent must be obtained, and the sample (other than urine) must be taken by a health-care professional. The failure to consent to provide an intimate sample without good reason can be used in evidence against the defendant at trial (s. 62(10) PACE 1984).

Evidence from samples obtained unlawfully remains admissible subject to the court's exclusionary discretion at common law and under s. 78 PACE 1984 (see Chapter 6).

7.13 DNA EVIDENCE

The UK has one of the most comprehensive DNA databases in the world. The forensic techniques involved in extracting an individual DNA profile and comparing it with other DNA samples have attracted considerable attention from scientists, lawyers and the media. The techniques are relatively new having been perfected in the late 1980s. Over the course of time, however, the techniques have grown increasingly sophisticated, such that DNA evidence can yield very compelling evidence. Every human being has a unique DNA make-up (apart from an identical twin). The profiling techniques enable a forensic scientist to compare two biological samples and to determine the likelihood that the two samples originated from the same source. DNA evidence is perceived as being particularly cogent evidence because of the statistical improbabilities that profiling produces. The process of extraction, extrapolation, interpretation and presentation of results is explained by Lord Justice Phillips in *R v Doheny* [1997] 1 Cr App R 369.

R v Doheny establishes the procedure the prosecution should follow in respect to the disclosure and presentation of DNA evidence. The defence may call their own expert witness to challenge the validity of the opinion provided by the prosecution's expert witness. Issues of sample degeneration, cross-contamination and deliberate planting of samples by prosecuting authorities can significantly diminish the probative value of the DNA evidence. Indeed, there may be a perfectly innocent explanation to account for a defendant's DNA being found at the crime scene. The ultimate evaluation of DNA evidence, as with other forensic opinion evidence, is a matter for the jury or magistrates. DNA technology today is approaching individualisation. When odds against a random match of one in 60 billion are quoted, DNA evidence all but positively identifies the person whose profile matches the crime stain obtained by the police.

7.13.1 RETAINING FORENSIC SAMPLES

The retention and use of a suspect's fingerprint/footwear impression and DNA samples is currently governed by s. 64 PACE 1984 (as amended). These samples may be retained even if the person from whom they were taken is acquitted of the offence or is not prosecuted. Retained samples may only be used for:

- a purpose related to the prevention or detection of crime; or
- the investigation of an offence; or
- the prosecution of a case.

The retention of samples of an acquitted suspect was challenged in *Chief Constable of South York-shire, ex p. Marper* [2004] 1 WLR 2196 under Article 8, the right to privacy. The domestic court held that even if the provision was an interference with Article 8, it was proportionate to the aim it sought to achieve. The decision was appealed to the European Court of Human Rights as *S and Marper v UK* [2008] *The Times*, 8 December, where it was decided that the blanket and indiscriminate retention of samples irrespective of the gravity of the offence or of outcome of the case, constituted a disproportionate interference with the applicants' rights under Article 8. The provision failed to strike a fair balance between competing public and private interests beyond any reasonable margin of appreciation and was not necessary in a democratic society.

 Looking Ahead

The implications of the *Marper* decision have been addressed with the enactment of the Protection of Freedom Act 2012. When the relevant provisions under the Act are brought into force, a new s. 63D PACE 1984 will, in the future, regulate the destruction of samples (known as 's. 63D material') taken during an investigation into an offence. In a number of subsections (s. 63E–T PACE 1984), the Act provides a very detailed and prescriptive statutory framework for the destruction of s. 63D material based on the 'Scottish' model.

Samples taken from a person not suspected of an offence (i.e. as part of mass screening) must be destroyed as soon as they have fulfilled their purpose. Where such samples should have been destroyed, they may not be used in evidence or for the purposes of investigation against such a person (s. 64(3) PACE 1984).

7.14 FACIAL MAPPING

Evidence about a defendant's involvement can be provided by other expert testimony including experts in facial mapping techniques, 'walking gait analysis' (see *Otway* [2011] EWCA Crim 3), and voice recognition experts. The admissibility of expert opinion evidence is considered in Chapter 17. Facial mapping might be required in a case where still photographs or a video image have been taken of the suspect and a comparison with the suspect is available. Experts in photographic technologies and anatomical features can enhance picture quality and offer an opinion as to the likelihood of the defendant and the person pictured being one and the same. In *R v Clare and Peach* [1995] 2 Cr App R 333, a police officer who had viewed a video recording some 40 times with lengthy and studious consideration was permitted to give evidence on whether persons shown on the recording committing acts of violent disturbance inside a football ground were the accused.

7.15 THE PRACTICAL ISSUES ASSOCIATED WITH IDENTIFICATION EVIDENCE

Identification evidence, whether based on eye-witness testimony or obtained through forensic procedures, is a significant evidential component in many cases and most commonly tendered as part of the prosecution's case.

The prosecutor is aware that, provided the proper procedures were complied with during the investigation of the offence, identification evidence has high evidential value in proving the case against the defendant. Identification obtained through forensic procedures usually requires the prosecutor to work closely with an expert witness. As noted at 7.12.1, provided there is no contamination of the forensic samples and the legal grounds for obtaining the evidence were correctly applied, forensic evidence found at the crime scene can provide compelling circumstantial evidence linking the defendant to the offence

For the prosecutor, provided the proper procedures under Code D were followed, eye-witness identification evidence has considerable probative value. The investigating officer's decision whether to convene an identification procedure requires careful consideration and may be a significant factor in the Crown Prosecutor's assessment of the reliability of the prosecution evidence in deciding whether the evidential test is satisfied under the Code for Crown Prosecutors (see Chapter 8, para. 8.2.5). Such important decisions illustrate the practical advantages of the close working relationship between the police and the CPS under the statutory charging scheme (see Chapter 8, para. 8.2), as a CPS lawyer either in person or by telephone through CPS Direct is available to advise the police on the practical evidential issues that arise during the police investigation. Finally where the eye-witness identification is likely to be challenged at trial by the defence, the prosecutor must closely examine the circumstances in which the prosecution witness purported to have identified the accused at the crime scene to ensure the identification will satisfy the 'Turnbull' guidelines (see Chapter 17, para. 17.6).

Just as prosecutors appreciate the potential probative value of identification evidence, defence lawyers are aware that identification evidence can be a weak link in a prosecution case where the proper procedures under Code D were not followed. The practical aspects of identification procedures are considered further in our online chapter 'Advising at the Police Station—Practical Steps'.

online resource centre

SELF-TEST QUESTIONS

Consider our case study *R v Lenny Wise*.

You will recall Lenny has been charged in connection with a burglary at the home of an old age pensioner. His defence is one of complete denial; however, he is linked to the crime by, *inter alia*, eye-witness identification. In discharging its legal burden of proof beyond reasonable doubt, the prosecution will be relying on evidence of identification in this case.

1. Assess the strength of the identification evidence against Lenny.

2. Consider how the evidence of identification in this case has actually materialised.

3. Can you point to any specific breaches of Code D in relation to the manner in which the evidence has been obtained and which would, in your view, enable the trial advocate to apply to have the evidence excluded under s. 78 PACE 1984 in the interests of ensuring a fair trial?

online resource centre

An analysis of the self-test questions can be found on the Online Resource Centre.

Figure 7.1 OBTAINING EVIDENCE OF IDENTIFICATION

Pre-trial safeguards under Code D—their purpose

- To ensure the quality and reliability of eye-witness identification, the detail of which can be found through:
  - video parade Annex A;
  - identification parade Annex B;
  - group parade Annex C;
  - confrontation Annex D;
  - showing photographs Annex E.

When can an eye-witness be shown photographs?

- When there is no known and available suspect in mind (Code D para. 3.3).

When must an identification procedure be convened?

- Where the suspect disputes being the person the witness claims to have seen, an identification procedure should be held unless:
  - it is not practicable; or
  - it would serve no useful purpose in proving or disproving the suspect was involved in the offence, Code D para. 3.12.

CHALLENGING THE ADMISSIBILITY OF EYE-WITNESS IDENTIFICATION

- Use s. 78 PACE 1984 on the basis that the admission of such evidence would have an adverse effect on the fairness of the proceedings.
- Relevant factors would be proven breaches of Code D, including:
  - failure to convene an identification procedure;
  - failure to properly record an identification procedure;
  - failure to disguise a prominent feature in the suspect's appearance;
  - allowing eye-witnesses contact with one another before a parade;
  - use of photographs in a case where the suspect was known;
  - a failure to properly conduct an identification procedure—see Annexes to Code D;
  - failure to secure access to legal advice beforehand.

8

THE DECISION TO PROSECUTE AND THE PROSECUTION'S DUTIES OF DISCLOSURE OF EVIDENCE

8.1   **INTRODUCTION**

CPS Statement—Shooting of Jean Charles de Menezes

Stephen O'Doherty, reviewing lawyer, CPS Special Crime Division, said today that following a review of evidence after the inquest into the death of Jean Charles de Menezes he had found insufficient evidence to prosecute any individual police officer.

Mr O'Doherty said:

'Following the inquest into the death of Jean Charles de Menezes and the subsequent open verdict returned by the jury, I conducted a further review of the case in light of the fresh evidence uncovered by the inquest.

I have now concluded that there is insufficient evidence that any offence was committed by any individual officers in relation to the tragic death of Mr de Menezes.

In reaching this decision, I considered whether the officers known as C2 and C12 acted in self-defence in shooting Mr de Menezes and also whether they lied to the inquest about what was said and done immediately before the shooting.

The answers the jury provided to specific questions they were asked by the coroner made it clear, albeit to a civil standard, that the jury did not accept the officers' accounts of what happened. However, although there were some inconsistencies in what the officers said at the inquest, there were also inconsistencies in what passengers had said. I concluded that in the confusion of what occurred on the day, a jury could not be sure that any officer had deliberately given a false account of events.

I also considered the actions of the individual officers in the police management team on that day and considered whether there was sufficient evidence to charge any of them with gross negligence manslaughter. There was no fresh evidence from the inquest which caused me to change my original decision that there was insufficient evidence to do so.

I have today written to the de Menezes family explaining my decision.'

Source: CPS Website (13 February 2009)

This chapter is divided into two parts. The first part explains the role of the Crown Prosecution Service (CPS) and the factors that are taken into account when deciding to charge a suspect or to divert him from prosecution. The second part of the chapter examines the very important obligations which are placed upon the CPS both at common law and under statute to serve pre-trial disclosure of evidence upon the defendant.

The CPS was set up in 1986 and is the main body which prosecutes criminal cases investigated by the police in England and Wales. In February 2010, the CPS published a Statement of Ethical Principles for the Public Prosecutor. The Statement can be accessed at: http://www.cps.gov.uk/legal/s_to_u/statment_of_ethical_principles_for_the_public_prosecutor/.

The principles require prosecutors to:

- act in accordance with the law in England and Wales in a way that is compatible with the Human Rights Act 1998;
- prepare and conduct cases in accordance with the Criminal Procedure Rules;
- at all times abide by the Code for Crown Prosecutors; and
- uphold the Code of Conduct set by professional regulators including the Solicitors Regulation Authority.

The statement sets out the professional conduct requirements generally expected of public prosecutors, which include the requirement for a prosecutor to be independent, fair and impartial. It further identifies specific professional conduct duties in the context of criminal proceedings. Most importantly, it reminds all public prosecutors of their 'duty to the court in question to act with independence in the interests of justice'. An important aspect of this duty is the requirement to 'endeavour to ensure that evidence which is favourable to the defendant or which undermines the prosecution case is disclosed as soon as reasonably practicable in accordance with the law.

8.2 STATUTORY CHARGING UNDER THE CJA 2003

Under the statutory charging procedure introduced by the Criminal Justice Act 2003 (CJA 2003) the decision to charge a suspect with a criminal offence rests, for the most part, with the CPS, although the police retain the right to charge in a range of circumstances outlined at para. 8.2.1. However mundane or high profile an investigation might be, the decision to charge is reached in each case by the CPS lawyer/police applying the full code test under the Code for Crown Prosecutors to the evidence gathered as part of the investigative process. As the CPS press release at the outset of this chapter shows, a decision not to charge needs as much justification as a decision to charge.

In a straightforward case, the suspect may be charged within a few hours after the commission of the alleged offence. The investigation of a more serious offence may take several days or weeks or even months.

As part of statutory charging, the police liaise with their local CPS counterparts who provide charging advice based on the available evidence. Out-of-hours and weekend access to the CPS is provided by prosecuting lawyers who work from home for CPS Direct, which provides a telephone and IT-based service to the police.

Important guidance on the operation of the statutory charging scheme can be found in a CPS document entitled *Director's Guide on Charging: Guidance to Police Officers and Crown Prosecutors issued by the Director of Public Prosecutions s. 37A PACE 1984* (Fourth Edition—January 2011). The guidance is accessible via the web-link section of our Online Resource Centre and at http://www.cps.gov.uk/publications/directors_guidance/dpp_guidance_5.html#a01.

8.2.1 OFFENCES WHERE THE POLICE CAN CHARGE THE SUSPECT

Under the *Director of Public Prosecution's (DPP) Guidance on Charging* (2013), the police may charge the suspect with any summary-only offence including an offence of criminal damage where the value of the damage or loss is less than £5,000 irrespective of anticipated plea; any offence of retail theft (shoplifting) or attempted retail theft irrespective of plea provided it is suitable for sentence in the magistrates' court; and any either-way offence anticipated as a guilty plea and suitable for sentence in a magistrates' court, provided it is not:

• a case requiring the consent to prosecute of the DPP;

• a case involving a death;

• connected with terrorist activity or official secrets;

• classified as hate crime or domestic violence under CPS policies;

• an offence of violent disorder or affray;

• causing grievous bodily harm or wounding, or actual bodily harm;

• a Sexual Offences Act offence committed by or upon a person under 18;

• an offence under the Licensing Act 2003.

In any case where the custody officer is uncertain about whether the police or the CPS should charge, the duty prosecutor should be consulted.

8.2.2 THE RESPONSIBILITY OF THE CPS TO CHARGE

Except for the situations outlined under 8.2.1, where the police may decide to charge or divert from prosecution, the Crown Prosecutor must decide the charge in every other case including indictable-only offences and either-way offences not suitable for sentence in a magistrates' court or not anticipated as a guilty plea.

The DPP's guidance provides that a *guilty plea is anticipated* where either:

- the suspect has made a clear and unambiguous admission to the offence and has said nothing that could be used as a defence, or

- the suspect has made no admission but has not denied the offence or otherwise indicated it will be contested and the commission of the offence and identification of the offender can be established by reliable evidence or the suspect can be seen clearly committing the offence on a good quality visual recording.

A case may be considered suitable for sentence in a magistrates' court unless:

- the loss or damage relating to the charge is more than £5,000 or would exceed that sum if more than one offence is charged (or taken into consideration), or

- the overall circumstances of the offence are so serious that the court may decide that a sentence of more than six months' imprisonment justifies sending the case to the Crown Court, or

- the offence has been committed whilst the suspect was subject to a Crown Court order then in force.

8.2.3 THE PROCEDURE WHERE THE POLICE CHARGE THE SUSPECT

In deciding whether to charge, the custody officer applies the Full Code Test to the facts of the offence. For a charge to be laid, the Full Test Code, which is found in section 4 of the Code for Crown Prosecutors (see para. 8.2.5), requires the custody officer to be satisfied that, first, 'there is sufficient evidence to achieve a realistic prospect of a conviction' and second, that 'it is in the public interest for the suspect to be charged'. If both elements are satisfied the suspect can be charged.

After charge, the police pass the case file to the Crown Prosecutor, who, under section 4 of the Code for Crown Prosecutors, is under a duty to review the file to confirm that the defendant has been charged with the correct offence and that the evidential and public interest criteria under the Full Code Test are satisfied (s. 10 Prosecution of Offences Act 1985).

8.2.4 THE PROCEDURE WHERE THE CROWN PROSECUTOR DECIDES THE CHARGE

Early advice about the charge at the police station enables the prosecutor to determine whether a simple or conditional caution (or a youth caution or a youth conditional caution for a young offender) can be offered as an alternative to prosecution or, if not, what the appropriate charge should be. It is the prosecuting lawyer's duty to advise the investigating police officer about the evidence and what, if any charge, the evidence supports and whether further evidence is required.

In many cases where the Crown Prosecutor decides to charge, the suspect will previously have been released on bail under s. 37B Police and Criminal Evidence Act 1984 (PACE 1984). Under s. 37(7)(a) PACE 1984, conditions may be attached to bail pending a decision whether to charge (see Chapter 14, para. 4.14).

After the suspect has been bailed, an officer involved in the investigation of the offence will refer the case file (known as MG3 'Report to Crown Prosecutor for a Charging Decision') to the Crown Prosecutor for a decision.

In deciding whether to charge, the Crown Prosecutor will apply the Full Code Test to decide whether the evidence discloses a realistic prospect of a conviction and if it is in the public interest for the suspect to be charged.

After applying the Full Code Test, the Crown Prosecutor will give the investigating officer written notice of his decision (s. 37B(4) PACE 1984). If the prosecutor decides that no charges shall be laid and no caution offered, the decision not to prosecute must be communicated in writing to the suspect by the custody officer (s. 37B (5) PACE 1984).

8.2.5 **THE FULL CODE TEST—SECTION 4, CODE FOR CROWN PROSECUTORS**

For the suspect to be charged, the two elements of the Full Code Test must be satisfied. The custody officer or the Crown Prosecutor must be satisfied that:

• there is sufficient evidence to provide for a realistic prospect of conviction; and

• that it is in the public interest to prosecute.

The Code is the basis for the prosecutor's work (and for the police when making charging decisions) to ensure that fair and consistent decisions are made about commencing and continuing with a prosecution. The most recent version of the Code came into effect in January 2013. As a public document it can be accessed from a number of sources, including our Online Resource Centre and via the CPS website.

In deciding whether to charge and what the appropriate charge should be, the Code will also be used in conjunction with other official documents including the DPP's Guidance on Charging (see 8.2) and any applicable prosecuting policies (see CPS website). A defence lawyer should have a good working knowledge of the Code and understand the way in which the local Crown Prosecutors and supporting staff apply its provisions. The CPS has an extremely informative website at http://www.cps.gov.uk/.

What is the evidential test? (Code sections 4.4–4.6)
The evidence in the case should provide a realistic prospect of conviction. The evidential test is satisfied where *an objective, impartial and reasonable jury or bench of magistrates or judge hearing a case alone, properly directed and acting in accordance with the law, is more likely than not to convict the defendant of the charge alleged.*

The evidential test requires the prosecutor to be satisfied that the evidence obtained by the police against the suspect can be used in court. This involves an assessment of whether each piece of evidence is likely to be admissible, the importance of each piece of evidence to the prosecution case as a whole, as well as the reliability and credibility of the evidence. Based on these factors, if the evidential test is satisfied, the Crown Prosecutor will then apply the 'public interest' test.

The 'public interest' test (Code sections 4.7–4.12)
The Code requires that the prosecution must be in the public interest. In 1951 Lord Shawcross, who was then the Attorney-General, made an important statement about the public interest in prosecuting criminal offences, which has been supported by Attorney-Generals ever since:

'It has never been the rule in this country—I hope it never will be—that suspected criminal offences must automatically be the subject of prosecution.'

Section 4.7 of the Code provides that where there is sufficient evidence to justify a prosecution, prosecutors must go on to consider whether a prosecution is required in the public interest. Reflecting the comments of Lord Shawcross, section 4.8 acknowledges that whilst a prosecution will normally take place, in some cases the public interest can sometimes be served by offering the offender an out-of-court disposal rather than a prosecution. The public interest factors that can affect the decision to prosecute are laid down in section 4.12(a) to (g) of the Code. These factors require the prosecutor to consider the following questions:

(a) How serious is the offence committed? The more serious the offence the more likely it is that a prosecution is required.

(b) What is the level of the suspect's culpability? The greater the suspect's level of culpability, the more likely it is that a prosecution is required. Culpability is likely to be determined by suspect level of involvement; the extent to which the offending was premeditated or planned or whether the defendant has previous criminal convictions or was on bail at the time of the offence.

(c) What were the circumstances of and the harm caused to the victim? The circumstances of the victim are highly relevant. The greater the vulnerability of the victim, the more likely it is that a prosecution is required. The Victims' Code is available from the CPS website.

(d) Was the suspect under the age of 18 at the time of the criminal offence? For further details on this consideration see Chapter 24, para. 24.9.

(e) What is the impact on the community? The greater the impact of the offending on the community, the more likely it is that a prosecution is required.

(f) Is prosecution a proportionate response? The prosecutor should also consider whether prosecution is proportionate to the likely outcome in the case by taking into account the cost to the CPS and the wider criminal justice system of any prosecution weighed against any likely penalty. A further consideration is whether the case can be prosecuted in accordance with the principles of effective case management. For example, in a case involving multiple suspects, a prosecution might be reserved for the main participants only to avoid excessively long and complex proceedings.

(g) Do sources of information require protecting? Special care should be taken when proceeding with a prosecution where information may be disclosed that could harm the UK's international relations, national security, or confidential sources of information.

8.3 CPS PROSECUTING POLICIES

In addition to the Code for Crown Prosecutors, the CPS has published policies for prosecuting certain types of offences, including, for example, offences of domestic violence. The policy document explains that while there is no statutory offence of domestic violence, the term is used to describe a range of behaviour often used by one person to control and dominate another, with whom there is or has been a close or family relationship. An offence involving domestic violence may arise out of the physical, sexual, psychological, emotional or financial abuse by one person against another. While most abuse is perpetrated by a male family member on a female, the policy recognises that abuse can also be inflicted on victims in same-sex relationships or the victims of abusive family members. The policy also recognises that members of certain minority ethnic groups, the disabled, lesbians and gay men may be reluctant to report abuse. Other factors which may prevent the reporting of domestic violence are religious, cultural or language barriers.

The CPS works closely with other criminal justice agencies such as the police, Victim Support and Refuge. In deciding whether to prosecute, the safety of the victim, any children in the case and any other person involved are given priority—although in more serious cases a prosecution may continue even where the victim has requested that no further action should be taken against the alleged perpetrator. In deciding whether a domestic violence case should be prosecuted or continue, the CPS will again apply the 'public interest' and the 'evidential' tests to the facts of the particular case.

8.4 THE THRESHOLD TEST

As noted at para. 8.2.4, in many cases, the suspect may be bailed under s. 37(7)(a) PACE 1984 to allow the Crown Prosecutor to make a charging decision. However, there will be cases where suspects present such a substantial bail risk that they should not be released from custody, even though there is insufficient evidence currently available to make an immediate charging decision. As some or all of the potential evidence in the case is not available, the 'realistic prospect of conviction test' under the Full Code Test cannot be met. In these circumstances, the prosecutor is entitled to apply the so-called Threshold Test (section 5.1 of the Code) where the following four conditions under the Code (section 5.2) are met:

(a) there is insufficient evidence currently available to apply the evidential stage of the Full Code Test; and

(b) there are reasonable grounds for believing that further evidence will become available within a reasonable period; and

(c) the seriousness or the circumstances of the case justifies the making of an immediate charging decision; and

(d) there are continuing substantial grounds to object to bail in accordance with the Bail Act 1976 and in all the circumstances of the case an application to withhold bail may properly be made.

Under the Threshold Test, the prosecutor will review the evidential requirements in the case (section 5.4 of the Code). First, the prosecutor must be satisfied that there is reasonable suspicion that the person to be charged has committed the offence, (sections 5.5–5.7) and second, that further evidence can be gathered to provide a realistic prospect of conviction (sections 5.8–5.11).

If both evidential requirements are satisfied under the Threshold Test, the prosecutor must then apply the public interest stage of the Full Code Test based on the information available at that time (section 5.11).

A decision to charge under the Threshold Test must be kept under review. The evidence must be regularly assessed to ensure that the charge is appropriate and that the continued objection to granting the defendant bail is justified. The Full Code Test must be applied as soon as is reasonably practicable and before the expiration of the defendant's custody time limit (section 5.12).

8.5 THE SELECTION OF CHARGES—SECTION 6, CODE FOR CROWN PROSECUTORS

Under section 6.1 of the Code, the Crown Prosecutor should select charges which:

- reflect the seriousness of the offence and the extent of the offending;
- give the court adequate powers to sentence and impose appropriate post-conviction orders; and
- enable a case to be presented in a clear and simple way.

Where there is a range of possible charges available (i.e. careless driving/dangerous driving, common assault/assault occasioning actual bodily harm) the CPS lawyer will review the available evidence against the CPS's Charging Practice for the particular offence (see Legal Guidance section of CPS website).

8.6 ALTERNATIVES TO PROSECUTION

Under section 7.1 of the Code, an out-of-court disposal may be given if this is considered to be an appropriate response to the offender and/or the seriousness and consequences of the offending. According to the Ministry of Justice, in the 12-month period to September 2012, 386,900 offenders were diverted from prosecution by receiving diversionary disposals such as a Penalty Notice or a Cannabis Warning. More formally, an adult may receive a simple caution or a conditional caution. A young person may be given a youth caution or a youth conditional caution, which, since April 2013 have replaced reprimands and final warnings (see Chapter 24). There are a number of ways in which a suspect may be diverted from formal criminal proceedings.

8.6.1 SIMPLE CAUTION

According to the Ministry of Justice, 212,000 cautions were administered by the police in the 12 months to June 2012.

The police retain the discretion to caution a suspect in all cases other than indictable-only offences. Only the CPS can allow a simple caution to be issued for an indictable-only offence. The decision to issue a simple caution must be made in accordance with the Director of Public Prosecutions Guidance (see earlier). The police may take advice from the CPS at any stage as to whether a simple caution might be appropriate. Detailed guidance on the use of the simple caution can be found at http://www.Justice.gov.uk/out-of-court-disposals (see link in the web-links section of our Online Resource Centre). The main points are as follows.

A simple caution will be appropriate where:

- the evidence is sufficient to warrant a prosecution (i.e. there is a realistic prospect of conviction based on the Full Code Test);
- the offender admits her guilt;
- it is in the public interest for a simple caution to be administered (the views of any victim should be sought); and
- the offender agrees to such a disposal after being made aware that the caution may be cited in court if she offends in the future.

An important precondition for a simple caution is that the offender must make a clear and reliable admission of guilt. The court may strike down a caution where no admission by the defendant has been obtained (see *Metropolitan Police Commissioner, ex p. P* [1995] TLR 305). A simple caution is formally administered at a police station by an officer of at least the rank of inspector. The offender will sign a form agreeing to the caution and that she admits her involvement in the offence.

A detainee should be advised that while a simple caution does not constitute a conviction, records are kept and the caution may be cited in court if she later re-offends. A simple caution issued for a sexual offence will require registration on the Sex Offenders' Register and must be disclosed. A simple caution may also have to be disclosed for certain types of employment. It is also important to advise that a caution does not prevent the possibility of future prosecution. The CPS may still instigate proceedings at a later date even after the detainee has been formally cautioned although the defence could strongly argue that this constitutes an abuse of process (see Chapter 6).

While any adult may be cautioned, in practice a 'vulnerable' person is more likely to receive a simple caution than other offenders, depending on the nature of the offence alleged. Included in the category of a vulnerable person are:

- the elderly;
- the infirm;
- a detainee suffering from a mental condition or impairment;
- a detainee suffering from a physical disability;
- a detainee under severe emotional distress.

Whilst the simple caution is more suited to low-level offending behaviour, it can exceptionally be used to deal with more serious offences. The Association of Chief Police Officers (ACPO) has developed a Gravity Factors Matrix which assists police officers to determine the seriousness of the offence and hence the suitability of a simple caution. Each offence included in the gravity matrix is scaled between 1 and 5, with 1 being the least serious. The presence or absence of aggravating features influences the overall score. A score of 5 requires the offence to be prosecuted.

8.6.2 CONDITIONAL CAUTION (CPS CODE SECTION 7)

A conditional caution is a disposal available under ss. 23–27 CJA 2003 and is appropriate where the prosecutor considers that there is sufficient evidence for a prosecution but it is in the interests of the offender, the victim and the community to require the offender to comply with specified conditions aimed at rehabilitation, reparation and punishment. A factor in deciding whether a conditional caution is required, as opposed to a simple caution or prosecution, is whether the specified conditions will be an appropriate and effective way of dealing with an offender's behaviour, or making reparation for the effects of the offence on the victim and on the community.

Under s. 23 CJA 2003, a conditional caution is available where:

- the authorised person (usually a police officer or prosecutor) must have evidence that the offender committed an offence; and

- the authorised person decides there is sufficient evidence to charge the offender with the offence and that a conditional caution should be given to the offender in respect of the offence; and

- the offender must admit committing the offence to the authorised person; and

- the authorised person must explain the effect of the conditional caution and warn the offender that failure to comply with any aspect of the conditions may result in the prosecution of the offence; and

- the offender must sign a document containing the details of the offence; an admission of guilt; consent to be cautioned and details of the conditions attached to the caution.

A conditional caution can be given by either a police officer or by a Crown Prosecutor. Detailed guidance on conditional cautioning can be found in the Code of Practice for Adult Conditional Cautions (April 2013), which can be accessed at http://www.justice.gov.uk/downloads/oocd/code-practice-adult-conditional-cautions-oocd.pdfA and CPS guidance can be found at: http://www.cps.gov.uk/publications/directors_guidance/adult_conditional_cautions.html. A link on our Online Resource Centre (web-links section: Guidelines) will take you there. Separate guidance on Youth Conditional Cautions can be found at http://cps.gov.uk/publications/directors_guidance/youth_conditional_cautions.html#a01 and at http://www.justice.gov.uk/out-of-court-disposals.

 online resource centre

In addition to the requirements of s. 23 CJA 2003, as explained above, in deciding whether a conditional caution is appropriate, regard should be had to a range of factors, including the seriousness of the offence, the circumstances of the case, the views of the victim, and the background, circumstances, and previous offending history of the offender. Conditional cautions are a proportionate response to low-level offending which allows the offender to make swift reparation to victims and communities.

8.6.3 CONDITIONS THAT CAN BE ATTACHED

The conditions attached to the caution must be:

- appropriate to the offence;
- achievable; and
- proportionate.

The conditions should have one or more of the following objectives which are aimed at the offender's rehabilitation, reparation and/or punishment. The rehabilitative element may require the offender to attend a drug or alcohol rehabilitation course or anger management classes. The reparative element might include repairing or making good any damage caused to property such as cleaning graffiti or simply apologising to the victim. A financial penalty is the only punitive element currently available and can include a fine or a compensation payment to the victim. The provision of a financial penalty condition are set out in s. 23A Criminal Justice Act 2003.

8.6.4 FAILING TO COMPLY WITH THE CONDITIONAL CAUTION

If the suspect fails to comply with the conditions of the caution, she is liable to be prosecuted for the original offence as the public interest test will have been satisfied. The conditional caution, although not a conviction, forms part of the offender's record and may be cited in any subsequent criminal proceedings.

8.7 THE DEFENCE SOLICITOR INFLUENCING THE DECISION TO CHARGE

The direct access between the police and their local CPS counterparts means that custody officers will usually be acting on the advice of the Crown Prosecutor. It should still be possible, however, for the defence solicitor/legal adviser to influence the decision to charge where the evidence that links the suspect to the offence appears to be weak or unreliable. In this situation, the solicitor should persuade the custody officer to release his client unconditionally or on police bail. Even where the evidence discloses a case to answer, the defence solicitor could persuade the Crown Prosecutor through the custody officer, to deal with his client by an alternative disposal to a formal prosecution.

In many cases, and especially where the police have made a full disclosure of the evidence against the suspect, it will be clear that the Full Code Test is satisfied and the defence solicitor's latitude for negotiation is limited. In some situations it might be in a detainee's interest to be charged as soon as possible where, for example, he has been in police detention for a long time or where the defence solicitor considers that it would not be in his client's interests to be interviewed again by the police.

As with all representations made in connection with a client's detention at the police station, it is vital to ensure that the custody officer's or Crown Prosecutor's responses are accurately recorded on the custody record and in the defence solicitor's contemporaneous notes.

8.8 THE CPS AND THE CRIMINAL CASE MANAGEMENT FRAMEWORK

Guidance on how adult cases should be prosecuted and managed is provided by the Criminal Case Management Framework (CCMF). The CCMF seeks to disseminate good practice and compliance with the Criminal Procedure Rules as well as underpinning the principles of a new initiative: 'Stop Delaying Justice' (SDJ) to ensure the efficient disposal of criminal cases by the courts working in partnership with the CPS and defence lawyers. Although the CCMF should be used by all criminal practitioners, the CPS is the organisation most likely to apply its guidance. Part 1 of the CCMF covers the conduct of adult cases in the magistrates' court. Part 2 relates to the conduct of cases in the Crown Court. The CCMF can be accessed at http://webarchive.nationalarchives.gov.uk/20100512160448/ccmf.cjsonline.gov.uk/ (see link in the web-links section of our Online Resource Centre). online resource centre

Reference will be made to the CCMF later in this chapter.

8.9 PRE-TRIAL DISCLOSURE OF EVIDENCE—AN INTRODUCTION

At a number of stages in a criminal case the rules governing the pre-trial disclosure of evidence impose extensive obligations on the CPS which are critical to a defendant's right to a fair trial. Clearly a defendant cannot be expected to defend allegations made against her unless she is aware of the evidence that will be given in support of those allegations. It would be morally wrong for the prosecution to withhold evidence that weakens the prosecution case or assists the defence case. Although the aim in the adversarial system is to win, there are wider obligations on the prosecution to assist the search for the truth and to ensure that a miscarriage of justice does not occur.

The right to the pre-trial disclosure of evidence is enshrined in the European Convention on Human Rights 1950 (ECHR 1950) as being fundamental to the right to a fair trial under Article 6(1). Article 6(3)(b) provides:

'Everyone charged with a criminal offence has the right to be informed promptly, in a language which he understands and in detail of the nature and cause of the accusation against him.'

As well as supporting the defendant's right to a fair trial, the pre-trial disclosure of evidence greatly assists the administration of justice by enabling the court and the parties to identify the issues that are likely to be disputed at trial. This is a key aspect of the court's case management duties under Part 3 Criminal Procedure Rules. There are also time-saving advantages in requiring pre-trial disclosure of evidence. On the basis of the disclosed evidence, a defendant may be advised to plead guilty at an early stage. Pre-trial disclosure may lead to the evidence of some prosecution witnesses being agreed in written form without the requirement for them to attend court, thereby saving time and expense.

A key piece of legislation in the context of disclosure is the Criminal Procedure and Investigations Act 1996 (CPIA 1996). The Act, which imposes onerous disclosure duties upon the prosecution as well as duties on the defendant, is supplemented by a detailed Code of Practice (Part II CPIA 1996 (s. 23)). The Code (which we will refer to as the Disclosure Code) can be accessed via the web-links section of the Online Resource Centre and at http://www.xact.org.uk/information/downloads/CPIA/Disclosure_code_of_practice.pdf. Section 26 CPIA 1996 makes the Code admissible in evidence where breach of its provisions is relevant to a question arising in the proceedings and further provides that a failure by the police to observe the Code will not result in civil or criminal liability. A failure by the CPS to comply with its disclosure obligations clearly affects the fairness of the proceedings and may be the subject of a defence application to stay the proceedings for abuse of process (see Chapter 6).

In complying with its disclosure obligations, the CPS lawyer will apply the guidance provided in the Attorney-General's Guidelines on Disclosure. The importance of these guidelines cannot be underestimated. They can be accessed from our Online Resource Centre, and at http://www.cps.gov.uk/legal/a_to_c/attorney_generals_guidelines_on_disclosure/.

8.10 USED AND UNUSED MATERIAL

Central to an understanding of the disclosure rules is the distinction between 'used' and 'unused' material. These words are not defined by statute but are adopted by us as convenient labels to assist understanding.

'Used' material refers to evidence that will form part of the prosecution's case against the defendant and is the evidence to be used to prove the defendant's guilt at trial. The prosecution is under a duty to disclose its used evidence at an early stage in the case. Our case studies (*R v Lenny Wise*, *R v Roger Martin*, *R v William Hardy*) include examples of 'used material'.

'Unused' material is evidence collected during the investigation into the offence but which is not part of the prosecution's case against the accused at trial. The prosecution's duty to disclose 'unused' material arises at a later stage in the case.

As the CPS can only make disclosure of evidence to the defence based on the evidence gathered or generated as part of the police investigation, what disclosure obligations fall on the police?

8.11 DISCLOSURE OBLIGATIONS ON THE POLICE/INVESTIGATOR

The obligations upon the police to record, retain and reveal to the prosecutor material obtained in a criminal investigation are contained in the CPIA 1996 and its accompanying Disclosure Code.

8.11.1 KEEPING TRACK OF INVESTIGATIVE MATERIAL

The Disclosure Code (para. 5) requires the recording and retention of all relevant information and material gathered or generated during an investigation. A disclosure officer must be appointed to each investigation and may be a member of the investigation team. There is a requirement to record all types of information, including evidence obtained during the investigation (the record of searches of the suspect's person and/or property), evidence generated by the investigation (incriminating admissions and no comment interviews, etc.) and information received verbally. Paragraph 5 of the Code specifies the types of relevant material which should be routinely retained in a criminal case. It includes:

- crime reports;
- custody records;
- records of telephone calls, e.g. 999 calls;
- final versions of witness statements (and draft versions, where their content differs from the final version);
- interview records;
- communications between the police and experts such as forensic scientists, reports of work carried out by experts, and schedules of scientific material prepared by the expert for the investigator, for the purposes of criminal proceedings;
- information provided by an accused person which indicates an explanation for the offence with which that person has been charged;
- any material casting doubt on the reliability of a confession;
- any material casting doubt on the reliability of a witness;
- records of first description of a suspect by each potential witness who purports to identify or describe the suspect, whether or not the description differs from that of subsequent descriptions by that or other witnesses.

Where there is any doubt about the relevance of material gathered or generated, the investigator must retain it.

Paragraph 3.5 of the Disclosure Code states that:

'In conducting an investigation, the investigator should pursue all reasonable lines of enquiry, whether these point towards or away from a suspect. What is reasonable in each case will depend on the particular circumstances.'

8.11.2 DISCLOSURE SCHEDULES

Paragraph 6 Disclosure Code requires material that is relevant to the investigation and which the disclosure officer thinks will not form part of the prosecution case to be listed in a schedule of non-sensitive material. If the disclosure officer believes the material is sensitive it must be listed on a separate schedule for sensitive material.

Sensitive material is material which the investigating officer believes would not be in the public interest to disclose, including evidence relating to national security or police informants, location of surveillance positions and material relating to children.

The schedules are then passed to the CPS. The schedules must be prepared in the following situations:

- where the offence is indictable only; or
- it is an either-way offence likely to be tried in the Crown Court; or
- where the defendant is likely to plead not guilty to a matter which is to be tried summarily.

The material must be listed in the schedule with sufficient detail to enable the prosecutor to decide whether he needs to inspect it before a decision is made to disclose it to the defence. In addition to the listing of material, the disclosure officer must provide the prosecutor with a copy of any material which undermines the prosecution's case, including records of first description of a suspect and information relating to any explanation by the defendant for the offence charged (para. 7). The schedules may require amending after the CPS lawyer has considered the evidence in the case.

8.12 **THE CPS OBLIGATION TO DISCLOSE 'USED' MATERIAL**

The CPS must disclose any 'used' material in a case that can be tried summarily before a magistrates' court in accordance with the 'Advance Information Rules' which are contained in Crim PR, Part 21 and which are reproduced in part below:

'Providing initial details of the prosecution case

21.2. The prosecutor must provide initial details of the prosecution case by—

  (a) serving those details on the court officer; and

  (b) making those details available to the defendant, at, or before, the beginning of the day of the first hearing.

Content of initial details

21.3. Initial details of the prosecution case must include—

  (a) a summary of the evidence on which that case will be based; or

  (b) any statement, document or extract setting out facts or other matters on which that case will be based; or

  (c) any combination of such a summary, statement, document or extract; and

  (d) the defendant's previous convictions.'

8.12.1 **WHEN MUST THE CPS COMPLY WITH CRIM PR PART 21?**

The prosecution's obligations to provide 'Advance Information' need to be understood in the context of the first hearing before a magistrates' court in connection with an either-way or summary offence which must be an 'effective' hearing. The Criminal Case Management Framework (see para. 8.8) states that an effective first hearing requires that:

(1) a plea be taken;

(2) the appropriate venue for trial is determined;

(3) the real issues are identified;

(4) the case (including sentence) can be concluded on the day or, if not, directions can be given so that it can be concluded at the next hearing or as soon as possible after that.

To ensure that the first hearing is effective an initiative known as CJ-SSS (Simple, Speedy, Summary, Criminal Justice) came into operation in all magistrates' courts in November 2007. The practices reflected by CJ-SSS are now being given new impetus by a further initiative, Stop Delaying Justice (SDJ), which re-states existing case management practice as required by the Criminal Procedure Rules and the Criminal Case Management Framework (see 8.8). Both CJ-SSS and SDJ are explained more fully in Chapter 9.

CJ-SSS requires the CPS to serve sufficient disclosure of the prosecution's case on the accused as early as possible and at the latest by 9 am on the day of the first hearing to enable the defendant to enter a firm plea. In compliance with SDJ the court will expect the defendant to enter or indicate a plea at the first hearing unless he is appearing in custody, in which case the prosecution may not be in possession of all the available advance information.

Once a case is charged and is to proceed to court, the prosecution file for the first hearing which is based on the 'Streamlined Process' and will be proportionate to the requirements of that hearing. It must provide the prosecutor with sufficient information to be able to conclude the case if the plea is guilty. It must also enable the prosecutor to conduct an effective case management hearing if a not guilty plea is entered. In preparation for the initial hearing of an offence which may be tried summarily, the CPS will serve the defence with 'Advance Information' based on the 'Streamlined Process'. It will comprise the charge sheet (MG4); the police report (MG5) which includes a police officer's summary of the key evidence (including copies of any hand-written key witness statements); a summary of the defendant's interview and a list of non-key witness evidence; and what each non-key witness contributes; plus a list of the defendant's previous convictions (see Appendix 1 Document 2 for an illustration of 'Streamlined Disclosure' in the context of our fictitious case study, *R v Lenny Wise*). If the case proceeds to summary trial or is sent to the Crown Court, the CPS file will be upgraded to take account of its more onerous disclosure duties in these circumstances.

With effect from April 2012, the CPS (which has traditionally complied with its disclosure obligations by serving hard copy documents) will be moving to the production and service of digital case files. It is a key stepping stone in the Government's ambition for the Criminal Justice System (CJS) to digitally exchange information between the core CJS agencies by April 2012. Defence practitioners need to get ready for the digital service revolution. For an account of the changes see: http://www.justice.gov.uk/about/justice/transforming-justice/criminal-justice-system-efficiency-programme2/criminal-justice-system-efficiency-programme/defence-practitioners.

8.12.2 ADVANCE INFORMATION IN INDICTABLE-ONLY CASES?

There are separate disclosure rules for offences that are triable only on indictment which arise once the offence has been sent to the Crown Court under s. 51 Crime and Disorder Act 1998 (CDA 1998). The rules are considered in Chapter 13. Although Crim PR, 21 has no application to an indictable-only offence, the CPS will normally serve available advance information at an early stage in an indictable-only case where a request is made and where fairness requires such disclosure. This is particularly important where the CPS has information that might affect a bail decision (see Chapter 10 and *R v DPP, ex p. Lee* [1992] 2 Cr App R 304).

8.13 CPS OBLIGATIONS TO DISCLOSE UNUSED MATERIAL (CRIM PR, PART 22)

The CPIA 1996 and the Disclosure Code impose duties on the CPS lawyer to disclose unused evidence that will not form part of the prosecution case.

At what point does the obligation to disclose unused material arise?

* When an either-way case is committed or sent to the Crown Court, the disclosure provisions relating to 'unused material' arise at this stage.

* If an either-way case is to be tried in the magistrates' court or the offence is summary-only and a not guilty plea has been entered, the disclosure of 'unused material' under the CPIA 1996 arises at this stage.

* For an offence triable only on indictment, unused material is included in the case sent bundle (see Chapter 13 which explains the procedural course of an offence triable only on indictment).

8.13.1 THE SPECIFIC DISCLOSURE DUTIES ON THE CPS UNDER THE CPIA 1996

Based on the disclosure schedules prepared by the disclosure officer in the case (see para. 8.11.2), the CPS lawyer must review the evidence on the file and decide whether any disclosure is required by s. 3 CPIA 1996.

8.13.2 INITIAL DISCLOSURE OF UNUSED MATERIAL—S. 3 CPIA 1996

'The prosecutor must—
(a) disclose to the accused any prosecution material which has not previously been disclosed to the accused and which might reasonably be considered capable of undermining the case for the prosecution against the accused or of assisting the case for the accused.'

In *R v Vasilou* [2000] 4 Archbold News 1, the Court of Appeal held this would include the disclosure of a prosecution witness's previous convictions.

The test to be applied under s. 3 CPIA 1996 is objective and requires the prosecutor to decide which evidence might reasonably undermine the prosecution case. In the Attorney-General's Guidelines on Disclosure (paras. 10–14), material that can reasonably be considered capable of undermining the prosecution case against the accused or assisting the defence case will include:

'10. . . . anything that tends to show a fact inconsistent with the elements of the case that must be proved by the prosecution. Material can fulfill the disclosure test:

   (a) by the use to be made of it in cross-examination; or

   (b) by its capacity to support submissions that could lead to:

      (i) the exclusion of evidence; or

      (ii) a stay of proceedings; or

      (iii) a court or tribunal finding that any public authority had acted incompatibly with the accused's rights under the ECHR, or

   (c) by its capacity to suggest an explanation or partial explanation of the accused's actions.

11. In deciding whether material may fall to be disclosed under paragraph 10, especially (b)(ii), prosecutors must consider whether disclosure is required in order for a proper application to be made. The purpose of this paragraph is not to allow enquiries to support speculative arguments or for the manufacture of defences.

12. Examples of material that might reasonably be considered capable of undermining the prosecution case or of assisting the case for the accused are:

- material casting doubt upon the accuracy of any prosecution evidence;

- material which may point to another person, whether charged or not (including a co-accused) having involvement in the commission of the offence;

- material which may cast doubt upon the reliability of a confession;

- material that might go to the credibility of a prosecution witness;

- material that might support a defence that is either raised by the defence or apparent from the prosecution papers;

- material which may have a bearing on the admissibility of any prosecution evidence.

13. It should also be borne in mind that while items of material viewed in isolation may not be reasonably considered to be capable of undermining the prosecution case or assisting the accused, several items together can have that effect.

14. Material relating to the accused's mental or physical health, intellectual capacity, or to any ill treatment which the accused may have suffered when in the investigator's custody is likely to fall within the test for disclosure set out in paragraph 8 above.'

Disclosure under s. 3 CPIA 1996 is limited to information in the prosecutor's possession or evidence which the prosecutor has inspected. The prosecutor's disclosure duty depends on the efficiency and honesty of the disclosure officer who prepares the schedule. Disclosure can be made by either giving a copy of the material to the defence or allowing the defence to inspect it at a reasonable time and place.

If initial disclosure is not available, the CPS must provide a written statement to the defendant confirming this. Along with initial disclosure the CPS must also disclose a copy of the schedule of non-sensitive material prepared by the disclosure officer in the case.

8.13.3 INITIAL DISCLOSURE OF UNUSED MATERIAL—TIME LIMITS

In the case of a summary trial, standard directions give the prosecution 28 days from the date of the defendant's not guilty plea to serve initial disclosure of unused material. For either-way offences sent to the Crown Court, standard directions will determine the date by which the CPS must serve any unused material. In indictable-only cases, the time limit for disclosure is directed by the trial judge at the preliminary case management hearing before the Crown Court (see Chapter 13).

8.13.4 DEFENCE DISCLOSURE

The defence obligations to make pre-trial disclosure of evidence are considered in greater detail in Chapter 13. For all cases that are tried on indictment, the defendant must serve a defence statement on the prosecution under s. 5 CPIA 1996 once the CPS has complied or has purported to comply with its disclosure duties under s. 3 CPIA 1996. Defence statements are considered in detail in Chapter 13. The service of a defence statement is optional in a case that is to be tried summarily (see Chapter 12). In addition to serving a defence statement, the defendant must also give written notice of his intention to call defence witnesses (s. 6C CPIA 1996) irrespective of whether the case is to be tried summarily or on indictment (see Chapters 12 and 13).

8.13.5 PROSECUTOR'S CONTINUING DUTY

Section 7A CPIA 1996 (as amended by the CJA 2003) provides that after the prosecutor has complied with initial disclosure under s. 3 CPIA 1996 and before the accused is acquitted or convicted or the prosecutor decides not to proceed with the case (and, in particular, following the service of a defence statement), the prosecutor must keep under review whether there is any further prosecution material that might reasonably be considered capable of undermining the prosecution case against the accused or of assisting the defence case. Following the service of a defence statement if the prosecution concludes there is no further evidence to disclose, this should be communicated to the defendant.

A summary and flowchart depicting the various stages of the disclosure regime in relation to the classification of criminal offences can be found at Figures 8.2. and 8.3.

8.14 DISCLOSING INFORMATION HELD BY THIRD PARTIES

The CPIA 1996 does not apply to potentially relevant evidence in the possession of a third party such as a local authority, hospital, school or a forensic science organisation but which is not directly involved in the case. The Attorney-General's Guidelines (paras. 51–54) deal with third party disclosure.

If a third party will not voluntarily disclose information, either side may issue a witness summons under the Criminal Procedure (Attendance of Witnesses) Act 1965 (Crown Court) and s. 97 Magistrates' Court Act 1980 (magistrates' court) requiring the third party to disclose the evidence. The third party may resist the application on the basis of public interest immunity in accordance with the procedure set out in s. 16 CPIA 1996 (*R v Brushett* [2001] Crim LR 471). The principles relating to public interest immunity are briefly discussed later.

8.15 WITHHOLDING RELEVANT EVIDENCE

Occasionally, the prosecution or a third party will resist the disclosure of otherwise relevant and admissible evidence on the basis that it is 'sensitive' and it is not in the wider public interest for it to be heard in the public domain of a criminal trial. Evidence covered by public interest immunity includes:

- documents and other material relating to national security;
- confidential information;

- the identity of police informants and undercover police officers;
- details of premises used for police surveillance; and
- information dealing with the welfare of children.

The defence advocate, however, may wish to see such evidence to evaluate it and perhaps challenge it. Where disclosure is opposed on this basis, the prosecution will claim the evidence is covered by public interest immunity (PII).

While many aspects of disclosure are regulated by statute, the principles relating to PII remain governed by the common law. The procedural rules governing public interest immunity applications are contained in Crim PR, Part 25 which take account of the leading case on PII, which is the House of Lords decision in *R v C; R v H* [2004] 2 WLR 335.

The overriding principle which governs a judge's or magistrates' decision whether to order disclosure is based on ensuring an innocent defendant is not convicted. This principle is derived from the judgment of Lord Taylor CJ in *R v Keane* [1994] 1 WLR 746:

> 'If the disputed material may prove the accused's innocence or avoid a miscarriage of justice, then the balance comes down resoundingly in favour of disclosing it.'

8.16 FURTHER INFORMATION ON DISCLOSURE

For further detailed consideration of pre-trial disclosure of evidence, take a look at the Disclosure Manual of the CPS (http://www.cps.gov.uk/legal/d_to_g/disclosure_manual/).

KEY POINT SUMMARY

- Understand the division of charging responsibilities between the police and the CPS.
- Know the procedures to be followed where the decision to charge is taken by the police or the CPS.
- Have a good working knowledge of the Full Code Test under the Code for Crown Prosecutors and an understanding of the ways in which the evidential and the public interest tests are applied in the decision to charge.
- Know when the Threshold Test applies.
- Understand the alternatives to prosecution and the applicable criteria for them.
- Understand that an accused is entitled to disclosure of the evidence the prosecution intends to rely on ('*used*' material) in discharging its burden of proof.
- The obligation to serve used material arises at a very early stage before the first hearing where the case can be tried before the magistrates' court.
- Understand the test that the CPS lawyer must apply in discharging his or her 'unused' material disclosure duties under s. 3 CPIA 1996.
- Entitlement to initial prosecution disclosure of unusued material under s. 3 CPIA 1996 only arises in a case to be tried summarily where a not guilty plea is indicated.
- The submission of a defence statement is voluntary in summary cases but mandatory in indictable cases (see Chapters 12 and 13).
- The prosecution is obliged to keep disclosure of unused material under constant review, particularly in the light of service of a defence statement.
- Where the prosecution seeks to withhold relevant/material evidence on the ground that it is sensitive, application must be made to a court to sanction the withholding of such material.
- Important detail as regards the operation and effect of the CPIA 1996 is contained in its accompanying Code of Practice and in the Attorney-General's Guidelines on Disclosure.

SELF-TEST QUESTIONS

Question 1

The following self-test questions are designed to test your understanding and application of the evidential and public interest tests applied by Crown Prosecutors. Before attempting the questions, consider the following example.

Wayne, aged 24, has been arrested on suspicion of assault occasioning actual bodily harm under s. 47 Offences Against the Person Act 1861. The offence occurred during Wayne's wedding reception, when Brian, the bride's brother, made insulting comments about Wayne. There are several witnesses to the offence who would be willing to testify in court. Wayne denies the offence and Brian has indicated to the CPS that he wishes further action to be taken against Wayne. Wayne has two convictions for violent disorder for separate offences outside a nightclub. Consider whether the evidential and public interest tests are satisfied as required by the Full Code Test under the Code for Crown Prosecutors.

Advice

In applying the Code for Crown Prosecutors to Wayne's case, it appears that the evidential test is satisfied as there are several witnesses to the offence who would be willing to testify in court. There is nothing to suggest that these witnesses would not give relevant and reliable testimony and that the *actus reus* and *mens rea* of the offence could be proven. In terms of the public interest test, there are factors in favour of continuing the prosecution, not least the use of violence and in his previous criminal conduct, Wayne appears to have a propensity to be violent. On the particular facts of the case, it is likely that Wayne will be charged and prosecuted.

By applying the Code for Crown Prosecutors, consider whether the 'evidential' test and the 'public interest' test are satisfied in the following cases. You might also consider whether there are alternative methods by which the potential defendant may be dealt with.

(a) Gerald, aged 75, has been charged with 14 counts of sexual assault arising out of his employment in a residential home for children. The alleged offences occurred between 1968 and 1973. The police have traced four victims of the offences who are willing to testify at Gerald's trial. Gerald, who has no criminal convictions, has recently been diagnosed with a serious heart complaint.

(b) Debbie, aged 35, is a single parent with three children. She has been arrested on suspicion of theft. It is alleged that she stole a pack of disposable nappies, a jar of coffee and a bottle of vodka from Cutcost Supermarket. Debbie is advised to make no comment in interview. The supermarket's policy is always to prosecute shoplifters. In support of the prosecution case, the store detective will testify at trial and there is a security video tape of the alleged offence. Debbie has no previous convictions apart from a conviction for careless driving. In a private discussion with her solicitor, Debbie discloses that she does not really know why she took the items and that she is recovering from a nervous breakdown having been in an abusive marriage which has recently ended in divorce.

(c) After Patrick, aged 14, tells his father, Frank, that he (Patrick) is in a gay relationship, Frank hits Patrick, causing him actual bodily harm. Patrick is attacked by his father on two further occasions. Frank also locks Patrick in his room preventing him from leaving the house to keep him away from his boyfriend. After a week, Patrick's mother, Marie, tells the police who intervene and arrest Frank. Patrick does not want any action to be taken against Frank. Frank has no previous convictions.

Question 2

The following scenario explores prosecution disclosure obligations. Try to attempt to answer the questions posed at the conclusion.

Barry (aged 28) is charged with rape contrary to s. 1 Sexual Offences Act 2003. His victim is Tina, aged 15. The attack is alleged to have occurred in some public toilets inside a park where Barry is employed as a park attendant. Tina reported the rape to staff at the care home where she resides some two days after it was alleged to have occurred. Tina is subjected to a full forensic examination which reveals visible bruising around the vaginal area.

Having identified Barry as being the man responsible, he is arrested. He too is subject to a full forensic examination. In interview Barry denies the offence, stating Tina approached him outside the public toilets in the park offering him sex in return for money. He refused her advances. She called him a paedophile and walked off.

The attack is said to have been witnessed by Leroy aged 15. He has given a statement to the police stating he witnessed a girl matching Tina's description emerge from some public toilets in the park in a state of distress claiming she had been raped. Kelly, a friend of Tina, has given a statement to the police claiming that Barry has asked Tina for sex on a number of occasions and became aggressive when Tina refused. Barry informs you that he has observed Tina in the company of males on numerous occasions while in the park and believes her to be sexually promiscuous. The allegations against him are a complete fabrication.

A defence witness has come forward who wishes to remain anonymous claiming that Tina is an attention seeker and that she has previously made a false accusation of rape against a male care-worker several months ago, having allegedly offered him sex. She later withdrew the allegation. Leroy is also a resident of the care home at which Tina resides and is very much under Tina's 'control'.

Chart the various stages of disclosure in this case by answering the following:

- What is the classification of the offence with which Barry is charged?

- Can you expect advance information in this case, and if so, what do you anticipate you are likely to receive? (Think in terms of what the investigative process is likely to yield.)

- At what stage will the prosecution come under an obligation to disclose 'unused' material?

- Will the defence need to serve a defence statement in this case, and if so, what will the content of that statement comprise?

- Do you anticipate there may be material that the prosecution might not wish to disclose? If so, on what basis and how would the situation be resolved in procedural terms?

online
resource
centre

Analysis of questions 1 and 2 is provided on our Online Resource Centre, where scenario 2 is further developed.

FIGURE 8.1 THE DECISION TO CHARGE

The decision to charge or to offer an alternative course is for the most part the responsibility of the CPS in conjunction with the custody officer under the CJA 2003 (s. 37B PACE).

The decision to charge is based on two tests contained within the CPS Code for Crown Prosecutors. The test comprises:

- evidential test—is there sufficient evidence to provide for a realistic prospect of conviction?

- public interest test—is it in the public interest that the defendant is prosecuted? (This requires the application of various factors listed in the Code.)

ALTERNATIVES TO PROSECUTION

Simple caution

- Defendant may be cautioned where:
  - evidence is sufficient to have warranted prosecution;
  - defendant admits guilt; and
  - defendant agrees to be cautioned (Home Office Circular 016/2008).

Conditional cautions: ss. 23–27 Criminal Justice Act 2003

- Defendant may receive a conditional caution where:
  - defendant admits the offence to an authorised person; and
  - in the opinion of the prosecutor there is sufficient evidence to charge, and the public interest is satisfied by the offer of a conditional caution.

- The condition(s) attached to the caution must be:
  - proportionate to the offence;
  - achievable; and
  - appropriate.

- The condition(s) might require the defendant:
  - to attend drug/alcohol rehabilitation course;
  - to attend anger management course;
  - to make good damage to property
  - to pay a fine.

FIGURE 8.2 PRE-TRIAL DISCLOSURE OF EVIDENCE

SUMMARY-ONLY OFFENCES

- Prosecution will disclose used material or 'Advance Information' under Crim PR, Part 21.

- If defendant pleads not guilty, any 'unused' material (initial disclosure) which might reasonably be considered capable of undermining the case for the prosecution or of assisting the case for the accused must be disclosed, s. 3 CPIA 1996.

- Within 14 days of initial disclosure, defence may voluntarily serve a defence statement, s. 6 CPIA 1996 but must serve a defence witness statement s. 6C CPIA 1996.

- Prosecution must serve any further 'unused' evidence which might reasonably be expected to assist the defence as disclosed in the defence statement under its continuing duty to review unused material, s. 7A CPIA 1996.

OFFENCES TRIABLE EITHER WAY

- Prosecution will disclose the substance of its case against the accused under the Advance Information Rules (Crim PR Part 21).

- The disclosure obligations on each party will then depend on whether the case is to be tried summarily or on indictment.

- If sent for trial to the Crown Court, initial disclosure of prosecution unused material should be served in accordance with standard directions.

- If being tried before a magistrates' court as per summary offences above.

- If being tried on indictment, as per indictable offences below.

INDICTABLE-ONLY OFFENCES AND CASES TO BE TRIED ON INDICTMENT

- Evidence and other material which the prosecution intends to use at trial will be disclosed to the defence under reg. 2 Crime and Disorder Act 1998 (Service of Prosecution Evidence) Regulations 2005 within 70 or 50 days of the case being sent to the Crown Court for trial under s. 51 Crime and Disorder Act 1998.

- Any 'unused' material (initial disclosure), which might reasonably be considered capable of undermining the case for the prosecution or of assisting the case for the accused must be disclosed, s. 3 CPIA 1996, thereafter in accordance with time limits.

- Within 28 days of initial disclosure, defence must serve a defence statement, s. 5 CPIA 1996 (note the possible drawing of adverse inferences under s. 11 CPIA 1996). The defendant must also serve a defence witness statement s. 6C CPIA 1996.

- Prosecution must serve any further 'unused' evidence which might reasonably be expected to assist the defence as disclosed in the defence statement under its continuing duty to review unused material, s. 7A CPIA 1996.

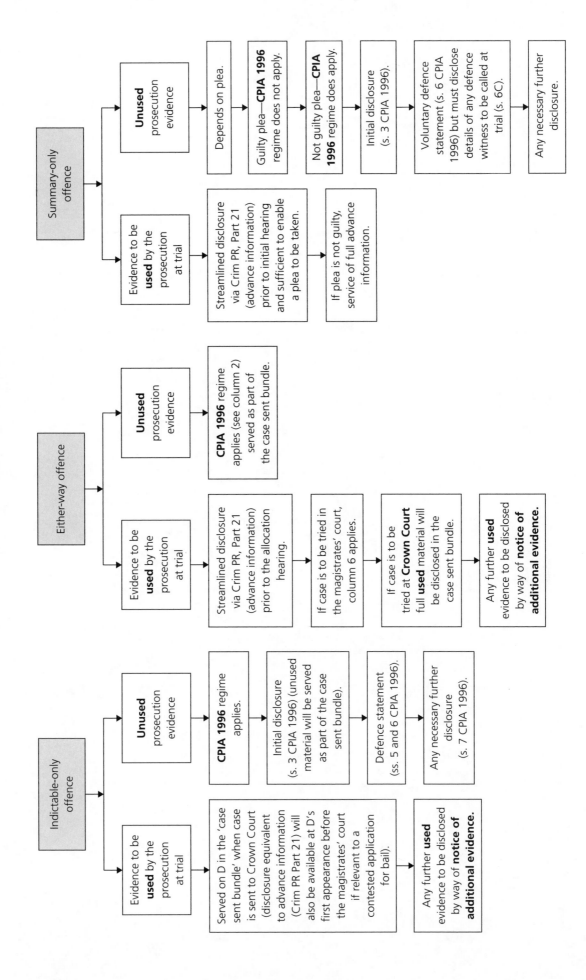

FIGURE 8.3 DISCLOSURE FLOWCHART

Part III

FROM CHARGE TO TRIAL

Part III considers the procedural stages between charge/ requisition and a defendant having to appear in court to answer the allegations made against him.

In Chapter 9 we consider public funding of criminal proceedings and the early stages of the criminal litigation process.

Chapter 10 explains the court's role in granting and refusing bail.

Chapter 11 considers the special procedure in relation to an either-way offence.

In Chapter 12 we consider summary trials and the steps to be taken in preparing for a trial in the magistrates' court.

Finally, in Chapters 13 and 14 we explain the procedural stages of a trial on indictment in the Crown Court.

FUNDING OF CRIMINAL DEFENCE SERVICES AND EARLY STAGES OF THE CRIMINAL JUSTICE PROCESS

9.1   INTRODUCTION

In this chapter we consider:

- the state funding of criminal defence work; and

- the early stages of a criminal case, including a defendant's first appearance before a magistrates' court and the steps a defence practitioner will take to prepare for this hearing.

9.2   LEGAL AID—A HUMAN RIGHT?

Every person charged with a criminal offence is entitled to defend himself in person or through legal assistance. Article 6(3)(c) European Convention on Human Rights 1950 enshrines this right and further stipulates that the entitlement to legal representation must be free where the person has insufficient means to pay and when the interests of justice require it.

A defendant faced with a criminal charge may pay privately for legal representation. This, however, is relatively rare because apart from road traffic offences the vast majority of defendants who retain a defence solicitor have their legal expenses met by the state under the Legal Aid, Sentencing and Punishment of Offenders Act 2012 (LASPO 2012), which has repealed and replaced the Access to Justice Act 1999. It is part of defence solicitors' professional duty to consider the provision of state-funded assistance for their clients (Solicitors Code of Conduct, Chapter 1 and *Principle 4*), which in part explains why approximately £1.2 billion is spent every year on criminal legal aid.

9.3   LEGAL AID AGENCY

From 1 April 2013, LASPO 2012 saw the creation of a new executive agency (replacing the Legal Services Commission). The responsibility for administering criminal and civil legal aid is to be assumed by the newly named Legal Aid Agency (LAA) working within the Ministry of Justice. The Standard Crime Contract with the LAA requires all client files to be opened and maintained in a quality assured way. Firms 'report' the work they have undertaken to the LAA and receive regular payments on that basis. Trainee solicitors, legal executives and paralegals working in franchised firms will be inducted into the procedures for opening and maintaining files to comply with LAA requirements. All of the CRM forms associated with the public funding of criminal defence services can be accessed from the LAA's website (http://www.justice.gov.uk/legal-aid). All files must contain a completed CRM1.

9.4   PRE-CHARGE ADVICE AND ASSISTANCE

9.4.1   AT THE POLICE STATION

Assistance at the police station is provided under the Police Station Advice and Assistance Scheme which is explained in Chapter 4, para. 4.7.4.

9.4.2   PRE-CHARGE ADVICE OUTSIDE THE POLICE STATION

Reference should also be made to the pre-charge advice and assistance scheme. Funding under this scheme requires the defence practitioner to complete forms CRM1 and CRMS2. The scheme is means tested. Defendants in receipt of certain welfare benefits (including income-based job seeker's allowance and income support) qualify automatically in terms of their means. Assistance can only be provided under this scheme where the defence practitioner believes there is sufficient benefit to the client to justify the work being carried out. The scheme covers a client who seeks advice outside the police station in connection with a matter for which the client is under investigation but has not been charged. It also covers representation in connection with an investigation by a non-police body such as the Department of Work and Pensions.

9.5 FUNDED REPRESENTATION IN COURT

A defendant charged with a criminal offence who wishes to be represented by a solicitor in court must either:

- seek representation by the Court Duty Solicitor;
- apply to the court for a representation order; or
- pay privately.

9.5.1 DUTY SOLICITOR SCHEME

Representation at court by a duty solicitor is completely free and not subject to a means or merits test. However, a duty solicitor can only represent a defendant who is:

- in custody;
- charged or requisitioned in connection with an imprisonable offence;
- applying for bail (unless the defendant has used a duty solicitor for a previous application);
- at risk of imprisonment for failing to pay a fine or failing to obey a court order.

A duty solicitor *may not* represent someone in connection with:

- a trial;
- a hearing to send or commit a case to the Crown Court;
- an application for bail (if that person has used a duty solicitor for a previous application); or
- a non-imprisonable offence (unless that person is in custody).

A duty solicitor is most likely to represent a defendant making a first appearance before a magistrates' court who wishes to plead guilty to a non-indictable-only offence(s) and be sentenced or who wishes to apply for bail, having been denied post-charge police bail and who therefore appears before the magistrates' court in custody. If further representation beyond the limited scope of the duty solicitor scheme is required, the defendant must either represent himself or instruct a solicitor to appear for him under a representation order.

9.6 REPRESENTATION ORDERS

If a defendant requires publicly funded representation in court, the defendant must obtain a representation order. For both magistrates' court and Crown Court proceedings a defendant must satisfy a means test and the interests of justice (merits) test.

9.6.1 APPLYING FOR A REPRESENTATION ORDER

The relevant forms are:

- CRM14 Application for Legal Aid in Criminal Proceedings;
- CRM15 Financial Statement for Legal Aid in Criminal Proceedings.

CRM14 must be completed in all cases whether tried summarily or on indictment and contains the interests of justice test and the applicant's relevant personal information. The applicant may additionally be required to complete CRM15 (statement of financial means). A representation order application is processed administratively by the magistrates' court at which the defendant will make his initial appearance. The forms can be handwritten. They currently cannot be completed electronically, but this is set to change in the future.

9.7 THE INTERESTS OF JUSTICE TEST (CRM14)

- The interests of justice (IoJ) test is automatically satisfied in a case where an accused is charged with an indictable-only offence which is sent to the Crown Court. The applicant needs only to tick the 'Indictable' box on the front page of CRM14 for it to be processed on this basis.
- Where an accused is charged with a summary-only or either-way offence, a representation order will only be granted if the IoJ criteria are met.
- If an either-way offence fails the IoJ test but is subsequently sent/committed to the Crown Court (see Chapter 11), the IoJ test is automatically satisfied by the sending/committal.
- The IoJ test must be met where a convicted defendant seeks publicly funded representation to appeal against conviction and/or sentence before the Crown Court.

The Legal Aid, Sentencing and Punishment of Offenders Act 2012 (Criminal Legal Aid (General) Regulations 2013) provides that if any of the following grounds apply, the IoJ test is satisfied and a defendant is entitled to a representation order:

- if proven the defendant is likely to lose his liberty or livelihood or suffer serious damage to his reputation;
- the case involves a substantial question of law;
- the defendant is under a mental or physical disability or has inadequate knowledge of English such that the defendant is unable to follow the proceedings or put his case;
- the defence involves the tracing and interviewing of witnesses or expert cross-examination of a prosecution witness;
- legal representation is desirable in the interests of someone other than the accused.

9.7.1 ARTICULATING THE INTERESTS OF JUSTICE TEST

How does the defence practitioner articulate the IoJ test?

Take a look at CRM14 (see the completed copy in relation to the *Lenny Wise* case study in Appendix 1). The interests of justice grounds are listed at Question 29 of the form. Defence practitioners should articulate as many of the grounds as possible, in sufficient detail to maximise the chances of a representation order being granted. A copy of CRM14 can be found on the LAA's website: http://www.justice.gov.uk/forms/legal-aid-agency/criminal-forms/applications. Helpful guidance on completing CRM14 and CRM15 can also be found on this page. Detailed guidance on completing the interests of justice test can be accessed at: http://www.justice.gov.uk/downloads/legal-aid/eligibility/guidance-on-consideration-of-defence-representation-order-applications.pdf. This is well worth reading and can be found in the web-links section (Funding) on our Online Resource Centre.

The articulation of the IoJ test will now be considered.

9.7.2 LOSS OF LIBERTY

Obviously the more serious the offence, the more likely the defendant could go to prison if convicted. There must be a real—as opposed to a theoretical—risk of imprisonment. Many offences carry a theoretical risk of imprisonment, for example, theft. However, a first-time conviction for theft of a small sum of money would not result in imprisonment.

The defence practitioner should research the relevant sentencing guidelines for the offence charged by reference to the Magistrates' Court Sentencing Guidelines (MCSGs) (extracts from which are reproduced at Appendix 2). The MCSGs indicate the starting point and the range of sentences based on the type of conduct in the commission of the offence. If the sentencing guidelines suggest that a custodial sentence is the appropriate starting point upon conviction, the guidelines should be cited to support the loss of liberty ground. You should also list any aggravating features in the alleged commission of the offence (i.e. vulnerable victim or a theft in breach of trust etc.).

If the guidelines suggest a sentencing starting point of a community penalty, the defence practitioner needs to consider whether any aggravating features in the offence makes custody more likely. This would include where the defendant has previous convictions for a similar offence or the offence was committed whilst on bail in connection with other criminal matters. Full details of previous offending and the sentence imposed should be given. If a copy of the defendant's criminal record is available this should be included in the application. If the defendant is subject to a suspended sentence of imprisonment, the risk of a prison sentence on conviction for the new offence is more likely. Similarly, if the defendant is subject to an existing community order, conviction for the current offence may result in that order being revoked and the defendant being re-sentenced for the earlier offence. By definition, being charged with a serious either-way offence gives rise to a real risk of imprisonment upon conviction; being charged with a summary-only offence does not.

9.7.3 LOSS OF LIVELIHOOD

Does the defendant stand to lose his job if convicted? If so, this needs to be carefully and fully articulated. The likely loss of livelihood should be a direct consequence of the conviction or sentence. Articulation of this ground depends on the defendant's job and the nature of the offence. If a defendant is at risk of a custodial sentence, the chances of him losing his employment are likely to be high. The prospect of lost employment would be particularly high where, for example, the offence involves an allegation of theft from an employer or the offence is of a sexual or violent nature and the defendant's job includes contact with children and young people. Loss of livelihood normally refers to current livelihood. Arguably, someone training for a profession may be eligible to be included in this ground.

Road traffic offences may result in loss of livelihood through disqualification from driving upon conviction. However, some driving offences are minor in nature and, consequently, it may be more difficult to obtain a representation order for minor driving offences. Assertions that mandatory disqualification from driving will result in a loss of livelihood will be examined critically. A right to representation would not normally be justified where a defendant seeks to avoid disqualification under the totting-up disqualification procedure having acquired 12 or more penalty points on his driving licence, or for a drink-driving offence. Where there is a strong argument for advancing special reasons for avoiding disqualification (see Sentencing in Road Traffic Cases—online chapter), the interests of justice might be met.

online resource centre

9.7.4 DAMAGE TO REPUTATION

If convicted, is the defendant likely to suffer serious damage to his reputation? If so, this needs to be articulated. Examples might include a conviction for a sexual offence, or a first-time conviction for dishonesty. If the defendant already has a previous conviction for a similar offence or has a conviction for a more serious offence, it will be difficult to argue that the defendant is likely to suffer damage to his or her reputation. A previous conviction of itself, however, does not preclude applying under this ground where, for example, the defendant has been convicted of a relatively minor offence, or a 'spent' conviction, but is now charged with a much more serious offence. The defendant's job and the precise nature of the offence are relevant when assessing loss of reputation.

9.7.5 SUBSTANTIAL QUESTION OF LAW

Does the applicant's case involve a substantial question of law? If it does, the defence practitioner needs to explain in detail what the point of law is. This includes a legal argument about the *actus reus* and *mens rea* elements of the offence, where, for example, a defendant is pleading not guilty to theft, submitting that she lacked dishonest intent in accordance with *R v Ghosh* [1982] 3 WLR 110. In this situation it is clearly in the interests of justice for the defendant to be legally represented.

A substantial question of law also covers challenging the admissibility of evidence including:

* arguments about whether it is appropriate to draw an adverse inference from an accused's silence at the police station under s. 34 Criminal Justice and Public Order Act 1994 (see Chapter 5);

* applying to have a confession excluded under ss. 76 and 78 Police and Criminal Evidence Act 1984 (PACE 1984) for breaches of Code C (see Chapter 6);

* applying to have identification evidence excluded under s. 78 PACE 1984 for breach of Code D (see Chapter 7);

* disputing the admissibility of hearsay evidence (see Chapter 18);

* disputing the admissibility of bad character evidence under the Criminal Justice Act 2003 (see Chapter 19).

The IoJ test requires the defence lawyer to explain precisely the point of law that applies to the applicant's case.

9.7.6 INADEQUATE KNOWLEDGE OF ENGLISH—PHYSICAL OR MENTAL DISABILITY AND CANNOT PUT CASE

This ground applies where the applicant has inadequate knowledge of English, or is unable to communicate (perhaps because of a speech impediment or lack of literacy), or suffers from a mental or physical disability. Clearly it is in the interests of justice for the defendant to be represented by a lawyer. Full details of the lack of knowledge of English or the disability must be given, for example: 'I have been diagnosed with clinical depression by my GP who has prescribed a tranquilliser', 'I speak Urdu and have a little knowledge of basic English but would be unable to understand the advance information or follow technical or legal phrases adequately'.

9.7.7 TRACING AND INTERVIEWING OF WITNESSES

If the accused's defence requires a witness to be traced and/or interviewed this should be explained and details provided. The reason for wanting to trace or interview a witness should be made clear, along with an indication of how the witness will assist the defendant's case. For example, a witness may provide the defendant with an alibi. Where a defence witness is known to the defendant, it is often better for the witness to be approached and interviewed by the legal representative in order to preserve the witness's independence. If a prosecution witness is to be interviewed on behalf of the defendant, this should also be undertaken by a lawyer, although it is unusual for a defence practitioner to interview a prosecution witness before the trial as this would raise professional conduct issues (see 1.11.6). This ground under the IoJ test can also be used where the defence seeks to instruct an expert witness.

9.7.8 EXPERT CROSS-EXAMINATION

This ground is not confined to the cross-examination of an expert witness but can be used for any defendant who is pleading not guilty as this will trigger the need to cross-examine witnesses. The defence practitioner should explain why the defendant would have difficulty in personally cross-examining the witnesses. The witness might be, for example, an expert or a police officer or an eye-witness whose evidence is crucial or someone with a purpose of their own to serve. The cross-examination may raise points of law which necessarily requires legal expertise.

9.7.9 THE INTERESTS OF SOMEONE OTHER THAN THE DEFENDANT

Is it in the interests of someone other than the defendant that the defendant should be represented by a solicitor?

This ground often causes confusion. The 'someone other' is largely restricted to those who are directly affected by the proceedings in their capacity as witnesses. It would clearly not be in the interests of justice if an accused charged with a sexual offence was to cross-examine the alleged victim in person. Similarly, in the case of a vulnerable prosecution witness, such as an elderly eye-witness to a burglary or a child witness, it might be argued that it is in the interests of justice for the accused to be represented by a solicitor rather than to allow the accused himself to cross-examine the witness. Sections 34–39 Youth Justice and Criminal Evidence Act 1999 prohibit a defendant from personally cross-examining a complainant in specified sexual offence cases and this prohibition extends to personally cross-examining a child witness in relation to an offence of a sexual or violent nature.

9.7.10 ANY OTHER REASON

This final, catch-all ground could include the need to skilfully examine a defence witness or to carefully review the evidence in the case or to seek further disclosure from the prosecution.

A defendant will be granted a representation order where the defendant's case satisfies one or more of the IoJ criteria already explained. Obviously it is more difficult to satisfy the test where the defendant is charged with a minor, summary-only offence and conversely the IoJ test is more easily satisfied in connection with a serious either-way offence. Remember that the IoJ test is automatically satisfied where the applicant is charged with an indictable-only offence.

9.8 MEANS TESTING (CRM15)

Means testing applies to representation orders in the Crown Court and in the magistrates' court. Some applicants are 'passported' which means they do not need to complete CRM15. 'Passported' applicants include those:

- under 18; and
- applicants in receipt of any of the following benefits: Income Support, Income Based Job-seeker's Allowance, Guaranteed State Pension Credit (note that the Universal Credit is set to replace all of these benefits in 2013).

Applicants must provide their national insurance number if aged over 16, or proof of benefit. The application cannot be processed without this information. All other applicants must complete the means test on CRM15. The applicant's financial eligibility is determined by the magistrates' court which receives and processes the application for a representation order. Criminal defence practitioners can give clients an indication as to whether they are likely to pass the means test by inputting their financial details on the LAA's Online Financial Eligibility Calculator, which can be accessed at http://www.justice.gov.uk/legal-aid/assess-your-clients-eligibility.

9.9 THE MEANS TEST AS APPLIED TO CASES TRIED IN THE MAGISTRATES' COURT

Means testing in magistrates' court proceedings is confined to an assessment of income alone. In contrast to Crown Court means testing, capital is not taken into account. The means testing scheme in the magistrates' court is said to be an 'in or out' scheme.

The applicant either qualifies in terms of his means, in which case (subject to satisfying the IoJ test) he qualifies for a representation order, or he does not, in which case he is ineligible. The assessment of an applicant's income eligibility threshold is the same for both magistrates' court proceedings and Crown Court proceedings except there is no upper limit in the Crown Court.

The magistrates' court means test comprises two elements: an initial assessment and a full means test. The initial assessment takes account of the applicant's gross annual income and adjusts it against the applicant's family unit size by applying a 'weighting' formula. Once the applicant's 'weighted' gross annual income figure is determined the applicant will either be:

- eligible; or
- ineligible; or
- a full means test will be required.

On current figures the thresholds are as follows:

- A 'weighted' gross annual income of less than £12,475: applicant passes the means test and need not complete CRM15.
- Greater than £22,325 CRM15 will need to be completed: applicant fails the means test and cannot therefore be granted a representation order to cover proceedings in the magistrates' court.
- If the applicant's 'weighted' income falls between the lower and upper threshold, a full means test must be undertaken CRM15 will need to be completed.

9.9.1 WHAT COUNTS AS INCOME?

Income for these purposes is total income from all sources, including wages; state benefits (unless specifically disregarded); maintenance payments; benefits in kind; income from savings and investments. The calculation is based on income received in the 12-month period before the application. Disregarded state benefits for this purpose include:

- attendance allowance;
- severe disablement allowance;
- carer's allowance;
- disability living allowance;
- housing benefit;
- council tax benefit;
- any payment made out of a social fund.

The applicant must produce proof of income. This can include the most recent wage slip or, where self-employed, the most recent tax return or set of accounts. Proof of income can be waived for an employed or self-employed applicant who has been produced before a magistrates' court in police custody and who is subsequently remanded into custody by the magistrates' court and who therefore cannot get access to financial information. This must be indicated on CRM15.

For the purposes of the initial assessment, the applicant's gross annual income is 'weighted' by applying a mathematical formula which takes account of a partner and children living as dependants in the same household.

9.9.2 IS A PARTNER'S INCOME INCLUDED?

A partner's income is included in the assessment of means. A partner is defined as anyone (including a person of the same sex) with whom the applicant lives as a couple. The applicant's partner is required to sign CRM14 and 15 where their means are aggregated. The requirement for a signature is waived if the applicant is remanded in custody by the court or the partner is indisposed in some way. A partner's income will not be aggregated where the partner has a contrary interest including where the partner is:

- the alleged victim; or
- a prosecution witness; or
- both are defendants and there is a conflict between them.

9.9.3 IS CAPITAL TAKEN INTO ACCOUNT?

An applicant's capital assets are completely ignored for means testing in relation to magistrates' court proceedings.

9.9.4 THE FULL MEANS TEST

The purpose of the full means test is to calculate the applicant's annual disposable income. This is based on the applicant's gross annual income (not 'weighted' annual income). Where the applicant's annual disposable income exceeds the current figure of £3,398, the applicant will be financially ineligible to receive public funding for proceedings in the magistrates' court.

In calculating the applicant's annual disposable income, deductions are made for:

- income tax and national insurance contributions (for the applicant and partner if partner's income is aggregated);
- housing costs (i.e. rent/mortgage);
- child care fees (excluding private education);
- maintenance to a former partner;
- an annual living allowance (calculated using a mathematical formula).

The calculations required for both the initial and full means test can be performed on the LAA's online financial calculator. You are reminded that it is the court which undertakes the means test to determine eligibility. For detailed guidance on all aspects of means testing for magistrates' court and Crown Court proceedings (see later) access a copy of the Criminal Legal Aid Manual (February 2012) published by the LAA at http://www.justice.gov.uk/legal-aid/criminal-legal-aid-eligibility.

9.9.5 PAYMENT FOR ASSISTING A CLIENT TO COMPLETE CRM14 AND 15

A defendant who wishes to apply for a representation order will require assistance to complete CRM14 and 15 if applicable. Where a representation order is granted, the defence practitioner can claim 30 minutes' worth of assistance under the representation order. Where a representation order is refused because the applicant fails the means test, the solicitor can claim a fixed fee of £75 under the *early cover scheme* provided the applicant instructed his solicitor before the first hearing and his solicitor submitted his application for a representation order within five days of being instructed. Where a representation order is refused under the IoJ test, the solicitor can claim one hour's preparatory work under the *pre-order cover scheme*. The work typically covered under these post-charge schemes includes:

- taking a client's instructions;
- assisting the client to complete an application for a representation order;
- routine letters and telephone calls to the court and the CPS.

9.9.6 **HARDSHIP REVIEW**

A hardship review application may be submitted when:

* a defendant is refused legal aid because he fails the means test; or
* a defendant thinks he will fail the means test but has exceptional financial circumstances perhaps due to unusually high outgoings or because defence costs are likely to be unusually expensive.

To apply for a hardship review, the applicant must complete CRM16.

9.9.7 **RIGHT OF APPEAL AGAINST A REFUSAL OF A REPRESENTATION ORDER?**

If the applicant fails the IoJ test, he has the right to submit a further application and thereafter a right of appeal to the magistrates' court.

If the applicant fails the means test there is no right of appeal. However, the applicant can ask for a re-assessment of his means if his circumstances have changed or a recalculation if the applicant thinks that an error has been made.

9.10 **THE MEANS TEST AS APPLIED TO CASES TRIED ON INDICTMENT**

A defendant charged with an indictable-only offence or charged with an either-way offence whose case is sent to the Crown Court will be means tested to determine how much the defendant will have to contribute towards the costs of his defence.

As already noted there is a significant difference between the means testing scheme applicable to magistrates' court proceedings and the scheme in the Crown Court. In the magistrates' court, means testing is restricted solely to the applicant's income. The Crown Court scheme is *contributory* and is assessed against the applicant's *income, capital and equity*. This requires the applicant to provide additional information on CRM15 relating not just to income but also to capital assets. There is no self-certification of income for employed or self-employed applicants who are remanded into custody by a court as there is for cases that are concluded in the magistrates' court. Whilst the application can be processed without proof of income, outgoings and capital, proof must be submitted within 14 days of the case being committed or sent to the Crown Court. An additional fee is available to defence solicitors who assist defendants to obtain the required evidence where they have been remanded in custody. If supporting evidence of income is not provided, an 'income evidence sanction' will be applied which can increase the amount to be paid under a contribution notice to £900 per month or more, depending on income. If evidence of capital assets is not provided the rules permit removal of the £30,000 allowance with the result that a convicted offender may be asked to pay his costs in full.

Subject to the outcome of the means assessment in the Crown Court, some defendants may have to contribute to some or all of their defence legal costs under a *contribution notice/order*. The contribution may be from income, capital or a combination of each.

The income threshold limits that apply in the magistrates' court (outlined at paras. 9.9.1–9.9.4) are the same for the Crown Court except there is no upper income threshold applied in the Crown Court. As in the magistrates' court, certain applicants automatically qualify in terms of their means. They include applicants under 18 and those in receipt of any of the following benefits: Income Support, Income Based Jobseeker's Allowance; Guaranteed State Pension Credit. Such applicants do not need to complete CRM15. An applicant whose annual household disposable income is greater than £3,398 will be subject to a contribution notice. Income-based contributions are set at 90% of disposable income (limited to a maximum contribution calculated according to the type of offence being tried) and are payable by six monthly instalments (five, if all instalment payments are paid on time). If the defendant is acquitted, all income-based payments made under a contribution notice will be refunded with interest.

The combined capital and equity threshold for Crown Court proceedings is £30,000. Any capital-based contributions under a contribution order are payable at the conclusion of the case if the applicant is convicted and his monthly contributions from income have not covered his defence costs in full.

Any applicant who is assessed as having to make a contribution towards his legal costs can submit a hardship review application and can ask for his contribution order to be reviewed and recalculated if he feels it has been computed in error or his circumstances have changed.

A Crown Court representation order will not be revoked or withdrawn for non-payment of a contribution order. However, there are enforcement measures available and non-payment will increase the overall cost liability.

9.10.1 PROVISION FOR AN EITHER-WAY CASE SENT TO THE CROWN COURT

When applying for a representation order to cover the proceedings before the magistrates' court, the applicant will need to complete CRM14 and (if applicable CRM15 including the property and capital aspect of the form). If the applicant failed the IoJ test initially but his case is subsequently sent to the Crown Court for trial, he will be passported through the IoJ test.

What happens to an applicant who is charged with an either-way offence who fails the means test in the magistrates' court but whose case is subsequently sent to the Crown Court? The applicant's means will be re-assessed to calculate any contribution order/notice. The applicant's representation order will then cover proceedings from the date after the case has been sent to the Crown Court.

9.10.2 PROVISION IN RELATION TO A CASE WHICH IS COMMITTED FOR SENTENCE

A representation order granted in the magistrates' court will cover proceedings subsequently committed for sentence to the Crown Court.

Any applicant who failed to apply for funding in the magistrates' court may apply to cover the proceedings in connection with a committal for sentence. Such an applicant would automatically satisfy the IoJ test but would be subject to a means test based on income only. If the applicant applied for a representation order before the magistrates' court but failed the means test, the regulations stipulate that such an individual will be ineligible for publicly funded assistance upon committal for sentence in the Crown Court unless there has been a change in circumstances. The applicant can submit a hardship review application using form CRM16.

9.10.3 PROVISION FOR AN APPEAL AGAINST CONVICTION AND/OR SENTENCE TO THE CROWN COURT

Where an appeal is made to the Crown Court against conviction and/or sentence in summary proceedings a further CRM14 application is required. If the appellant was granted a representation order by the magistrates' court and his financial circumstances have not changed and he indicates this on CRM14, he need not submit a further CRM15. The IoJ test will need to be satisfied where a convicted applicant seeks publicly funded representation on appeal before the Crown Court. Financial eligibility is based on the 'in or out' scheme that applies in the magistrates' court. However, where an applicant's income is above the threshold and the appeal is abandoned or the appeal is partly or wholly unsuccessful, the applicant will have to make a contribution ranging from £250 to £500.

9.10.4 **A SUMMARY OF KEY DIFFERENCES BETWEEN MEANS TESTING IN THE MAGISTRATES' COURT AND CROWN COURT**

MAGISTRATES' COURT	CROWN COURT
Must meet the interests of justice test.	'Passported' through interests of justice test (except for appeals).
Income only means test.	Income, capital and equity are means tested.
Simple in/out test (if means tested is failed, no representation order).	Contribution-based scheme (if income/capital is above a certain level a representation order will still be granted subject to a contribution notice/order).
Representation order issued for eligible defendants.	Contribution order/notice issued alongside representation order.
Evidence of income required.	Evidence of income and capital required.
Self-certification of income for defendants remanded in custody.	No self-certification of income/capital for defendants remanded in custody.

9.11 **WHAT WORK CAN BE DONE UNDER A REPRESENTATION ORDER?**

A representation order covers the entire proceedings in the magistrates' courts including an application for bail before the Crown Court. It covers advice about a possible appeal to the Crown Court against conviction and/or sentence. For representation at an appeal, a further application for a representation order has to be made to either the magistrates' court or the Crown Court (see 9.10.3).

Where a representation order is granted to cover cases triable on indictment, the order will cover the costs of representation in the Crown Court and will extend to obtaining advice when appealing against conviction and/or sentence to the Court of Appeal.

9.12 **DISBURSEMENTS**

It may be necessary for the accused's lawyer to incur disbursements in preparing the defence case. This might include instructing an expert witness, an interpreter or enquiry agent or obtaining the transcript of an interview. Solicitors should always seek prior authorisation from the LAA to incur expenditure in excess of £100 using Form CRM4. It will be necessary to show that this course of action is in the client's best interests and that it is reasonable to incur the disbursement and that the amount to be incurred is reasonable. The defence practitioner should therefore ascertain in advance the amount of expenditure that will be needed. In the *R v Lenny Wise* case study (the complete version of which can be accessed in the Online Resource Centre), as part of the case preparation, Lenny Wise's solicitor obtains the LAA's prior authorisation to obtain an expert report from Lenny's consultant psychiatrist.

online
resource
centre

9.13 **ACQUITTED DEFENDANTS**

An acquitted defendant who has incurred expenditure in conducting his defence (which clearly applies to a privately funded acquitted defendant) is generally entitled to costs from central funds for such an amount as the court considers reasonably sufficient to compensate for costs incurred (s. 16 Prosecution of Offenders Act 1985). While such orders are at the court's discretion they should normally be awarded unless it is felt that the accused brought suspicion on himself by his conduct and misled the prosecution into thinking the evidence against him was stronger than it was. Guidance can be found in Practice Direction (Crime: Costs) [1991] 1 WLR 498. A legally aided acquitted defendant's costs will be met under the representation order. Provision in LASPO 2012 has seen the amount payable to a privately paying acquitted defendant out of central funds capped to legal aid rates for magistrates' court cases and with no order for costs in the Crown Court (this will effectively compel some defendants to accept legal aid with a contribution rather than paying privately).

9.14 WASTED COSTS

Where a defence solicitor or the CPS has wasted the court's time by an improper, unreasonable or negligent act or omission, s. 19 Prosecution of Offenders Act 1985 permits the court to make a wasted costs order.

9.15 THE FUTURE OF PUBLIC FUNDING

The Coalition Government has announced that further efficiencies are required in the criminal justice system to allow for the 'swifter resolution of cases before the courts'. Ministry of Justice reforms are set to strengthen the effectiveness of the Crown Court means testing scheme which, from July 2013, will include powers to seize and if necessary sell a defen-dant's motor vehicle if convicted. From April 2013, the LAA will have additional powers to actively pursue convicted offenders for their full legal costs if they refuse to provide the financial information necessary to perform a means test. Provision has also been made to amend legal aid contribution orders if hidden assets or earnings later come to light.

The Coalition Government has re-affirmed its commitment to introduce competitive price tendering in the criminal legal aid market and has decided to accelerate the timetable in this regard. An eight-week consultation exercise will run until April 2013. The process could well see a significant reduction in the number of firms who are able to provide publicly funded criminal defence services. Competitive tendering competitions will commence in the autumn 2013, with new contracts being awarded to the firms that are successful in the bidding process. A condition of the new contract will be a requirement to work digitally as part of the move to a digital criminal justice system.

9.16 FIRST APPEARANCE BEFORE THE MAGISTRATES' COURT

This next section should be read in conjunction with Chapter 8.

Irrespective of the classification of the offence, once charged or requisitioned/summonsed, the defendant's first appearance will be before a magistrates' court. The procedure at the first hearing will depend on whether the defendant is listed to appear at an early administrative hearing (EAH); early first hearing (EFH); or before the remand court. Before the purpose and procedure of these hearings is explained, consideration needs to be given to two recent initiatives, namely CJ-SSS and SDJ, which are aimed at reinforcing the case management responsibilities of the courts and of the parties and thereby ensuring the more efficient disposal of cases in the magistrates' court.

9.16.1 CJ-SSS AND SDJ

A defendant's first appearance in the magistrates' court when charged or requisitioned with an offence that may be tried summarily is governed by the principles of CJ-SSS and SDJ. CJ-SSS is an acronym for Simple, Speedy, Summary, Criminal Justice and SDJ for Stop Delaying Justice.

In November 2007 an important initiative known as CJ-SSS was introduced in all magistrates' courts. CJ-SSS attempted to streamline the conduct of cases before a magistrates' court by reducing the time between arrest and the conclusion of the case by ensuring that the first hearing before a magistrates' court is always an effective hearing, thereby avoiding unnecessary adjournments. A further, important initiative, SDJ, which enhances CJ-SSS, was introduced in all magistrates' courts on 1 January 2012. SDJ is an initiative from the senior judiciary which aims to ensure that all contested trials in the magistrates' court are fully case managed from the first hearing and disposed with at the second hearing.

Where an offence may be tried summarily, CJ-SSS and SDJ require a magistrates' court to (a) take a plea from the accused at the first hearing; and (b) where a not guilty plea is entered, for the trial to be fully case managed at the first hearing and listed for trial to be held within six to eight weeks of the defendant's first court appearance. Both CJ-SSS and SDJ adopt a near zero tolerance to adjournments in cases that can be tried summarily.

The CJ-SSS and SDJ initiatives do not apply to a defendant making his first appearance in connection with an indictable-only offence as the offence will be sent immediately to the Crown Court under s. 51 CDA 1998 (see Chapter 13). Nor do they, strictly speaking, apply to a defendant making his first appearance before a magistrates' court in custody because, having been charged, police bail was refused. In this latter instance, if the defendant is in a position to indicate his plea, a court will enter a plea and move to the next stage.

The success of CJ-SSS/SDJ depends on co-operation between the police, the CPS and the defence, together with robust case management by the court. CJ-SSS/SDJ requires the CPS to serve sufficient disclosure of the prosecution's case (see Chapter 8, para. 8.12.1 and Appendix 1, Document 2) on the accused before the first hearing to enable the defendant to enter or indicate a firm plea. Indeed, under SDJ, the court will expect and insist that a defendant enter or indicate a plea at the first hearing. If the defence solicitor has been instructed at the last minute and has been handed prosecution disclosure at court, the court will expect the solicitor to have reviewed the disclosed evidence and advised his client, before coming into court.

If, at the first hearing, the defendant enters a guilty plea to either a summary-only or either-way offence, the case will immediately proceed to sentence (see Part V). It is therefore entirely possible and not unusual, for the prosecution of an offence that may be tried summarily to be concluded at the first hearing before the magistrates' court.

If the defendant enters a not guilty plea to a summary-only matter, CJ-SSS and SDJ require that the case is listed for summary trial within six to eight weeks.

If the defendant indicates a not guilty plea or chooses to give no indication as to plea in relation to an either-way offence (this is known as the plea before venue (PBV)), the case will immediately proceed to the mode of trial enquiry/allocation hearing (see Chapter 11).

Defence lawyers commonly complain about insufficient prosecution material being served before the first hearing in connection with a summary offence. The SDJ initiative makes it clear that, notwithstanding any such representations by the defence, a plea must still be entered at the first hearing. Neither can the defence use the excuse that an application for public funding (representation order) has not yet been processed and granted and therefore the defendant is not able to enter a plea. If such an argument is advanced, the court will refer to Crim PR Part 3.8, which requires the court at every hearing to take a plea or indication of plea (if it has not already been done). The obligation to take a plea does not depend on the extent of disclosure or the grant of legal aid.

The CPS will prepare its files according to the defendant's anticipated plea and whether the defendant appears before the magistrates' court at an early first hearing (EFH) or an early administrative hearing (EAH).

Early first hearing (EFH)

Cases that are likely to be listed for an EFH are straightforward summary-only or either-way matters where the police anticipate a guilty plea will be entered. In such cases, the CPS will prepare an expedited streamlined file to be served on the defendant in accordance with the prosecution's disclosure obligations under Crim PR, Part 21 (see Chapter 8, para. 8.12). This should contain enough information to enable the defence solicitor to advise on plea.

Having spoken with a solicitor before making a first appearance in court the defendant may not wish to enter a plea at this early stage and may seek an adjournment. In this situation, in accordance with CJ-SSS/SDJ, the magistrates' court will record a not guilty plea and proceed to the next stage (mode of trial enquiry/allocation in relation to an either-way offence) and/or set a date for summary trial.

Early administrative hearings (EAH)

Early administrative hearings will cover indictable-only cases and all other offences where the plea at this early stage is uncertain. In accordance with the principles under CJ-SSS/SDJ, the CPS should serve on the defence sufficient disclosure of its evidence to enable a firm plea to be taken or indicated (except in an indictable-only offence). If the defendant chooses to plead guilty at an EAH, the court will proceed to sentence immediately. If the plea is not guilty and the offence is triable either-way, the magistrates' court will expect to proceed to the mode of trial enquiry/allocation hearing (see Chapter 11). If the offence is summary-only and a not guilty plea is entered, the magistrates' court will expect each party to be in possession of sufficient information (including witness availability) to enable the date to be fixed for a summary trial. Where the case is adjourned the defendant will either be released unconditionally, or be remanded on bail or in custody.

Remand court

A defendant appearing for the first time before a magistrates' court in custody (having been denied bail by the police upon being charged (see Chapter 4, para. 4.14.2)) will appear before the remand court of the magistrates' court. Such a court has a secure dock facility. CJ-SSS does not apply to such cases, although if the defendant is prepared to indicate a plea, the magistrates' court will happily progress the case to the next stage. Unless a guilty plea is entered to all matters and the defendant is sentenced immediately, the case will be adjourned for no longer than eight days to enable the service of prosecution evidence, or, if the offence is an indictable-only offence, it will be sent immediately to the Crown Court.

9.16.2 CASE MANAGEMENT OF TRIAL AT FIRST HEARING

A key part of the efficient case management under SDJ is the mandatory requirement for all magistrates' courts to use the trial preparation form (http://www.justice.gov.uk/courts/procedure-rules/criminal/forms/formspage) wherever a not guilty plea is entered to a case that is to be summarily tried.

Prior to the defendant's first appearance, the prosecution will have provided the District Judge or the legal adviser sitting with a lay bench of magistrates, with a copy of the evidence that will form the basis of the prosecution's case. This will of course also have been served on the defence prior to a plea being taken. To assist the court to complete the trial preparation form, the defendant will be asked to explain why he is pleading not guilty and what aspects of the prosecution's case he disputes. Both the defence and the prosecution will be expected to identify what is in issue between them (Crim PR Part 3.3) and whether any point of law arises. If the defence fails or refuses to identify the real issues in dispute the defendant is unlikely to be allowed to advance at trial a defence he has not disclosed on the case management form. The court will want to know how many witnesses each side will be calling; whether any witness statements can be agreed and be read at court under s. 9 CJA 1967 (see Chapter 12, para. 12.8.9); whether any live witnesses are likely to need special measures (see Chapter 16); and whether hearsay (see Chapter 18) or bad character (see Chapter 19) applications are envisaged. When taking the parties through the case management form, the court will actively enquire as to why it is necessary for a particular witness to attend and whether, in the light of the issues that are in dispute, the witness's evidence can be agreed and read to the court. The parties will be encouraged to draft appropriate admissions under s. 10 CJA 1967 (see Chapter 15, para 15.8) as a way of avoiding calling unnecessary witnesses and to identify the core issues in the case. The case management aspect of SDJ is entirely consistent with the overriding objective in Crim PR Part 1 that cases will be dealt with justly, efficiently and expeditiously taking into account the gravity of the offence alleged, the complexity of what is in issue, the severity of the consequences for the defendant and others affected and the needs of other cases. For consideration of the professional conduct obligations which are placed on criminal defence practitioners as a consequence of active case management by the courts, see 1.11.8.

'Virtual' courts

Section 57C Crime and Disorder Act 1998 (CDA 1998) permits a magistrates' court to direct that a preliminary hearing before a court be conducted via live-link from a police station. Currently there are a small number of local justice areas where a 'virtual' first hearing from a police station may be conducted. This applies both to defendants who are detained at the police station under s. 57C(3) CDA 1998 and to defendants who have been bailed to return to the police station for a live-link appearance in connection with the offence ('live-link bail') (s. 57C(4) CDA 1998). Section 57C(7) contains an express requirement for the defendant's consent to be given before the court makes a live-link direction. An accused answering to live-link bail is to be treated as having surrendered to custody of the court from the time when it makes a live-link direction in respect of him.

Section 57D CDA 1998 provides that where the accused attends a preliminary hearing over a live link and is convicted in the course of it, and the court proposes to proceed immediately to sentence, the accused may continue to attend over the link provided that he or she agrees and the court is satisfied that it is not contrary to the interests of justice.

The Law Society has issued a Practice Note on Virtual Courts accessible at http://www.lawsociety.org.uk/productsandservices/practicenotes/virtualcourts.page, which explains what a defence practitioner should have regard to when advising a client whether to consent to appear via live-link from a police station.

9.17 PREPARING FOR THE FIRST APPEARANCE BEFORE THE MAGISTRATES' COURT

Typical steps to be undertaken in preparation for an accused's first appearance before a magistrates' court include:

* conducting an initial interview with the defendant (this interview may take place at the police station, in the solicitor's office or at court);
* opening a file;
* completing an application for a representation order;
* requesting advance information from the CPS (if there is time before the first hearing);
* anticipating problems with bail.

Opening a file

Every publicly funded defence practitioner is required to open a file for each new client and to complete a standard CRM1 form. Every file has to be allocated a Unique File Number (UFN), a requirement under the General Criminal Contract. All fee-earning time spent on the matter must be recorded.

Initial interview

If the defendant has been charged and released on police bail or has received a requisition/summons, the defendant should be in possession of a summons/requisition or charge sheet which will enable the defence practitioner to check the precise nature of the allegations which her client is facing. The initial interview is important for extracting information whilst events are hopefully still fresh in the defendant's mind. The defence practitioner should obtain all the defendant's personal details as well as an accurate list of previous convictions and details of the defendant's financial circumstances.

During the first interview, the defence practitioner must discuss funding issues with her client. If representation in court is needed, a representation order should be applied for without delay. If the defendant is required to produce evidence of income in support of his application for a representation order, he must be instructed to produce this information without delay.

General advice about the likely progress of the case and the possible plea/sentence might be offered to the defendant at this stage. Unless the matter is very clear cut, however, defence practitioners should wait until they are in possession of the prosecution's evidence (advance information) before offering any firm advice as to plea.

At the conclusion of the initial interview, the defence practitioner will typically:

- submit an application for a representation order;
- write to her client confirming his instructions;
- request disclosure of the prosecution's case (advance information);
- contact any potential defence witnesses with a view to taking a statement.

Each of these will now be briefly considered.

Submit an application for a representation order
The application for a representation order will be sent to or handed to the magistrates' court at which the defendant is to appear.

Write to her client confirming his instructions
At an early stage the defence practitioner will send her client a client care letter in accordance with Chapter 1 SRA Code of Conduct 2011 which should confirm her client's instructions and provide information about costs. It is customary for a file to hold a client's proof of evidence. A proof of evidence is a statement of the facts recounted at the client's initial interview. In due course (and especially where a not guilty plea is anticipated) the proof of evidence will be an important source of information to the advocate representing the defendant at trial. If an initial proof of evidence is drafted, the client should be given the opportunity to review its content, sign and date it (see Appendix 1, Document 6).

Request disclosure of the prosecution's 'used' material
The rules relating to the pre-trial disclosure of evidence against a defendant are of considerable importance and have been considered in greater detail in Chapter 8. Crim PR Part 21 requires the CPS to serve 'advance information' on the accused in all cases that are triable summarily. This will comprise streamlined disclosure as explained in Chapter 8, para. 8.12. The CPS is moving towards the digital service of evidence in 2012, although paper copies will still be served in custody cases. In indictable-only offences, further comprehensive disclosure is made later in the proceedings. Under CJ-SSS/SDJ, advance information should be available on the defendant's first appearance before a magistrates' court.

The importance of obtaining advance information in all but the most straightforward cases cannot be overstated. A defence practitioner cannot properly advise a client on his plea/venue for trial unless she is in possession of and has evaluated the advance information.

The defendant will need to be taken through the advance information and advised on plea. In accordance with CJ-SSS/SDJ, if the plea is not guilty, the magistrates' court will want to proceed to the mode of trial enquiry/allocation hearing in the case of an either-way offence and set a firm date for summary trial if required. If a not guilty plea is entered to an offence that can only be tried summarily, the defence must assist the court with its duties to actively manage cases under Crim PR Part 3 and SDJ (see 9.16.2 for an account of what will be expected from the defence). Given the need for the case to be fully case managed for trial at the first hearing, this requires the defence practitioner to work fast and to have the necessary information about witness availability to hand (if possible) before the first hearing.

Approaching potential defence witnesses

If a not guilty plea is anticipated, potential defence witnesses should be approached as soon as possible whilst events are still fresh. Where required an enquiry agent may be used to track down a potential witness. Witness statements should be taken in the absence of the defendant and without the witness having seen any prosecution witness statements in advance. It is important to obtain the witness's honest, unrehearsed account of the events witnessed.

KEY POINT SUMMARY

- Be able to differentiate between the various funding schemes for the different criminal defence services that can be offered to a client.

- When articulating the interest of justice test for a representation order use as many aspects of the criteria as you can and articulate them fully and accurately.

- Understand the means testing process as it applies to cases in the magistrates' court and in the Crown Court.

- Understand the importance of keeping and maintaining accurate file notes and efficient time recording on LAA client files.

- The defence practitioner should use the initial interview with the client to take a detailed statement and to apply for public funding.

- Understand that in the magistrates' court the defendant will be expected to enter a plea at the first hearing and that the magistrates' court will want to progress the case to the next stage (mode of trial enquiry or allocation hearing and set a firm date for summary trial if necessary) unless the offence is triable only on indictment. A defendant should not be advised on plea unless the defence practitioner or duty solicitor has had the opportunity to consider streamlined advance information served by the prosecution, which should be available in time for the first hearing.

SELF-TEST QUESTIONS

Case studies: *R v Roger Martin*; *R v William Hardy*; *R v Lenny Wise*

You are familiar with the issues in relation to *R v Roger Martin, R v Lenny Wise* and *R v William Hardy.* Having regard to each client's proof of evidence try to complete an application for a representation order on behalf of each of them. You will find a completed application for a representation order in Appendix 1 in so far as Lenny Wise is concerned. Roger Martin's and William Hardy's applications for a representation order can be found in the case study section of the Online Resource Centre.

 online resource centre

The complete version of the all three case studies can be accessed on the Online Resource Centre where you can see all the steps described in the second part of this chapter (including initial file notes and early correspondence) illustrated on the solicitor's file.

Figure 9.1 CRITERIA FOR AN APPLICATION FOR A REPRESENTATION ORDER

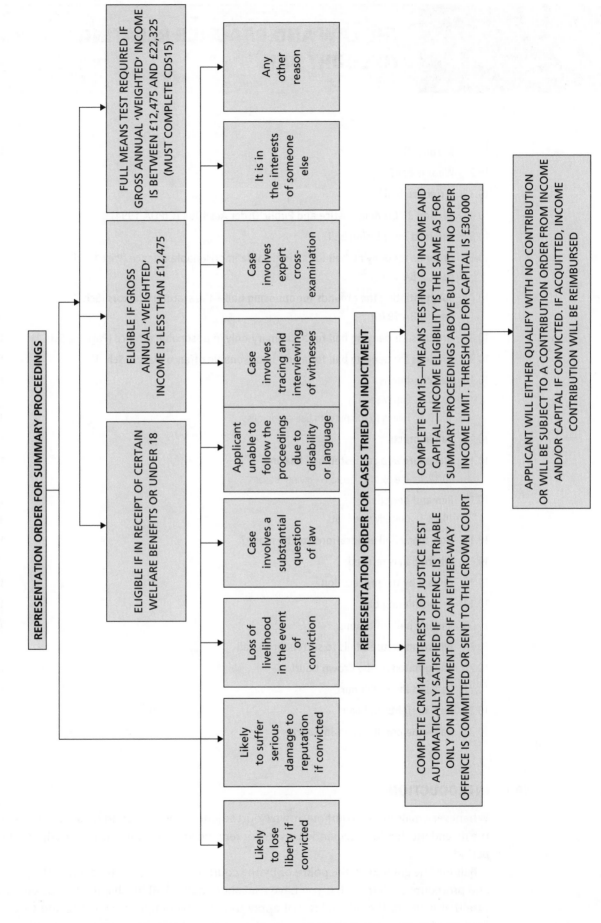

10 THE LAW AND PRACTICE RELATING TO COURT BAIL

10.1 INTRODUCTION

Whenever a magistrates' court or Crown Court adjourn a case, the court must decide whether the defendant should be remanded on bail or remanded in custody during the adjournment period.

Bail may be granted by the police or by the court. In this chapter, we explain the practice and procedure of court bail. If you have read about police bail in Chapter 4, you will recognise that many of the principles that apply to police bail under s. 38 Police and Criminal Evidence Act 1984 (PACE 1984) (see Chapter 4, para. 4.14.2) also apply to court bail.

In this chapter we examine:

- the grounds upon which bail might be refused;
- the factors a court can have regard to when deciding whether bail should be granted;
- the procedure at a contested bail application;
- appeals against bail decisions;
- bail and Article 5 European Convention on Human Rights 1950 (ECHR 1950).

Rules of court relevant to bail are contained in Crim PR, Part 19.

10.2 WHAT IS BAIL?

Bail is the release of the defendant subject to a duty to surrender to the court at a specified time and date. Bail may be granted to a defendant unconditionally or with conditions attached.

The provisions governing court bail are contained in the Bail Act 1976 (BA 1976). In many cases a defendant's bail status will be negotiated between the prosecution and the defence subject to the court giving consent. Where the prosecution opposes bail, a contested bail hearing will be held. Most bail hearings are conducted in magistrates' courts.

After being charged, where a defendant is refused police bail under s. 38 PACE 1984, the refusal is often an indication that bail will be opposed by the Crown Prosecution Service (CPS) when the defendant makes his first court appearance. For the court, the enquiry into bail requires a speculative exercise. Bail is essentially a question of trust. Can the court trust this defendant to be released back into the community on bail? Occasionally this trust can be abused, as in the case of ex-Metropolitan Police Inspector, Gary Weddell, who, in January 2008, was granted conditional bail on a charge of murdering his wife, and whilst on bail murdered his mother-in-law before killing himself.

10.3 A RIGHT TO BAIL?

Section 4 BA 1976 gives the defendant a *prima facie* right to bail (a presumption in favour of bail) when charged with a criminal offence irrespective of how serious the offence is. Where the prosecution seek to rebut this presumption by objecting to the defendant being granted bail, the court will invite both the prosecution and the defence to make submissions on the matter. In deciding whether the accused should be granted bail, the court will carefully consider whether the grounds for objecting to bail put forward by the prosecution and challenged by the defence are established by having regard to the statutory factors outlined at para. 10.6.

The presumption in favour of bail under s. 4 BA 1976 generally applies at all stages of the court proceedings from post-charge to immediately before conviction and continues to apply post-conviction where a court adjourns for the preparation of a pre-sentence report. Strictly speaking, s. 4 BA 1976 has no application:

- to police bail when the defendant is charged at the police station—s. 38 PACE 1984 (see Chapter 4);
- on summary conviction where the offender appeals against conviction or sentence;
- on summary conviction where the magistrates' court decides to commit the defendant to the Crown Court for sentence.

Although the presumption to bail does not apply in these situations, the court retains discretion to grant bail where the defendant appeals to the Crown Court and where the defendant is committed to the Crown Court for sentence. In deciding bail the magistrates will apply the criteria under the BA 1976.

The presumption in favour of bail puts the onus on the prosecution to show a good reason why bail should be withheld. The presumption in favour of bail is subject to s. 25 CJPOA 1994.

10.4 **SECTION 25 CRIMINAL JUSTICE AND PUBLIC ORDER ACT 1994 (CJPOA 1994)**

Section 25 CJPOA 1994 provides that where the accused is charged with or convicted of murder, attempted murder, manslaughter, rape or attempted rape and has been previously convicted of any of these offences, the accused shall be granted bail only if a court is satisfied that there are exceptional circumstances which justify it. Section 25 CJPOA 1994 effectively creates a presumption against granting bail in these circumstances.

10.5 **GROUNDS FOR REFUSING BAIL**

Notwithstanding the general presumption to grant bail under s. 4 BA 1976, a court may withhold bail if one or more statutory grounds under the BA 1976 apply.

The BA 1976 draws a distinction between grounds for refusing bail in relation to:

* an indictable imprisonable offence (Part 1, Sch. 1 BA 1976);
* a summary-only imprisonable offence (Part 1A, Sch. 1 BA 1976);
* a non-imprisonable offence (Part II, Sch. 1 BA 1976).

10.6 **GROUNDS FOR DENYING BAIL FOR AN INDICTABLE IMPRISONABLE OFFENCE (PART 1, SCH. 1, PARA. 2 BA 1976)**

Where the accused is charged with an imprisonable offence triable on indictment (this includes an either-way offence), Part 1 of Sch. 1, para. 2 to BA 1976 provides for a number of instances where the accused need not be granted bail. Note, however, important changes to Part 1, Sch. 1, para. 2 in the box below.

Important recent change restricting a court's power to withhold bail

Provisions under the Legal Aid, Sentencing and Punishment of Offenders Act 2012 (LASPO 2012) have inserted a new para. 1A into Sch. 1, Part 1 which restricts a court's powers to remand an adult defendant in custody prior to conviction where there is *no real prospect of the defendant receiving a custodial sentence* if convicted.

* The para. 1A restriction applies to the three main exceptions to bail outlined below: para. 2(1) (failure to surrender/commission of further offences or interfering with witnesses etc.); para. 2A (refusal of bail where defendant appears to have committed indictable or either way offence whilst on bail; and para. 6 (refusal of bail where defendant has been arrested for breaking conditions of bail or failing to surrender to previously granted bail).

* Paragraph 1A does not, however, apply to a defendant who needs to be kept in custody for his own protection or where there is a risk of further offending that may take the form of domestic violence. The restriction only affects cases where the alleged offence, taken in combination with the relevant circumstances (such as the defendant's previous convictions) does not justify a custodial sentence. In such a case the CPS will not seek a remand in custody. In less clear cut cases, the CPS may make representations against bail but invite the court to consider whether the no 'real prospect' restriction applies. The court is not expected to engage in a sentencing exercise in advance of trial but merely to form a view on the facts. If it is not clear to the court that there is no real prospect of custody, the restriction does not apply.

---

(1) Paragraph 2(1)

The accused need not be granted bail where the court is satisfied that there are *substantial grounds for believing* that, if released on bail (conditional or otherwise), the accused would:

'(a) fail to surrender to custody, or

(b) commit an offence while on bail, or

(c) interfere with witnesses or otherwise obstruct the course of justice, whether in relation to himself or any other person.'

In practical terms, the first three substantive grounds set out in para. 2(1)(a)–(c) of Sch. 1 are the most important and account for 95% of refusals of bail. Given the frequency with which these grounds are commonly cited, we consider them in detail at 10.12.

(2) Paragraph 2(2ZA) (inserted by Sch. 11 LAPSOA 2012)

The defendant need not be granted bail if the court is satisfied that there are substantial grounds for believing that the defendant, if released on bail (whether subject to conditions or not), would commit an offence while on bail by engaging in conduct that would, or would be likely to, cause—

(a) physical or mental injury to an associated person; or

(b) an associated person to fear physical or mental injury (an associated person is defined by s. 2 Family Law Act 1996).

(3) Paragraph 2A

'2A The defendant need not be granted bail if—

(a) the offence is an indictable offence or an offence triable either way; and

(b) it appears to the court that he was on bail in criminal proceedings on the date of the offence.'

Therefore if X is presently on police bail in connection with an allegation of vehicle interference (summary-only) and is subsequently arrested and charged with burglary (either-way) as X was on police bail at the date of the burglary offence, the court need not grant him bail in accordance with para. 2A.

There are currently two versions of para. 2A, both of which are in force. The original version of para. 2A is as already set out. It is prospectively repealed by s. 14 CJA 2003. The 'new' version, which was enacted under s. 14 CJA 2003, effectively creates a presumption against bail being granted by providing that bail *may not* be granted to a suspect aged over 18 who is already on bail on the date of the offence unless there is no significant risk of the suspect committing an offence on bail. This provision came partially into force on 1 January 2007 but only in relation to offences carrying life imprisonment.

Therefore if X is on bail for an alleged assault and is subsequently arrested and charged with robbery (an offence which carries a life sentence) the prosecutor should refer the court to the application of s. 14 CJA 2003.

(4) Paragraph 2(3)

'The defendant need not be granted bail if the court is satisfied that he should be kept in custody for his own protection or if he is a child or young person, for his own welfare.'

Defendants are likely to be remanded in custody for their own protection where they pose a danger to themselves or are charged with an offence that incites considerable public revulsion, e.g. child sexual abuse/paedophilia.

(5) Paragraph 2(4)

'The defendant need not be granted bail if he is already serving a custodial sentence.'

Obviously a defendant who is already serving a custodial sentence for another crime will not be granted bail in connection with new matters and should not apply for bail. The court should, however, ascertain the earliest date of release to ensure a defendant is not remanded in custody beyond that date.

(6) Paragraph 2(5)

'The defendant need not be granted bail where the court is satisfied that it has not been practicable to obtain sufficient information to take a decision in relation to bail.'

There may be cases where the police have charged a suspect but have insufficient details regarding the suspect's identity and address or his previous convictions. In this situation a court can refuse bail until information is available although it must be said that para. 5 is used sparingly in practice.

(7) Paragraph 2(6)

> 'Having been released on bail in connection with the same offence, the defendant has been arrested under s. 7 Bail Act 1976 (for absconding or breaking bail conditions).'

If a defendant is granted bail (whether by the court or the police) and fails to surrender to bail or breaks any bail conditions, the defendant can be arrested and held in custody (s. 7 BA 1976). If the failure to surrender is admitted or proved, the defendant commits the criminal offence of absconding. Where a breach of bail conditions is admitted or proved, this does not constitute an offence. However, in both situations, a court can choose to withhold bail under para. 6.

As with para. 2A earlier, there are two versions of para. 6 currently in force. The original version is as already outlined. It is prospectively repealed by s. 15 CJA 2003. The 'new' version which was enacted under s. 15 CJA 2003 effectively creates a presumption against bail being granted in that it provides that bail *may not* be granted to a suspect aged over 18 who it appears, having been released on bail in connection with the proceedings, has failed to surrender to custody, unless the court is satisfied that there is no significant risk that if released on bail, the defendant would fail to surrender to custody. This provision came partially into force on 1 January 2007 but only in relation to offences carrying life imprisonment.

(8) Paragraph 2(6A–6C) Positive drug testing at the police station

Bail *may not* be granted in the circumstances specified by s. 19(4) CJA 2003 (inserting paras. 6A–6C into Sch. 1 Part 1 to BA 1976) unless the court is satisfied there is no significant risk of the accused committing an offence while on bail (whether subject to conditions or not). The relevant circumstances are that the accused must:

- be over 18;
- have tested positive for the presence of a Class A drug;
- be charged with a Class A related drug offence or the court must have substantial grounds for believing that the misuse of a Class A drug caused or contributed to the offence with which the accused is charged; and
- refuses (a) to undergo an assessment of his dependency on or propensity to misuse drugs, or (b) having undergone such an assessment, and having had follow-up action proposed to address his dependency/propensity, refuses to undergo such follow-up action.

Where bail is granted under s. 6B, it must be subject to a condition that the defendant undergoes an initial assessment or participates in any follow-up treatment. The power of the police to take a drug sample at the police station and to require a defendant to undergo an initial assessment where he has tested positive is considered in Chapter 4, para. 4.14.3.

(9) Paragraph 2(6ZA) Special provision in relation to murder cases

A special provision relating to bail in murder cases came into force on 1 February 2010 (s. 114 Coroners and Justice Act 2009 inserting s. 6ZA into Sch. 1 Part 1 BA 1976). Section 6ZA BA 1976 provides that a defendant who is charged with murder may not be granted bail unless the court is of the opinion that there is no significant risk that, if released on bail, the defendant would commit an offence that would be likely to cause physical or mental injury to another person.

Section 115 C&JA 2009 provides that a defendant who is charged with murder may not be granted bail except by a Crown Court judge. The power of a magistrates' court to consider bail in murder cases at any stage is therefore removed. A bail decision in a murder case must be made as soon as reasonably practicable, and in any event within 48 hours (excluding public holidays) beginning the day after the defendant's appearance in the magistrates' court. If necessary the defendant must be committed to the Crown Court whilst in custody to enable a bail decision to be made, whether he or she is at the same time sent for trial under s. 51 Crime and Disorder Act 1998 (see Chapter 13).

(10) Paragraph 2(7)

'Where the case has been adjourned for enquiries or a report, it appears to the court that it would be impracticable to complete the enquiries or make a report unless the accused is kept in custody.'

This ground applies where a defendant has been convicted of an offence or has pleaded guilty but there are concerns that the defendant may not co-operate with the probation service in the preparation of a pre-sentence report. A common example is where defendants are unable to offer a fixed address to which they can be bailed and contacted.

10.7 SUBSTANTIATING THE GROUNDS FOR OPPOSING BAIL—THE STATUTORY FACTORS (SCH. 1 PARA. 9 BA 1976)

The BA 1976, Sch. 1 Part 1 para. 9 requires a court to have regard to a number of factors in determining whether the grounds for denying bail under paras. 2(1), 2A, 2ZA, 6A, and 6ZA are made out. These include:

• the nature and the seriousness of the offence and the probable method of dealing with it;
• the defendant's character, record, associates and community ties;
• the defendant's bail record;
• the strength of the evidence against the defendant;
• if the court is satisfied that there are substantial grounds for believing that the defendant, if released on bail (whether subject to conditions or not), would commit an offence while on bail including the risk that the defendant may do so by engaging in conduct that would, or would be likely to cause physical or mental injury to any person other than the defendant; and
• any other relevant factor.

Many of the factors listed in para. 9 of Sch. 1 Part 1 are self-explanatory. In practice, the more serious the offence, the greater the risk of a custodial sentence being imposed and therefore the greater the risk the defendant will abscond. In completing the case file for the CPS, the police will provide details of the defendant's past criminal record and personal circumstances. The CPS will therefore be aware of the type of person the defendant is and whether the defendant has family, a job or other commitments in the area. Clearly the defendant's previous bail record will be of considerable importance to the court.

It is the interrelationship between the grounds for refusing bail and the applicable factors which determine the grant or refusal of bail. In para. 10.12 we consider bail in practice and illustrate the interrelationship between the grounds for refusing bail and the factors the court takes into account.

10.8 GROUNDS FOR DENYING BAIL FOR A SUMMARY-ONLY IMPRISONABLE OFFENCE (PART 1A, SCH. 1)

Bail can be refused in connection with a summary-only imprisonable offence on one or more of the following grounds (note that paras. 2, 3, and 7 do not apply to an accused who is 18 and who has not been convicted in the case if it appears to the court that there is no real prospect of the defendant receiving a custodial sentence in the event of conviction):

• if, having been previously granted bail, the defendant has failed to surrender to custody and the court believes that, if released on bail, he would do so again (para. 2);
• if the defendant was on bail on the date of the offence and the court has substantial grounds to believe that, if released, he would commit an offence on bail (para. 3);

- there are substantial grounds for believing that, if released on bail, the defendant would commit an offence by engaging in conduct that would be likely to cause physical or mental injury to an associated person (as defined by s. 2 Family Law Act 1996) or cause an associated person to fear physical or mental injury (para. 4);

- the court is satisfied the defendant should be kept in custody for his own protection (para. 5);

- the defendant is already serving a custodial sentence (para. 6);

- having been released on bail in connection with the present offence, the defendant has been arrested for absconding or breaking bail conditions under s. 7 BA 1976 and there are substantial grounds for believing that the defendant, if released on bail (whether subject to conditions or not) would fail to surrender to custody, commit an offence on bail or interfere with witnesses or otherwise obstruct the course of justice (para. 7);

- lack of sufficient information (para. 8).

The provisions in relation to drug testing outlined at para. 10.6 apply to a defendant charged with a summary-only imprisonable offence.

10.9 GROUNDS FOR DENYING BAIL FOR A NON-IMPRISONABLE OFFENCE (PART II, SCH. 1)

Where the accused is charged with a non-imprisonable offence, Sch. 1 Part II to BA 1976 provides that the accused need not be granted bail where:

- it appears to the court that, having been previously granted bail, the defendant has failed to surrender to custody and the court has substantial grounds to believe, in view of that failure, that if released on bail (whether subject to conditions or not) the defendant would fail to surrender (para. 2); or

- the court is satisfied that the accused should be kept in custody for his own welfare or protection; (para. 3); or

- the defendant is already in custody in respect of any sentence; (para. 4); or

- having been released on bail in connection with the present offence, the defendant has been arrested for absconding or breaking bail conditions under s. 7 BA 1976, there are substantial grounds for believing that the defendant, if released on bail (whether subject to conditions or not) would fail to surrender to custody, commit an offence on bail or interfere with witnesses, or otherwise obstruct the course of justice (para. 5); or

- having been released on bail in connection with the present offence, the defendant has been arrested for absconding or breaking bail conditions under s. 7 BA 1976, there are substantial grounds for believing that, if released on bail, the defendant would commit an offence by engaging in conduct that would be likely to cause physical or mental injury to an associated person (as defined by the Family Law Act 1996, s. 2) or cause an associated person to fear physical or mental injury (para. 6).

10.10 BAIL CONDITIONS

A defendant may be granted conditional or unconditional bail. It is very common for the court to impose conditions under s. 3 BA 1976 on a defendant when granting bail. Common bail conditions include:

- reporting to a police station (perhaps two or three times a week or even daily);

- living at a specified/alternative address (including a bail hostel);

- avoiding contact with prosecution witnesses;

- avoiding a particular area (this could require a defendant not to enter a particular building or area or go within a specified radius of it);

- avoiding a particular activity (this could include a condition that the defendant does not visit licensed premises or sit in the front seat of any vehicle);
- imposing a curfew (requiring a defendant to remain at a specified address between certain hours—for example, 8 pm to 7 am—it could also include a 'doorstep' condition or electronic tagging);
- requiring a surety (see later);
- surrendering a passport.

In accordance with s. 8 BA 1976, conditions may only be attached to bail where it is necessary to ensure either that a defendant:

- will surrender to custody;
- does not commit further offences;
- does not interfere with witnesses or obstruct the course of justice; or
- for the person's own protection; or
- in the case of a convicted offender, to ensure the accused is available to enable enquiries for the purposes of a report to be made to the court.

To reduce the risk of absconding, a court can impose a condition that the defendant reside at a specified address and/or report to a police station. A condition that the defendant surrenders his passport and/or provides a surety is also designed to reduce the risk of an accused failing to surrender.

Where a court is concerned that a defendant might commit further offences, it could impose a curfew, where, for example, a defendant is accused of committing night-time burglaries.

A condition could also be imposed to prevent the accused from entering a specified place; for example, a supermarket from which he habitually steals merchandise. Where there is a risk of an accused committing further offences because of the accused's relationship with a particular victim, a condition could require that the accused resides at an alternative address and must not contact the injured party. These final two conditions are appropriate to prevent an accused from interfering with a witness or obstructing the course of justice.

The decision to impose one or more conditions must be a proportionate measure to reduce the risk(s) identified by the court. In negotiating bail with the CPS, the defence solicitor may need to offer or agree to certain conditions subject to his client's consent. The defence solicitor should discuss this with his client either at the police station or in the holding cell at court. Where an alternative address is likely to be needed, the defence solicitor may have to find alternative accommodation. If a bail hostel place is required, the defence solicitor will liaise with the probation service to see if a place is available and it is suitable for the defendant. This option would not be suitable, for example, for a mentally unstable or drug-dependent defandant.

Where a court grants bail to someone charged with murder in circumstances outlined at para. 10.6(8), then unless a satisfactory report on the defendant's mental condition has been obtained, the court must impose a condition requiring the defendant to undergo examination by two medical practitioners, including a psychiatrist.

Where the court grants bail in the circumstance outlined at para. 10.6(7), it must be subject to a condition requiring the defendant to undergo an initial drug assessment or to participate in follow-up treatment.

10.10.1 SURETY/SECURITY

A court may require a defendant to provide a suitable surety or sureties before granting bail. A surety is a person who promises to forfeit a sum of money fixed by the court (known as a recognisance) if the defendant fails to attend court as directed. It is the surety's solemn duty to ensure the defendant's future attendance at court. The amount of recognisance is determined by the court and depends on the surety's financial resources. If the defendant fails to answer his bail, any surety is liable to forfeit whole or part of the recognisance.

A surety must be a suitable person who will be required to attend court and give evidence on oath, confirming, amongst other things, his financial resources, his character and any previous convictions, and his relationship and proximity to the defendant. Such a condition can be imposed where the defendant is at risk of failing to surrender, perhaps because the defendant has links to a foreign jurisdiction.

A court can require a defendant to deposit a security before being released. This is rather like a bail bond. It requires the defendant or someone on his behalf to deposit a sum of money or other valuable security as a guarantee to ensure attendance. The sum can be forfeited if the defendant absconds.

10.10.2 FAILING TO COMPLY WITH BAIL CONDITIONS

If bail is granted subject to conditions, the importance of complying with the conditions will be explained to the defendant in court. The defence solicitor should remind his client of their importance.

A failure to abide by any condition of bail can lead to a defendant's arrest and reappearance before the court in custody (s. 7 BA 1976). A power of arrest is available where a police constable has reasonable grounds for believing that a person has broken, or is about to break, a bail condition. If the breach is proved or admitted, then although the defendant does not commit a further offence by breaking a bail condition, the court may decide the defendant has had his chance and should be remanded in custody for the duration of the proceedings (para. 10.6 (7)). Alternatively, the court might impose more onerous conditions or give the defendant a stern warning about the importance of abiding by conditions of bail.

Having been arrested for suspected breach of bail conditions, s. 7 BA 1976 requires the defendant to be brought before a magistrate within 24 hours of arrest, excluding Sundays.

Where a breach of bail conditions is denied, the Divisional Court held in *R (on the application of the DPP) v Havering Magistrates' Court* [2001] 2 Cr App R 2, that the breach proceedings fall within Article 5 ECHR 1950 and do not invoke the right to a fair trial provisions in Article 6. Although the proceedings do not constitute a trial, the need for the hearing to be adversarial with each side enjoying equality of arms, means the prosecution has to adduce some evidence of the breach (this can include hearsay evidence). In turn the defendant must have a full and fair opportunity to contest the allegation if he denies it.

10.11 BAIL IN PRACTICE

The most commonly cited reasons for opposing court bail are contained in Sch. 1 para. 2(1)(a)–(c), namely that there is a substantial risk that if released on bail the defendant will:

- abscond; or
- commit further offences; or
- interfere with witnesses and obstruct the course of justice.

These grounds are further strengthened in the circumstances outlined at para. 10.6.

On a daily basis magistrates' courts hear arguments based on these grounds. It is not enough for the prosecution to suggest that the defendant might abscond, or might commit further offences, there must be *substantial grounds* for the belief.

Here, we provide some typical arguments put forward by the CPS when opposing bail on the grounds set out in Sch. 1 para. 2. You will see how the statutory factors listed in para. 9 (see para. 10.7) are used to substantiate the prosecution's grounds for opposing bail. We further consider how the defence advocate might counter the prosecution's objections.

Examples

The risk of absconding from the prosecution perspective

Why can the defendant not be trusted to remain in the local area? What incentive does the defendant have to abscond? Perhaps the defendant is charged with a serious offence and risks a substantial sentence of imprisonment if convicted or is currently subject to a suspended sentence of imprisonment. Even if a prison sentence for the new offence is not a certainty, a further conviction would put the defendant in breach of a suspended prison sentence and may provide the incentive to abscond. Perhaps the defendant has previous convictions for failing to surrender. If the defendant has poor community ties such as no immediate family in the area, what incentive is there for the defendant to remain in the jurisdiction of the court?

The prosecuting advocate might address the court in this way:

'Sir, you and your colleagues will be aware that this defendant has three previous convictions for absconding.'

'Madam, this defendant was granted bail on an earlier occasion and has failed to surrender. He appears before you this morning pursuant to a warrant for his arrest.'

'Sir, this defendant's community ties are poor. He is unable to offer a stable address in the area. He has no job and no reason to stay here.'

'The accused is a foreign national whose family resides abroad. She poses a flight risk.'

Risk of absconding from the defence perspective

It does no harm to remind the court of the presumption in favour of bail (s. 4 BA 1976) if it applies. If the defendant has a record for absconding, it is important for the defence solicitor to find out about the circumstances of the absconding offences. Were they deliberate? How long ago were they committed? Did the defendant ultimately surrender and plead guilty or was he arrested? If the defendant has a good bail record, this should be stressed! The defence solicitor should examine his client's community ties. Does he have a job, a mortgage, family or anything to keep him in the area?

It is pertinent to ask whether the defendant is going to be convicted of the offence he is charged with. This requires the defence solicitor to examine the strength of the evidence against his client. The defendant may indicate he is pleading not guilty and wishes to challenge the evidence against him. In these circumstances it is legitimate to point out that the defendant will not abscond because he wishes to clear his name of the charges faced. If the defendant is likely to plead guilty, the defence solicitor should consider whether a custodial sentence is a certainty. If not, he should make the appropriate representations.

Finally, the defence solicitor needs to consider what conditions to offer in order to allay the court's fear of the defendant absconding. Possibilities might include a condition of residence at a fixed address or at a bail hostel. In addition, the court may want the defendant to report to a police station on specified days and at certain times. A court may require the defendant to surrender his passport if he poses a flight risk. Less frequently, the court may only grant bail subject to the defendant providing a suitable surety or security.

The commission of further offences from the prosecution perspective

The prosecutor must ask himself why this particular defendant is likely to commit further offences if released on bail. This may be due to the defendant's extensive criminal record indicating that he is a prolific offender or because the defendant has a particular need to commit offences, for example to feed a drug addiction. Added to this the defendant may not have a stabilising influence in his life and even no fixed address. In some cases the risk of the commission of further offences may be due to the defendant's close proximity to the victim, for example in a domestic assault where the injured party fears reprisals if the defendant remains under the same roof.

The prosecuting advocate may address the court on these issues in this way:

'Madam, the defendant was already on bail for another similar offence when arrested in connection with these matters.'

'The defendant has a substantial criminal record for theft and burglary . . .'

'The defendant is a substance abuser who steals to fund his habit . . .'

'Sir, this defendant cannot keep out of trouble—you only have to examine his criminal record. You will also see he is the subject of an anti-social behaviour order made three months ago . . .'

'The defendant has committed offences whilst subject to a sentence of this court—in short, he cannot be trusted.'

Commission of further offences from the defence perspective

The defence solicitor should carefully consider the defendant's criminal record. Are the defendant's previous convictions recent? Have circumstances changed so that there is now a stabilising influence in the defendant's life? Does the defendant have responsibilities such as the care of a child who is likely to be taken into care if the defendant is remanded? Once again, what evidence connects the defendant to the offence with which he is charged? Does the defendant admit the charge for which he is already on bail? Looking at the defendant's past criminal record, is it possible to say whether no offences have been committed by the defendant whilst on bail?

Will imposing suitable conditions help to allay the magistrates' fears that this defendant will commit further offences? Possibilities might include imposing a curfew where a defendant has a history of committing offences at night. A condition that excludes the defendant from engaging in particular behaviour or going to a certain place may be effective, i.e. a condition not to visit licensed premises or to go within a certain radius of a particular shop. The availability of an alternative address away from the area where the crime is alleged to have occurred may alleviate the risk.

Interference with witnesses or obstructing the course of justice from the prosecution perspective

This ground might be argued where, for example, there is more than one co-accused who is still at large. It could also cover the situation where the defendant is implicated in a burglary or robbery and there is stolen property that has yet to be recovered. It also extends to those situations where a defendant may know or be related to a victim or witness and may well wish to contact that person. Perhaps the defendant is predisposed to use violence or has a previous conviction for witness intimidation or harassment.

The prosecuting advocate may address the court on these issues in the following way:

'Sir, this defendant has previous convictions for violence.'

'Sir, this defendant has a previous conviction for perverting the course of justice.'

'Sir, there is as you can imagine a lot of ill-feeling in the area where the defendant resides. If released on bail the danger that the defendant might be embroiled in further confrontation cannot be ignored . . .'

'Madam, there is a large amount of stolen property that has still to be recovered and a co-accused still at large.'

Interference with witnesses or obstructing the course of justice from the defence perspective

Once again, if the defendant is not admitting the offence, assess the strength of the evidence against her. Point out that the defendant would not wish to make matters worse for herself by doing the things suggested. What was the date on which the offence is alleged to have occurred? Stolen property that is not immediately recovered is unlikely ever to be recovered. Consider whether there is any evidence that the defendant will threaten or interfere with a witness. Look at the defendant's record in this respect. Can conditions be suggested to allay the magistrates' or District Judge's fears? Possibilities include a condition that the defendant does not contact a witness or does not go within a certain radius of a particular area. The availability of alternative accommodation away from the witness or the area may greatly assist.

One of the factors a court should consider when deciding bail is the strength of the evidence against a defendant. From the defence perspective, if the defendant has not made damaging admissions and intends to plead not guilty, it is always worth challenging the evidence linking the defendant to the offence. It would be wholly unjust for a court to remand into custody on weak evidence, so consider whether to advance a defence at this stage.

10.12 PROCEDURE AT A CONTESTED BAIL HEARING

There is no prescribed procedure at a contested bail hearing. The usual practice after a court has decided to adjourn the case is for the prosecution to make representations against bail being granted. This will be based on the information contained in the police file. The defendant is then given an opportunity to put any relevant considerations before the court. This will usually be done through the defendant's solicitor or the duty solicitor in court.

Neither the prosecution nor the defence advocate is likely to have much time to prepare for the bail hearing. The principles of CJ-SSS and SDJ (which apply to summary-only and either-way offences and which are outlined in Chapter 9, para. 9.16.1) should mean that the defence advocate or duty solicitor is in possession of sufficient disclosure of prosecution evidence at the first hearing before a magistrates' court to enable a bail application to be made. Even though CJ-SSS and SDJ do not strictly apply to indictable-only offences, the CPS will normally serve advance information at an early stage in an indictable-only case where fairness requires such disclosure for the purpose of a bail hearing (*R v DPP, ex p. Lee* [1999] 2 Cr App R 304).

A contested bail hearing takes the form of a mini-trial at which the rules of evidence are relaxed. The BA 1976 gives each side the framework for their representations. The prosecuting advocate will refer to the witness statements he has on file and the account the defendant gave at the police station in making the court aware of how the defendant came to be charged in connection with the matter(s) for which he appears. The prosecutor will outline his objections and hand in a copy of the defendant's previous convictions. The defence solicitor will then make his submissions, countering the arguments put by the prosecution. If the defendant has a job or an offer of work that is likely to be lost if remanded, the defence solicitor should try to obtain a letter from the employer to confirm this. If residence is likely to be a problem, the defence solicitor should have enquired about alternative accommodation.

Any available witnesses such as a surety or a person giving evidence of an alternative address will be put before the court. Having heard the representations from both sides, the magistrates will decide on the matter and announce their decision. You are able to view a contested bail hearing in the video clip section of our Online Resource Centre in the *R v Lenny Wise* case study.

Before you do this you might attempt the exercise we have set in conjunction with the case study at the end of this chapter, together with two other scenarios designed to test your understanding of bail.

10.12.1 THE COURT'S DECISION—GIVING REASONS

Section 5 BA 1976 provides that where a court withholds bail or grants conditional bail, the reason(s) for doing so must be announced in open court. Where bail is refused, the defendant must be given a notice setting out the reason(s) for the magistrates' decision. It is the usual practice in magistrates' courts to give reasons for granting bail in all cases where bail has been opposed.

It should be stressed that bail is a decision for the court and it should be considered at every remand hearing, whether it is applied for or not. Magistrates can grant bail, notwithstanding prosecution objections, and may also remand a defendant in custody where there is no objection from the prosecutor.

A defendant who is 21 or over will be remanded to a prison if bail is denied. Between the ages of 17 and 20, remand is normally to a remand centre or an adult prison if no places are available at a remand centre.

It is important to remember that if convicted, the sentencing court can take into account the time served on remand when sentencing an offender to a period of imprisonment.

Instead of remanding the accused in custody, s. 128 Magistrates' Courts Act 1980 (MCA 1980) enables a magistrates' court to remand the defendant to a police station for a period not exceeding three clear days. This may be done only if it is necessary for enquiries to be made into any offence other than the one(s) for which he is appearing before the court. The defendant must be brought back to the magistrates' court as soon as the need to remand him at the police station ceases. Whilst on remand at the police station, the defendant is entitled to the same range of protections afforded by PACE 1984 and the Codes of Practice as any detainee who has been arrested on suspicion of having committed an offence (see Chapter 4).

10.13 REMAND PERIODS

When a magistrates' court remands a defendant in custody at his first appearance, the remand period must not exceed eight days.

It may be several weeks or even months before a case is ready for trial or for sending to the Crown Court. Provision is made in s. 128A MCA 1980 for an accused to be remanded for up to 28 days without his consent. The power only applies once a magistrates' court has set a date for the next stage of the proceedings to take place and decides the accused should be remanded in custody until that date. The power does not apply on a first remand. An accused is therefore allowed two bail applications before this power can be exercised. If the defendant is to be further remanded after 28 days, he must be produced at the next court hearing. The increasing use of TV video-links from prisons to some magistrates' courts and Crown Courts means prisoners do not have to be physically produced (see Chapter 9, para. 19.16.1 and 'virtual' courts).

After conviction a court may remand a defendant pending sentence where a pre-sentence report or some other report is required before sentence can be properly imposed. Where a court grants a defendant bail after conviction, the maximum period is four weeks. Where a defendant is remanded in custody pending completion of reports the maximum period is three weeks.

10.13.1 CUSTODY TIME LIMITS

When an accused has been refused bail, s. 22 Prosecution of Offenders Act 1985 (POA 1985) imposes the following maximum time limits during which an accused may be remanded in custody between various stages in the proceedings before trial:

(a) 70 days between an accused's first appearance in the magistrates' court and sending to the Crown Court (see Chapter 11);

(b) 70 days between first appearance and summary trial for an offence triable either way (reduced to 56 days if the decision for summary trial is taken within 56 days);

(c) 56 days between first appearance and trial for a summary-only offence; and

(d) 112 days between sending for trial and arraignment in the Crown Court (where committal proceedings still apply).

Where an indictable offence is sent straight to the Crown Court under s. 51 Crime and Disorder Act 1998 (see Chapter 13), the maximum custody time length is 182 days with time running from the date the case is sent up by the magistrates, less any time already spent in custody.

If the prosecution fails to comply with the custody time limits, the defendant has an absolute right to bail. A court can impose some conditions on the defendant's bail, such as reporting or a condition of residence, but cannot require the defendant to provide a surety or security as a condition of release.

The prosecution can apply for an extension of the custody time limit before it expires. The criteria for granting an extension are laid down in s. 22 POA 1985. For a detailed explanation of the extension of custody time limits, see the most recent edition of *Blackstone's Criminal Practice*.

10.14 HOW MANY BAIL APPLICATIONS CAN BE MADE?

While a court is under a duty to consider the grant of bail at each hearing after it has been refused, the defendant is prevented from making repeated applications by Sch. 1 Part IIA to BA 1976 (as amended by s. 154(2) CJA 1988). This provides:

> 'At the first hearing after that at which the court decided not to grant the defendant bail he may support an application for bail with any further argument as to law or fact that he desires . . . At subsequent hearings the court need not hear arguments as to fact or law which it has heard previously . . .'

Where an accused has been refused bail at a previous hearing, the accused may make one further application only based on the same facts/arguments. Thereafter, unless there has been a 'change of circumstances' (i.e. new arguments as to the law or to facts are advanced), the court need not hear further argument at a subsequent hearing.

Consider the following examples of the operation of Part IIA:

X makes an unsuccessful application for bail on his first appearance. He makes a further unsuccessful application for bail on his second appearance. Thereafter Part IIA applies and the court need not hear a further application on his appearance unless there has been a change in circumstances.

X chooses not to make an application for bail on his first appearance. He makes an unsuccessful application for bail on his second appearance. Under Part IIA the court need not hear a further application on X's next appearance unless there has been a change in circumstances.

X makes an unsuccessful application for bail on his first appearance. He chooses not to make a further application on his second appearance. Part IIA applies and the court need not hear a further application on X's next appearance unless there has been a change in circumstances.

A change of circumstances need not be a major change either in the defendant's personal circumstances or in the proceedings connected with the case. So, for example, where an accused has been charged with an indictable offence and has been refused bail at two previous hearings, the fact that the case against the accused appears less strong when full pre-trial disclosure is made during the course of the proceedings, may amount to a change of circumstances. For judicial guidance on what may amount to a 'change in circumstances', please see *Nottingham Justices ex p Davies* [1981] 1 QB 38 and *R (B) v Brent Youth Court* [2010] EWHC 1893 (Admin).

10.15 WHERE BAIL IS REFUSED

Where magistrates have heard a full application for bail, the court must issue a full argument certificate. A copy must be given to the accused. Armed with this, an accused refused bail by the magistrates can apply to a Crown Court judge under s. 81 Senior Courts Act 1981. The procedure for applying to the Crown Court is set out in Crim PR, Part 19.18. Applications are usually dealt with within 48 hours of the initial refusal, although the defendant must give 24 hours' notice to the CPS of his intention to appeal. The 'appeal' will be conducted before a Crown Court judge in chambers and will take the form of a complete rehearing. Trainee solicitors and paralegal staff have full rights of audience before a Crown Court judge in chambers. The application to the Crown Court will be covered by an existing representation order.

10.16 APPEAL BY THE PROSECUTION

If bail is opposed by the prosecution but is granted to a person charged with or convicted of an offence carrying imprisonment or an offence of taking a vehicle without consent or aggravated vehicle-taking, s. 1 Bail (Amendment) Act 1993 gives the prosecution the right to appeal against the grant of bail to a Crown Court judge. There are strict procedural requirements governing the prosecution's right to appeal which are set out in Crim PR, Part 19.16. The prosecution must give oral notice of appeal at the conclusion of the proceedings in which bail was granted and before the defendant is released from custody. The oral notice must be confirmed in writing within two hours after the end of the proceedings. Pending the appeal, the magistrates must remand the defendant in custody. The Crown Court must hear the appeal within 48 hours and it will be a complete rehearing. Crim PR, Part 19.17 permits a defendant to be present at the hearing of the prosecution's appeal against the grant of bail.

The prosecution now has a right to appeal to the High Court against the decision of a Crown Court judge to grant bail to a person charged with or convicted of an imprisonable offence (Sch. 11 LAPSO 2012). This new route of appeal has no application to a decision of a judge of the Crown Court that was on appeal from the Magistrates' Court under the 1993 Act. The procedures are much the same as for appeals under the 1993 Act, requiring:

• prosecuting counsel to inform the Crown Court at the end of the hearing, before the defendant is released from custody, that the CPS intend to appeal, and to serve written notice of appeal on the Crown Court within two hours;

• the Crown Court to remand the defendant in custody until the appeal is determined or otherwise disposed of.

10.17 **RECONSIDERING BAIL**

Section 5B BA 1976 (inserted by the CJPOA 1994) allows a court to reconsider the grant of bail on application by the prosecution. The power only applies if the offence with which the defendant is charged is indictable only or triable either way. The application must be based on information that was not available to the court or the police at the last hearing. Therefore new information must have come to light since the last bail hearing which puts the question of bail in a new light. Under s. 5B the court can vary the bail conditions imposed last time or impose new ones or remand in custody.

10.18 **VARYING BAIL CONDITIONS**

Under s. 8(a) and (b) BA 1976 either side can apply to have bail conditions varied or, in the prosecution's case, to have conditions imposed on the grant of unconditional bail. It is not uncommon for a defendant to apply to have bail conditions varied. This requires an application to the court that imposed the conditions or to the Crown Court if a matter has already been sent there for trial or sentence.

Circumstances may have changed since the defendant was conditionally bailed that make the conditions impracticable or unworkable, i.e. securing a job outside the immediate area or the need to change address. The CPS may or may not make a submission in relation to the application. In a domestic violence prosecution where the alleged victim retracts her complaint and the defendant seeks to vary bail conditions (which may well exclude him from the family home), the CPS may call the complainant to testify on oath to her position in relation to bail.

Section 16 CJA 2003 amended BA 1976 to allow a defendant to appeal to the Crown Court against the imposition of any of the following conditions:

• residence away from a particular place;

• surety;

• curfew.

Such an appeal may not be brought if the defendant or the prosecution has already applied to a magistrates' court to have bail conditions varied and the matter has been dealt with or, in the case of the prosecution, it has applied for bail to be reconsidered in accordance with s. 5B BA 1976 and the matter has been determined.

10.19 WHERE AN ACCUSED FAILS TO SURRENDER TO BAIL

Section 6(1) BA 1976 creates the offence of absconding where the accused has been released on bail (whether by the police or by a court) and fails, without reasonable excuse, to surrender to custody at the time and date specified in the bail notice. Section 6(2) makes it an offence for a defendant who has a reasonable excuse for failing his bail, not to have then surrendered himself as soon as was thereafter reasonably practicable. Where the accused fails to surrender, the burden will be on the accused to prove that he had reasonable cause for failing to surrender.

Where the defendant is found guilty, absconding is punishable by up to three months' imprisonment and/or a maximum fine of £5,000 in the magistrates' court. Where bail was imposed by the Crown Court, the offence of absconding is treated as criminal contempt and is punishable by a maximum sentence of 12 months' imprisonment and/or an unlimited fine. A BA 1976 offence committed during the proceedings gives the court further grounds for refusing bail (see para. 10.6). Where an accused fails to surrender or having surrendered disappears before the case is heard, the court must decide what to do. Where there is no explanation for the accused's failure to appear, the court is likely to issue a warrant for the accused's immediate arrest. If the case has been listed for trial, the accused may be tried in his absence. Where some explanation is forthcoming to account for a defendant's absence, e.g. the defendant manages to contact his solicitor alerting him of a family emergency, the court is likely to grant bail in absence or issue a warrant backed with bail. The court will require proof for the absence, such as a medical certificate, to be produced on the next occasion.

10.20 BAIL GRANTED BY THE CROWN COURT

The Crown Court has an inherent jurisdiction (s. 81 Senior (previously Supreme) Courts Act 1981) to grant bail and can exercise its jurisdiction when:

- the defendant has been remanded in custody by a magistrates' court prior to the case being sent or committed to the Crown Court or summary trial and appeals to the Crown Court;
- the defendant has been sent or committed to the Crown Court for trial or has been committed for sentence;
- the defendant has been summarily convicted, imprisoned and denied bail pending an appeal to the Crown Court;
- the defendant has been convicted and sentenced before a Crown Court and now wishes to appeal to the Court of Appeal.

10.21 BAIL AND THE HIGH COURT

The High Court may grant bail in the case of a convicted and imprisoned offender appealing against conviction or sentence by way of case stated or by judicial review.

10.22 HUMAN RIGHTS AND BAIL

The Law Commission in its Report No. 269, *Bail and the Human Rights Act 1998*, concluded that the existing law governing bail was broadly compliant with the ECHR 1950. Article 5 and not Article 6 governs decisions about bail. Article 5 guarantees an individual's right to liberty and security and therefore has clear relevance to bail decisions. Article 5(1) allows the right to be abrogated in defined circumstances and in accordance with a procedure prescribed by law. The prescribed circumstances include the lawful detention of a person after conviction by a competent court (Article 5(1)(a)) and the lawful arrest or detention of a person effected for the purpose of bringing him before a court on reasonable suspicion of having committed an offence or when it is reasonably necessary to prevent that person committing an offence or fleeing after having done so (Article 5(1)(c)).

10.23 BAIL—THE PRACTICAL CONSIDERATIONS

The prosecutor is most likely to oppose bail in a case where the accused has been remanded in police custody upon being charged or is appearing before the magistrates' court in custody, either because it is alleged the accused has broken the conditions of his bail or has failed to surrender to the court's custody. The prosecutor must quickly assimilate the information on the police file and construct an argument opposing bail based on the grounds under BA 1976. Where bail is opposed but is granted by the magistrates, the prosecutor must be ready to give immediate notice of appeal if this is appropriate.

For the defence, it is important to realise that defendants tend to think of the short term. For them, gaining bail may be of considerable importance—more important than the final outcome.

The defence advocate must ensure he has sufficient disclosure of the prosecution's case (including a list of any previous convictions) to be able to deal with the prosecution's objections. The defence advocate should respond to each of the prosecutor's objections in turn and be prepared to advise his client on the further opportunities for applying for bail if it is refused. Bail conditions, such as an alternative address, should be canvassed with the client and if conditional bail is granted, the defence advocate should explain the importance of abiding by those conditions.

KEY POINT SUMMARY

- Be able to distinguish between the grounds for opposing bail and the factors used to substantiate the grounds.
- Know the circumstances where there is effectively a presumption against bail, making it more difficult for an accused to be granted bail.
- The defence advocate should anticipate the likely objections to bail and see what conditions the client can offer in an attempt to overcome the likely objections.
- Remember the rules of evidence are relaxed at a contested bail hearing.
- Be aware that the strength or weakness of the evidence against the accused is a relevant factor for the court to have regard to when reaching a decision on bail.
- Remember that an accused has more than one opportunity to apply for bail, including the option of applying to a Crown Court judge in chambers where bail is refused by a magistrates' court.
- The prosecution has the right to appeal against the grant of bail in certain circumstances.

SELF-TEST QUESTIONS

To test your knowledge and understanding of the substantive law of bail, consider the following scenarios. Formulate what you consider would be your objections to bail being granted, having regard to the grounds for opposing bail and the factors the court is likely to have regard to. What submissions would you put forward to counter these objections to try and ensure bail is granted? An analysis of the scenarios is provided on the Online Resource Centre.

online resource centre

Exercise 1: *R v Karl Green*

Karl Green is charged with wounding with intent, contrary to s. 18 of the Offences Against the Person Act 1861 (OAPA 1861). He appears before the magistrates' court. The prosecution seeks the usual eight-day adjournment to enable the case to be sent to the Crown Court. It is alleged that Karl assaulted David

Murphy outside a public house on the housing estate where both the men live. The offence occured two days ago. The injured party is presently in a coma. One witness, who is a friend of the injured party, has provided the police with a statement in which he identifies Karl Green as the person who punched his friend. In his statement he refers to the two men exchanging words. In one swift movement, he alleges, Green punched his friend with such force as to cause him to fall unconscious to the ground. An independent witness has provided a statement giving a similar account of the incident and a description of the man responsible being consistent with Green's appearance. The witness also states he observed the man who threw the punch flee the scene.

Karl Green is presently on conditional bail for a serious s. 18 OAPA 1861 assault on a police constable, alleged to have occurred six weeks earlier. He was seriously drunk at the time and one of the conditions of his bail, which includes him reporting to his local police station, prohibits him from visiting licensed premises. He appeared before the magistrates' court last week admitting a breach of his bail condition not to visit licensed premises. The magistrates were prepared to renew his bail, having regard to the explanation offered by Green which had been to fetch his sister who works at a public house as her baby was sick. According to his list of antecedents, Karl Green lives apart from his wife and is out of work. He has six previous convictions. The most recent relates to an assault occasioning actual bodily harm (s. 47 OAPA 1861) last year, for which Green received a six-month prison sentence suspended for 18 months. He has further convictions for assault dating some three and four years ago, two previous convictions for theft and a conviction for a public order offence. He was convicted of absconding three years ago.

In interview with his solicitor, Karl Green admits to throwing the punch. He maintains, however, that he acted in self-defence. Green claims the injured party was the aggressor and that, in self-defence, he threw one punch. When the injured party did not get up, Green panicked. His brother was with him when the incident occurred and will testify on his behalf. Green lives with his mother. He and his ex-wife are attempting a reconciliation. She had been dating the injured party but had terminated the relationship in recent weeks, believing she could salvage her marriage. She and Green have a son, Stephen, who is four years old. Karl says he is currently in work—he works for his cousin's skip-hire company. If remanded in custody he is likely to lose his job. His previous failure to surrender was due to sickness; however, no medical evidence was ever obtained. Green voluntarily surrendered himself and was fined for the offence of failing to answer his bail. So far as the assault on the policeman is concerned, he will be pleading guilty to a less serious charge of assault. He was seriously intoxicated at the time and does not recall much of what happened. He has expressed his deep remorse. Green tells his solicitor that he has a sister who may be prepared to offer him accommodation ten miles outside the area of the estate where he and his victim live.

Exercise 2: *R v Daniel Phillips*

Daniel Phillips has been charged with arson contrary to s. 1(1) of the Criminal Damage Act 1971 and with resisting a constable in the execution of his duty. The allegation is that he deliberately set fire to his former partner's house, causing extensive damage. He has been remanded into police custody pending his initial appearance before a magistrates' court. The case should be adjourned.

Daniel is 26. His former partner, Rachel Hughes, is 22. She has made a statement to the police. The couple have a child aged three who Rachel cares for. The relationship ended two years ago but Daniel has been reluctant to accept it. Rachel refused Daniel access to their son but this was resolved 18 months ago by court order. In recent weeks Rachel has formed a new relationship.

The police were called to Rachel Hughes's home at 6 am three days ago (a Saturday). Her property was on fire. Initial forensic tests have revealed the fire was started deliberately by someone pouring an accelerant through the front door letterbox and igniting it with a match. The finger of suspicion points to Daniel.

Daniel collected his son from Rachel for an access visit on the Saturday afternoon. She asked him to deliver their son back to her mother—the child was going to spend the night with his grandmother. She told Daniel Phillips that she would be staying with a friend of hers overnight. Her friend received a telephone call at 5.30 am. A male voice, which she thinks she recognised as Daniel, requested her to inform Rachel that her house was on fire.

Daniel was arrested three days later as the police were unable to locate him immediately—he was no longer living at his mother's address. There is no forensic evidence to link him to the crime scene as yet, but tests are continuing. Daniel made no comment in interview on the advice of his solicitor.

Rachel maintains she is absolutely terrified of Daniel, who has four previous convictions. He was convicted of criminal damage two years ago. Following an argument with Rachel he damaged her car. He was conditionally discharged for this offence for a period of one year. Six months later he was convicted of assault occasioning actual bodily harm and breach of a conditional discharge. The incident followed the breakdown of his relationship with Rachel. She started to date another man. When Daniel found out, he assaulted the man. He denied involvement but was found guilty by magistrates. He was given a community supervision order for two years. Last year Daniel was convicted of an offence under s. 2 of the Harassment Act 1997. He pleaded guilty before a Crown Court judge and was sentenced to six months' imprisonment, suspended for 18 months to run alongside his existing community supervision order. Daniel was also subject to a restraining order of five years forbidding him to contact or communicate with Rachel except when and for the sole purpose of collecting his son for an access visit. The harassment had taken the form of obscene text messages. Rachel was also bombarded with dozens of pictures taken of her, some of which were cut up. She started to receive menacing telephone calls in the early hours of the morning, which were eventually traced to a mobile telephone registered to Daniel.

In interview with his solicitor, Daniel steadfastly denies setting fire to the property. He maintains he has no axe to grind so far as Rachel is concerned. In fact he has formed a new relationship in recent months. His new girlfriend, Anita, aged 19, is pregnant with his baby. He was with her at the time of this alleged incident, at her mother's house. She and her mother will verify this. He left his mother's home several weeks ago, as he could not cope with her alcoholic mood swings. Daniel maintains the access visit with his son went off without problem and that he would not do anything to jeopardise his relationship with his son. Furthermore he is complying with the requirements of the community supervision order which is helping him to address the reason for his earlier offending. He is residing on a permanent basis with his new girlfriend and has a job as a mechanic. He denies resisting the police constable in the course of his arrest, maintaining the officer was much too heavy-handed.

Case study: *R v Lenny Wise*

Consider the advance information in relation to this case study, together with Lenny Wise's list of previous convictions (located in Appendix 1, Document 2). Assume you are the CPS lawyer and that this is Lenny's second appearance before a magistrates' court. He has been remanded in custody since being charged. Upon what grounds will you oppose bail and what factors will you have regard to in substantiating your objections? The prosecution's submission in this case can be viewed on the video section of our Online Resource Centre. A transcript of the prosecuting solicitor's submission can be located on our Online Resource Centre in the case study section. For general consideration of the skills of advocacy, see Chapter 2.

Now look at this file from the perspective of the defence. Having regard to the advance information and to Lenny's statement (Document 6 , located within Appendix 1), construct a defence submission in this case countering the prosecution's objections. How are you going to convince the court to grant bail in this case? The defence submission in this case can be viewed on the video section of our Online Resource Centre. A transcript of the defence solicitor's submission can be located on our Online Resource Centre in the case study section.

An account of the magistrates' decision in relation to bail is contained in Document 15. You will see that Lenny appeals the refusal of bail to a judge in chambers in the Crown Court and is subsequently granted conditional bail (Document 20). Documents 17–19 can be found in the case study section of our Online Resource Centre, which contains a complete set of the documentation forming the *R v Lenny Wise* case study.

Case studies: *R v Roger Martin* and *R v William Hardy*

With regards to *R v William Hardy* and *R v Martin*, although there have been adjournments in each of these cases, there is no contentious issue as regards bail and each defendant is remanded on conditional bail during the proceedings.

FIGURE 10.1 COURT BAIL

EXCEPTIONS TO THE RIGHT TO BAIL

The Bail Act 1976 (s. 4) generally presumes the defendant should be granted bail. However:

- bail should only be granted exceptionally where a defendant is charged with murder, manslaughter, rape (or attempts) and he has previous convictions for one of these offences (s. 25 CJPOA 1994);

- bail may not be granted to a defendant charged with murder unless there is no significant risk that, if released, the defendant would commit an offence that would be likely to cause physical or mental injury;

- the defendant need not be granted bail if he is over 18 and is already on bail unless there is no signifcant risk of him committing an offence on bail (currently applies only to offences carrying life imprisonment (s.14 CJA 2003));

- the defendant need not be granted bail if he is over 18 and has previously been granted bail in the proceedings and has failed to surrender unless the court is satisfied there is no signifcant risk of the defendant failing to surrender if released on bail (currently applies only to offences carrying life imprisonment (s. 15 CJA 2003));

- the defendant need not be granted bail if he has tested positive to a Class A drug and is charged with an offence involving a specifed Class A drug under Misuse of Drugs Act 1971, or the court is satisfied that his offending is due to his drug dependency and the defendant refuses to undergo an assessment or follow-up treatment for his dependency (s. 19 CJA 2003).

REBUTTING THE PRESUMPTION TO BAIL

- the presumption to bail may be rebutted where the defendant is charged with an indictable imprisonable offence and where there is a real prospect of imprisonment; and

- the court is satisfied (Sch. 1 Part 1 Bail Act 1976) there are **substantial grounds** for believing the defendant will:

  - fail to surrender to custody; or
  - commit an offence while on bail; or
  - interfere with witnesses or obstruct the course of justice; or

- the defendant is already on bail for another offence and has been charged with an indictable offence; or

- the court is satisfied that the defendant should be kept in custody for his protection (or welfare where a juvenile); or

- the defendant is already serving a custodial sentnce; or

- the defendant, having been released on bail, fails to surrender to bail or breaks a condition of that bail; or

- the court is satisfed it has not been practicable to obtain suffcient information to take a decision under the Bail Act 1976; or

- where the case has been adjourned for preparation of a report, it appears impracticable to complete the enquiries or report unless the defendant is in custody.

PARAGRAPH 9 FACTORS

- In deciding whether the ground(s) for refusing bail are made out, the court takes into account para. 9 Bail Act 1976 factors:

  - the nature and seriousness of the offence;
  - defendant's character, antecedents, community ties;
  - bail record;
  - strength of the evidence;
  - the risk that the defendant would engage in conduct that would be likely to cause physical or mental injury to another person; and
  - any other relevant matter.

BAIL CONDITIONS

- bail can be unconditional or conditional;
- conditions ensure that the defendant:
  - will surrender to custody; or
  - will not commit further offences; or
  - will not interfere with witnesses or obstruct the course of justice; or
  - is available to assist with preparation of a pre-sentence report.

- conditions include:
  - reporting to a police station;
  - living at a specifed address (possibly bail hostel);
  - curfew;
  - surety;
  - the defendant should not contact a specifc individual;
  - exclusion from specified locality or place.

APPEALING BAIL DECISIONS

- defence can 'appeal' against refusal of bail or bail conditions to Crown Court judge in chambers;

- prosecution can appeal to Crown Court against allowing bail where offence is punishable with imprisonment.

11 PROSECUTING AN EITHER-WAY OFFENCE

11.1 INTRODUCTION

The wide range of either-way offences includes assault occasioning actual bodily harm, theft and burglary. Sections 17–21 Magistrates' Courts Act 1980 (MCA 1980) provide that where a defendant aged 18 or over is charged with an either-way offence, mode of trial proceedings must be held to determine whether the defendant should be tried summarily or on indictment before any evidence is called.

Either-way offences can be committed with varying degrees of seriousness depending on the aggravating or mitigating features in the particular case. The more aggravating features, the more serious the offence will be regarded. Magistrates' court powers of sentence are limited compared to the Crown Court. If a magistrates' court considers its maximum sentencing powers (six months for a single either-way offence, increasing to 12 months where consecutive custodial sentences are imposed for two or more either-way offences) to be insufficient, the case will be sent to the Crown Court. Theft offences provide a good illustration. Theft can range from simple shoplifting to the appropriation of property worth millions of pounds.

Clearly, the offender charged with shoplifting would be most appropriately dealt with summarily while the more serious, high-value theft should be dealt with in the Crown Court.

In this chapter we examine:

- the procedure for deciding where an either-way offence should be tried;
- the relative merits of summary trial and trial on indictment; and
- for those either-way offences that are to be tried in the Crown Court, the next stage of the proceedings.

11.2 NEW DEVELOPMENTS WARNING

Either-way offences which are to be tried in the Crown Court have until recently been sent there through 'committal proceedings' held in the magistrates' court following an adjournment of what used to be known as the mode of trial enquiry. In December 2011, it was announced that Sch. 3 Criminal Justice Act 2003 (CJA 2003) would be brought into force. Schedule 3 abolished committal proceedings substituting in its place the 'sending' procedure under s. 51 CDA 1998 which applies to indictable-only offences. Schedule 3 has also made significant reforms to the mode of trial enquiry, which is now known as the allocation hearing. The change to 'allocation' and the abolition of committal hearings have been introduced on a phased basis and are expected to be completed nationwide by the end of May 2013. This chapter therefore has been written from a post-Sch. 3 CJA 2003, perspective. We have removed reference to the mode of trial enquiry, although we suspect that the term will be heard in magistrates' courts for some considerable time to come.

11.3 PLEA BEFORE VENUE

online resource centre

All defendants charged with an either-way offence are subject to the plea before venue procedure which precedes any allocation hearing (s. 17A MCA 1980/s. 50A(3) CDA 1998). The procedure provides the defendant with an opportunity to indicate how he intends to plead. The plea before venue is illustrated in the video section of our Online Resource Centre in the *R v Lenny Wise* case study, which was filmed under the old pre-Sch. 3 CJA 2003 (mode of trial) procedure.

You are reminded that a defendant charged with an either-way offence is entitled to receive pre-trial disclosure of the prosecution's evidence in accordance with Crim PR, Part 21 (Advance Information). Unless the matter is clear-cut, the defence lawyer should obtain this advance information before advising on plea. Under CJ-SSS/SDJ (see Chapter 9, para. 9.16), the Crown Prosecution Service (CPS) is required to serve advance information on the defendant prior to his first appearance before a magistrates' court to enable a plea to be indicated. In accordance with SDJ, the magistrates' court will expect to conduct the allocation hearing at the first hearing. Where the defendant is making his first appearance in custody, some magistrates' courts will relax this requirement and grant a short adjournment if a plea cannot be taken.

11.3.1 PROCEDURE AT PLEA BEFORE VENUE

The court's legal adviser will check with the parties whether a plea can be indicated. If it can, the legal adviser will explain to the accused in ordinary language that he will be asked to indicate to the court whether he intends to plead guilty or not guilty. The legal adviser will also explain that if the defendant indicates a guilty plea, the magistrates' court will proceed to sentence and deal with him as if he had been found guilty and there will be no trial and no evidence will be called. The defendant will also be warned that notwithstanding an indication of a guilty plea, the magistrates' court may still commit him for sentence to the Crown Court under s. 3 Powers of Criminal Court (Sentencing) Act 2000 (PCC(S)A 2000) if the court considers its sentencing powers are insufficient or if the 'dangerousness' provisions explained in Chapter 22 apply (s. 3 PCC(S)A 2000). The legal adviser will then read the charge to the accused, who is asked to indicate his plea. A defendant has four possible responses. The defendant can:

- indicate a guilty plea;
- indicate a not guilty plea;
- give no indication of plea; or
- enter an equivocal plea.

11.3.2 WHERE THE DEFENDANT INDICATES A GUILTY PLEA

If the defendant indicates that he would plead guilty, he is taken to have pleaded guilty. Consequently, the magistrates' court will proceed to sentence him immediately or following an adjournment for the preparation of a pre-sentence report. The procedure upon sentence for a guilty plea and the possibility of committal for sentence to the Crown Court following the indication of a guilty plea to an either-way offence is explained in greater detail in Chapter 21.

11.3.3 WHERE THE DEFENDANT INDICATES A NOT GUILTY PLEA, GIVES NO INDICATION OF PLEA OR MAKES AN EQUIVOCAL PLEA

If at the plea before venue, the defendant indicates that he will plead not guilty or makes no indication as to plea or makes an equivocal plea, the court will proceed to the allocation hearing. An equivocal plea is where the defendant's response to the charge is ambiguous. Where the court is uncertain about the defendant's plea, a not guilty plea will be entered on his behalf.

11.4 THE ALLOCATION HEARING—SS. 17–20 MCA 1980 (AS AMENDED)

In some cases the CPS lawyer and the defence may agree the appropriate trial venue. The only time there is likely to be disagreement between the parties is where the prosecution invites the court to decline to try the matter summarily because in its view the magistrates' sentencing powers would be insufficient but the defendant seeks to persuade the court to retain jurisdiction. In outlining the alleged facts of the case, the prosecution should either represent that the case is suitable for summary trial or it will make representations as to why the case would be more appropriately dealt with in the Crown Court. The magistrates' court will listen to any representations from the defence advocate before coming to a decision about where the case should be dealt with.

It is important to remember that in the first instance the decision where the case will be tried lies with the magistrates hearing the case. In reaching their decision, the magistrates will take into account all of the following:

- the submissions made by the parties;
- the statutory position under s. 19 MCA 1980 (as amended);
- the allocation guideline issued by the Sentencing Council for England and Wales (SC);
- specific sentencing guidelines issued by the SC including the Magistrates' Court Sentencing Guidelines (MCSGs) explained in Chapter 21.

11.4.1 REVISED S. 19A MCA 1980 PROCEDURE

Section 19 MCA 1980 (as amended) sets out the procedure in relation to allocation. It provides as follows:

(1) The court shall decide whether the offence appears to it more suitable for summary trial or for trial on indictment.

(2) Before making a decision under this section, the court—

    (a) shall give the prosecution an opportunity to inform the court of the accused's previous convictions (if any); and

      (b) shall give the prosecution and the accused an opportunity to make representations as to whether summary trial or trial on indictment would be more suitable.

(3) In making a decision under this section, the court shall consider—

      (a) whether the sentence which a magistrates' court would have power to impose for the offence would be adequate; and

      (b) any representations made by the prosecution or the accused under subsection (2)(b) above, and shall have regard to any allocation guidelines (or revised allocation guidelines) issued as definitive guidelines under section 170 of the Criminal Justice Act 2003.

The position as regards the allocation hearing is as follows:

- The magistrates' court will invite the prosecution to disclose any previous convictions the defendant may have (this is a significant change from the previous practice under the mode of trial enquiry).

- The prosecution will present a full outline of what the defendant is alleged to have done and will make representations as to whether summary trial or trial on indictment is more suitable.

- The defence may agree with the prosecution's representation, make contrary representations or no representations at all.

- In making a decision, the magistrates' court will have regard to the allocation guideline formulated by the SC and to any representations made by the prosecution or the accused.

- The decision to accept summary jurisdiction will be based, for the most part, on the adequacy of the court's sentencing powers, taking into account the seriousness of the offence(s) charged.

- Having accepted jurisdiction to try a case summarily, the magistrates' court will still be able to commit for sentence on conviction if their powers are insufficient or if the offence is a specified offence and the 'dangerousness' provisions apply (see Chapter 22).

- Where the magistrates' court accepts summary jurisdiction, the defendant may seek an indication as to whether a non-custodial or custodial sentence would be imposed in the event of a guilty plea before making a choice. This is another significant change from the previous position under the mode of trial enquiry. Any indication of sentence given may influence a defendant as to the appropriate venue for trial and possible plea. However, a court is not bound to give an indication.

- Where an indication of sentence is given, the defendant will be asked whether he wishes to reconsider any indication given or declined to be given at the earlier plea before venue.

- If the defendant then indicates a guilty plea, the court may not impose a custodial sentence unless such a sentence was indicated or the offence is a specified offence and the defendant is committed for sentence as a dangerous offender under s. 3A PCC(S)A 2000 (see Chapter 22).

- Where the magistrates' court declines jurisdiction to try a case or the defendant chooses trial by jury, the case will be sent forthwith to the Crown Court.

Of central importance to the allocation hearing are the magistrates' sentencing powers on conviction. The crucial importance of this will be more fully appreciated and understood after you have covered sentencing law and practice in Part V.

    The maximum sentence a magistrates' court can impose on conviction for an either-way offence is six months' imprisonment. This increases to a maximum of 12 months where the defendant is convicted of two or more either-way offences. The maximum fine that a magistrates' court can impose is currently £5,000 per offence, unless the statutory maximum for the offence prescribes a lesser amount. When making representations about the appropriate venue for trial for an either-way offence, the CPS advocate should provide the magistrates' court with accurate information on any sentencing guidelines for the offence under consideration.

In applying the s. 19A MCA 1980 statutory factors to the specific facts of the case before it, the magistrates' court will consider whether any aggravating features in the commission of the offence, identified by the prosecuting advocate, may justify the case being tried in the Crown Court which has higher sentencing powers. Common aggravating features in the commission of an offence include where a defendant has acted in a premeditated way; where the victim of the crime was vulnerable; or where the property damaged or stolen was of high economic or sentimental value.

The MCSGs (see Appendix 2 for sample extracts) identify sentencing starting points and a sentence range (moving up and down from the starting point) for offences triable in the magistrates' court based on varying levels of seriousness in the ways in which an offence might be committed. When passing sentence, a court must follow any relevant sentencing guideline unless it would be contrary to the interests of justice. The starting point identified in the MCSGs for a particular offence might be committal for sentence to the Crown Court or committal might be within the range of sentences available. The guidelines also identify aggravating features in the commission of an offence which might lead the court to sentence at a higher starting point or beyond the range of disposals available. Whilst the MCSGs are primarily applied when passing sentence, they are also highly relevant to the allocation hearing. They will be used by the prosecution and the defence in making their representations as to venue for trial and they will be used by the magistrates' court in reaching a decision about allocation for trial based on its maximum sentencing powers.

11.4.2 ALLOCATION GUIDELINE

In addition to the statutory factors in s. 19 MCA 1980 (as amended) already outlined, the magistrates' court will also be required to have regard to the allocation guideline issued by the SC which came into force on 11 June 2011 in determining the most appropriate venue for trial.

A copy of the guideline is available from the SC's website: http://sentencingcouncil.judiciary.gov.uk/.

The guideline cautions that:

'It is important to ensure that all cases are tried at the appropriate level. In general, either way offences should be tried summarily unless it is likely that the court's sentencing powers will be insufficient. Its powers will generally be insufficient if the outcome is likely to result in a sentence in excess of six months' imprisonment for a single offence.

The court should assess the likely sentence in the light of the facts alleged by the prosecution case, taking into account all aspects of the case including those advanced by the defence.

The court should refer to definitive guidelines to assess the likely sentence for the offence.'

The guideline reminds those who decide allocation that if the court determines that the case can be tried summarily, under s. 3 PCC(S)A 2000 it still has the power, on conviction, to commit the defendant for sentence to the Crown Court if it is of the opinion that the offence or combination of offences, is so serious that greater punishment should be inflicted than the court has power to impose.

It should be clear that the allocation decision is closely related to the likely sentencing outcome in the event of conviction. Consequently, both the prosecution and defence should attend the allocation hearing with a clear understanding of the sentencing guidelines for the either-way offence the accused is charged with. If the prosecution seeks to persuade the court that the case is not suitable for summary trial, this contention must be substantiated by reference to the sentencing guidelines in the MCSGs for the offence charged (see Chapter 21 for an explanation of sentencing guidelines). In the exceptional case where an either-way offence is not covered by the MCSGs, the prosecution should refer to any relevant Court of Appeal sentencing guidelines. The magistrates' legal adviser will additionally advise lay magistrates on likely sentencing outcomes if advice is sought. Relevant sentencing guidelines can be researched in a practitioner text such as *Blackstone's Criminal Practice*.

If the defence oppose the prosecution's assertion and seek to persuade the court to try the case in the magistrates' court, the defence will also need to make representations. If the defendant has already decided to elect trial by jury, the defence may choose to make no representations.

Whilst the presumption is in favour of summary trial, if the alleged offence is serious and has aggravating features, the magistrates' court may conclude that its maximum sentencing powers would be insufficient. This is the most common reason for a magistrates' court to decline jurisdiction to try an either-way offence.

11.4.3 POSSIBLE OUTCOMES OF THE ALLOCATION HEARING

(a) The magistrates' court declines jurisdiction

Where the magistrates' court decides that trial on indictment is more appropriate, the defendant has no right of election and the magistrates' court decision is communicated to him. The allocation hearing is adjourned and the defendant is sent forthwith to stand trial before the Crown Court (s. 51 CDA 1998). A date is set for the defendant's first appearance before the Crown Court. Pending the adjournment, the CPS will prepare and serve the case sent bundle on the defence (comprising used and unused prosecution evidence—see Chapters 8 and 13).

(b) The magistrates' court accepts jurisdiction

Where the magistrates' court decides that the case should be tried summarily, the legal adviser will explain to the defendant that he now has a choice. He can consent to be tried summarily (i.e. before the magistrates' court) or he can elect trial by jury in the Crown Court (i.e. trial on indictment). It will be explained to the defendant that if he chooses to be tried summarily and is convicted, he could still be committed to the Crown Court for sentence if the magistrates' court concludes, in the light of everything it has heard, that its sentencing powers are insufficient. It is at this point that the defendant can seek an indication of sentence if he were to be tried and convicted summarily.

If the defendant consents to summary trial, the magistrates' court will adjourn the allocation hearing and set a date for summary trial. If the defendant elects trial on indictment, the allocation hearing will be adjourned and the case will be sent forthwith to the Crown Court and a date set for the defendant's first appearance before the Crown Court. Pending the adjournment, the CPS will prepare and serve the case sent bundle on the defence as previously explained under (a). To assist further understanding of this important area and the roles undertaken by the prosecutor, defence lawyer and the court, consider this example.

 Example

Patryk, aged 35, is charged with assault occasioning actual bodily harm (s. 47 Offences against the Person Act 1861) and criminal damage (s. 1(1) Criminal Damage Act 1971), and is due to make his initial appearance before the magistrates' court. His defence advocate has been served with advance information of the prosecution's evidence at court. From the evidence disclosed, it is alleged that Patryk assaulted a 45-year-old male with a baseball bat. The victim lives close to Patryk and there is bad feeling between them. The victim alleges that Patryk approached him in the street and started an argument.

When the victim threatened to call the police, it is alleged that Patryk went back into his house and emerged with a baseball bat. He proceeded to smash the windscreen of the victim's car, causing damage of £400. When the victim tried to prevent Patryk from causing any further damage, it is alleged that Patryk swung the bat at the victim's head causing a wound near to the victim's left eye, which required four stitches, and the loss of three teeth as well as severe bruising to the cheekbone and jaw. The wound will not leave any permanent scarring but dental treatment will be ongoing for some time.

Patryk, who exercised his right to remain silent at the police station, denies both offences. In relation to the assault, Patryk tells his solicitor that his neighbour started an argument and in the course of it he picked up a house brick and threatened Patryk with it. Patryk accepts he returned to his house to arm himself with a baseball bat because he feared further confrontation. When he re-emerged from his house, Patryk alleges that the victim started to verbally abuse him and in a fit of temper Patryk raised his baseball bat and aimed it at the victim's car resulting in the windscreen being smashed. Patryk maintains that he was then charged at by the victim and in self-defence he struck the victim with the bat not intending to cause serious injury. Patryk would prefer the matter to be dealt with summarily. Patryk has several previous convictions for drug-related offences and assault.

The prosecuting advocate will know that assault occasioning actual bodily harm is an either-way offence and that criminal damage below £5,000 is a summary-only offence. Consequently, the maximum custodial sentence that the magistrates' court could pass in this case is six months' imprisonment. The CPS advocate will consider the sentencing guidelines for the offence of assault occasioning actual bodily harm. The guideline for assault contained in the MCSGs is reproduced in Appendix 2. *[Note the appearance of this offence-specific guideline is different from the others that appear in the MCSGs because it has recently been revised by the Sentencing Council for England and Wales, which adopts a different format from its predecessor, the Sentencing Guidelines Council.]* The prosecutor will say that based on what is alleged (premeditation, use of a weapon and serious injury), the magistrates' court sentencing guidelines suggest the assault should be sent to the Crown Court as it should be classed as a Category 1 s. 47 ABH. The prosecutor will disclose Patryk's previous convictions.

The defence advocate will use the sentencing guidelines to argue that the injury is not that serious and is non-permanent and therefore the magistrates' court would have sufficient sentencing powers on conviction as it could be classed as a Category 2 assault with a sentence starting point of 26 weeks in custody.

The magistrates conducting this allocation hearing will consider the representations made by the prosecution and the defence. On balance, they are likely to decline jurisdiction on the basis that their sentencing powers, in accordance with their sentencing guidelines, will be insufficient. In this event, Patryk will have no choice about where the case is heard.

11.5 THE REASONS FOR ELECTING TRIAL IN THE MAGISTRATES' COURT OR IN THE CROWN COURT

Where the magistrates believe the case is suitable for summary trial, the defendant has the right to elect trial by jury before the Crown Court or to consent to being tried summarily in the magistrates' court.

At a very early stage in the proceedings after receiving advance information from the CPS, the defendant's solicitor should assess the nature of the prosecution evidence against her client and be prepared to advise her client about the relative advantages of summary trial or trial on indictment if a plea of not guilty is to be entered. Part of this advice will be based on a number of practical factors including how the defendant's case is funded and the defendant's personal circumstances. Clearly, if a defendant is privately funded or would be subject to a contribution order in the Crown Court, summary trial will be much cheaper than trial on indictment. If the defendant is vulnerable or has an anxious disposition, he may not be capable of dealing with the considerable pressures of a Crown Court trial.

In addition to any practical considerations, the defence lawyer should also consider the relative advantages and disadvantages of both types of proceedings having regard to the particular facts of her client's case. While it is part of the defence solicitor's professional duty to advise her client where his case should be tried, the decision ultimately lies with the client.

11.5.1 **RELATIVE MERITS OF TRIAL ON INDICTMENT**

Higher acquittal rate

In spite of inconclusive evidence, most defence lawyers believe that trial by jury provides a better chance of their client being acquitted. There is a commonly held perception that magistrates can be 'case-hardened' because they sit on a regular basis and often hear the same defence arguments. This is especially relevant in cases involving disputed police evidence, as magistrates may be more prepared to accept the evidence of the police in preference to that of the defendant. There is a widely held perception that jurors come to a case with a more open mind. For a defendant charged with theft who pleads not guilty because he lacked dishonest intent, 12 jurors hearing this defence for the first time may be more likely to give him the benefit of the doubt.

Disputed evidence

Where the case involves disputed evidence, the judge, as a legally qualified professional, is clearly much better placed to deal with points of law. A Crown Court judge will be more confident about excluding a disputed piece of evidence than a Bench of lay magistrates. Also the separation of functions between judge and jury makes defence challenges about the admissibility of prosecution evidence during the trial much more effective as the jury is excluded from hearing arguments about the disputed point of law. Where the case involves disputing the admissibility of the prosecution's evidence (for example challenging the admissibility of a confession or evidence of identification), trial on indictment should be advised. Apart from the problems that some lay magistrates may experience in fully appreciating the advocate's legal submissions about the admissibility of prosecution evidence, if the defence submission is upheld, lay magistrates are required to put the excluded evidence to the back of their minds and continue trying the case. The increasing use of pre-trial hearings in the magistrates' court at which binding rulings on disputed evidence can be made means this problem arises less frequently than it used to. Of course some of these observations do not apply to summary trials conducted before a District Judge sitting in the magistrates' court.

Delay

It can take months before a case finally comes to trial in the Crown Court. Delay can be both an advantage and a disadvantage. The defence advocate might use the inevitable delay of trial in the Crown Court to prepare her client's case and to test the prosecution case.

Cost

Cost will be a significant factor for some defendants when deciding which trial venue to choose. Representation orders for summary proceedings are means tested. As explained in Chapter 9, the magistrates' court means test is an 'in or out' scheme. If the defendant qualifies for a representation order, he knows he will not have to contribute to any of his defence legal costs. If he does not qualify for a representation order, however, he will either have to represent himself or pay for legal representation out of his own funds. If acquitted, the defendant will be able to recover his privately paid costs out of central funds.

Means testing also now applies to proceedings before the Crown Court. A Crown Court trial is considerably more expensive than a magistrates' court trial. Unless the defendant is 'passported' through the Crown Court means test or falls within the threshold for income and capital entitlement, he will be subject to a contribution order in the Crown Court (see Chapter 9, para. 9.10).

A further aspect of costs will arise if the defendant is convicted. In the event of conviction, prosecution costs (which most convicted defendants will be ordered to pay unless sentenced to custody) will be higher in the Crown Court than in the magistrates' court.

Powers of sentence

The Crown Court's powers of punishment greatly exceed those available to the magistrates' court. The Crown Court can impose a sentence up to the statutory maximum for the particular offence. Fines are also likely to be considerably higher in the Crown Court. This may be an important factor for a defendant.

11.5.2 RELATIVE MERITS OF SUMMARY TRIAL

Powers of sentence

If convicted in summary proceedings, the defendant is likely to receive a more lenient sentence, as the magistrates' court sentencing powers are limited compared to the Crown Court. As a matter of good practice, however, the defence advocate should remind her client about the magistrates' court power to commit to the Crown Court for sentence under s. 3 PCC(S)A 2000.

Delay

The delay in Crown Court proceedings may be a highly relevant consideration for some defendants, especially if the defendant is anxious or has been remanded in custody after being refused bail. The time between the date of the alleged offence and the date set for trial is often considerably shorter in summary cases enabling the case to be completed much sooner.

Publicity

Trial in the Crown Court will usually involve the defendant being exposed to greater publicity. Representatives of the local press and sometimes the national media will often take a greater interest in Crown Court proceedings. This is an important factor where the defendant is a public figure or the case is of particular public interest, for example, where a teacher is charged with a sexual offence.

Stress

The relative informality of summary proceedings makes the magistrates' court more appropriate for a nervous client. By contrast, the atmosphere of the Crown Court is considerably more formal and intimidating.

Cost

As outlined above, a trial in the magistrates' court can be conducted much more cheaply than a trial conducted before the Crown Court. For a defendant who does not pass the means test in the magistrates' court but who will be subject to a contribution order in the Crown Court, this will be an important consideration.

Defence pre-trial disclosure of evidence

Under the Criminal Procedure and Investigations Act 1996 (CPIA 1996), there is no obligation on the accused to serve a defence statement in summary proceedings (see Chapter 12, para. 12.7.5). In trials on indictment, after the prosecution has served 'initial' disclosure of 'unused' evidence, the accused is required to serve a defence statement (see Chapter 13, para. 13.6.3). In summary proceedings, the service of a defence statement is voluntary.

Presenting advocate

If the defendant's trial is in the magistrates' court, the defendant is likely to have met his advocate before the trial. It is more likely that the advocate will be fully conversant with the facts, whereas at the Crown Court, instructions delivered to counsel are sometimes delivered at a very late stage and often there is no guarantee that the barrister instructed by the solicitor will be the person who represents her client at trial.

Appeal

An appeal from a Crown Court decision must be made to the Court of Appeal and requires leave. An appeal against summary conviction is made to a Crown Court. Leave is not required and the appeal is a complete re-hearing of the case including, where appropriate, the admission of fresh evidence. The only disadvantage of an appeal to the Crown Court is that the sentence imposed by the magistrates' court can be increased if the appeal is unsuccessful but the appeal process is much more straightforward.

11.6 THE SPECIAL PROCEDURE IN CRIMINAL DAMAGE CASES

Where a defendant is charged with criminal damage contrary to s. 1 Criminal Damage Act 1971 unless the offence involves damage by fire, there are special rules regarding allocation. If the value of the damaged property is £5,000 or less, the case should be tried summarily. The defendant has no right of election to the Crown Court. The maximum sentence that a magistrates' court can impose for such an offence is three months' imprisonment and/or a £2,500 fine. If the damage to the property is over £5,000, the court is required to hold an allocation hearing in the normal way.

11.7 SPECIAL RULES RELATING TO CERTAIN EITHER-WAY OFFENCES

In the context of a third burglary offence, any previous convictions for burglary are important. If a defendant is charged with a third offence of domestic burglary the court will apply s. 111 PCC(S)A 2000, which requires a person convicted of a third domestic burglary offence (where all three of the offences were committed after 30 November 1999) to be given a custodial sentence of three years unless there are circumstances that do not justify imposing such a sentence. As this sentence is clearly in excess of the magistrates' court sentencing powers, it has no choice but to treat the offence as triable only on indictment, with the result that it must be sent to the Crown Court (s. 51 Crime and Disorder Act 1998, see Chapter 13).

11.8 SENDING AN EITHER-WAY OFFENCE TO THE CROWN COURT

Where the magistrates' court has decided at the allocation hearing that the case is more suitable for trial in the Crown Court or where the accused has elected trial on indictment after the magistrates' court has accepted jurisdiction to hold a summary trial, the case is sent forthwith to the Crown Court under s. 51 CDA 1998. The defendant's next appearance in connection with the either-way offence will be before the Crown Court at a Plea and Case Management Hearing (PCMH). The conduct of the PCMH is covered in Chapter 13. The s. 51 CDA 1998 'sending' procedure is the same procedure that is used to send an indictable-only offence and any related offence to the Crown Court following the accused's first appearance in connection with the matter before the magistrates' court. The s. 51 CDA 1998 procedure is outlined more fully in Chapter 13.

11.8.1 LINKED EITHER-WAY OR SUMMARY-ONLY OFFENCES

If the defendant is sent for trial in connection with an either-way offence, s. 51(3) CDA 1998 requires the magistrates' court also send a 'related' either-way (s. 51(3)(a)) or summary-only offence (s. 51(3)(b)) for trial on indictment. An either-way offence is 'related' where it can be joined in the same indictment because it is founded on the same facts or forms part of a series of offences of the same or similar character (s. 51E CDA 1998).

The magistrates' court must also send any related summary offence for which the defendant appears at the same time (s. 51(3)(b) CDA 1998). A related summary offence must arise out of circumstances which are the same as or connected with the indictable-only offence and be punishable with imprisonment or disqualification (s. 51(11) CDA 1998). If the accused is convicted on indictment for the either-way offence, then if the judge considers that the summary-only offence is related to the indictable offence, the accused will be asked to enter a plea. If the accused pleads guilty, the Crown Court will pass sentence but its sentencing powers will be limited to those of the magistrates' court. If the defendant pleads not guilty and the prosecution wishes to proceed, the matter will have to be remitted back to the magistrates' court.

 Example

Brian is charged with burglary. At the allocation hearing, the magistrates' court determines that the offence should be heard on indictment. When the case sent papers are prepared, it appears that in order to escape from the crime scene Brian took a car without the owner's consent (a summary-only offence). The summary-only matter can be added to the indictment. Brian will be asked to plead to each count. If he pleads not guilty the jury will be sworn and the prosecution will present evidence to the court in respect of the burglary matter. If Brian is convicted of the burglary matter, he will be asked to enter a plea in relation to the vehicle-taking matter.

Where a defendant appears before a magistrates' court on a separate occasion charged with a related either-way or summary offence, the magistrates have discretion to send the matter(s) up to the Crown Court so that they may be joined with the indictable-only matter(s) (s. 51(4) CDA 1998).

11.8.2 POSITION OF CO-ACCUSED JOINTLY CHARGED WITH AN EITHER-WAY OFFENCE

Suppose that A and B are jointly charged with an either-way offence. At the PBV, A indicates a guilty plea but B indicates a not guilty plea. In these circumstances, A will be sentenced by the magistrates' court (subject to possible committal for sentence to the Crown Court) and B will proceed to the allocation hearing.

What if both A and B indicate a not guilty plea? Both will be subject to the allocation hearing. If the magistrates' court declines summary jurisdiction, both will be sent forthwith to the Crown Court under s. 51 CDA 1998. If the magistrates' court accept summary jurisdiction, do A and B have an individual right of election? With the implementation of s. 51 CDA 1998 in relation to either-way offences, if either A or B elects trial on indictment, both will be sent forthwith to the Crown Court (s. 51(5) CDA 1998) irrespective of whether the other would have preferred summary trial.

11.8.3 CO-ACCUSED FACING AN EITHER-WAY OFFENCE RELATED TO AN INDICTABLE-ONLY OFFENCE OR SENT EITHER-WAY OFFENCE

Where B is charged with an either-way offence which is related to an indictable-only offence with which A is charged, the either-way matter must be sent to the Crown Court in accordance with the requirements of s. 51 CDA 1998 (see Chapter 13). In these circumstances, the defendant (B) facing the either-way offence has no individual right of election. Any further related either-way offence or summary-only offence punishable with imprisonment or disqualification with which B is charged will also be sent.

Example

A is charged with causing grievous bodily harm with intent contrary to s. 18 Offences Against the Person Act 1861 (indictable-only). B is charged with affray (triable either way). The affray allegation arises out of the s. 18 assault. A will be sent for trial in the Crown Court in connection with the indictable-only matter. If B appears before magistrates at the same time as A, B's case must also be sent to the Crown Court.

Where A, charged with an either-way offence, is sent for trial under s. 51 CDA 1998 and another adult (B), appears before the court, either on the same or subsequent occasion, charged jointly with A in connection with an either-way offence which appears to be related to the offence for which A was sent for trial, s. 51(5) CDA 1998 provides that where B appears on the same occasion as A, the court must also send B for trial to the Crown Court. Where B appears on a different occasion, the court has discretion to send the case. Any further related either-way offence or summary-only offence punishable with imprisonment or disqualification with which B is charged will also be sent.

11.9 POST-ALLOCATION MATTERS WHERE CASE IS TO BE SENT TO THE CROWN COURT

A number of important ancillary matters need to be considered once the either-way offence has been sent to the Crown Court.

11.9.1 BAIL

When the case is adjourned after the allocation hearing, the issue of a defendant's bail might well arise. Where the defendant has previously been refused bail, a fresh application for bail might be made depending on how many previous bail applications have been made (see Chapter 10, para. 10.15). Application may be made to the Crown Court. Generally the defendant's case being sent for trial at the Crown Court does not amount to a change in circumstances supporting a third application for bail, unless the evidence disclosed in the case sent bundle suggests the prosecution's case is not as strong as it originally appeared. This situation may satisfy the 'change of circumstances' test. The defence advocate should ensure bail is extended to cover the Crown Court proceedings where her client is currently subject to bail (conditional or otherwise).

11.9.2 REPRESENTATION ORDERS

If the defendant has qualified for a representation order before the magistrates' court, the representation order will cover the Crown Court proceedings upon the case being sent for trial. If the defendant applied for a representation order before the magistrates' court but failed the means test, he will qualify for a representation order at this point but will be subject to a contribution order/notice based on his income and capital, declared on CRM15. If the defendant failed the interests of justice test initially but his case is subsequently sent to the Crown Court for trial, he will be passported through the interests of justice test.

11.9.3 DISCLOSURE OF EVIDENCE AND STANDARD CASE PROGRESSION DIRECTIONS

On sending a case for trial under s. 51 CDA 1998, a date will be set for a PCMH (see Chapter 13) in the Crown Court. In accordance with the Crim PR Part 3, standard case progression directions apply which enable the parties to work towards the PCMH and ensure that the PCMH is an effective hearing. The standard directions make provision for the service of evidence (both used and unused material) by the CPS.

Following the abolition of committal hearings, it is assumed that the disclosure of evidence rules that apply to an either-way offence that has been sent to the Crown Court for trial will follow the same procedure as adopted in indictable-only offences. This means that the prosecution will be required to serve the case sent bundle on the defence (see Appendix 1, Documents 25–28) within 50 days if the defendant is in custody and 70 days in non-custody cases.

The case sent bundle will include:

- the draft indictment;
- all 'used' material including witness statements (primary prosecution disclosure);
- the schedule of unused material; and
- initial prosecution disclosure of unused material in accordance with s. 3 Criminal Procedure and Investigations Act 1996 (CPIA 1996).

Within 14 days of the service of the case sent bundle, the defence must notify the prosecution of their witness requirements (i.e. which prosecution witnesses the defence wish to attend court).

Within 28 days of the prosecutor completing or purporting to complete the disclosure obligations under s. 3 CPIA 1996, the defence must serve a defence statement (pursuant to s. 5 CPIA 1996), and details of any defence witnesses must be notified to the prosecution (s. 6C CPIA 1996). The rules on the disclosure of unused material and the requirement on the part of the defendant to serve a defence statement are considered in Chapter 13, which explores the conduct of trials on indictment.

Provision is also made in the standard case management progression form for the service of:

- any application for a special measures direction (see Chapter 16);
- notice to admit hearsay or evidence of bad character (see Chapters 18 and 19);
- defence notice objecting to the admission of hearsay or evidence of bad character.

11.10 APPLICATION FOR DISMISSAL OF THE EITHER-WAY OFFENCE SENT TO THE CROWN COURT

Committal hearings in either-way cases served as a mechanism for weeding out evidentially weak cases before they were committed to the Crown Court. Prior to the abolition of committal hearings, the prosecution was required to establish a *prima facie* case against the accused based on the evidence disclosed in the committal bundle. What is the position under the s. 51 CDA 1998 sending procedure? Once the accused has been served with the case sent bundle then, in accordance with Sch. 3, para. 2(1) CDA 1998, the defence can apply to the Crown Court to have the charge/s dismissed. The application to dismiss is identical to the procedure that applies to indictable-only offences. The procedure is covered in greater detail in Chapter 13, para. 13.7.1. Reporting restrictions (limited to details of the defendant's name, age and bail arrangements) in relation to applications for dismissal of charges apply automatically but can be lifted.

What is the position where, because of some amendment to the charge/s or a successful application to have charges dismissed before the Crown Court (outlined previously), an accused no longer faces the charge for which he was sent for trial? If he still faces an either-way offence, the Crown Court has to go through the plea before venue/mode of trial/ allocation enquiry as outlined at the start of this chapter.

11.11 CHANGING THE ALLOCATION DECISION

The abolition of committal proceedings for either-way offences means that it will no longer be possible to switch between committal proceedings and summary trial or vice versa. The power that previously permitted a switch from summary trial to committal is replaced by a new power under s. 25(2A) MCA 1980 for the prosecution to apply for an either-way offence which has been allocated for summary trial to be tried on indictment instead. The application must be made before the summary trial begins and before any application or issue in relation to the summary trial is dealt with. The court may grant the application if it is satisfied that the sentence which a magistrates' court would have power to impose would be inadequate.

KEY POINT SUMMARY IN RELATION TO EITHER-WAY OFFENCES

- In relation to all either-way offences, a defendant will be required to give an indication of his or her plea—this is known as the 'plea before venue'.
- The plea before venue will invariably be conducted at the defendant's initial appearance before the magistrates' court in accordance with CJ-SSS/SDJ.
- If the defendant indicates a guilty plea, the magistrates must accept jurisdiction to deal with the defendant summarily but can commit the defendant to the Crown Court for sentence if it concludes its maximum sentencing powers are insufficient.
- Where a not guilty plea or no plea is indicated, an allocation hearing must be held and the initial decision as to where the case shall be tried lies with the magistrates.
- If the magistrates' court declines summary jurisdiction, the defendant will have no choice—he will be tried on indictment in the Crown Court.
- If the magistrates' court accepts jurisdiction, the defendant will have the choice between a Crown Court trial or a trial before the magistrates' court.
- In reaching a decision as regards allocation, the magistrates will apply the statutory provisions under s. 19 MCA 1980 (as amended), the allocation guideline and specific sentencing guidelines and will consider, in particular, whether their maximum sentencing powers are likely to be sufficient in the event of conviction.
- When advising a client about allocation, the defence practitioner should not only consider the legal merits of advising in favour of summary trial or trial on indictment but also consider the client's personal circumstances and whether the client could cope with the considerable demands of a Crown Court trial.
- The defence advocate needs to find out in advance the prosecution's views on allocation and, if necessary, be prepared to argue against the CPS.

SELF-TEST QUESTIONS

Consider the following short scenarios.

- What representations do you consider the prosecution might make as regards allocation in each case?
- Applying s.19 MCA 1980 factors, the allocation guideline and any applicable sentencing guidelines, do you consider the magistrates will accept or decline jurisdiction?
- Outline the procedure in relation to each possibility and consider, if the accused in each of the following exercises were given the choice as to election, what advice you would give in this regard?

 online resource centre

Analysis can be found on the Online Resource Centre.

Exercise 1

Gunnar Erikson is 45 years old. He is charged with sexually assaulting a 12-year-old schoolgirl, contrary to s. 7 Sexual Offences Act 2003. It is alleged that he sat next to the girl when her friends left the bus they were all travelling on, leaving the girl and him alone on the upper deck. The girl alleges that Erikson tried to stroke her inner thigh and that he forcefully placed her hand on his clothed but erect penis. The girl promptly pushed him aside and quickly moved downstairs. The girl complained to her mother later that evening. Erikson was arrested several days later. He denies the offence and claims he is the victim of mistaken identification. Erikson has several previous convictions for theft and child sex offences. The girl turned 13 six days after the alleged offence.

Exercise 2

Sinead Hogan is a 36-year-old pharmacist. She is charged with 16 offences of false accounting (s. 17 Theft Act 1968) and fraud worth £21,830 (s. 1 Fraud Act 2006) against the Prescription Pricing Authority. It is alleged that over a period of eight months she claimed expenditure for dispensing ordinary purpose syringes when her records show that she in fact dispensed a cheaper plastic disposable syringe. Sinead is a woman of impeccable character and denies the allegation.

Case study: *R v Lenny Wise*

Allocation—*R v Lenny Wise*

online resource centre

Take a look at *R v Lenny Wise* in the video section of our Online Resource Centre. You will recall that Lenny is charged with domestic burglary. [We would ask you to note that the Lenny Wise scenario was filmed under the pre-Sch. 3 CJA 2003 procedure and thus refers to the mode of trial enquiry. Consequently, Lenny's previous convictions were not disclosed for the purposes of what would have been mode of trial decision. They would have been disclosed under the new allocation hearing procedure.] The plea before venue takes place at Lenny's second appearance before Lyme Magistrates. Lenny's solicitor gives him advice as regards mode of trial/allocation. The advice of Lenny's solicitor is contained in a file note (see Document 7 in Appendix 1).

On the video you can see Lenny indicates a not guilty plea at the plea before venue followed by his mode of trial enquiry/allocation hearing. You will also see the outline by the CPS lawyer inviting the court to decline jurisdiction to try the matter. At the conclusion of the mode of trial enquiry/allocation the magistrates decline jurisdiction and adjourn the matter and send the case to the Crown Court. Lenny is given the date for his Plea and Case Management Hearing before the Crown Court. The reason for their decision is that they do not believe their sentencing powers would be sufficient in the event of conviction having regard to a number of aggravating factors. Lenny need not concern himself with means testing in the Crown Court. He will not be made the subject of a contribution order as he qualifies automatically in terms of his means (see Chapter 9).

FIGURE 11.1 EITHER-WAY OFFENCE—GENERAL SEQUENCE OF EVENTS

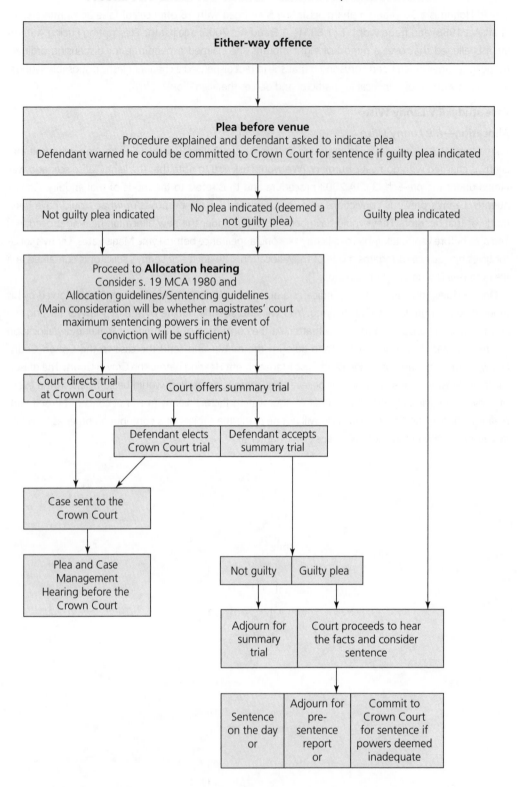

PROSECUTING SUMMARY OFFENCES

12.1 INTRODUCTION

In this chapter we consider the steps in preparing for a summary trial. A summary trial will be held where a defendant pleads not guilty to a summary-only offence or pleads not guilty to an either-way offence where the magistrates' court has accepted jurisdiction to try the offence at the allocation hearing and the defendant has consented to summary trial.

This chapter should be read in conjunction with the latter part of Chapter 9 which provides an account of the early stages of a summary/either-way offence. In this chapter we specifically consider:

- pleading guilty by post;
- the circumstances in which a defendant can be summarily tried in her absence;
- the rules governing the drafting of a written charge/information;
- the pre-trial disclosure of evidence in a summary case;
- case management;

- the steps when preparing for summary trial;
- the procedure at a summary trial on a not guilty plea.

12.2 COMMENCING A PROSECUTION FOR A SUMMARY-ONLY MATTER

Criminal proceedings are commenced either by the police charging an individual at the police station, or by the Crown Prosecution Service issuing a 'written charge and postal requisition' in accordance with s. 29 Criminal Justice Act 2003 (CJA). Prior to s. 29 CJA coming fully into force, the alternative method of commencing a prosecution to charging the suspect at the police station, was to 'lay an information' before a magistrates' court and have the court issue a 'summons' requiring the defendant to attend court on a given date and time to answer the information/s (charge/s) laid against him. The 'information' and 'summons' method of commencing criminal proceedings will continue to be used for private prosecutions only.

The required content of the written charge/information is set out in Crim PR, Part 7(3)(1). It is the formal accusation against the defendant. Crim PR r 7 (3) provides that a 'written charge' or 'information' must contain:

(a) notice of when and where the defendant is required to attend the court; and

(b) a statement of the offence which describes in ordinary language and (if the offence is created by statute) identifies the legislation that creates it and sufficient particulars of the conduct constituting the commission of the offence to make clear what the prosecutor alleges against the defendant.

In the case of a 'requisition', the prosecutor must ensure service of both the 'written charge and the requisition' which may be contained within a single document on the defendant. Service is usually made by sending it by first class post to an address where it is reasonably believed that the accused will receive it (Crim PR r. 4). If the accused fails to appear and satisfactory service can be established, the court can adjourn the case or proceed in the defendant's absence or issue an arrest warrant for the accused either backed or not backed for bail.

12.2.1 TIME LIMITS FOR THE PROSECUTION OF SUMMARY-ONLY OFFENCES

A magistrates' court may not try a defendant for a summary offence unless the requisition/information was laid within six months of the commission of the alleged offence (s. 127(1) Magistrates' Courts Act 1980 (MCA 1980)). This provision applies to most summary-only offences, although the time limit can be expressly overridden by statute.

12.3 PLEADING GUILTY BY POST

In some summary cases the defendant need not initially attend court where, under s. 12 MCA 1980, the defendant pleads guilty by sending a letter to the court in the following circumstances:

(a) the offence is summary-only; and

(b) the proceedings have been started by requisition/summons.

It is up to the prosecution (in the exercise of its discretion) to determine whether the accused should be given the option of pleading guilty by post.

Where the defendant pleads guilty by post, the prosecution must serve on the defendant:

(i) the requisition/summons;

(ii) a brief statement of the facts upon which the prosecution is to rely, or a copy of any statements written in compliance with s. 9 Criminal Justice Act 1967 (CJA 1967); and

(iii) any information relating to the defendant that will be put before the court; and

(iv) a notice explaining the procedure.

If the defendant wishes to plead guilty, she must notify the court and may submit a written statement in mitigation of sentence. The court proceeds on the basis of the written statements submitted by both sides which must be read to the court. The magistrates may refuse to accept a guilty plea if the statement in mitigation reveals a defence or the plea is unclear. If the guilty plea is accepted, the magistrates can sentence immediately, depending on the type of sentence or following an adjournment requiring the defendant's attendance.

12.4 DEFENDANT UNAWARE OF COURT PROCEEDINGS

If the defendant was unaware of the proceedings then, within 21 days of finding out about the proceedings, s. 14 MCA 1980 permits the defendant to make a statutory declaration that she knew nothing of the proceedings. The declaration may be made before the court or a solicitor. The effect of the declaration is that the requisition/summons and all the proceedings are void. The written charge/information, however, is still valid.

12.5 JOINDER OF OFFENCES AND DEFENDANTS IN THE INFORMATION

At the commencement of a summary trial, the defendant is asked to plead guilty or not guilty to the information containing the charge(s).

The general rule is that a written charge/information may only charge one defendant with a single offence (Crim PR, Part 7.3) unless the prosecution alleges that the offence was committed jointly by more than one defendant.

 Example

> Ben and Chris are charged with common assault arising out of a fight outside a nightclub on 23 January. The prosecution alleges both defendants assaulted the victim. As both defendants committed the offence jointly, each will be tried on the same written charge.

A written charge or information which charges more than one offence is bad for duplicity and the prosecutor must decide which charge he wishes to proceed with.

In some situations, where the defendant faces more than one charge or several accused are charged in separate written charges/informations, the court may try the charges together. Written charges/informations may be tried together where:

• the defence agree to the charges being tried together; or

• the court orders the offences to be tried together because it is in the interests of justice to do so and the offences form part of a series of offences of the same or similar character.

If the defence do not agree to the charges being tried together, for the alternative ground to apply the court must be satisfied that the offences are part of a series of offences of the same or similar character. This requires, first, that there should be some connection between them in time and place and the nature of the offences. Secondly, the court will take into account whether it is in 'the interests of justice' for the written charges to be tried together. Guidance on the application of the interest of justice test is provided by the House of Lords in *Chief Constable of Norfolk v Clayton* [1983] 2 AC 473. When applying the interests of justice test, the court must consider the convenience to the prosecution of having the charges/informations tried together against any injustice that might arise to the defendant. In most cases the defence will resist having the charges/informations tried together. A common submission is that it is not in the interests of justice as the evidence from one offence might unfairly prejudice the magistrates in deciding a defendant's guilt in respect to the other offence.

Example

(i) Over the course of three days Leah commits four offences of theft and obtaining property by deception by going from shop to shop and obtaining goods from each of them using a false credit card.

(ii) In a domestic dispute over the course of two weeks, Neil commits common assault against his ex-girlfriend, her new boyfriend and his ex-girlfriend's mother.

(iii) Julie steals two books from the library. The following day she commits an offence of careless driving.

In examples (i) and (ii) the two conditions for the written charges to be tried together appear to be satisfied. First, the offences are part of a series of offences of the same or similar nature. There is also proximity between them in terms of time. Second, the court would rule that it is in the interests of justice for the charges to be tried together after considering the balance of convenience to the prosecution and the potential prejudice to Leah and Neil.

In example (iii) the grounds for trying the charges together are not satisfied. As the defence will not agree and the offences are not the same or of a similar nature, Julie will be tried separately on each charge.

12.5.1 AMENDING THE WRITTEN CHARGE/INFORMATION

If the details contained in the written charge/information are incorrect or inconsistent with the evidence called by the prosecution, s. 123 MCA 1980 permits it to be amended at any stage of the proceedings provided the error has not caused injustice to the defendant. Examples of minor errors which would not cause injustice are where the defendant's name or the location of the offence is misspelt in the written charge. Where the error is regarded as 'substantial', the court may allow the amendment but will also grant an adjournment to allow the defence to deal with any issues arising out of the amendment (s. 123 MCA 1980).

 Example

Rashid is requisitioned with driving a motor vehicle with a defective tyre. The written charge details the defective tyre to be 'on the rear offside of the vehicle'. In fact, the defective tyre was on the rear nearside of the vehicle. In this situation, amending the written charge will be permitted and it is unlikely that the error would be regarded as substantial.

Majinder is requisitioned for common assault, which is wrongly specified in the written charge as having been committed on 23 March. In fact the alleged offence occurred on 26 March. As Majinder has an alibi for his whereabouts on 23 March, it is likely that the proposed amendment is 'substantial' and the court will adjourn the proceedings to enable the defence to deal with the amendment.

12.6 THE EARLY STAGES OF A SUMMARY-ONLY/EITHER-WAY OFFENCE

As we saw in Chapter 9, in the early stages of a summary-only or either-way offence the defence solicitor will advise the client about her plea. Before giving advice, the defence solicitor will need to:

- interview the client;
- obtain and evaluate prosecution advance information (Crim PR, Part 21); and
- obtain a representation order on behalf of the client.

12.6.1 TAKING A PLEA

In accordance with CJ-SSS and now SDJ (see Chapter 9, para. 9.16), the defendant is expected to enter a plea at the first hearing before the magistrates' court. To facilitate this, the CPS must serve sufficient disclosure of the prosecution's case on the accused as early as possible and at the latest by 9 am on the day of the first hearing to enable the defendant to enter a firm plea (see Chapter 8, para. 8.12). A guilty plea will require the court to pass sentence either on the day or following an adjournment for a pre-sentence report. Sentencing practice is considered in Part V.

Where the defendant indicates a not guilty plea in a summary case, the Stop Delaying Justice (SDJ) initiative aims to ensure that all contested trials in the magistrates' court are fully case managed from the first hearing and disposed with at the second hearing.

The court is required to actively manage the case by making standard directions, as explained later. A summary case should normally be listed for trial within six to eight weeks. This may be longer if, for example, the case is likely to involve defence expert evidence. The defendant will be remanded on bail or in custody to the trial date. Having set the trial date, some magistrates' courts additionally list the case for a pre-trial review/case management hearing usually one week before the date set for trial to avoid last minute difficulties which may lead to the trial being vacated on the day.

12.6.2 CASE MANAGEMENT OF A SUMMARY TRIAL

All parties are obliged to assist the court in its active management of cases under Crim PR Part 3 which provides:

'(a) the court must establish, with the active assistance of the parties, what disputed issues they intend to explore; and

(b) the court may require a party to identify—

   (i) which witnesses that party wants to give oral evidence,

   (ii) the order in which that party wants those witnesses to give their evidence,

   (iii) whether that party requires an order compelling the attendance of a witness,

   (iv) what arrangements are desirable to facilitate the giving of evidence by a witness,

   (v) what arrangements are desirable to facilitate the participation of any other person, including the defendant,

   (vi) what written evidence that party intends to introduce,

   (vii) what other material, if any, that person intends to make available to the court in the presentation of the case,

   (viii) whether that party intends to raise any point of law that could affect the conduct of the trial or appeal, and

   (ix) what timetable that party proposes and expects to follow.'

In setting a firm date for a summary trial at the first hearing, the magistrates' court will expect both the prosecution and the defence to assist in the completion of a trial preparation form (see Part 3 Case Management: *Preparation for Trial in a Magistrates' Court*: http://www.justice.gov.uk/courts/procedure-rules/criminal/forms/formspage).

The case management aspect of SDJ is entirely consistent with the overriding objective in Crim PR Part 1 that cases will be dealt with justly, efficiently and expeditiously taking into account the gravity of the offence alleged, the complexity of what is in issue, the severity of the consequences for the defendant and others affected and the needs of other cases.

In accordance with Crim PR Part 3 and to effectively manage the case, the magistrates' court will require the parties to confirm:

- what the real issues in the case are;
- whether any point of law arises as part of their case;

- what witness evidence can be agreed and read out to the court under s. 9 CJA 1967 (see 18.4.1);

- whether any evidence can be adduced by way of formal admissions in accordance with s. 10 CJA 1967;

- how many witnesses need to be called for each side and have dates for their availability (witnesses should only attend trial if they can testify on issues in dispute between the parties and the court must actively consider whether the witnesses' evidence can be agreed under ss. 9 or 10 Criminal Justice Act 1967);

- whether the record of interview at the police station (ROTI) can be agreed;

- whether any applications for special measures or to admit evidence of bad character or hearsay are anticipated;

- what is a realistic time estimate for the trial.

Once the case has been listed for trial, the parties must comply with any directions that are given as regards the service of unused evidence and applications to make or oppose bad character/hearsay. Although the Criminal Procedure Rules provide timescales for the service of a notice to admit bad character, SDJ provides that the court is entitled to allow the application to be made orally at the case management stage (i.e. the first hearing), and will want to do so where it is obvious that an application could or should be made. Contested applications for special measures/bad character and hearsay will usually be listed for a pre-trial hearing at which binding rulings under s. 45 Courts Act 2003 can be made.

Where any party anticipates there could be a problem with being ready by the trial date (this may be due to witness unavailability), Crim PR Part 3 imposes a duty on the party to notify the court's case progression officer in good time so that an application can be made to vacate the date set for the trial.

With CJ-SSS and more so now with SDJ, an application by either side seeking an adjournment will be rigorously scrutinised. The near zero tolerance approach to adjournments advocated by SDJ means that if the defence has complied with all its responsibilities and is fully ready for trial, but the prosecution has failed to comply with its responsibilities, then normally it would not be in the interest of justice for the prosecution to be allowed an adjournment and the prosecution may fail. If the failure lies with the defence and an adjournment is granted, the defence can expect to be subject to a wasted costs order.

Can the defence refuse to co-operate with the court's case management responsibilities?

What if the defendant simply indicates to the court when completing the case management form that he pleads not guilty and intends to put the prosecution to proof of his guilt? Can a defendant refuse to disclose the nature of his defence on the basis that it requires him to waive legal professional privilege or it violates his privilege against self-incrimination? If this is what the client instructs his solicitor to do, how does the solicitor reconcile his duties under the SRA Code of Conduct 2011 (*Principle 1*) to uphold the proper administration of justice with (*Principle 4*) his duty to act in the best interests of his client?

The position is that the defence solicitor is under a duty to actively assist the court in its case management responsibilities under Crim PR Part 3. This is re-affirmed by the Law Society in its recently issued revised Practice Note on the Criminal Procedure Rules 2011 (accessible at: http://www.lawsociety.org.uk/advice/practice-notes/criminal-procedure-rules-2011/). The guidance makes it clear that whilst a court cannot require a solicitor to act in a way which would override the presumption of innocence, the right to silence and the privilege against self-incrimination or legal professional privilege, a solicitor can be required by the Crim PR, or by a direction of the court (Crim PR 3.5) made under its case management duties arising from Crim PR Part 3, to provide information that will enable the court process to proceed efficiently.

It is well established by case law, and is re-affirmed by SDJ, that a defendant who advances a positive defence at trial having not previously disclosed it on the case management form can gain no advantage from ambushing the prosecution and failing to comply with his obligations under Cr PR Part 3.3 to assist the court in its case management duties (see *Director of Public Prosecutions v Chorley Justices* [2006] EWHC 1795 (Admin)).

12.7 PREPARING FOR TRIAL (DEFENCE PERSPECTIVE)

Where the case is listed for trial (and having regard to the matters in Crim PR, Part 3 previously outlined), the defence solicitor should begin preparing for a summary trial as soon as possible. This may include some or all of the following.

12.7.1 VISITING THE CRIME SCENE

Visiting the crime scene can give the defence lawyer a better understanding of the location where the offence occurred. It is often useful to prepare a plan or take photographs, especially in road traffic collision cases where there is a dispute between the prosecution and the defendant about, for example, the position of the vehicle(s) on the road.

12.7.2 TRACING AND INTERVIEWING POTENTIAL DEFENCE WITNESSES

The practical effect of the stricter case management duties imposed by the courts places enormous pressure on a defence advocate to prepare for summary trial at the outset. Any potential defence witness should be contacted at the earliest opportunity for a statement to be taken. Sometimes, this may require the defence to make enquiries to identify the names and addresses of potential witnesses.

Whilst there is no property in a witness, it would be unusual for the defence to interview a prosecution witness before trial, and regard should always be had to the potential dangers that this could give rise to under the SRA Code of Conduct 2011 outlined in Chapter 1, para. 1.11.6. In this situation the guidance contained in the 'old' 2007 Code remains valid:

'To avoid such allegations it would be wise, when seeking to interview a witness for the other side, to offer to interview them in the presence of the other side's representative.'

12.7.3 INSTRUCTING AN EXPERT WITNESS

Many summary offences do not require expert evidence but in those cases where expert evidence is required, the defence advocate should instruct an expert at the earliest opportunity. If the defendant has a representation order, the defence should obtain the written authority of the Legal Aid Agency (LAA) using Form CRM4, before formally instructing the expert. It is common practice to support the application with an explanation of why an expert is required and what the fee will be.

Where either the prosecution or the defence intends to call expert evidence at trial, Crim PR, Part 33 requires the pre-trial disclosure of the expert's report both to the court and to the other party (see Chapter 17, para. 17.9.3).

12.7.4 THE PRE-TRIAL DISCLOSURE OF EVIDENCE

Once an accused has pleaded not guilty to a matter that is to be tried summarily, the prosecution will come under further obligations to make pre-trial disclosure of evidence. This will include any 'used' material that the prosecution intends to rely on at trial which has not previously been disclosed and any 'unused material' under the Criminal Procedure and Investigations Act 1996 (CPIA 1996).

12.7.5 'UNUSED' MATERIAL AND DEFENCE STATEMENTS

Section 3 CPIA 1996 requires the prosecution to serve the defendant with initial disclosure of any evidence not previously disclosed, which might reasonably be considered capable of undermining the case for the prosecution or of assisting the case for the accused. For a full explanation of the rules on disclosure of 'unused material' see Chapter 8, para. 8.9 onwards.

The prosecution's obligation to serve 'unused' material arises in cases to be tried summarily where the defendant pleads not guilty. Standard directions in the case management form make provision for the service of 'unused material' by the prosecution on a specified date.

On receiving initial prosecution disclosure 'unused material' the defendant may choose to file a defence statement under s. 6 CPIA 1996, indicating on which matters the defendant takes issue with the prosecution case and for what reasons and giving particulars of any defence or alibi the defendant intends to rely on at trial. The detailed rules governing the service of defence statements are explained in Chapter 13, which outlines the steps for preparing for trial on indictment.

While the service of a defence statement is voluntary in summary cases, s. 6C CPIA 1996 requires the defendant to serve a defence witness notice giving details of all defence witnesses (other than an expert witness) he intends to call at trial. The provision is considered in more detail in Chapter 13, para. 13.6.13. The time limit for service of the defence witness notice in summary cases is 14 days after the prosecution's compliance or purported compliance with its initial disclosure duties under s. 3 CPIA 1996.

In those very exceptional situations when a defence statement is served in a summary case, the prosecution must fulfil its ongoing obligation to keep disclosure under review in accordance with s. 7A CPIA 1996. In particular the CPS must disclose any 'further' material which has not previously been disclosed and which might reasonably be expected to assist the accused's case as disclosed in the defence statement.

Apart from complying with the obligation highlighted above under s. 6C CPIA 1996 to disclose details of any witness to be called at trial, in view of the potential sanctions that apply to the service of a defence statement, why would a defence solicitor serve a defence statement in a summary trial?

12.7.6 DEFENCE STATEMENTS AND SUMMARY TRIALS

The answer to the question stated comes down to tactical considerations. The defence advocate knows that serving a defence statement will force the prosecutor to look again at the 'unused' material (s. 7A CPIA 1996) to see whether there is any previously undisclosed material that might assist the case for the defendant. The defence advocate therefore needs to carefully consider the disclosure schedule which is served with initial disclosure of unused material under s. 3 CPIA 1996, and decide whether serving a defence statement might unearth further useful disclosure. However, the service of a defence statement in summary proceedings remains rare as usually there is nothing to be gained by it.

12.7.7 EVALUATING THE EVIDENCE

Having obtained full disclosure of the prosecution's case and an updated proof of evidence from the defendant and any defence witnesses, the defence solicitor should begin to evaluate the strength of the prosecution's case and to formulate a strategy for defending the case in court. In preparing for trial the elements of the offence(s) charged must be researched so the advocate knows the facts in issue which the prosecution must prove to secure the defendant's conviction. Research may also be necessary where the defence intends to challenge prosecution evidence at trial. The defence advocate should come to court prepared to cite relevant statutory provisions and case law in support of his submission to have prosecution evidence excluded.

Where the prosecution has served an application to allow one or more of its witnesses to give evidence under a special measures direction (see Chapter 16), or it has served an application to admit hearsay evidence (see Chapter 18), or to admit the defendant's bad character (see Chapter 19), the defence advocate must decide whether to oppose the application. If the application is opposed, the defence advocate should serve a notice in accordance with the standard directions or make an application to serve notice out of time, if necessary.

12.7.8 SECURING THE ATTENDANCE OF WITNESSES AT TRIAL

SDJ reinforces the responsibility of each party under the Crim PR to ensure their witnesses attend the trial, Crim PR Part 3.8(2)(b). As the trial approaches, the defence advocate will have formulated a strategy of how he intends to defend his client in court. An important part of the preparation is to decide which of the witnesses from whom he has taken a proof of evidence will be called to give evidence for the defence. Initially, the defence advocate will write to a prospective witness giving full details of the time and location of the court hearing asking the witness to attend voluntarily or to produce a document. If the witness does not reply or indicates that she is not willing to appear voluntarily it will be necessary to apply to the court for a witness summons to be issued.

The rules on the issue and service of a witness summons, which apply both to the prosecution and the defence, are contained in Crim PR, Part 28.

The application for a witness summons can be made orally or in writing. Special rules apply to a witness summons that seeks to have a witness produce a document.

Some witnesses will be reluctant to attend even where they have been served with a witness summons. In this situation, s. 97(2) MCA 1980 authorises an arrest warrant to be issued against the witness to ensure attendance.

12.7.9 DISPUTED EVIDENCE

Disputes about the admissibility of evidence do not arise as frequently in the magistrates' courts as at trials in the Crown Court. However, where evidence is disputed, the matter will be decided by the magistrates/District Judge at the beginning of the trial or during the trial. In some circumstances a *voir dire*, or trial within a trial, will be held (*R v Liverpool Juvenile Court, ex p. R* [1987] 2 All ER 668). At a *voir dire*, evidence may be called and legal submissions made as to why the disputed evidence should be excluded. If the magistrates decide the evidence is inadmissible, no further mention will be made of it and no reliance can be placed on it. A *voir dire* will commonly be held where the defendant disputes the admissibility of a confession or seeks to have identification evidence excluded for breaching Code D. The *voir dire* is much more effective in the Crown Court where there is a strict division of functions between the judge and the jury and issues of law and evidence are decided in the absence of the jury. This is not possible in the magistrates' court as the magistrates are arbiters of both fact and law. The use of pre-trial binding rulings under the Courts Act 2003 (highlighted at para. 12.6.2) goes some way to reducing the potential prejudice arising from the *voir dire* procedure in summary proceedings as the trial Bench will be differently composed.

12.7.10 PREPARING TO MITIGATE ON CONVICTION

Unless the defendant is acquitted on all charges the defence advocate should be ready to make a plea in mitigation of sentence. Sentencing practice and procedure is explained in detail in Part V.

12.8 PREPARING FOR TRIAL (PROSECUTION PERSPECTIVE)

In preparing for trial, the prosecutor is likely to follow the same steps as the defence advocate. The CPS lawyer will prepare for trial in accordance with the Manual of Guidance (see Chapter 8, para. 8.2).

In the short time available to prepare for summary trial, the prosecution advocate will have determined whether:

- an application for a special measures direction for one or more of its witnesses is required (see Chapter 16);
- an application to admit hearsay (see Chapter 18) or bad character evidence is required (see Chapter 19).

The prosecuting lawyer will, amongst other things, also:

- serve any unused material that is required to be disclosed in accordance with s. 3 CPIA 1996 (see para. 12.7.5);
- try to agree evidence with the defence in accordance with ss. 9 and 10 CJA 1967 (see para. 12.6.2 and Chapter 15, para. 15. 8);
- research the elements of the offence so that she is clear what needs to be proved (see Chapter 15);
- determine which witnesses to call and in what order;
- ensure attendance of her witnesses with the assistance of the police and witness liaison;
- ensure any exhibits are available for production in court;
- be prepared to resist a defence argument to have prosecution evidence excluded;
- be prepared to assist the court on passing sentence if the accused is convicted, by referring the court to any of the defendant's relevant previous convictions and ask for ancillary orders where appropriate.

12.9 RIGHTS OF AUDIENCE BEFORE MAGISTRATES' COURT AND TERMS OF ADDRESS

Only solicitors/barristers, licensed ILEX advocates and associate prosecutors (to a very limited degree) have a right of audience to conduct trials in a magistrates' court. If you are training to be a lawyer, although you may not have rights of audience at this stage, the magistrates' court is an invaluable learning experience—take full advantage to watch and learn.

When addressing a District Judge, the address is 'Sir' or 'Madam'. A lay Bench can be addressed collectively as 'Your Worships'. Alternatively an advocate may choose to address the chairperson of the Bench and say 'Madam and your colleagues' or 'Sir and your colleagues'. When referring to the magistrates' adviser, it is customary to state 'Your learned legal adviser' and when referring to your opposing advocate, you might say 'My friend for the prosecution' or, in the case of a barrister, 'My learned friend'.

12.10 FAILURE OF THE DEFENDANT TO ATTEND TRIAL

Unless it would be contrary to the interests of justice, s. 11(1)(b) MCA 1980 requires the trial to go ahead in the absence of an adult defendant. Much will depend on what explanation, if any, is advanced for the defendant's absence.

If the explanation is that the defendant is too ill to attend trial or has been faced with a family emergency, the court may accept a defence request for the trial to be adjourned to a later date and for bail to be extended. If the court decides to try the defendant in her absence and the defendant is represented, his solicitor can still put the prosecution to prove its case and make submissions and a closing speech. A trial in the defendant's absence, particularly an unrepresented defendant, is most likely to result in a conviction as the evidence against the defendant is not contradicted.

Having convicted an absent defendant, a court may also sentence in her absence or adjourn sentence and issue a warrant for the defendant's arrest. Where an offender is sentenced to imprisonment in her absence, she must be brought before the court before being taken to prison.

12.11 **THE PROCEDURE AT A SUMMARY TRIAL ON A NOT GUILTY PLEA**

Where the defendant pleads not guilty, the whole prosecution case is put in issue. The relevant rules of court relating to the conduct of summary trials are contained in Crim PR, Part 37(3).

(1) The hearing begins with the defendant's full name, address and date of birth and the name of her solicitor being given to the court.

(2) The charge(s) will be put to the defendant by the justices' legal adviser and the defendant confirms that she pleads not guilty to the charge(s).

(3) The prosecutor may make an opening speech by addressing the court with regard to:

— the prosecution's version of the facts;

— the witnesses to be called in support of the prosecution case; and

— any legal issues that will arise.

(4) The first prosecution witness is questioned by the prosecutor in examination-in-chief, the purpose of which is to obtain answers from the witness which supports the prosecution case. All factual witnesses must remain outside the courtroom until they have given their evidence. Each witness called will firstly take the oath or affirmation and state their name. It is customary to point out to the witness that they should speak clearly and at a slow pace, addressing their answers to the Bench. Certain witnesses may give their evidence with the benefit of special measures. The rules relating to witness testimony are explained in Chapter 16.

Note: As part of its duties to robustly manage summary trials in accordance with Crim PR Part 3 and SDJ, the court must ensure that the 'live' evidence, questions and submissions are directly related to the disputed issues. It is anticipated that greater use will be made by the court of Crim PR 37.4(4)(e). This permits a party calling a witness to ask that a witness's earlier statement stand as his evidence in chief. The two preconditions for this to apply are that the parties agree and that the court permits this to be done. It is a useful case management tool as it reduces the time a witness will spend in the witness box and therefore enables the court to ensure that cases are dealt with efficiently and expeditiously and that the evidence is given in the shortest possible way (Crim PR 1(2)(e) and 3.2(1)(d)).

(5) The witness may then be cross-examined by the defence with a view to undermining the accuracy or truthfulness of what the witness said during examination-in-chief and/or to undermine the witness's credibility.

(6) The prosecution may re-examine the witness to repair any damage that may have been inflicted on the witness during cross-examination.

(7) The magistrates may ask the witness questions at any time but in most courts the convention applies that the witness will be questioned after the parties have finished asking questions.

The process of witness testimony of examination-in-chief, cross-examination and re-examination continues until all the prosecution witnesses have testified.

(8) As well as calling witnesses to give oral evidence, the prosecution may also put its case to the court by presenting evidence in other forms including statements of witnesses who are not in court under s. 9 CJA 1967 (see earlier), or under the hearsay provisions, video recordings, tape recordings or real evidence such as an exhibit presented in court.

(9) At the conclusion of the prosecution's case, the defence may submit that there is no case to answer. Under Crim PR, Part 37(3)(c), the court may acquit on the ground that the prosecution evidence is insufficient for any reasonable court properly to convict. The test was more specifically defined under the now defunct Practice Direction (*Submission of No Case*) [1962] 1 WLR 227 as being a failure by the prosecution to establish an

essential element of the alleged offence, or the prosecution evidence has been so discredited in cross-examination or is so manifestly unreliable that no reasonable tribunal could safely convict on it.

(10) Where a submission of no case to answer is not made or is unsuccessful, the defence may put its case to the court. The defence advocate may make an opening speech, but, as he is normally allowed only one speech, it is usual practice to reserve this to the end of the defence case so that he may have the advantage of the 'last word'.

(11) The defence calls its first witness, subjecting the witness to an examination-in-chief. Where the accused exercises her right to testify under s. 79 PACE 1984, the accused must be the first defence witness and has the right to leave the dock and give evidence from the witness box (*R v Farnham Justices, ex p. Andrew Gibson* [1991] Crim LR 642).

(12) The defence witness may then be cross-examined by the prosecution and any co-accused.

(13) The defence advocate may re-examine the witness to repair any damage that may have been inflicted on the witness during cross-examination.

(14) After any evidence called by the defence, the court may permit the prosecution or other party to adduce further evidence.

(15) The prosecution and the defence will usually close the proceedings by making a closing speech. The defence will have the last word.

(16) The court will then announce its decision of guilty or not guilty after retiring to consider the evidence. On finding the defendant guilty, the court will consider whether it is necessary to obtain a pre-sentence report. Where a pre-sentence report is ordered, the case will be adjourned to enable the report to be prepared. Before proceeding to sentence, the prosecution will disclose to the court the defendant's previous convictions (if any). The defence advocate will make a plea in mitigation. The court then passes sentence. In relation to an either-way offence, the court can commit the defendant for sentence to the Crown Court under s. 3 Power of Criminal Courts (Sentencing) Act 2000 (PCC(S)A 2000) where it is of the view that its powers of sentence are insufficient. Section 6 of the same Act enables the court to also commit any summary offence for which the defendant has been convicted alongside the either-way offence. The practice and procedure of sentencing, including the power to commit for sentence are considered in Part V.

(17) Where the defendant is found not guilty, the defendant is free to leave. If the defendant is not legally aided she may apply to have her costs met out of central funds under s. 16 Prosecution of Offenders Act 1985. Such orders are at the discretion of the court but should normally be awarded unless it is felt that the accused brought suspicion on herself by her conduct and/or misled the prosecution into thinking the evidence against her was stronger than it in fact was. Guidance can be found in *Practice Direction (Crime: Costs)* [1991] WLR 498. A legally aided acquitted defendant's costs will be met under the representation order.

We further consider trial advocacy in the context of trials before the Crown Court in Chapter 14.

In conducting a summary trial you are reminded of the various rules of professional conduct that could arise under the solicitors' code of conduct (2011), which are considered in Chapter 1. They include:

- duties owed to the court (Chapter 5: *Outcome 1*);
- duties as an advocate (Chapter 5: *Indicative Behaviours*);
- core duties to uphold the proper administration of justice (*Principle 1*);
- conflict of interest if representing more than one defendant (*Chapter 3*);
- confidentiality (*Chapter 4*).

See reference to the Law Society's Practice Note at 12.6.2.1.

KEY POINT SUMMARY

- Be aware of the circumstances in which a defendant can be tried in his or her absence.
- Know the law which permits two or more written charges to be tried together and how you might challenge the 'interests of justice' test.
- Know the responsibilities of each side in the pre-trial disclosure of evidence.
- Know the procedure for securing the attendance of witnesses at trial.
- Know the practice for admitting a witness's written statement in hearsay form under s. 9 CJA 1967.
- Be aware of the purpose of and the issues that will be covered by standard directions for trial and the duty of the parties to assist the court in the active management of cases under Crim PR, Part 3.
- Know the sequence of events where the defendant pleads not guilty.
- Know the test to support a submission of no case to answer.

SELF-TEST QUESTIONS

1. What is the test to determine whether a defendant can be tried for two or more written charges at the same time where the defendant does not consent?
2. Explain how the defence solicitor will find out what the prosecution's evidence comprises in advance of trial.
3. How can the solicitor ensure the attendance of witnesses?
4. What is the role of the legal adviser in a summary case (see Chapter 1)?
5. At what point might a submission of no case to answer be made and what is the test to support such a submission?

Analysis of these questions can be found on our Online Resource Centre.

 online resource centre

FIGURE 12.1 THE PROSECUTION OF A SUMMARY OFFENCE AND SUMMARY TRIAL

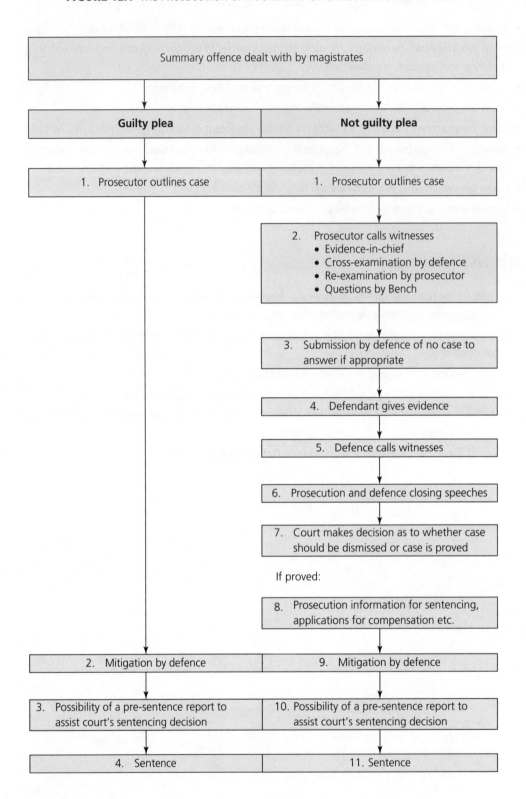

13   CROWN COURT PROCEEDINGS PRE-TRIAL

13.1 **INTRODUCTION**

Although indictable offences usually involve more complex issues of law, evidence and fact than summary cases, much of the preparatory work is the same. With much greater powers of punishment available to the Crown Court however, the potential consequences for a defendant are much more serious if the case is not properly prepared.

You may wish to read this chapter in conjunction with the latter part of Chapter 9 which explains the provision of public funding for indictable-only cases and the initial preparatory steps that will occupy the defence practitioner when dealing with a client charged with an indictable-only offence.

This chapter deals with pre-trial practices and procedures of indictable-only offences. It covers:

• sending indictable-only cases to the Crown Court under s. 51 Crime and Disorder Act 1998 (CDA 1998);

• preparing for the preliminary hearing in the Crown Court;

• preparing for trial on indictment;

• pre-trial disclosure issues and defence statements;

• instructing counsel;

• pre-trial hearings including the Plea and Case Management Hearing (PCMH).

You will be aware that either-way offences can also be tried on indictment in the Crown Court. As explained in Chapter 11, with the abolition of committal hearings, either-way cases are also sent to the Crown Court using the s. 51 CDA 1998 procedure. Once an either-way offence is sent to the Crown Court, a date is set for the PCMH. Before considering the PCMH and other general preparatory steps we explain some specific provisions governing indictable-only offences.

13.2 **THE DEFENDANT'S FIRST COURT APPEARANCE FOR AN INDICTABLE-ONLY OFFENCE—S. 51 CRIME AND DISORDER ACT 1998**

Despite being charged with an indictable-only offence, the defendant will make his first appearance before a magistrates' court at which his entitlement to bail will be decided. Bail is more likely to be opposed by the prosecution in an indictable-only offence because of the seriousness of the offence and the greater risk of the defendant absconding.

While the rules relating to the pre-trial disclosure of advance information do not strictly apply to indictable-only offences, the Crown Prosecution Service (CPS) will normally provide this information before the defendant's first appearance (see Chapter 8, para. 8.12).

Having made an initial appearance before a magistrates' court, s. 51(1) CDA 1998 requires the case to be formally sent forthwith to the Crown Court. The case will usually then be listed for a preliminary hearing which should be held within 14 days of the case being sent or eight days if the defendant is remanded in custody.

Whether or not the case is listed for a preliminary hearing, a PCMH must be held 14 weeks after the case has been sent where a defendant is in custody and within 17 weeks where a defendant is on bail. In sending the case, the magistrates' court is required, as part of its case management powers, to complete a case progression form which imposes standard directions on the parties relating to the service of prosecution evidence and defence statements. Standard directions include deadlines for the service of applications for special measures, hearsay evidence and bad character and responses thereto. The standard directions form can be accessed at: http://www.justice.gov.uk/courts/procedure-rules/criminal/forms/formspage (Part 3: Case Management-Magistrates' Court Directions for Case Sent to the Crown Court).

13.2.1 SENDING 'RELATED' OFFENCES TO THE CROWN COURT FOR TRIAL

Section 51(3) CDA 1998 provides that where an adult defendant is sent for trial under s. 51 in connection with an indictable-only offence, the magistrates' court must also send any related either-way offence for which the defendant appears at the same time. An either-way offence is 'related' where it can be joined in the same indictment because it is founded on the same facts or forms part of a series of offences of the same or similar character (s. 51E CDA 1998). The magistrates' court must also send any related summary offence for which the defendant appears at the same time (s. 51(3)(b) CDA 1998). A related summary offence must arise out of circumstances which are the same as or connected with the indictable-only offence and be punishable with imprisonment or disqualification (s. 51(11) CDA 1998).

Consider the following examples of how linked summary or either-way offences may also be sent to the Crown Court for trial.

 Example 1

Sanjeev is charged with grievous bodily harm with intent, contrary to s. 18 Offences Against the Person Act 1861 (an indictable-only offence). He also faces an allegation of affray, contrary to s. 3 Public Order Act 1986 (either-way offence). Both incidents arise out of a brawl in the centre of town involving football supporters from rival clubs. The either-way offence is founded on the same facts as the indictable-only offence (s. 51E) and must therefore be sent to the Crown Court along with the indictable-only offence under s. 51(3)(a) CDA 1998.

 Example 2

Denis is charged with driving while disqualified (a summary-only offence). In the course of the investigation into the offence he gives false particulars to the police leading to the arrest of someone other than himself. He is therefore charged with perverting the course of justice (an indictable-only offence). As the summary-only offence arises out of circumstances connected with the indictable-only offence and is punishable with imprisonment, both offences must be sent for trial to the Crown Court under s. 51(3)(b) CDA 1998.

Where a defendant appears before a magistrates' court on a separate occasion charged with a related either-way or summary offence, the magistrates have discretion to send the matter(s) up to the Crown Court so that they may be joined with the indictable-only matter(s) (s. 51(4) CDA 1998).

13.2.2 SENDING A LINKED CO-DEFENDANT TO THE CROWN COURT

 Example 3

What is the position where a co-accused is charged with an either-way offence which is related to the indictable-only offence? To take the example of Sanjeev, assume that Tom is also charged with affray arising out of the brawl. In these circumstances, s. 51(5) CDA 1998 requires the magistrates' court to send Tom's case to the Crown Court along with Sanjeev's indictable-only offence if Tom appears at the same time as Sanjeev. Co-defendants facing an either-way offence which is related to an indictable-only offence therefore have no right of election in these circumstances. If Tom, who is charged with affray, appears in court after Sanjeev's initial appearance, the magistrates would have discretion to send Tom's either-way offence to the Crown Court.

13.2.3 SENDING YOUNG OFFENDERS TO THE CROWN COURT

Where a young offender, aged under 18, is jointly charged with an indictable-only offence, s. 51(7) CDA 1998 provides that the magistrates' court shall send the young person for trial in the Crown Court along with the adult if it is in the interests of justice. If this power is exercised, the magistrates can also send any 'related' either-way or summary matter which the young person faces. (For an explanation of the interests of justice test and for full consideration of the young person in the criminal justice system, see Chapters 24, 25 and 26.)

13.3 PRELIMINARY HEARING BEFORE THE CROWN COURT

The principal purpose of the preliminary hearing is to enable the judge to draw up a timetable for the service of prosecution evidence and a defence statement.

In a recent judicially led initiative, Crown Courts have been directed to introduce early guilty plea schemes, the intention being that where a defendant intends to plead guilty at the Crown Court, his case should be dealt with at the earliest possible time (that being the preliminary hearing) and attract the full sentencing discount available for a timely guilty plea (see Chapter 21, para. 21.13). A defendant who intends to plead guilty at the preliminary hearing will be arraigned (see Chapter 14, para . 14.7) and subjected to an early guilty plea hearing. If the case is suitable for a fast delivery report by the Probation Service (see Chapter 21, para. 21.16.1) it will be sentenced on the day. If a full pre-sentence report is required, the matter will be adjourned for preparation and the case will be listed for sentence no less than three weeks thereafter.

Where it is clear that the defendant will not enter a guilty plea at the preliminary hearing the judge will set a date for a Plea and Case Management Hearing (PCMH). A substantial amount of work will be undertaken by both the prosecution and the defence to prepare for the PCMH (see below).

13.3.1 CROWN COURT BAIL

As the preliminary appearance before the Crown Court will most likely end in an adjournment, the question of the defendant's bail may arise again. The defendant can make two contested bail applications, after which Part IIA Sch. 1 Bail Act 1976 applies (see Chapter 10, para. 10.15). Under this provision a court need not hear argument on the question of bail unless there has been a change in circumstances. The defendant may already have made an unsuccessful bail application at a previous appearance before the magistrates' court. A second application is permitted before the Crown Court. If this is unsuccessful and the defendant is remanded in custody, the trial judge and the prosecution should be aware of the custody time limits when setting the timetable for the PCMH (see Chapter 10).

13.4 PREPARATORY STEPS IN THE EARLY STAGES OF AN INDICTABLE-ONLY OFFENCE

The preparatory work undertaken in the early stages of all criminal cases, including indictable cases, are considered in Chapter 9. The early stages of an indictable-only matter will require the defence lawyer to:

- interview her client;
- prepare a proof of evidence based on the initial interview;
- contact the CPS to:
  - obtain advance information;
  - request a copy of her client's criminal record;
  - obtain a record of any police interviews with her client;
  - obtain a copy of her client's custody record;
- interview potential defence witnesses;
- visit the crime scene if thought to be helpful;
- instruct an expert witnesses if necessary.

For an illustration of these steps please refer to the *R v Lenny Wise* case study in our Online Resource Centre.

13.5 DISCLOSING 'USED' MATERIAL AT TRIALS ON INDICTMENT

In indictable-only cases, the defence lawyer will not usually be in a position to advise her client on plea until the prosecution has made a full disclosure of the case against him. The standard directions which apply to a case sent for trial by a magistrates' court under s. 51 CDA 1998, require the service of prosecution case papers ('case sent bundle') to be made within 50 days where the defendant is in custody and within 70 days in other cases.

The 'case sent bundle' will include:

- the draft indictment;
- all 'used' material including witness statements (primary prosecution disclosure);
- list of exhibits;
- the schedule of unused material; and
- initial prosecution disclosure in accordance with s. 3 Criminal Procedure and Investigations Act 1996 (CPIA 1996).

See the *R v Lenny Wise* case study in our Online Resource Centre which includes a sent bundle and Chapter 11.

Once the prosecution has served the 'case sent bundle', an important part of the defence solicitor's case preparation will be to carefully scrutinise the prosecution witness statements and other evidence to assess the strength of the case against her client. This assessment will be very important when advising a client whether to plead guilty or not guilty.

13.6 DISCLOSING 'UNUSED' MATERIAL—CPIA 1996

In addition to the prosecution's obligation to disclose evidence it intends to rely on at trial, the CPIA 1996 requires the prosecution to disclose the evidence which it will not use at trial. This is known as 'unused' material. The prosecution's obligation to serve 'used' and 'unused' material is explained in detail in Chapter 8. For the purpose of this chapter we briefly remind you of the key provisions. You may find it helpful to review the flowchart on disclosure which can be found at the end of Chapter 8 (Figure 8.3).

13.6.1 INITIAL PROSECUTION DISCLOSURE OF UNUSED MATERIAL IN CROWN COURT TRIALS

Section 3 CPIA 1996 requires the prosecution to provide the defendant with initial disclosure defined as any evidence not previously disclosed, which might reasonably be considered capable of undermining the case for the prosecution or of assisting the case for the accused.

13.6.2 INITIAL DISCLOSURE TIME LIMITS

Practice differs between CPS areas. In some areas the CPS will comply with its obligations under s. 3 CPIA 1996 when it serves the 'case sent bundle' in an indictable-only offence or in an either-way offence to be tried on indictment. In other areas, s. 3 CPIA 1996 disclosure is made in accordance with standard directions upon the sending of the case or as directed by the trial judge at the preliminary case management hearing before the Crown Court.

13.6.3 DEFENCE DISCLOSURE OBLIGATIONS UNDER THE CPIA 1996

After initial disclosure, s. 5 CPIA 1996 requires that a defence statement should be served on the court and the CPS. The defence statement must be served within 28 days of initial disclosure. A defence statement is mandatory in cases to be tried on indictment. Failure to serve the defence statement can lead to adverse comment and inferences being drawn by the court under s. 11 CPIA 1996. The importance of correctly drafting a defence statement cannot be overstated and is considered here.

Section 5 CPIA 1996 allows defence statements to be served on a co-accused on the application of any party or by the court of its own motion.

13.6.4 THE TIME LIMIT TO SERVE THE DEFENCE STATEMENT

The accused has 28 days to file a defence statement under s. 5 CPIA 1996 for trials on indictment. Time runs from the date on which the prosecution complies or purports to comply with its initial disclosure obligations under s. 3 CPIA 1996. The inclusion of the words 'purporting to comply' is worth highlighting. It implies partial disclosure is enough to trigger the defence disclosure obligation under s. 5. The defence can apply to the court for an extension of the time limit before it expires.

13.6.5 WHAT MUST A DEFENCE STATEMENT CONTAIN?

Section 6A CPIA 1996 requires that a defence statement must be in writing and must:

* set out the nature of the accused's defence including any particular defences on which he intends to rely;
* indicate the matters of fact on which the accused takes issue with the prosecution;
* set out, in the case of each matter, why the accused takes issue with the prosecution case;
* set out the particular facts on which the accused intends to rely for his defence; and
* indicate any point of law (including any point as to the admissibility of evidence) which the accused wishes to take, and any authority on which he intends to rely for that purpose.

A defence statement that discloses an alibi must give particulars including the witness's name, address and date of birth or as many of these details that are known to the accused when the statement is given, including any information in the accused's possession which might be of material assistance in identifying or finding the alibi witness. There is a continuing duty on the accused to provide this information if it comes to light after service of the defence statement.

Progessive reforms now mean that defence statements must be much more detailed than was previously required. This level of detail no doubt causes considerable practical difficulties for defence solicitors who may sometimes struggle to obtain clear instructions from a client within a very tight time frame. In addition to the specific requirements under s. 6A CPIA 1996, further disclosure requirements under s. 6C (highlighted at para. 13.6.13) came into force on the 1 May 2010.

13.6.6 DRAFTING A DEFENCE STATEMENT TO AVOID AN ADVERSE INFERENCE BEING DRAWN

Section 11 CPIA 1996 states that where the accused:

* fails to serve a defence statement (where this is compulsory);
* fails to serve a defence statement within the time limit;
* sets out inconsistent defences in the defence statement;
* puts forward at his trial a different defence than that set out in the defence statement;
* adduces evidence in support of alibi without having given the necessary particulars of the alibi

the court or any other party (with the court's leave) may make such comment as appears appropriate and the court or jury may draw such inferences as appear proper in determining the defendant's guilt in connection with the offence for which he is being tried.

In practical terms, s. 11 CPIA 1996 is very important. Whether a defence statement is compulsory (indictable cases) or voluntary (summary cases), careful drafting is needed to avoid comment and an adverse inference being drawn.

Section 11(5) gives a court discretion to decide whether comment is permitted and as a consequence whether an inference might be drawn. Importantly, under s. 11(10), a person cannot be convicted solely on an adverse inference drawn under s. 11 CPIA 1996.

In exercising discretion under s. 11(5) what must the court take into account? The defendant is entitled to put forward an explanation as to why an adverse inference should not be drawn. Section 11(8) specifically requires a court to have regard to the defendant's reasons where the defendant has set out inconsistent defences before making or permitting comment. The nature of the inference drawn will therefore depend on the type of omission under s. 11 CPIA 1996 and the reasons for it. It may be that an alternative defence is put forward at trial because of a change in the prosecution's case from that indicated in the service of the case sent papers. It must be assumed that in this situation no adverse comment would be made. In other circumstances, the probable effect of an adverse inference drawn under s. 11 CPIA 1996 will be to cast doubt on the accused's defence. The evidential effect is similar to an adverse inference drawn from a suspect's silence under the Criminal Justice and Public Order Act 1994, which was considered in Chapter 5, and for this reason it is compatible with Article 6 European Convention on Human Rights 1950 (*R v Essa* [2009] EWCA Crim 43).

13.6.7 DRAFTING A DEFENCE STATEMENT—TACTICAL CONSIDERATIONS

In the light of s. 11 CPIA 1996, great care should be taken when drafting a defence statement if an adverse inference is not to be drawn. The defence practitioner must avoid putting forward inconsistent defences so she always needs to ensure that her client's instructions will not change or the trial advocate will not adopt an alternative approach. Disclosing a client's defence has implications for legal professional privilege which should be discussed with the client. The client needs to be given comprehensive and accurate advice regarding his defence statement and its implications before he checks, signs and dates it.

A tactical judgement has to be made about how much information the defence statement should contain. The more detail, the easier it is to facilitate further disclosure and the less the risk of an adverse inference being drawn from non-disclosure. Conversely, a more detailed defence statement will assist the prosecution in identifying the potential lines of cross-examination that may be raised against prosecution witnesses at trial. It is doubtful, in the light of the changes brought about by the Criminal Justice Act 2003 (CJA 2003) requiring a greater degree of specificity, that simply stating 'self-defence', or 'no dishonest intent' or 'mistaken identity' would be sufficient to avoid an adverse inference under s. 11 (*R v Tibbs* [2001] 2 Cr App R 309).

Assistance is given to defence practitioners in the Attorney-General's Guidelines:

'A defence statement must comply with the requirements of section 6A of the Act. A comprehensive defence statement assists the participants in the trial to ensure that it is fair. The trial process is not well served if the defence make general and unspecified allegations and then seek far-reaching disclosure in the hope that material may turn up to make them good. The more detail a defence statement contains the more likely it is that the prosecutor will make an informed decision about whether any remaining undisclosed material might reasonably be considered capable of undermining the prosecution case or of assisting the case for the accused, or whether to advise the investigator to undertake further enquiries. It also helps in the management of the trial by narrowing down and focusing on the issues in dispute. It may result in the prosecution discontinuing the case. Defence practitioners should be aware of these considerations when advising their clients. Whenever a defence solicitor provides a defence statement on behalf of the accused it will be deemed to be given with the authority of the solicitor's client (s. 6E CPIA 1996).'

An important decision on whether a defence statement is compulsory in cases to be tried on indictment is *GR* [2010] EWCA Crim 1928 in which the Court of Appeal stated that defence advocates should never advise a client not to serve a defence statement and should always explain to a client what the statutory obligation is and what the consequences will be if a defence statement is not served or if something is omitted from the statement. Where the defence case is simply to put the prosecution to proof, a defence statement must still be served, stating the defendant does not admit the offence, putting the prosecution to strict proof and that the defendant will not be advancing a positive case at trial.

13.6.8 **PROSECUTOR'S CONTINUING DUTY TO KEEP DISCLOSURE UNDER REVIEW**

Section 7A CPIA 1996 (as amended by the CJA 2003) provides that after the prosecutor has complied with initial disclosure under s. 3 CPIA 1996 and before the accused is acquitted or convicted or the prosecutor decides not to proceed with the case (particularly following service of the defence statement), the prosecutor must keep under review whether there is any further prosecution material that might reasonably be considered capable of undermining the prosecution case against the accused or of assisting the defence case. Following the service of a defence statement, if the prosecution concludes there is no further evidence to disclose, this should be communicated to the defendant.

13.6.9 **APPLYING FOR FURTHER DISCLOSURE**

Under s. 8 CPIA 1996 the accused can apply to the court for further disclosure if he has grounds to believe there may be material which satisfies the objective test for disclosure provided he has filed a defence statement in accordance with the requirements of s. 5 or s. 6 of the Act. The defendant must prove to the court that he reasonably believes there is prosecution material which may assist his defence. The defendant must have settled grounds for the application and may not use s. 8 CPIA 1996 as a 'fishing expedition'.

13.6.10 **DISCLOSURE AND PRACTICAL CONSIDERATIONS**

Both the prosecution and the defence should be aware of disclosure issues at all stages in the prosecution of an indictable offence. The defence must always pursue legitimate requests for disclosure. A failure by the prosecution to disclose material within the definition of initial disclosure will give grounds for an appeal against conviction based on a material irregularity at trial—although there is no guarantee the conviction will be quashed (*R v Craven* [2001] 2 Cr App R 181). The prosecutor will be keen to scrutinise the defence statement for any deficiencies.

The practical aspects of disclosure under the CPIA 1996 are considered further in the context of our case study, *R v Lenny Wise*. The scenario includes illustrations of used and unused material and an example of a defence statement. The full documentation supporting this case study can be found on the Online Resource Centre.

online resource centre

13.6.11 **LOOKING AHEAD**

 Looking Ahead

There are a number of significant reforms relating to defence disclosure contained in the CJA 2003 which will amend s. 6 CPIA to include ss. 6A, 6B, 6C, 6D and 6E.

13.6.12 **SERVING AN UPDATED DEFENCE STATEMENT (NOT YET IN FORCE)**

There will be a requirement on the accused to serve an updated defence statement nearer the start of the trial (s. 6B CPIA 1996, inserted by s. 33 CJA 2003). Alternatively, the defendant may provide a witness statement stating that he has made no changes to the defence statement that has been served.

13.6.13 **NOTIFYING THE PROSECUTION OF INTENDED WITNESSES (IN FORCE)**

Section 34 CJA inserts s. 6C into the CPIA 1996 and requires a defendant to indicate whether he intends to call any witnesses. This statutory requirement is in addition to the requirement to file a defence statement (which of course is mandatory for a case to be tried on indictment) and it applies to both Crown Court and magistrates' court proceedings.

What are the specific requirements under s. 6C CPIA 1996?

The defence witness notification must:

(a) give the name, address and date of birth of each proposed witness, or as many of those details as are known to the accused when the notice is given;

(b) provide any information in the accused's possession which might be of material assistance in identifying or finding any such proposed witness in whose case any of the details mentioned in paragraph (a) are not known to the accused when the notice is given.

What is the time limit for compliance?

It is the same time limit as for the service of a defence statement (i.e. 28 days for a Crown Court case and 14 days for a case that is to be tried summarily). Time starts to run from when the prosecutor complies or purports to comply with her duty to serve initial disclosure (see Chapter 13, para. 13.6.1).

What are the consequences of failing to comply with s. 6C CPIA 1996?

If the accused serves his s. 6C CPIA 1996 notice late, or at his trial calls a witness (other than himself) not included, or not adequately identified, in the witness notice, an adverse inference under s. 11 CPIA 1996 may be drawn by the magistrates or jury.

If things change, must an amended notice be served?

Yes. Section 6C(4) CPIA 1996 imposes a duty to serve an amended notice when:

• the defence decides not to call a witness, or

• the defence decides to call other witnesses, or

• the discovery of further information that may enable the identifying or finding any proposed witness.

In response to this new obligation, the Law Society has issued a Practice Note which all defence lawyers should read: http://www.lawsociety.org.uk/productsandservices/practicenotes/defwitnessnotice.page.

The rationale behind s. 6C CPIA 1996 is that it enables the police to run checks on the character of a proposed defence witness in advance of trial and, if considered appropriate, enables the police to interview the witness, which is somewhat controversial. A Code of Practice governing the conduct of such an interview also came into force on 1 May 2010 (http://www.opsi.gov.uk/acts/acts1996/related/ukpgacop_19960025_en.pdf). The Code requires the police to:

• ask the witness whether she/he is prepared to consent to be interviewed;

• inform the witness that she/he is not obliged to attend the interview and that he/she is entitled to be accompanied by a solicitor (though this will not be publicly funded); and

• ask whether the witness consents to a solicitor attending the interview on behalf of an accused as an observer.

The Code requires the police to inform the accused or his legal representative that an interview has been requested and to indicate whether the witness has consented to be interviewed in the presence of a solicitor attending on behalf of the accused as an observer. The police must notify the accused of the date, time and place of the interview. The interview must be recorded and a copy must be served on the accused.

13.6.14 NOTIFICATION OF THE DECISION TO INSTRUCT AN EXPERT WITNESS (NOT YET IN FORCE)

Section 6D has also been added to the CPIA 1996 and provides that if an accused instructs an expert witness with a view to providing opinion evidence at trial, the accused must give to the court and the prosecutor a notice specifying the person's name and address unless included in the defence statement. Curiously, no sanctions are prescribed for non-compliance with this provision.

13.7 WHAT IF THE PRE-TRIAL DISCLOSURE OF EVIDENCE REVEALS A WEAK PROSECUTION CASE?

Where the 'case sent bundle' indicates a weak prosecution case, the defence may apply to the Crown Court to dismiss the charge(s).

13.7.1 MAKING AN APPLICATION TO DISMISS THE CHARGE

Under Sch. 3 CDA 1998, the defence may make an oral or a written application to the Crown Court to dismiss the charge(s) against the defendant. In most cases, the application will be decided on the basis of written submissions unless the defendant requests that oral evidence should be heard and the judge considers that it is in the interests of justice that oral evidence should be heard. In this situation, prosecution witnesses may be required to attend the hearing and be cross-examined. (The option to call oral evidence is prospectively repealed by Sch. 3 CJA 2003.) The defence may also seek to have disputed evidence excluded under s. 76 or s. 78 PACE 1984 (see Chapter 6). The detailed rules relating to an application to dismiss charges to be tried in the Crown Court are contained in Crim PR, Part 13. On hearing the representations from each side, the judge will dismiss the charge(s) where there is insufficient evidence for a jury to properly convict the accused. Where the application to dismiss is unsuccessful, the date will be confirmed for the PCMH. Reporting restrictions will apply at a hearing to dismiss although a defendant can apply to have reporting restrictions lifted (Sch. 3, para. 3 CDA 1998).

13.7.2 WHAT HAPPENS TO ANY RELATED CHARGES IF THE INDICTABLE-ONLY OFFENCE IS DISMISSED LEAVING ONLY AN EITHER-WAY OR SUMMARY OFFENCE?

The procedure under Sch. 3, paras. 7 to 15 to the CDA 1998 requires the Crown Court to conduct the plea before venue procedure in relation to an either-way offence. If the defendant indicates a not guilty plea or makes no indication at all, the allocation hearing must be conducted. If it is decided to deal with the either-way offence summarily, the case will be remitted to the magistrates' court. A summary-only offence would also be remitted to the magistrates where the linked indictable offence has been dismissed.

13.8 PRE-TRIAL HEARINGS IN THE CROWN COURT

Before the case proceeds to trial, both the prosecution and the defence will be required to attend one or more pre-trial hearings. Pre-trial hearings are designed to prevent ineffective trials. They enable the trial judge to fulfil the obligation under Crim PR, Part 3 to actively manage the case. The trial judge can make directions at the hearing, hear argument and give a binding ruling on a matter relating to the trial.

13.8.1 PLEA AND CASE MANAGEMENT HEARING—SS. 39–43 CPIA 1996

All cases to be tried on indictment will have a Plea and Case Management Hearing (PCMH).

The main purpose of the PCMH is to arraign the accused, i.e. to receive his plea or pleas to the count or counts contained in the indictment. The PCMH then proceeds on the basis of whether the defendant pleads guilty or not guilty.

13.8.2 PLEADING NOT GUILTY AT THE PCMH

Where the defendant pleads not guilty to some or all of the counts in the indictment necessitating a trial, the PCMH ensures that any steps necessary for trial will be taken and that the court is provided with sufficient information to fix a trial date. This process is facilitated by the advocates completing a detailed PCMH questionnaire (see Crim PR Forms—Part 3 Form—Plea and Case Management Hearing Form: http://www.justice.gov.uk/courts/procedure-rules/criminal/formspage). The issues the judge will require details of include:

- the number of witnesses who will give oral evidence;
- the number of witnesses whose evidence can be agreed and read to the jury;
- any facts formally admitted under s. 10 CJA 1967;
- any exhibits or schedules;
- any expert evidence to be relied on;
- any disputed points of law or evidential issues that will be put before the court together with the authorities relied upon;
- details of any alibi evidence which has been disclosed to the prosecution;
- the estimated length of the trial; and
- the dates on which the witnesses and the advocates are available.

The PCMH questionnaire covers many of the aspects of case management covered by Crim PR, Part 3.10 and the parties are expected to comply with all directions made as part of the PCMH. One very important step that the defence solicitor is required to take is to provide the CPS with a full list of all the prosecution witnesses the defence requires to attend trial. The standard 'case sent' directions stipulate this should be done within seven days of receiving disclosure of the prosecution's case as this gives the police the chance to check witness availability in advance of the PCMH. At the conclusion of the PCMH, the judge will normally fix the date for trial or direct that it will be placed in the 'warned list' at some point in the near future. The listing of the case for trial needs to take account of custody time limits where the defendant has been remanded in custody throughout the proceedings. Complex cases may need to be listed for a further pre-trial hearing.

13.8.3 PLEADING GUILTY AT THE PCMH

If it is the defendant's intention to plead guilty at the PCMH to some or all of the counts on the indictment, the defence should notify the court and the prosecution as soon as possible and not less than 14 days before the hearing. Notification enables the court to order a pre-sentence report in time for the PCMH. Where the defendant pleads guilty at the PCMH, the judge may proceed to sentence or adjourn the sentencing hearing for the preparation of a pre-sentence report. Advance notification of an intention to plead guilty may not be possible. The decision to enter a guilty plea or pleas may be the subject of ongoing negotiation between the prosecution and the defence. If the defendant offers to plead guilty to some counts but not others or offers to plead guilty to a less serious alternative offence, it will be for the prosecution to decide whether the plea or pleas are acceptable. The defendant may wish to seek a *Goodyear* direction from the trial judge before deciding whether to plead guilty. All of these possibilities may be canvassed before the PCMH or on the first day of trial (see further Chapter 14, paras. 14.6 and 14.7).

13.8.4 **PREPARATORY HEARINGS**

A preparatory hearing (see ss. 28–38 CPIA 1996 and Crim PR, Part 15) is appropriate for long and complex cases to be heard in the Crown Court. The judge decides whether there should be a preparatory hearing following an application by either party or by the court's own motion. In practice, the decision whether to hold a preparatory hearing is likely to be made at the PCMH.

Where a preparatory hearing is held, it takes place before the jury is sworn, and may clarify any difficult or contentious issue which will assist the jury's understanding of any matter in the case, identify issues which are likely to be material to the jury's verdict and expedite the proceedings or assist the judge's management of the trial. The preparatory hearing is part of the trial process.

13.8.5 **PRE-TRIAL RULINGS**

Sections 31–39 CPIA 1996 provides that a judge may make a binding ruling at any pre-trial hearing (including the PCMH) on matters relating to the admissibility of evidence and/or a question of law. Where a disputed point of law arises between the parties, the judge may well direct each party to serve skeleton arguments on the matter in dispute within prescribed time limits prior to giving a ruling on the matter.

Where a pre-trial ruling has been made, it may only be varied or discharged where it is in the 'interests of justice'. An application to vary a binding ruling will not be heard unless there has been a 'material change of circumstances' since the making of the original ruling. The CPIA 1996 provides a right of appeal to the Court of Appeal against a pre-trial ruling.

Matters of law and evidence likely to be determined at a pre-trial hearing could include:

* determining the competency of a witness;
* ruling on a special measures direction for a vulnerable or intimidated witness (see Chapter 16);
* deciding whether to hold a joint trial for two or more accused or whether to sever an indictment in a case where an accused faces more than one charge;
* resolving disputes as to the admissibility of hearsay evidence (see Chapter 18) or bad character evidence (see Chapter 19);
* determining a public interest immunity (PII) application to withhold evidence (see Chapter 8);
* making a ruling as to the admissibility of disputed confession evidence or evidence of identification (see Chapter 6).

The benefit of these rulings is that they should enable the trial to proceed on the day. An unfavourable pre-trial ruling may also influence an accused to change his plea to guilty. A judge is not obliged to give a pre-trial ruling on a disputed point of law in advance of trial and in some instances will wait until the prosecution has opened its case.

13.9 **PREPARING FOR TRIAL**

Much of the prosecution and defence lawyer's time when preparing for trial will be in connection with the PCMH. Typical preparatory matters are considered here.

13.9.1 **WITNESSES**

Both the defence and the prosecution must ensure the attendance of its witnesses at trial. Where it appears that a witness will not attend voluntarily, an application to summons the witness's attendance can be made under ss. 2–4 Criminal Procedure (Attendance of Witnesses) Act 1965. The rules relating to the issue of a witness summons are contained in Crim PR, Part 28.

13.9.2 **BRIEFING THE TRIAL ADVOCATE**

The defendant will need to be represented at the PCMH by a barrister or a solicitor-advocate. The CPS will also need to instruct a prosecuting advocate unless an in-house higher rights advocate is to appear. The trial advocates must be formally instructed or 'briefed'. The task of briefing counsel or a solicitor-advocate is commonly given to a trainee solicitor/paralegal or CPS caseworker. A properly drafted brief is a disciplined exercise requiring you to organise the materials in a file and to think very carefully about the issues in the case.

When to brief

The date set for the PCMH will dictate the time by which the brief should be delivered.

If the defence solicitor requires assistance in completing the defence statement, counsel should be instructed at an even earlier stage. It will obviously be easier to organise a conference with counsel in advance of the PCMH if the brief is sent in plenty of time.

It is preferable that the advocate who represents the defendant at the PCMH will also represent the defendant at trial. The CPS will instruct in-house barristers or solicitor-advocates or will use independent counsel based on their seniority. For the defence, unless a firm employs a solicitor-advocate with higher rights of audience, the instructing lawyer will have a preferred choice of barrister. All barristers' services are engaged through the clerk at the barrister's chambers. All the papers in the case and the instructions will be sent to the barrister in a brief to counsel.

What should a brief contain?

Whilst there is an etiquette to briefing the advocate, the precise practice may vary from firm to firm and your firm may have a preferred style. The brief we have drafted in conjunction with the *R v Lenny Wise* case study (see Appendix 1, Document 39) is written in the third person.

The brief should contain a back sheet with details of the case, the date and type of hearing, with the instructing solicitor's details on the right-hand side of the page. The left-hand side of the back page is left blank to enable counsel to handwrite endorsements onto it. If the case is legally aided, the back page of the brief should make this clear.

Where appropriate the brief may cover the advocate's representation at both the PCMH and at trial. In other cases separate briefs will be sent.

The front page of the brief should contain the case heading and a numbered list of enclosures. The list of enclosures depends entirely on the particular case you are dealing with, but would typically include:

- defendant's proof of evidence;
- draft indictment;
- case sent bundle;
- relevant correspondence with CPS;
- expert report(s).

The brief should begin with an introduction which deals with the defendant's personal details, the charge(s), the history of the case and any bail arrangements.

The brief should provide an analysis of the prosecution case by cross-referencing to the prosecution witness statements and other evidence that has been disclosed under the pre-trial disclosure rules and which will be included with the brief as enclosures. Any strengths or weaknesses in the prosecution case should be identified, as should the admissibility of items of prosecution evidence which may be challenged at trial.

The brief should also contain a summary of the defence case and identify any strengths or weaknesses.

The advocate should also be clearly directed on what advice is sought. This might relate to witness requirements, points of evidence, advice on plea or assistance with drafting a defence statement. The advocate's attention should also be directed to the factors that might be raised in mitigation in the event of your client being convicted.

Commonly, the brief will ask whether the advocate believes a conference with instructing solicitors will assist in the case preparation.

The brief will be sent to the advocate who should respond within the return date. At this stage, the solicitor needs to be mindful of key dates, particularly in relation to serving a defence statement, notifying the CPS which prosecution witnesses are required to attend trial to be cross-examined and responding to notices to admit bad character or hearsay. The advocate may send written advice in advance of the PCMH. It is important that the advocate's advice is followed up. This may involve further interviews with the defendant or witnesses or further correspondence with the CPS. If the barrister suggests a conference is needed, this must be organised by the instructing solicitor. This involves contacting counsel's clerk for available dates as well as contacting the defendant. The conference usually takes place at counsel's chambers.

KEY POINT SUMMARY

- Understand that all indictable-only offences must be sent to the Crown Court along with related (either-way/summary) offences in accordance with s. 51 CDA 1998 following an initial appearance before a magistrates' court.
- Trials on indictment cover not just indictable-only offences but either-way offences which have been sent for trial by a magistrates' court.
- Be aware of the rules dealing with the pre-trial disclosure of evidence by both the prosecution and the service of a defence statement under the CPIA 1996.
- The submission of a defence statement is mandatory in a case tried on indictment.
- Great care needs to be taken when drafting a defence statement in order to avoid an adverse inference from being drawn under s.11 CPIA 1996.
- Currently, the disclosure obligations on the defence are limited compared to those on the prosecution but will become more onerous under the CJA 2003 when all the relevant provisions are fully implemented.
- Know the conventions about instructing counsel.
- Understand the purpose of the PCMH and the procedures where the defendant pleads guilty or not guilty at the arraignment.

SELF-TEST QUESTIONS

1. What is the purpose of the initial hearing in the magistrates' court where the defendant is charged with an indictable-only offence?
2. What obligation does the prosecution have in relation to the pre-trial disclosure of evidence in an indictable-only offence?
3. Explain the procedure at the application to dismiss the charge in the Crown Court.
4. Explain the purpose of the PCMH.
5. In which type of case will it normally be appropriate to hold a preparatory hearing?
6. Consider once more Question 2 at the end of Chapter 8.

Case study: *R v Lenny Wise*

You will recall that Lenny Wise has been sent to stand trial on the burglary allegation and a date has been set for his Plea and Case Management Hearing before Lyme Crown Court. Initial prosecution disclosure of unused material, in compliance with s. 3 CPIA 1996, is made (see Document 27). Before you look at the defence statement in relation to Lenny Wise you may wish to attempt a draft of your own. The defence statement submitted in this case is at Document 32. Further disclosure, in compliance with the CPS's duties under s. 7A CPIA 1996, are made in Documents 34, 35 and 36. Subject to the prosecution's duty to keep disclosure under review, the pre-trial disclosure of evidence in relation to *R v Lenny*

Wise is complete. You will see that Lenny's solicitor has obtained a psychiatric report from Lenny's consultant, see Document 37. The requirement under Crim PR, Part 24 for the disclosure of expert reports to be adduced in court has been complied with.

You now have all the necessary information to undertake a brief to counsel. Our suggested brief to counsel in this case is included at Document 39.

You will see on Lenny Wise's file an account of his PCMH before Lyme Crown Court (Document 41). In correspondence between Lenny's solicitors and the CPS leading up to the PCMH (see Document 31), the defence suggests a further pre-trial hearing will be needed to address the issues surrounding the admissibility of Lenny's confession and the admissibility of Lenny's record of past criminal convictions. At the PCMH, counsel for the CPS concede that Lenny Wise's confession has been obtained in breach of PACE and Code C and that the CPS will not be relying on it. The matter is then listed for trial. A further, very short brief to counsel to represent Lenny Wise at trial is subsequently sent (see Document 44).

FIGURE 13.1 THE PROSECUTION OF INDICTABLE-ONLY OFFENCES AND TRIAL ON INDICTMENT

Defendant will make initial appearance before magistrates' court; matters relating to bail will be determined; advance information ought to be available.

Defendant's case is sent to the Crown Court under s. 51 CDA 1998 together with any related either-way offence or related summary offence if punishable with imprisonment or disqualification.

Defendant will make his initial appearance before Crown Court judge where he can plead guilty if he chooses otherwise the judge will devise a timetable for the pre-trial disclosure of evidence and will set a date for a Plea and Case Management Hearing **(PCMH)**.

- Prosecution will serve case sent bundle comprising used and unused material, the latter in compliance with s. 3 CPIA 1996;
- defence will be required to serve a defence statement in compliance with ss. 5 and 6 CPIA 1996 plus a defence witness notification (s. 6C CPIA 1996);
- prosecution will serve any further unused material in accordance with s. 7A CPIA 1996;
- defence can apply to have charges dismissed for insufficient evidence;
- case may need to be listed for a pre-trial hearing.

- Defendant will be asked to plead at his **PCMH**;
- defence should brief trial advocate in sufficient time to ensure attendance at **PCMH** and to advise on plea;
- if plea is to be not guilty, defence must notify CPS as to which witnesses it wants to cross-examine so that availability can be checked before **PCMH**.

PCMH	**PCMH**
defendant pleads guilty; sentence will follow immediately unless pre-sentence is required.	defendant pleads not guilty; date will be set for Crown Court trial; defence and prosecution will prepare for trial.

14 TRIAL BEFORE THE CROWN COURT

14.1 **INTRODUCTION**

Where the defendant pleads not guilty when arraigned at the Plea and Case Management Hearing (PCMH), the judge will set the date for the trial in the Crown Court. This chapter considers the procedural and practical steps at a trial on indictment by examining the following:

- the rules dealing with the indictment;
- supporting counsel at trial;
- empanelling the jury;
- the presentation of the prosecution and defence cases;
- the judge's summing-up; and
- the jury's verdict.

14.2 **THE INDICTMENT**

Where the accused has been sent for trial in the Crown Court, the prosecution is required to draw up the indictment. The indictment is the formal document that contains the charge(s) the accused will plead to at trial, and is often included in the case sent bundle. Each charge on the indictment is known as a count, and the defendant will plead guilty or not guilty to each count at the PCMH or at trial.

The provisions that govern the drafting and use of indictments are principally to be found in Crim PR, Part 14 and the Indictments Act 1915 (IA 1915):

'(1) The heading should consist of the word "indictment", followed by the name of the place where the Crown Court is sitting and the name of the case.

(2) After the name of the case ("The Queen v John Smith and Adrian Green") should be written the presentment ("John Smith and Adrian Green are charged as follows:").

(3) It must include a paragraph headed "count".

(4) There must be a statement of the offence charged which:

- describes the offence in ordinary language, and
- identifies any legislation that creates it; and
- identifies particulars of the conduct constituting the commission of the offence as to make clear what the prosecutor alleges against the defendant.

(5) More than one incident relating to the commission of the offence may be included in a count if, by having regard to the time, place or purpose of those incidents taken together they amount to a single course of criminal conduct.

(6) An indictment may contain more than one count if all the offences charged are founded on the same facts; or form or are part of a series of offences of the same or similar character.

(7) If there is more than one count the counts are required to be numbered consecutively.

(8) An indictment may contain any count charging substantially the same offence as one specified in the notice of the offence or offences for which the defendant was sent for trial.

(9) Two or more accused persons may be charged in one count where the allegation is that they acted together to commit the offence.

(10) Two or more accused persons, not alleged to have acted together, may be charged in a single indictment (but in separate counts).

(11) The indictment must be signed by an appropriate officer of the Crown.'

The prosecution must draw up the indictment within prescribed time limits. The draft indictment should be served on an appropriate officer of the Crown Court within 28 days of the case being sent there. After being signed by a court officer, the draft indictment becomes the indictment on which the defendant is tried. An example of a draft indictment is featured in our Online Resource Centre in our case study *R v Lenny Wise* (see Appendix 1, case sent bundle).

While the detailed rules about drafting indictments are outside the scope of this *Handbook,* some important general principles are here explained.

14.2.1 WHAT COUNTS MAY BE INCLUDED ON THE INDICTMENT?

Subject to the rules on 'joinder' of offences, a draft indictment may include charges for any indictable offence disclosed by the evidence after it has been sent for trial under s. 51 CDA 1998.

In addition to indicting the accused for those offences for which he has been sent for trial, the indictment may also include counts for certain summary offences (see Chapter 13, para. 13.2.1).

An indictment may contain several counts but each count must allege only one offence. If the wording of the count shows that it is alleging two or more offences, the count is said to be 'bad for duplicity' and will be quashed. Should the judge wrongly reject a defence motion to have a duplicitous count quashed, the accused will have a good ground for appeal against conviction if found guilty.

The rules on 'joinder' determine what counts may be properly joined in the same indictment. Before the rules on 'joinder' of counts are briefly considered, when would a single count be bad for duplicity?

14.2.2 DUPLICITY

Each count in an indictment must allege only one offence. A single count alleging that Ian Brown stole razor blades belonging to Tesco on 13 July, and stole a DVD player from Asda on the 14 July would be bad for duplicity. It discloses two different offences allegedly committed on different days involving different victims. A count charging Ian with theft of razor blades and a DVD player from Tesco on 14 July would be perfectly valid. Although it might be said that two separate thefts have been committed, a degree of pragmatism is applied. Several criminal acts may be alleged in one count if they are so closely linked together as to form one activity or transaction (*DPP v Merriman* [1973] AC 584) or they 'amount to a course of conduct' within the meaning of Crim PR, Part 14 2 (2). For example, where a defendant is accused of stealing cash or property from the same victim on several unspecified occasions, it is permissible to state in a single count that D stole £2,500 from V on a day or days unknown during a period between May 2012 and July 2013.

14.2.3 JOINDER OF COUNTS IN AN INDICTMENT

Crim PR, Part 14.2(3) provides that charges may be joined in the same indictment where the offences are either:

• founded on the same facts; or

• form, or are part of, a series of offences of the same or a similar character.

In *R v Mansfield* [1977] 1 WLR 1102, M was charged in an indictment containing 10 counts. Three counts were for arson at various hotels over the course of a week. The remaining counts were for murder, based on the fact that seven people had died in one of the fires. The three arson counts formed part of a series of offences of the same or similar character and the seven murder counts were founded on the same facts as the arson counts and so were all properly joined in the indictment. In *R v Barrell and Wilson* (1979) 69 Cr App R 250, two appellants were charged with affray and assault occasioning actual bodily harm arising out of an argument outside a disco. One defendant subsequently attempted to bribe one of the victims and a further charge of attempting to pervert the course of justice was preferred. Defence counsel made an unsuccessful application to sever the count of attempting to pervert the course of justice from the counts alleging affray and assault occasioning actual bodily harm. The Court of Appeal indicated that the matters were essentially of the same factual origin and therefore could be validly included on the same indictment.

The meaning of the phrase 'offences which form, or are part of, a series of offences of the same or a similar character' (see Crim PR, Part 14.2(3)(b)) was given a wide interpretation by the House of Lords in *Ludlow v MPC* (1970) 54 Cr App R 233. For offences to be similar, there must be some nexus between them both in terms of law and fact. In *Ludlow*, L was charged in Count 1 with attempted theft and in Count 2 with robbery. There was therefore a similarity in law between the two offences. The attempted theft in Count 1 was alleged to have been committed in Acton (a London suburb) in a private part of a public house. The Count 2 offence was alleged to have been committed 16 days after the Count 1 offence and also at a public house in Acton. The House of Lords held there was a sufficient similarity to justify the 'joinder' of the counts in one indictment.

If the judge believes that the accused may be 'prejudiced or embarrassed in his defence' through a single trial of all the counts against him in an indictment, or for any other reason he considers that separate trials of at least some of the counts is desirable, he may make an order to that effect under s. 5(3) Indictment Act 1915 (IA 1915). This is commonly referred to as severing the indictment. Where the indictment is invalid, however, because it contains counts which are neither founded on the same facts nor form part of a series of the same or similar character, the invalidity cannot be cured by an application to sever the indictment see *R v Newland (MA)* [1988] QB 402.

The approach to be taken by a judge when being asked to consider an application to sever the indictment was explained by the House of Lords in *Ludlow v Metropolitan Police Commissioner* (see earlier). Prejudice or embarrassment might arise where there is a danger that the jury might wrongly take into account evidence in relation to one count and use it when deciding the defendant's guilt in relation to another count or where one of the counts raises particularly scandalous behaviour by the accused. In this situation any potential prejudice to the accused can be avoided by the judge giving the jury a clear direction to treat the counts and the evidence in support of each count separately.

14.2.4 JOINDER OF DEFENDANTS

An indictment can, of course, charge two or more defendants jointly either as principal offenders or as secondary parties and an indictment can charge defendants in separate counts but in the same indictment, providing there is a linking factor between the counts. The defendants might have been acting in concert, for example, but committing separate offences. In *R v Assim* [1966] 2 QB 249, two defendants were charged in a single indictment, one with unlawfully wounding X and the other with assaulting Y occasioning him actual bodily harm. They could not be charged in a single count because their respective acts of violence had separate victims. However, both assaults were perpetrated on the same night at the same nightclub where the two defendants were both employed.

For further guidance the classic exposition of 'joinder' of the defendants is to be found in Lord Diplock's judgment in *DPP v Merriman* [1973] AC 584.

All parties to a single offence may be jointly charged in a single count, but it remains open to the jury to acquit some defendants but convict others. Similarly, the trial judge has a discretionary power to order the separate trial of defendants jointly charged in a single count, although this should be exercised exceptionally as a single trial saves times and spares witnesses.

Consider the following example of the joinder of counts and defendants on a single indictment.

Example

Arif is charged with Count 1, affray. William is charged with wounding, Count 2. Both charges arise out of a disturbance when both defendants were refused entry to a nightclub.

All counts may be joined in the same indictment under Crim PR, Part 14.2(3), as they are founded on the same facts.

14.2.5 AMENDING THE INDICTMENT

The power to amend an indictment, once it has been served, is provided by s. 5 Indictment Act 1971, and may be exercised unless the judge considers that such amendment would cause 'injustice'. The power to amend may be exercised at any stage during the trial. Any defect can be remedied by amendment whether the defect is trivial or more fundamental. Amendment may also take the form of inserting new counts in the indictment either in substitution for or in addition to those originally drafted.

For detailed analysis of the rules on drafting indictments, see *Blackstone's Criminal Practice*.

14.3 SUPPORTING THE ADVOCATE AT TRIAL

Supporting the prosecution or defence counsel or a solicitor-advocate is a task that is commonly allocated to a trainee solicitor, paralegal or Crown Prosecution Service (CPS) caseworker. In defence firms and in the CPS, the staff member is often handed a file at short notice and told to act as a 'watching brief' in the Crown Court. This role requires the staff member to quickly assimilate the information contained in the file.

As a result of changes to the funding of criminal cases, a defence representative is only paid for attending the advocate at trial where the proceedings come within one of the following categories:

- very serious indictable offences;
- serious fraud cases;
- where the defendant is a child or a young person;
- where the defendant will not be able to follow the proceedings because of illness, disability or inadequate command of English; or
- on the day that the client is likely to be given a custodial sentence.

If the accused's case falls outside one of the above categories, a paralegal or trainee solicitor's attendance for the defence at the Crown Court may still be paid for where the judge issues a litigator certificate. A litigator certificate is likely to be issued where:

- there are a significant number of defence witnesses to be marshalled on any given day; or
- there are a significant number of defence documents; or
- the defence advocate is representing more than one accused; or
- the accused is likely to be disruptive if the advocate appeared alone; or
- the advocate will need notes taken for the proper conduct of the defence; or
- there are any other exceptional circumstances.

14.4 LAST-MINUTE CHECKLIST

In the period leading up to the trial date a member of the prosecution or the defence team should ensure, where appropriate, that:

- any matters arising out of counsel's written advice or raised in conference have been complied with;
- there are sufficient copies of the defence and prosecution documentation (trial bundles) for the judge and jury;
- from the prosecution perspective, there is an obligation to keep disclosure of evidence under review (see Chapters 8 and 13) and if further evidence is to be relied on at trial that has not previously been disclosed the prosecution must serve a notice of additional evidence on the defence complying with the requirements of s. 9 CJA 1967. If the defence do not object within seven days, the statement will be read to the court as evidence at the trial without calling the witness;
- the prosecution will also need to ensure that any exhibits have been properly packaged and are available;
- each witness has been warned to attend trial or summonsed if necessary; and
- any domestic arrangements for the witnesses have been made, for example, that hotel accommodation has been booked.

14.4.1 **WHICH WITNESSES MUST THE PROSECUTION CALL?**

As a matter of practice and as a general rule, the prosecution must ensure the attendance of all witnesses 'whose names are on the back of the indictment' (i.e. those witnesses whose statements have been served as part of the case sent bundle). The service of a witness statement is an indication that the prosecution will call that witness and will secure the attendance of the witness at trial even if the prosecutor now believes the evidence the witness will give may be unhelpful to the prosecution case.

It is unnecessary, however, for the prosecution to call a witness whose evidence is to be given as hearsay either under s. 9 CJA 1967 or s. 114 CJA 2003: see Chapter 18.

14.5 **FIRST DAY OF THE TRIAL**

On the first day of the trial you should arrive at court as early as possible. Ensure that you have all the relevant documentation and contact numbers for your barrister and witnesses in case of emergencies. Confirm with the court staff in which court the case is being heard. If you have any immediate concerns, the court usher is usually an invaluable source of information. When representing the accused, you will look out for the defendant and the defence witnesses. This is a time when you will need good interpersonnel skills to allay any of your side's apprehension. The prosecution witnesses will normally be met by Witness Support staff.

Contact your advocate and confirm that he has everything he needs. It is common immediately before the start of the trial to be given last-minute tasks such as:

- photocopying;
- providing witnesses with copies of their statements to enable them to refresh their memory before testifying;
- liaising with witnesses, as the advocate cannot talk directly to the witnesses who are to be called;
- if assisting the defence advocate, you may be asked to take a proof of evidence from a defence witness whose identity has just come to light or to take a further proof of evidence with a view to clarifying some aspect of a witness's evidence;
- familiarising the witnesses with the layout of the courtroom; and
- undertaking last minute legal research.

14.5.1 **CONFERENCE WITH THE ADVOCATE**

The defence advocate will wish to speak with the defendant. This may be the first time the defendant has met her advocate. You will be required to make the introductions and to keep a careful note of the matters covered in the conference.

The advocate may give advice that a client does not wish to hear—most commonly that she should consider pleading guilty to some or all of the charges. Negotiations between opposing trial advocates on plea bargaining is not uncommon on the first day of a trial.

14.6 **PLEA BARGAINING**

There is no formal system of plea bargaining in England and Wales, and it remains of central importance that a defendant has a genuine choice whether to plead guilty or not guilty. It is common for the prosecution and the defence to negotiate about the gravity of the charge and the defendant's plea. Where a guilty plea to a lesser alternative charge is acceptable to all sides, the prosecution will offer no evidence on the more serious charge or ask for the charge to lie on the court file. Where a defendant faces multiple counts and indicates guilty pleas to some of those counts which are acceptable to the prosecution, the remaining counts can either be withdrawn or allowed to lie on file.

A Crown Court judge cannot be party to any plea bargaining as a defendant's decision to plead guilty must be unfettered. In *R v Goodyear* [2005] 3 All ER 117, the Court of Appeal stated that a trial judge can, at the invitation of the defence, give a binding indication of the maximum sentence in the event of a guilty plea. Any indication of the maximum sentence must be on an agreed basis of plea and not on hypothetical facts or charges. The court went on to give guidance on the procedure to be adopted when giving an indication of sentence.

'(1) An indication should not be given unless requested by the defendant.

(2) The indication request should not be made unless the legal representative obtains signed authority from his client.

(3) The judge should refuse to consider the indication if he has not been provided with a written basis of plea.

(4) The hearing should be conducted in open court.

(5) The judge should not do anything that would constitute a 'plea bargain'.

(6) The judge has discretion without stating his reasons not to give an indication of sentence or can decide that he will give an indication at a later stage in the proceedings.

(7) Advance indication should be limited to the maximum sentence if a guilty plea was given at the time of the request.'

For full guidance on plea bargaining see the *Goodyear* judgment.

14.7 **ARRAIGNMENT AND PLEAS**

The trial formally begins with the defendant's arraignment. If the defendant has already been arraigned at the PCMH (which is the normal practice) and has pleaded not guilty, the count(s) in the indictment will simply be read out to the defendant again. Where a not guilty plea is maintained and a trial is to be held, the jury is empanelled. Only in exceptional circumstances will a defendant be arraigned at the start of the trial where, for example, he was not arraigned at the PCMH. A defendant would only be re-arraigned at the start of a trial if the indictment has been amended in a significant way or the defendant has decided to change his plea.

14.7.1 PLEADING GUILTY

A guilty plea entered by the accused must be unambiguous and voluntary. If a plea remains ambiguous, a not guilty plea must be entered instead. A voluntary plea must be of the accused's own free will and not the result of any external pressure. Such pressure, which will result in the quashing of a conviction, may come from either the judge or from counsel (*R v Turner* [1970] 2 QB 321 and *R v Barnes* (1970) 55 Cr App R 100). As outlined at para. 14.6, the defendant may choose to plead guilty having been given an indication as to the likely maximum sentence following a *Goodyear* direction. It is not uncommon for defendants to plead guilty to matters after being advised by counsel whom the defendant may be meeting for the first time either at the PCMH or on the day of trial.

Where the accused pleads guilty to a lesser alternative charge or only to some counts on a multiple count indictment, the decision to accept the plea, therefore avoiding the need for a trial, rests with the prosecution. If the plea is not acceptable to the prosecution, a jury is empanelled and evidence is then called in the normal way. If the defendant pleads guilty to a lesser offence (i.e. guilty to manslaughter but not guilty to murder) and the plea is accepted by the prosecution, the defendant stands acquitted of the offence charged and the court proceeds to sentence him for the lesser matter.

14.7.2 PROCEDURE FOLLOWING A GUILTY PLEA

If a defendant pleads guilty, a jury will not be empanelled and the court may sentence immediately or adjourn for the preparation of a pre-sentence report (see Chapters 20 and 21 for a full account of sentencing practice and procedure). If the accused pleads guilty to one count but will be tried on other counts, the judge will postpone sentence on the guilty plea until the outcome of his trial on the outstanding counts.

14.7.3 CHANGING A PLEA

An accused may change his plea from not guilty to guilty at any stage of the trial prior to the jury returning their verdict.

The judge has discretion to permit an accused to change a guilty plea to a plea of not guilty at any time until the court passes sentence. In practice, however, this discretion is used very sparingly (see *Revitt v DPP* [2006] 1 WLR 3172).

14.8 DURING THE TRIAL

In your supporting role in the Crown Court, you will sit behind the advocate taking a careful note of the proceedings and will be available to give any assistance. If the defendant wishes to communicate with her advocate, this often has to be done through the support staff. It is especially important to keep an accurate note of the answers given by the prosecution witnesses during cross-examination and by the defence witnesses during examination-in-chief, as the advocate is unlikely to make a written record of the witness's answers whilst asking questions. The same practices apply to the prosecution support staff, who are the point of contact between the advocate and the lead investigating police officer.

There may be times during the trial when the advocate has missed an important point or you have an idea that might be useful to your party's case. Write a legible note summarising the point and slide it forward to bring it to the advocate's attention. If a more serious issue arises, it may be necessary to hold a conference with the advocate at the end of the day or even at an adjournment during the main proceedings.

14.8.1 **EMPANELLING THE JURY**

The jury will be empanelled or selected from a jury in waiting of 20 or more people who have been summonsed for jury service at the Crown Court. The clerk of the court calls out the potential jurors' names from a recently shuffled pack of cards, each card bearing a juror's name. This fulfils the requirement under s. 11 Juries Act 1974 that jurors should be selected randomly.

Once 12 names have been selected, the individuals are called forward to take the jury oath. Before being sworn, each juror may be asked to 'stand by' by the prosecution or challenged 'for cause' by either the prosecution or the defence.

14.8.2 **ASKING A JUROR TO 'STAND BY'**

The prosecutor can ask a juror to 'stand by' as the juror is about to take the oath. Although the prosecutor does not have to give a reason to ask a juror to 'stand by', most commonly it is as the result of the jury panel being vetted by the police. The practice of asking a juror to 'stand by' has been severely curtailed by the Attorney-General's Guidelines on Exercise by the Crown Court of its Right of Stand-by (2012).

14.8.3 **CHALLENGE FOR CAUSE**

Both the prosecution and the defence may challenge a juror for cause (s. 12(3) Juries Act 1974). This is done orally immediately before the juror is sworn. The party making the challenge has the burden of proving that:

• the juror is not qualified to serve;
• the juror is biased; or
• the juror may reasonably be suspected of being biased.

14.8.4 **JUDICIAL CHALLENGES**

The judge has a residual power to remove a juror where, for example, the juror is illiterate or otherwise is deemed unsuitable or incapable of sitting as a juror. A juror may be discharged by the judge during the trial where, for example, the juror is ill or for 'any other good reason'.

14.8.5 **THE COMPOSITION OF THE JURY**

An empanelled jury should consist of 12 jurors, although cases are regularly heard with 11 or even 10 jurors.

14.8.6 **CAN THE DEFENDANT BE TRIED ON INDICTMENT IN HIS ABSENCE?**

As a general principle, an accused should be present throughout his trial. Attendance is secured by a remand into custody or release on bail (see Chapter 10). In exceptional circumstances the accused's presence in court may be dispensed with because of the accused's misbehaviour or through his voluntary absence or ill health. Where the accused fails to surrender to bail or escapes from custody, the judge has discretion to hold the trial in the accused's absence. See the guidance on this point from the Court of Appeal in *R v Hayward* [2001] 3 WLR 125 and by the House of Lords in *R v Jones (Anthony William)* [2003] 1 AC 1.

14.9 **THE PROSECUTION CASE**

After the jury has been empanelled, the formal part of the trial begins with the prosecution advocate making an opening speech. The presentation of evidence in a criminal trial is governed and shaped by rules of evidence which are explained in Chapters 4–7 and 15–20.

The opening speech by the prosecution is best understood in the context of the rules which determine the burden of proof, explained in Chapter 15.

It is no part of the prosecutor's role to win the case at all costs, and in *R v Gonez* [1999] All ER (D) 674, the Court of Appeal endorsed the prosecutor's role as a minister of justice.

14.9.1 THE OPENING SPEECH

The purpose of the opening speech is to outline the case in a simple, narrative form by explaining the alleged facts and the evidence the prosecution intends to rely on. The opening speech gives the advocate the opportunity to advance the prosecution's theory of the case.

In the opening speech, the prosecutor will:

* outline the facts;
* instruct the jury that it is the prosecution which brings the case and that the prosecution must prove the defendant's guilt;
* a brief explanation of the relevant points of law, whilst acknowledging that the judge is the sole arbiter on points of law;
* identify the witnesses to be called and provide an outline of what each witness is expected to tell the court.

Most disputes about the admissibility of evidence will have been dealt with at a pre-trial hearing and be the subject of a binding ruling by the trial judge. Where items of disputed evidence remain to be decided, the prosecutor must not refer to the disputed evidence during the opening speech. Any outstanding evidential issues will be decided in a *voir dire*, i.e. at a trial within the main trial conducted in the absence of the jury.

14.10 THE COURSE OF TRIAL—PRESENTING EVIDENCE

Having been sworn or affirmed, each prosecution witness gives evidence in the following order:

* examination-in-chief by the prosecution advocate;
* cross-examination by the defence advocate;
* re-examination (where appropriate) by the prosecution advocate.

Where the prosecution do not call a witness whose name appears on the back of the indictment (see para. 14.4.1), the prosecution has a duty to ensure that the witness is present at court for the trial so that the defence may call him if they wish. As an alternative to calling a witness and subjecting him to examination-in-chief, it is open to the prosecuting advocate to simply make the witness available for cross-examination. The advocate would, in these circumstances, call the witness, establish his name and address and then invite the defence to ask questions.

Evidence may also be presented by the prosecution in written form, through formal admissions and by adducing exhibits.

Questioning of witnesses through examination-in-chief or cross-examination must be conducted in accordance with the rules of evidence and in compliance with the advocate's professional conduct responsibilities (see Chapter 1 with specific reference to *Principle 1* and *Chapter 5* of the *Solicitors' Code of Conduct 2011*).

An effective examination of all witnesses requires the trial advocate to:

* always be in control of the witness;
* have clear objectives when examining the witness and an awareness of how those objectives can be achieved;
* know what the witness is going to say and how the witness is going to say it—the examination of a witness at trial is not about ascertaining the truth—it is about getting the witness to say something that supports the advocate's case. Whether in a summary trial or

a trial on indictment, pre-trial preparation based on the disclosure of evidence will have alerted the advocate to the questions that should be put to witnesses in examination-in-chief or in cross-examination.

It should not be forgotten that a witness may be giving evidence with the benefit of a special measures direction (see Chapter 16).

14.10.1 EXAMINATION-IN-CHIEF

The purpose of examination-in-chief is to obtain evidence in support of the party calling the witness. It must be conducted in accordance with the rules of evidence. The mechanics of conducting an examination-in-chief and the applicable rules of evidence are considered in Chapter 16, para. 16.8. We briefly illustrate the process of examination-in-chief in our case study of *R v Lenny Wise* with the inclusion of an extract from the examination of the eye-witness Shirley Lewis (see Document 45 on our Online Resource Centre).

14.10.2 CROSS-EXAMINATION

Cross-examination has a number of purposes, and provides the opportunity to:

* obtain helpful replies or concessions from a witness;
* expose errors, weaknesses or inconsistencies in the witness's account;
* undermine the witness's personal credibility—subject to the permissible limits allowed by the rules of evidence.

The rules relating to cross-examination are explained in Chapter 16 (paras. 16.9–16.12). Great importance is attached to cross-examination in the adversarial system of criminal justice. It may seem an obvious point, but witnesses are far from infallible. Witnesses may be biased. They may not come to court to tell the truth, the whole truth and nothing but the truth. Memory fades over time. The witness's actual perception of the event may not have been made in ideal circumstances. All of these fallibilities can be exposed and explored in cross-examination. Cross-examination also gives the advocate a chance to put his case to the opponent's witness. We briefly illustrate the process of cross-examination in our case study of *R v Lenny Wise*. At Document 45, located on our Online Resource Centre in the case study section, we have included an extract from the examination of the eye-witness Shirley Lewis.

Where two or more defendants are separately represented, each may cross-examine prosecution witnesses in the order in which they appear on the indictment.

14.10.3 RE-EXAMINATION

In asking questions of his witness in re-examination, the advocate is restricted to matters that have arisen in cross-examination. The advocate cannot introduce new matters which he omitted to ask the witness in examination-in-chief. Re-examination is generally regarded as a damage limitation exercise. It can be used to rehabilitate the witness in the eyes of the court where this is necessary.

14.11 DEFENCE SUBMISSION OF NO CASE TO ANSWER

At the close of the prosecution case, the defence may make a submission of 'no case to answer'. The decision is made by the judge in the absence of the jury. The basis of a submission of no case to answer in the Crown Court was explained by Lord Lane in *R v Galbraith* [1981] 2 All ER 1060, in the following terms:

> 'How then should the judge approach a submission of "no case"? (1) If there is no evidence that the crime alleged has been committed by the defendant, there is no difficulty. The judge of course will stop the case.

(2) The difficulty arises where there is some evidence but it is of a tenuous character, for example because of the inherent weakness or vagueness or because it is inconsistent with other evidence. (a) Where the judge comes to the conclusion that the Crown's evidence, taken at its highest, is such that a jury properly directed could not properly convict on it, it is his duty, on a submission being made, to stop the case. (b) Where however the Crown's evidence is such that its strength or weakness depends on the view to be taken of a witness's reliability, or other matters which are generally speaking within the province of the jury and where on one possible view of the facts there is evidence on which a jury could properly come to the conclusion that the defendant is guilty, then the judge should allow the matter to be tried by the jury.'

Where the submission of no case to answer is rejected by the court, or a submission is not made, it is likely that the defence will call evidence to support the accused's plea of not guilty.

Whilst the defence would normally make a submission of no case to answer at the close of the prosecution case there is also nothing to prevent a submission being made at the conclusion of the defence case (*R v Anderson* (1998) *The Independent*, 13 July 1998).

14.12 THE DEFENCE CASE

- The defence advocate may make an opening speech which will outline the defence case and/or seek to undermine the prosecution evidence.
- The defence will then call evidence in support of its case—beginning with the accused where the accused elects to testify.

Each defence witness gives evidence in the following order:

- examination-in-chief by the defence advocate;
- cross-examination by the prosecution advocate and co-accused (if applicable);
- re-examination (where appropriate) by the defence advocate.

If the defendant chooses to give evidence on oath, the defendant will be the first defence witness to testify (s. 79 PACE 1984). Whether the defendant should give evidence at his trial or not requires careful consideration. The evidential consequences of the defendant choosing not to give evidence on oath and the factors that influence the decision are considered in Chapter 19, para. 19.4.1.

Where there are two or more defendants separately represented, each may be cross-examined by the other and then by the prosecution.

14.13 THE CLOSING SPEECHES

At the close of the defence case, the prosecution advocate and then the defence advocate make a closing speech to the judge and jury. The closing speech is the advocate's final opportunity to persuade the jury of the merits of his party's case and therefore needs to be delivered with full persuasive effect using a combination of logic and emotion. Each advocate will attempt to present his case in the most favourable light by identifying any evidence that supports his case and discrediting evidence that undermines it. In the course of making their speeches, the prosecution will obviously emphasise points in its favour (including, if applicable the accused's failure to give evidence or to have mentioned his defence at the police station); the defence advocate may suggest to the jury inconsistencies, improbabilities and other weaknesses in the prosecution case. If, for example, prosecution witnesses have had their previous convictions admitted in evidence during the trial, the defence advocate may suggest that their credibility is such that they cannot be believed on oath. The defence advocate may also remind the jury of the prosecution's opening speech and highlight any disparities between what was said by the prosecutor at the start of the trial and how the prosecution evidence was presented at trial. Finally the defence advocate should remind the jurors that if they are left in any doubt about the defendant's guilt, they must acquit.

14.14 **THE SUMMING-UP**

Following the defence advocate's closing speech the judge will sum up the case to the jury. The judge directs the jurors on points of law and evidence, and helps them to consider the facts. The following issues are commonly referred to in the summing-up:

• an explanation that the jury are the sole arbiters of the facts in the case, but they must accept the judge's direction on points of law and evidence;

• an explanation of the offence(s) charged including an examination of each of the elements;

• a clear direction on the burden and standard of proof;

• an assessment of the evidence put before the court. The judge may comment on the evidence presented by each party as counsel might have done in their closing speeches. The judge may direct the jurors' attention to any answers from a witness which might appear to be implausible or to examine why a particular witness might have a motive to lie;

• depending on the issues in the case, the trial judge may be required to direct the jury on the following evidential issues:

— the dangers of relying on identification evidence;

— the dangers of relying on certain types of uncorroborated evidence;

— the use that can be made of evidence of a defendant's bad character;

— the use that can be made of the defendant's good character;

— the precise circumstances in which an adverse inference from the defendant's silence might be drawn under ss. 34, 35, 36 and 37 Criminal Justice and Public Order Act 1994;

— the special considerations that apply to expert evidence;

— the need to consider the evidence in relation to each count separately unless the rules of evidence dictate otherwise;

— the rules relating to confession evidence;

— the dangers of relying on hearsay evidence;

— the significance of lies told by the defendant.

Many of the directions the judge is required to give are explained in the Crown Court Bench Book (see http://www.judiciary.gov.uk/Resources/JCO/Documents/Training/benchbook_criminal_2010.pdf. Quite often the trial judge will discuss her directions with the advocates before directing the jury.

When attending with counsel or a solicitor-advocate in the Crown Court, it is very important that you take a verbatim record of the trial judge's directions. An error in the summing-up or appearance of bias in favour of the prosecution can provide a defendant with grounds for appeal in the event of a conviction.

At the end of the summing-up the judge advises the jury to appoint a foreman and instructs the jury to retire to seek a unanimous verdict.

On occasions, after the jury retires to make its decision, the jury may ask the judge for further explanation of matters of law or to remind them of any part of the evidence. If the jury ask for information about a point on which no evidence has been given, the judge must tell them there is no evidence on the matter and they must reach their verdict on the basis of the evidence they have heard. Where the jury have a question, it will be delivered by the jury bailiff (see later), who passes it on to the judge. The judge then asks for the trial advocates and the accused to return to court. The note is then read out and the advocates will be invited to make representations as to how the judge should deal with the question. The jury are brought back in to court whereupon the judge will confirm the question asked and the answer that is given along with any further direction deemed necessary.

For further information on jury related issues, see *Blackstone's Criminal Practice*.

14.15 **THE VERDICT**

When the judge has concluded her summing up, a court usher (jury bailiff) takes the oath to keep the jury in some 'private and convenient place'. The jury deliberates in private, free from outside interference. If the jury reaches a unanimous verdict the jurors return to the courtroom and the judge asks whether they have reached such a verdict. If the answer is 'Yes', the jury foreman reads out the verdict to each count on the indictment. The jury must return a verdict on each count and in respect of each accused joined in the count, unless they are discharged from giving a verdict on a certain count. Where the indictment contains alternative counts, for example, counts of handling stolen goods or theft, the jury will only return a verdict on one count. An indictment may expressly, or impliedly, include a lesser alternative offence such as manslaughter in place of murder. The jury may find the defendant not guilty of the count charged but guilty of the lesser offence. The decision to leave alternative counts to the jury is a matter for discussion between the advocates and the trial judge.

14.15.1 **A UNANIMOUS OR A MAJORITY VERDICT?**

In her summing-up the judge will direct the jury to try to reach a unanimous verdict. However, where it is not possible for all the jurors to agree, s. 17 Juries Act 1974 allows for majority verdicts of 11:1 or 10:2 or, if the jury is reduced below 12, a majority 10:1 or 9:1. The defendant may either be convicted or acquitted by a majority verdict.

Before a majority verdict can be considered, the jury must have retired for at least two hours or such longer period as is reasonable, having regard to the nature and complexity of the case. If at the end of that time the jury indicates there is no possibility of reaching a unanimous verdict, the judge may send them out for a further period. If the judge decides that she is willing to accept a majority verdict, the jurors are directed they should continue to reach a unanimous verdict but if they cannot, a majority verdict will be accepted.

There is a great deal of authority which stresses that no pressure should be placed on a jury to arrive at a verdict. If there is such pressure, any conviction is liable to be quashed.

14.15.2 **WHAT IF THE JURY CANNOT REACH A VERDICT?**

If a jury cannot agree on a verdict, the judge discharges them from giving a verdict. The accused is not acquitted and may be re-tried before a different jury. It is for the prosecution to determine whether there should be a re-trial. In the absence of reasons to the contrary, it is the practice to have a retrial following a failure by one jury to agree.

14.16 **THE PROCEDURE AFTER THE JURY'S DECISION**

Where the accused is found guilty, the court will sentence either on the day or, more likely, the proceedings will be adjourned, for a pre-sentence report to enable the court to enquire into the accused's background. Part V of this *Handbook* covers sentencing. Where the defendant is remanded in custody pending sentence, it will be necessary for defence counsel and whoever may be assisting him to see the defendant in the cells to discuss the verdict and any possible grounds for appeal. The defence representative may also be required to provide emotional support to the defendant and his family about the outcome.

If the convicted defendant was granted a representation order subject to a capital-based contribution (see Chapter 9), the specified capital sum will now be payable. If you are representing an acquitted defendant, this is the time to express your relief and to celebrate the result!

Depending on the verdict it may be necessary for the CPS staff member to meet with the prosecution advocate and the police investigating team to discuss any further action in the case.

At the conclusion of the case both CPS and defence support staff should write a full note of the court's decision and ensure that the brief is properly endorsed and that all the accompanying papers are received back from counsel.

14.17 ACQUITTED DEFENDANTS

Privately funded defendants who are acquitted are generally entitled to an award of costs from central funds under s. 16 Prosecution of Offenders Act 1985. Such orders are at the discretion of the court but should normally be awarded unless it is felt that the accused brought suspicion on herself by her own conduct or misled the prosecution into thinking the evidence against her was stronger than it in fact was. The Legal Aid, Sentencing and Punishment of Offenders Act 2012 (LASPO 2012), however, has both curtailed and prohibited the amount of costs that can be recovered. A defence cost's order can no longer be made in the Crown Court. Thus, an acquitted defendant who has privately funded his defence in the Crown Court will not be reimbursed his defence legal costs. Where a privately paying defendant is acquitted in the magistrates' court, s. 16 POA 1985 applies, but the amount recoverable is limited to legal aid rates. A legally aided acquitted defendant's costs will be met under the representation order. Any income-based contributions will be reimbursed with interest.

14.17.1 THE DOUBLE JEOPARDY RULE

Brief mention is made of s. 75(1) CJA 2003 which abolishes the rule against double jeopardy in respect of certain serious qualifying offences that resulted in acquittal following trial on indictment. The rules apply whether the acquittal was by a jury or where a conviction was quashed on appeal. The 'qualifying offences' are listed in Sch. 5 CJA 2003 and include murder, manslaughter, kidnapping, rape, serious sexual offences, certain drugs offences, arson, genocide, terrorist offences and conspiracy to commit a qualifying offence.

The procedure, which includes obtaining the consent of the DPP and leave of the Court of Appeal, is set out in ss. 76–80 CJA 2003. The DPP must be satisfied that there is new and compelling evidence, and that it is in the public interest to proceed with an application to the Court of Appeal. 'New' means evidence that was not adduced at the previous trial; 'compelling' evidence must be highly probative of the case against the acquitted person (s. 78). The Court of Appeal must be satisfied that there is evidence of such quality and relevance as to create a very real chance of conviction and that it is in the interests of justice to order a second trial.

14.18 THE PROSECUTION'S RIGHT OF APPEAL

In relation to trials on indictment, the prosecution enjoys a right of interlocutory appeal against binding rulings made by a trial judge at a preparatory hearing in accordance with ss. 35 and 36 Criminal Procedure and Investigations Act 1996 (Crim PR, Part 66).

Under s. 58 Criminal Justice Act 2003 the prosecution may appeal to the Court of Appeal against a terminating ruling made by the judge in relation to an issue at a trial on indictment and which cannot otherwise be the subject of an appeal to the Court of Appeal. The appeal can be against any judicial ruling made during the trial until the beginning of the summing-up to the jury. The prosecution's right to appeal arising out of decisions in the Crown Court is considered in more detail in Chapter 23, para. 23.11.

14.19 **JUDGE-ONLY TRIALS ON INDICTMENT**

Sections 43–50 CJA 2003 and s. 17 Domestic Violence, Crime and Victims Act 2004 (DVCVA 2004) introduced trial on indictment without a jury. Where these sections apply the defendant can, on application by the prosecution, be tried by a judge. These are known as judge-only trials.

Judge-only trial arises in three different circumstances.

'(1) Section 43 CJA 2003—on application by the prosecution where the case is a serious and complex fraud. This is not yet in force.

(2) Section 44 CJA 2003—on application by the prosecution where there is a risk of "jury tampering". This provision came into force 24 July 2006. There are two different types of application.

(a) An application made before the start of the trial. The prosecution will need to demonstrate that there is evidence of a real and present danger of jury tampering and that the risk of jury tampering is so substantial that it is necessary in the interests of justice for the trial to be conducted without a jury, notwithstanding any steps (e.g. police protection) that might reasonably be taken to prevent the risk.

(b) An application, made after the discharge of the jury where the discharge is a result of jury tampering, to continue the trial as a judge-only trial. The judge must hear representations from both the defence and the prosecution. The judge will consider the same issues as set out above.'

Under ss. 45 and 47 CJA 2003 both the prosecution and the defence have the right of appeal to the Court of Appeal regarding any decision implementing a judge-only trial. If the defendant is convicted the judge must, under s. 48 CJA 2003, give reasons for the decision.

The first ever trial without jury before the Crown Court against four men charged with a £1.75 million robbery at a warehouse in Heathrow committed in 2005, commenced on 13 January 2010. The four were subsequently found guilty by the judge.

Guidance on the use of judge-only trials was provided by the Court of Appeal in *R v J, S and M* [2011] 1 Cr App R 5.

'(3) Section 17 DVCVA 2004—on application by the prosecution the jury try only sample counts and a judge sitting alone tries the remaining counts. This provision came into force on 8 January 2007. The prosecution must satisfy the following conditions, that:

(a) the number of counts in the indictment is such that a trial of them all by jury would not be practicable;

(b) each count tried by the jury is a sample of counts which could for their part be tried by judge-only trial; and

(c) that it is the interests of justice to make the s. 17 DVCVA 2004 order.'

KEY POINT SUMMARY

- Be aware of the circumstances in which a defendant can be tried for more than one offence and can be tried jointly with others.
- On the day of trial the trainee solicitor/paralegal's role is to support the trial advocate and (if the defence representative) support the accused and his family.
- Be aware that although there is no formal system of plea bargaining, the defence advocate may, with the defendant's express consent, negotiate or take up an offer to plead guilty to a less serious alternative offence or seek a binding indication of sentence from the judge in the event of a guilty plea being entered.
- Keep clear written notes of the conduct of the proceedings including what is said by counsel in conference and what is said during the course of the evidence.
- Understand the various stages of the trial on indictment and the verdicts which a jury can return.

SELF-TEST QUESTIONS

1. What is a draft indictment?

2. What is the test for joining more than one count in an indictment?

3. What test does the defence have to meet in order to successfully make a submission of no case to answer at a trial in the Crown Court?

4. What procedure should be adopted in the Crown Court if a point of law arises?

5. Why is the trial judge's summing-up so important?

6. What is an attendance/litigation certificate?

Analysis of these questions can be found on our Online Resource Centre.

Part IV

PROVING THE CASE—THE RULES OF CRIMINAL EVIDENCE

In Part IV we consider further the rules of criminal evidence. In doing so, we build on those rules of criminal evidence already covered in Chapters 5–7.

We begin in Chapter 15 by considering the rules that determine which party has the legal and evidential burdens of proving the issues in a contested case either before a Crown Court or before a magistrates' court. In Chapters 16 and 17 we consider a number of rules associated with witnesses giving evidence at trial. Chapter 18 address the admissibility of hearsay evidence, whilst Chapter 19 explores the important area of the admission of a defendant's bad character. We conclude Part IV with a brief consideration of the rules on private privilege.

Part IV

PROVING THE
CASE—THE RULES
OF CRIMINAL EVIDENCE

15 THE BURDEN OF PROOF

15.1 INTRODUCTION

In this chapter we explain the rules governing the legal and evidential burdens of proof that decide which party has the responsibility of proving a fact in issue to the court. We then explain the degree of persuasiveness the evidence must attain to satisfy the appropriate standard of proof and briefly consider the human rights issues in those exceptional situations where the accused has the legal burden of proof. For both the prosecution and the defence, the rules that allocate the burden of proof and the degree of proof are fundamental to the outcome of a case at trial.

15.2 THE LEGAL BURDEN OF PROOF—THE GENERAL RULE

Generally the prosecution has the legal burden of proving a defendant's guilt. This fundamental rule was famously enshrined in *Woolmington v DPP* [1935] AC 463 and is known as the '*Woolmington*' principle.

As a practical illustration of the *Woolmington* principle, remind yourself of the example in Chapter 2 of the theft offence under s. 1 Theft Act 1968. The prosecution has the legal burden of proving the facts in issue in the case—the *actus reus* of the offence, i.e. the defendant appropriated property belonging to another and the *mens rea,* i.e. that the defendant was dishonest and had the intention to permanently deprive. Where the defendant is pleading not guilty and is not putting forward a defence, the defence has neither a legal nor an evidential burden to prove anything.

15.3 **EXCEPTIONS TO *WOOLMINGTON*—REVERSE BURDEN CLAUSES**

Whilst the *Woolmington* principle applies in most criminal cases, including the most serious offences such as murder and robbery, a number of exceptions apply at common law or under statute where the defence has the legal burden of proving one or more of the facts in issue. These are known as reverse burden clauses because they effectively reverse the presumption of innocence. Where a reverse burden clause applies, human rights considerations will almost inevitably arise at trial. These are considered at para. 15.7.

15.3.1 **THE REVERSE BURDEN CLAUSE AT COMMON LAW**

At common law where the accused submits that at the time of the offence he was insane within the meaning of *McNaghten's Rules* (1843) 10 Cl & F 200, the defence has the legal burden of proving insanity at trial.

15.3.2 **EXPRESS STATUTORY REVERSE BURDEN CLAUSES**

In a number of statutes, Parliament has expressly passed the legal burden to the accused to prove one or more facts in issue. For example, s. 139 Criminal Justice Act 1988 (CJA 1988) prohibits a person from possessing a knife in a public place. Under s. 139(4) CJA 1988, the accused has a defence where he can show 'good reason or lawful authority' for possessing the knife in a public place. Once the prosecution has discharged the legal burden of proving that the accused was found in possession of a knife in a public place, the defence then has the legal burden of proving that he had good reason or lawful authority for possessing the knife.

Another example is s. 2 Homicide Act 1957 (HA 1957) as amended, where Parliament has expressly provided that the accused has the legal burden of proving the partial defence of diminished responsibility under s. 2 HA 1957 on a charge of murder.

15.3.3 **IMPLIED STATUTORY REVERSE BURDEN CLAUSES**

In other statutes, Parliament has impliedly placed the legal burden on the accused to prove a fact in issue. In summary cases s. 101 Magistrates' Courts Act 1980 (MCA 1980) provides:

> 'Where the defendant to an information or complaint relies for his defence on any exception, exemption, proviso, excuse or qualification, whether or not it accompanies the description of the offence or matter of complaint in the enactment creating the offence or on which the complaint is founded, the burden of proving the exception, exemption, proviso, excuse or qualification shall be on him; and this notwithstanding that the information or complaint contains an allegation negating the exception, exemption, proviso, excuse or qualification.'

An example of s. 101 MCA 1980 is provided by s. 143 Road Traffic Act 1988 which makes it an offence to drive a motor vehicle without insurance. Once the prosecution has discharged its legal burden by proving that on the date specified in the information or written charge the defendant drove a motor vehicle on the public highway, the legal burden passes to the accused to prove that at the time he was driving he was insured to do so. If the defendant successfully discharges the legal burden on this issue, he will be acquitted. Section 101 most commonly applies to regulatory offences which prohibit or restrict certain activities such as selling alcohol unless the defendant has a licence to do so or is permitted to engage in a specified activity that is otherwise illegal.

The rationale behind the common law and statutory exceptions to the *Woolmington* principle is that the facts in issue which are covered by a reverse burden clause are within the defendant's exclusive knowledge or control and it is therefore easier for the defendant to prove the fact(s) in issue rather than for the prosecution to disprove them.

15.4 THE STANDARD OF PROOF REQUIRED TO DISCHARGE THE LEGAL BURDEN

Where the legal burden falls on either the prosecution or the defence the evidence presented to support the fact must have the necessary degree of persuasiveness to convince the court. This is known as the standard of proof. If the prosecution has the legal burden of proving a fact in issue, the standard of proof is 'beyond a reasonable doubt'. This phrase is defined in the Judicial Studies Board specimen directions in the following terms:

> 'How does the prosecution succeed in proving the defendant's guilt? The answer is—by making you sure of it. Nothing less than that will do. If after considering all the evidence you are sure that the defendant is guilty, you must return a verdict of "Guilty". If you are not sure, your verdict must be "Not Guilty".'

Where the defence has the legal burden, the standard is on the balance of probabilities. In *Re H (Minors) (Sexual Abuse: Standard of Proof)* [1996] 1 All ER 1, Lord Justice Nicholls suggested the phrase meant the following:

> 'The balance of probability standard means that the court is satisfied an event occurred if the court considers that, on the evidence, the occurrence of the event was more likely than not.'

15.5 THE EVIDENTIAL BURDEN

A party will prove its case and discharge its legal burden, by putting evidence before the court to support its version of the facts and interpretation of the law. This is known as discharging the evidential burden. Generally, the party which has a legal burden of proof will have an evidential burden. To state the obvious: the legal burden of proof cannot be discharged without adducing evidence!

The evidential burden will be discharged in a number of ways by:

- calling witnesses to give oral evidence;
- tendering documentary evidence;
- showing photographs or video evidence;
- producing items of real evidence, e.g. the murder weapon at a trial for murder or CCTV/ mobile telephone records;
- producing expert opinion evidence to prove, e.g. the presence of the defendant's DNA at the crime scene.

15.5.1 THE EVIDENTIAL BURDEN AND THE PROSECUTION

It is always open to the defence to make a submission of no case to answer at the close of the prosecution's case. Where the submission is successful the defendant will be acquitted. Such a submission will succeed in the Crown Court if the test outlined in Chapter 14, para. 14.10 is met. To paraphrase the '*Galbraith*' test: if, at the close of its case, the prosecution has failed to prove an essential element of its case or its evidence has been so thoroughly discredited such that no jury, properly directed on it could properly convict, a submission of no case to answer will be upheld. Quite simply, the prosecution will have failed to discharge its evidential burden. Even an unsuccessful submission does not mean that the prosecution has discharged its legal burden of proof, since this is determined by the jury/magistrates at the conclusion of the case on all the evidence presented by both sides in deciding the defendant's guilt.

15.5.2 THE EVIDENTIAL BURDEN AND THE DEFENCE

Where the accused merely pleads not guilty and does not put forward a defence, the defence advocate may cross-examine the prosecution witnesses to instigate reasonable doubt in the mind of the magistrates or jurors about the accused's guilt. In this sense the defendant does not bear an evidential burden.

However where the defence puts forward an affirmative defence such as self-defence or duress, it has an evidential burden to put some evidence in support of the defence before the court. The evidential burden will be discharged where, if believed and left uncontradicted, the evidence would induce a reasonable doubt in the mind of the magistrates or the jury as to whether the defence case might be true or not. Where the defendant has discharged the evidential burden, the prosecution then has the legal burden to disprove the accused's defence. If the accused has not adduced any evidence of his defence, the trial judge is not obliged to leave the defence to the jury.

The example in para. 15.6 provides a practical illustration of the rules governing the allocation of the legal and evidential burdens of proof.

15.6 DISCHARGING THE LEGAL AND EVIDENTIAL BURDENS OF PROOF—AN EXAMPLE

 Example

Ali is charged with robbery. He pleads not guilty by suggesting that he is the victim of mistaken identification. The Crown Prosecutor knows that to discharge the legal burden of proof, the prosecution will have to prove in accordance with s. 8(1) Theft Act 1968, that Ali dishonestly appropriated property belonging to another with the intention to permanently deprive and that before or at the time of doing so and in order to do so, Ali used force on any person or put any person in fear of force being used.

To discharge the legal burden of proof, the prosecution must adduce evidence (i.e. discharge its evidential burden) by calling, for example, the investigating officers to testify. The officers will give evidence in examination-in-chief about the investigation including whether incriminating items were found in Ali's possession linking him to the robbery. The officers will also be able to tell the court if Ali had made incriminating admissions to the police during the investigation or at the police station. Other prosecution witnesses might be called to testify in examination-in-chief that immediately before the robbery they saw Ali at the crime scene. The victim is likely to be an important prosecution witness. She may give evidence in examination-in-chief about the property that was stolen from her and the force that was used against her.

Other types of evidence may also be tendered by the prosecution including real evidence, footage of CCTV recordings and documentary evidence, and quite possibly forensic evidence in the form of expert opinion evidence.

The defence will try to undermine the prosecution case by cross-examining each defence witness by challenging the witness's factual evidence and/or attempt to undermine the witness's personal credibility as a witness. The defence may also put evidence before the court in support of Ali's defence. If, for example, Ali is pleading not guilty because he has an alibi, evidence should be put before the court to prove Ali's alleged whereabouts at the time of the offence. However, in this case there is no legal burden of proof on Ali and, as he is not advancing an affirmative defence, there is no evidential burden on him either. His only burden is a tactical one which is to adduce some evidence to raise a reasonable doubt in the mind of the jury.

Where the prosecution fails to adduce evidence in support of an element of the actus reus or the mens rea of robbery, at the close of the prosecution case, the defence may make a submission of no case to answer, as outlined in *R v Galbraith* [1981] 2 All ER 1060.

Assuming a submission of no case to answer is not made in this case or, if it is made, it is unsuccessful following a direction from the judge, the jury will decide whether Ali is guilty on the evidence presented.

15.7 CHALLENGES TO REVERSE BURDEN CLAUSES UNDER ARTICLE 6 EUROPEAN CONVENTION ON HUMAN RIGHTS 1950 (ECHR 1950)

Imposing a legal burden of proof on a defendant to prove one or more of the facts in issue effectively requires the defendant to prove his innocence. At first reading this requirement appears incompatible with Article 6(2) ECHR 1950 which explicitly provides that everybody charged with a criminal offence shall be presumed innocent until proven guilty.

In several prominent cases since the implementation of the Human Rights Act 1998, defence lawyers have argued that imposing a legal burden on the defendant to prove a fact in issue infringes the presumption of innocence under Article 6(2) ECHR 1950. The principles identified here suggest the courts are dealing with these arguments on a case-by-case basis. In a case where a court concludes that imposing a legal burden on a defendant violates the presumption of innocence under Article 6, it will use its interpretive power under s. 3 Human Rights Act 1998 (see Chapter 1, para. 1.9.1), to read the statutory provision down so as to impose only an evidential burden of proof on the accused (*R v Lambert* [2002] 2 AC 545).

15.7.1 REVERSE BURDEN CLAUSES—THE GUIDING PRINCIPLES

The following guiding principles can be distilled from the cases decided on this issue so far:

- A reverse burden clause is not automatically incompatible with the presumption of innocence under Article 6(2) provided the legal burden imposed on the defence is not unreasonable and is proportionate to the aim of the provision (*Salabiaku v France* (1988) 13 EHHR 370).

- A reverse burden clause is more easily justified where the overall burden to prove the essential ingredients of the offence remains on the prosecution.

- A reverse burden clause imposing an evidential burden only on the accused will not contravene the presumption of innocence under Article 6(2).

- A legal burden is more easily justified where the defendant is required to prove something within his own knowledge so that it is easier for the defendant to prove the fact than for the prosecution to disprove it.

- The stronger the public interest in preventing the type of harm covered by the legislation, the more likely that a legal burden will be placed on the accused provided it is proportionate to the aims of the legislation, for example:

  — imposing a legal burden of proof on the defendant under s. 139 CJA 1988 was a proportionate response to the social problem of people carrying knives in public (*R v Matthews* [2004] QB 690 and *L v DPP* [2002] 1 Cr App R 32);

  — s. 11(1) Terrorism Act 2000 was not proportionate, given the extraordinary breadth of the provision and the practical difficulty an accused would have in establishing a defence (*Attorney-General's Reference (No. 1 of 2004)* [2004] 1 WLR 2111).

- The more severe the penalty available to the court on conviction the more reasonable it would be to impose an evidential burden only on the accused.

- It is easier to justify the imposition of a legal burden of proof in a regulatory offence, e.g. *R (on the application of Grundy and Co. Excavations Ltd and the Forestry Commission) v Halton Division Magistrates Court* (2003) 167 JP 387.

For further judicial guidance on reverse burden clauses and the presumption of innocence, see the following cases: *R v Lambert* [2002] 2 AC 545; *R v Mathews* [2004] QB 690; *R v Drummond* [2002] 2 Cr App R 352; *R v Johnstone* [2003] 2 Cr App R 33; *Attorney-General's Reference (No. 1 of 2004)* [2004] 1 WLR 2111; and most authoritatively the House of Lords decision in *Attorney-General's Reference (No. 4 of 2002); Sheldrake v DPP* [2005] 1 AC 264.

15.8 FORMAL ADMISSIONS—S. 10 CJA 1967

Under s. 10 CJA 1967, an admission can be made by either the prosecution or the defence before or at the trial. If made before the trial, the admission must be in writing and, where the defendant is legally represented, must be made by his solicitor or barrister. Where a party formally admits a fact in issue, the fact does not have to be proved at trial by relevant and admissible evidence.

15.9   **BURDENS OF PROOF—PRACTICAL CONSIDERATIONS**

The incidence of the legal and evidential burdens of proof play a highly practical role at all stages of a criminal case for both the prosecution and the defence.

Prosecution perspective

*   A vital early task for the CPS lawyer when advising the police about charge, is to research the elements of the offence(s) for which the suspect has been detained and then to assess the evidence obtained by the police during the police investigation. This is necessary to enable the CPS lawyer to form a view about whether there is sufficient evidence to charge and if so, with which offence.

*   This exercise will be repeated more formally by the Crown Prosecutor when applying the 'evidential' test under the Code for Crown Prosecutors to ensure there is a 'realistic' prospect of a conviction in the case (see Chapter 8).

*   The principles covering the incidence of the legal and evidential burdens of proof are also fundamentally important at trial. On a not guilty plea, the prosecution will only be able to prove the defendant's guilt by fully discharging its legal and evidential burdens of proof.

*   When opening the case for the prosecution at trial, the Crown Prosecutor should explain what the prosecution has to prove in the case and the meaning of 'beyond reasonable doubt'.

*   The Crown Prosecutor must be prepared to defend a possible submission of no case to answer which could arise at the close of its case, having presented the evidence in support of the prosecution's case.

Defence perspective

*   The defence lawyer at the police station must also carefully consider the essential elements of the offence(s) when assessing the strength of the evidence against her client before offering advice about whether, for example, her client should remain silent in the police interview or to negotiate her client's release from custody. These considerations also extend to where the offence(s) impose a legal burden and/or an evidential burden on the client.

*   If the client is subsequently charged, the legal adviser's assessment of the evidence will form the basis of advising her client about whether to give an early indication of a guilty plea to attract a 'full' sentencing discount.

*   At trial, the defence should be alert to the possibility of making a submission of no case to answer at the close of the prosecution's case where the prosecution has not established a *prima facie* case against the accused.

*   The defence advocate needs to be aware if the trial judge in the Crown Court misdirects the jury on the burden and standard of proof and a conviction results as this will provide grounds to appeal against conviction.

▌ **KEY POINT SUMMARY**

*   The rules relating to the incidence of legal and evidential burdens of proof are of considerable practical importance.

*   Know the general rule about the incidence of the legal burden of proof in a criminal case.

*   Know the exceptions to the *'Woolmington'* principle.

*   Be able to explain the relationship between the legal burden and the evidential burden.

*   Be aware of the standard of proof that a party has to satisfy in order to discharge its legal burden.

*   Understand that where a legal burden of proof is imposed on a defendant an issue of compatibility with Article 6(2) ECHR 1950 might arise.

- Know the evidential effect of a formal admission in a criminal case.
- Be able to apply these basic evidential rules to your client's case.

SELF-TEST QUESTIONS

1. What is the general rule about the incidence of the legal burden of proof in a criminal case?
2. Explain the meaning of the phrase 'reverse burden clause'.
3. What factors do the courts take into account in deciding the compatibility of a reverse burden clause with Article 6(2) ECHR 1950?

 online resource centre

Analysis of these questions can be found on our Online Resource Centre.

FIGURE 15.1 THE LEGAL AND EVIDENTIAL BURDENS OF PROOF

THE LEGAL BURDEN OF PROOF

- as a general rule and as a fundamental component of Article 6 the prosecution has the legal burden of proving the defendant's guilt (*Woolmington v DPP*);
- the prosecution will not know whether it has succeeded in discharging its legal burden of proof until the jury/magistrates return a verdict.

↓

EXCEPTIONS TO THE *WOOLMINGTON* PRINCIPLE WHERE THE DEFENDANT HAS A LEGAL BURDEN OF PROOF (REVERSE BURDEN CLAUSES)

- at common law where the defendant pleads insanity under the *McNaghten Rules* 1843;
- express or implied statutory exceptions (e.g. s. 2 Homicide Act 1957, s. 101 Magistrates' Courts Act 1980 in summary proceedings);
- reverse burden clauses give rise to a potential Article 6 argument.

↓

THE STANDARD OF PROOF

- the legal burden of proof must be discharged 'beyond reasonable doubt';
- 'on the balance of probabilities' wherever legal burden falls on the defence, i.e. the court considers that, on the evidence, the occurrence of the event was more likely than not (*Re H (Minors) (Sexual Abuse: Standard of Proof)*).

↓

THE EVIDENTIAL BURDEN OF PROOF

- the general rule is that the party with the legal burden also has an evidential burden;
- it is a burden to adduce some evidence;
- a failure by the prosecution to discharge its evidential burden at the close of the prosecution's case will result in a successful submission of no case to answer by the defence (*R v Galbraith* for Crown Court trials; *Practice Direction (Submission of No Case)* in summary cases);
- there is always a tactical burden on the defendant to exploit the 'reasonable doubt';
- where the defendant raises an affirmative defence, there is an obligation to adduce some evidence of it.

16 WITNESS EVIDENCE

16.1 INTRODUCTION

This chapter deals with the important topic of witness evidence. Where a defendant pleads not guilty, the law governing witness evidence plays a vital part in assisting the court to decide the ultimate issue in the case—the defendant's guilt or innocence.

From their earliest involvement, both prosecution and defence lawyers will formulate their strategies and advice with the trial in mind. Is the prosecution evidence sufficiently strong and credible for the Crown Prosecution Service (CPS) to prove its case at trial beyond reasonable doubt? Can the defence successfully challenge the prosecution evidence to induce reasonable doubt in the minds of the jury or magistrates about the defendant's guilt? All the preparatory work in the case, research, interviews, the taking of witness statements, written correspondence, meetings with the defendant client or the investigating police officers and conferences with expert witnesses have one aim in mind—to prepare their party's case for the trial.

This chapter explains the law, procedure and the practical issues associated with witness evidence. (The special position of a defendant as a witness in his own defence is considered in Chapter 19.) In this chapter, the following issues are addressed:

- the use of out-of-court memory-refreshing documents;
- the tests to decide a witness's competence to give evidence;
- the compellability of a witness;
- the assistance available to 'vulnerable' or 'intimidated' witnesses to give evidence under a special measures direction;
- a witness taking the oath or affirming;
- the rules associated with examination-in-chief;
- the rules associated with cross-examination and re-examination.

16.2 DEALING WITH WITNESSES BEFORE TESTIFYING

On the day of the trial both prosecution and defence teams have a number of duties in relation to their witnesses. These tasks are often given to a trainee defence solicitor or a paralegal, or for the CPS, a caseworker or a person from the witness support service.

First, each side must ensure that its witnesses are present at court and available to give evidence. A witness remains out of court until called to testify to ensure she is not influenced by hearing other evidence. This practice is subject to two exceptions. First, an expert witness will usually be in court before testifying, and second, the police officer in charge of the case may also be in court provided the defence consent as this recognises the officer's position as the prosecution client. The officer is available to advise the prosecutor on any issues arising during the trial.

Second, a witness should be encouraged to refresh his memory. As the witness is likely to have written or dictated his statement some months earlier to the police or a member of the defence team, while waiting to give evidence the witness should read over his statement to remind himself of the matters about which he is going to testify (see *R v Richardson* [1971] 2 QB 484). The witness should be reminded not to compare or discuss his evidence with other witnesses.

Third, a witness should be available to give evidence when called. Both sides have discretion in which order to call its witnesses, subject to s. 79 Police and Criminal Evidence Act 1984 (PACE 1984), which requires that the defendant should be called before any other defence witness.

16.3 WITNESS EVIDENCE—THE PRELIMINARY ISSUES

Once called to give evidence a number of preliminary issues will be dealt with by the court before the witness begins to testify.

16.3.1 THE PRESUMPTION IN FAVOUR OF COMPETENCY

Before a witness can testify, the court must be satisfied that the witness is competent to give evidence. A witness is competent where, as a matter of law, the court can receive his evidence. Section 53(1) Youth Justice and Criminal Evidence Act 1999 (YJCEA 1999) presumes that all witnesses are competent to testify by providing: *'At every stage in criminal proceedings all persons are (whatever their age) competent to give evidence.'* A witness may give sworn or unsworn evidence depending on age, emotional maturity and understanding. Under s. 55(2) YJCEA 1999, a witness aged 14 years and over is presumed competent to give sworn evidence where the witness has sufficient appreciation of the solemnity of the occasion and the particular responsibility of telling the truth which is involved in taking an oath. Where a witness aged 14 years and over fails the sworn evidence test, he may give unsworn evidence (s. 56(1) YJCEA 1999).

A 'child' is a witness under the age of 14 years and is presumed competent to give unsworn evidence where it appears to the court that he is able to understand questions put to him and give answers to them which can be understood. This satisfies the test of 'intelligible testimony' (s. 53(3) YJCEA 1999).

16.3.2 CHALLENGING THE COMPETENCE OF A WITNESS—S. 54 YJCEA 1999

It is rare for a party (or the court) to challenge a witness's competence and is only likely to be made against a very young or a mentallly impaired witness. The application is usually made pre-trial in summary proceedings or at the Plea and Case Management Hearing in the Crown Court. If made at trial, the challenge is likely to be either immediately before or after the witness has begun to testify. The challenge may relate to the witness's competence *per se* or competence to give sworn evidence. In the Crown Court the issue is determined in the jury's absence.

In deciding the issue of competence, the court may hear expert evidence and take into account whether the witness is eligible for a 'special measures direction' under s. 19 YJCEA 1999 (see paras. 16.4 and 16.5).

The issue of a child's competence to give evidence was graphically illustrated in April 2009 when a four-and-a half year-old girl, known as X became the youngest witness ever to testify at the Old Bailey. X gave evidence under a special measures direction about being anally raped when she was under the age of three by the defendant. The charges were denied. X's examination-in-chief was received via pre-recorded video interview conducted by a specially trained police officer (see para. 16.5.5.). X was cross-examined via a live-link (see para. 16.5.2.). The trial judge had considered X's competence before the trial commenced. Having reviewed X's pre-recorded video and having heard evidence from experts on both sides, he concluded that X was a competent witness. In the course of the trial, X was subject to cross-examination. It is evident from the transcript of the proceedings that X struggled to answer some of the questions put in cross-examination. At the conclusion of cross-examination, defence counsel invited the judge to revisit X's competency because X's age had made it impossible to effectively cross-examine X and to put his client's case to her. The trial judge concluded that when X had been asked simple questions she had been able to answer them and was therefore competent. In summing up, the trial judge directed the jury about the issue of the child's age, emphasising that X's reliability, credibility and truthfulness should be assessed in the same way as any other witness.

The defendant was convicted and appealed against his conviction and sentence. In dismissing the appeal, the Court of Appeal in *R v Barker* [2010] EWCA Crime 4 stated that issues about the competence of a witness to give evidence under s. 53 YJCEA 1999 was not limited to child witnesses. The provisions equally applied to the infirm or those of unsound mind. The Lord Chief Justice stated:

'The question is entirely witness or child specific. There are no presumptions or preconceptions. The witness need not understand the special importance that the truth should be told in court, and the witness need not understand every single question or give a readily understood answer to every question. Many competent adult witnesses would fail such a competency test. Dealing with it broadly and fairly, provided the witness can understand the questions put to him and can also provide understandable answers, he or she is competent. If the witness cannot understand the questions or his answers to questions which he understands cannot themselves be understood he is not. The questions come, of course, from both sides. If the child is called as a witness by the prosecution he or she must have the ability to understand the questions put to him by the defence as well as the prosecution and to provide answers to them which are understandable . . . The trial process must, of course, and increasingly has, catered for the needs of child witnesses, as indeed it has increasingly catered for the use of adult witnesses whose evidence in former years would not have been heard, by, for example, the now well understood and valuable use of intermediaries. In short, the competency test is not failed because the forensic techniques of the advocate (in particular in relation to cross-examination) or the processes of the court (for example, in relation to the patient expenditure of time) have to be adapted to enable the child to give the best evidence of which he or she is capable. At the same time the right of the defendant to a fair trial must be undiminished. When the issue is whether the child is lying or mistaken in claiming that the defendant behaved indecently towards him or her, it should not be over-problematic for the advocate to formulate short, simple questions which put the essential elements of the defendant's case to the witness, and fully to ventilate before the jury the areas of evidence which bear on the child's credibility.'

In upholding Barker's conviction, the Court of Appeal concluded that the trial judge's ruling on competence had been correct.

16.3.3 **COMPELLABLE WITNESSES**

Where a person is competent to testify, he will also generally be compellable. A witness is compellable if, as a matter of law, he can be made to give evidence, and a failure to testify can result in the person being committed to prison for contempt of court.

There are two main exceptions to the general rule about a witness's compellability. The first exception relates to the defendant, whose position is explained in Chapter 19. The second exception relates to the defendant's spouse under s. 80 PACE 1984 which establishes that:

- The defendant's spouse or civil partner is competent and compellable to give evidence for the defence unless the spouse or civil partner is jointly charged in the proceedings (s. 80(4) PACE 1984).

- The defendant's spouse or civil partner is a competent but not a compellable prosecution witness except where the defendant is charged with:
  — an assault on, or injury or a threat of injury to, the wife, husband or civil partner or on a person who was at the material time under the age of 16; or
  — is charged with a sexual offence alleged to have been committed in respect of a person who was at the material time under the age of 16 *except* where the spouse or civil partner is jointly charged with such an offence unless he or she no longer stands to be convicted (s. 80(3) PACE 1984).

 Example

Gordon is pleading not guilty to separate offences of assaulting Rob, aged 37, and assaulting Lucy, his 15-year-old step-daughter.

Moira, who is Gordon's wife, is a competent and a compellable *defence* witness for both offences. If the *prosecution* wishes to call Moira to give evidence against Gordon, she will be a competent but not a compellable witness at Gordon's trial for assaulting Rob. If the prosecution wishes to call Moira to give evidence against Gordon at his trial for assaulting Lucy, Moira will be both competent and compellable. She will be compellable as the offence of assault on a person under the age of 16 falls within s. 80(3) PACE 1984.

16.4 TESTIFYING UNDER A SPECIAL MEASURES DIRECTION

To reduce the trauma of giving evidence, the prosecution or the defence or the court can apply under Crim PR, Part 29 for the witness to testify under a special measures direction. (The availability of special measures is also taken into account by the court when deciding a witness's competence, see para. 16.3.1.)

Special measures will be ordered where the witness is either 'vulnerable' (s. 16 YJCEA 1999) or 'intimidated' (s. 17 YJCEA 1999) and the court is satisfied that it will improve the quality of the witness's evidence (s. 19(2) YJCEA 1999). Several amendments to the provision of special measures have been made under the Coroners and Justice Act 2009 (C&JA 2009).

16.4.1 VULNERABLE WITNESSES

Section 16 YJCEA 1999 defines a vulnerable witness as:

- a person under 18 at the time of the court hearing; or
- a person who has a significant impairment of intelligence and social functioning, mental disability, mental or physical disorder or a physical disability.

A vulnerable witness automatically attracts a special measures direction entitling him to a range of facilities to assist him to give oral evidence. Section 21 YJCEA 1999 provides additional safeguards for all child witnesses whilst s. 22A YJCEA 1999 makes special provision for complainants in a sexual offence where the case is to be tried in the Crown Court.

In the *Barker* case noted at 16.3.2, the 4-year-old rape victim testified at the Old Bailey under a special measures direction by a pre-recorded video interview (admitted as her evidence-in-chief) and cross-examination through a closed circuit television link. When conducting the witness examination the barristers removed their wigs and used their first names.

16.4.2 INTIMIDATED WITNESSES

To be eligible for a special measures direction as an intimidated witness under s. 17 YJCEA 1999, the court must be satisfied that the quality of the witness's evidence would be diminished by his fear or distress connected with testifying in the proceedings. In determining this, a court shall have regard to the following under s. 17(2):

- the nature and facts of the alleged offence;
- the witness's age;
- the witness's social and cultural background and ethnic origin;
- the witness's domestic and employment circumstances;
- the witness's religious and political beliefs;
- the behaviour of the accused and/or his family and/or his associates towards the witness; and
- any views expressed by the witness.

A complainant in a sexual offence and a witness in proceedings relating to a 'relevant' offence (this includes a wide range of violent crimes involving the use of a gun or knife) automatically fall within this section and therefore the court does not need to be satisfied that the quality of the witness's evidence will be diminished for the purposes of establishing eligibility to special measures as an intimidated witness. A witness to a 'relevant offence' can inform the court that he or she does not wish to be eligible for assistance.

Irrespective of whether the witness falls within s. 16 or s. 17, under s. 19 YJCEA 1999, the court must be sure that the special measures will improve the quality of the witness's evidence and if so decide which of the measures available will maximise the quality of the witness's testimony and whether any such measure(s) might inhibit the evidence being effectively tested.

16.5 **TYPES OF SPECIAL MEASURES**

The facilities available under a special measures direction depend on whether the witness is a child, a vulnerable adult or an intimidated witness and whether the appropriate facilities are available in either the Crown Court or in the magistrates' court.

16.5.1 **GIVING EVIDENCE FROM BEHIND A SCREEN—S. 23 YJCEA 1999**

- Prevents the witness from being seen by the accused while testifying.
- The witness will be seen by the judge and jury or the justices and the advocates.
- The facility is available for a child, a vulnerable adult or an intimidated witness in both the Crown Court and in the magistrates' court.

16.5.2 **GIVING EVIDENCE THROUGH A LIVE TELEVISION LINK—S. 24 YJCEA 1999**

- This facility is available to all vulnerable and intimidated witnesses in the Crown Court and in the magistrates' court.
- A witness testifying through a live television link does not infringe the defendant's right to a fair trial under Article 6 European Convention on Human Rights 1950 (ECHR 1950) (see the House of Lords decision in *Camberwell Green Youth Court, ex p D and Others* [2005] 2 Cr App R 1).
- The C&JA 2009 provides that when making a live-link direction, a court can also direct that a person specified by the court can accompany the witness when the witness is giving evidence by live link. The court must take the witness's wishes into account when it determines who is to accompany the witness.

16.5.3 **GIVING EVIDENCE IN PRIVATE—S. 25 YJCEA 1999**

- This provision excludes from the court those persons specified in the direction where:
  — the proceedings relate to a sexual offence; or
  — it appears to the court that there are reasonable grounds for believing that any other person than the accused has sought or will seek to intimidate the witness in connection with testifying in the proceedings.
- The defendant or the defendant's legal representatives or an interpreter appointed to assist the witness or a court reporter cannot be excluded.
- Giving evidence in private is available for all vulnerable witnesses and intimidated witness in both the Crown Court and in the magistrates' court.

16.5.4 **REMOVAL OF WIGS AND GOWNS—S. 26 YJCEA 1999**

- Available for a child, a vulnerable adult or an intimidated witness in the Crown Court.

16.5.5 **VIDEO-RECORDED EVIDENCE-IN-CHIEF—S. 27 YJCEA 1999**

- This special measure provides for the video-recording of an interview with the witness which may be admitted as the evidence-in-chief of that witness, unless it would not be in 'the interests of justice' to allow the recording to be admitted.
- A s. 27 special measure is potentially available to all vulnerable and intimidated witnesses—but special rules require such a measure to mandatorily apply to child witnesses and complainants in respect of sexual offences which are to be tried in the Crown Court.
- Section 21 YJCEA 1999 (as amended by C&JA 2009) creates a primary rule requiring all child witnesses to give evidence-in-chief by a video-recorded statement and any further

evidence by live link, unless the court is satisfied that to do so will not improve the quality of that child's evidence. A child witness is allowed to 'opt out' of this 'primary rule' provided the court is satisfied, after taking into account certain factors, that not giving evidence in that way will not diminish the quality of the child's evidence.

- The C&JA 2009 creates a new s. 22A YJCEA 1999 for complainants in sexual offences tried in the Crown Court. It requires the complainant's video-recorded statement to be admitted under s. 27 where it would maximise the quality of the complainant's evidence.

 Looking Ahead

When s. 137 Criminal Justice Act 2003 (CJA 2003) comes into force, wider use may be made of video-recorded eye-witness evidence in cases involving serious crimes permitting a court to authorise a video-recording of an interview with a witness (other than the accused) to be admitted as the evidence-in-chief provided subject to compliance with certain conditions.

16.5.6 VIDEO-RECORDED CROSS-EXAMINATION OR RE-EXAMINATION—S. 28 YJCEA 1999

- Where the video-recording is admitted as the witness's evidence-in-chief, the direction may also provide that any cross-examination or re-examination should be video-recorded.
- The recording must be made in the presence of the judge or justices and the legal representatives acting in the proceedings but not the accused.
- **This provision is not currently in force.**

16.5.7 EXAMINATION OF A WITNESS THROUGH AN INTERMEDIARY—S. 29 YJCEA 1999

- Permits the witness to be examined through an interpreter or through any other person as the court may direct.
- Available to all vulnerable witnesses in the Crown Court and in certain magistrates' courts.

16.5.8 AIDS TO COMMUNICATION—S. 30 YJCEA 1999

- This facility permits the witness while testifying to be provided with such a device as the court considers appropriate to enable questions to be put to the witness or receive answers from him to overcome any disorder or disability or other impairment.
- Available to all vulnerable witnesses in the Crown Court and a magistrates' court.

16.5.9 ANONYMOUS WITNESS EVIDENCE

The Criminal Evidence (Witness Anonymity) Act 2008 permitted a witness to give evidence anonymously in a criminal trial under an anonymous witness order. The legislation was enacted to deal with the growing problem of witness intimidation and arose specifically out of the decision in *R v Davis* [2008] UKHL 36. In *R v Davis* the House of Lords had ruled that a trial was likely to be unfair if anonymous witness evidence constitutes the sole or decisive evidence against an accused. The House further decided that there is no common law rule which allowed the prosecution to withhold the identity of a witness from the accused. To overrule the decision in *Davis*, the Criminal Evidence (Witness Anonymity) Act 2008 enjoyed a very rapid legislative passage through Parliament. The 2008 Act, which was a temporary measure, has been re-enacted under s. 86 Coroners and Justice Act 2009 and provides as follows:

- The court may make an anonymous witness order where it considers appropriate to ensure the identity of a witness in the proceedings is not disclosed (s. 86(1)).

- The order will specify the type of special measures to be made under s. 86(1) to secure the witness's anonymity including:
  — withholding a witness's name (s. 86(2)(a));
  — permitting the witness to use a pseudonym (s. 86(2)(b));
  — screening the witness (s. 86(2)(d)); and
  — disguising the witness's voice by modulation (s. 86(2)(d)).
- Section 86(4) requires a witness who is subject to an anonymous witness order to be seen by the judge and other members of the court, the jury (if there is one) and any other person appointed to assist the court such as an interpreter.
- Section 87 permits an application for an anonymous witness order to be made by either the prosecution or by the defence although a defence application would require the identity of the witness to be disclosed to the prosecution.
- The conditions for making an order are set out in s. 88: an order may be made if three conditions are met:
  — Condition A (s. 88(3)): that the order is necessary to:
    (a) protect the safety of the witness or another person or to prevent any serious damage to property (a court must have regard to the witness's reasonable fear of these consequences if identified); or
    (b) prevent real harm to the public interest;
  — Condition B (s. 88(4)): that having regard to all the circumstances the measures would be consistent with a defendant receiving a fair trial; and
  — Condition C (s. 88(5)): the importance of the witness's testimony is such that the witness ought to testify; and:
    (a) the witness would not testify unless the order was made; or
    (b) there would be real harm to the public interest if the witness were to testify without the order being made.
- In deciding whether Conditions A–C are met, s. 88(2) requires a court to have regard to:
    (a) the defendant's general right to know a witness's identity;
    (b) the extent to which a witness's credibility is a relevant factor in the case;
    (c) whether evidence given by the witness may be the sole or decisive evidence;
    (d) whether the witness's evidence may be properly tested without his identity being disclosed;
    (e) whether there is any reason to believe that the witness:
        (i) has a tendency to be dishonest, or
        (ii) has any motive to be dishonest in the circumstances of the case, having regard (in particular) to any previous convictions of the witness and to any relationship between the witness and the defendant or any associates of the defendant;
    (f) whether it would be reasonably practicable to protect the witness by any means other than by making a witness anonymity order specifying the measures that are under consideration by the court.
- In jury trials a further safeguard is provided by s. 90 where the judge is required to give the jury an appropriate warning to ensure that the defendant is not prejudiced by a witness giving evidence anonymously.

For the first judicial guidance on witness anonymity orders see *R v Mayers and Others* [2008] EWCA Crim 1418.

16.5.10 PROCEDURE FOR SEEKING A SPECIAL MEASURES DIRECTION

Detailed rules on the procedure and time limits for applying for a special measures direction are contained in Crim PR, Parts 29–31. In the Crown Court, the prosecution should serve the notice of application on the defendant and the court within 28 days of the case sent bundle. In summary cases, the notice should be served within 14 days of the defendant indicating a not guilty plea. A party opposing the application must serve the notice of opposition within 14 days of the date upon which the application was served on him. Applications for a special measures direction can be made out of time and can be made orally at the trial. The application for a special measures direction can be found in the forms section on the Criminal Procedure Rules web pages.

Limited special measures are available to some eligible defendants and are considered in Chapter 19, para. 19.3.1.

16.5.11 USE OF LIVE LINK OTHER THAN FOR VULNERABLE WITNESSES

Section 51 CJA 2003 permits a court to allow any witnesses (other than the defendant) to give evidence by a live link from any suitable facility (it is not limited to those in a court building) if the court is satisfied that it is in the interests of the efficient and effective administration of justice and where the necessary facilities are already available. In deciding whether to give a direction the court must consider all the circumstances of the case and a list of statutory factors under s. 51(7). The provision is appropriate for witnesses with limited availability, such as professional witnesses, or those with mobility issues who do not qualify for live links under the 1999 Act. The written application requesting a witness to give evidence via live link should be made at the earliest opportunity, stating the grounds upon which such application is made by reference to the factors listed in s. 51(7).

16.6 THE PRACTICAL ISSUES OF WITNESS EVIDENCE

Good case preparation will have identified and anticipated any problems that might arise about the competence of a witness and the need for special measures.

The difficulties encountered with the competence and credibility of the main prosecution witness during the first well-publicised Damilola Taylor murder trial is a good illustration of what might happen when potentially important issues relating to witnesses are not properly addressed during case preparation. Damilola Taylor was a 10-year-old schoolboy who bled to death in November 2000 on the stairwell of a block of flats on the North Peckham Estate in south London. Two 16-year-old brothers were charged with murder. In pleading not guilty, the defence claimed the boy had injured himself accidentally.

A key prosecution witness was a 14-year-old girl, known only as witness Bromley, who claimed that she had witnessed the attack. However, the reliability of her testimony was tainted after it was suggested in cross-examination that she was only giving evidence to claim a £50,000 reward offered by the *Daily Mail* in connection with the conviction of Damilola's murderers. As a result of the attacks on the witness's credibility, the prosecution case collapsed and the brothers were acquitted. Since 2008, a CPS lawyer can carry out an audio-taped pre-trial witness interview, if felt to be necessary, and in accordance with the prescribed guidelines. It is easier for a defence solicitor to assess credibility issues in relation to a defence witness as the defence team will have direct contact with the witness.

16.7 TAKING THE OATH OR AFFIRMING

Once any preliminaries have been dealt with but before testifying, the witness will take the oath or affirm. Where the witness is a religious observer, s. 1 Oaths Act 1978 allows the oath to be taken on the New Testament or in the case of a Jewish witness, on the Old Testament. The witness will be required to state: 'I swear by Almighty God . . .' and then the appropriate form of words as prescribed by law.

Where the witness follows another faith, an appropriate form of oath will be taken. For example, a Muslim witness is sworn on the Koran 'I swear by Allah . . .'. A Sikh will swear on the Sunder Gutka 'I swear by Waheguru . . .'

If the witness refuses to take an oath or the oath is contrary to his religion, s. 5 Oaths Act 1978 allows the witness to make a solemn affirmation in the following form: 'I [name] do solemnly, sincerely and truly declare and affirm . . .'

Having been sworn or affirmed, the party calling the witness will begin the examination-in-chief.

16.8 EXAMINATION-IN-CHIEF

This is the stage where the advocate questions her own witness with the following purposes:

- to obtain answers from the witness about his factual evidence which supports the party's case;
- to put questions to the witness which enhance the witness's personal credibility;
- to raise any matters which the advocate anticipates might be raised in cross-examination.

Having previously taken the witness's statement when events were fresh in the witness's memory, the advocate expects the answers to be consistent with his written statement. A question should not be asked in examination-in-chief to which the witness or the advocate does not know the answer!

16.8.1 LEADING QUESTIONS

Leading questions are not generally permitted in examination-in-chief. A leading question either suggests to the witness the answer desired by the advocate or assumes the existence of disputed facts that have not yet been satisfactorily proven.

 Example

Consider these examples of leading questions.

'The car you saw the defendant drive away from the crime scene was a blue Ford Escort, wasn't it?'

'Is it correct to suggest that when you saw the defendant she was acting suspiciously?'

These questions clearly offend the rule against leading questions, as the witness is led into giving the answer the advocate desires.

Where a leading question is asked in error, the judge or the magistrates' adviser will suggest to the advocate that the question should be put differently. There are two situations where leading questions are permitted. First, at the start of a witness's testimony leading questions are permitted about introductory matters, such as the witness's name, address and occupation. Second, leading questions can be asked to establish a fact that is not in dispute between the parties.

Consider the following short illustration of an examination-in-chief.

 Example

In a prosecution for a domestic assault the prosecutor could start his examination-in-chief of the complainant in the following way:

Q: Mrs Dougherty, can you recall what you were doing in the early evening of 6 April?

A: Yes. I was at home preparing supper.

Q: Who else was at home with you?

A: My children. They were upstairs playing with their computer games.

Q: Was your husband home at this time?

A:	No. He was down the pub.
Q:	What time did your husband come home?
A:	He came home at around 7.30 in the evening.
Q:	Can you describe your husband's demeanour when he came in?
A:	I'm sorry, I don't understand the question.
Q:	Can you tell the court what you observed about your husband when he walked in?
A:	I could tell he was drunk.
Q:	How could you tell he was drunk?
A:	He was unsteady on his feet and he smelt of alcohol.
Q:	In your own words can you tell the court what happened next . . .

16.8.2 **THE WITNESS REFRESHING HIS MEMORY**

Under s. 139 CJA 2003, a witness can refresh his memory from a document or transcript of a sound recording at any stage while testifying, provided:

• the document was made or verified by the witness on an earlier occasion; and

• the witness states in his oral evidence that the document records his recollection of the matter at the earlier time; and

• his recollection of the matters about which he is testifying is likely to have been significantly better at that time than it is at the time of his oral evidence.

Before the witness uses the document, it must be produced for inspection by the court and by the opposing advocate. Where the witness is cross-examined on those parts of the document which the witness used to refresh his memory, the document does not form part of the evidence in the case.

Where the cross-examiner strays outside those parts of the document that the witness used to refresh his memory, the whole document may be put in evidence to be considered by the jury/magistrates as evidence of the truth of what it states (s. 120(3) CJA 2003).

 Example

The most commonly encountered memory-refreshing document is a police officer's notebook. Where the officer wishes to refresh his memory during examination-in-chief, it is customary for the following exchange to take place between the advocate and the officer.

Police officer:	'May I refer to my pocket book?'
Advocate:	'When did you make up your pocket book, officer?'
Police officer:	'When I returned to the police station.'
Advocate:	'Were the events still fresh in your mind when you made up your pocket book?'
Police officer:	'Yes they were.'

The court usher will then pass the notebook to be inspected by the court and the defence advocate. The defence advocate should carefully note the parts used by the officer to refresh his memory and should restrict cross-examination to those parts to avoid the whole document becoming part of the evidence in the case.

16.8.3 **ADMITTING A WITNESS'S PREVIOUS CONSISTENT STATEMENT**

In a criminal trial the 'best' evidence is a witness giving oral testimony in court of facts within the witness's personal knowledge. There is a general common law rule excluding previous consistent (or self-serving) statements. Such previous consistent statements are deemed to have little or no evidential value. However, there are several exceptions to the general rule where a witness's previous consistent statement may be admitted. The exceptions have largely been codified by s. 120 CJA 2003.

Under s. 120 CJA 2003 a witness's previous consistent statement can be admitted as evidence in several situations including:

- to rebut the allegation that the witness's evidence has been recently fabricated, s. 120(2) CJA 2003 (this is dealt with at para. 16.11 in the context of re-examination);

- a previous statement identifying or describing a person, object or place (the obvious application of this would be a witness's previous identification of an accused at an identification procedure); and

- where the victim of the alleged crime has made a previous statement about the commission of the alleged offence against her to another person and the statement was not made as a result of a threat or promise (s. 120(7) CJA 2003). This is known as making a previous complaint. A prior complaint can only be admitted into evidence if the complainant gives oral evidence in connection with its subject matter.

A previous consistent statement admitted under s. 120 CJA 2003 can be admitted as evidence of the truth of its content as well as evidence of the witness's consistency. It will be a matter for the jury or magistrates to determine how much weight should be attached to the earlier statement.

 Example

Gill is the victim of a street robbery. Heavily traumatised by the incident, she goes home and tells her brother Chris about the robbery and describes the assailant.

Under s. 120(7) CJA 2003, evidence of the conversation may be admitted in evidence at the trial of the person accused of robbing Gill, providing Gill gives a first-hand account of what occurred. Where Gill's previous consistent statement is admitted under s. 120(7) CJA 2003, it is admissible as evidence of the truth of the statement's contents—i.e. that Gill was the victim of a street robbery committed by the person Gill described to her brother.

Debbie claims to have been raped by a man she met over the internet. Two days after the alleged rape, Debbie confides to her best friend Rosie that she has been raped but begs her not to tell anyone because she (Debbie) cannot come to terms with what has happened. Debbie makes a formal complaint to the police several weeks later leading to Robert being arrested and charged. Robert's defence is consent. At trial, and assuming Debbie gives evidence, the prosecution will be able to call Rosie to give evidence of Debbie's earlier complaint under s. 120(7) CJA 2003.

16.8.4 UNFAVOURABLE OR HOSTILE WITNESS

At an early stage in the proceedings the prosecution and the defence will take a proof of evidence from each witness it intends to call to give evidence to support its case at trial. Most witnesses will give the answers expected of them and their oral evidence will be consistent with their earlier statement. In this situation, a witness is said to 'come up to proof'. Where a witness does not give the answers expected of him during examination-in-chief he may be either 'unfavourable' or 'hostile'.

An unfavourable witness is a witness who does not 'come up to proof'. This means the witness cannot, for whatever reason, recall a fact(s) about his testimony even after refreshing his memory. The advocate cannot assist the witness by asking leading questions or by prompting him—even though the witness's inability to answer his questions may damage his side's case. It is good practice to get an unfavourable witness out of the witness box as soon as possible—subject to the other party's right to cross-examine the witness.

While an unfavourable witness can be damaging, a more serious situation arises for the advocate when a witness turns hostile. A witness is hostile where he shows no desire to tell the truth in support of the party calling him. An example would be where, in his oral testimony, the witness deliberately and maliciously changes his evidence from what was contained in his written statement or conveniently can 'no longer recall the incident'.

In the Crown Court, if the advocate believes his witness is hostile, the advocate will apply to the judge in the jury's absence for leave to treat the witness as hostile. In summary proceedings a submission is made to the District Judge or magistrates.

The judge or magistrates will then be shown the witness's previous written statement to support the application to have the witness ruled as hostile. The court will then decide whether the witness is hostile or merely unfavourable by considering the witness's demeanour, attitude and any other relevant factor.

Where the witness is ruled hostile:

- the advocate may cross-examine his witness; and/or
- the advocate may ask his witness whether or not he has made an earlier statement which is inconsistent with his present oral testimony—s. 3 Criminal Procedure Act 1865.

Where the witness adopts his earlier written statement as his evidence or the written statement is proven against him, the statement becomes evidence of any matter stated in it of which oral evidence would have been admissible (s. 119(1) CJA 2003).

 Example

Josef is being prosecuted for assaulting his wife, Sandra. The police were called to the couple's home and witnessed Sandra in a state of distress with a split, bleeding lip. In her initial statement to the police Sandra states that Josef assaulted her whilst he was in a drunken rage. Shortly before summary trial, Sandra and Josef are reconciled. Having taken the oath in the witness box, Sandra testifies that she cannot recall the incident. What can the prosecutor do in this situation?

The prosecutor can apply to the magistrates to have Sandra declared hostile. The magistrates will be shown Sandra's earlier signed statement and will have observed her demeanour in the witness box. If Sandra is declared to be a hostile witness, the prosecutor will ask Sandra if she has made a statement on an earlier occasion which is inconsistent with what she is now saying on oath. Sandra may say that the content of her earlier statement is untrue. Having established that Sandra made the earlier inconsistent statement, it will be a matter for the magistrates trying the case to decide where the truth lies and whether, in the circumstances, they can convict Josef beyond reasonable doubt on the basis of the earlier statement alone.

16.9 CROSS-EXAMINATION

Cross-examination is where the advocate questions the other side's witness and has the following purposes:

- to obtain factual evidence from the witness which supports the case of the cross-examiner; and
- to test the truthfulness of the evidence the witness has given in examination-in-chief or to cast doubt on the witness's evidence; and
- to undermine the witness's credibility.

16.9.1 CHALLENGING THE WITNESS'S FACTUAL EVIDENCE

Where in cross-examination the advocate contradicts the witness's factual evidence, the cross-examiner should put his client's version of the facts to the witness to give the witness the opportunity to explain the contradiction. A failure to cross-examine a witness on his factual evidence is taken by the court as accepting the witness's evidence-in-chief on that issue.

Questions asked in cross-examination are not restricted to issues arising in examination-in-chief but may be directed to any fact in issue or to attacking the witness's credibility.

Leading questions are not only allowed but are essential for effective cross-examination. Consider the following example of cross-examination.

A further example of the way in which witness testimony is obtained in court is provided in the *R v Lenny Wise* case study in relation to the eye-witness, Shirley Lewis. The complete version can be accessed on our Online Resource Centre.

online resource centre

Example

Continuing the example of the domestic violence assault highlighted earlier in the context of examination-in-chief, the defence advocate might cross-examine the complainant as follows:

Q: It's simply not true is it, Mrs Dougherty, that your husband launched an unprovoked attack on you?

A: He did.

Q: In fact it was you who had been drinking, hadn't you Mrs Dougherty?

A: No.

Q: Your husband says there was a half empty bottle of vodka on the kitchen table.

A: It's not true.

Q: Is it true that you have had counselling for drink problems in the recent past?

A: I have been depressed. I wasn't drunk.

Q: So you accept you sometimes drink to escape your problems?

A: I sometimes have a drink but I wasn't drunk.

Q: In fact you have been having a lot of problems in your marriage recently, haven't you?

A: Yes.

Q: Your husband has been seeing someone else, hasn't he, and that must have made you feel very angry and hurt.

A: He assaulted me.

Q: Your husband was intending to leave you that night, wasn't he?

A: I don't know.

Q: When he came in to the house it was with the intention of collecting some personal belongings, wasn't it?

A: No—he asked me why his supper wasn't ready. He started shouting at me like he always does.

Q: No—that's not how it happened, is it? You tried to stop him getting past you. He pushed you to one side and you lost your temper, didn't you?

A: No.

Q: You lost your temper and attacked him. In defending himself he pushed you back and you fell against the kitchen sink—that's how you cut your head, isn't it?

16.9.2 **ATTACKING THE WITNESS'S CREDIBILITY**

The cross-examiner may also attack the witness's credibility to persuade the jury or the magistrates to give little or no weight to the witness's oral evidence by suggesting the witness is biased or has previous convictions. Matters affecting the credibility of a witness's evidence are said to be collateral issues in the case and subject to the finality rule which means that evidence cannot be called to rebut the witness's answer.

However, as exceptions to the finality rule, the cross-examining advocate is allowed to adduce evidence to contradict the answer given by the witness where he has suggested the witness:

- is biased; or
- has made a previous inconsistent statement; or
- has previous convictions (s. 100 CJA 2003); or
- suffers from a physical or mental disability.

16.9.3 **PROVING A PREVIOUS INCONSISTENT STATEMENT**

In cross-examination the defence advocate will have a copy of the prosecution witness's earlier statement disclosed under the pre-trial disclosure of evidence rules (see Chapter 8) and will expect answers that are consistent with the witness's written statement. However, where the witness gives answers that are inconsistent with his earlier written statement, s. 5 Criminal Procedure Act 1865 permits the witness to be cross-examined about those parts of his written statement that are inconsistent with his oral evidence.

If the witness denies that he made a written statement that is inconsistent with his present oral testimony and the advocate wishes to contradict the witness, the advocate must draw the witness's attention to those parts of his statement that are inconsistent with his oral testimony. The witness will then be asked whether he wishes the court to adopt the version of his evidence contained in the written statement or his oral evidence.

Section 4 Criminal Procedure Act 1865 provides a similar provision in relation to an inconsistency between a witness's previous oral statement and his oral testimony in court. The cross-examiner can point out the inconsistencies to the witness and ask him which version he wishes the court to adopt as his evidence.

Section 119(1) CJA 2003 provides that where a previous inconsistent statement is proved, the statement becomes evidence of any matter stated in it of which oral evidence would have been admissible. The jury or magistrates must decide where the truth lies. Whether the witness offers an explanation for the inconsistency or not, his credibility is undermined.

16.9.4 **ADMISSIBILITY OF A NON-DEFENDANT'S BAD CHARACTER—S. 100 CJA 2003**

Either party may adduce evidence of a witness's previous convictions or other bad character evidence to undermine the witness's credibility. The rules governing the admission of bad character of both the defendant and non-defendants were substantially reformed by the CJA 2003. The provisions that apply to a defendant can be found in s. 101 CJA 2003 and are considered at length in Chapter 19. The rules relating to the admissibility of non-defendant bad character are contained in s. 100 CJA 2003, which provides:

'(1) In criminal proceedings evidence of the bad character of a person other than the defendant is admissible if and only if—

(a) it is important explanatory evidence;

(b) it has substantial probative value in relation to a matter which—

(i) is a matter in issue in the proceedings, and

(ii) is of substantial importance in the context of the case as a whole;

or

(c) all parties to the proceedings agree to the evidence being admissible.'

Section 100 applies not only to the witnesses in the case but to any person other than the defendant. In most cases an application under s. 100 will relate to a witness and can be made by either the prosecution or the defence.

The following conditions apply before the evidence of a non-defendant's bad character can be admitted.

(1) The evidence must fall within the definition of bad character under s. 98 CJA 2003

Bad character is defined in s. 98 CJA 2003 as:

- evidence of or a disposition towards misconduct other than evidence which has to do with the alleged facts of the offence for which the defendant is charged, or

- evidence of misconduct in connection with the investigation or prosecution of that offence.

Section 98 clearly covers a witness's previous convictions or other disreputable conduct which, if heard by the court, would undermine the witness's credibility. As s. 98 specifically excludes conduct related to the facts of the offence being tried, it would not be necessary for the defence to seek leave to question the investigating police officer that she planted the evidence on the defendant or that she fabricated the defendant's confession. These suggestions clearly relate to evidence of misconduct during the investigation. Arguably, no leave is required where a defendant suggests the witness committed the crime as this would be questioning to do with the alleged facts of the offence.

(2) Leave must be granted by the court to admit the evidence

If the evidence falls within s. 98, the court's leave must be granted before evidence of a non-defendant's bad character may be adduced—unless the parties agree to the bad character evidence being disclosed (s. 100(1)(c) CJA 2003).

A party seeking leave will be required to give notice to the court in accordance with Crim PR, Part 35.2. The party who receives the notice may oppose the application by giving notice in writing. Such matters can be dealt with at trial or more likely at a pre-trial hearing.

(3) The reasons for admitting a non-defendant's bad character

Leave will only be granted if the court is satisfied that the bad character evidence should be admitted because:

- it is important as explanatory evidence (s. 100(1)(a) CJA 2003); or

- it has substantial probative value in relation to a matter raised in the proceedings and is of substantial importance in the context of the case as a whole (s. 100(1)(b) CJA 2003).

(a) Important as explanatory evidence (s. 100(1)(a) CJA 2003)

A non-defendant's bad character will only be admitted as explanatory evidence where, without it, the court would find it impossible or difficult to properly understand the other evidence in the case and its value for understanding the case as a whole is substantial. In some situations it will be necessary for a party to give explanatory background information to the offence, which may result in part or the whole of the witness's bad character being disclosed.

 Example

Nigel is charged with arson by starting a fire in the hostel for resettling young offenders in which he was living at the time of the alleged offence. Nigel has previous convictions for dishonesty and drug-related offences. He denies the offence.

Wasswa testifies for the prosecution that on the day of the fire, he saw Nigel storing five large containers of barbeque fuel and firelighters under his bed. In providing the court with the background facts of the arson offence, the prosecutor will refer to the fact that Wasswa was residing at the hostel. This will obviously imply that Wasswa has a criminal record. In this situation it will be unnecessary for the prosecution to disclose full details of that criminal record.

(b) The evidence has substantial probative value in relation to a matter in the proceedings (s. 100(1)(b) CJA 2003)

Section 100(1)(b) permits the admission of a non-defendant's bad character into evidence only where it satisfies the test of enhanced relevance. Evidence relating to the credibility of a witness falls within s. 100 (*R v Weir* [2006] 1 WLR 1885). Evidence that has only marginal value or no real significance or goes to a trivial or minor issue in the case may not be admissible.

In deciding the 'substantial probative value' test, s. 100(3)(a), (b) and (c) CJA 2003 set out a non-exhaustive list of factors for the court to consider, including:

• the nature and number of the events or other things to which the evidence relates;

• when those events or things are alleged to have happened or existed;

• that it is evidence of the person's misconduct and it is suggested that the evidence has probative value by reason of the similarity between that misconduct and other misconduct.

To highlight some of the potential difficulties in the operation of s. 100, we include some worked examples for you to consider.

 Example 1

Consider the earlier example of Nigel, accused of starting a fire in a hostel for young offenders. Nigel denies the offence and states Wasswa is responsible. Wasswa has previous convictions for arson. Nigel wishes to adduce evidence of Wasswa's previous convictions. Arguably, Nigel does not require leave to accuse Wasswa of having committed the offence, since it has to do with the alleged facts (s. 98 CJA 2003). In substantiating that allegation, Nigel would want to adduce evidence of Wasswa's propensity to cause damage by fire as Wasswa's propensity is clearly relevant to Nigel's defence. If this falls within the definition of s. 98 CJA 2003, leave will not be required. If it does not and the parties do not agree, leave will be required.

Alternatively Nigel might deny the offence and simply accuse Wasswa of lying when he states he saw Nigel storing lighter fuel under his bed. If Wasswa's previous convictions relate to criminal damage and drug misuse, it is difficult to see how these can be said have substantial relevance in relation to the issues in this case. If Wasswa's previous convictions, however, related to theft and burglary, they would arguably assume the necessary substantial probative value as they cast Wasswa's credibility as a witness in a different light.

 Example 2

Dominic is on trial for burglary. He calls Andrew to give evidence of alibi. Andrew has two recent convictions for dishonesty. Will the prosecution be able to put these convictions to Andrew? If the defence does not agree, the prosecution will seek leave under s. 100 CJA 2003. Arguably the previous convictions cast doubt on the credibility of Andrew who is obviously an important defence witness.

Guidance on the application of s. 100(1)(b) CJA 2003 is provided by *R v Brewster and Cromwell* [2010] EWCA Crim 1194. The Court of Appeal observed:

'. . . the purpose of section 100 was to remove from the criminal trial the right to introduce by cross-examination old or irrelevant or trivial behaviour in an attempt unfairly to diminish in the eyes of the tribunal of fact the standing of the witness or to permit unsubstantiated attacks on credit.'

In relation to the test that ought to be applied, the Court of Appeal further observed:

'The first question for the trial judge under section 100(1) (b) is whether creditworthiness is a matter in issue which is of substantial importance in the context of the case as a whole. This is a significant hurdle. Just because a witness has convictions does not mean that the opposing party is entitled to attack the witness' credibility. If it is shown that creditworthiness is an issue of substantial importance, the second question is whether the bad character relied upon is of substantial probative value in relation to that issue. Whether convictions have persuasive value on the issue of creditworthiness will, it seems to us, depend principally on the nature, number and age of the convictions. However, we do not consider that the conviction must, in order to qualify for admission in evidence, demonstrate any tendency towards dishonesty or untruthfulness. The question is whether a fair-minded tribunal would regard them as affecting the worth of the witness' evidence.'

(c) Practical issues associated with s. 100 CJA 2003

Unless the parties agree to the admission of a non-defendant's bad character, s. 100(1)(a) or (b) CJA 2003 is triggered. When considering a defence application to admit the bad character of a prosecution witness, the judge will be mindful of the risk of appeal in the event of conviction if the application is refused. It should be remembered that generally there is no burden of proof on the defendant. All the defendant has to do to be acquitted is to raise a reasonable doubt and for this reason it is likely to be easier for the defence to demonstrate that the line of questioning has substantial probative value in support of the defence case to undermine the credibility of a prosecution witness (*R v Weir* [2006] 1 WLR 1885).

More significantly, both prosecutors and defence advocates will be aware that if leave is granted and evidence of a prosecution witness's bad character is admitted, on the tit-for-tat principle, the defendant's previous convictions may be disclosed under s. 101(1)(g) CJA 2003 (see Chapter 19). A steady stream of case law on bad character is emerging. If it is relevant to your core Criminal Litigation course or to your elective in Advanced Criminal Litigation you can access the 'Bad Character Case Compendium' which is held on the student resource section of our Online Resource Centre. The compendium contains a summary of the most important cases on bad character to date, including some recent cases on s. 100 CJA 2003.

Finally, you should be aware that questioning a witness with a view to exposing wrongdoing is subject to *Principle 1*, Chapter 5—Indicative Behaviours of the Solicitors Code of Conduct 2011.

16.10 CROSS-EXAMINING THE WITNESS ON HIS PHYSICAL OR MENTAL DISABILITY

Medical evidence may be introduced during cross-examination to prove that the witness suffers from a physical or mental disability that may undermine the accuracy of his testimony (*Toohey v Metropolitan Police Commissioner* [1965] AC 595). The law requires the evidence of unreliability to come from a recognised medical specialist so that if you intend to challenge an aspect of a witness's physical or psychiatric fitness to give evidence, you will have to instruct an expert witness to testify.

> **Example**
>
> The witness states that she saw the defendant at a distance of 100 metres breaking into a car. There is evidence to suggest the witness was not wearing her glasses at the time. To rebut this identification, evidence could be introduced by the defence to prove that the witness is short-sighted and cannot see any further than 40 metres without corrective lenses.

16.11 RE-EXAMINATION

The third stage of witness testimony is re-examination, where the party calling the witness may ask further questions of the witness following cross-examination. Re-examination enables the advocate to repair the damage done to the witness's credibility during cross-examination and to explain any confusion or ambiguities in the witness's evidence. Leading questions are not permitted because, as with examination-in-chief, the advocate is dealing with his own witness.

Re-examination is confined to matters arising out of cross-examination. The advocate cannot ask the witness about a matter he omitted to cover in examination-in-chief.

As noted in para. 16.8.3, an issue that may arise during re-examination is where, in cross-examination, it was suggested that the witness has recently made up or fabricated his evidence. This is a potentially serious attack on the witness's credibility and re-examination provides an opportunity to rebut this allegation of recent fabrication. Section 120(2) CJA 2003 permits the witness's previous statement to be admitted in evidence to show that his evidence has not been recently made up. Where the previous consistent statement is admitted, it becomes evidence of the truth of the matters stated in it. See *R v Oyesiku* (1971) 56 Cr App R 240 for an example of where an allegation of recent fabrication was rebutted.

16.12 CROSS-EXAMINING THE COMPLAINANT IN A SEXUAL OFFENCE

Special rules apply to the cross-examination of a complainant in a sexual offence. The rules contained in ss. 41–43 YJCEA 1999 prohibit a defendant from asking a complainant about any of his/her past sexual behaviour involving the defendant or any other person, except with the leave of the court in defined circumstances. The law was unsuccessfully challenged as being incompatible with a defendant's right to a fair trial in the leading authority of *A (No 2)* [2002] 1 AC 45. These complex rules are outside the scope of this work but may be researched in the current edition of *Blackstone's Criminal Practice*.

KEY POINT SUMMARY

- All witnesses are presumed to be competent to give evidence.
- Know the test that a witness has to satisfy to be competent and to be able to give sworn evidence or unsworn evidence.
- Anticipate and be prepared to argue against any challenges to the competence of your witnesses and to raise argument as to the competency of an opposing party's witness.
- Be aware that special measures and/or anonymous witness orders are available to assist vulnerable or intimidated witnesses to give evidence.
- Know the practice and procedure for applying for a special measures direction and/or an anonymous witness order and the facilities that are available.
- Be aware of the purposes of examination-in-chief and the need to prepare questions that will elicit answers from the witness that are favourable to your case.
- Know the general rule against asking leading questions in examination-in-chief and the limited circumstances in which leading questions are permitted.
- Be aware of the purpose of cross-examination and the purpose of the advocate being permitted to ask leading questions.
- Understand that s. 100 CJA 2003 now regulates the admissibility of evidence of a non-defendant's bad character and that, in the absence of agreement between the parties, leave of the court in accordance with s. 100 is required.
- Be aware of the purpose of re-examination and its limitations.

SELF-TEST QUESTIONS

1. David is charged with sexual assault on his step-daughter, Florence, aged 14. Florence has learning difficulties. David is pleading not guilty. The prosecution has witness statements from Susie, David's wife, and their son, Aaron aged 7.

   (a) Is Susie a competent and compellable witness for the prosecution?

   (b) Which type of evidence will Florence be presumed competent to give?

   (c) Consider why there may be doubts about Florence's competence to give this type or any other type of evidence.

   (d) Which type of evidence will Aaron be presumed competent to give?

   (e) What provisions are there to assist Florence and Aaron to give evidence?

2. Are leading questions permitted during examination-in-chief?

3. What conditions are required by s. 139 CJA 2003 for a document to be used by a witness to refresh his memory during examination-in-chief?

4. Explain the purposes of cross-examination.

5(a) Kyle is on trial for grievous bodily harm. The incident occurred in a nightclub. The victim is Ben. Chris, a key witness for the prosecution, is a good friend of Ben. Kyle states he acted in self-defence when he was attacked by Ben and Chris. Ben has a recent previous conviction for affray committed during a disturbance in a town centre. Chris has recent previous convictions for public order offences and assault. Should Kyle be allowed to adduce evidence of these previous convictions?

5(b) If the facts in the scenario in 5(a) are changed such that Chris has a previous conviction for perverting the course of justice (he gave false particulars to the police in order to avoid a driving-related prosecution), would leave be granted to put this conviction to the witness?

Case study: *R v Lenny Wise*

With reference to the *R v Lenny Wise* case study, consider whether any of the potential witnesses in this case might qualify in terms of a special measures direction.

Analysis of all the above questions can be found on our Online Resource Centre.

 online resource centre

FIGURE 16.1 WITNESS COMPETENCE AND COMPELLABILITY

COMPETENCY

- a witness is competent where as a matter of law his evidence can be received by the court;

- all witnesses are presumed competent to give evidence (s. 53(1) YJCEA 1999);

- a witnesses aged 14 years and above will be presumed competent to give sworn evidence;

- a witness aged under 14 years will be presumed competent to give unsworn evidence;

- where a witness's competence is challenged, s. 54 YJCEA 1999 lays down the procedure for the court to decide the issue;

- the court must be satisfied that the witness is able to understand questions put to him and give answers to them which can be understood (s. 53(3) YJCEA 1999);

- a witness may be granted the benefit of a special measures direction before a determination as to competency is made (s. 54(3) YJCEA 1999).

COMPELLABILITY

- a witness is compellable where he can be made to give evidence and a failure to testify may result in him suffering a penalty;

- generally, all witnesses are competent and compellable for the prosecution, except
  - the defendant and co-defendant; and
  - the defendant's spouse BUT see s. 80(3) PACE 1984.

SPECIAL MEASURES DIRECTION, S. 19 YJCEA 1999

- a special measures direction seeks to reduce the trauma of a 'vulnerable' or an 'intimidated' witness to give evidence;

- s. 16 YJCEA 1999 defines a 'vulnerable' witness as:
  - a witness under 18 years; or
  - a witness who suffers from significant impairment of intelligence and social functioning;

- s. 17 YJCEA 1999 defines an intimidated witness as:
  - a witness whose quality of evidence is diminished by fear or distress associated with testifying;

- where a special measures direction is made under s. 19 YJCEA 1999, the court may order the following, subject to availability:
  - witness may give evidence from behind a screen, s. 23 YJCEA 1999;
  - witness may give evidence through a live TV link, s. 24 YJCEA 1999;
  - witness may give evidence in private, s. 25 YJCEA 1999;
  - removal of lawyers' wigs, s. 26 YJCEA 1999;
  - witness may video-record his evidence-in-chief, s. 27 YJCEA 1999;
  - witness may video-record his cross-examination and re-examination, s. 28 YJCEA 1999;
  - witness may give evidence through an intermediary, s. 29 YJCEA 1999;
  - witness may give evidence with the benefit of a communication aid, s. 30 YJCEA 1999;

- witness anonymity orders are subject to special rules.

FIGURE 16.2 WITNESS TESTIMONY

EXAMINATION-IN-CHIEF

- Purpose of questions in examination-in-chief is to:
  - elicit factual evidence which supports the party's case;
  - enhance the witness's personal credibility;
  - anticipate issues to be raised in cross-examination.
- Leading questions are generally not permitted.

Memory refreshing by a witness

- s. 139 CJA 2003 permits a witness to refresh his memory from a document made or verified by him if he states:
  - the document records his recollection at an earlier time; and
  - his recollection of the matter is likely to have been significantly better at that time.

Admissibility of previous consistent statements by a witness

- s. 120 CJA 2003 permits evidence of the witness's previous consistent statement to be admitted as evidence of its truth, including where the victim of the crime made a voluntary complaint to another person, s. 120(7) CJA 2003.

Unfavourable witness

- is a witness who cannot recall some facts about his testimony and simply does not come up to proof.

Hostile witness

- is a witness who shows no desire to tell the truth at the behest of the party calling him:
  - where the witness is ruled hostile, the advocate can cross-examine his own witness and under s. 3 Criminal Procedure Act 1865 put his previous statement to the witness;
  - where the previous statement is proven against the witness; or
  - where the witness adopts his previous statement, s. 119(1) CJA 2003 makes his statement evidence of the truth of any matter stated in it.

CROSS-EXAMINATION

- The purpose of cross-examination is to:
  - elicit factual evidence which supports the cross-examiner's case;
  - test the truthfulness of the witness's evidence in examination-in-chief; and
  - undermine the witness's credibility.
  Leading questions are permitted.

- Proving the witness has made a previous inconsistent statement, s. 4 Criminal Procedure Act 1865
  - where the previous statement is proven against the witness; or
  - the witness adopts his previous statement,
  - s.119(1) CJA 2003 makes his statement evidence of the truth of any matter stated in it.

- Undermining the witness's general credibility
  Such questioning is subject to the finality rule in that the cross-examiner must take the witness's answer as being final unless the cross-examiner submits the witness:
  - is biased;
  - has previous convictions;
  - has a physical or mental disability which undermines the reliability of his evidence.

- Adducing evidence of a witness's bad character
  - usually raised in cross-examination;
  - under s.100(1)(a) CJA 2003, the court may only grant leave to admit evidence of the bad character of someone other than the accused if:
    - it is important explanatory evidence;
    - it has substantial probative value in relation to a matter which is a matter in issue in the proceedings *and* is of substantial importance in the context of the case as a whole; or
    - all parties agree;
  - s. 100 CJA 2003 has no application if the witness's misconduct is connected with the investigation or prosecution of the present offence, see s. 98 CJA 2003;
  - adducing evidence of another person's bad character can result in the accused's bad character being revealed to the court (s. 101(1)(g) CJA 2003).

RE-EXAMINATION

- The purpose of re-examination is to:
  - repair any damage inflicted during cross-examination.
- Leading questions are not permitted.
- A witness may rebut an allegation of recent fabrication by adducing evidence of an earlier previous inconsistent statement, which (if admitted) will be evidence of what it states (s. 120(2) CJA 2003).

17 CORROBORATION, THE 'TURNBULL GUIDELINES' AND OPINION EVIDENCE

17.1 INTRODUCTION

There is a link between the first two evidential rules explained in this chapter. The law governing corroborative or supporting evidence and the application of the 'Turnbull guidelines' in cases involving disputed evidence of eye-witness identification seek to ensure the court reaches its verdict on 'reliable' evidence to prevent miscarriages of justice or convictions being overturned on appeal as 'unsafe'.

This chapter considers:

- the nature of corroborative evidence;
- the situations where corroborative evidence is required as a matter of law;
- the situations where a corroboration warning might be given as a matter of judicial discretion;
- the application of the 'Turnbull guidelines' in cases where eye-witness identification is disputed.

Finally, the rules relating to opinion evidence and to expert opinion evidence in particular are explained.

17.2   WHAT IS MEANT BY CORROBORATION?

Corroborative evidence is independent evidence which supports or confirms other evidence in the case.

Evidence that requires corroboration is said to be unreliable or deficient or tainted in some way. A common example is where a witness may have a purpose of his own to serve by testifying for the prosecution against the accused.

When evaluating the evidence in a case, both prosecution and defence lawyers should always assess their witness's credibility. How will the witness appear to the jury/magistrates? Is the witness likely to be believed? Does the witness have a motive for giving false evidence? These all involve considerations of weight. Where a witness's evidence may be questionable, a corroboration warning might be appropriate. Such a warning alerts the jury/magistrates to the dangers of relying solely on the witness's testimony and the need for independent evidence which is capable of supporting what the witness has to say.

17.2.1   WHEN IS CORROBORATIVE EVIDENCE REQUIRED?

While corroboration has assumed less formal significance in criminal trials in recent years, corroborative evidence may still be encountered in two situations:

- where the offence charged requires corroborative or supporting evidence as a matter of law before the accused can be convicted; and

- where the court considers it appropriate as a matter of discretion to give a warning about the evidence of an 'unreliable' witness.

17.3   CORROBORATION REQUIRED AS A MATTER OF LAW

A limited number of statutes require prosecution evidence to be corroborated as a matter of law before the defendant can be convicted of the offence, including perjury (s. 13 Perjury Act 1911) and treason (s. 1 Treason Act 1795).

The only offence in this category which you might encounter is where a defendant is charged with speeding. Section 89(2) Road Traffic Regulation Act 1984 (RTRA 1984) requires that the defendant cannot be convicted of speeding on the opinion evidence of one witness. The vehicle's speed has to be corroborated by the opinion evidence of another witness. In practice, s. 89 RTRA 1984 has been superseded by modern technology, as in most prosecutions the vehicle's speed is proved by an electronic device such as a radar gun or the police vehicle's speedometer reading which do not need to be supported by independent evidence.

17.4   CORROBORATION AND THE EXERCISE OF JUDICIAL DISCRETION

Traditionally, the evidence of certain witnesses such as children, the complainant in a sexual offence and an accomplice (a person initially charged in the proceedings but who has pleaded guilty and testifies for the prosecution against the accused) was regarded as less reliable than the testimony of other witnesses. When directing the jury about the evidence of these witnesses, the judge was required, as a matter of law, to give a mandatory warning about the dangers of convicting the accused on the unsupported evidence of these witnesses.

The mandatory requirement to give a corroboration warning in relation to these three types of witnesses has been abolished. The present position is that a corroboration warning is discretionary and depends on the facts of each case. The key case on corroboration is *R v Makanjuola; R v Easton* [1995] 3 All ER 730, where the Court of Appeal laid down the following general guidelines:

- A corroboration warning is not a mandatory requirement because the witness is a child giving unsworn evidence or an accomplice or the complainant of a sexual offence.

- It is matter for the judge's discretion what, if any, warning is considered appropriate in relation to the evidence of a particular witness.

- In some cases, it may be appropriate for the judge to warn the jury to exercise caution before acting on the unsupported evidence of a witness. There will need to be an evidential basis for suggesting that the evidence of the witness may be unreliable.

- If any question arises whether a special warning should be given in respect of a witness, it is desirable that the question be resolved with counsel in the absence of the jury before final speeches.

- Where the judge decides to give a warning in respect of a witness, it will be appropriate to do so as part of the judge's review of the evidence and the manner in which the judge gives a direction is a matter for the judge's discretion.

- The Court of Appeal will not interfere with the trial judge's discretion except where the judge acted in an 'unreasonable' way as explained in *Associated Picture Houses Ltd v Wednesbury Corporation* [1948] 1 KB 223.

17.4.1 WHEN MIGHT A CORROBORATION WARNING BE GIVEN?

Both prosecution and defence advocates must be alert to the need for a corroboration warning in the case where a witness's evidence might be regarded as unreliable or tainted. The defence advocate might try to persuade the judge to give a corroboration warning to the jury, or raise it as a relevant consideration before a magistrates' court in her closing speech in any of the following situations:

- a prosecution witness has an 'axe to grind' against the defendant or stands to profit from the defendant's conviction, including an accomplice (see *R v Cheema* [1994] 1 WLR 147) and a co-defendant who runs a cut-throat defence against another co-accused (see *R v Jones* [2004] 1 Cr App R 5);

- a prosecution witness who has a propensity to be untruthful;

- there is evidence to suggest collusion between witnesses or some ulterior motive for the evidence that has been given;

- the witness is mentally unstable or is otherwise regarded as unreliable.

A trial judge cannot be compelled to give a corroboration warning as the decision is discretionary. However, an unreasonable failure to give a warning, in a case where a conviction results, may give the defendant grounds for an appeal against conviction. Where a warning is considered appropriate, the *Makanjuola* guidelines give the court discretion to tailor the warning to the specific facts of the case.

17.5 THE REQUIREMENTS OF CORROBORATIVE EVIDENCE

For evidence to be corroborative, it needs to be:

- admissible in its own right; and
- independent of the evidence to be corroborated.

Corroborative evidence may come from any other evidence in the case, including:

- the oral testimony of another witness;
- an incriminating admission made by a defendant;
- documentary evidence;
- real evidence;
- other circumstantial evidence in the case;

- lies told by the defendant can support the prosecution, where:

  — the lie is deliberate and is material to an issue in the case; and

  — the lie is motivated by a realisation of guilt and fear of the truth; and

  — the lie can be proved to be a lie by other evidence;

  — the jury should be reminded that some people may lie for reasons other than perhaps hiding their guilt for the present offence, including where the accused may lie out of shame, or to bolster a defence, or out of a wish to conceal their disgraceful behaviour from their family (see *R v Lucas* [1981] QB 720);

- forensic evidence such as DNA linking the defendant to the crime scene;

- the defendant's refusal, without good cause, to consent to give an intimate sample under s. 62 Police and Criminal Evidence Act 1984 (PACE 1984);

- inferences from a defendant's silence under Criminal Justice and Public Order Act 1994 (CJPOA 1994), ss. 34–37 (see Chapter 5);

- a defendant's previous convictions where they show a propensity for the defendant to behave in a way that is relevant to proving the facts of the present offence (see Chapter 19).

17.6 THE 'TURNBULL GUIDELINES'

The Turnbull guidelines are of considerable practical importance in trials where the defendant claims to be the victim of mistaken eye-witness identification.

In Chapter 7 we explained the pre-trial safeguards in Code D of the Codes of Practice in dealing with identification procedures used by the police during the investigation to confirm or exclude the defendant's involvement in an offence. Identification evidence obtained in breach of these procedures is vulnerable to challenge under s. 78 PACE 1984.

Disputed evidence of eye-witness identification is treated with caution as extensive psychological research has highlighted the errors eye-witnesses make when they observe, interpret and recall information. An honest witness may be a very convincing witness but may still be mistaken in identifying the defendant at the crime scene. In order to minimise the risk of a miscarriage of justice based on mistaken identification, the Court of Appeal has developed guidelines about how the courts should deal with evidence of disputed eye-witness identification. The guidelines were formulated in *R v Turnbull* [1977] QB 224.

The Turnbull guidelines apply in a case where the defendant disputes the accuracy of eye-witness identification and are fundamental to ensuring that the defendant enjoys a fair trial.

A slightly abridged version of the Turnbull guidelines appears here. The trial judge must adapt the guidelines, when directing the jury, to the particular facts of the case. The guidelines provide:

> 'First, whenever the case against an accused depends wholly or substantially on the correctness of one or more identifications of the accused which the defence alleges to be mistaken, the judge must warn the jury of the special need for caution before convicting the accused in reliance on the correctness of the identification . . . In addition he should instruct them as to the reason for the need for such a warning and should make some reference to the possibility that a mistaken witness can be a convincing one and that a number of such witnesses can all be mistaken.
>
> Secondly, the judge should direct the jury to examine closely the circumstances in which the identification by each witness came to be made. How long did the witness have the accused under observation? At what distance? In what light? Was the observation impeded in any way, as for example by passing traffic or a press of people? Had the witness ever seen the accused before? How often? If only occasionally, had he any special reason for remembering the accused? How long elapsed between the original observation and the subsequent identification to the police. Was there any material discrepancy between the description of the accused given to the police by the witness when first seen by them and his actual appearance? . . . Finally, he should remind the jury of any specific weaknesses which had appeared in the identification evidence.

Recognition may be more reliable than identification of a stranger; but even when a witness is purporting to recognise someone he knows, the jury should be reminded that mistakes in recognition of close relatives or friends are sometimes made.

All these matters go to the quality of the identification. If the quality is good at the close of the accused's case, the danger of a mistaken identification is lessened; but the poorer the quality, the greater the danger.

. . . when the quality is good, as for example when the identification is made over a long period of observation, or in satisfactory conditions by a relative or neighbour, a close friend, a workmate and the like, the jury can safely be left to assess the value of the identifying evidence even where there is no other evidence to support it; provided always, however, that an adequate warning has been given about the special need for caution.

When, in the judgment of the trial judge, the quality of the identifying evidence is poor, as for example a fleeting glimpse of a witness or a longer observation made in difficult conditions, the situation is very different. The judge should then withdraw the case from the jury and direct an acquittal unless there is other evidence which goes to support the correctness of the identification. This may be corroboration in the sense lawyers use that word; but it need not be so if its effect is to make the jury sure that there has been no mistaken identification . . .

The judge should identify to the jury the evidence capable of supporting the identification. If there is any evidence or circumstances which the jury might think was supporting when it did not have this quality, the judge should say so . . .

Care should be taken by the judge when directing the jury about the support for an identification which may be derived from the fact that they have rejected an alibi. False alibis may be put forward for many reasons: an accused, for example, who has only his own truthful evidence to rely on may stupidly fabricate an alibi and get lying witnesses to support it out of fear that his own evidence may not be enough. Further, alibi witnesses can make genuine mistakes about dates and occasions like any other witnesses can. It is only when the jury is satisfied that the sole reason for the fabrication was to deceive them and there is no explanation for its being put forward can fabrication provide any sort of identification evidence. The jury should be reminded that providing the accused has told lies about where he was at the material time does not of itself prove that he was where the identifying witness says he was.'

The Turnbull guidelines require the judge to make an initial qualitative assessment of the eye-witness identification. If the trial judge concludes the identification evidence is poor and is unsupported by any other evidence in the case, the judge must withdraw the case from the jury and direct an acquittal. If the trial judge concludes the evidence is poor but is supported by other evidence in the case or the identification evidence is good, the judge can leave the case to the jury but must direct the jury in accordance with the Turnbull guidelines and stress the special need for caution. In a case where the evidence of identification is poor but supported, the judge must point out the evidence that is capable of providing the support. Supporting evidence will be similar to corroborative evidence as outlined in para. 17.5.

In accordance with the guidelines, the judge must explain why there is a special need for caution with such evidence and direct that, while an honest witness may be a very convincing witness, the witness may nevertheless be mistaken. The judge should invite the jury to consider the circumstances in which the witness purportedly identified the defendant and point out any specific weaknesses in the identification including:

- a witness's failure to make a positive identification;

- a breach of Code D, such as a failure to convene a formal identification procedure;

- inconsistencies between witnesses' original descriptions.

17.6.1 EYE-WITNESS IDENTIFICATION IN 'GOOD' CONDITIONS

The Turnbull guidelines give examples of identification in 'good' conditions including where:

- the identification is made over a long period of observation; or
- the identification is made by a relative or neighbour or a close friend or a workmate etc.

17.6.2 EYE-WITNESS IDENTIFICATION IN 'POOR' CONDITIONS

The Turnbull guidelines give examples of identification in 'poor' conditions including where:

- the witness has a fleeting glimpse of the crime scene; or
- the observation is made in difficult lighting or weather conditions; or
- the witness has only a distant view of the crime scene.

17.6.3 THE TURNBULL GUIDELINES IN SUMMARY PROCEEDINGS

The Turnbull guidelines equally apply to trials in the magistrates' court. In a summary case involving disputed identification evidence of the accused, the legal adviser will remind the magistrates of the guidelines in open court and the special need for caution.

17.6.4 FAILURE TO GIVE A TURNBULL WARNING

The failure to give a Turnbull warning in cases of disputed eye-witness identification will invariably provide a convicted defendant with a ground for appeal against conviction on the basis that his conviction is 'unsafe'.

17.6.5 WHEN DO THE TURNBULL GUIDELINES NOT APPLY?

The Turnbull guidelines should be followed in all cases where the possible mistaken identification of the accused is in issue. The guidelines will not apply to:

- cases involving the identification of motor vehicles;
- the evidence of police officers who base their identification on long periods of observation or surveillance;
- cases in which there has been no formal identification of the defendant, only evidence of a description;
- cases where the accused maintains that the eye-witness is fabricating his evidence (*R v Cape* [1996] 1 Cr App R 191).
- in most cases where the accused admits his presence at the crime scene but note the guidance in *R v Thornton* [1995] 1 Cr App R 578.

17.6.6 TURNBULL—THE PRACTICAL CONSIDERATIONS

The application of the Turnbull guidelines to the facts of the case is a significant consideration for the prosecuting lawyer in a number of situations. These include giving pre-charge advice to the police or when applying the evidential test under the Code for Crown Prosecutors. A further consideration will be whether the prosecution can prove its case if the identification evidence is critically scrutinised under the Turnbull guidelines at trial.

The guidelines are also a relevant consideration for the defence advocate in a contested case based on mistaken identification where the examination-in-chief and cross-examination of eye-witnesses will be based around the guidelines. The defence advocate should also carefully scrutinise the trial judge's direction to the jury to ensure it complies with the requirements laid down in *R v Turnbull*.

You are reminded that our fictional case study *R v Lenny Wise* is a case based on alleged mistaken identification.

Example

Francis is 21 and has been arrested on suspicion of burglary of commercial premises. He is white, of medium build, 6' tall with bleached white hair. The break-in occurred at 3.30 am. A description of the alleged assailant is provided by a security guard. He explains that when the alarm bell was activated, he chased the assailant across the yard of the factory for approximately 40–50 seconds before the assailant climbed over a wall. The yard was partially illuminated and he saw the person from a distance of approximately 30 yards. The security guard describes the youth as white, average height (about 5'10") and build, aged in his early twenties. The youth had fair hair and was wearing denims and a black short jacket. The assailant ripped his clothing on wire meshing covering the top of the wall.

At 3.45 am on the night in question, two officers in a police patrol vehicle arrested Francis. At the time of the arrest, Francis was wearing dark trousers and blue tee-shirt. No jacket was found.

Francis chose not to be represented by a solicitor at the police station and proceeded to deny any involvement in the burglary. He agreed to participate in a video identification procedure. In interview he refused to answer questions and failed to account for a large tear in his jeans. Francis was released on police bail. Four days after witnessing the incident, the security guard attended the identification suite to view the video parade. After some hesitation he selected Francis's image. Francis was subsequently charged with burglary. Francis denies the offence and calls evidence of alibi at his trial.

At Francis's trial, a Turnbull direction would be given about the evidence of the security guard's eye-witness identification. The judge or magistrates would be required to assess the quality of the security guard's identification evidence. If the judge concludes the evidence is poor quality and is unsupported by other evidence, the case will be withdrawn from the court. If the identification evidence is supported by other independent evidence, it can be left to the jury or the magistrates to assess the reliability of the evidence by examining the circumstances in which the identification was made.

In this case the judge may conclude that the evidence is weak but is supported by the fact that Francis refused to answer questions at the police station and failed to give an account of the tear in his jeans. If the case is left to the jury, the judge will invite them to consider the fact that the initial observation of the assailant was in less than ideal circumstances. The security guard had the person under observation for only a short period of time, and at a distance. The lighting was good, however, although it does not appear that Francis is known to the security guard. Although an honest witness, the security guard may nevertheless be mistaken. The judge should remind the jury that the security guard was hesitant before making a formal identification of Francis.

17.7 OPINION EVIDENCE

In a criminal case a witness is called to court to give factual evidence based on what the witness perceived with his own senses. The general rule in criminal proceedings is that opinion evidence is inadmissible. A witness is not permitted to state orally or to write that the 'defendant is obviously guilty' or the 'defendant was up to no good'. In addition to being inadmissible, a witness's opinion is irrelevant and offends the 'ultimate issue' rule. The 'ultimate issue' relates to the defendant's guilt or innocence, which must be decided by the magistrates or the jury on the basis of all the evidence in the case.

There are two important exceptions to the general rule where opinion evidence is admissible: facts personally perceived by the witness, and opinion evidence given by expert witnesses.

17.8 FACTS PERSONALLY PERCEIVED BY THE WITNESS

A lay witness may give an opinion on a fact that she has personally perceived not requiring expertise. For example, it would be admissible for the witness to state that 'the defendant was drunk', or 'the defendant's car was speeding as it approached the road junction'.

In each example, the witness is giving her opinion on a matter within her personal knowledge and experience that does not require expertise or training. In effect these statements are statements of fact and are necessary to communicate to the court an accurate impression of the events the witness is testifying about.

17.9 EXPERT WITNESSES

An expert witness may give her opinion on an issue that goes beyond the ordinary competence of the court. The list of matters upon which expert evidence is required in criminal proceedings continues to grow and includes:

- accident investigation;
- ballistics;
- blood and breath tests;
- blood-alcohol levels;
- fingerprints;
- handwriting;
- computer technologies;
- facial mapping and facial identification;
- the defendant's state of mind when pleading insanity or diminished responsibility;
- medical, psychological, scientific and forensic investigations.

Although these are highly technical matters of which the court has no knowledge or experience, expert evidence is like any other evidence in the case and is subject to an assessment of the weight to be accorded to it by the jury/magistrates.

17.9.1 WHO IS AN EXPERT?

Whether a witness is competent to give 'expert' evidence is a matter of law to be decided by the court. In deciding this issue, reference will be made to the witness's education, academic qualifications and professional experience. In the cases of *R v Clare and Peach* [1995] 2 Cr App R 333 and *R v Hodges and Walker* [2003] 2 Cr App R 247, the witnesses qualified as an expert because of their practical experience as police officers.

At the trial of Hodges and Walker for supplying heroin, expert evidence was admitted from a detective constable in the drugs squad with 17 years' experience. The officer testified that the drugs paraphernalia, the large quantity of heroin and the amount of money discovered at W's property was inconsistent with W's claim that the drugs were for his personal use. On appeal, the Court of Appeal held that the officer's testimony had correctly been admitted as expert evidence. While the officer did not have medical or toxicological qualifications, he was entitled to refer to his expertise as a result of talking to drug users and to drug dealers.

Therefore, one of the first questions to be asked in examination-in-chief of an expert will be to establish the witness's credentials as an expert in his particular field.

17.9.2 THE EXPERT'S DUTIES

The duties of an expert witness are set out in Crim PR, Part 33.

(1) An expert must help the court to achieve the overriding objective by giving an unbiased opinion on matters within his expertise.

(2) This duty overrides any obligation to the person from whom he receives instructions or by whom he is paid.

(3) This duty includes an obligation to inform all parties and the court if the expert's opinion changes from that contained in a report served as evidence or given in a

statement under Crim PR, Part 24 or Part 29 (to support an application for a special measures direction).

The required content of an expert's report is set out in Part 33.3.

Under Part 33.5 the court may direct that the experts instructed by both parties should discuss the issues within their area(s) of expertise and prepare a statement for the court of the matters on which they agree and disagree, giving their reasons.

The court also has the power under Part 33.7 to direct the use of a single joint expert in the case of co-defendants both seeking to instruct different experts.

17.9.3 THE PRE-TRIAL DISCLOSURE OF EXPERT EVIDENCE

Crim PR Part 33.4 has simplified the rules on the service of expert evidence.

Part 33.4 applies as follows:

'(1) A party who wants to introduce expert evidence must—

    (a) serve it on—

        (i) the court officer, and

        (ii) each other party;

    (b) serve it—

        (i) as soon as practicable, and in any event

        (ii) with any application in support of which that party relies on that evidence; and

    (c) if another party so requires, give that party a copy of, or a reasonable opportunity to inspect—

        (i) a record of any examination, measurement, test or experiment on which the expert's findings and opinion are based, or that were carried out in the course of reaching those findings and opinion, and

        (ii) anything on which any such examination, measurement, test or experiment was carried out.

(2) A party may not introduce expert evidence if that party has not complied with this rule, unless—

    (a) every other party agrees; or

    (b) the court gives permission.'

Therefore, under Crim PR, Part 33.4, where either party proposes to rely on expert evidence at a summary trial or a trial on indictment it must be served in advance of trial and as soon as is practicable on the court and any other party in the case. A failure to comply with the rules may result in the expert evidence not being admitted unless the court gives permission or the other parties in the case agree.

The rules do not detract from the prosecutor's general duty of disclosure in relation to used material and to unused material under the Criminal Procedure and Investigations Act 1996 (CPIA 1996) (see Chapter 8) and it is usual for the prosecution's expert evidence to be disclosed under the general disclosure rules.

Section 30 Criminal Justice Act 1988 permits an expert's report to be admitted in evidence whether or not the report's author attends to give oral evidence.

Disclosing an unfavourable expert's report

As Crim PR, Part 33.4 does not override legal professional privilege, the defence is not obliged to disclose an unfavourable expert report which is not to be used at trial. The prosecution's position, however, is different, as an unhelpful report which is not to be used at trial will be disclosed under the 'unused' material rules on the pre-trial disclosure of evidence explained in Chapter 8.

Note that when s. 6(D) CPIA 1996 (as amended by the Criminal Justice Act 2003) comes into force, an accused who instructs an expert witness with a view to providing an opinion for use as evidence at trial, must give to the court and the prosecutor a notice specifying the person's name and address unless specified in the defence statement (see Chapter 13, para. 13.6.14).

17.10 **EXPERT EVIDENCE—PRACTICAL CONSIDERATIONS**

The decision to instruct an expert witness rests entirely with the parties. During the criminal investigation the police may instruct several expert witnesses including forensic scientists. The provision of expert evidence may be a significant factor for the prosecuting lawyer in determining whether to charge. Reliable and credible expert evidence as part of the prosecution case can be a significant factor in persuading a defendant to plead guilty.

Funding is obviously a highly relevant consideration for a privately paying defendant. If the defendant is publicly funded, the defence lawyer should obtain the Legal Services Commission's authorisation before incurring the expense of instructing an expert witness (see Chapter 9, para. 9.11). As there is no definitive directory of defence expert witnesses, defence lawyers tend to instruct on the basis of a recommendation or/and having instructed the expert in an earlier case.

Both parties should always have in mind that if they intend to rely on expert evidence at trial, disclosure of the expert's report must be made in accordance with Crim PR, Part 33.

KEY POINT SUMMARY

- Understand and be able to recognise the circumstances in which a corroboration warning might be called for.

- Understand and be able to recognise the circumstances in which the Turnbull guidelines are applicable.

- The decision to give a corroboration warning lies with the judge/magistrates, with the relevant guidance provided by the decision in *R v Makanjuola*.

- A failure to give a Turnbull warning in a case where it must be given affords a convicted defendant strong grounds for appeal against conviction.

- Expert opinion evidence is admissible in relation to an issue which is outside the competency of the court.

- An expert witness's competency is determined by his qualification and or relevant experience.

- Wherever a party seeks to rely on expert evidence, rules of court require that party to give notice.

SELF-TEST QUESTIONS

Consider this factual scenario and answer the questions that follow.

You act for Stefan who has been charged with causing grievous bodily harm with intent, contrary to s. 18 Offences Against the Person Act 1861 (OAPA). The assault is alleged to have been racially motivated. He pleads not guilty at his trial, giving evidence on oath that he was not involved in the crime. He calls his girlfriend to substantiate his defence of alibi.

The assault occurred outside a public house at 11.30 pm in a busy city centre street. Witnesses describe two white youths attacking an Asian youth. Eye-witnesses provided varying descriptions of the attackers. An anonymous witness has told the police that Stefan and Andrew (also charged in connection with the proceedings) were involved. Upon his arrest and having been confronted with positive identification evidence, Andrew admitted his limited involvement and implicated Stefan as being the principal instigator of the attack and of being completely out of control.

Stefan was subsequently arrested. His solicitor advised him not to answer police questions as he considered the evidence against Stefan to be very weak. Stefan followed his advice. In the interview, Stefan was cautioned and asked to account for visible bruising to his nose. He offered no explanation. Stefan consented to participating in a video identification procedure.

It was several days before the victim was able to assist the police. Shortly after being hospitalised, the victim was shown several sets of photographs of convicted offenders (which included a photograph of Stefan) to see if he could spot his attacker. He selected Stefan's photograph. Three weeks later the victim was well enough to view the video parade and selected Stefan's image.

At trial, the prosecution accepts Andrew's guilty plea to a much less serious offence of assault occasioning actual bodily harm (s. 47 OAPA 1861) and agrees to withdraw the s. 18 charge. Andrew gives evidence for the prosecution, putting the blame on Stefan as being the person responsible for kicking the youth while he was on the ground.

Stefan maintains Andrew is lying in order to cover up his own involvement in a serious offence. Stefan denies being at the scene. Andrew is to be married in a few weeks time to a woman whose brother is a member of the investigative team.

In evidence, Stefan states that, while he and his girlfriend were in the city centre on the evening in question and had a drink with Andrew and some of his friends, they left before any trouble occurred.

CCTV footage is available of the incident. Sergeant Peter Taylor is called for the prosecution to give evidence of the fact that the blurred image on one of the stills is that of Stefan. The sergeant has studied the stills for a number of hours using video enhancing equipment.

Questions

- Do you have any concerns as regards the manner in which the evidence of identification has been obtained in this case? If so, is there anything you can do about this?

- On what basis will Sergeant Taylor's evidence be admitted?

- Is this a case which calls for a Turnbull direction? If so, explain why. What will the requirements of that warning be?

- Is this is a case which calls for a corroboration warning? If so, explain why.

Case study: *R v Lenny Wise*

Consider whether a Turnbull warning would need to be given in *R v Lenny Wise*, and whether any issues in relation to expert opinion evidence arise in this case.

Analysis on the above can be found on our Online Resource Centre.

online
resource
centre

FIGURE 17.1 CORROBORATION

CORROBORATIVE EVIDENCE

- What is it?

  Corroborative evidence is independent evidence which supports or confirms other evidence in the case (see *R v Baskerville*).

- What type of witness might it apply to?

  Where there is reason to doubt the reliability/truthfulness of a prosecution witness (perhaps because the witness has a purpose of his own to serve in giving false/unreliable evidence), a corroboration warning about the dangers of relying upon the unsupported evidence of the witness may be required.

- Where might supporting evidence come from?
  - another witness's oral testimony; or
  - documentary or real evidence; or
  - forensic evidence; or
  - the defendant's lies or admissions (*R v Lucas*).

- Corroboration as a matter of judicial discretion

  A judge may choose to give a corroboration warning to a jury (or magistrates can warn themselves) about the dangers of relying on the uncorroborated evidence of a 'suspect' witness where 'there is an evidential basis for it' (see *R v Makanjuola and Easton*).

THE 'TURNBULL GUIDELINES'

- Guidelines laid down by the decision in *R v Turnbull*.
- 'Turnbull' applies to evidence of eye-witness identification where the defendant disputes his presence at the crime scene.
- Turnbull guidelines require:
  - the court to proceed with caution as an honest witness may be a mistaken witness;
  - the jury or magistrates' court should consider the circumstances of the eye-witness identification, including:
    - the length of time the witness allegedly observed the defendant;
    - the light and distance etc. in which the identification occurred;
    - did the witness have a special reason for remembering/recognising the defendant etc.
- Where the identification took place in 'good' conditions, the jury or magistrates may assess the value of the identifying evidence.
- Where the identification take place in poor conditions, the evidence should be withdrawn unless there is supporting evidence about the correctness of the identification.
- Jury/magistrates should be reminded of any specific weakness in the evidence of identification, including breaches of Code D (under PACE 1984).

OPINION EVIDENCE

- Generally inadmissible in a criminal case, except:
  - facts personally perceived by the witness which does not require expertise; or
  - expert evidence on an issue beyond the ordinary competence of the court, including:
    - forensic science;
    - facial mapping;
    - accident investigation.
- The expert's role is to provide impartial information to assist the court reach a decision in the case.
- If a party wishes to rely on expert evidence at trial, a copy of the expert's report must be served (Crim PR, Part 33).

18 HEARSAY EVIDENCE

18.1 INTRODUCTION

Hearsay evidence is often described as 'second-hand' evidence and offends the preferred way in which evidence is presented at a criminal trial which requires witnesses to attend court to give oral evidence about facts of which they have personal knowledge. This is the most reliable evidence on which the court decides the defendant's guilt or innocence. Hearsay evidence is therefore inferior to the original witness's direct oral testimony, because it cannot be tested by cross-examination.

Hearsay evidence in criminal cases most often arises in two situations:

- if a witness testifies about facts of which he has no personal knowledge because the facts were communicated to the witness by another person who is not in court; and

- where a witness's written statement is put before the court because the witness is unable to attend court to give oral evidence.

Consider the following example of hearsay evidence.

 Example

Magda witnesses a robbery in which a pensioner's handbag is stolen. She tells her friend Ainsley that the person responsible was a white male of average height, wearing a black jogging top and baggy black trousers with a tattoo on the left-hand side of his face. If Magda cannot attend court to give a first-hand account of what she witnessed, can Ainsley be called to repeat what Magda told him about the circumstances of the robbery? The answer is no because Ainsley's evidence infringes the rule against admitting hearsay evidence as Ainsley has no personal knowledge of the facts about which he is testifying, as he did not see the man alleged to be responsible for the robbery. As Ainsley is relying on what Magda has told him, he cannot be effectively cross-examined.

Alternatively, if Magda makes a written witness statement to the police but is unable to attend trial to give oral evidence, can the prosecution adduce Magda's written statement in place of her oral testimony? The written statement constitutes hearsay evidence. As in the first example, it will not be possible to cross-examine Magda to test the reliability and truthfulness of her evidence, and once again, the court would be relying on 'second-hand' evidence.

Hearsay evidence can be first-hand hearsay or multi-hand hearsay where a statement has gone through more than one intermediary. Suppose in this example that Ainsley is unable to attend trial but tells Toby what Magda told him. If Toby is called to give evidence, this would constitute multi-hand hearsay. The same would be true if a written statement by Ainsley, recounting what Magda said to him was to be admitted as evidence, as this would be two steps removed from the original source.

18.2 HEARSAY EVIDENCE—THE GENERAL RULE

The general rule in criminal cases is that hearsay evidence is inadmissible for the reasons explained in the introduction to this chapter. Unless the hearsay comes within a recognised common law or statutory exception it is inadmissible, although the Criminal Justice Act 2003 (CJA 2003) has *considerably* widened the basis for admitting hearsay evidence.

18.3 IDENTIFYING HEARSAY EVIDENCE

Hearsay has been defined as follows:

'Any statement other than one made by a person while giving oral evidence in the proceedings is inadmissible to prove the truth of any fact stated in it.' (*R v Kearley* [1992] 2 AC 228)

To come within the definition of hearsay, the evidence will consist of the following elements:

(1) The evidence must be contained in a 'statement' and covers all forms of communication including:

— a written witness statement;

— a document compiled in the course of a business or by a public authority;

— a witness's oral evidence;

— a witness's evidence recorded on an audio or video tape;

— evidence on a computer disc;

— a gesture by a witness (*R v Gibson* [1887] LR 18 QBD).

(2) The statement must have been made by the witness other than while giving evidence in the present proceedings.

(3) The statement must be put in evidence to prove the truth of the statement's contents and not for any other reason, for example, to prove the statement was made or to show the witness's state of mind at the time the statement was made.

A confession is a good illustration of evidence containing the constituent elements of a hearsay statement:

- the confession will be contained in a 'statement'—i.e. a written transcript of the interview with the police or a tape-recording of the interview;

- the confession will be made on an occasion other than while the defendant gives evidence in the present proceedings—i.e. the defendant will confess at the police station during the investigation of the alleged crime; and

- the purpose of putting the statement before the court is to prove its truth—i.e. that the accused admits his involvement in the offence as charged.

Confession evidence is admissible as an exception to the hearsay rule in accordance with the principles explained in Chapter 6.

18.3.1 DEFINITIONAL DIFFICULTIES WITH HEARSAY EVIDENCE

Not every out-of-court statement is hearsay. If the earlier out-of-court statement is adduced for a reason other than proving the truth of facts asserted, the statement will not be hearsay. In *R v Davis* [1998] Crim LR 659, the defendant attempted to prevent adverse inferences being drawn against his silence under s. 34 Criminal Justice and Public Order Act 1994 (see Chapter 5) by trying to repeat on oath the advice his legal adviser had given him at the police station to remain silent. The defendant was prevented from doing so by the judge who ruled it as hearsay. The Court of Appeal held the trial judge was wrong as the evidence was not hearsay because the defendant was not seeking to prove the truth of anything his legal adviser had said, but was merely trying to show the effect the advice had on him in explaining his decision to remain silent.

18.3.2 IMPLIED ASSERTIONS

An implied assertion is a statement which is not intended by its maker to explicitly assert a fact but does so by implication. Implied assertions are excluded from the definition of hearsay by s. 115(3) CJA 2003. The hearsay provisions under the CJA 2003 only apply to a statement that appears to have been made:

'to cause another person to believe the matter, or to cause another person to act or a machine to operate on the basis that the matter is as stated . . . '.

In practice, unless the statement's maker intended to assert a fact, the hearsay rule does not apply and the evidence may be admitted as direct evidence of a fact provided it is relevant to the particular case.

18.3.3 STATEMENTS PRODUCED BY MECHANICAL DEVICES—HEARSAY OR REAL EVIDENCE?

Section 115(2) CJA 2003 confines the hearsay provisions to statements made by a person. Would CCTV images, photographic stills and audio recordings fall within the hearsay rule?

These forms of recording events, which are commonly admitted in evidence, are examples of real evidence and are excluded from the hearsay rule. The provenance of the evidence will still need to be proven and therefore it is necessary to adduce evidence of when the video was filmed and by whom.

18.3.4 STATEMENTS PRODUCED BY A COMPUTER—HEARSAY OR REAL EVIDENCE?

Does a document created by a computer constitute hearsay? Where the computer performs an entirely automated process which does not involve any human input of information, the printout reading or calculation that the computer performs is real evidence. This means that readings from a speedometer, police radar gun and Intoximeter are not hearsay. Similarly, the automated telephone exchange records which log the dates, times and numbers of telephone calls made and received are frequently admitted in evidence as items of real evidence. Section 129(2) CJA 2003 creates a rebuttable presumption as to the correct functioning of a mechanical device.

Where a computer is used to perform a task based on information inputted by a human being, the evidence is likely to come within the hearsay rule if the purpose of using the computer printout is to prove the truth of some fact asserted by the person who entered the information. Such computer-generated evidence is admissible under s. 129(1) CJA 2003 which provides that:

'where a representation of fact:

(a) is made otherwise than by a person, but

(b) depends for its accuracy on information supplied (directly or indirectly) by a person,

the representation is not admissible in criminal proceedings as evidence of the fact unless it is proved that the information was accurate.'

For other types of information stored on computers such as e-mail correspondence, business records, invoices etc., which comprise statements made by a person, their admissibility is subject to s. 116 or s. 117 CJA 2003 (see later).

Having considered the constituent elements of a hearsay statement, we will examine the common law and statutory exceptions to the general exclusionary rule which allow hearsay evidence to be admitted at trial.

18.4 THE STATUTORY EXCEPTIONS TO THE HEARSAY RULE

Most statutory exceptions to the hearsay rule are contained in the CJA 2003, which has codified the most important exceptions to the rule—although some cases from the 'old' law under the CJA 1988 continue to be relevant. Before we consider the CJA 2003 provisions, two other important statutory exceptions to the hearsay rule should be noted.

18.4.1 SECTION 9 CJA 1967

In practice s. 9 CJA 1967 is the most important exception to the hearsay rule, and is in daily use in all Crown Courts and magistrates' courts. Section 9 CJA 1967 permits a witness's written statement to be read to the court without the witness attending the trial where:

- the statement is signed by the maker; and
- contains a declaration in specified words as to the statement's truth; and
- the statement has been served on the opposing party; and
- within seven days of its service the opposing party has not objected to the statement being admitted as hearsay.

The key point about a 'section 9 statement' is the other side's consent must be obtained before the statement may be admitted as hearsay unless the statement falls within another admissible hearsay provision. If the other side objects, for whatever reason, the court has no power to overrule the objection and admit the statement in evidence. An advocate is only likely to agree to a witness's evidence being read to the court under s. 9 CJA 1967 if she does not wish to cross-examine the witness because nothing the witness says in their statement is disputed.

When preparing a case for trial and, in accordance with Crim PR, Part 3, both prosecution and defence lawyers should consider whether there are any witnesses whose evidence could be read to the court under s. 9 CJA 1967. In our *R v Lenny Wise* case study, you will see that in preparing for trial, several prosecution witness statements have been agreed and will be admitted as 'section 9 statements'. For further guidance see Chapter 12, para. 12.8.9.

18.5 HEARSAY EVIDENCE UNDER THE CJA 2003

Section 114 CJA 2003 regulates the admissibility of hearsay evidence under the CJA 2003. The section provides:

> 'a statement not made in oral evidence in the proceedings is admissible as evidence of any matter stated if it comes within one of the four exceptions'.

Section 114(1)(a)–(d) identifies the following four situations where hearsay will be admissible under the Act:

- s. 114(1)(a)—hearsay will be admissible where it comes within one of the categories of admissible hearsay evidence under the Act (mainly where a witness is unavailable to give evidence—ss. 116 and 117 CJA 2003) and any other preserved statutory section (s. 9 CJA 1967 and Sch. 2 CPIA 1996, see earlier);

- s. 114(1)(b)—hearsay will be admissible where it comes within one of the preserved common law rules (s. 118);

- s. 114(1)(c)—hearsay will be admissible where the parties agree to the evidence being admitted;

- s. 114(1)(d)—hearsay will be admissible where the court is satisfied that it is in the 'interests of justice' for the hearsay statement to be admitted (the so-called safety-valve).

The main statutory gateways for admitting hearsay are provided by ss. 116 and 117 CJA 2003.

18.5.1 THE UNAVAILABLE WITNESS—S. 116 (FIRST-HAND HEARSAY)

A statement will only be admissible under s. 116(1) CJA 2003 where:

- the person could have given oral evidence if he had attended court; and

- the person who made the statement is identified to the court's satisfaction; and

- the person who made the statement had the requisite capability (s. 123 CJA 2003) at the time he made the statement.

The definition of capability is the same as the competence test to give oral evidence under s. 53 Youth Justice and Criminal Evidence Act 1999, i.e. can the witness understand questions put to him and give answers that can be understood (see Chapter 16).

Section 116 CJA 2003 permits a statement to be admitted where the witness is unable to attend court for one of the following reasons:

- the witness is dead or is unfit because of his bodily or mental condition (s. 116(2)(a) and (b));

- the witness is outside the UK and it is not reasonably practicable for him to attend (s. 116 (2)(c));

- the witness cannot be found although such steps as it is reasonably practical to take to find him have been taken (s. 116(2)(d));

- that through fear the witness does not give evidence (or does not continue to give evidence) (s. 116(2)(e)).

Under s. 116 CJA 2003 it is immaterial whether the hearsay statement is contained in a document or was made orally. Once the condition for admitting the statement is proved under s. 116, the evidence can be admitted.

The burden of proving the relevant condition rests on the party seeking to adduce the hearsay evidence. Disputes about the statement's admissibility are likely to be determined at a pre-trial hearing.

18.5.2 THE REASONS FOR A WITNESS'S UNAVAILABILITY

Reason 1—the witness is dead or unfit

R v Setz-Dempsey [1993] 92 Cr App R 98 confirms that an assessment of the witness's 'unfitness to attend' can include mental or physical capacity. A death certificate or medical report should discharge the burden of proving this ground.

Reason 2—the witness is (a) outside the UK and (b) it is not reasonably practicable to secure his attendance

If the witness's statement is to be given as hearsay, both conditions have to be satisfied by the party seeking to rely on s. 116(2)(d) CJA 2003. In *R v Castillo* [1996] 1 Cr App R 438, the Court of Appeal identified a number of factors that should be considered in determining whether it is practicable for the witness to attend, including:

- the importance of the evidence the witness could give;

- the expense and inconvenience of securing the attendance of the witness;

- the seriousness of the offence;

- whether the witness's evidence could be given via live television link; and

- the prejudice likely to be caused to the defendant given that the defendant would have no opportunity to cross-examine.

Reason 3—all reasonable steps have been taken to find the witness, but he cannot be found

The party seeking to use the hearsay at trial must prove that all reasonable steps have been taken to find the witness including indicating the steps taken to trace the witness (see *R v T(D)*, 4 June 2009, unreported).

Reason 4—the witness does not give evidence through fear

Fear is widely defined in s. 116(3) to include fear of death or injury of another person or financial loss. The witness's fear must be genuine and should be proved by admissible evidence. In *R v Rutherford* [1998] Crim LR 490, fear was proved by a signed written statement from the witness. A witness may still be in fear notwithstanding that the fear was not induced by or on behalf of the accused (*R v Horncastle and Others* [2009] EWCA Crim 964).

Where a party relies on the 'fear' ground under s. 116(2)(e), the court may grant leave under s. 116(4) where it would be in the interests of justice to admit the statement having regard to:

(1) the statement's contents;

(2) any risk that its admission or exclusion will result in unfairness to any party (with particular reference to how difficult it will be to challenge the statement if the relevant person does not give evidence);

(3) in appropriate cases, the fact that a special measures direction could be made in relation to the relevant person (see Chapter 16);

(4) any other relevant circumstance.

The requirement to seek leave under this ground is an important safeguard in protecting the defendant's right to a fair trial under Article 6. The relationship between hearsay evidence and Article 6 is considered at para. 18.13.

Consider the following examples of admitting hearsay under s. 116 CJA 2003.

 Example 1

Ethel, aged 84, is the victim of a burglary. She describes the burglar to her daughter Dianna. Ethel suffers a stroke soon after and is unable to provide a formal written statement to the police or indeed to attend trial. Can the prosecution call Dianna so that she may repeat in court what her mother told her about the burglar? This would clearly constitute hearsay evidence. Hearsay evidence is generally inadmissible unless it comes within the exceptions under the CJA 2003. Assume Ethel was capable at the time she spoke with her daughter. On the face of it, the conditions for admissibility under s. 116 CJA 2003 would appear to be satisfied. The identity of the maker of the statement is not in dispute and Ethel is unable to attend trial for a prescribed reason under s. 116(2)(b).

 Example 2

Serge is the victim of a homophobic assault. He gives the police a detailed description of his attackers in a written witness statement. Serge refuses to give evidence in court as he fears for his personal safety. Can the prosecution adduce Serge's written statement as hearsay evidence? Serge's statement would appear to be admissible under s. 116(2)(e) CJA 2003. Serge is clearly identifiable as the maker of the statement and is unavailable to give oral evidence out of fear. In choosing to admit Serge's statement the court must have regard to the factors set out in s. 116(4) CJA 2003, including the availability of special measures to assist witnesses like Serge to give evidence.

18.6 BUSINESS DOCUMENTS—S. 117

Business documents are admissible under s. 117 CJA 2003 and take into account modern business practice where millions of documents are created on a daily basis. As it is impossible to require every person who had personal knowledge of the document's contents to testify in court, s. 117(2) makes business documents admissible as hearsay where the following conditions are satisfied:

- the document was created or received in the course of a trade, business, profession or other occupation, or as the holder of a paid or unpaid office (s. 117(2)(a)); and
- the person who supplied the information contained in the statement (the relevant person) had or might reasonably be expected to have had personal knowledge of the matters dealt with in the statement (s. 117(2)(b)); and
- each person (if any) through whom the information was supplied from the relevant person received the information in the course of a trade, business, profession or other occupation or as the holder of a paid or unpaid office (s. 117(2)(c)).

Section 117 permits the admission at trial of multiple hearsay which satisfies the requirements of the section. In each case:

- the person creating or receiving the document must be acting in the course of a trade, business, profession, or as the holder of a paid or unpaid office; and
- the person who supplied the information contained in the statement must reasonably be supposed to have personal knowledge of the matters dealt with; and
- if the information came through an intermediary, the information must have been received by a person in the course of a trade, business, profession or as the holder of a paid or unpaid office.

Business records, ledgers, invoices and hospital records etc. will all be admissible under s. 117(2).

18.6.1 **DOCUMENTS PREPARED FOR A CRIMINAL INVESTIGATION OR CRIMINAL PROCEEDINGS— SPECIAL RULES**

Section 117(4) provides documents prepared for pending or contemplated criminal proceedings and which are to be admitted as hearsay, must satisfy the conditions laid down in s. 117(5). Such statements are admissible providing any of the five conditions set out in s. 116(2) CJA 2003 relating to the absence of the relevant person is satisfied (see para. 18.5.1), or, as an additional reason, the relevant person (the person who supplied the information contained in the document) cannot reasonably be expected to have any recollection of the matters dealt with in the statement having regard to the length of time since he supplied the information and all other circumstances (s. 117(5)(b)).

Section 117(7) CJA 2003 incorporates an important safeguard to documents to be admitted under s. 117 in providing that a court may make a direction to exclude a statement if the statement's reliability as evidence for the purpose for which it is tendered is doubtful in view of:

- its contents;
- the source of the information contained in it;
- the way in which or the circumstances in which the information was supplied or received; or
- the way in which or the circumstances in which the document concerned was created or received.

Consider the following example of admitting hearsay under s. 117(4) CJA 2003.

 Example

Take the example of Ethel which we considered earlier in the context of s. 116. Assume Ethel has been able to provide the police with a written statement, but is then unable to attend trial. Her written statement would be admissible under s. 117(4)–(5) CJA 2003. It comprises a document prepared for the purposes of criminal proceedings and a prescribed reason for not calling Ethel is made out, namely she is not well enough to attend trial (s. 116(2)(b)). There would appear to be no obvious reason for doubting the reliability of her statement (s. 117(7)).

18.7 **HEARSAY ADMISSIBLE UNDER THE PRESERVED COMMON LAW RULES— S. 118 CJA 2003**

The CJA 2003 specifically preserves some common law exceptions to the hearsay rule including the most important—*res gestae* and confessions.

18.7.1 *RES GESTAE* **STATEMENTS—S. 118(4)(A)–(C) CJA 2003**

Res gestae means transaction, or series of events. There are various situations which cover the admission of evidence under the *res gestae* rule under s. 118(4) CJA 2003 including the 'spontaneous utterance rule'. The leading case on the 'spontaneous utterance rule' is *R v Andrews* [1987] AC 281, where the House of Lords held that a statement made by a fatally stabbed man naming his two attackers soon after he was attacked was properly admitted under the *res gestae* rule.

Section 118(4)(a) CJA 2003 preserves the 'spontaneous utterance rule' and allows an earlier out-of-court statement to be adduced in evidence providing the statement was made by a person 'so emotionally overpowered by an event that the possibility of concoction or distortion can be disregarded'.

A *res gestae* statement can also be admitted where the witness is available to give evidence. The admissibility of hearsay evidence under the *res gestae* principle remains subject to the court's discretion to refuse to admit the statement under s. 78 Police and Criminal Evidence Act 1984 (PACE 1984) on the grounds of unfairness (s. 126(2) CJA 2003).

In *R v W* [2003] 2 Cr App R 29 the defendant was accused of a very serious assault on his mother. She had been pushed down the stairs and had her hair set on fire. There were several witnesses to the aftermath of the attack during which the victim told each of them that her son had gone berserk and attacked her. Later, however, the victim refused to give a statement to the police and gave a deposition before a magistrates' court in which she retracted her oral allegation, claiming she had accidentally fallen downstairs. She declined to comment on how her hair had been burned.

Realising that there would be little point in calling the victim to testify, the prosecution called the witnesses to whom the victim had spoken immediately after the assault to give evidence under the *res gestae* principle. The Court of Appeal held there was nothing in *R v Andrews* which prohibited a *res gestae* statement being admitted, even though the witness to the facts was available to give evidence. As with other prosecution evidence, the *res gestae* statement was subject to the court's exclusionary discretion under s. 78 PACE 1984. However, on the facts and given the importance of this witness to the prosecution's case and the inability of the defendant to cross-examine the hearsay witness, the defendant could not have enjoyed a fair trial as required by Article 6 European Convention on Human Rights 1950 (ECHR 1950).

18.7.2 STATEMENTS IN PUBLIC DOCUMENTS—S. 118(1) CJA 2003

Statements contained in a public document or certified true copies are admissible at common law as evidence of the truth of their contents. This exception to the hearsay rule has long been recognised because such evidence was considered to be reliable and very often the public official who compiled the document would have no recollection of the facts, or be dead, or be unfit to testify. Many statutes provide for the admissibility of certain classes of documents, such as certified true copies of entries in a register of deaths compiled by the Registrar of Births, Deaths and Marriages, as evidence of the date of a person's death where this is a relevant fact in issue in any proceedings.

In addition to such specific provisions, most statements in public documents will be admissible in criminal cases by virtue of s. 117 CJA 2003.

18.7.3 CONFESSION EVIDENCE—S. 118(5) CJA 2003

A confession is a statement made on an earlier out of court occasion which is being relied on in court to prove the truth of facts asserted in it. For that reason it comprises hearsay evidence. Confession evidence has always been admissible as a common law exception to the hearsay rule. Having read Chapter 6, you will be aware that the defendant may oppose the admission of confession evidence under ss. 76 and 78 PACE 1984. It is normally the prosecution that seeks to have the defendant's confession adduced into evidence. Sometimes however, a co-accused will seek to adduce another co-accused's confession into evidence because it assists his defence.

Suppose co-accused A makes a confession, which in whole or in part exonerates B. The prosecution do not propose to rely on A's confession in evidence. Can B adduce A's confession as hearsay? The answer is 'yes'. This scenario arose in the case of *R v Myers* [1998] AC 124, where the House of Lords effectively created a further exception to the hearsay rule by allowing B to adduce evidence of A's confession provided it had not been obtained by means of 'oppression' and was not 'unreliable'. As a consequence of the decision in *Myers* s. 76 PACE 1984 (the main statutory section which regulates the admissibility of disputed confession evidence—see Chapter 6) was amended to allow one co-defendant *charged in the same proceedings* to admit in evidence a confession made by a second co-defendant where the confession supports the defence of the first co-defendant (s. 76A PACE 1984).

18.8 ADMITTING HEARSAY BY AGREEMENT—S. 114(1)(C) CJA 2003

This ground is self-explanatory.

18.9 THE 'SAFETY-VALVE'—S. 114(1)(D) AND S. 121 CJA 2003

Section 114(1)(d) gives a court discretion to admit hearsay evidence which does not come within one of the other specified categories for admitting hearsay evidence under the CJA 2003. A court may only admit such evidence where it is in the interests of justice.

In applying the discretionary 'interests of justice' test the court will apply the following factors laid down in s. 114(2)(a)–(i):

(a) how much probative value the statement has (assuming it to be true) in relation to a matter in issue in the proceedings, or how valuable it is for the understanding of other evidence in the case;

(b) what other evidence has been, or can be, given on the matter or evidence mentioned in paragraph (a);

(c) how important the matter or evidence mentioned in paragraph (a) is in the context of the case as a whole;

(d) the circumstances in which the statement was made;

(e) how reliable the maker of the statement appears to be;

(f) how reliable the evidence of the making of the statement appears to be;

(g) whether oral evidence of the matter stated can be given and, if not, why it cannot;

(h) the amount of difficulty involved in challenging the statement;

(i) the extent to which that difficulty would be likely to prejudice the party facing it.

The 'safety-valve' gives the court a limited inclusionary discretion to admit hearsay where it is in the interests of justice. The section is meant to be used exceptionally where hearsay evidence cannot be admitted under any other provision and is applied on a case-by-case basis. The case law, however, shows the courts are using s. 114(1)(d) to extend the boundaries of admissible hearsay. For example, in *RL v R* [2008] 2 Cr App R 18, L was charged with four counts of rape and five counts of indecent assault against his daughter. L attempted to explain the presence of a towel with his semen on it at the crime scene by suggesting that it had been left in his daughter's flat after L and his wife had had sex during an earlier visit. The police obtained a statement from Mrs L in which she stated she could not remember having sex with L as he had alleged. As L's wife was not a compellable prosecution witness at trial (see Chapter 16), the prosecution sought to put Mrs L's statement in evidence under s. 114(1)(d) CJA 2003 as being in the interests of justice. The trial judge admitted the statement and L was convicted. On appeal, the Court of Appeal ruled that the evidence had been properly admitted under s. 114(1)(d) CJA 2003.

In *R v Stewart John Burton* [2011] EWCA Crim 1990, B appealed against his conviction for sexual activity with a child. B had been arrested following the discovery of letters from him to a 14-year-old girl (X). Gifts from B and pregnancy test kits were also found in X's bedroom. The letters referred to them having kissed and cuddled. X refused to discuss the matter with her mother but told a police officer that she and B had been boyfriend and girlfriend. She said they had kissed and cuddled but denied having had sexual intercourse with him. She later refused to provide a statement or be interviewed. The Crown sought to adduce evidence of what X had said to the police officer, under s. 114(1)(d) CJA 2003. The conversation between X and the police officer could not be admitted under s. 116 CJA 2003 because she, at age 14, was available to give evidence albeit she refused to do so. The prosecution could have witness summonsed X but concluded that would have been counterproductive. The only basis upon which the conversation between X and the police officer could have been admitted was under s. 114(1)(d). B objected on the basis that the Crown was trying to circumvent the restrictions on admitting hearsay evidence under s. 116 CJA 2003. The judge concluded that the Crown was right not to force X to give oral evidence given her age, and admitted the evidence in the interests of justice.

Upholding the conviction, the Court of Appeal concluded that this was an exceptional case and therefore it was in the interests of justice that the evidence be admitted. Particular emphasis was placed on the fact that the absent witness was a child of 14 who clearly had feelings for the accused. She was not best placed to assess what was in her best interests and there was a clear public interest in protecting young people from sexual exploitation by older men.

 Example 1

Recall the earlier example of Ethel aged 84 who is the victim of the burglary. If Ethel gives a description of the perpetrator to her neighbour Arthur and Arthur relays the information to his son Thomas, will the prosecution be able to call Thomas to give evidence of what Ethel said to Arthur which in turn was said to him if both Ethel and Arthur are unable through illness to give oral evidence at trial?

This example raises the issue of multiple hearsay evidence. The original statement has gone through more than one stage of reporting. It cannot therefore be admitted under s. 116 CJA 2003 and it is not admissible under s. 117 CJA 2003 as that section is restricted to documentary hearsay. The only possibility in this instance is the safety-valve. Assume there is no reason to doubt the credibility of any of the witnesses. The statement is of importance to the prosecution. There is a good reason for Ethel's inability to give oral evidence and the defence can still challenge the evidence. On balance, the court might choose to admit the evidence given its reliability and probative value.

18.10 MISCELLANEOUS HEARSAY PROVISIONS

The CJA 2003 has formally brought into the hearsay rules a number of miscellaneous provisions dealing with a witness's written statement where the witness testifies at trial.

- Section 119 CJA 2003 provides that where a witness admits making a previous inconsistent statement or it has been proved that he has made such a statement, the statement can now be admitted as evidence of the truth of what it asserts. (For the rules on proving a previous inconsistent statement, see Chapter 16, para. 16.9.3.)

- Section 120 CJA 2003 enables a witness's previous consistent statement to be admitted as evidence of the truth of what it asserts. This includes previous consistent statements used to rebut a suggestion of recent fabrication, recent complaints, and statements used to refresh a witness's memory upon which the witness is cross-examined, resulting in the statement being put in evidence (see Chapter 16).

- Section 120(4) CJA 2003 provides that a witness's previous statement may be admissible as evidence of the facts stated, if while giving evidence the witness indicates that to the best of his belief he made the statement, that it states the truth and the statement falls within one of the prescribed categories under s. 120(5), (6) and (7) (see Chapter 16).

18.11 IMPORTANT SAFEGUARDS WHEN ADMITTING HEARSAY EVIDENCE

Although the CJA 2003 introduces a more liberal regime for admitting hearsay, even where the conditions for admissibility are satisfied, the Act provides safeguards to limit multiple hearsay and provisions for challenging the capability and credibility of a hearsay witness. The availability of these safeguards will be taken into account by the court when determining disputes between the prosecution and defence regarding the CJA 2003 hearsay provisions and their compatibility with the defendant's right to a fair trial under Article 6 (see para. 18.13).

18.11.1 RESTRICTING MULTIPLE HEARSAY—S. 121 CJA 2003

Multiple hearsay occurs when a statement passes through more than one intermediary.

Section 121 provides that a hearsay statement is not admissible to prove the fact that an earlier hearsay statement was made unless:

- either of the statements is admissible under s. 117 CJA 2003; or under s. 119 as a previous inconsistent statement; or under s. 120 as a previous consistent statement; or
- the parties agree to it being admitted (s. 121(1)(b)); or
- the court is satisfied that the value of the evidence, taking into account how reliable the statement appears to be, is so high, that the interests of justice require it to be admitted (s. 121(1)(c)).

Section 121(1)(c) is regarded as a second safety-valve. In assessing the interests of justice under s. 121(1)(c), a court should additionally consider the factors set out in s. 114(2)(a)–(i) (see *Maher v DPP* [2006] EWHC 1271 (Admin)). The factors in s. 114(a)–(i) are outlined at para. 18.9.

18.11.2 THE WITNESS'S CAPABILITY TO MAKE THE STATEMENT—S. 123 CJA 2003

Nothing in ss. 116, 119 or 120 makes a statement admissible as evidence if it was made by a person who did not have the requisite capability at the time when he made the statement. The same requirement applies to statements admitted under s. 117(2) in relation to the person who supplied or received the information or created or received the document.

18.11.3 CHALLENGING THE WITNESS'S CREDIBILITY—S. 124 CJA 2003

Section 124 CJA 2003 permits the opposing party to challenge the hearsay witness's credibility in the same way as if the witness had given oral evidence.

18.11.4 STOPPING THE CASE WHERE EVIDENCE IS UNCONVINCING—S. 125 CJA 2003

Section 125 requires the court to stop the case and to acquit the defendant where the case against him is based wholly or partly on an out-of-court statement which is so unconvincing that, considering its importance to the case, a conviction would be unsafe. This provision applies only to trials on indictment.

18.11.5 EXCLUDING UNNECESSARY HEARSAY—S. 126 CJA 2003

Section 126(1) CJA 2003 gives the court discretion to exclude hearsay evidence where the court is satisfied that the value of the evidence is substantially outweighed by the undue waste of time which its admission would cause.

18.11.6 DISCRETION TO EXCLUDE HEARSAY—S. 126 CJA 2003

Section 126(2) CJA 2003 preserves the discretion under s. 78 PACE 1984 (unfairness) and at common law under s. 82(3) PACE 1984 (probative value outweighed by prejudicial effect) to exclude hearsay evidence. This is a very important safeguard to ensure that a defendant continues to enjoy a fair trial under the CJA 2003 hearsay provisions.

18.11.7 DIRECTING THE JURY

In accordance with the guidance provided to judges in the Crown Court Bench Book, and as an important safeguard the judge should point out to the jury the limitations of hearsay evidence, namely, the jury has not had the benefit of seeing or hearing the witness, nor has the witness been subject to cross-examination. In a summary trial, the advocate against whom the hearsay evidence has been adduced should remind the magistrates of the limitations of such evidence in his closing speech.

18.12 PROCEDURE FOR ADMITTING HEARSAY EVIDENCE—CRIM PR, PART 34

A party seeking to introduce hearsay evidence must give notice to the court and all other parties in advance of trial, on a prescribed form, in accordance with time limits laid down in Crim PR, Part 34. Where the case is to be tried summarily, notice is usually served at the same time that the prosecution complies with its obligations to serve 'unused' material (see Chapter 8). Where a case has been sent for trial under s. 51 Criminal Disorder Act 1998, a hearsay notice must be served in accordance with standard case progression directions or, in the case of an indictable-only offence, directions given by the judge at the preliminary hearing. Having received notice of hearsay evidence, a party may oppose its admission by giving notice within 14 days on a prescribed form. Provision is made in the rules to allow a court to vary the notice requirements or even dispense with them (Crim PR, Part 34.7). A dispute between the parties is likely to result in a pre-trial ruling on the matter.

18.13 HEARSAY EVIDENCE AND THE ECHR 1950

Article 6(3)(d) confers on a defendant the right to examine or have examined witnesses against him and to obtain the attendance and examination of witnesses on his behalf under the same conditions as the witnesses against him. Where evidence is admitted as hearsay, the defendant is unable to cross-examine the witness. Is the admission of hearsay evidence intrinsically unfair?

The case law of the ECHR 1950 suggests that hearsay does not automatically conflict with Article 6, provided there are counterbalancing measures in place which enable the defendant to effectively challenge the evidence (*Kostovski v Netherlands* [1990] 12 EHHR 434). In *Luca v Italy* [2003] 36 EHHR 46, the European Court of Human Rights (ECtHR) observed that Article 6 would invariably be breached in a case where hearsay evidence is the sole or decisive evidence against the defendant. This proposition was rejected by the Court of Appeal in *R v M* [2003] 2 Cr App R 21 and *R v Sellick and Sellick* [2005] 1 WLR 3257. In both cases there was evidence to suggest that the accused was directly or indirectly responsible for the hearsay witness being unavailable to give evidence.

In a number of domestic cases, including *R v Sellick and Sellick*; and *R v Al-Khawaja* [2006] 1 Cr App R 184, the Court of Appeal has acknowledged the wide range of safeguards (see para. 18.11) in relation to the admission of hearsay evidence, including the specific preservation of s. 78 PACE 1984, by s. 126 CJA 2003, as important protections to ensure the defendant's right to a fair trial. Recent attention has however been paid to the important decision of the ECtHR in *Al-Khawaja and Tahery v UK* (20 January 2009). Al-Khawaja was a doctor who was convicted of sexually assaulting two female patients. One of his victims committed suicide before the trial. Her evidence, which was of particular importance to the prosecution's case, was admitted at trial as hearsay. Following Dr Al-Khawaja's unsuccessful appeal against his conviction, he took his case to the ECtHR which, following the principle in *Luca v Italy*, declared that the admission of hearsay evidence at his trial did violate Article 6(1), specifically Article 6(3)(d). The British Government appealed the decision of the ECtHR in this case to the Grand Chamber of the court.

In the meantime in *Horncastle and Others v R* [2009] EWCA Crim 964, a powerfully composed Court of Appeal with five members considered the practical effects of *Al-Khawaja and Tahery v UK* and concluded that provided the hearsay safeguards in CJA 2003 were observed, a conviction based solely or decisively on hearsay evidence would not in fact breach Article 6(3)(d). The key element in assessing the fairness of the trial was whether in admitting the hearsay a trial court was satisfied the hearsay evidence was reliable and its reliability had been properly tested and assessed. Following the Court of Appeal's decision in *Horncastle and*

Others v R, leave to appeal to the then House of Lords was granted on a point of law of public importance as to whether a defendant could enjoy a fair trial under Article 6(1) and (3)(d) where the evidence against him was wholly or to a decisive extent based on the evidence of witnesses whom the defendants had no opportunity to cross-examine.

In *R v Horncastle and Others* [2009] UKSC 14, in its reconstituted form as the Supreme Court, the Court strongly affirmed the approach taken by the Court of Appeal. In giving the judgment of the Court, Lord Phillips, whilst acknowledging the important protections provided to a defendant by Article 6(3)(d), held the principle was not absolute. There were sufficient safeguards in the rules for admitting hearsay under the Criminal Justice Act 2003 to ensure that prosecution hearsay evidence would not be admitted in contravention of the defendants' right to a fair trial under Article 6. Accordingly the sole or decisive evidence test propounded by the ECtHR in *Al-Khawaja* was rejected.

Following the Supreme Court's judgment in *Horncastle*, the long anticipated Grand Chamber judgment in the case of *Al-Khawaja and Tahery* was delivered ([2011] ECHR 2127). Reversing the decision of the ECtHR in Al-Khawaja's case (by concluding overall that Al-Khawaja had enjoyed a fair trial in accordance with Art. 6), but affirming its decision in Tahery's case (where the absent witness did not attend trial out of fear not orchestrated by the defendant or his associates). The Grand Chamber concluded that the 'sole and decisive rule' articulated in previous judgments of the ECtHR was not to be applied in an inflexible manner, and that where hearsay evidence is the sole or decisive evidence against a defendant, its admission as evidence will not automatically result in a breach of Art. 6. However, 'sufficient counterbalancing factors, including the existence of strong procedural safeguards' are required so as to permit a fair and proper assessment of the reliability of that evidence to take place. In the view of the Grand Chamber, the safeguards under CJA 2003 outlined at para. 18.11 and the requirement for leave where fear is relied on as the reason for a witness's absence are, in principle, strong safeguards/counterbalancing factors designed to ensure fairness.

The Grand Chamber also held that when an absent witness's fear is attributable to the defendant or those acting on his behalf, the defendant is taken to have waived his Art. 6 rights, no matter how important the absent witness is to the prosecution's case.

In the light of the Grand Chamber's decision in *Al-Khawaja and Tahery v UK* (2011) and the Supreme Court in *Horncastle* (2009), further clarification has been provided by the Court of Appeal in a series of conjoined appeals in *Riat, Doran, Wilson, Claire, Bennett* [2012] EWCA Crim 1509. In giving judgment, the Vice-President set out five crucial propositions about the relationship between the CJA 2003 hearsay provisions and the right to a fair trial:

- The law to be applied is that in the 2003 Act.

- If there is any difference, on close analysis, between the judgment of the Supreme Court in *Horncastle* and that of the European Court of Human Rights in *Al-Khawaja and Tahery v UK*, the obligation of a domestic court is to follow the guidance of the Supreme Court.

- There is no overarching rule, either under Convention law or in domestic law, that hearsay evidence which is 'sole or decisive' evidence against an accused automatically conflicts with the fair trial requirements under Article 6.

- In deciding whether to admit hearsay evidence, a trial judge need not ordinarily look further than the provisions of the CJA 2003 and the guidance in *Horncastle*.

- Neither under the statute, nor under *Horncastle*, can hearsay simply be treated as if it were first-hand evidence and automatically admissible.

18.14 HEARSAY EVIDENCE—TRIAL CONSIDERATIONS

Whilst the rules governing the admission of hearsay apply equally to both prosecution and the defence, in most cases hearsay evidence is usually admitted as part of the prosecution case. Having read Chapter 16 you will be aware that there are a number of special measures that are open to some vulnerable and intimidated witnesses. It is for the police and the Crown Prosecution Service lawyer to identify these witnesses and to make an application for special measures on their behalf. However, it is far from uncommon for a witness to fail to attend trial. Where either party becomes aware of a problem before trial, consideration should be given to the possible admission of the witness's evidence under the hearsay provisions. If time permits, an application should be made in accordance with Crim PR, Part 34.

Where the defence is served with notice to admit hearsay evidence, either in advance or at trial, the defence must serve notice to oppose the admission (time permitting) if the hearsay is opposed. Opposition may be based on the fact that the prosecution cannot establish a ground for its admission or, more likely, that the admission of hearsay evidence will lead to an unfair trial.

For all parties it may be appropriate for hearsay to be admitted by agreement either under s. 9 CJA 1967 or under s. 114(1)(c) CJA 2003.

KEY POINT SUMMARY

- Understand what hearsay evidence is. It is any out-of-court statement which is repeated in court for the purpose of proving the truth of a fact or facts asserted in the earlier out-of-court statement. In other words, the earlier statement is being relied on 'testimonially'.

- Understand that as a general rule, hearsay evidence is inadmissible in criminal cases unless it falls within a recognised common law or statutory exception. (Note: the categories for admission have been significantly broadened by the CJA 2003.)

- Recognised common law exceptions admitting hearsay evidence include statements admitted as part of the spontaneous utterance rule (*res gestae*) and confession evidence.

- Hearsay evidence can be admitted with the agreement of the parties under s. 9 CJA 1967 (agreement will be confined to those written statements that do not contain contentious facts requiring the witness to be cross-examined).

- The main statutory basis for admitting hearsay is contained in s. 114 CJA 2003.

- The statutory requirements of ss. 116 (unavailable witness) and 117 CJA 2003 (business documents) must be proved before hearsay evidence can be admitted.

- Understand the categories for admission of hearsay under the CJA 2003 include the safety-valve s. 114(1)(d), which covers hearsay that is not capable of being admitted under any other provision in the Act providing it is in the interests of justice.

- Be aware of the statutory safeguards that will apply in the context of the CJA 2003 and the need to ensure the admission of hearsay evidence does not prejudice a defendant's right to a fair trial in accordance with Article 6.

SELF-TEST QUESTIONS

The CPS is prosecuting an armed robbery involving several defendants. Duane (who has provided the police with a detailed statement during the investigation) is a key prosecution witness. He has received a number of menacing telephone calls warning him against testifying. He has a young family and tells the police he will not testify in court. What evidential problem does this development give rise to and how can the prosecution get around it?

For analysis, see our Online Resource Centre.

 online resource centre

FIGURE 18.1 HEARSAY EVIDENCE

THE GENERAL RULE

- Hearsay is any statement made on an earlier out-of-court occasion which is being adduced in court to prove the truth of facts asserted in that earlier out-of-court statement.
- Section 114 CJA 2003 provides that hearsay evidence being: 'a statement not made in oral evidence in the proceedings, is admissible as evidence of any matter stated in it, if it comes within one of the four exceptions', s. 114 CJA 2003.
- The exceptions which permit the reception of hearsay evidence in criminal cases are set out in s. 114(1)(a)–(d) CJA 2003.
- The exceptions include:
  - s. 116 CJA 2003 (unavailable witness providing the witness is identified);
  - s. 117 CJA 2003 (business documents);
  - s. 114(1)(b) CJA 2003 (it comes within one of the preserved common law exceptions);
  - s. 114(1)(c) CJA 2003 (the parties agree to the hearsay being admitted); or
  - s. 114 (1)(d) CJA 2003 (court decides that it is 'in the interests of justice' for the hearsay to be admitted);
  - s. 9 CJA 1967 (agreed witness statements).
- The CJA 2003 contains a number of safeguards, including the application of s. 78 PACE to ensure use of hearsay evidence is compatible with Article 6 and special provisions as regards multiple hearsay.

REASONS FOR WITNESS UNAVAILABILITY (S. 116 CJA 2003)

- witness is ill, s. 116(2)(a) CJA 2003; or
- is dead, s. 116(2)(b) CJA 2003; or
- cannot be found, s. 116(2)(c) CJA 2003; or
- is outside the UK and it is not reasonably practicable for him to attend, s. 116(2)(d) CJA 2003; or
- witness is in fear, s. 116(2)(e) CJA 2003 (leave required).

ADMITTING A BUSINESS DOCUMENT AS HEARSAY

- under s. 117 CJA 2003, a business document may be admitted as hearsay where:
  - the document was created or received in the course of a business or trade or profession etc.; and
  - the person who supplied the information contained in the statement had or might reasonably be expected to have had personal knowledge of the matters dealt with in the statement; and
  - if the document passed through an intermediary, each intermediary was acting in the course of a trade, profession etc.

PRESERVED COMMON LAW EXCEPTIONS TO THE HEARSAY RULE

- Hearsay is admissible under s. 118 CJA 2003 where the statement falls within one of the preserved common law exceptions, including:
  - the *res gestae* rule;
  - public documents.

ADMITTING HEARSAY WHERE IT IS 'IN THE INTERESTS OF JUSTICE'

- Where a hearsay statement does not come within one of the recognised exceptions under s. 114(1)(a)–(c) CJA 2003, the court may admit the statement under s. 114(1)(d) CJA 2003 where 'it is in the interests of justice'.
- The following factors under s. 114(2) must be taken into account when exercising discretion, including:
  - the credibility of the statement's maker;
  - the statement's probative value;
  - the reason why oral evidence cannot be given;
  - the statement's importance to the party's case;
  - the difficulty to the other side in challenging the hearsay.

19 CHARACTER EVIDENCE AND THE ACCUSED AS A WITNESS AT TRIAL

19.1 INTRODUCTION

In this chapter we examine the evidential rules that apply to the defendant at trial, including:

- the defendant's competence and compellability;

- the course of the defendant's evidence;

- drawing an adverse inference under s. 35 Criminal Justice and Public Order Act 1994 (CJPOA 1994) from the defendant's silence at his trial;

- disclosure of a defendant's past character;

- should the defendant give evidence—arguments for and against.

19.2   THE ACCUSED AS A COMPETENT DEFENCE WITNESS

Under s. 53(1) Youth Justice and Criminal Evidence Act 1999 (YJCEA 1999), the defendant is a competent witness in his defence at every stage of the proceedings and, as a matter of law, can testify at his own trial.

While the defendant is a competent defence witness, he is not a compellable witness—i.e. he has the right not to give evidence and unlike any other witness who refuses to testify he will not be in contempt of court (s. 1(1) Criminal Evidence Act 1898 (CEA 1898)). However, if the defendant remains silent, adverse inferences may be drawn from his silence under s. 35 CJPOA 1994, which is considered at para. 19.4. An accused is a competent but a non-compellable witness for a co-accused under s. 53 YJCEA 1999.

19.2.1   THE DEFENDANT AS A PROSECUTION WITNESS

The defendant is not a competent prosecution witness, whether he is charged alone or jointly with another defendant (s. 53(4) YJCEA 1999). In practice, s. 53(4) YJCEA 1999 is only relevant where one accused (X), is jointly charged with another (Y). A co-accused cannot give evidence for the prosecution while he remains a party to the proceedings. Under s. 53(5) YJCEA 1999, however, where co-accused (X) ceases to be a party in the proceedings, he becomes a competent and compellable prosecution witness against any other person who has been charged in the same proceedings. This occurs where:

- X has been acquitted or has pleaded guilty at an earlier hearing and has been sentenced by the court; or
- X makes a successful submission of no case to answer at the close of the prosecution's case; or
- proceedings against X are discontinued; or
- X is tried separately from Y as a result of a successful application to sever a joint trial.

In any of these situations X may give evidence for the prosecution against Y and anyone else charged in the proceedings. X's status will then change from a co-accused to an accomplice. The defence advocate may submit to the judge or magistrates that the accomplice's evidence should be accompanied by a corroboration warning in accordance with the principles in *R v Makanjuola* [1995] 1 WLR 1348 (see Chapter 17).

19.3   THE COURSE OF THE DEFENDANT'S EVIDENCE

Section 79 PACE 1984 stipulates that if a defendant is to give evidence, he must normally testify before any other defence witness. The defendant's evidence follows the same course as any other witness, including swearing an oath or affirming: examination-in-chief; cross-examination; and, where appropriate, re-examination.

19.3.1   CAN THE DEFENDANT GIVE EVIDENCE UNDER A SPECIAL MEASURES DIRECTION?

A 'vulnerable' defendant can apply to the court to give evidence on oath through a live TV link under s. 47 Police and Justice Act 2006 (PJA 2006). A court will only grant leave if it is in the interests of justice and the conditions under s. 47(4) or (5) are met. Where the defendant is under the age of 18, the conditions under s. 47(4) are:

(a) his ability to participate effectively in the proceedings as a witness giving oral evidence in court is compromised by his level of intellectual ability or social functioning; and

(b) use of a live link would enable him to participate more effectively in the proceedings as a witness (whether by improving the quality of his evidence or otherwise).

Where the defendant is over the age of 18, the conditions under s. 47(5) are:

(a) he suffers from a mental disorder (within the meaning of the Mental Health Act 1983) or otherwise has a significant impairment of intelligence and social function;

(b) for that reason he is unable to participate effectively in the proceedings as a witness giving oral evidence in court; and

(c) the use of a live link would enable him to participate more effectively in the proceedings as a witness (whether by improving the quality of his evidence or otherwise).

Section 33BA(3) YJCEA 1999 permits an accused to testify through an intermediary where under s. 33BA(2) the accused:

• suffers from a mental disorder within the meaning of the Mental Health Act 1983 or otherwise has a significant impairment of intelligence and social function; and

• for that reason is unable to participate effectively in the proceedings as a witness giving oral evidence in court, s. 33BA(6); and

• the order is necessary to ensure the accused enjoys a fair trial, s. 33BA(2)(b).

An order can be made on behalf of an accused under the age of 18, where his ability to effectively participate in the proceedings as a witness is compromised by his intellectual ability or social functioning.

19.4 ADVERSE INFERENCES FROM THE DEFENDANT'S SILENCE AT TRIAL—S. 35 CJPOA 1994

Where the defendant does not testify, s. 35 CJPOA 1994 permits the prosecution to comment on the defendant's silence and, where appropriate, call for inferences to be drawn by the court. Section 35 CJPOA provides:

'(1) At the trial of any person for an offence, subsections (2) and (3) below apply unless—

(a) the accused's guilt is not in issue; or

(b) it appears to the court that the physical or mental condition of the accused makes it undesirable for him to give evidence; . . .

(2) Where this subsection applies, the court shall, at the conclusion of the evidence for the prosecution, satisfy itself (in the case of proceedings on indictment, in the presence of the jury) that the accused is aware that the stage has been reached at which evidence can be given for the defence and that he can, if he wishes, give evidence and that, if he chooses not to give evidence, or having been sworn, without good cause refuses to answer any question, it will be permissible for the court or jury to draw such inference as appears proper from his failure to give evidence or his refusal, without good cause, to answer any question.

(3) Where this subsection applies, the court or jury, in determining whether the accused is guilty of the offence charged, may draw such inferences as appear proper from the failure of the accused to give evidence, or his refusal without good cause to answer any question.

(4) This section does not render the accused compellable to give evidence on his own behalf, and he shall accordingly not be guilty of contempt of court by reason of a failure to do so.'

Before adverse inferences can be drawn under s. 35 CJPOA 1994, the following conditions must be satisfied if the defendant is to enjoy a fair trial:

(1) At the close of the prosecution's case, the judge is required to put the following question to the defence advocate:

'Have you advised your client that the stage has now been reached at which he may give evidence and, if he chooses not to do so, or having been sworn without good cause refuses to answer any question, the jury may draw such inferences as appear proper from his failure to do so?' *(Practice Direction (Criminal: Consolidated)* [2002] 3 All ER 904).

(2) If the defendant remains silent, the jury (or the magistrates) should be directed in the following terms in accordance with the guidance laid down by the Court of Appeal in *R v Cowan, Gayle and Riccardi* [1995] 4 All ER 939:

— the legal burden of proof remains on the prosecution;

— the defendant is entitled to remain silent;

— before drawing an adverse inference from the defendant's silence, the jury/magistrates have to be satisfied that there is a case to answer on the prosecution evidence; and

— if the jury or magistrates conclude that the only sensible explanation for the accused's silence is that he has no answer to the prosecution's case, or none that would stand up to cross-examination, adverse inferences may be drawn.

An adverse inference drawn from the accused's failure to give evidence cannot be the sole finding of guilt (s. 38(3) CJPOA 1994).

It is common for a defendant to submit that a particular physical or mental condition prevented him from testifying. A 'physical condition' would include an epileptic attack. A mental condition would include latent schizophrenia. If after the defence has discharged an evidential burden to prove the condition, it appears to the judge in the *voir dire* that the defendant's physical or mental condition makes it undesirable for him to give evidence, the jury will be directed that adverse inferences should not be drawn (see *R v Friend* [1997] 2 Cr App R 231).

19.4.1 **ADVISING A DEFENDANT WHETHER TO TESTIFY AT TRIAL**

As the defendant is a competent but not a compellable witness at his trial an important part of the defence case preparation is to advise their client whether to give evidence. The advice will be based on both practical considerations and the potential legal implications of testifying or remaining silent.

The practical considerations include:

(1) The nature of the prosecution and defence case

Some offences, for example, a sexual offence, may involve only two participants—the victim and the defendant. In this situation it is almost inevitable that the defendant must testify, as there is no other way in which the defence evidence can be put to the court. This may also apply where one co-accused blames the other. If there are credible and reliable witnesses who can give evidence in support of the defendant's case, it might not be necessary to call the defendant.

(2) Where a legal burden of proof is placed on the defendant

Where a legal burden of proof is placed on a defendant to establish his innocence (see Chapter 15), often the accused is the only person who can testify in support of that defence.

(3) Will the defendant be a credible witness?

Sometimes the best prosecution witness is the defendant! The defence advocate will assess how her client will come across in the witness box. Will she appear believable and credible? Will she cope with cross-examination? Is the defendant sufficiently articulate to create a good impression? Does she have the mental strength to cope with testifying, as appearing as a witness in a criminal trial is highly stressful?

(4) Strength of the prosecution's case

Where objectively assessed the prosecution's evidence is unlikely to persuade a jury of the defendant's guilt beyond reasonable doubt, the defence advocate may not wish to assist the prosecution by calling her client to testify if she has doubts about her client's ability to cope with cross-examination. The decision about whether to allow the defendant to testify may have to wait until after the cross-examination of the prosecution witnesses.

(5) The legal considerations

As well as the practical factors, the decision whether the defendant should testify also involves an important legal consideration because if the defendant does not give evidence, adverse inferences may be drawn under s. 35 CJPOA 1994 (see para. 19.4).

19.5 DISCLOSING EVIDENCE OF THE DEFENDANT'S CHARACTER

While most attention is directed towards the admission of a defendant's past bad character, a defendant's good character also has important evidential value.

19.5.1 THE DEFENDANT'S GOOD CHARACTER

Evidence of the defendant's good character is admissible to show that he is not the type of person who would commit the offence(s) charged and/or it may be relevant to assessing the defendant's credibility (i.e. whether the defendant is likely to be telling the truth).

'Good character' will usually mean the absence of a criminal record, but particularly praiseworthy activities such as a good military service record, public service or charitable acts may also be used to enhance a defendant client's character.

The approach taken by the courts when dealing with a defendant's good character was laid down by the Court of Appeal in *R v Vye and Others* [1993] 97 Cr App R 134:

- A defendant with no convictions is entitled to a good character direction as to his propensity (i.e. the defendant is less likely to have committed this offence because he is a person of past good character). This direction must be given irrespective of whether or not the defendant gives evidence in the case.

- A defendant with no convictions is also entitled to a good character direction as to his credibility where, before trial, he has asserted his innocence either at the police station and/or has given evidence on oath at his trial.

In the Crown Court, the trial judge is required to direct the jury in accordance with the principles in *R v Vye*. A failure to give a good character direction will provide a defendant with a good ground to appeal against his conviction. In a summary trial, the defence advocate should remind the magistrates of the relevance of good character evidence.

The court retains discretion whether to give a good character direction in a case where an accused has a previous conviction albeit for a minor or dated offence and where he has no previous convictions, but admits to past disreputable conduct (*R v Aziz* [1995] 3 WLR 53). In *R v Hamer* [2010] EWCA Crim 2053, the Court of Appeal held that an accused who had no previous convictions or cautions but who had been issued with a fixed penalty notice for disorder (PND) was entitled to an unfettered '*Vye*' direction.

19.5.2 OBTAINING EVIDENCE OF GOOD CHARACTER

When preparing the defence case for trial, it is necessary to obtain character evidence in support of a client with good character. Character evidence can be presented orally by calling a witness to give evidence on oath, or in a witness statement admitted with the prosecution's agreement, under s. 9 Criminal Justice Act 1967 (CJA 1967) (see Chapter 12, para. 12.8.9). The defendant's previous convictions (if any) will have been disclosed under the prosecution's pre-trial disclosure of evidence obligations, enabling the defence advocate to assess whether the accused is entitled to a good character direction.

19.6 **ADMITTING EVIDENCE OF THE DEFENDANT'S BAD CHARACTER**

Part 11 of the CJA 2003 provides a comprehensive statutory framework for admitting the bad character evidence of both the defendant and non-defendant. The provisions covering non-defendants are explained in Chapter 16.

The 2003 Act undermines many of the traditional immunities which generally gave the defendant a shield, or protection against having evidence of his bad character disclosed to the court.

The 'old law' (abolished by s. 99 CJA 2003) was based on an exclusionary approach. Evidence of a defendant's bad character was generally inadmissible to show that because of past offending, the defendant was guilty of the current offence and was limited to a number of exceptions which included the admission of a defendant's bad character under the 'similar fact' evidence rule.

The justification for the former exclusionary approach was to protect the defendant from the prejudice that such knowledge would engender in the minds of the jury or magistrates. The knowledge that X has previous convictions for theft and burglary, on a current charge of burglary, would make it much more likely that X would be convicted as it was thought that juries and magistrates would attach too much significance to the defendant's criminal record and insufficient attention to the evidence linking the defendant to the present offence.

The CJA 2003 considerably extends the boundaries for admitting evidence of a defendant's bad character with fewer safeguards.

19.6.1 **STATUTORY DEFINITION OF BAD CHARACTER**

Section 98 CJA 2003 defines evidence of a person's bad character as 'evidence of, or of a disposition towards, misconduct on his part . . .'.

The term 'misconduct' is further defined by s. 112 CJA 2003, as the commission of an offence or other 'reprehensible' behaviour.

The definition of bad character under the Act is wide and includes:

• evidence of the defendant's previous convictions;

• evidence relating to an offence(s) with which the defendant was charged but not convicted;

• evidence relating to an offence(s) with which the defendant has been charged but acquitted;

• evidence not amounting to criminal conduct but which constitutes 'reprehensible' behaviour.

While the definition of bad character under the CJA 2003 is generally clear, there is uncertainty about the precise limits of what amounts to 'reprehensible behaviour'.

Section 98 further provides that the Act *does not* apply to evidence of, or of a disposition towards, misconduct on his part which:

'(a) has to do with the alleged facts of the offence with which the defendant is charged, or

(b) is evidence of misconduct in connection with the investigation or prosecution of that offence.'

Evidence of misconduct going directly to the facts of the offence for which the defendant is being tried is excluded from the CJA 2003 bad character provisions. The admissibility of this evidence is governed by its relevance to the issues in the current case. Consider the following examples:

 Example 1

Nigel is charged with arson by starting a fire in a hostel for resettling young offenders in which he was living at the time of the alleged offence. The fire occurred shortly after a dispute between Nigel and a member of the hostel staff who accused Nigel of breaking the hostel's curfew rules. In proving the facts, the prosecutor will have to refer to the fact that Nigel was residing at a hostel for the resettling of young offenders. It has to do with the facts of the offence and therefore does not trigger the character provisions under the Act (s. 98(a)).

 Example 2

Gina is accused of a serious offence of assault. The prosecution wishes to adduce evidence that Gina has tried to bribe a prosecution witness not to give evidence. The evidence of the bribe is admissible as it is evidence connected with the prosecution of the offence (s. 98(b)).

19.7 GATEWAYS TO ADMISSION

Section 101(1) CJA 2003 is very significant and is reproduced below in full. It provides seven gateways through which evidence of a defendant's bad character can be admitted.

'**101 Defendant's bad character**

(1) In criminal proceedings evidence of the defendant's bad character is admissible if, but only if—

    (a) all parties to the proceedings agree to the evidence being admissible,

    (b) the evidence is adduced by the defendant or is given in answer to a question asked by him in cross-examination,

    (c) it is important explanatory evidence,

    (d) it is relevant to an important matter in issue between the defendant and the prosecution,

    (e) it has substantial probative value in relation to an important matter in issue between the defendant and a co-defendant,

    (f) it is evidence to correct a false impression given by the defendant, or

    (g) the defendant has made an attack on another person's character.

(2) Sections 102 to 106 contain provisions supplementing subsection (1).

(3) The court must not admit evidence under subsection (1)(d) or (g) if, on an application by the defendant to exclude it, it appears to the court that the admission of the evidence would have such an adverse effect on the fairness of the proceedings that the court ought not to admit it.

(4) On an application to exclude evidence under subsection (3) the court must have regard, in particular, to the length of time between the matters to which that evidence relates and the matters which form the subject of the offence charged.'

Each of the gateways are explained in detail later but before we do so, we will consider the following important question—does the court retain discretion to exclude evidence of a defendant's bad character?

19.7.1 THE STATUTORY DISCRETION TO EXCLUDE BAD CHARACTER EVIDENCE

Under s. 101(3) CJA 2003 the defence may apply to the court to exclude evidence of bad character under either gateway (d) or (g) ONLY if the admission of the evidence would have an adverse effect on the fairness of the proceedings. Section 101(3) specifically provides:

'The court must not admit evidence under subsection 1(d) or (g), if on application by the defendant to exclude it, it appears to the court the admission of the evidence would have such an adverse effect on the fairness of the proceedings that the court ought not admit it.'

In *R v Hanson; R v Gilmore; R v Pickstone* [2005] 2 Cr App R 21, the Court of Appeal stated that the discretion under s. 101(1)(3) was stronger than under s. 78 PACE 1984 as under the former the court 'must not admit' the evidence where its admission would have such an adverse effect on the fairness of the proceedings whereas under s. 78 PACE 1984, the court 'may refuse to allow' the evidence.

In exercising discretion under s. 101(3) CJA 2003 the court is specifically required to have regard to the length of time that has passed since the bad character sought to be admitted was committed (s. 101(4) CJA 2003).

While the discretion to exclude bad character evidence under s. 101(3) is specific to gateways (d) and (g), what is the position under the other gateways? In the absence of an express provision excluding the operation of s. 78 PACE 1984, it must be assumed that it applies to the admission of the defendant's bad character under the 2003 Act. This proposition is supported by statements in the Court of Appeal's decision in *R v Highton; R v Van Nguyen; R v Carp* [2005] 1 WLR 3472.

19.7.2 ADMITTING BAD CHARACTER BY AGREEMENT—S. 101(1)(A) CJA 2003

All parties to the proceedings agree to the defendant's bad character being admitted in evidence.

19.7.3 VOLUNTARILY DISCLOSING BAD CHARACTER—S. 101(1)(B) CJA 2003

Evidence of the defendant's bad character is given by the defendant himself or is given in answer to a question asked by him in cross-examination with the intention of disclosing his bad character.

Section 101(1)(a) and (b) is largely self-explanatory. In relation to s. 101(1)(b), there may be tactical advantages to a defendant choosing to adduce evidence of his bad character where the prosecution has chosen not to put the bad character in evidence as part of its case.

19.7.4 BAD CHARACTER AS IMPORTANT EXPLANATORY EVIDENCE—S. 101(1)(C) CJA 2003

This gateway is further defined in s. 102, and is available only to the prosecution. It is not relied on in practice to any significant extent.

'**102 Important explanatory evidence**

For the purposes of s. 101(1)(c) evidence is important explanatory evidence if—

(a) without it, the court or jury would find it impossible or difficult properly to understand other evidence in the case, and

(b) its value for understanding the case as a whole is substantial.'

In some cases it will be necessary for the prosecution to give background information about the offence, which may result in part or the whole of the defendant's bad character being disclosed. Section 101(1)(c) CJA 2003 gives statutory effect to the previous position at common law.

The Court of Appeal in *R v Edwards; Fysh; Duggan and Chohan* [2006] 1 Cr App R 3 (specifically the appeal of Chohan) provides a useful illustration of gateway (c). Chohan was charged with burglary. He denied the offence. The main prosecution evidence came from an eye-witness who identified him at an identification parade. The identification of Chohan was based on recognition as the eye-witness claimed Chohan had been her drug dealer. Chohan denied involvement in the burglary and accused the eye-witness of fabricating her evidence because he had terminated a sexual relationship with her. Chohan denied supplying drugs to her. The trial judge permitted the evidence to be adduced under gateway (c) as the supply of drugs clearly constituted reprehensible behaviour and it comprised important explanatory evidence. It explained the basis of the eye-witness's identification and why she was so confident that her identification of Chohan was accurate.

19.7.5 BAD CHARACTER AS AN IMPORTANT ISSUE BETWEEN THE DEFENDANT AND THE PROSECUTION—S. 101(1)(D) CJA 2003

Evidence of the defendant's bad character is relevant to an important matter in issue between the defendant and the prosecution. This is an important gateway for the prosecution.

Gateway (d) is further defined in s. 103 and is available only to the prosecution.

'103 Matter in issue between the defendant and the prosecution

(1) For the purposes of section 101(1)(d) the matters in issue between the defendant and the prosecution include—

    (a) the question whether the defendant has a propensity to commit offences of the kind with which he is charged, except where his having such a propensity makes it no more likely that he is guilty of the offence;

    (b) the question whether the defendant has a propensity to be untruthful, except where it is not suggested that the defendant's case is untruthful in any respect.

(2) Where subsection (1)(a) applies, a defendant's propensity to commit offences of the kind with which he is charged may (without prejudice to any other way of doing so) be established by evidence that he has been convicted of—

    (a) an offence of the same description as the one with which he is charged, or

    (b) an offence of the same category as the one with which he is charged.

(3) Subsection (2) does not apply in the case of a particular defendant if the court is satisfied, by reason of the length of time since the conviction or for any other reason, that it would be unjust for it to apply in his case.

(4) For the purposes of subsection (2)—

    (a) two offences are of the same description as each other if the statement of the offence in a written charge or indictment would, in each case, be in the same terms;

    (b) two offences are of the same category as each other if they belong to the same category of offences prescribed for the purposes of this section by an order made by the Secretary of State.

(5) A category prescribed by an order under subsection (4)(b) must consist of offences of the same type.

(6) Only prosecution evidence is admissible under section 101(1)(d).'

An important matter in issue between the prosecution and the defence includes:

- the question whether the defendant has a propensity to commit offences of the kind with which he is currently charged (unless the propensity makes him no more likely to be guilty of the offence with which he is charged); and/or

- the question whether the defendant has a propensity to be untruthful (unless it is not suggested that the defendant's case is untruthful).

Section 144 Coroners and Justice Act 2009 extended the application of s. 103 CJA 2003 to include a defendant's conviction(s) from a foreign jurisdiction where the conviction(s) would have been admissible in England and Wales.

Gateway (d) is very significant because it makes it considerably easier for a defendant's bad character to be admitted than previously at common law under the similar fact evidence rule. Previous convictions and other 'reprehensible behaviour' will be admitted against the defendant under gateway (d) provided they are relevant to an important matter in issue between the prosecution and the defence, subject to the discretion to exclude under s. 101(3).

In the light of the more relaxed rules governing the admission of the defendant's bad character in *R v Hanson; R v Gilmore; R v Pickstone* [2005] 2 Cr App R 21 the Court of Appeal warned prosecutors that bad character applications should not be routinely made simply because a defendant has previous convictions.

(1) Propensity to commit offences of the kind with which the defendant is charged

Under s. 103(2) CJA 2003, propensity to commit offences of the kind with which the defendant is charged *may* be established by evidence that the defendant has been convicted of an offence of the same description or an offence of the same category as the offence(s) with which he is charged. Section 103(2) does not apply if a court concludes that by reason of length of time since conviction or for any other reason, it would be unjust to infer propensity from the defendant's criminal record (s. 103(3)).

(2) An offence of the same description/category

An offence will be of the same description if the statement of offence would in each case be the same (s. 103(4)(a)). For example, if X is charged with assault occasioning actual bodily harm contrary to s. 47 Offences Against the Person Act 1861 and has a previous conviction for a s. 47 assault, this would constitute an offence of the same description and would therefore be admissible to show X's propensity to commit violent assault.

Offences of the same category have to be prescribed in an Order made by the Secretary of State (s. 103(4)(b)). Currently the two categories of offences that fall within the same category are theft and child sex offences.

Theft offences of the same category include theft, robbery, burglary, aggravated burglary, taking a motor car without consent, aggravated vehicle-taking, handling stolen goods, going equipped to steal, making off without payment and inchoate offences of the same description. In relation to sexual offences against persons under the age of 16, the Order includes a full list of all such offences in Part 2 including rape, indecent assault, unlawful sexual intercourse and incest, together with the new offences involving children under the Sexual Offences Act 2003.

Where the defendant is on trial for either a theft or child sex offence and has a conviction(s) for an offence(s) which fall within the same category, there is a strong presumption that the conviction(s) should be revealed to the jury.

(3) Proving propensity to commit an offence of the kind in other ways

Proof of propensity to commit an offence of the kind with which the defendant is charged is not confined to previous convictions for offences of the same description or category. For example, Letitia is charged with a serious assault arising out of an incident in a nightclub. She claims to have acted in self-defence maintaining she was the victim of an unprovoked attack. She has previous convictions for affray and for a public order offence under s. 5 Public Order Act 1986. Although Letitia's previous convictions are not of the same description or category as the current charge, the prosecution could legitimately argue that they indicate a propensity on Letitia's part to engage in acts of violence and public disturbance, making her defence less credible. Her previous convictions are therefore relevant to an important matter in issue between the prosecution and the defence.

In *Elliott* [2010] EWCA Crim 2378 bad character evidence disclosed in letters written to E whilst he was on remand in custody suggesting S was a member of a criminal gang involved in drug crime and the use of firearms was used by the prosecution to rebut an assertion of innocent association. Guns and drugs were found in a store cupboard outside S's home. S denied possession, stating the items had been deposited by others. The Court of Appeal held the evidence 'was plainly capable' of assisting the jury in resolving the disputed issue.

Evidence of a defendant's propensity is not restricted solely to proof of previous convictions and can be proved in other ways (s. 103(2) CJA 2003). In *R v Weir* [2005] EWCA

Crim 2866, the Court of Appeal held that propensity could be established by proof that the defendant had been given a police caution.

Propensity can be established by proof of conduct that is not criminal (provided it is reprehensible). In the pre-2003 Act case of *R v Butler* (1987) 84 Cr App R 12, B denied committing a very degrading sexual assault on a woman in the back of the woman's car after he had flagged her car down, maintaining the woman's identification of him was mistaken. The prosecution was allowed to adduce evidence from the defendant's former girlfriend of the degrading and very similar sexual acts she had allowed him to perform on her. Although the evidence disclosed no criminal acts on the defendant's part, as his former girlfriend had consented, it provided significant probative value on the issue of the accuracy of the victim's identification of her attacker.

Propensity can also be established by unproven past allegations of misconduct, even where this resulted in an acquittal, provided the evidence is relevant. In the pre-2003 Act case of *R v Z* [2000] 3 WLR 117, the defendant denied a charge of rape, maintaining his victim had consented. At his trial evidence was heard that he had previously been tried and acquitted of rape in three separate trials, having used the same defence in each case. The victims in each of the previous cases were permitted to give evidence against Z as their evidence was relevant to the issue of consent in the case being tried. In *R v Smith* [2005] EWCA Crim 3244, a case heard under the 2003 Act, the Court of Appeal endorsed the approach taken in *R v Z* about the admissibility under gateway (d) of earlier allegations against the accused for which he was not prosecuted but which showed propensity to commit the offences charged in the later proceedings. To ensure the defendant is not unfairly prejudiced by this approach the Court of Appeal specifically emphasised that the defendant's protection comes through the judge's discretion to exclude the evidence of bad character under s. 101(3) or, where appropriate, through s. 78 of the Police and Criminal Act 1984.

For a more detailed consideration of the difficulties of establishing propensity from unproven past accusations, see *R v McKenzie* [2008] EWCA Crim 758 and *R v O'Dowd* [2009] EWCA Crim 905 in our Bad Character Case Compendium, which is found in the student resource section of our Online Resource Centre.

 online resource centre

(4) *R v Hanson* and its importance in relation to propensity and the exercise of discretion under s. 101(3)

In one of the first key decisions on the bad character provisions under the CJA 2003, the Court of Appeal provided the following guidance in *R v Hanson; R v Gilmore; R v Pickstone* [2005] 2 Cr App R 21:

(1) Where the prosecution relies on the defendant's propensity to commit offences, there are three questions to be answered:

    (i) Does the history of conviction(s) establish a propensity to commit offences of the kind charged?

    (ii) Does that propensity make it more likely that the defendant committed the offence charged?

    (iii) Is it unjust to rely on the conviction(s) of the same description or category; and, in any event, will the proceedings be unfair if they are admitted?

(2) Propensity is not confined to offences of the same description or category. As such s. 103(2) is not exhaustive of the types of convictions which might be relied on to show evidence of propensity to commit offences of the same kind. Equally, simply because an offence falls within the same description or category is not necessarily sufficient to show a propensity.

(3) There is no minimum number of events that are required to show propensity. The fewer the number of convictions, the weaker the evidence of propensity is likely to be. A single previous conviction may show evidence of propensity where the offence

discloses unusual tendencies or the *modus operandi* discloses significant features such as to give the previous misconduct probative force.

> 'Child sexual abuse or fire setting, are comparatively clear examples of such unusual behaviour but we attempt no exhaustive list. Circumstances demonstrating probative force are not confined to those sharing striking similarity. So, a single conviction for shoplifting will not, without more, be admissible to show propensity to steal. But if the modus operandi has significant features shared by the offence charged, it may show propensity.'

(4) Having regard to the exercise of judicial discretion under s. 101(3), and under s. 103(3), the court should take into consideration:

   (i)   the degree of similarity between the previous conviction and the offence charged, albeit they are both within the same description or prescribed category. For example, theft and assault occasioning actual bodily harm may each embrace a wide spectrum of conduct. This does not, however, mean that what used to be referred as striking similarity must be shown before convictions become admissible;

   (ii) the respective gravity of the past and present offences;

   (iii) a key factor will be an assessment of the strength of the prosecution's case. If there is little or no evidence, it is unlikely to be just to admit a defendant's previous convictions.

(5) The date of the commission of an offence will often be more significant than the date of conviction. Old convictions, with no special features shared with the offence charged, are likely to have an adverse effect on the fairness of the proceedings.

(6) It will often be necessary, before determining admissibility and even when considering offences of the same description or category, to examine each individual conviction rather than merely to look at the name of the offence or at the defendant's record as a whole.

(7) The sentence passed will not normally be probative or admissible at the behest of the Crown, though it may be at the behest of the defence.

(8) Where past events are disputed, the judge should be careful not to permit the trial to drift into satellite litigation by a prolonged investigation into the circumstances of the past misconduct:

> ' . . . the Crown needs to decide, at the time of giving notice of the application, whether it proposes to rely simply upon the fact of conviction or also upon the circumstances of it. The former may be enough when the circumstances of the conviction are sufficiently apparent from its description, to justify a finding that it can establish propensity, either to commit an offence of the kind charged or to be untruthful and that the requirements of ss. 103(3) and 101(3) can, subject to any particular matter raised on behalf of the defendant, be satisfied. For example, a succession of convictions for dwelling-house burglary, where the same is now charged, may well call for no further evidence than proof of the fact of the convictions. But where, as will often be the case, the Crown needs and proposes to rely on the circumstances of the previous convictions, those circumstances and the manner in which they are to be proved must be set out in the application. There is a similar obligation of frankness upon the defendant, which will be reinforced by the general obligation contained in the new Criminal Procedure Rules to give active assistance to the court in its case management (see r. 3.3). Routine applications by defendants for disclosure of the circumstances of previous convictions are likely to be met by a requirement that the request be justified by identification of the reason why it is said that those circumstances may show the convictions to be inadmissible. We would expect the relevant circumstances of previous convictions generally to be capable of agreement, and that, subject to the trial judge's ruling as to admissibility, they will be put before the jury by way of admission. Even where the circumstances are genuinely in dispute, we would expect the minimum indisputable facts to be thus admitted. It will be very rare indeed for it to be necessary for the judge to hear evidence before ruling on admissibility under this Act.'

(9) The importance of correctly directing the jury is also stressed. In any case where bad character is admitted, the jury should be instructed not to place undue reliance on bad character evidence:

> 'Evidence of bad character cannot be used simply to bolster a weak case, or to prejudice the minds of a jury against a defendant. In particular, the jury should be directed; that they should not conclude that the defendant is guilty or untruthful merely because he has these convictions; that, although the convictions may show a propensity, this does not mean that he has committed this offence or been untruthful in this case; that whether they in fact show a propensity is for them to decide; that they must take into account what the defendant has said about his previous convictions; and that, although they are entitled, if they find propensity as shown, to take this into account when determining guilt, propensity is only one relevant factor and they must assess its significance in the light of all the other evidence in the case.'

(10) If a judge has directed himself or herself correctly, the Court of Appeal will be slow to interfere with a ruling as to admissibility.

What of the specific appeals in Hanson?

In *Hanson*, the charge was theft of money from the living accommodation above a public house. The circumstantial evidence linking Hanson to the crime clearly indicated he had a case to answer, although it was not overwhelming. He denied the offence but had previous convictions for dishonesty, including dwelling-house burglary, theft from premises, a previous conviction for robbery and aggravated vehicle-taking. On the facts in this case, the Court of Appeal observed:

> 'Convictions for handling and aggravated vehicle taking, although within the theft category, do not, in our judgment, show, without more pertinent information, propensity to burgle as indicted or to steal, to which the applicant pleaded guilty. The applicant's robbery conviction, albeit also within the theft category, might, had it been analysed, have been regarded as being so prejudicial as to adversely affect the fairness of the proceedings in relation to the offence charged. But the applicant had a considerable number of convictions for burglary and theft from private property that were plainly properly admissible to show propensity to commit an offence of the kind here charged.'

In *Gilmore,* an offence of theft was denied. Gilmore was arrested in the early hours of the morning. He had in his possession a bag containing very recently stolen items. Gilmore claimed to have come across the items innocently, believing them to be rubbish. The evidence linking him to the theft was strong. Three recent previous convictions for theft were properly admitted. They were indicative of a recent propensity to steal.

In *Pickstone,* the charges included the rape and indecent assault of P's step-daughter. P denied the offences. There was medical evidence to support the fact of sexual interference. P stated the girl was making up the allegation against him. The respective credibility of the complainant and the defendant was very much in issue. Nine years previous to the current allegation, P had been convicted of the indecent assault of an 11-year-old girl. The trial judge admitted the previous conviction under gateways (d) and (g). He expressly took into account the length of time since the previous conviction, concluding the 'defendant's sexual mores and motivations are not necessarily affected by the passage of time'. In this context, the admission of the evidence under gateways (d) and (g) would not adversely affect the fairness of the proceedings.

(5) Can an old or single previous conviction prove propensity?

In *R v Sully* (2007) 151 SJLB 1564, two convictions for sexual assault on children which were over 30 years old were correctly admitted on a charge of sexual assault of a female under 13. Similarly in *R v Cox* [2007] EWCA Crim 3365, on a charge of sexually assaulting a 13-year-old babysitter, the defendant's previous convictions for sexual assault and attempted unlawful sexual intercourse with a 12-year-old girl, committed 20 years previously, were admitted. By contrast, in *R v Michael M* [2007] Crim LR 637, a 20-year-old conviction for possessing a sawn-off shotgun was wrongly admitted as evidence of propensity on a charge of possession of a firearm with intent to cause fear of violence. These cases show that what constitutes propensity is a question of fact in each case but that the dicta in *R v Hanson* are being applied in the context of offences showing 'unusual features', for example sexual offences involving children.

(6) Propensity to be untruthful—s. 103(1)(b)

Section 101(1)(d) CJA 2003 further permits the prosecution to adduce evidence of a defendant's bad character where the defendant's propensity to be untruthful is an important matter in issue between the prosecution and the defence. In *R v Hanson* [2005] 2 Cr App R 21, the Court of Appeal observed that a propensity to be untruthful is not the same as a propensity to dishonesty (s. 103(1)(b)) and therefore the prosecution should not simply adduce evidence of previous convictions for dishonesty with the explicit purpose of showing the accused has a propensity for untruthfulness.

This statement must now be read in the light of the comments made by Lord Phillips CJ, in *R v Campbell* [2007] 1 WLR 2798 which appear to render s. 103(1)(b) virtually obsolete. Lord Phillips observed that a defendant's truthfulness is likely to be in issue in any case where he pleads not guilty and so propensity to be untruthful cannot normally be described as being an important matter in issue.

> 'A propensity for untruthfulness will not of itself, go very far to establishing the committal of a criminal offence. To suggest that a propensity for untruthfulness makes it more likely that a defendant has lied to the jury is not likely to help them. If they apply common sense they will conclude that a defendant who has committed a criminal offence may well be prepared to lie about it, even if he has not shown a propensity for lying whereas a defendant who has not committed the offence charged will be likely to tell the truth, even if he has shown a propensity for telling lies. In short, whether or not a defendant is telling the truth to the jury is likely to depend simply on whether or not he committed the offence charged. The jury should focus on the latter question rather than on whether or not he has a propensity for telling lies. For these reasons, the only circumstance in which there is likely to be an important issue as to whether a defendant has a propensity to tell lies is where telling lies is an element of the offence charged. Even then, the propensity to tell lies is only likely to be significant if the lying is in the context of committing criminal offences, in which case the evidence is likely to be admissible under section 103(1)(a).'

Lord Phillips' reasoning appears to ignore the clear wording in s. 103(1)(b) CJA 2003 which deems a propensity to be untruthful to be a matter in issue between the prosecution and the defence and is contrary to the dicta in *R v Hanson* [2005] which give guidance as to what types of previous convictions are relevant to a determination of a defendant's propensity to be untruthful. In a case where the jury is required to assess the credibility of two conflicting accounts (the defendant's version and the version of a prosecution witness), the fact that the defendant has convictions for fraud or deception is surely relevant to an important matter in issue?

(7) Evidence of propensity—the practical issues

For the CPS, gateway (d) is the most common route for the defendant's bad character to be disclosed under the CJA 2003. The reason for this is the wide test under gateway (d), which admits evidence of the defendant's propensity to commit offences or to be untruthful where it is 'relevant to an important issue between the prosecution and the defence'. Most CPS applications involve disclosing previous convictions to prove propensity. In practice the reprehensible ground is not frequently invoked by the CPS due, in part, to uncertainty about what constitutes reprehensible behaviour. Included in this ground might be where the defendant had previously harassed his rape victim or reported incidents of earlier domestic violence in a later offence of serious domestic assault. Note has also been taken of the Court of Appeal's warning in *R v Hanson; R v Gilmore; R v Pickstone* [2005] Cr App R 21, urging restraint by prosecutors not to routinely make bad character applications to bolster an otherwise weak evidential case.

Even though the test for admitting evidence under gateway (d) is interpreted widely, a prosecution application to show propensity should not go unchallenged by the defence. The defence should require the court to ask itself: 'Is the defendant's propensity (as identified by the prosecution) truly relevant to the facts in issue?' or: 'Does the defendant's propensity make it more likely that he committed the offence?' Even if the answer to either question is yes, the defence should still apply to have the evidence excluded under s. 101(3) CJA 2003 (see para. 19.7.1) on the basis that it would have an adverse effect on the fairness of the proceedings. The nature of the defence relied on will be significant in determining the relevance and therefore the admissibility of bad character evidence.

Issues of propensity to commit offences of the kind with which the defendant is charged will involve difficult questions of fact for the judge/magistrates. It may be insufficient for the prosecution to rely on the defendant's criminal record as the court may need to hear the facts behind the conviction to determine its true relevance and whether it is indicative of the defendant's propensity. Suppose a defendant is facing a disputed allegation of common assault but has a previous conviction for assault contrary to s. 47 Offences Against the Person Act 1861 (OAPA 1861). This is an offence of the same description, but an assault can be committed in different ways and for many different reasons.

The following examples illustrate the possible application of gateway 101(1)(d).

 Example 1

Barry is charged with assault occasioning actual bodily harm on his neighbour. He pleads not guilty, maintaining he acted in self-defence. Barry has a previous conviction for a violent assault, contrary to s. 20 OAPA 1861, six years earlier. He was involved in a fracas in a public house following a football match and pleaded guilty. The prosecution would say that he has a previous conviction for an offence of the same description/type which shows Barry has a propensity to use violence. The defence should oppose the application to have this previous conviction admitted. Applying the dicta in *Hanson* (this being one previous conviction only with no special feature), can this single previous conviction amount to propensity? It should also be noted that the manner in which the earlier assault came to be committed is somewhat different from the present alleged assault. In addition, regard should be had to s. 103(3)—this previous conviction is six years old. Aside from challenging propensity, the defence should make an application under s. 101(3) to have it excluded on the basis that its admission would have an adverse effect on the fairness of the proceedings.

In exercising discretion regard should be had to the guidance in *Hanson*. In particular, the previous offence was more serious than that current offence and the circumstances were different. A pertinent factor will be an assessment of how strong the prosecution's case is, as bad character evidence should not be adduced to bolster an evidentially weak case. If the evidence was admitted, the judge would need to carefully direct the jury not to place too much reliance on the fact of previous convictions. If the evidence is not admitted under gateway (d) it might be admitted under gateway (g) if Barry's defence involves an attack on a prosecution witness. It would be up to the judge to decide how to direct the jury in terms of the relevance of the evidence (see para. 19.12).

In the above example, assume instead that Barry has three previous convictions for theft. Could these convictions be admitted as evidence of Barry's propensity to be untruthful?

In the light of the statements in *Hanson*, the answer is arguably no. A propensity towards dishonesty is not the same thing as a propensity to be untruthful. It would be important to ascertain whether Barry pleaded guilty to any or all of his previous offences or was found guilty after having given evidence on oath. In the light of Lord Phillips' statement in *R v Campbell* [2007], the evidence would appear to assume no relevance at all. The evidence could, however, be admitted under gateway (g) if Barry's defence involves an attack on a prosecution witness (see later).

Example 2

Deepak is charged with burglary. He denies the offence, maintaining a defence of mistaken identity. He intends to call his girlfriend as an alibi. Deepak has an extensive criminal record which includes a conviction for violent robbery four years ago, and several previous convictions for theft, burglary and possession of drugs over the past 12 years. Will the fact of these previous convictions be admissible?

The prosecution will want to adduce Deepak's previous convictions for dishonesty related offences under s. 101(1)(d), both as evidence of Deepak's propensity to commit offences of the kind with which he is charged and as evidence of his propensity to be untruthful. The previous convictions for robbery, theft and burglary are all offences of the same description/category as the current offence. The assumption will therefore be that they show Deepak's propensity to commit offences of dishonesty.

What can the defence argue in this situation? How relevant is Deepak's propensity to the issue of whether the witness's identification is correct or not, especially as Deepak denies being at the scene? Would it not adversely affect the fairness of the proceedings if they were to be admitted? Wouldn't the jury inevitably disregard the evidence of identification and conclude Deepak is guilty because of his track record? If Deepak's defence is mistaken identity, in what sense is he putting forward an untruthful defence? While the previous convictions for theft and burglary may be admitted on the issue of his propensity, the admission of the robbery conviction might be regarded as being particularly prejudicial. *Hanson* suggests the court should have regard to the respective gravity of past and present offences and the strength of the prosecution's case. Applying the dicta in *Hanson* (and subject to the caveat raised by Lord Phillips in *R v Campbell*), previous convictions for offences of dishonesty do not necessarily indicate a propensity to be untruthful.

Once again, if the evidence was admitted, the judge should carefully direct the jury not to place too much reliance on the fact of previous convictions.

 Example 3

Frank is charged with sexually assaulting his nine-year-old nephew. He denies the offence, maintaining that the child is lying. Frank received a caution 18 months earlier for possession of indecent photographs of young boys which were found on his computer. He only accepted the caution because he felt under pressure and wanted to avoid unwanted publicity as he was working as a teacher. He does not know how the images appeared on his computer. Can the prosecution use this fact in evidence against him at his trial for sexual assault?

The prosecution would argue that the caution suggests Frank has a paedophilic disposition, making it less likely that the nephew is making up the allegation. Although he has only a caution recorded against his name, *Hanson* suggests that sex offences involving children are indicative of unusual behaviour.

The defence advocate might argue that the earlier offence is very different to that currently alleged, and for this reason its relevance in the context of the current case must be doubted. Furthermore, there is doubt as to the safety and reliability of the previous caution. Consequently, the admission of such evidence would prejudice Frank's right to a fair trial on the basis that its prejudicial value exceeds its probative effect. Does it make it more likely that the boy is telling the truth?

19.8 BAD CHARACTER ADMITTED BETWEEN CO-DEFENDANTS— S. 101(1)(e) CJA 2003

Evidence of a defendant's bad character has substantial probative value to an important issue between the defendant and a co-defendant.

Section 101(1)(e) CJA 2003 is defined further in s. 104, and applies only to a co-defendant.

'104 Matter in issue between the defendant and a co-defendant

(1) Evidence which is relevant to the question whether the defendant has a propensity to be untruthful is admissible on that basis under section 101(1)(e) only if the nature or conduct of his defence is such as to undermine the co-defendant's defence.

(2) Only evidence—

    (a) which is to be (or has been) adduced by the co-defendant, or

    (b) which a witness is to be invited to give (or has given) in cross-examination by the co-defendant
       is admissible under section 101(1)(e).'

This subsection may apply where co-accused (A) wishes to lead evidence of a fellow co-accused's (B's) propensity to commit offences of a certain kind to show that it was more likely that B committed the offence in question. A good example of this gateway is provided by *R v Randall* [2004] 1 Cr App R 26 where it was not entirely clear which of the co-accused had inflicted the final, fatal injury in an allegation of murder. Each blamed the other. Co-accused A sought to introduce B's previous convictions for serious violence to suggest that B was more likely to have inflicted the fatal injury. By contrast, A's previous convictions were for minor offences. The House of Lords quashed A's conviction for murder, maintaining the trial judge should have directed the jury that B's criminal past was relevant to A's defence, and that they could consider B's past when determining the involvement of each in the offence. The key factor is whether the evidence has substantial probative value on an important matter in issue between co-defendants.

Where one co-accused wishes to adduce evidence of the other's propensity to be untruthful, s. 104(1) specifically stipulates that this will only be allowed where the nature and conduct of the co-accused's defence undermines the defence of his fellow co-accused. In *R v Lawson* [2007] 1 WLR 1191, it was suggested that convictions for shoplifting and stealing are relevant to untruthfulness and that the statements in *R v Hanson,* which suggest there is a difference between dishonesty and untruthfulness (see para. 19.7.5(6)), should not be applied to gateway (e).

The following guidelines are taken from the pre-2003 Act case of *R v Varley* [1982] 2 All ER 519 which continue to apply to gateway (e).

- It has to be decided objectively whether the evidence either supports the prosecution case in a material respect or undermines the defence of the co-accused.

- In relation to undermining a co-accused's defence, care must be taken to see that the evidence clearly undermines the defence. Inconvenience to or inconsistency with the other's defence is not of itself sufficient.

- Mere denial of participation in a joint venture is not of itself sufficient to rank as evidence against the co-defendant. Such denial must lead to the conclusion that if the witness did not participate then it must have been the other who did.

The following should be noted about s. 101(1)(e) CJA 2003:

- Where the grounds for admitting evidence of a co-accused's bad character are satisfied, there is no discretion to disallow cross-examination (provided the safeguard that the evidence must have substantial probative value in relation to an important matter in issue between the co-accused is satisfied).

- Evidence of a bad character disclosed under this gateway is not limited to undermining a co-accused's credibility as a witness, and may (subject to how the judge chooses to direct the jury) be used as evidence going towards the co-accused's guilt.

Consider this example of the operation of s. 101(1)(e) CJA 2003.

 Example

Wayne and Jordan are jointly charged with murder. The prosecution alleges that the victim was fatally wounded as a result of being knifed by one or both of the defendants. Wayne and Jordan are pleading not guilty and are running cut-throat defences by blaming each other. Wayne has several previous convictions. Last year he was convicted of possession of an offensive weapon, namely a knuckle-duster. Five years previously, following a trial at which he gave evidence on oath, he was convicted of robbery, during which an iron bar was used to inflict a serious injury on a security guard. Wayne has several previous convictions for theft, deception and burglary over a 10-year period. In his examination-in-chief, Wayne states that it was Jordan who knifed the victim. Jordan has one recent previous conviction for theft and a conviction for affray four years previously in respect of which she pleaded guilty.

Jordan's counsel may seek to cross-examine Wayne about his previous convictions on the basis that:

- Wayne's previous convictions have substantial probative value in relation to an important issue between the co-accused—i.e. the identity of the person who inflicted the fatal knife injury on the deceased; and

- in giving evidence, Wayne has undermined Jordan's defence.

Provided these conditions are satisfied, the court has no discretion to prevent Jordan from adducing evidence of Wayne's previous convictions. The bad character evidence is arguably relevant both to undermining Wayne's credibility as a witness (as his previous convictions show that he has a propensity to be dishonest) and to the likelihood that it was more likely to have been Wayne who inflicted the fatal stab wound as his previous recent conviction for possession of an offensive weapon and his conviction for a violent robbery indicate a propensity to commit violent assaults.

For a case that illustrates the application of gateway (e), see *R v Edwards; Rowlands; McClean; Gray and Smith* [2005] EWCA Crim 3244.

19.9 **BAD CHARACTER TO CORRECT A FALSE IMPRESSION GIVEN BY THE DEFENDANT—S. 101(1)(F) CJA 2003**

Evidence of the defendant's bad character is admissible to correct a false impression given by the defendant.

Section 101(1)(f) CJA 2003 is further defined by s. 105 and is available only to the prosecution:

'105   **Evidence to correct a false impression**

(1) For the purposes of section 101(1)(f)—

  (a) the defendant gives a false impression if he is responsible for the making of an express or implied assertion which is apt to give the court or jury a false or misleading impression about the defendant;

  (b) evidence to correct such an impression is evidence which has probative value in correcting it.

(2) A defendant is treated as being responsible for the making of an assertion if—

  (a) the assertion is made by the defendant in the proceedings (whether or not in evidence given by him);

  (b) the assertion was made by the defendant—

    (i) on being questioned under caution, before charge, about the offence with which he is charged, or

    (ii) on being charged with the offence or officially informed that he might be prosecuted for it, and evidence of the assertion is given in the proceedings,

  (c) the assertion is made by a witness called by the defendant;

  (d) the assertion is made by any witness in cross-examination in response to a question asked by the defendant that is intended to elicit it, or is likely to do so; or

  (e) the assertion was made by any person out of court, and the defendant adduces evidence of it in the proceedings.

(3) A defendant who would otherwise be treated as responsible for the making of an assertion shall not be so treated if, or to the extent that, he withdraws it or disassociates himself from it.

(4) Where it appears to the court that a defendant, by means of his conduct (other than the giving of evidence) in the proceedings, is seeking to give the court or jury an impression about himself that

is false or misleading, the court may if it appears just to do so treat the defendant as being responsible for the making of an assertion which is apt to give that impression.

(5) In subsection (4) 'conduct' includes appearance or dress.

(6) Evidence is admissible under section 101(1)(f) only if it goes no further than is necessary to correct the false impression.

(7) Only prosecution evidence is admissible under section 101(1)(f).'

A defendant gives a false impression if he makes an express or implied assertion which gives the court a false or misleading impression about him. A defendant can create a false impression through an assertion made at the police station or by what he says on oath at trial or through his conduct in the proceedings (s. 105(4)). As with all the gateways, it applies irrespective of whether the defendant gives evidence in his defence. Gateway (f) may be avoided if the defendant withdraws or disassociates himself from the assertion (s. 105(3)). In *Renda* [2005] EWCA Crim 2826, gateway (f) was triggered at the police station when R made false statements regarding his work history. The Court of Appeal held that a concession extracted from a defendant in cross-examination will not amount to a withdrawal or disassociation from a previously made misleading statement.

The prosecution may only introduce evidence of the defendant's bad character sufficient to rebut the false impression that was made about the defendant's character (s. 105(6)). It may not be necessary, therefore, for the whole of the defendant's bad character to be disclosed.

There is nothing in the Act which suggests that, having adduced evidence of the defendant's bad character under this gateway, the court cannot use the information to infer guilt. Equally, there is nothing to prevent the judge from directing the jury to make limited evidential use of such evidence. As the discretion under s. 101(3) does not apply to this gateway, the admissibility of the defendant's bad character can be challenged under s. 78 PACE 1984 and the common law discretion under s. 82(3) PACE 1984.

 Example

Saeeda is charged with handling a consignment of stolen designer clothes. Both during the police investigation and at trial, Saeeda asserts that she would never do anything dishonest where her business interests are concerned. To rebut this false assertion about her unimpeachable business ethics, the prosecution wish to put in evidence Saeeda's conviction for a VAT fraud committed while she was a director of an unrelated business venture six years ago. The prosecution would be able to put Saeeda's conviction into evidence to rebut the misleading impression she has created about her business affairs. Had Saeeda made her assertion solely in the course of the interview, the gateway could still be triggered by the investigating officer giving evidence of the assertion in interview. In either instance, Saeeda should be advised to withdraw the statement she made in interview before trial. In these circumstances the gateway under s. 101(1)(f) would not be triggered.

19.10 BAD CHARACTER ADMITTED UNDER S. 101(1)(g) CJA 2003

Evidence of the defendant's bad character is admissible after the defendant has made an attack on another person's character.

This is another significant gateway for the prosecution and is further defined in s. 106:

'**106 Attack on another person's character**

(1) For the purposes of section 101(1)(g) a defendant makes an attack on another person's character if—

(a) he adduces evidence attacking the other person's character, or

(b) he (or any legal representative appointed under section 38(4) of the Youth Justice and Criminal Evidence Act 1999 to cross-examine a witness in his interests) asks questions in cross-examination that are intended to elicit such evidence, or are likely to do so, or

(c) evidence is given of an imputation about the other person made by the defendant—

    (i) on being questioned under caution, before charge, about the offence with which he is charged, or

    (ii) on being charged with the offence or officially informed that he might be prosecuted for it.

(2) In subsection (1) "evidence attacking the other person's character" means evidence to the effect that the other person—

    (a) has committed an offence (whether a different offence from the one with which the defendant is charged or the same one), or

    (b) has behaved, or is disposed to behave, in a reprehensible way; and "imputation about the other person" means an assertion to that effect.

(3) Only prosecution evidence is admissible under section 101(1)(g).'

19.10.1 WHAT AMOUNTS TO AN ATTACK?

Gateway (g) replaces the old law under s. 1(3)(ii) CEA 1898 which gave a defendant a shield against the revelation of past bad character whilst giving evidence on oath. The defendant would lose his shield if his defence led to the character of a prosecution witness being impugned. In *R v Hanson* [2005] 2 Cr App R 21, the Court of Appeal observed:

'As to s. 101(1)(g), the pre-2003 Act authorities will continue to apply when assessing whether an attack has been made on another person's character, to the extent that they are compatible with s. 106.'

This means that authorities such as *Selvey v DPP* [1970] AC 304 and *R v Britzman* [1983] 1 WLR 350 on what constitutes an 'attack' continue to apply. In *Selvey* it was held that a defendant still loses his shield notwithstanding that attacking the character of another is a necessary part of his defence. Some latitude was given to defendants under the 1898 Act in that a denial of guilt, however emphatic, would not amount to an attack. The cases at common law went so far as to suggest that even calling a witness a liar would not amount to an attack, but a suggestion that the witness had a motive for lying would do so. Based on the pre-2003 Act authorities, the following situations would constitute an 'attack' on another:

- an allegation that a prosecution witness is biased;
- an allegation that the police have fabricated evidence;
- cross-examining a prosecution witness on any previous convictions they might have;
- accusing a prosecution witness of perjury;
- accusing the investigating officers of deliberately flouting PACE and the Codes of Practice.

It will probably not amount to an 'attack' to suggest that:

- a prosecution witness is mistaken, confused or simply wrong;
- the police have got some aspect of the Codes of Practice wrong;
- a prosecution witness is lying, subject to the latitude the court gives an accused in accordance with the decision in *R v Britzman*.

Gateway (g) is wider than its Criminal Evidence Act 1898 predecessor. It refers to attacking another person's character and is therefore not limited to witnesses in the case. It is irrelevant whether the defendant testifies.

Of particular concern is that gateway (g) extends to the defendant's comments at the police station. In *R v Ball* [2005] EWCA Crim 2826, B used the word 'slag' during a police interview when seeking to defend an allegation of rape which was held to be sufficient to trigger gateway (g). Suppose the investigating officer says to the suspect '. . . so are you saying that witness X is lying . . . ?' If the suspect answers this affirmatively, he might be regarded as attacking another person's character, triggering the admission of his previous convictions at any subsequent trial. This provision makes the already difficult role of the legal adviser at the police station (considered in the online chapter 'Advising at the Police Station') considerably more challenging.

online
resource
centre

You will recall that the defendant will only be able to 'attack' the character of a witness if he is granted leave under s. 100 CJA 2003, see Chapter 16, para. 16.9.4. Even where a defendant is granted leave to adduce evidence disclosing the character of another under s. 100 CJA 2003, gateway (g) will still be triggered, as this is regarded as making an attack on the character of another person.

19.10.2 THE EXERCISE OF DISCRETION IN RELATION TO GATEWAY (g)

As with s. 101(1)(d), the defence can apply to have the evidence excluded under s. 101(3) CJA 2003 on the basis of 'unfairness'. Under the pre-2003 Act, the discretion to exclude evidence of a defendant's previous convictions following the loss of his shield, even where his previous convictions were similar to the offence for which he was being tried, was exercised restrictively. In *R v Burke* (1986) 82 Cr App R 156, while acknowledging that 'cases must occur in which it would be unjust to admit evidence of a character gravely prejudicial to the accused, even though there may be some tenuous grounds for holding it technically admissible', the Court of Appeal nevertheless went on to say that:

'In the ordinary and normal case the trial judge may feel that if the credit of the prosecutor or his witnesses has been attacked, it is only fair that the jury should have before them material on which they can form their judgment whether the accused person is any more worthy to be believed than those he has attacked. It is obviously unfair that the jury should be left in the dark about an accused person's character if the conduct of his defence has attacked the character of the prosecutor or the witnesses for the prosecution.'

 Example

Consider the following example of s. 101(1)(g) CJA 2003. Lim is charged with assaulting his cohabitee on two separate occasions. The couple have a volatile relationship. Lim denies the allegation and claims he acted in self-defence, maintaining the injured party flew at him in a drunken rage. Lim has previously obtained a civil injunction against his partner. Lim seeks leave under s. 100 CJA 2003 to adduce evidence of his partner's violent acts against him. This is clearly an attack on her character. As a consequence, the prosecution serves notice under s. 101(1)(g) to admit Lim's previous convictions for wounding with intent, assault occasioning actual bodily harm and assault on a police officer (the most recent committed eight years ago), offences of theft, handling and deception committed 12 years ago and two drink-related driving offences (failing to provide a specimen and driving with excess alcohol) committed in the last five years. None of his assaults were perpetrated on females. If leave is granted under s. 100 CJA 2003, it is inevitable that gateway (g) will be opened. The defence could apply to have the evidence excluded (s. 101(3) CJA 2003) on the basis that to admit them would be unduly prejudicial. Lim will say that his previous convictions for violence are considerably dated and that none of them involved him using violence against women. If admitted, Lim might persuade the court to confine their relevance to an assessment of his credibility only. However, given the statements in *Highton* and *Campbell,* there is nothing to prevent the court from using the previous convictions on the issue of Lim's propensity if they are relevant. Previous convictions for deception may well be used as evidence indicating a propensity to be untruthful subject to the statements in *Campbell* on this point.

19.11 THE PRACTICE AND PROCEDURE FOR ADMITTING EVIDENCE OF A DEFENDANT'S BAD CHARACTER

With the exception of gateways (a), (b) and (e), it is the Crown Prosecutor's decision whether to make a bad character application.

Where a bad character application is made, the police will provide evidence of the defendant's bad character from the Police National Computer (PNC) which details a person's previous offending.

The procedure for applying is set out in Crim PR, Part 35. On receiving the defendant's antecedents from the PNC the prosecution must serve the notice in the prescribed form when seeking to admit evidence of the defendant's bad character under gateways (c)–(g), excluding (e). Most applications are in writing and in accordance with strict time limits. However, Part 35 enables an application to be made orally and out of time where the interests of justice require it. Where the application is opposed by the defence, the notice to oppose must be served on the prescribed form and returned within set time limits.

In the Crown Court, the bad character application will initially be considered by the judge at the Plea and Case Management Hearing along with other pre-trial issues. The prosecution and defence advocates will usually have submitted a skeleton argument in support of their applications. The full application will then usually be left to be heard on the day of the trial before the jury is empanelled.

Both prosecutors and defence advocates will be aware that a binding ruling in favour of admitting evidence of a defendant's bad character made before the trial may persuade a defendant to plead guilty.

In cases that are to be tried before the magistrates' court, a contested application is normally listed for consideration at the pre-trial hearing where a District Judge or magistrates will hear legal arguments and make a binding ruling.

When making a binding ruling on the admissibility of bad character evidence, the court must give written reasons for reaching its decision (s. 110 CJA 2003).

In assessing the evidence and preparing the case for trial the CPS lawyer requires an excellent understanding of the statutory framework and the leading case law because where bad character is admissible, in most cases it will significantly enhance the prosecution's case and increase the chance of a successful prosecution.

The defence lawyer should also be similarly vigilant and be prepared to rigorously persuade the court that either the test for admitting the bad character under the gateway specified by the CPS in the application is not made out or argue persuasively that the court should exercise its exclusionary discretion under s. 78 PACE 1984 and/or s. 101(1)(3) CJA 2003.

Our case study *R v Lenny Wise* includes an application by the prosecution to admit evidence of Lenny Wise's criminal convictions under s. 101(1) CJA 2003. The relevant documentation can be accessed from our Online Resource Centre.

19.12 RELEVANCE AND USE THAT CAN BE MADE OF BAD CHARACTER ADDUCED UNDER S. 101

The CJA 2003 makes no stipulation as to the use that can be made of bad character under the Act. In *R v Highton; R v Van Nguyen; R v Carp* [2005] 1 WLR 3472 the Court of Appeal stated:

> 'In the case of gateway (g), for example, admissibility depends on the defendant having made an attack on another person's character, but once the evidence is admitted, it may, depending on the particular facts, be relevant not only to credibility but also to propensity to commit offences of the kind with which the defendant is charged.'

This view is supported by statements made in *R v Campbell* [2007] 1 WLR 2798. Lord Phillips observed that once bad character is admitted it can be used for any purpose for which it assumes relevance. Thus bad character admitted through gateway (g) may be used by a jury as evidence of the defendant's propensity even though the bad character has not been admitted under gateway (d) and vice versa. The importance of correctly directing the jury on the relevance of the evidence and the need not to place undue reliance upon it is stressed in *Highton.*

19.13 MISCELLANEOUS MATTERS

Under s. 107 CJA 2003 power is given to a trial judge to stop a trial on indictment at any time before the close of the prosecution's case where evidence has been admitted under s. 101(1)(c)–(g) CJA 2003 and the court is satisfied that the evidence is contaminated, with the result that any conviction would be regarded as being unsafe. There are also special rules relating to childhood convictions under s. 108 CJA 2003, which provide that where a person (aged 21 or over) is being tried, evidence of any previous convictions committed by him under the age of 14 shall not be admissible unless both of the offences are triable on indictment and the court is satisfied that the interests of justice require the evidence to be admitted.

Postscript

A steady stream of case law on bad character is emerging. If it is relevant to your core Criminal Litigation course or to your elective in Advanced Criminal Litigation you can access the 'Bad Character Case Compendium' which is held on the student resource section of our Online Resource Centre. The compendium contains further analysis of bad character evidence and a summary of the most important cases on bad character to date. A number of recent decisions are illustrative of the arguments typically advanced at first instance.

online resource centre

Some decisions show how far the pendulum has swung in favour of the prosecution in admitting evidence of the defendant's bad character. This has serious implications for defendants because if bad character is admitted, it can significantly strengthen the prosecution's case. However, only a handful of cases go to appeal and most decisions on admitting bad character are made at first instance by judges, District Judges and magistrates on the facts in each case. A defence advocate can therefore influence the way in which law is applied and developed on a day-to-day basis.

Further postscript

In the Lecturers' Resource section of the Online Resource Centre, you will find a free-standing video case study entitled *R v Nicholas Jones*. The case involves applications to admit both defendant and non-defendant bad character. The applications were not scripted and were argued before a judge of the Crown Court, who gives a detailed ruling on each application. Full instructions on how you might use this learning resource are given.

online resource centre

KEY POINT SUMMARY

- Be aware of the evidential value of a defendant's good character. Evidence of a defendant's past good character should always be advanced.

- The admissibility of evidence of a defendant's past bad character is regulated by the provisions of the CJA 2003.

- Bad character is very widely defined to include any reprehensible behaviour and is not confined to previous convictions.

- Understand that there are seven gateways in s. 101 through which evidence of a defendant's bad character may be adduced, and that each gateway is further defined in ss. 102–106.

- The application of judicial discretion under s. 101(3) CJA 2003 may prove to be a crucial safeguard in ensuring the defendant can enjoy a fair trial as it gives the court discretion (at least in the context of the most frequently engaged gateways (d) and (g)) to exclude bad character evidence if it would have an adverse effect on the fairness of the proceedings.

- Guidance on what constitutes propensity to commit offences of the kind charged and how judicial discretion to exclude evidence of propensity might be exercised has been provided by the Court of Appeal in *Hanson* and *Highton*.

- The defence must oppose the application of bad character if it is to be excluded—the decision to admit or exclude such evidence may well depend on the quality of the arguments put forward by opposing advocates!

- The defendant is not a compellable witness in a criminal case, but a failure to give evidence without good cause is subject to the risk of having an adverse inference drawn under s. 35 CJPOA 1994.

- Understand the factors that may be taken into consideration when advising clients about whether or not to testify at their trial.

1. Aaron is charged with possession of drugs with intent to supply. The drugs were found under the bonnet of a car he was driving. Aaron pleads not guilty, maintaining he had no knowledge of the presence of the drugs having borrowed the car. Twelve months ago, Aaron was convicted of possession of crack cocaine with intent to supply. He pleaded guilty on the basis that he was a mere custodian of the drugs for a friend. He was given a community sentence which is considered lenient for such an offence. Upon what basis do you feel the prosecution would seek admission of Aaron's previous conviction? If you were the defence advocate, what arguments would you advance in opposition?

2(a) Brian is charged with the rape of a 15-year-old girl. His defence is that the girl consented. He was convicted five years ago of an offence of unlawful sexual activity with a 14-year-old girl following a guilty plea. Will the prosecution be able to rely on this earlier conviction? What representations would the defence make opposing the prosecution application to adduce his previous conviction?

2(b) Vary the facts slightly. Brian is still charged with the rape of a 15-year-old. His defence is that his victim consented. Brian has a previous conviction for raping his former 26-year-old partner, eight years ago. On that occasion, he ran the same defence. Would this previous conviction be admissible? If so, on what basis?

3. Barry and Tina are accused of the murder of Sean, aged 3. Barry was Sean's step-father and Tina was his natural mother. The child died as a result of head injuries. Barry denies murder and states that the child died while in his mother's care and that she has a vicious temper and punched the child while in a drunken stupor. Tina denies murder and claims Barry struck Sean about the head while high on drugs. She maintains she is terrified of Barry and was powerless to do anything. The pathologist's report discloses that the child was malnourished and that his body was covered in bruises and cigarette burns. Barry has several previous convictions for drug-related offences and theft, a previous conviction for criminal damage and one previous conviction for assault occasioning actual bodily harm. Tina has a previous conviction for theft. She will give evidence in support of her defence. Should Barry give evidence? Does the conduct of his defence give you cause for concern? If so, why?

4. Danielle is charged with causing grievous bodily harm with intent. It is alleged she 'glassed' a man in the face causing facial injuries. She denies the offence. She has no previous convictions. What evidential use can be derived from the last-mentioned fact?

Analysis of the above questions can be found on our Online Resource Centre.

Case study: *R v Lenny Wise*

You are reminded that the complete documentation in relation to this case study can be accessed from our Online Resource Centre.

You will be aware of the issues in this case. The prosecution have served notice to admit Lenny Wise's previous convictions under s. 101(1)(d) CJA 2003. The defence have served notice opposing their admission.

Do you consider that Lenny's previous convictions would be admissible?

Consider whether it would be advisable for Lenny to give evidence in his defence. What factors would have a bearing on your advice?

FIGURE 19.1 EVIDENTIAL RULES RELEVANT TO THE ACCUSED

COMPETENCE AND COMPELLABILITY OF THE ACCUSED

- The accused is:
  - a competent but non-compellable witness for the defence, s. 53 YJCEA 1999;
  - neither a competent or compellable witness for the prosecution, s. 53(4) YJCEA 1999.

- A co-accused is also not a competent or compellable witness for the prosecution unless he ceases to be a party to the proceedings (s. 53(5) YJCEA 1999).

THE COURSE OF THE ACCUSED'S EVIDENCE

- Section 79 PACE 1984 requires the accused to testify as the first defence witness.
- Where the accused does not give evidence at his trial, adverse inferences may be drawn against his silence under s. 35 CJPOA 1994, providing:
  - the accused is made aware of his right to testify and the possible consequences of remaining silent, Practice Direction (Criminal Consolidated) [2002]; and the jury or magistrates are reminded that:
    - the legal burden of proving the accused's guilt lies with the prosecution; and
    - the defendant is entitled to remain silent; and
    - the prosecution must have established a *prima facie* case against the accused; and
    - adverse inferences cannot be the sole reason for finding the accused guilty, s.38(3) CJPOA 1994; and
    - adverse inferences may only be drawn where the only explanation for the accused's silence is that he has no answer to the prosecution case; or none that would stand up to cross-examination (see *R v Cowan, Gayle and Riccardi* [1995]).

GOOD CHARACTER

- A defendant with good character is entitled to a good character direction, see *R v Vye and Others* [1993] as to:
  - propensity (a defendant of good character is less likely to have committed the offence); and
  - credibility as a witness (where the defendant before trial asserts his innocence and/or gives evidence at trial).

ADDUCING THE DEFENDANT'S BAD CHARACTER

- Bad character is defined by s. 98 CJA 2003 as evidence of or a disposition towards misconduct or other reprehensible behaviour.
- Section 101(a)–(g) CJA 2003 provides seven gateways through which evidence of a defendant's bad character can be admitted:
  (a) all parties agree to the evidence being admitted;
  (b) the evidence is adduced by the defendant or is given in answer during the defendant's cross-examination;
  (c) it is important explanatory evidence;
  (d) it is relevant to an important matter in issue between D and P;
  (e) it has substantial probative value in relation to an important matter in issue between a defendant and co-defendant;
  (f) it is evidence to correct a false impression given by a defendant; or
  (g) the defendant has made an attack on another person's character.
- Evidence of bad character sought to be admitted under s. 101(1)(d) and (g) is subject to exclusionary discretion in s. 101(3) CJA 2003 based on the fairness of admitting the evidence which is triggered by the defence.
- *R v Hanson* [2005] provides important guidance on what constitutes propensity to commit offences of the kind and propensity to be untruthful.
- In exercising discretion in terms of what is just under s. 103(3) and the fairness of the proceedings under s. 101(3), *Hanson* says the following factors are important:
  - the similarity between past and present offences;
  - the respective gravity of past and present offending;
  - the age of any previous convictions;
  - the strength of the prosecution's case.

20 PRIVATE PRIVILEGE

20.1 INTRODUCTION

The term 'private privilege' relates to separate privileges that prevent evidence from being disclosed in litigation, or witnesses from being compelled to answer questions at trial. In a criminal case, privilege may be claimed in two situations:

• legal professional privilege;

• the privilege against self-incrimination.

While it is generally in the public interest for cases to be decided on all available admissible and relevant evidence, private privilege recognises that in certain situations it is in the wider public interest to maintain the confidentiality of communications between a lawyer and his client even where the court is denied the benefit of otherwise admissible and relevant evidence.

In this chapter we consider:

• legal professional privilege in criminal cases;

• legal professional privilege and the courts;

• waiving legal professional privilege;

• the privilege against self-incrimination;

• the privilege against self-incrimination and the European Convention on Human Rights 1950.

Whilst the evidential effect of claiming private privilege is the same as claiming public interest immunity (see Chapter 8, para. 8.15), an important difference between them is that private privilege is a personal right belonging to the client or to a witness and cannot be claimed by any other person. Conversely public interest immunity seeks to protect the 'confidentiality' of the work of organisations operating in the 'public' domain, such as the police, security services and HM Revenue and Customs.

20.2 **LEGAL PROFESSIONAL PRIVILEGE IN CRIMINAL CASES**

Legal professional privilege in criminal cases is defined by s. 10(1) Police and Criminal Evidence Act 1984 (PACE 1984), to include:

'(a) communications between a professional legal adviser and his client or any person representing his client made in connection with the giving of legal advice to the client;

(b) communications between a professional legal adviser and his client or any person representing his client or between such an adviser or his client or any such representative and any other person made in connection with or in contemplation of legal proceedings and for the purpose of such proceedings; and

(c) items enclosed with or referred to in such communications and made—

    (i) in connection with the giving of legal advice; or

    (ii) in connection with or in the contemplation of legal proceedings and for the purposes of such proceedings;

when they are in the possession of a person who is entitled to possession of them.'

Under s.10(2) PACE 1984, legal professional privilege does not apply to communications between legal adviser and client where it is used to commit or to conceal the commission of a crime.

It is immaterial whether the lawyer was aware of the illicit purpose of the communication and the 'crime' may relate to an offence either under United Kingdom law or in a foreign jurisdiction, see *R v Cox and Railton* [1884] 14 QBD 153.

Legal professional privilege applies in the following two situations.

20.2.1 **COMMUNICATIONS BETWEEN THE LAWYER AND CLIENT—S. 10(1)(A) PACE 1984**

All communications between the lawyer and client in 'the giving or obtaining of legal advice', and within the proper scope of the lawyer's professional work, will be privileged from disclosure. According to the Court of Appeal in *Balabel v Air India* [1988] 2 All ER 246, 'giving legal advice' is not restricted to communications that specifically request or give legal advice, but also includes communications and correspondence that are part of the ongoing relationship between the lawyer and the client.

Therefore, legal professional privilege will attach to:

- all communications between a lawyer and his client;
- communications with counsel;
- communications to salaried legal advisers whether or not they hold a formal legal qualification; and
- communications to foreign lawyers.

The most obvious example of the privilege is that a client cannot be compelled to disclose any oral or written advice given to her by her lawyer or counsel in connection with the case.

While the phrase 'giving legal advice' is broadly interpreted, the courts will not apply the principle to all client–lawyer communications.

Legal professional privilege does not apply to:

- a record of a conveyancing transaction (*R v Crown Court at Inner London Sessions, ex p. Baines and Baines* [1987] 3 All ER 1025);
- a solicitor's documentary records of time spent with a client;
- time sheets;
- fee records;
- the record of a client's appointment in a solicitor's appointment diary (see *R v Manchester Crown Court, ex p. R (Legal Professional Privilege)* [1999] 1 WLR 832).

These documents are not covered by legal professional privilege as they are not concerned with the giving of legal advice.

20.2.2 COMMUNICATIONS WITH THIRD PARTIES—S. 10(1)(b) PACE 1984

Legal professional privilege will attach to communications between the client, the legal adviser and a third party where the sole or dominant purpose of the communication was in connection with actual or pending litigation.

In deciding the 'dominant purpose test', the court will adopt an objective view of all the evidence, taking into account the intention of the document's author and the purpose of preparing the document. The key requirement in maintaining the privileged status of communications with third parties is that the communication must relate to pending or contemplated litigation.

20.3 THE PURPOSE OF LEGAL PROFESSIONAL PRIVILEGE

The purpose of the privilege is that it is in the public interest that when seeking the advice of her lawyer, a client should be able to openly discuss her case, and to make a full disclosure of all relevant information to her lawyer in the knowledge that she cannot be compelled to disclose the content of those discussions, nor will she be compelled to give evidence about them in court.

20.4 LEGAL PROFESSIONAL PRIVILEGE AND THE COURTS

As legal professional privilege underpins the administration of criminal justice, the courts adopt a strict approach to enforcing its application. The position is illustrated by the House of Lords in *R v Derby Magistrates' Court, ex p. B* [1996] AC 487.

R v Derby Magistrates' Court, ex p. B [1996] AC 487

A 16-year-old girl was murdered. The appellant was arrested and made a statement to the police that he alone was responsible for the murder. He later retracted the statement and alleged that although he had been present at the scene of the crime, it was his step-father who had killed the girl. Relying on this second statement, the appellant was acquitted in the Crown Court.

Later, the appellant's step-father was charged with the murder. At the step-father's committal, the appellant was called as a witness for the prosecution and repeated the statement that his step-father had killed the girl. He was cross-examined by the defence about the instructions he had given to his solicitor concerning the murder. The appellant claimed legal professional privilege but the magistrates issued a summons (s. 97 Magistrates' Courts Act 1980) directing the appellant and his solicitor to produce the relevant proofs of evidence as they would be 'likely to be material evidence'.

On appeal, the House of Lords held that a summons could not be issued under s. 97 Magistrates' Courts Act 1980 to compel the production of documents protected by legal professional privilege unless the privilege had been waived, which in the present case, it had not. In reaffirming its status, the House of Lords stated that legal professional privilege is much more than an ordinary rule of evidence; it is a fundamental condition on which the administration of justice rests.

The importance that the European Court of Human Rights attaches to the right of a client to consult a lawyer in private has been stressed on a number of occasions.

20.5 WAIVING/LOSING LEGAL PROFESSIONAL PRIVILEGE

Privileged material may be relied on by an opposing party if the privilege is waived or lost. As legal professional privilege vests in the client, only she can waive it, either at the pre-trial stage or during the trial. If the client expressly or impliedly waives the privilege a lawyer can be compelled to reveal the contents of the communications between himself and the client, or between himself and a third party. As explained in Chapter 5 the question of waiver commonly arises where the accused is required to explain her silence in response to questions at the police station, by disclosing the reasons that she was given by her lawyer for refusing to answer. In this situation both the accused and the legal adviser may be cross-examined about the content of the advice given at the police station.

The rules on legal professional privilege attaching to communications to an expert witness should be read in conjunction with the obligation on both the prosecution and the defence to disclose any expert report either side intends to rely on at trial (see Chapter 17). Disclosing a report automatically waives any privilege attached to the report. An expert's report which the defence does not use in evidence at trial is covered by legal professional privilege and therefore does not have to be disclosed.

Legal professional privilege may be lost accidentally (see *R v Tompkins* (1977) 67 Cr App R 181).

20.6 POWERS OF SEARCH AND LEGAL PROFESSIONAL PRIVILEGE

While the police have extensive powers of search during an investigation (see Chapter 3), Parliament has been careful to exclude items that are subject to legal professional privilege from the ambit of a search warrant issued under s. 8 PACE 1984. This general principle is qualified in part by the exception recognised under the Regulation of Investigatory Powers Act 2000 (RIPA 2000) and confirmed by the House of Lords in the combined appeals of *In re McE and Others* [2009] UKHL 15 in which a majority held that on a proper construction s. 27 RIPA 2000 was intended to override a suspect's right to have a private consultation with a solicitor.

Although the House of Lords was not called upon to decide whether evidence lawfully obtained in breach of legal professional privilege would be admissible at trial, Lord Carswell observed that the principle expounded in *R v Derby Magistrates' Court, ex p B*, which prohibits the use of evidence obtained in breach of legal professional privilege, remained absolute.

20.7 THE PRIVILEGE AGAINST SELF-INCRIMINATION

The privilege against self-incrimination is an important right enjoyed by all United Kingdom citizens. The right to silence (see Chapter 5) is an important component of this privilege. The privilege against self-incrimination applies throughout the investigation process and continues through to trial. Once a defendant has chosen to give evidence on oath in support of his defence, he cannot refuse to answer questions in cross-examination on the ground that it would incriminate him as to the offence charged! However, no witness (including the defendant) need answer any question or produce documents or items at trial which would expose the witness to the possibility of future prosecution under United Kingdom law.

20.7.1 ASSERTING AND WAIVING THE PRIVILEGE

The privilege belongs to the witness and must therefore be claimed by the witness during the proceedings. Only the witness may waive the privilege. If answering a question or producing a document could potentially violate a witness's privilege not to self-incriminate, the modern practice is for the judge or the magistrates' legal adviser to warn the witness that she does not have to answer the question. Once the court is satisfied that the privilege applies, the witness will not be compelled to answer even if her motive for remaining silent is based in bad faith or she has a motive of her own to serve.

Where the witness waives the privilege or does not assert the privilege, her answers can be used in evidence against her in subsequent criminal proceedings.

20.7.2 **STATUTORY EXCEPTIONS TO THE PRIVILEGE AGAINST SELF-INCRIMINATION**

Various statutes compel an individual to answer questions and provide information in a criminal investigation. A failure to comply with the statutory requirement will lead to the designated person being liable to a penalty. A commonly invoked provision is s. 172 Road Traffic Act 1988. Section 172(2)(a) Road Traffic Act 1988 requires the keeper of a motor vehicle to answer questions as to the identity of the driver of the vehicle where the driver is suspected of being involved in a road traffic offence. Failure to provide such information is an offence under s. 172(3) Road Traffic Act 1988, punishable with a fine and the endorsement of penalty points on the driver's licence. A similar example is provided by s. 31 Theft Act 1968, which states that a witness may not refuse to answer any questions in proceedings for the recovery or administration of property or the execution of a trust on the ground that to do so might incriminate him or his spouse (or civil partner) of an offence under the Act. The point raised by defence lawyers in this area is that where an individual is compelled to answer questions or provide evidence which could later be used in evidence against him, is the use of such evidence compatible with Article 6 and the right to a fair trial? The point is considered here.

20.7.3 **THE PRIVILEGE AGAINST SELF-INCRIMINATION AND THE ECHR 1950**

In *Saunders v United Kingdom* (1997) 23 EHRR 313, the defendant had been compelled to answer questions about his business dealings during an investigation by the Department of Trade and Industry. The statute containing the compulsory powers did not prevent the answers obtained from being used in evidence in subsequent criminal proceedings. In fact, they were used against Saunders in a later prosecution under the Companies Act 1985. In finding that there had been a violation of Article 6, the European Court of Human Rights observed:

> 'The Court recalls that, although not specifically mentioned in Article 6 of the Convention, the right to silence and the right not to incriminate oneself are generally recognised international standards which lie at the heart of the notion of a fair procedure under Article 6. Their rationale lies, *inter alia*, in the protection of the accused against improper compulsion by the authorities thereby contributing to the avoidance of miscarriages of justice and to the fulfilment of the aims of Article 6. The right not to incriminate oneself, in particular, presupposes that the prosecution in a criminal case seek to prove their case against the accused without resort to evidence obtained through methods of coercion or oppression in defiance of the will of the accused. In this sense the right is closely linked to the presumption of innocence contained in article 6(2) of the Convention.'

The *Saunders* decision was relied on in the case of *Brown v Stott* [2001] 2 WLR 817, which concerned s. 172 Road Traffic Act 1988 and which requires the keeper of a motor vehicle to answer questions as to the identity of the driver of the vehicle where the driver is suspected of being involved in a road traffic offence. Failure to provide such information is an offence under s. 172(3) Road Traffic Act 1988, punishable with a fine and endorsement.

Brown v Stott [2001] 2 WLR 817

The police were called to an all-night superstore, where B was suspected of having stolen a bottle of gin. The officers thought that B had been drinking and asked her how she had got to the store. She replied that she had driven there and pointed to a car that she said was hers. At the police station, car keys were found in her handbag, and pursuant to s. 172(2) Road Traffic Act 1988, the police required her to say who had driven the car to the store. B replied that she had driven the car. A breath test was administered that proved positive. B was charged with driving after consuming excess alcohol under s. 5(1)(a) Road Traffic Act 1988.

On appeal, the Privy Council held that evidence of B's admission that she had driven the vehicle to the all-night store did not infringe her privilege against self-incrimination or her right to a fair hearing under Article 6 for the following reasons:

- the rights under Article 6 are not absolute and may be qualified in respect to a proper clear public objective such as road safety;

- there was a clear public interest in enforcement of road traffic legislation and that properly applied, s. 172 Road Traffic Act 1988 did not represent a disproportionate response to this serious social problem:
  - — s. 172 Road Traffic Act 1988 permitted the police to ask a suspect a simple question, the answer to which does not incriminate the accused *per se*;
  - — the penalty for refusing to answer the question is moderate and non-custodial;
  - — if there was evidence of coercion by the police, the court had discretion to exclude the suspect's answer.

The same conclusion was reached by the European Court of Human Rights in *O'Halloran v UK* (2007) 47 EHRR 397. Whilst the privilege against self-incrimination is an important human right, it is not an absolute right.

KEY POINT SUMMARY

- Know the situations where legal professional privilege can be claimed.
- Be aware of the circumstances in which legal professional privilege may be lost.
- Understand the privilege against self-incrimination and its limitations.

SELF-TEST QUESTIONS

1. Are all communications passing between a solicitor and his or her client privileged from disclosure?
2. What is the dominant purpose test for legal privilege to attach to communications between the client, solicitor and a third party?
3. In whom does legal privilege vest?
4. Explain the privilege against self-incrimination.

Analysis of these questions can be found on our Online Resource Centre.

online resource centre

FIGURE 20.1 PRIVATE PRIVILEGE

LEGAL PROFESSIONAL PRIVILEGE

- Prevents the disclosure of all communications between the lawyer/client in connection with the giving or obtaining of legal advice, including (s. 10(1)(a) PACE);
  - letters, memoranda containing legal advice; and
  - communications with counsel.

- Prevents the disclosure of all communications between the client, lawyer and a third party where the sole or dominant purpose is in connection with actual or pending litigation including communications in connection with advice sought from an expert witness (s. 10(1)(b) PACE).

- The courts take a strict approach to enforcing the privilege, see *R v Derby Magistrates' Court, ex p. B.*

- The privilege will be lifted where:
  - it is waived by the client; or
  - it used to further a crime; or
  - it is lost accidentally.

PRIVILEGE AGAINST SELF-INCRIMINATION

- Permits a witness to refuse to answer a question on oath where the answer would expose to the possibility of a criminal charge being laid against him.

- The privilege applies to individuals who are compelled to answer questions by investigating bodies, the answers to which are then used in evidence against that individual in criminal proceedings.

- The privilege belongs to the witness.

- The witness may waive the privilege.

- The privilege is not an absolute right under Article 6 European Convention on Human Rights and may be qualified where:
  - there is a clear public interest in the privilege not applying; and
  - it is proportionate to the aim of the legislation, see *Brown v Stott.*

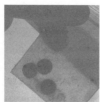

Part V

POST-CONVICTION: SENTENCING AND APPEALS

Part V covers all aspects of sentencing in the Crown Court and magistrates' court.

In Chapter 21 we consider the procedure on passing sentence and the general principles that inform the process of sentencing.

In Chapter 22 we explain specific types of sentence and provide guidance on how a defence solicitor might prepare and deliver a plea in mitigation.

The final chapter in this section, Chapter 23, considers the process of appeal against sentence and conviction.

online resource centre

The special considerations that apply to the sentencing of road traffic offences are covered in a separate chapter which can be found on the Online Resource Centre. Only consider this specialist chapter after you have digested Chapters 21 and 22.

21

SENTENCING PROCEDURE AND THE GENERAL PRINCIPLES OF SENTENCING

21.1 INTRODUCTION

A defendant will be sentenced before the Crown Court or magistrates' court upon conviction, either after pleading guilty or having been found guilty after a trial. As the vast majority of defendants plead guilty to some or all of the charges against them, a considerable amount of a prosecutor's time and even more of a defence lawyer's time is taken up with the question of sentence.

A criminal defence practitioner will:

(1) advise his client on the likely sentence after a guilty plea or on conviction;

(2) represent his client at a sentencing hearing by making a plea in mitigation;

(3) advise his client on the prospects of a successful appeal against sentence.

In dealing with any of the above tasks, the well-prepared defence advocate will require a thorough knowledge of sentencing principles and practice. It is worth highlighting that sentencing considerations are also relevant to the grant of a representation order (Chapter 9) the grant of bail (Chapter 10) and, of course, allocation (Chapter 11).

Sentencing law and practice is complex and for this reason the subject is covered in two chapters to assist understanding. In this chapter we explain the procedure on passing sentence and consider the general principles that govern a court's decision when passing sentence. In Chapter 22 specific types of sentence are explained and strategies suggested for preparing and delivering an effective plea in mitigation are explored.

21.2 NEW DEVELOPMENTS—WARNING

Sentencing is a fast-changing area of criminal practice. The Sentencing Council for England and Wales regularly issues new and revised sentencing guidelines. Also the Court of Appeal hands down sentencing guidance when deciding appeals against sentence. The Legal Aid, Sentencing and Punishment of Offenders Act 2012 (LASPO 2012) has made a number of changes to sentencing. Keeping up to date with developments in sentencing is therefore important for the well-informed law student and the busy criminal practitioner.

21.3 THE ROLE OF THE CPS ON SENTENCE

Whilst the prosecutor does not take an active role in sentencing, she represents the public interest. In deciding whether to accept a guilty plea, the prosecutor must apply the guidance summarised at para. 21.4.3 and in the Attorney-General's guidance on the acceptance

of guilty pleas (see web-links section of the Online Resource Centre). So far as the prosecutor's role in the sentencing exercise is concerned, the prosecutor must assist the court in reaching an appropriate sentence by drawing the court's attention to:

- any victim impact statement;
- any evidence of the impact the offending has had on the community;
- any relevant sentencing guidelines or guideline cases;
- the aggravating and mitigating factors of the offence;
- any other relevant sentencing provisions and ancillary orders sought.

The prosecutor should also challenge any assertion by the defence in mitigation that is derogatory to a person's character.

21.4 THE PROCEDURE ON SENTENCING

The procedure is generally the same whether the offender is sentenced in the Crown Court or magistrates' court.

The court will pass sentence where the defendant has pleaded guilty or after being found guilty. Sentence may be adjourned to obtain a pre-sentence report (see para. 21.16.1), or to await the conclusion of other outstanding criminal proceedings against the defendant where it would make good sense to sentence on the totality of the defendant's criminal behaviour.

21.4.1 PROCEDURE FOLLOWING A FINDING OF GUILT

Where a defendant has been found guilty, the court will know the circumstances of the offence and the defendant's involvement. The prosecutor's role in this situation is largely restricted to reading out any victim impact statement in the case; referring the court to the defendant's antecedent history; detailing any requests for compensation; and asking for ancillary orders, including prosecution costs.

The defence advocate will be invited to make a plea in mitigation of sentence. If the advocate or the court believes that further information about the defendant is required before sentence can be passed, the hearing will be adjourned for a pre-sentence report (PSR) (see para. 21.16.1) prepared by the probation service. In this situation, the defence advocate will often reserve what he wishes to say by way of mitigation until the full sentencing hearing.

Where a court adjourns sentence for a PSR, it can remand the defendant in custody or on bail. In these circumstances, a court can adjourn sentence for no more than three weeks. Bail may be conditional or unconditional and can include a condition that the defendant co-operates with the probation service in the preparation of the report. An adjournment in these circumstances can be for no more than four weeks or to avoid an adjournment, a magistrates' court will ask for a fast delivery pre-sentence report wherever possible (see para. 21.16.1).

21.4.2 PROCEDURE FOLLOWING A GUILTY PLEA

Although the procedure is broadly similar in both the Crown Court and the magistrates' court, the relevant rules governing the procedure that a magistrates' court should follow upon conviction are laid down in Crim PR, Part 37.10. Where a defendant pleads guilty, avoiding the need for a trial, the sentencing hearing will begin with the prosecution outlining the circumstances of the offence. This will be based on the evidence contained in witness statements and the defendant's interview and/or any agreed basis of plea between the parties. Sometimes, the prosecution may include CCTV footage as part of its outline and may also refer the court to any victim impact statement.

The prosecutor will then provide the court with a copy of the defendant's criminal record, drawing attention to any relevant previous convictions. If the current conviction places the defendant in breach of an existing court order, the prosecutor should provide details of the earlier offence. The same applies following conviction after trial. If the offence involves injury to an individual or damage to property, the prosecutor should provide full details and hand in any applications for compensation. In the case of an injury or damage, the prosecutor may refer the court to any photographs of the injured party or the damaged caused.

The prosecutor should present the facts fully and fairly. If there are any offences to be taken into consideration (see para. 21.18), these will be referred to by the prosecutor and an agreed schedule submitted to the court. Finally, the prosecutor will ask for any ancillary order and prosecution costs in a specified sum.

Having heard the prosecution, the defence will then submit a plea in mitigation. Once again, if the defence solicitor feels a PSR might be required, she will invite the court to adjourn for the report to be prepared before addressing the court in any great detail on the matter of sentence.

21.4.3 NEWTON HEARINGS

Before an accused enters a guilty plea it is good practice for the defence advocate to discuss the basis of his client's plea with the prosecution, as a guilty plea does not necessarily mean that the accused accepts everything outlined by the prosecution. A defendant may wish to plead guilty to some charges but not others. A defendant may be prepared to plead guilty to assault but deny the use of a weapon in the commission of the assault. In deciding whether to accept a guilty plea, the prosecutor must apply section 9 of the Code for Crown Prosecutors, which provides:

> 'Crown Prosecutors should only accept the defendant's plea if they think the court is able to pass a sentence that matches the seriousness of the offending, particularly where there are aggravating features. Crown Prosecutors must never accept a guilty plea just because it is convenient.

In considering whether the pleas offered are acceptable, Crown Prosecutors should ensure that the interests of the victim and, where possible, any views expressed by the victim or victim's family, are taken into account when deciding whether it is in the public interest to accept the plea. However, the decision rests with the Crown Prosecutor.

It must be made clear to the court on what basis any plea is advanced and accepted. In cases where a defendant pleads guilty to the charges but on the basis of facts that are different from the prosecution case, and where this may significantly affect sentence, the court should be invited to hear evidence to determine what happened, and then sentence on that basis.'

If a basis of plea is accepted, the defence advocate must make sure that the court sentences her client on the agreed basis of plea which should be in writing and signed by all the parties. Where, despite a guilty plea, there is a significant dispute between the prosecution and the defence about the facts of the offence which cannot be resolved and the dispute would materially affect the sentence, a Newton hearing (*R v Newton* (1982) 77 Cr App R 13) may be required to determine the disputed fact. A Newton hearing takes the form of a trial of the disputed issue. Witnesses will be called and the formal rules of evidence apply. The burden of proof on the disputed issue rests with the prosecution and the standard of proof is beyond reasonable doubt. Where the prosecution case is believed, the defendant may lose some or all credit for pleading guilty (see para. 21.13). If the contested issue is resolved in the defendant's favour, the credit due to him should not be reduced.

The case law on Newton hearings is covered in *Blackstone's Criminal Practice*. Once the court has heard the outline of the facts from the prosecution and has considered the defendant's plea in mitigation, it is in a position to determine the appropriate sentence in accordance with the principles outlined later.

21.5 HIERARCHY OF SENTENCES

The magistrates' court and the Crown Court can pass a range of sentences under the Criminal Justice Act 2003 which we list here in decreasing order of severity:

- custody—immediate/suspended;
- community sentence (combining requirements such as unpaid work/supervision/curfew);
- fine/compensation order;
- discharge (conditional or absolute).

We consider the specifics of each sentence in Chapter 22.

In addition, upon conviction for certain offences, a court may and in some cases must also endorse the offender's driving licence or disqualify him from driving or order the destruction or confiscation of property acquired by criminal activities or order the seizure of criminal assets. In sexual offences the court will require the offender to register on the Sex Offenders' Register.

21.6 SENTENCING AIMS

When a sentence is passed on an offender over the age of 18, s. 142 CJA 2003 requires the court to have regard to one or more of the following purposes of sentencing. They include:

(a) the punishment of offenders;

(b) reduction in crime (including its reduction by deterrence);

(c) the reform and rehabilitation of the offender;

(d) the protection of the public;

(e) the making of reparation by the offender to people affected by their offences.

The CJA 2003 does not indicate that any one purpose is more important than any other. In formulating a realistic sentencing objective for the plea in mitigation, the defence solicitor should consider what the court's sentencing aims are likely to be.

Punitive sentences include custody and certain types of community sentence where the offender must undertake unpaid work or abide by a curfew. These sentences deprive the offender of his liberty. In some cases a large fine can be punishment. In particularly serious cases where an offender has used violence, perhaps not for the first time, or has committed a serious sexual offence, there will be a need to protect the public, and the offender can expect a lengthy custodial sentence.

Where the offence is less serious and there are underlying reasons for an offender's behaviour, a rehabilitative sentence might be appropriate which aims to prevent further offending. The most obvious example is a community sentence with a supervision requirement, or a drug rehabilitation requirement. For a first-time offender whose offence is not serious, a conditional discharge might be appropriate.

In terms of reparation as a sentencing objective, a court ordering an offender to pay compensation to his victim for injury, loss or damage is a good example.

21.7 THE BASIS OF SENTENCING UNDER THE CJA 2003

The CJA 2003 adopts the fundamental principle that a sentence should not be more severe than the seriousness of the offence warrants. The sentence a court chooses to impose should therefore reflect the seriousness of the offence.

21.7.1 THE TOTALITY PRINCIPLE

In sentencing an offender for more than one offence, a court must have regard to the totality principle which requires that the sentence passed must not be disproportionate to the seriousness of the overall offending behaviour. Statutory effect is given to this principle in s. 66(3) CJA 2003 which applies to custodial sentences, community orders and fines. A defendant who has committed several similar offences over a relatively short period may receive a single sentence which reflects the seriousness of his overall offending behaviour rather than separate (consecutive) sentences for each offence. The Sentencing Council for England and Wales (see para. 21.8) has issued guidance on the application of the totality principle which came into force in June 2012.

21.7.2 DEFINING THE SERIOUSNESS OF AN OFFENCE

Section 143(1) CJA 2003 states that in assessing the seriousness of any offence, the court must consider:

* the offender's culpability in committing the offence; and
* any harm which the offence has caused or was intended to cause or might foreseeably have caused.

Culpability includes such matters as the defendant's intention when committing an offence, whether he acted recklessly or had knowledge of the risk he was taking. Harm and risk of harm can include harm to the victim but also to the wider community.

Statutory aggravating factors affecting the seriousness of an offence are identified in ss. 143–146 CJA 2003.

* Section 143(2) requires a court to treat an offender's previous convictions as an aggravating factor if the court considers it reasonable to do so, having regard to the nature of the offence and the time that has elapsed since conviction. Recent and relevant previous convictions will therefore be regarded as aggravating the seriousness of the current offence before the court.

- Section 143(3) requires the court to treat any offence committed while on bail as being an aggravating factor in determining the seriousness of the offence.
- Sections 145 and 146 provide that where an offence is either racially or religiously motivated or is motivated out of hostility towards a person's sexual or presumed sexual orientation or transgender identity or presumed transgender identity, disability or presumed disability, this shall be regarded as an aggravating feature in determining the seriousness of the offence.

In addition to any statutory aggravating factors, the court will also consider any aggravating and mitigating features of the offence itself with reference to any applicable sentencing guidelines for the offence.

In its publication *Overarching Principles: Seriousness*, the Sentencing Guidelines Council (see later) provides general guidance on assessing an offender's culpability for the purposes of s. 143 CJA 2003. Culpability is determined by such matters as the offender's motivation in committing the offence; whether it was planned or spontaneous and whether the offender was in a position of trust. A further relevant factor includes the deliberate targeting of a vulnerable victim by reference to their age, disability or by virtue of their job. The guidance offers an extensive list of typical aggravating and mitigating features to an offence.

- To remind you—the starting point when sentencing an offender is an assessment by the court of the seriousness of the offence.

21.8 SENTENCING COUNCIL FOR ENGLAND AND WALES

Sentencing practice in England and Wales is underpinned by sentencing guidelines formulated by the Sentencing Council for England and Wales (SC) and its predecessor, the Sentencing Guidelines Council (SGC). The SGC was created under the CJA 2003 with a statutory duty to provide authoritative guidance on sentencing to be applied by the courts, a role which had traditionally been undertaken by the Court of Appeal in relation to sentencing in the Crown Court.

To assist in the development of a consistent approach to sentencing across England and Wales, the SGC issued a number of definitive general sentencing guidelines and offence-specific guidelines including:

- *Overarching Principles: Seriousness* (December 2004);
- *New Sentences: CJA 2003* (December 2004);
- *Reduction in Sentence for a Guilty Plea (Revised)* (July 2007);
- *Manslaughter by Reason of Provocation* (November 2005);
- *Definitive Sentencing Guideline on Robbery* (July 2006);
- *Overarching Principles: Domestic Violence* (December 2006);
- *Breach of a Protective Order* (December 2006);
- *Guidelines on Sexual Offences Act 2003* (April 2007);
- *Definitive Sentencing Guideline: Fail to Surrender to Bail* (November 2007);
- *Overarching Principles: Assault on Children and Cruelty to a Child* (February 2008);
- *Causing Death by Driving* (July 2008);
- *Theft and Burglary in a building other than a dwelling* (December 2008);
- *Breach of Anti-Social Behaviour Order* (December 2008);
- *The Magistrates Court Sentencing Guidelines 2008;*
- *Attempted Murder* (July 2009);
- *Statutory Offence of Fraud* (October 2009);
- *Overarching Principles—Sentencing Youths* (November 2009);
- *Corporate Manslaughter and Health and Safety Causing Death* (February 2010).

The SGC was abolished by the Coroners and Justice Act 2009 (C&JA 2009), and replaced by the Sentencing Council for England and Wales (SC) which began work on 6 April 2010.

The primary role of the Council is to issue sentencing guidelines which, under s. 125 C&JA 2009, courts *must follow unless it is in the interest of justice not to do so*. To date, the Council has issued definitive offence-specific sentencing guidelines on assault offences, burglary, drug offences and offences relating to dangerous dogs.

All existing SGC guidelines (see the list just mentioned) now come under the ownership of the SC. Until such time as a SGC guideline is revised by the SC, it will remain applicable, including the Magistrates' Court Sentencing Guidelines which are fundamental to sentencing practice in the magistrates' court (see para. 21.11).

The importance of the SC in terms of sentencing practice cannot be overstated. Final and draft guidelines produced by the SC/SGC can be accessed at http://sentencingcouncil. judiciary.gov.uk/sentencing-guidelines.htm. Our Online Resource Centre includes a link to the SC in the web-links section.

online resource centre

21.8.1 HOW ARE OFFENCE-SPECIFIC GUIDELINES ISSUED BY THE SENTENCING COUNCIL APPLIED?

Offence-specific guidelines identify a sentencing starting point and a range of sentences either side of the starting point based on varying degrees of seriousness in the ways in which an offence might be committed. If there are aggravating features in the commission of the offence (offence-specific guidelines will include a non-exhaustive list of aggravating features) and/or statutory aggravating features are present on the facts of the case, this will increase the seriousness of the offence and may result in the court adopting a higher sentencing starting point or even considering a sentence outside the range of sentence available under the guideline. If more mitigating factors outweigh the aggravating features in the commission of the offence, this may result in the court choosing to adopt a lower sentencing starting point. Having determined a provisional sentence based on an assessment of the seriousness of the offence as prescribed by the sentencing guidelines, the court may adjust its initial position on hearing any personal offender mitigation and on any timely guilty plea (if applicable) when arriving at a final sentence.

Section 121 C&JA 2009 provides for a higher degree of specificity in the formulation of offence-specific guidelines issued by the Sentencing Council than was previously the position under the SGC. The format of SC guidelines is best illustrated by reference to its guideline on 'Assault'. In Appendix 2, you will find a copy of the guideline applicable to the sentencing of an offender under s. 47 Offences against the Person Act 1861 (ABH).

Each guideline identifies the range of sentences available (*'the offence range'*) which, in the opinion of the Council, it may be appropriate for a court to impose on an offender convicted of that offence. The *offence range* identified by the SC for a s. 47 ABH is from a fine at the lowest end of the range to three years' imprisonment if tried on indictment. The guideline describes different categories of cases involving the commission of the offence (*'the category range'*) which illustrate in general terms the varying degrees of seriousness with which the offence may be committed. The category into which a particular offence falls is decided by reference to the offender's culpability and/or the harm caused by the offence(s) and any other specifically relevant factor(s). The guideline specifies both a *starting point* for each *category range* and a *range* of sentence either side of the *starting point*. The *starting point* is the sentence the SC considers to be appropriate for all offenders in all cases. This contrasts with SGC guidelines where the sentencing starting point is based on a first-time offender who has pleaded not guilty.

As assault occasioning actual bodily harm contrary to s. 47 OAPA 1861 is triable either way, the guideline for sentencing this offence applies both to cases that are sentenced before the Crown Court and the magistrates' court. The applicable guideline is reproduced in Appendix 2.

The guideline defines three offence *categories* for all the assault offences within the guideline. The most serious is category 1. A category 1 assault (whether it be a s. 18 GBH or a common assault) will involve *greater harm* (serious injury must normally be present) and *higher culpability*. A category 2 assault will involve *greater harm* (serious injury must normally be present) and *lower culpability* or *lesser harm* but *higher culpability*. A category 3 assault involves *less harm* and *lower culpability*. The guideline identifies factors specific to greater and lesser harm and factors specific to higher culpability and lower culpability. A court should have regard to these aggravating/mitigating factors in deciding which *category* of offence the present case falls within. Identifying the correct *category range* enables the court to identify the sentencing *starting point* and *range* of sentence available. The guideline then requires the court to consider whether there are any additional statutory or other aggravating factors or whether there are any mitigating factors in the commission of the offence or personal offender mitigation which should result in an upward or downward adjustment from the starting point. The court then takes into account any reduction applicable for a guilty plea, as well as the totality principle and any time spent on remand in custody in reaching its final sentencing outcome.

 Example

Do you recall the example of Patryk in Chapter 11, para. 11.3.4 in the context of the mode of trial enquiry/allocation hearing? As explained in Chapter 11, sentencing guidelines are inextricably linked with mode of trial/allocation decision. Patryk is sent for trial before the Crown Court and decides to plead guilty. It is accepted by the prosecution that there has been long-standing ill feeling between Patryk and his neighbour and Patryk, who had been subjected to a substantial degree of provocation, had armed himself with the bat with the intention to only damage his neighbour's car. His victim is not 'vulnerable' and, whilst dental treatment will continue for the next three months, the wound will heal with no permanent scarring and there is no lasting psychological injury. A pre-sentence report has been prepared which suggests Patryk is remorseful for the injuries he has caused. He has written a letter of apology to his victim. The report describes Patryk as a reformed drug addict who was recently bereaved and is receiving treatment from his doctor for chronic depression. Since the offence he has left his flat and lives elsewhere. In determining mode of trial/allocation, we concluded that this could be a category 1 offence due to greater harm and higher culpability caused by several aggravating factors (use of a weapon; premeditation; serious injury). This is why the magistrates' court declined jurisdiction. In determining the actual sentence, the Crown Court will apply the s. 47 ABH guideline. The category range for this offence is as follows:

Offence category	Starting point	Category range
Category 1	1 year 6 months' custody	1–3 years' custody
Category 2	26 weeks' custody	Low level community order–51 weeks' custody
Category 3	Medium level community order	Band A—High level community order

Therefore the sentencing starting point based on a category 1 assault occasioning actual bodily harm sentenced before a Crown Court is 1 year and 6 months' custody. Given that the injuries are non-permanent and given that it is accepted that there was a substantial degree of provocation by the victim, a judge may be persuaded that this is a category 2 offence with a sentencing starting point of 26 weeks in custody but with a range that takes it down to a community order. Aggravating factors include Patryk's previous convictions. Mitigating factors include Patryk's remorse and clinical depression. If the judge concludes that the custody threshold is passed (see Chapter 22, para. 22.2.1) which it is whether it is classed as a category 1 or 2 ABH, she might choose to impose a suspended sentence of imprisonment based on the mitigating factors in this case, which would be within the range of sentence suggested under the guideline for this offence. Credit will be given for the guilty plea.

21.9 SENTENCING GUIDELINES IN THE CROWN COURT

Sentencing in the Crown Court has historically been informed by decisions of the Court of Appeal. Whilst the role of formulating sentencing guidelines now belongs to the SC, in cases where there is no definitive SGC or SC guideline, Court of Appeal decisions continue to apply. Most decisions are reported in the Criminal Appeal Sentencing Reports and summarised in *Blackstone's Criminal Practice*, making it an excellent starting point for your research into the relevant sentencing guidelines applicable to cases to be sentenced before the Crown Court.

The SGC/SC has regularly published a useful compendium of all current Court of Appeal sentencing guidelines cases which can be accessed through the SC's web-pages at http://sentencingcouncil.judiciary.gov.uk/guidelines/other-guidelines.htm.

21.10 HOW DOES THE DEFENCE SOLICITOR ASSESS THE SERIOUSNESS OF AN OFFENCE?

Defence solicitors must consider their client's role in the particular offence and consider which factors aggravate and which factors mitigate the seriousness of the offence. These include the statutory aggravating factors identified at para. 21.7.2 and in the SGC's publication on seriousness and the factors identified in the Magistrates' Court Sentencing Guidelines for specific offences.

21.11 MAGISTRATES' COURT SENTENCING GUIDELINES (MCSGs)—A STRUCTURED APPROACH TO SENTENCING

The MCSGs, issued by the SGC in 2008, cover virtually all offences that are commonly dealt with in the adult magistrates' court. The effect of the MCSGs has been to make the sentencing exercise before a magistrates' court a much more prescriptive and predictable exercise. At Appendix 2 in this *Handbook* we include a small number of offence-specific sentencing guidelines taken from the MCSGs. The s. 47 assault revised sentencing guideline, referred to earlier, looks different from the other offence-specific guidelines in Appendix 2 as it adopts the format for all future sentencing guidelines issued by the Sentencing Council. When a new SC is issued, it is incorporated into the MCSGs if the offence can be sentenced there.

The guidelines require a magistrates' court to take a structured approach to sentence based on the seriousness of the offence or offences. Similar to the approach explained in para. 21.8.1, the structured approach requires the court to first assess the seriousness of the offence in order to arrive at a provisional sentence. The court must then consider any personal offender mitigation before determining its actual sentence. If a sentencing discount is available for a guilty plea, it is applied at this point. The structured approach to sentencing in the magistrates' court is illustrated in the diagram that appears at the end of this chapter.

21.11.1 USING THE MCSGs TO ASSESS THE SERIOUSNESS OF AN OFFENCE

With the exception of sentencing guidelines that have recently been issued by the SC and which have been incorporated into the MCSGs, the starting point in terms of sentence in the MCSGs are based on a first-time offender convicted after trial. The guidelines, which apply to all offenders irrespective of plea or previous convictions, provide a *starting point* in terms of sentence based on examples of the nature of activity which may constitute the particular offence progressing from less to more serious conduct. The nature of the activity that best describes what the offender is said to have done enables the court to identify the appropriate *starting point* in terms of sentence and also specifies a sentence *range* that can fall either side of the starting point. The court may depart from the *starting point* to reflect any aggravating or mitigating features of the offence itself (beyond those identified to determine the starting point) in order to reach a provisional sentence. To illustrate the concept of seriousness under the MCSGs, consider the offence of dangerous driving. The guideline for this offence is reproduced in Appendix 2.

In relation to dangerous driving, a single incident involving little or no damage or risk of personal injury attracts a sentencing starting point of a medium level community order but with a range of sentences from a low level community order to a high level community order. For an offence of dangerous driving involving excessive speed in a built-up area, the starting point rises to a custodial term of 12 weeks with a sentencing range from a high level community order to a custodial term of 26 weeks. For an offence of dangerous driving which involves prolonged bad driving and deliberate disregard for the safety of others or excessive speed in a built-up area, the starting point and the range is committal for sentence to the Crown Court.

Having established the starting point in terms of sentence, the court must then consider any statutory aggravating features and any aggravating or mitigating features of the offence under consideration. Aggravating features of dangerous driving as specified in the offence-specific guideline include:

- evidence of alcohol or drugs;
- aggressive driving such as driving much too close to the vehicle in front or racing;
- carrying out other tasks while driving.

Mitigating features of dangerous driving include:

- genuine emergency;
- speed not excessive;
- offence due to inexperience rather than irresponsibility.

The more aggravating factors there are, the more likely the starting point for the sentence will increase with the possibility that a court may adopt a starting point outside the suggested sentencing range.

21.12 PERSONAL OFFENDER MITIGATION

The seriousness of an offence may indicate a particular type of sentence. However, every offender must be sentenced on an individual basis. The court must therefore have regard to any personal offender mitigation that might apply in the case. It is the combination of the seriousness of the offence, and any personal offender mitigation that will determine the appropriate sentence. The seriousness of the offence may indicate a custodial sentence but there may be strong personal mitigating factors which suggest a community-based disposal as the most appropriate sentence. Personal offender mitigation will clearly be highlighted by the defence in the plea in mitigation (which we consider in Chapter 22) and in any pre-sentence report.

21.13 DISCOUNT FOR TIMELY GUILTY PLEAS

Section 144 CJA 2003 provides as follows:

'(1) In determining what sentence to pass on an offender who has pleaded guilty to an offence in proceedings before that or another court, a court shall take into account—

(a) the stage in the proceedings for the offence at which the offender indicated his intention to plead guilty, and

(b) the circumstances in which this indication was given.'

Section 174(2)(b) CJA 2003 provides that in passing sentence on an offender, the court must state in open court in ordinary language that it has given the offender the benefit of a discount under s. 144 CJA 2003.

Timely guilty pleas save cost, court time and, most importantly, spare victims and witnesses from having to give evidence. Section 144 CJA 2003 does not specify the amount of discount a court might award. In its guideline on the effect of pleading guilty, the SGC recommended a sliding scale, ranging from a maximum of one–third (where the guilty plea was entered at the first reasonable opportunity), reducing to a maximum of up to one–quarter (where a trial date has been set) and up to a maximum of one–tenth (for a guilty plea entered at the 'door of the court'). The application of the sentencing discount may influence the type of sentence passed and might take the disposal below the range suggested by the MCSGs. It is expected that the Sentencing Council will produce new guidelines on reduction of sentence for a guilty plea in the near future.

Sentencing discounts do not apply to ancillary orders which include compensation orders or to the minimum periods of disqualification and the mandatory imposition of penalty points.

21.14 WHAT CONSTRAINS SENTENCING?

There are a number of factors that constrain sentencing, including:

- the statute creating the offence (statutes creating an offence will specify a maximum penalty for the particular offence);
- whether the sentence is being imposed in the Crown Court or in the magistrates' court (magistrates' courts' powers of sentence are limited);
- statutory sentencing requirements laid down by Parliament (in some instances Parliament has removed judicial discretion and requires the imposition of a mandatory sentence of imprisonment or other ancillary penalty);
- the defendant's age (the sentencing of offenders under the age of 18 is considered in Chapter 26);
- whether the defendant pleaded guilty or was found guilty (timely guilty pleas attract a reduction in the length of sentence).

21.14.1 THE LIMITS OF THE MAGISTRATES' COURT'S SENTENCING POWERS

The maximum custodial sentence that a magistrates' court can currently pass for an imprisonable offence is six months upon conviction of a summary matter (s. 78 Powers of Criminal Courts (Sentencing) Act 2000 (PCC(S)A 2000) and s. 133 Magistrates' Courts Act 1980 (MCA 1980)) unless the statute creating the offence specifies a lesser maximum sentence. It does not matter that a defendant is convicted of two or more summary matters on the same occasion: the maximum prescribed by statute is six months. The six months maximum can rise to 12 months where consecutive prison sentences of six months are imposed on a defendant convicted of two or more either-way matters (proviso to s. 133(1) and (2) MCA 1980), although a court would need to have regard to the totality principle, highlighted at para. 21.7.1. The magistrates' court is further constrained in terms of the size of the fine it can impose. The maximum fine is £5,000 for each offence. This cap will be removed when the relevant provisions of LASPO 2012 come into force. Some offences, however, specify a maximum fine of less than £5,000.

The magistrates' sentencing jurisdiction is closely related to the allocation hearing for either-way offences as one of the principal reasons for a magistrates' court declining jurisdiction to try an either-way matter is that the magistrates consider their maximum sentencing powers, in the event of conviction, are insufficient. See Chapter 11 for further details.

21.14.2 **POWER TO COMMIT FOR SENTENCE UNDER S. 3 PCC(S)A 2000**

Upon summary conviction for an either-way offence, magistrates have the power to commit a defendant to the Crown Court for sentence under s. 3 PCC(S)A 2000 where they consider their maximum powers of punishment to be insufficient, having regard to the seriousness of the offence. Where this power is exercised, magistrates can also commit the offender for sentence on any other offences for which the defendant has been convicted (s. 6 PCC(S)A 2000). This enables the Crown Court to deal with all outstanding matters including any other less serious either-way or summary matters the defendant has been convicted of and any suspended sentence or breach of a community penalty or conditional discharge imposed by a magistrates' court for which the accused now stands to be dealt with. However, the Crown Court's sentencing powers are limited to those of the magistrates and the summary offence(s) must be punishable with imprisonment or disqualification.

The power to commit for sentence is more likely to be used where a defendant indicates an intention to plead guilty to an either-way offence which requires the magistrates' court to accept summary jurisdiction. Where a full mode of trial enquiry/allocation hearing has been conducted, the power to commit for sentence under s. 3 PCC(S)A 2000 might be exercised where the evidence disclosed at trial shows the offence to be more serious than was suggested at the mode of trial enquiry/allocation hearing, or it is revealed, upon conviction, that the accused has an extensive criminal record and/or is asking for other offences to be taken into consideration. If the defendant is committed for sentence under s. 3 PCC(S)A 2000, the Crown Court will proceed to deal with the defendant as if he had been convicted on indictment.

Although the point has not been definitively determined by case law, the Divisional Court in *North Sefton Magistrates' Court, ex p. Marsh* (1994) 16 Cr App R (S) 401 held that s. 3 discretion is unfettered and that because magistrates had decided to accept jurisdiction to try a case does not constrain the court from subsequently deciding to commit the defendant for sentence upon conviction. The SC's recently issued allocation guideline states that where the court decides that the case is suitable to be dealt with in the magistrates' court, it should remind the defendant that all sentencing options remain open, including committal to the Crown Court for sentence at the time it informs the defendant of this decision.

The funding provisions to cover representation before the Crown Court upon committal for sentence are outlined in Chapter 9 at para. 9.10.2.

21.14.3 **COMMITTAL FOR SENTENCE UNDER S. 4 PCC(S)A 2000**

Where an accused has indicated a guilty plea to an either-way offence but has been committed for trial in the Crown Court on a related either-way offence, the magistrates' court can commit the defendant to the Crown Court for sentence on the matter to which he has indicated a guilty plea under s. 4 PCC(S)A 2000. If the Crown Court convicts the defendant on the related either-way matter, or if the magistrates' court, on committal for sentence under s. 4, states that it also had the power to do so under s. 3, the Crown Court can sentence on the offence as if the defendant had been convicted on indictment; otherwise its powers are limited to those upon summary conviction.

21.15 **THE CROWN COURT'S SENTENCING POWERS**

The Crown Court's sentencing powers are considerably greater than those of the magistrates' court. Theft is a good illustration of this point. Conviction for a single offence of theft under the Theft Act 1968 in a magistrates' court currently carries a maximum six months' custodial sentence. Conviction on indictment in the Crown Court carries a maximum custodial sentence of seven years and an unlimited fine.

The more extensive sentencing powers available to the Crown Court are an important factor in an accused's decision whether to elect trial in the Crown Court if he is given the choice at the allocation hearing (see Chapter 11).

Where a Crown Court passes sentence on a defendant who has been convicted of or has pleaded guilty to a summary offence which has been committed to the Crown Court alongside an either-way offence under s. 51(3)(b) CDA 1998, the powers of the Crown Court are limited to those of a magistrates' court.

21.15.1 MANDATORY SENTENCES IN THE CROWN COURT

Recent reforms have removed the discretionary element in sentencing in favour of mandatory sentences which have primarily affected sentencing in the Crown Court. Sections 110 and 111 PCC(S)A 2000 require a minimum sentence of seven years for a third conviction of Class A drug trafficking and a minimum three years for a third conviction of domestic burglary. In relation to domestic burglary the defendant must have committed his second burglary after being convicted of his first and, in addition, both burglary convictions must post-date 1 December 1999. The court need not impose the minimum term if it is of the opinion that it would be unjust to do so. A court may go below the minimum sentence in order to grant a discount for a timely guilty plea.

Life imprisonment is mandatory for murder. It is up to the court to fix the minimum term in accordance with s. 269 CJA 2003 and *R v Jones* [2005] EWCA Crim 3115.

Sections 224–229 CJA 2003 make special provision for 'dangerous' offenders. These are considered in more detail in Chapter 22, para. 22.8.

21.16 WHAT INFORMS THE PROCESS OF SENTENCING?

The sentencing process is informed by the sentencing guidelines, pre-sentence reports and personal offender mitigation.

It is essential to realise that before a client can be advised about the possible sentence and before any plea in mitigation is prepared, the relevant sentencing guidelines for the offence charged must be researched. In serious cases, a defence solicitor may wish to take the advice of counsel or a solicitor-advocate on the question of sentence.

21.16.1 PRE-SENTENCE REPORTS—S. 156 CJA 2003

The importance of a pre-sentence report cannot be underestimated. When the court requires more information about an offender before it decides the appropriate sentence, the information may be provided by a pre-sentence report (PSR), prepared by a probation officer. The report will be compiled with the offender's assistance and any other relevant source, e.g. the offender's doctor or employer. The report's purpose is to assist the court to find the most appropriate sentence for the offender and commonly includes an assessment of the offender's attitude to the offence and his awareness of the consequences of his actions, the offender's personal history, previous convictions, education, employment position and health. Importantly the report will assess the offender's risk of re-offending based on the current offence and his attitude to it, and address such matters as the defendant's suitability for certain types of sentence. The report will propose what the probation service considers to be the most appropriate sentence for the offender, consistent with any sentencing aims expressed by the court. A court is not bound to follow the proposal. If the proposal is helpful to the defendant, however, his solicitor or barrister will no doubt place much emphasis on it.

Pre-sentence reports are usually ordered when the court is considering a custodial or community sentence, although s. 156 CJA 2003 empowers the courts to sentence persons over 18 without the benefit of a PSR if a report is considered 'unnecessary'.

When requesting a PSR, the court will often state that it is keeping all of its sentencing options open. This means the court is not ruling out custody. If, in connection with an either-way offence, a magistrates' court wishes to retain the option of committing the offender to the Crown Court for sentence, it should specifically mention this when ordering the PSR. A failure to do so can give the defendant a legitimate expectation that committal for sentence as an option has been ruled out (*Feltham Justices, ex p Rees* [2001] 2 Cr App R (S) 1).

When a court requests a PSR, the probation officer in court will consider whether a standard delivery report (SDR) or a fast delivery report (FDR) should be provided. A SDR will take the probation service three to four weeks to prepare and will require an adjournment. A FDR can be prepared within two hours of the defendant being convicted or pleading guilty and therefore requires a much shorter adjournment. The introduction of CJ-SSS and SDJ (see Chapter 11) has resulted in the much greater use of FDRs, resulting in more offenders being sentenced on the day of their first appearance before the magistrates' court after pleading guilty.

21.17 VICTIM IMPACT STATEMENTS

There has been a significant move to acknowledge victims' rights within the criminal justice system in recent years. Since October 2001, it has been possible for victims to make a 'victim impact statement' detailing the effect that the offence has had on them. Guidance on the use of such statements is contained in the MCSGs and the Consolidated Criminal Practice Direction Part III, 28.

21.18 TAKING OTHER OFFENCES INTO CONSIDERATION

> 'The defendant pleads guilty to the offence of theft charged against him and asks that you take a further 26 offences of a like nature into consideration . . .'

A defendant is normally sentenced on those offences for which he has been convicted except for offences which the defendant asks to be 'TIC'd'—i.e. taken into consideration. The defendant is not convicted of these offences but admits the offences in court and asks for them to be taken into consideration upon passing sentence.

There are mutual benefits to this arrangement. For the prosecution, it assists in the clear-up rate for crimes. For the defendant, although he receives a higher sentence because of the increased number of offences, he knows he cannot be later prosecuted for the offences 'TIC'd'.

Any offences to be taken into consideration should be listed on a schedule which is signed by the defendant. In court, the defendant will be asked to confirm he is admitting the offences listed on the schedule and that he wishes for them to be taken into consideration when the court passes sentence. The procedure can be initiated by the police during the defendant's detention and by the prosecutor in court after a finding of guilt.

The procedure does not apply to driving offences which carry endorsement and/or disqualification. Courts should not allow offences of a different nature to be taken into consideration, and a magistrates' court should not take into consideration indictable-only offences.

Important guidance on sentencing in relation to offences taken into consideration is provided in the Divisional Court's decision in *R v Miles* [2006] EWCA 256.

The Sentencing Council has issued guidance on taking offences into consideration which will come into force in June 2012.

KEY POINT SUMMARY

- An understanding of the way in which a court will reach sentence in a particular case is a necessary pre-requisite of being able to advise a defendant client about sentence and in constructing a plea in mitigation of sentence.

- Sentencing practice requires courts to sentence on the basis of the seriousness of the offence.
- Seriousness is based on the offender's culpability and the harm caused as well as on any aggravating or mitigating features within the offence itself and any statutory aggravating factors.
- The court's assessment of offence seriousness will:
  - — determine which of the sentencing thresholds has been crossed;
  - — indicate whether a custodial, community or other sentence is the most appropriate;
  - — be a key factor in deciding the length of a custodial sentence, the number and nature of requirements to be incorporated in a community sentence and the amount of any fine imposed.
- Research and utilise available sentencing guidelines—including any specific offence sentencing guidelines issued by the SC/SGC and, Court of Appeal decisions for sentencing in the Crown Court and the Magistrates' Court Sentencing Guidelines for cases that are to be sentenced summarily—as these will provide you with a broad indication of likely sentence.
- Understand that although an offence might be regarded as serious and warrant a particular sentence, a court will have regard to personal offender mitigation in arriving at the most appropriate sentence.
- Anticipate the need for a pre-sentence report (PSR) and understand why such a report is often influential in informing the sentencing process.
- If a defendant client accepts he is guilty but disputes a material aspect of the prosecution's version of events, anticipate the need for a Newton hearing.
- Guilty pleas always attract a sentencing discount: the more timely the guilty plea, the greater the discount.

SELF-TEST QUESTIONS

Consider the following scenario and then try to answer the questions that follow by taking the structured approach to sentencing as explained in this chapter.

Scott is charged with assault occasioning actual bodily harm contrary to s. 47 Offences Against the Person Act 1861. It is alleged that Scott, aged 23, was drunk, and while at a kebab takeaway he and a group of other youths started shouting racial abuse at a group of Asian youths. A fight broke out and it is alleged Scott punched and head-butted one of the Asian youths causing a cut just above the young man's eye and a fracture to his nose. The cut did not require stitches and the fracture will heal in a few weeks.

Scott initially denies the offence in interview but pleads guilty at his first appearance in connection with the matter.

At the time of this offence Scott was on bail for an alleged offence of theft but was later acquitted. Scott's previous convictions include:

- 15 months ago: assault occasioning actual bodily harm—s. 47 Offences against the Person Act 1861 (Community Order, 12 months);
- 24 months ago: public order—threatening behaviour—s. 5 Public Order Act 1968 (fine);
- 36 months ago: theft—s. 1 Theft Act 1968 (conditional discharge).

Questions

- What is the starting point in terms of sentencing for an assault contrary to s. 47 according to the Magistrates' Court Sentencing Guidelines? The relevant guideline is included in Appendix 2.
- Try to gauge the seriousness of this offence—what factors aggravate the seriousness of this assault?
- Is this a case where a pre-sentence report is likely to be requested?
- Is Scott entitled to a sentencing discount?

Case studies: *R v Roger Martin; R v Lenny Wise; R v William Hardy*

In relation to *R v Hardy* and *R v Martin*, you will be able to see the plea in mitigation and the sentencing process on the video clips contained within our Online Resource Centre. Before you view these, however,

online resource centre

it is important that you engage in the process which culminates in the plea in mitigation. This can only be done by considering this chapter and Chapter 22 and attempting to engage in the tasks we have set in relation to the case studies throughout this chapter and Chapter 22.

R v Roger Martin

If you have considered the documentation in relation to this web-based only case study, you will be aware that Roger Martin has been advised to plead guilty to the offences of common assault, careless driving and failing to stop and report after an accident. All these matters are summary only and Roger Martin must therefore be sentenced before a magistrates' court. You will note that the solicitor's ability to negotiate a reduced charge of dangerous driving down to careless driving has been of enormous benefit to Roger Martin. He no longer faces the risk of a committal to the Crown Court and of course, dangerous driving carries with it a mandatory disqualification period of 12 months.

- **Ignoring the driving penalties for the time being, assess the level of seriousness of the common assault. Research any relevant sentencing guidelines.**
- **Try to ascertain what you consider will be the worst outcome for Roger Martin in terms of sentence.**
- **Do you consider a pre-sentence report should be obtained in these circumstances?**

 online resource centre

The questions posed in relation to *R v Roger Martin* are considered further on our Online Resource Centre.

R v William Hardy

It will be recalled that William Hardy has been advised to plead guilty to an offence of engaging in sexual activity with a child contrary to s. 9(2) Sexual Offences Act 2003. The offence is indictable-only.

- **What is the maximum sentence for this offence?**
- **Research any relevant sentencing guidelines for this offence in an attempt to gauge the level of seriousness and the likely sentence.**
- **Do you consider a pre-sentence report should be obtained in this case?**

 online resource centre

All of the above matters are considered on the Online Resource Centre.

R v Lenny Wise

You will be aware that Lenny Wise was acquitted of the offence of domestic dwelling burglary. Had Lenny Wise been convicted before the Crown Court, what would have been the maximum sentence the judge could have passed? Research the relevant sentencing guidelines for burglary offences tried on indictment. You will find the guideline specific to the offence of domestic dwelling burglary in the 'Sentencing Guidelines' section of the Sentencing Council's website: http://sentencingcouncil.judiciary. gov.uk/guidelines/guidelines-to-download.htm.

- **What sentence do you consider Lenny would have received?**
- **Would it have been necessary for a pre-sentence report to have been ordered?**

FIGURE 21.1 SENTENCING PROCEDURE

Sentencing procedure where defendant is found guilty

- Procedure generally same in Crown Court and magistrates' court.

- Court will be aware of facts of case and the defendant's role; defendant's criminal record will be disclosed to the court by the prosecutor who will seek any ancillary orders.

- The case may be adjourned for a pre-sentence report (SDR or FDR).

- Defendant may be bailed or remanded in custody pending preparation of reports.

- Defence make a plea in mitigation.

- Defendant sentenced with court giving reasons.

Sentencing procedure where defendant pleads guilty

- Procedure generally same in Crown Court and magistrates' court.

- Where dispute between prosecution and defence about facts of the offence, which would materially affect sentencing outcome, a Newton hearing (*R v Newton*) may be held.

- Prosecution outline facts of the offence and the defendant's role, seeking any ancillary orders.

- Defendant's criminal record will be disclosed to the court.

- The case may be adjourned for pre-sentence report (SDR or FDR).

- Defence make plea in mitigation.

- Defendant sentenced with court giving reasons.

FIGURE 21.2 STRUCTURED APPROACH TO SENTENCING UNDER MCSGs

Structured approach to sentencing under MCSGs

- Sentence is based on the seriousness of the offence defined by the offender's culpability in committing the offence and the risk of harm caused (s. 143 CJA 2003).

- A court will have a sentencing purpose in mind (s. 142 CJA 2003) when imposing a particular sentence.

- The seriousness of the offence/s is determined by:

↓

Statutory aggravating factors which include

- offence committed while on bail (s. 143);

- previous offending (s. 143);

- religiously aggravated (s. 145);

- racially aggravated (s. 145);

- motivated by a person's sexual orientation, transgender identity or disability (s. 146).

↓

Aggravating and mitigating features of the offence itself as identified by Sentencing guidelines

(whether they be Magistrates' Court Sentencing Guidelines/Court of Appeal judgments/Sentencing Council general and specific guidelines) will give an indication of the starting point in terms of the type of sentence and length, i.e. custody/community sentence/fine/discharge.

↓

Court will consider personal offender mitigation based on the plea in mitigation and addressed in any pre-sentence report.

↓

Court arrives at a sentence.

↓

Court applies any sentencing discount to take account of a guilty plea (s. 144 CJA 2003).

↓

Court passes sentence and explains its reasons (s. 174 CJA 2003).

22 SPECIFIC TYPES OF SENTENCE AND THE PLEA IN MITIGATION

22.1 INTRODUCTION

Having considered the general principles of sentencing practice in Chapter 21, this chapter explains the range of disposals available to a court when passing sentence on an adult offender and provides guidance about making a plea in mitigation.

22.2 WHEN CAN A DISCRETIONARY CUSTODIAL SENTENCE BE IMPOSED?

Even where an offence carries a custodial sentence this does not mean that custody will be automatically imposed. Section 152(2) Criminal Justice Act 2003 (CJA 2003) defines the custody threshold test by providing that:

> 'The court must not pass a custodial sentence on the offender unless it is of the opinion that the offence, or combination of the offence and one or more offences associated with it, was so serious that neither a fine alone or a community sentence can be justified for the offence.
>
> (3) Nothing in subsection (2) prevents the court from passing a custodial sentence on the offender if—
>
> (a) he fails to express his willingness to comply with a requirement which is proposed by the court to be included in a community order and which requires an expression of willingness; or
>
> (b) he fails to comply with an order under s. 161(2) (pre-sentence drug testing).'

Section 152(2) CJA 2003 acknowledges that custody should be a sentence of last resort.

In passing a custodial sentence, s. 174(2)(b) CJA 2003 requires a court to state in open court why it is of the opinion that the offence is so serious that no other sentence apart from custody is justified.

22.2.1 THE CUSTODY THRESHOLD TEST—S. 152(2) CJA 2003

As noted, s. 152(2) CJA 2003 establishes the 'custody threshold test': 'Is the offence so serious that neither a community sentence nor fine can be imposed?' Only if this question is answered affirmatively can a custodial sentence be imposed. As we saw in the previous chapter, the seriousness of an offence is assessed according to the defendant's culpability and the harm caused and the presence of aggravating and/or mitigating factors, as defined in the relevant sentencing guidelines. Where the court considers the offence is so serious that it merits a custodial sentence, there may be personal offender mitigation which requires a less draconian disposal than custody.

It is obvious that in many cases where an offender is convicted of a serious indictable offence, a custodial sentence is almost inevitable. Sentencing guidelines will help the defence advocate to determine whether the custody threshold is likely to be met in a particular case.

22.2.2 WHAT IF THE THRESHOLD TEST IS FINELY BALANCED?

Where the custody threshold test is finely balanced, the defence advocate has everything to play for in his plea in mitigation. In support of the defence advocate's argument that his client should not receive a custodial sentence, assistance may be provided by case law. For example, in *R v Kefford* [2002] 2 Cr App (S) R 106, the Court of Appeal reduced the original sentence of 12 months imposed on a building society employee for several dishonesty-related offences totalling £11,120 to four months because of prison overcrowding. More recently the problem of prison overcrowding and its effect on sentencing has been further highlighted by the Court of Appeal in *R v Seed* [2007] 2 Cr App R (S) 69.

22.3 CUSTODY BETWEEN THE AGES 18 AND 21

An offender under the age of 21 cannot be sentenced to a term of imprisonment in an adult prison (s. 89(1) Powers of Criminal Courts (Sentencing) Act 2000 (PCC(S) A 2000)). Offenders under the age of 21 but over 18, who are subject to a custodial sentence, will serve their time at a young offenders' institution. This will change when s. 61 Criminal Justice and Court Service Act 2000 is implemented which permits the term of imprisonment to be served in an adult prison. A minimum custodial sentence of 21 days must be imposed for offenders aged 18–20.

22.4 LENGTH OF CUSTODIAL SENTENCE

Section 153(2) CJA 2003 requires a custodial sentence to be for the shortest term that is commensurate with the seriousness of the offence, or the combination of the offence and one or more offences associated with it—although this does not apply to a sentence fixed by law and indeterminate and extended sentences for certain violent and sexual offences passed under ss. 224–229 CJA 2003 (see para. 22.8).

Guidance from the Court of Appeal in several cases including *R v Ollerenshaw* [1999] 1 Cr App R (S) 65; *R v Kefford* [2002] 2 Cr App R (S) 495 and *R v Seed* [2007] 2 Cr App R (S) 69 require courts to keep custodial sentences as short as possible, consistent with the court's duty to protect the public interest and to punish and deter the offender. The well-publicised concern about prison overcrowding reinforces the point.

22.4.1 THE TOTALITY PRINCIPLE AND CUSTODIAL SENTENCES

Section 153(2) CJA 2003 states that when imposing custody for more than one offence, a court must have regard to the totality principle which requires that the sentence passed must not be disproportionate to the seriousness of the overall offending behaviour. The totality principle most often arises in deciding whether two or more custodial sentences should be served concurrently or consecutively.

Assume a sentence of three months' imprisonment is imposed for possessing an offensive weapon and a further custodial sentence of three months for driving whilst disqualified. The sentences are ordered to run consecutively which means the offender is required to serve a total of six months' imprisonment. Had the two sentences been passed to run concurrently, the offender would be required to serve a total of three months in custody. In deciding whether to impose consecutive custodial sentences, the court must have regard to the totality of the defendant's actions and the need to sentence proportionately (see Chapter 21, para. 21.7.1).

22.4.2 **RELEASE FROM CUSTODY ON LICENCE**

The CJA 2003 draws a distinction between custodial terms of less than 12 months and custodial terms of more than 12 months. In relation to custodial terms of 12 months or more, relevant provisions are contained in ss. 237–268 CJA 2003. A prison sentence of 12 months or more is served in full, although half the sentence is served on licence in the community with the offender being subject to requirements. In passing sentence, the court will be able to recommend certain licence requirements, although they will not be binding on the Probation Service. The Probation Service will be able to attach specific requirements to the second half of the custodial sentence to prevent reoffending and to protect the public. A failure to abide by the requirements will result in the offender being recalled to custody. The provisions do not apply to 'dangerous' offenders nor to those offenders subject to extended sentences (see para. 22.8).

Where a court passes a custodial sentence of less than 12 months (which obviously covers the magistrates' court), half the sentence is served in custody. For the remainder of the term, the offender is on unconditional licence in the community. If the offender commits a further offence whilst on licence she can be ordered to return to custody to serve the balance of the original sentence.

22.4.3 **CREDIT FOR GUILTY PLEA**

As noted in Chapter 21, para. 21.13, where a custodial sentence is to be imposed, s. 144 CJA 2003 requires that the defendant should be given credit for a timely guilty plea and the court should reduce the term to take account of the guilty plea.

In its definitive guideline on 'Reduction in Sentence for a Guilty Plea' (July 2007), the SGC suggests:

'Where a sentencer is in doubt as to whether a custodial sentence is appropriate, the reduction attributable to a guilty plea will be a relevant consideration. Where this is amongst the factors leading to the imposition of a non-custodial sentence, there will be no need to apply a further reduction on account of the guilty plea.'

Thus the application of the reduction principle may therefore result in a non-custodial sentence where the custody threshold test is finely balanced. Section 174(2)(d) CJA 2003 imposes a duty on the court to state in open court that as a result of the guilty plea, the court has imposed a less severe sentence than it otherwise would have done.

22.4.4 **TIME SPENT REMANDED IN CUSTODY**

Time spent on remand in prison or on bail subject to an electronically monitored curfew of nine hours is to count as time served by the offender as part of the sentence (s. 108 Legal Aid Sentencing and Punishment of Offenders Act 2012 (LASPO 2012)).

22.5 **SUSPENDED SENTENCE OF IMPRISONMENT**

A suspended sentence of imprisonment can be imposed on an offender aged 18 or over where the custody threshold is met.

A suspended sentence is available in the Crown Court for a custodial sentence of 24 months or less and in the magistrates' court for a custodial sentence of six months or less. Custodial sentences of less than 14 days cannot be suspended. The period of suspension can be between six months and two years. As part of the suspended sentence, the court can order the offender to undertake requirements in the community during the supervision period. The list of requirements is the same as that for a community order (see para. 22.10). Any requirements must be commensurate with the seriousness of the offence. If the offender fails to comply with the requirements, or commits a further offence (whether or not punishable with imprisonment), the court has a number of options under Sch. 12 para. 8 CJA 2003. It can order that the suspended sentence be activated for the original custodial term or a lesser term unless it would be unjust to do so having regard to the extent to which the offender has complied with the community requirements of the suspended order, or amend the order extending the operational period or impose more onerous requirements. It can impose a fine for breach if it decides not to imprison.

22.6 CONCLUDING REMARKS ON DISCRETIONARY CUSTODIAL SENTENCES

We end this section on discretionary custodial sentences with reference to the guidance issued by the Sentencing Guidelines Council (SGC): *Overarching Principles: Seriousness* (December 2004). The SGC suggests at para. 1.33 that under the sentencing framework contained in the CJA 2003, the court should adopt the following structured approach when imposing a discretionary custodial sentence:

(a) Has the custody threshold been passed?

(b) If so, is it unavoidable that a custodial sentence be imposed?

(c) If so, can that sentence be suspended?

(d) If not, impose a sentence which takes immediate effect for the shortest term commensurate with the seriousness of the offence.

22.7 FIXED LENGTH SENTENCES

In some cases the length of a custodial sentence is fixed by law. This applies to a conviction for murder and mandatory minimum sentences (under ss. 110 and 111 PCC(S)A 2000) for a third conviction in connection with Class A drug trafficking and burglary. Mandatory minimum periods also apply to certain firearms offences. For each of these offences, a court is required to impose the minimum statutory term unless it would be 'unjust' to do so. Where the offender has been assessed as a 'dangerous' offender within s. 226 CJA 2003 (see later), a mandatory sentence of life or an indeterminate sentence for public protection must be passed.

22.8 SENTENCING DANGEROUS OFFENDERS

Sections 224–229 CJA 2003 introduced changes to sentencing 'dangerous' offenders. These provisions have been significantly amended by LASPO 2012. A significant part of LASPO's sentencing reforms includes the repeal of ss. 225 and 226 CJA 2003 (s. 123 LASPO 2012) which made provision for sentences of imprisonment for public protection (indeterminate sentences) and detention for public protection (the equivalent sentence for persons under 18). The indeterminate sentence for public protection is replaced with a life sentence upon conviction for a second 'serious' offence in the case of an offender aged 18 and over and a revised approach to extended sentences for offenders assessed as 'dangerous' has been brought into force.

The provisions apply to adults as well as young offenders aged under the age of 18. The application of the dangerousness provisions in relation to young offenders is considered in Chapter 26, para. 26.18. An essential part of the dangerousness provisions is the distinction between 'specified' and 'serious' offences.

A 'specified offence' is a violent or a sexual offence specified in Sch. 15 to the 2003 Act and which carries a sentence of between two and 10 years' imprisonment. A 'serious offence' is a violent or sexual offence specified in Sch. 15 which carries a sentence of 10 or more years' imprisonment in the case of an adult.

A sentence under the 'dangerousness' provisions can only be passed in the Crown Court which is a relevant consideration for a magistrates' court in determining allocation and possible committal for sentence (see Chapter 11 and Chapter 21, para. 21.14.2).

An extended sentence comprises two parts: a custodial sentence for the offence for such length as the seriousness of the offence demands which must be at least 4 years, and an extended period on licence for such length as the court considers necessary to protect the public from serious harm.

Who qualifies for a life sentence under the dangerousness provisions?

Section 225(1) and (2) CJA 2003 provide the following conditions:

- where an offender is aged 18 or over and is convicted of a 'serious offence'; AND
- the court considers that the offender is dangerous (that is there is a significant risk to members of the public of serious harm (which includes death or serious personal/psychological injury) occasioned by the commission of further 'specified offences'); AND
- the offence carries a life sentence; AND
- the court considers that the seriousness of the offence is such as to justify imposing a sentence of life imprisonment,

the court MUST impose a sentence of life imprisonment.

Guidance on imposing a discretionary life sentence is provided by the Court of Appeal in *R v Kehoe* [2008] EWCA Crim 819. Unless the offence is so serious that imprisonment for a whole life term is justified, a minimum term which the offender will serve in custody must be set. The minimum term is normally one-half of the notional determinate sentence which is set by taking into account the seriousness of the offence and any reduction for a guilty plea. Once the offender has served the minimum term, he will not be released on licence unless the Parole Board is satisfied that it is no longer necessary for the protection of the public that the offender be confined. The offender remains on licence for the rest of his life.

Life sentences to be imposed on conviction for a second serious offence

A new s. 224A CJA 2003 provides that a court *must* impose a life sentence on a person aged 18 or over who is convicted of an offence listed in Part 1 of Sch. 15B of the Act committed after 3 December 2012 which is *serious enough to justify a sentence of imprisonment of 10 years or more, if* that person has *previously* been convicted of an offence listed in any Part of Sch. 15B and was sentenced to imprisonment for life or for a period of 10 years or more in respect of that previous offence. However, the court *is not obliged to impose a life sentence* where it is of the opinion that there are particular circumstances which relate to the offence, the previous offence or the offender which would make it *unjust to do so* in all the circumstances.

Step 1: Was the offence committed on or after 3rd December 2012?
If the answer is NO then the provisions do not apply.

Step 2: Is the offence listed in Part 1, Sch. 15B CJA 2003?
If the answer is NO then the provisions do not apply.

Step 3: At date of conviction was the offender aged at least 18 years?
If the answer is NO then the provisions do not apply.

Section 224A (3) CJA 2003 sets out the *sentence condition*. The present offence must be serious enough to justify a sentence of imprisonment of 10 years or more. The court must consider what sentence it would have imposed but for s. 224A (taking into account any guilty plea made by the offender, as well as any aggravating or mitigating factors, and ignoring the extended sentence available under s. 226A CJA 2003).

Section 224A(4) sets out the previous *offence condition*. The offender must have been previously convicted of an offence listed in any part of Sch. 15B, and, on conviction, must have received a *relevant life sentence* or a *relevant determinate sentence*.

Step 4: But for consideration of these provisions, would the offence otherwise merit a determinate sentence (ignoring s. 226A CJA 2003) of at least 10 years or more?
If the answer is NO then the provisions do not apply.

Step 5: At the time this offence was committed had the offender previously been convicted of an offence listed in Sch. 15B CJA 2003?

If the answer is NO then the provisions do not apply.

Step 6: Was that previous offence punished with either a relevant life sentence (see s. 224A(5) CJA 2003) or a relevant sentence of imprisonment/detention for a determinate period (see s. 224A (6)– (11)) CJA 2003?

If the answer is NO then the provisions do not apply.

Section 224A(5) CJA 2003 sets out what is meant by a *relevant* life sentence. A relevant life sentence is one where the offender was not eligible for release during the first five years of the sentence (not taking into account any period spent on remand or bail). The term 'life sentence' includes a sentence of imprisonment or detention for public protection.

Section 224A(6) and (7) CJA 2003 set out when an extended sentence is relevant. An extended sentence is relevant if the custodial term was 10 years or more.

Section 224A(8) CJA 2003 provides that any other determinate sentence of imprisonment or detention of 10 years or more is a *relevant* sentence.

Step 7: The court must impose a life sentence unless factors relating to this offence, the previous offence, or the offender would make it unjust to do so.

New extended sentences

Section 226A(1) CJA 2003 provides that an extended sentence may be passed where

(a) an offender aged 18 is convicted of a specified offence (whenever that offence was committed);

(b) the court considers that the offender presents a significant risk to members of the public of serious harm through the commission by the offender of further specified offences;

(c) the court is not obliged to impose a life sentence because of the seriousness of the offence by virtue of section 224A (life sentence for second listed offence) or 225(2) CJA 2003 (life sentence for dangerous offenders); *and*

(d) either condition A **or** condition B is met.

Section 226A(2) CJA 2003 sets out condition A, which is that when the current offence was committed, the offender had a previous conviction for an offence listed in Sch. 15B.

Section 226A(3) CJA 2003 sets out condition B, which is that the current offence is serious enough that, if the court imposed an extended sentence under this section, it would specify an appropriate custodial term of at least four years.

Section 226A(5) CJA 2003 sets out the structure of the new extended sentence. It consists of the appropriate custodial term followed by an extension period, which is a further period during which the offender is to be subject to a licence. The offender will normally be released on a licence when he has served two-thirds of the custodial term.

Section 226A(6) CJA 2003 provides that the court must determine the custodial term.

Section 226A(7) CJA 2003 stipulates that the extension period must be a period of such length as the court considers necessary to protect the public from serious harm caused by the offender's commission of further offences listed in Sch. 15.

Section 226A(8) CJA 2003 sets out the maximum extension periods of five years for a violent offence and eight years for a sexual offence.

Section 226A(9) CJA 2003 stipulates that the appropriate custodial term and the extension period must not together exceed the maximum term of imprisonment that may be imposed for the offence.

How is an offender assessed as being dangerous?

In determining whether the offender is 'dangerous' the court must ask itself, does the offender pose a *significant* risk to members of the public of *serious harm* including death or serious personal/psychological injury occasioned by the commission of further '*specified offences*'?

Section 229 CJA 2003 provides that the court:

• *must* take into account all such information as is available as to the nature and circumstances of the offence;

- may take into account all available information about the nature and circumstances of any other offence(s) of which the offender has been convicted by a court anywhere in the world;

- may take into account any information it has about any pattern of behaviour of which any of the offences form part;

- may take into account any information it has before it about the offender.

It is the prosecutor's responsibility to direct the court to the possible application of the 'dangerousness' provisions. The pre-sentence report and any psychiatric report, as well as an offender's previous convictions and mental condition, will be essential in helping the court to determine whether someone is 'dangerous' within the meaning of s. 229 CJA 2003.

Important guidance was provided by the Court of Appeal in *R v Lang and Others* [2005] EWCA Crim 2864. Thirteen appeals were heard based on the 'dangerousness provisions' *as originally drafted under the CJA 2003,* prior to amendment by the Criminal Justice and Immigration Act 2008 (CJIA) and LASPO 2012. In all but three cases, the Court of Appeal varied the sentence either because it felt 'dangerousness' was not established on the facts, or a sentence of public protection (now abolished by LASPO 2012) was more appropriate than a life sentence. The judgment contains the following guidance on the assessment of dangerous and its consequences:

'(i) The risk identified must be significant. This is a higher threshold than mere possibility of occurrence and in our view can be taken to mean (as in the Oxford Dictionary) "noteworthy, of considerable amount or importance."

(ii) In assessing the risk of further offences being committed, the sentencer should take into account the nature and circumstances of the current offence; the offender's history of offending including not just the kind of offence but its circumstances and the sentence passed, details of which the prosecution must have available, and, whether the offending demonstrates any pattern; social and economic factors in relation to the offender including accommodation, employability, education, associates, relationships and drug or alcohol abuse; and the offender's thinking, attitude towards offending and supervision and emotional state. Information in relation to these matters will most readily, though not exclusively, come from antecedents and pre-sentence probation and medical reports . . . The sentencer will be guided, but not bound by, the assessment of risk in such reports . . .

(iii) If the foreseen specified offence is serious, there will clearly be some cases, though not by any means all, in which there may be a significant risk of serious harm. For example, robbery is a serious offence. But it can be committed in a wide variety of ways many of which do not give rise to a significant risk of serious harm. Sentencers must therefore guard against assuming there is a significant risk of serious harm merely because the foreseen specified offence is serious. A pre-sentence report should usually be obtained before any sentence is passed which is based on significant risk of serious harm. In a small number of cases, where the circumstances of the current offence or the history of the offender suggest mental abnormality on his part, a medical report may be necessary before risk can properly be assessed.

(iv) If the foreseen specified offence is not serious, there will be comparatively few cases in which a risk of serious harm will properly be regarded as significant. The huge variety of offences in Schedule 15 includes many which, in themselves, are not suggestive of serious harm. Repetitive violent or sexual offending at a relatively low level without serious harm does not of itself give rise to a significant risk of serious harm in the future. There may, in such cases, be some risk of future victims being more adversely affected than past victims but this, of itself, does not give rise to significant risk of serious harm.

(v) In relation to the rebuttable assumption to which section 229(3) gives rise, the court is accorded a discretion if, in the light of information about the current offence, the offender and his previous offences, it would be unreasonable to conclude that there is a significant risk. The exercise of such discretion is, historically, at the very heart of judicial sentencing and the language of the statute indicates that judges are expected, albeit starting from the assumption, to exercise their ability to reach a reasonable conclusion in the light of the information before them. It is to be noted that the assumption will be rebutted, if at all, as an exercise of judgment: the statute includes no reference to the burden or standard of proof. As we have indicated above, it will usually be unreasonable to conclude that the assumption applies unless information about the offences, pattern of behaviour and offender show a significant risk of serious harm from further offences. [*Note: the presumption of dangerousness referred was repealed by the amendments made to the dangerousness provisions under CJIA 2008.*]

(vi) In relation to offenders under 18 and adults with no relevant previous convictions at the time the specified offence was committed, the court's discretion under section 229(2) is not constrained by any initial assumption such as, under section 229(3), applies to adults with previous convictions. It is still necessary, when sentencing young offenders, to bear in mind that, within a shorter time than adults, they may change and develop. This and their level of maturity may be highly pertinent when assessing what their future conduct may be and whether it may give rise to significant risk of serious harm.

(vii) In relation to a particularly young offender, an indeterminate sentence (since abolished by LASPO 2012) may be inappropriate even where a serious offence has been committed and there is a significant risk of serious harm from further offences (see for example, *R v D* [2005] EWCA Crim 2282).

(viii) It cannot have been Parliament's intention, in a statute dealing with the liberty of the subject, to require the imposition of indeterminate sentences (since abolished by LASPO 2012) for the commission of relatively minor offences.

(ix) Sentencers should usually, and in accordance with section 174(1)(a) of the Criminal Justice Act 2003, give reasons for all their conclusions: in particular, that there is or is not a significant risk of further offences or serious harm; where the assumption under section 229(3) arises for making or not making the assumption which the statute requires unless this would be unreasonable; and for not imposing an extended sentence under sections 227 and 228. Sentencers should, in giving reasons, briefly identify the information which they have taken into account.'

22.9 COMMUNITY SENTENCES

As the name suggests, a community sentence is served in the community. Courts are encouraged to use community-based sentences as alternatives to custody. They are commonly proposed by the Probation Service in pre-sentence reports.

The CJA 2003 introduced significant changes to the structure and enforcement of community-based sentences. Courts now pass a generic community order with one or more specified requirements.

Contrary to popular perception, community-based sentences are demanding and rigorously enforced.

22.9.1 THE THRESHOLD FOR IMPOSING A COMMUNITY SENTENCE

As with custodial sentences, there is a threshold test for imposing a community order which must be met before a court can impose a community sentence. Section 148 CJA 2003 provides:

'A court must not pass a community sentence on an offender unless it is of the opinion that the offence, or the combination of the offence and one or more offences associated with it, is serious enough to warrant such a sentence.'

A community-based sentence can only be imposed for an offence which is considered to be 'serious enough' to warrant it. It cannot be imposed for an offence which is not punishable with imprisonment (s. 150A CJA 2003).

22.9.2 IS THE OFFENCE SERIOUS ENOUGH?

In assessing whether an offence is serious enough to warrant a community sentence, the MCSGs provide assistance. If you consult the guidelines, you will see there are several offences, including theft from a person and handling stolen goods, which suggest a sentencing range to include a community order. As previously indicated the balance of aggravating and mitigating features in the particular case may tilt the sentence down towards a fine or upwards beyond the community sentence threshold. The sentencing guidelines indicate the basic starting point.

22.10 COMMUNITY SENTENCES UNDER THE CJA 2003

Section 177 CJA 2003 creates a single, generic community order which will impose one or more requirements on the offender. The community order is available for all offenders aged 18 or over and can last for up to three years. The order must specify an end date, which can be no longer than the longest requirement.

The requirements that can be imposed under a community order include:

- unpaid work—s. 199;
- an activity requirement—s. 201;
- a programme requirement—s. 202;
- a prohibited activity requirement—defined s. 203;
- a curfew requirement—s. 204;
- an exclusion requirement—s. 205;
- a residence requirement—s. 206;
- a foreign travel prohibition requirement—s. 206 (A);
- a mental health requirement—s. 207;
- a drug rehabilitation requirement—s. 209;
- an alcohol treatment requirement—s. 212;
- an alcohol abstinence and monitoring requirement—212 (A) (currently being piloted);
- a supervision requirement—s. 213; and/or
- in the case of an offender under 25, an attendance centre requirement—s. 214.

Where a court makes a community order imposing a curfew requirement or an exclusion requirement, the court must also impose an electronic monitoring requirement (s. 177(3)).

22.10.1 HOW WILL THE TYPE OF ORDER BE DETERMINED?

Section 148(3) CJA 2003 provides that where the court passes a community sentence:

'(a) the particular requirement or requirements forming part of the order must be such as, in the opinion of the court is, or taken together are, the most suitable for the offenders; and

(b) the restrictions on liberty imposed by the order . . . are commensurate with the seriousness of the offence, or the combination of the offence and one or more offences associated with it.'

In determining the requirements for a community order, the court will have regard to one or more of the sentencing objectives contained in s. 142(1) CJA 2003 (see Chapter 21).

The seriousness of the offence and the risk of harm posed by the offender will determine the nature and combination of requirements and the intensity of those requirements.

Useful guidance on community orders is provided by the SGC in its publication: *New Sentences: CJA 2003* (December 2004) accessible through the Sentencing Council's website. The 'seriousness' of the offence is an important factor in deciding whether the court chooses a low, medium or high range of requirements. Proportionality and suitability will be the guiding principles.

Generally the guidelines suggest the lowest range of community sentence should be reserved for low level type of offences. Such an order might contain just one requirement for a short duration. The most requirements would be reserved for those offenders whose offences fall just short of the custodial threshold. The nature and severity of the requirements to be imposed should be guided by:

    (i) the assessment of the offence's seriousness (low/medium/high);

    (ii) the purpose(s) of sentencing the court wishes to achieve;

    (iii) the risk of reoffending;

    (iv) the ability of the offender to comply; and

    (v) the availability of requirements in the local area.

The SGC publication includes examples of the type of requirements that might be imposed based on an offence of low/medium/high seriousness.

The guidelines stress the importance of obtaining a pre-sentence report to help determine the particular requirements or combination of requirements in a specific case. Further guidance on seriousness in the context of the community order is contained in the MCSGs (2008), accessible via the SC's website.

22.11   THE REQUIREMENTS

22.11.1   UNPAID WORK—S. 199 CJA 2003

The offender is required to perform unpaid work in the community under the supervision of a responsible officer. A court cannot impose an unpaid work requirement unless the court is satisfied that the offender is a suitable person to perform such work. For this reason, a court will invariably require a pre-sentence report to assess the offender's suitability.

When imposing a community order with an unpaid work requirement, the court gives the offender the chance to make amends to the community in which the offence has been committed. It is punitive in nature. A supervising officer oversees the community work placement which might involve painting, decorating or gardening for organisations or individuals.

The number of hours of unpaid work must not be less than 40 and not more than 300 hours and should be proportional to the seriousness of the offence(s) committed. An unpaid work requirement may be combined with any further requirement(s) as the court deems fit.

22.11.2   ACTIVITY REQUIREMENT—S. 201 CJA 2003

This requires the offender to be present at a specified place and participate in specified activities. A pre-sentence report is normally required if the court is considering this as a requirement. The aggregate number of days of an activity order must not exceed 60.

The activities can include day centre attendance, education and basic skills training and reparation to victims with their consent.

22.11.3   PROGRAMME REQUIREMENT—S. 202 CJA 2003

An offender would be required to participate in an activity programme which has been accredited by a body established by the Secretary of State. A pre-sentence report would be required in order to check the offender's suitability and the availability of such an accredited programme.

The aims of these programmes are to:

- make offenders accept responsibility for their offences;
- avoid further offending;
- attempt to resolve any difficulties linked to offending behaviour, e.g. homelessness, marital or relationship breakdown, unemployment, illiteracy, addiction.

Such programmes have traditionally included:

- Enhanced Thinking Skills Programme. This requires the offender to participate in group work with a view to enabling poorly educated offenders to attain basic literacy and numeracy skills.

- Sex Offender Programme. This is aimed at offenders convicted of sexual offences who have been assessed as suitable for the programme.

- Drink Impaired Drivers Programme. This is aimed primarily at offenders convicted of drink-driving offences.

A programme requirement will invariably be combined with a supervision requirement (undertaken by a probation officer) under the community order.

22.11.4 PROHIBITED ACTIVITY REQUIREMENT—S. 203 CJA 2003

This requires the offender to refrain from participating in specified activities named in the order on any day or days specified during the requirement period. The requirements that may be included in a prohibited activity requirement are not limited and may include the prohibition of activities that would otherwise be lawful. Possibilities include prohibiting the defendant from visiting a particular place, for example nightclubs, or undertaking a particular activity such as driving, drinking alcohol or attending football matches.

22.11.5 CURFEW REQUIREMENT—S. 204 CJA 2003

A curfew requires a convicted offender to stay at an agreed address for a specified time of between two and 16 hours, e.g. between 7 pm and 7 am for a period of between one and seven days. A curfew can be imposed for a total of twelve months.

Curfew orders are enforced by electronic 'tagging' and are intended make it harder for an offender to commit further crimes by helping to break patterns of offending behaviour by forcing the offender to stay at the specified address.

A tag is attached to the offender's wrist or ankle and is linked to a monitoring machine installed in the place where the offender is living. The machine is linked via a telephone line to a monitoring centre. Monitoring centre staff become immediately aware if the curfew is broken.

In imposing a curfew requirement, the court will take account of the offender's religious beliefs, employment or attendance at an educational establishment and its compatibility with any other requirements imposed as part of the community order. A pre-sentence report may well be required in order for the court to be satisfied that suitable accommodation is available to the offender.

22.11.6 EXCLUSION REQUIREMENT—S. 205 CJA 2003

This directs the offender not to enter a place or an area specified in the order. An exclusion requirement must not exceed two years and will be monitored electronically. The order can provide for the prohibition to operate only during specified periods and may specify different periods or days during the order.

22.11.7 RESIDENCE REQUIREMENT—S. 206 CJA 2003

This requires the offender to reside at a place specified in the order. It could include a hostel or institution recommended by a probation officer.

22.11.8 MENTAL HEALTH TREATMENT REQUIREMENT—S. 207 CJA 2003

Rehabilitative in nature, a mental health requirement requires the offender to be treated by a medical practitioner or psychologist. Before a court can impose such a requirement it must be satisfied that the offender is in need of such treatment and the offender is willing to comply.

22.11.9 DRUG REHABILITATION REQUIREMENT—S. 208 CJA 2003

A drug rehabilitation requirement (DRR) involves assessment and treatment for drug dependency. The treatment and testing period must be a minimum of six months and a maximum of three years. Before a court can impose a drug treatment requirement, it must be satisfied the defendant is dependent on drugs and can be treated. The defendant must consent to the order. The pre-sentence report must include an assessment from a treatment provider and a place must be available to the defendant. A DRR is a high-intensity community order designed to get offenders to change their drug use, thereby reducing their offending. The order will involve frequent drug testing and a high level of contact and supervision coupled with a regular monthly review by the courts.

22.11.10 ALCOHOL TREATMENT REQUIREMENT—S. 212 CJA 2003

This requirement is specifically aimed at offenders who are dependent on alcohol and whose dependency may respond to treatment. The offender must be willing to comply with the requirement. The period of treatment cannot be for less than six months.

22.11.11 SUPERVISION REQUIREMENT—S. 213 CJA 2003

Under a supervision requirement the offender must, during the relevant period, attend appointments with the responsible probation officer at times and places determined by the officer to assist the offender's rehabilitation.

22.11.12 ATTENDANCE CENTRE REQUIREMENT (WHERE OFFENDER IS AGED UNDER 25)—S. 214 CJA 2003

An attendance centre requirement obliges the offender to attend at a centre for between 12 and 36 hours. Attendance is limited to one occasion a day and for not more than three hours at any time. The attendance centre must be reasonably accessible to the offender.

22.12 GUILTY PLEA CREDIT AND COMMUNITY ORDERS

Where a community sentence is to be imposed, the court should take account of s. 144 CJA 2003. This may be reflected in the number of requirements or duration of requirements under a community order. In its definitive guideline on 'Reduction in Sentence for a Guilty Plea' (July 2007), the SGC suggested that, where an offence crosses the threshold for imposing a community sentence, the application of the reduction principle under s. 144 CA 2003 may properly form the basis for imposing a fine or discharge instead.

22.13 ENFORCEMENT OF COMMUNITY ORDERS UNDER THE CJA 2003—SCH. 8

The court will explain the consequence of the offender's failure to comply with a community order. An offender can breach a community order by failing to comply with its requirements or by committing further offences while subject to a community order.

Where a breach occurs the Probation Service will issue a single warning about a failure to comply and any further failure will result in breach proceedings being commenced against the offender. The Probation Service can apply to have the order revoked by requiring the offender to be returned to court. In dealing with an offender for breaching the requirements, the court must take into account the extent to which the offender has complied with the order.

The court has a range of powers including to fine; take no action; impose more onerous requirements on the existing order; revoke the order if it is in the interest of justice to do so and resentence the offender for the original offence; and in the case of an offender aged over 18 (who was convicted of an imprisonable offence in the first instance and has wilfully and persistently failed to comply with the requirements of the order), the court may impose a prison sentence not exceeding six months.

In its guidelines, the SGC cautions that, in dealing with a breach of a community sentence, the primary objective should be to ensure that the requirements of the sentence are completed. In other words, custody should be the last resort, reserved for those who deliberately and repeatedly breach the requirements of their order.

22.14 DEFERRING SENTENCE—SS. 1 AND 2 PCC(S)A 2000

Section 1:

> 'The Crown Court or magistrates' court may defer passing sentence on an offender for the purposes of enabling the court, or any court to which it falls to deal with him, to have regard in dealing with him to . . .
>
> (a) his conduct after conviction (including, where appropriate, the making by him of reparation for his offence) or;
>
> (b) any change in his circumstances . . .'

Deferment can only be imposed with the offender's consent and if it is in the interests of justice to do so, having regard to the nature of the offence and the character and circumstances of the defendant.

Deferment may be for up to six months and results in an adjournment of the proceedings. The power to defer sentence is most appropriately exercised where there has been an offer by the offender to make reparation to her victim or a change is expected in the offender's life which may produce a stabilising influence, e.g. a new job or marriage.

The power to defer should be exercised sparingly. In accordance with Sch. 23 to the CJA 2003 courts will be able to impose requirements on the offender (similar to those imposed on a community order) during the period of deferment, including, if appropriate, supervision by a probation officer. If the court is satisfied that the offender has failed to comply with one or more requirements, the offender can be brought back to court to be sentenced. The expectation is that, if the offender stays out of trouble and does what is required of her, she will not receive a custodial sentence for the offence for which she has been convicted.

22.15 FINES

Fines are frequently imposed in the magistrates' courts. The power to impose a financial penalty is contained in ss. 126–129 PCC(S)A 2000. Fines are suitable punishment for offences which are not serious enough to merit a community sentence, nor so serious that a custodial sentence must be considered. A high fine can be regarded as punitive and aimed at deterring an offender from repeat offending.

Magistrates' courts can impose a maximum fine of £5,000 per offence (subject to the statutory maximum for the offence, if it is less) and subject to the totality principle, discussed at para. 22.4.1, in the context of consecutive custodial sentences. The £5,000 cap will be lifted when the relevant provisions under LASPO 2012 come into force. The Crown Court's power to impose a fine is unlimited.

Section 164 CJA 2003 importantly provides:

> '(1) Before fixing the amount of any fine to be imposed on an offender who is an individual, a court shall inquire into his financial circumstances.

(2) The amount of any fine fixed by the court shall be such as, in the opinion of the court, reflects the seriousness of the offence.

(3) In fixing the amount of any fine to be imposed on an offender (whether an individual or other person), a court shall take into account the circumstances of the case including, among other things, the financial circumstances of the offender so far as they are known, or appear, to the court . . .'

Section 162 CJA 2003 enables the court to order an offender to disclose his financial means when considering imposing a fine.

It is good practice for the defence lawyer to obtain a written statement of his client's means which can be handed to the court including a full breakdown of his client's income and outgoings.

The MCSGs provide detailed guidance on the imposition of fines in the magistrates' court. Some offences in the guidelines have a fine as the initial starting point when passing sentence. For the purposes of the MCSGs a fine is based on one of three bands (A, B or C).

	Starting point	Range
Fine Band A	50% of weekly income	25–75% of relevant weekly income
Fine Band B	100% of weekly income	75–125% of relevant weekly income
Fine Band C	150% cent of weekly income	125–175% of relevant weekly income

The choice of the fine band and the position of the offence within the range for that band is decided by the court's assessment of the overall seriousness of the offence. The size of the fine is then determined by the application of the defendant's relevant weekly income (RWI) to the choice of fine band and the position within it. The MCSGs include guidance on the definition of relevant weekly income based on the offender's income from employment or self-employment after deduction of tax and national insurance. Payments received from tax credits, housing and child benefits are excluded from determining the relevant weekly income. The minimum relevant weekly income for an offender in receipt of welfare benefits or generally in receipt of a very low income is £110. Where there is no reliable information on relevant weekly income, the guidelines require the court to assume the offender has a relevant weekly income of £400. In deciding the proportions of relevant weekly income that are starting points and ranges for each fine band, account has been taken of reasonable living expenses.

Credit must be given to take account of a guilty plea in accordance with principles previously discussed.

 Example

Bupinda pleads guilty to an offence of careless driving. She was driving too quickly in wet conditions and failed to notice a pedestrian stepping into the road. Bupinda applied her brakes but collided with the pedestrian causing minor injury. Bupinda has a previous conviction for speeding. Applying the MCSGs for this offence (see Appendix 2), the starting point for a fine based on what occurred would appear to be Band B. Aggravating features of the offence include injury to a pedestrian and the fact that Bupinda has a previous conviction for speeding. The magistrates' court decides that Band B is the appropriate band but that the fine should be calculated at 110% of relevant weekly income to take account of the aggravating features. Bupinda has a weekly income of £200. She can expect a fine in the region of £220 and she will be entitled to a one-third reduction for her timely guilty plea. She will therefore have to pay a fine of £150 plus a victim surcharge (see later).

Financial penalties (including fines/compensation orders/victims' surcharge/prosecution costs) may be paid by instalments. Where a financial penalty cannot be discharged immediately, a fines collection order will be made with the court setting the rate of payment. Court-appointed fines collection officers may take enforcement proceedings in the event of default.

Whilst a fine is usually imposed as a sentence in its own right it can be combined with a community order, a compensation order and with disqualification from driving. It cannot be combined with a discharge as a sentence for a single offence. In theory, a fine can be combined with custody but in practice this is rare as imprisonment will deprive the offender of the ability to pay.

22.15.1 VICTIM SURCHARGE

Whenever a court imposes a fine it must order the offender to pay a victim surcharge in accordance with the table below:

Sentence imposed	Victim surcharge
conditional discharge	£15
fine	10% of total fine, but minimum £20, maximum £120
community order	£60
custodial sentence (but see * below)	6 months or less: £80 over 6 months: £100
suspended custodial sentence	as custodial sentence above

22.16 COMPENSATION ORDERS

It is a legitimate expectation for a victim of a criminal offence to receive compensation for any injury, loss or damage suffered as a result of a convicted individual's actions. Section 130 PCC(S)A 2000 imposes a duty on the court to order compensation unless it gives reasons for not doing so. This obligation is further strengthened by s. 63 LASPO 2012. It is immaterial whether the victim has made an application for compensation.

Magistrates can award compensation of up to £5,000 per offence. In the Crown Court, the amounts are unlimited. The MCSGs contain a table of guideline compensation awards for personal injury. In fixing the level of compensation, the offender's means must be taken into account. Priority is given to compensation orders over victims' surcharge; fines and prosecution costs.

 Example 1

Johan is convicted of assault. The victim sustains a broken nose requiring some manipulation. Based on the guidelines, Johan can expect to be ordered to pay compensation in the region of £2,000. Clearly, if Johan is in receipt of welfare benefits this sum is likely to be substantially reduced.

 Example 2

Zara is convicted of resisting a police constable in the execution of his duty. The officer falls to the floor during the arrest, sustaining bruising to both knees. The court is considering a fine for the offence. Based on the MCSGs, compensation in the region of £50–£100 may well be ordered. If Zara is in receipt of welfare benefits and cannot afford to pay a fine as well as compensation, the court will give priority to the compensation element.

 Example 3

Luke is convicted of criminal damage. He pleads guilty to breaking a door. The cost of replacing the door is estimated at £150. Luke can expect to be asked to pay some or all of this sum by way of compensation, depending on his means.

Compensation can be awarded for psychological injury. For the purposes of a compensation order, the injured party can be an individual or a company/organisation.

Where injury or damage has occurred through a road traffic offence, compensation is not awarded by the courts. Such compensation is left to compulsory driving insurance schemes.

If the offender is uninsured and the Motor Insurers' Bureau will not cover the loss, an award can be made in these circumstances.

The prosecution should normally have compensation details to hand at the point of sentencing. Where personal injury has resulted, the CPS should have the necessary details, including photographic evidence, if available. Where damage has occurred the court will expect to see an invoice for repairs or an estimate for replacement.

Where a defendant disputes the amount of compensation requested, the court will hear representations. If the matter is incapable of being resolved, the question of compensation may be adjourned for further enquiries to be made or a possible Newton hearing (see Chapter 21, para. 21.4.3).

Where more than one offender caused the victim's injury, loss or damage, the court may apportion the compensation to be paid according to each offender's culpability and his or her ability to pay.

Can the court order compensation when it sends the offender to prison? Whilst it is not usual to do so, it is possible and the Court of Appeal has stated that such an order is not wrong in principle providing the court is satisfied the offender has the means to pay or will have sufficient earning capacity when released from prison (*R v Jonge* [1999] 2 Cr App R (S) 1).

22.17 CONDITIONAL DISCHARGE

A conditional discharge may be ordered under s. 12 PCC(S)A 2000 and is a common disposal in the magistrates' courts but may also be imposed by a Crown Court. The offender can be conditionally discharged for a period of up to three years. There is no minimum period specified.

It must be explained to the defendant that, if she does not reoffend during the period of the conditional discharge, she will not be punished for the offence for which she has been convicted. However, if she is convicted of a further offence, especially if it is of a similar type, the conditional discharge can be revoked and the defendant will be sentenced not only in connection with the new matter, but could also be resentenced for the offence for which she received the conditional discharge.

A conditional discharge therefore has a deterrent element. It would not be imposed for a serious offence, but it is particularly suitable for first-time offenders, and those who may not have offended in the recent past whose offence is not serious enough to warrant a community sentence. A conditional discharge is usually passed as a sentence in its own right but can be combined with an award of compensation and/or costs.

22.18 ABSOLUTE DISCHARGE

An absolute discharge may be imposed under s. 12 PCC(S)A 2000—although the sentence is rarely passed. In effect, the defendant is not being punished, although the conviction is recorded against her. It might be imposed on a defendant who, although technically guilty, is morally blameless, or in connection with a very trivial offence. Where the offence is very trivial the prosecutor may be required to explain why the prosecution was brought at all.

22.19 BIND OVER

The bind over is an ancient power available to the criminal courts. A bind over does not rank as a conviction. The power to bind over can arise either on complaint or of the court's own motion under common law powers and is also contained in s. 1(7) Justices of the Peace Act 1968. It enables a magistrates' court to bind over an individual to keep the Queen's Peace for a specified period of time and in a sum of money. It can be imposed where the court is satisfied that there has been a breach of the peace or there is a real risk of a breach in the future. The offender must consent to be bound over. No money is taken from the offender but it must be explained to the offender that, if she fails to keep the peace, she will be required to forfeit all or part of the sum specified. In court, it would be expressed in the following way:

Chair: 'Stand up—You will be bound over in the sum of £100 for a period of 12 months to keep the peace towards X. This means that you do not have to pay any money now. But if you break the order, you can be ordered to pay all or part of that sum. Do you agree to be bound over?'
Defendant: 'Yes . . .'

In practice, a bind over is a matter of negotiation between the defence and the prosecution. They are most commonly imposed in connection with less serious matters such as minor domestic disputes or disputes between neighbours which have resulted in court proceedings. In these cases, the defendant may feel aggrieved that she is the one being prosecuted when others might be regarded as being equally culpable. The offer of a bind over may therefore be the most pragmatic way of resolving the proceedings. The substantive offence which led the defendant to appear before the magistrates is then withdrawn when a bind over is imposed. The precise terms of the bind over must be explained. This could include refraining from specified types of conduct or activities.

If the defendant does not consent to the bind over and pleads not guilty to the substantive offence a trial date will be fixed and the matter tried. The benefits of a bind over ought to be explained to the defendant, as a guilty verdict will result in a criminal record and most probably an order that the defendant pays the prosecution's costs.

22.20 **ANCILLARY ORDERS**

22.20.1 **PROSECUTION COSTS**

It is common for courts to award some or all of the prosecution's costs in the event of a conviction (s. 17 Prosecution of Offences Act 1985) although priority is given to the payment of compensation orders and fines.

R v Northallerton Magistrates' Court, ex p Dove [2000] 1 Cr App R (S) 136 provides the guidance on awarding prosecution costs:

- The purpose of an award is to compensate the prosecution and not to punish the defendant.
- An award should not exceed the sum which the prosecutor has actually and reasonably incurred.
- Account must be taken of the offender's ability to pay, particularly having regard to any other financial penalties to be imposed, i.e. compensation/fine.

The amount sought by the prosecution depends on the nature of the offence and the degree of preparation that the prosecutor has had to undertake. The court may order all or part of the costs asked for, or make no order as to costs.

22.20.2 **CONFISCATION AND FORFEITURE**

We briefly refer to confiscation and forfeiture orders as the detail falls outside the scope of this text. The provisions are contained in the Proceeds of Crime Act 2002 and are notoriously complex and draconian. The Act gives the Crown Court powers to confiscate assets which are the result of the particular criminal conduct of which the defendant has been convicted. The most obvious example would be the proceeds of drug trafficking. However, the Act also permits a court to confiscate assets which it believes have been acquired as a result of general criminal conduct in circumstances where the offender is enjoying a 'criminal lifestyle'. There is a protracted procedure requiring the prosecution to provide a statement of information to which the defendant must respond. The provisions are not restricted to particular offences and can apply whenever a defendant is convicted before a Crown Court or if the defendant has been committed to the Crown Court for sentence. Although the court of its own motion can initiate the process, the application is likely to be made by the prosecution.

Section 143 PCC(S)A 2000 gives a court the power to order forfeiture of any property lawfully seized from the defendant (or which is in the defendant's possession or under her control at the time she was apprehended) which has been used for the purpose of committing or facilitating the commission of an offence or which was intended by the defendant to be used for such purpose. In utilising this power, a court should have regard to the totality of sentence for the particular offence. Provision is included in s. 145 PCC(S)A 2000 to allow the sale of property connected with an offence in order to pay compensation to the victim, but only where the offender's means are such that she would otherwise not be in a position to discharge the compensation figure.

22.20.3 ANTI-SOCIAL BEHAVIOUR ORDERS (ASBOS)

ASBOs can be made on a civil application or as an ancillary order after conviction in a criminal case, most usually at the invitation of the prosecutor. The power to impose an ASBO in criminal proceedings (popularly referred to as being a CrASBO) is contained in s. 1 Crime and Disorder Act 1998 and the Anti-social Behaviour Act 2003. The behaviour complained of must be anti-social in that it causes alarm, harassment or distress. The minimum duration of an ASBO is two years. There is no specified maximum.

A court should only make an order for as long as it considers necessary to protect the community from the named offender. The prohibitions expressed in the order must be specific in time and place and must be necessary to protect the public from further anti-social acts by the defendant in the locality. They must be reasonable and proportionate, clear, concise and enforceable. Guidance on the imposition of an ASBO in criminal proceedings was recently provided by the Court of Appeal in the case of *R v Parkin* [2004] Crim LR 490:

'In our judgment the following principles clearly emerge:

(1) The test for making an order is one of necessity to protect the public from further anti-social acts by the offender.

(2) The terms of the order must be precise and capable of being understood by the offender.

(3) The findings of fact giving rise to the making of the order must be recorded.

(4) The order must be explained to the offender.

(5) The exact terms of the order must be pronounced in open court and the written order must accurately reflect the order as pronounced.'

For an account of best practice in relation to ASBOs, consult the Home Office Guide to Anti-Social Behaviour Orders: https://www.gov.uk/government/policies/reducing-and-preventing-crime—2.

22.20.4 SEX OFFENDERS' REGISTER—NOTIFICATION REQUIREMENTS

Under the Sex Offenders Act 1997, the requirement to register is mandatory where an offender is convicted of a specified sexual offence. Under the Sexual Offences Act 2003, the requirement to register has become a requirement to notify. The defendant must notify the police at a specified police station within three days of the notification order being made, or within three days of being released, if the defendant is sent to prison for the sex offence. The defendant must inform the police of his name, date of birth and home address and of any later change of address or absence from the country. The minimum period of notification is for five years (two years for a caution), increasing to 10 years depending on the sentence imposed.

Other ancillary orders that can be imposed include football banning orders, restraining orders and deportation in some instances. More details can be researched in *Blackstone's Criminal Practice.*

22.20.5 **RESTRAINING ORDER**

Reforms introduced under s. 12 Domestic Violence Crime and Victims Act 2004 enable a court to impose a restraining order upon an individual. In the past the power to impose such an order was restricted to cases where the offender had been convicted of an offence under the Harassment Act 1977. As a consequence of the 2004 Act, restraining orders can be imposed in relation to any offence and even in the case of an acquittal. A restraining order can be imposed upon conviction for any offence for the purpose of protecting a person from conduct which amounts to harassment or will cause a fear of violence. Such an order can be imposed in the event of an acquittal where the court concludes that it is necessary to protect the person from harassment by the defendant. Recent guidance on imposing a restraining order following an acquittal can be found in the Court of Appeal decision in *R v Tara Major* [2010] EWCA Crime 3016.

The terms of a restraining order must be clear, precise and easily understood. The order must also be proportionate to the nature of the harassment and can be imposed for a specified period or until a further order is issued.

It is an offence to do anything prohibited by a restraining order without reasonable excuse, (s. 5(5)). The maximum penalty for breach of an order is five years' imprisonment following conviction on indictment and six months summarily, (s. 5(6) of the 1997 Act).

An application for a further order to vary or discharge the existing order can be made by the prosecution, defendant or any person mentioned in the order (s. 5(4) of the 1997 Act).

Having covered all the necessary background information relevant to the sentencing process, we finally consider how the defence solicitor might construct and deliver a plea in mitigation.

22.21 **THE PLEA IN MITIGATION**

As previously explained, the sentence a defendant receives will largely be determined by the seriousness of the offence. However, in arriving at the most appropriate sentence, the court will consider the defendant's personal circumstances and any personal offender mitigation.

The plea in mitigation is important because it should assist the court to determine the seriousness of the offence and direct the court's attention to any relevant personal offender mitigation.

22.21.1 **DELIVERING AN EFFECTIVE PLEA IN MITIGATION**

An effective plea in mitigation requires the defence advocate to combine a thorough knowledge of sentencing law and practice with good advocacy skills. There are, in our view, three fundamental requirements for a competent plea in mitigation.

First, the advocate must understand the theory of sentencing and the importance of researching the relevant sentencing guidelines.

Secondly, the advocate must have in mind a realistic sentencing objective, having regard to the theory behind sentencing and after considering the relevant sentencing guidelines. Formulating a realistic sentencing objective requires a combination of common sense and experience of sentencing.

Thirdly, the advocate needs good advocacy skills.

An effective plea in mitigation should be well thought through, carefully constructed and persuasively delivered. Preparation is the key.

22.21.2 **PREPARING A PLEA IN MITIGATION**

The starting point for a plea in mitigation is an awareness of the sentence a court can impose for the particular offence(s) and any applicable sentencing guidelines.

The defence advocate will know the prosecution's version of the facts having considered the pre-trial disclosure of evidence (advance information) and from hearing the prosecutor's submission to the court outlining the circumstances of the offence. Assuming you are acting for the defendant, you will have taken your client's detailed instructions about the offence and considered and discussed with him the contents of any pre-sentence. You should be able to assess the balance of any aggravating and mitigating features and be able to assess the seriousness of the offence with reference to any applicable offence-specific guideline.

As sentencing is based on the seriousness of the offence, you need to make an assessment of seriousness by asking 'What would I like to achieve for my client?'. Then put yourself in the court's position and consider what sentencing objective the court is likely to follow. Will it want to punish your client/rehabilitate him/prevent the commission of further offences/ protect the public/put your client on trust as to his future behaviour? By engaging in this exercise you should arrive at a realistic sentencing objective which gives you the basis upon which to build your plea in mitigation.

If you conclude that a custodial sentence is a possibility for your client, consider whether the custody threshold test is met on the case facts. Consider *R v Kefford* [2002] 2 Cr App R (S) 495 and other cases that are relevant to passing a custodial sentence. Can you use them in your plea in mitigation?

If your preparation leads you to conclude that the court might impose a community sentence, consider whether the criteria for such sentence are met.

If a financial penalty or a compensation order is likely, make sure you have an up-to-date statement of your client's financial means.

22.21.3 USING THE PRE-SENTENCE REPORT IN PREPARATION

In preparing a plea the defence advocate must discuss the content of any pre-sentence report (PSR) with his client. Advocates should be selective and refer the sentencing court to relevant portions of the pre-sentence report which assist the plea being put forward.

22.21.4 PRESENTING CHARACTER EVIDENCE OR OTHER EVIDENCE IN A PLEA IN MITIGATION

The defence advocate should consider whether personal testimonial evidence will assist the plea in mitigation by presenting the court with background information about your client. If your client is of good character and is charged with an offence which is likely to damage her reputation, it is useful to hand in to the court a short character reference. If your client has a medical condition that is relevant to sentencing, consider obtaining a written note from her GP, or if your client has a job offer or a helpful letter from an employer, it is good mitigation to obtain written confirmation to present to the court.

22.22 STRUCTURING A PLEA IN MITIGATION

There is no approved structure for a plea in mitigation as every plea in mitigation must be tailored to the individual case. Having regard to all that has been said in this and the preceding chapters, we include a checklist of the possible factors an advocate might have regard to in preparing a plea in mitigation.

Introduction

If your client has pleaded guilty, you may wish to introduce yourself to the Bench before beginning your plea in mitigation. You may also want to say a few words to introduce your client:

'Madam . . . my client is a young woman. She is 24. She has a job and resides with her partner . . . '

Acknowledge the prosecution's presentation of the facts

Consider thanking the prosecution for its fair outline of the facts of the case, if this is appropriate:

'Madam, I am grateful to my friend for fairly outlining the facts in this case . . .'

If there are aspects of the prosecution's presentation with which you disagree, highlight them at this stage. You might continue:

'There is, however, one matter which I feel I ought to clarify/bring to your attention at the outset and before going any further . . .'

Using a pre-sentence report

If a pre-sentence report has been prepared, ascertain from the Bench at an early stage in your plea whether they have had the opportunity to consider its content. If not, politely suggest that the Bench may wish to do so before you continue with your plea. Think about court etiquette. Be polite:

'Madam, I wonder if you have had the opportunity to consider the pre-sentence report that has been prepared in connection with this matter? You have; I am grateful for that indication . . .'

Use the pre-sentence report selectively, if it is to your benefit:

'I wonder if I might direct Madam's attention to paragraph 12 of the pre-sentence report where Miss James speaks favourably of a community-based disposal in this matter . . .'

Acknowledge your client's predicament

'Madam, let me say at the outset that my client is a deeply anxious individual . . . my client fully appreciates that she stands to be sentenced today for a serious offence/that she could be sent to prison for these offences today . . . she expresses her complete remorse for her wrongdoing . . . understands the need for punishment but also seeks the help of the court in dealing with her offending behaviour . . .'

Can you play down the seriousness of the offence?

Can you use the MCSGs, or other applicable guidelines to play down the seriousness of the offence? Consider the aggravating and mitigating factors. Are you absolutely clear as to the basis of your client's guilty plea if your client is pleading guilty?

If your client has pleaded guilty to an offence of assault, relevant mitigating factors may include provocation, a minor injury, etc. If your client has been found guilty of a theft offence, relevant mitigating features would include the fact that it was committed spontaneously, the amount involved is small or that the theft or deception was not committed for personal gain. If the offence to be sentenced was burglary, relevant factors would include the fact that the property was empty or disused and that no damage was caused in the course of the burglary. Have the stolen items been recovered? Was the crime committed in a sophisticated way?

Be tactful when exploring the victim's role in the commission of the offence. You do not want to score an own goal. It is your client who stands to be punished for the offence, not the victim.

If custody is a distinct possibility

Consider the applicable criteria. Is the offence 'so serious' that only custody can be justified? Be prepared to make representations based on the aggravating and mitigating features. Once again, refer to the sentencing guidelines and the case law considered in Chapter 21 and make the point that if a custodial sentence is to be imposed, its length should be commensurate with the seriousness of the offence (s. 153 CJA 2003). You might refer to the current problems of prison overcrowding highlighted in *Kefford* [2002] 2 Cr App (S) R 106 and *Seed* [2007] 2 Cr App R (S) 69, with a view to trying to persuade the court to keep any custodial sentence to as short a length as possible. You might ask the court to suspend a period of imprisonment.

Can you play down your client's role in the offence?

Was your client led into temptation? Perhaps your client was not the instigator or 'ring leader'. Was your client provoked? Was your client intoxicated or under the influence of an unlawful substance? You have to be careful with regard to the aforementioned. Drink and drugs do not excuse an offender's behaviour, but they may go some way to explain why your client acted in the way she did.

Can you offer an explanation as to why your client has offended?
Do not seek to excuse the offence, but see if you can offer an explanation for your client's offending. Common factors include low self-esteem, mental health issues, complete lack of self-control, dire financial straits, homelessness and addictive behaviour such as alcoholism, drug abuse, gambling.

Are there any personal factors at work that might put the offending behaviour into context?
Is your client getting divorced? Maybe your client is in the grips of an acrimonious break-down of a relationship. Perhaps your client is frustrated because she cannot gain access to her children resulting in a sense of frustration and anger. Is your client presently facing an uncertain future? Maybe she is ill, bereaved, redundant or about to be made redundant, being sued or going through some personal crisis. Consider whether any of the above can be substantiated by evidence, perhaps in the form of a short medical report or letter from an employer.

What is your client's attitude to the offence?
Some clients will give you more scope in this respect than others. Attitude may be reflected in a timely guilty plea and co-operation with the police. A guilty plea spares witnesses. You will want to remind the Bench that it should give credit for a timely guilty plea.

Your client's attitude might be expressed in a pre-sentence report if one is ordered and you should highlight this and bring it to the attention of the court. How candid has your client been in engaging with the probation service?

Most advocates will express their clients' regret and remorse and perhaps offer an apology. Of course, actions speak louder than words. If your client has sought to make reparation to the victim (by paying compensation or repairing any damage) or has personally expressed an apology this is very useful mitigation.

What effect will the conviction have on your client?
Will this conviction result in a damaged reputation? This will be of particular relevance in the case of a first-time offender, especially if convicted of an offence relating to dishonesty. A first-time conviction for a sexual offence will result in damage to your client's reputation.

What has been the effect of court proceedings on your client's family? Is the court sentencing a mother who has the sole care of her children? What effect have the proceedings had on your client? Has your client been put under stress by the court appearances? What were the circumstances of your client's arrest? Was it public? Did your client have to spend a night or two in a police cell? Is it an experience your client wishes to repeat? Does your client face the loss of her job as a result of this conviction?

No previous convictions?
The fact that your client has no previous convictions is excellent mitigation. It means that this offence is completely out of character and is a one-off. The court may want to place your client on trust as to her future behaviour, depending on the seriousness of the offence.

What if your client has a criminal record?
Can you use your client's criminal record to your advantage? Perhaps the last conviction was some time ago. Consider whether your client has been subject to a community order and has found it to be beneficial. Has your client made brave attempts to rehabilitate himself in the meantime? Maybe steps have been taken to overcome drug addiction. Should your client be given the benefit of the doubt on this occasion? Can you detect a trend in the nature of the offences that have been committed that now needs to be addressed?

Do you have any character witnesses you might call to give evidence or to submit in written form to the court?
Your preparation for the plea in mitigation should have alerted you to this possibility. Ensure you have enough copies of any character references to distribute to the court.

What has your client done since to assist matters?

Has your client made good any damage or offered to pay voluntary sums of compensation? Has your client been able to obtain employment? Has your client begun to address the reason for her offending? If alcoholism or drug abuse is the problem, has your client sought help from professionals? If the offending behaviour is set against the backdrop of a marital or relationship breakdown, consider whether your client has come to terms with matters and is seeking help, perhaps from a solicitor or a counselling agency.

In short, is there evidence you can point to which suggests your client has some insight into her offending behaviour and wants to do something about it?

Finances

Given that the fine is a popular sentencing option in magistrates' courts (see para. 22.15), you must be in a position to provide the court with details of your client's finances, including weekly income and outgoings, savings and debts. A fine should always reflect an individual's ability to pay, and you may need to make representations on this basis. Imposing a fine could of course have a detrimental effect on your client's family. Where your client has an outstanding account with the court, you can expect the legal adviser to check whether your client's existing payments are up to date.

Miscellaneous considerations

Do not overlook the fact that if the current conviction puts your client in breach of an existing penalty, you will need to address this and the circumstances pertaining to that previous offence, as your client is likely to be re-sentenced or punished in some way for it. If your client has admitted an offence of absconding during the currency of the proceedings you will need to address the court on this as it constitutes a separate offence. Remember that if you are mitigating on a driving matter, different considerations might apply. You might need to argue special reasons or mitigating circumstances such as exceptional hardship (see the online chapter 'Sentencing in Road Traffic Cases').

Finally your conclusion . . .

What are you seeking to persuade the sentencing court to do? Are you looking for leniency, or a sentence to address your client's needs and the need to punish? Close your submission:

> 'Unless I can assist you further Madam . . . those are my submissions . . .'

The foregoing checklist assumes your client has pleaded guilty to the offence, obviating the need for a trial. If your client has been found guilty following a trial, whilst you can still address the court on the mitigating features of the offence, it is pointless to disagree with the verdict and to seek to minimise your client's role. By finding your client guilty, the court has already made up its mind about your client's involvement. You must, however, explain your client's personal circumstances so that the court is appraised of the sort of individual it is sentencing.

22.23   ADVOCACY AND THE PLEA IN MITIGATION

Please refer to our comments in respect of advocacy skills in Chapter 2. We highlight a handful of key features in relation to pleas in mitigation.

Use powerful words

Use words that are inclusive:

> 'Let us examine the circumstances surrounding the commission of this offence . . . you will see . . . you will no doubt appreciate the position my client found herself in . . .'

Use a structure

There is no predetermined structure to a plea in mitigation. Consequently, you will need to devise a structure that gives coherence to your submission. Use the checklist above as your starting point. Consider ways in which you can link the various portions of your submissions:

'Madam, having looked at the circumstances of the offence, let us now turn to my client's personal situation . . .'

Remember, if you find yourself making a plea in mitigation before a District Judge, you will need to be succinct. An experienced District Judge may well indicate at the outset what sentence they are thinking of imposing on your client. Be prepared to hold your ground.

22.24 PROFESSIONAL CONDUCT

In submitting a plea in mitigation, the defence advocate should bear in mind the professional conduct rules with specific reference to *Principle 1,* the duty to uphold the rule of law and the administration of justice and *Chapter 5* of the *Solicitors' Code of Conduct* (2011) (see Chapter 1). When delivering a plea in mitigation the advocate must not attempt to deceive or knowingly or recklessly mislead the court and must not be complicit in another person deceiving or misleading the court.

KEY POINT SUMMARY

- A custodial sentence is the most draconian sentence a court can pass.
- For a custodial sentence to be imposed, the custody threshold test defined in s. 152 CJA 2003 must be met.
- The threshold test under the CJA 2003 requires the offence to be so serious that neither a fine alone, nor a community order, can be justified.
- The duration of a custodial sentence must be commensurate with the seriousness of the offence.
- A custodial sentence can be immediate or suspended.
- A suspended sentence may only be imposed where the custody threshold test is met. The offender may have one or more requirements imposed upon him to complete during the period of suspension.
- The threshold test for a community sentence is whether the offence is 'serious enough'. Community sentences involve one or more requirements based on the seriousness of the overall offending behaviour.
- Understand the range of sentencing options available to a court and the requisite criteria for each of them.
- When acting for the defendant, try to formulate a realistic sentencing objective for your client having regard to the offence your client has committed and the range of sentencing disposals available to the court.
- Try to think in terms of the worst case scenario for your client, and what you feel you can and would realistically like to achieve.
- If a custodial sentence is a distinct possibility, consider whether the custody threshold test is met: be prepared to cite supporting case law on this. Consider whether a community penalty might be a constructive alternative to custody.
- Given that a financial penalty is common, be sure to have a statement of means from your client and be prepared to make appropriate representations based on those means.
- Anticipate an ancillary order such as prosecution costs.
- All of the above underscore the importance of researching the penalties for the offence you are considering and any specific sentencing guidelines.

SELF-TEST QUESTIONS

1. Explain the basis upon which a court can impose a term of imprisonment upon a convicted offender.
2. What principles determine the length of a custodial sentence?
3. What types of custodial terms may be imposed?

4. Consider the short scenarios below and try to answer the following questions:

- What sentence do you feel the court is likely to pass, and why? Research the applicable sentencing guidelines (see Appendix 2 for assistance, although note that you may have to look up some of the offence-specific guidelines using the Magistrates' Court Sentencing Guideline which can be accessed via the Sentencing Council's website: http://sentencingcouncil.judiciary.gov.uk/).

- If you were the defence solicitor, what would you hope to persuade the court to do in terms of sentence?

 Exercise 1

Celia appears before the magistrates' court represented by the duty solicitor. She pleads guilty to stealing a gold bracelet worth £150 from a counter display. Without trying to conceal anything she picked up the bracelet, tried it on her wrist and left the shop without paying, prompting the sale's assistant to call shop security. She was stopped a few yards from the shop and admitted the theft. When interviewed by the police, she was co-operative but very tearful and frightened as to what her husband would say. She has no idea why she took the item. She had her credit cards on her at the time and could have paid.

Celia is married. She is 52. She has two grown-up children who live away from the family home. Her husband is a well-respected professional person. Celia has no employment. She has rheumatoid arthritis and has felt depressed of late. Celia is well thought of in her community and is an active member of a number of charitable concerns. Six months ago, Celia was conditionally discharged for 12 months for stealing items of underwear from a department store. She is in breach of this order by virtue of the current offence.

 Exercise 2

Louise pleads guilty to theft before the magistrates' court. She worked as a trainee in a hairdresser's shop. She had access to the till and took small amounts (£150 in total) over a period of several weeks. The thefts caused a bad atmosphere as everyone in the salon was under suspicion. Louise says she took the money because an acquaintance was putting pressure on her to repay a debt. She says she fully intended to repay the money from her tips. Louise is 18, has no previous convictions and pleads guilty at the first opportunity. She is now unemployed and receiving income support and housing benefit. She lives in a bedsit.

 Exercise 3

Andrew was found cultivating five cannabis plants in his bedroom. He says he was growing them for personal use and for the use of his disabled partner who suffers from a chronic illness and finds the effects alleviate some of his discomfort. Andrew pleaded guilty before the magistrates' court at the first opportunity. He has several previous convictions for theft and possession of drugs. Andrew and his partner receive invalidity benefit of £130 per week.

 Exercise 4

Darren is charged with assaulting a police constable in the execution of his duty contrary to s. 89 Police Act 1996. Darren and some of his friends had been celebrating their football team's win. They had been drinking and were rowdy. They were stopped by police on the High Street who asked them to calm down. While most of the youths dispersed, Darren (who accepts he was drunk) entered into an argument with one of the police officers. A scuffle ensued in which the police officer fell over. While the officer lay on the ground, he was kicked several times by Darren. The officer suffered a bloody nose and extensive bruising to his face and left arm and was off sick for three weeks. A pre-sentence report assesses Darren's risk of reoffending as being medium. It highlights Darren's alcohol consumption as being the motivation for the offence. Darren is deemed suitable for a community sentence including an unpaid work requirement. Darren is 21 and has previous convictions for possession of an offensive weapon and common assault. He completed a community order with a 60-hour unpaid work requirement for the offensive weapon offence last year. He pleads guilty before the magistrates' court to the assault on the officer and expresses his remorse. Darren is employed as a shop assistant and brings home £150 per week. He will lose his job if sent to prison. He lives with his mother and gives her £25 per week towards his keep. He owns a car and therefore has related car expenditure.

Analysis can be found on our Online Resource Centre.

Case study: *R v William Hardy*

You will recall that William Hardy has pleaded guilty to the offence of unlawful sexual activity with a child, which is an indictable-only offence.

Your file to date contains:

- William Hardy's proof of evidence;
- advance information;
- pre-sentence report;
- character references;
- an agreed basis of plea;
- your research of the relevant sentencing guidelines for an offence of this type (see analysis of self-test question in relation to Chapter 21).

In the light of all that we have considered in relation to sentencing, we invite you to draft a plea in mitigation on behalf of William Hardy.

You can see the full sentencing hearing in relation to *R v William Hardy* in the video section of our Online Resource Centre. In the video clips you will see the outline of the case presented by the solicitor-advocate for the CPS, followed by the plea in mitigation delivered by William Hardy's solicitor-advocate. A transcript (based for the most part on the plea) is included and analysis of the proceedings is provided on the video. You will also see the Crown Court Judge pass sentence on William Hardy.

Case study: *R v Roger Martin*

Taking into consideration our study of sentencing theory and practice, it is your turn to draft a plea in mitigation on behalf of Roger Martin.

You are able to see the final determination of the *R v Roger Martin* case study by viewing his sentencing hearing in the video section of our Online Resource Centre. In the video clips you will see the outline of the case presented by an associate prosecutor for the CPS, followed by the plea in mitigation delivered by Roger Martin's solicitor. Analysis of the proceedings is provided in the video. You will see the sentence passed by the magistrates. We would ask you to note that this scenario was filmed before the Criminal Justice Act 2003 came into force and before the SC's 'Assault' guideline came into effect. Were the same facts to be sentenced under the CJA 2003, Roger Martin would have been subject to a generic community order with specified requirements, which would include an element of supervision and unpaid work in the community.

FIGURE 22.1 THE CONDITIONS FOR IMPOSING A CUSTODIAL SENTENCE ON AN ADULT

- A custodial sentence may only be imposed if the threshold test is satisfied where:
  - the offence, or combination of offences; or associated offences
  - is so 'serious' that neither a fine alone nor a community sentence can be justified, s. 152(2) CJA 2003; or
  - where the offender fails to consent to a requirement to be included in a community order.
- Discount for pleading guilty will be applied, s. 144 CJA 2003.
- The length of custody should be commensurate with the seriousness of the offence, s. 153(2) CJA 2003.
- The length of custodial sentences passed by a magistrates' court is restricted compared to the Crown Court.
- The court should give reasons in open court for imposing the sentence passed, s. 174(2) CJA 2003.
- Before deciding to suspend a prison sentence, the custody threshold test must be met.
- Time spent on remand shall count as time served when imposing a custodial sentence, s. 240 CJA 2003.
- A magistrates' court can pass a maximum custodial sentence of six months (12 months for two or more either-way offences).
- Custodial sentences can be suspended for a period of between six months and two years and requirements may be imposed on the offender during the period of suspension.

FIGURE 22.2 NON-CUSTODIAL SENTENCES

COMMUNITY SENTENCES UNDER THE CJA 2003

- Imposed where the court is satisfied the:

  – offence; or
  – combination of offences; or
  – associated offences

  is/are 'serious enough' to warrant it, s. 148(1) CJA 2003.

- Section 177 CJA 2003 creates a single community sentence which will impose one or more requirements on the offender, e.g.:
  – unpaid work, s. 199 CJA 2003;
  – curfew requirement, s. 204 CJA 2003;
  – exclusion requirement, s. 205 CJA 2003;
  – residence requirement, s. 206 CJA 2003;
  – drug and/or alcohol rehabilitation requirement, ss. 209 and 221 CJA 2003.

- The requirement(s) imposed on the offender should be:

  – suitable for the offender; and
  – where the offender's liberty is restricted, commensurate with the 'seriousness' of the offence, s. 148(3) CJA 2003.

- Sentencing discount for guilty plea will apply.

- Pre-sentence report will invariably be required.

FINES

- Court must consider offender's financial circumstances before imposing a fine, s. 162(1) CJA 2003.
- Fine must reflect the 'seriousness' of the offence, s. 164(2) CJA 2003.
- Sentencing discount will apply for a guilty plea.
- Fines are higher in the Crown Court.

OTHER TYPES OF SENTENCE

- conditional discharge;
- absolute discharge.

ANCILLARY ORDERS

- Compensation orders:
  – on conviction s. 130 PCC(S)A 2000 requires court to order compensation for any injury, loss, damage etc.;
  – court must give reason for not making compensation order;
  – magistrates can order compensation up to £5,000;
  – see Magistrates' Court Sentencing Guidelines for compensation for personal injury;
  – compensation in Crown Court is unlimited;
  – priority given to compensation orders over fines, prosecution costs etc.

- Defendant pays prosecution costs:
  - purpose to compensate prosecution;
  - sum should not exceed costs reasonably incurred;
  - court must account for offender's ability to pay;
  - consfiscation and forfeiture orders, see Proceeds of Crime Act 2002.
- Anti-Social Behaviour Orders.
- Notification under Sex Offenders' Register.
- Football banning order.
- Restraining order.
- Deportation.

23.1 INTRODUCTION

This chapter examines the practice and procedure involved in appealing against a decision of the magistrates' court or the Crown Court. In most cases, the defendant will appeal against the 'safety' of the conviction and/or the severity of the sentence. Some procedures for challenging the trial court's decision, such as appeal by way of case stated or judicial review are available to both the prosecution and the defence. An increasing number of appeal procedures are available only to the prosecution. The procedures explained in this chapter include:

- reopening a case—s. 142 Magistrates' Courts Act 1980 (MCA 1980);
- appeal from the magistrates' court to the Crown Court;
- appeal by way of case stated;
- judicial review;
- appeal to the Court of Appeal;

- Attorney-General's Reference;
- Criminal Cases Review Commission;
- appeals under the Criminal Justice Act 2003 (CJA 2003).

The rules of court relating to appeals are now contained in Crim PR, Parts 63–75.

23.2 REOPENING A CASE—S. 142 MCA 1980

Following conviction by a magistrates' court, s. 142(2) MCA 1980 enables a defendant to ask the magistrates to set the conviction aside or to vary or rescind a sentence. The application may be made whether the defendant pleaded guilty or not guilty at the original trial.

In deciding whether to grant the application, the court will exercise its wide discretion under s. 142 MCA 1980 where it is 'in the interests of justice' to do so. Factors considered include the interests of the court and the inconvenience to other parties of reopening the case.

There is no time limit for making an application under s. 142 MCA 1980 but an unreasonable delay will be taken into account in determining the interests of justice test.

If the conviction is set aside, the case is reheard by a different set of magistrates.

A common use of s. 142(2) MCA 1980 is to rectify an obvious mistake made during the defendant's trial. It is also used to reopen cases where a defendant has been convicted in her absence. The defence lawyer may advise his client to make an application under s. 142 MCA 1980 if it will provide a speedier remedy than an appeal to the Crown Court.

Section 142(1) allows a magistrates' court to vary or rescind its decision as to sentence if it is in the interests of justice to do so. This power is frequently used to reopen sentencing decisions (most notably the imposition of a fine or penalty points) following a conviction in the defendant's absence.

 Example

Kemal is summonsed for careless driving. He fails to respond to the summons and is convicted by the magistrates' court in his absence. He applies under s. 142 MCA 1980 to have his conviction set aside. In deciding the interests of justice test, the magistrates will consider the inconvenience to the prosecution, the prosecution witnesses and to the court of the case being reheard. These interests will be balanced against the defendant's general right to have the opportunity to defend himself.

If Kemal has strong mitigating reasons for failing to attend trial because, for example, he was out of the country or was genuinely preoccupied with family or business problems the court may decide that it is in the interests of justice to rehear the case. If Kemal simply forgot to attend court, it is likely that his application under s. 142 MCA 1980 will fail.

23.3 APPEAL TO THE CROWN COURT—S. 108 MCA 1980 (CRIM PR, PART 63)

A defendant convicted before a magistrates' court may appeal against conviction and/or sentence to the Crown Court. Where the defendant pleaded guilty, the defendant may only appeal against the sentence imposed. Appeal to the Crown Court is not available to the prosecution.

If the defendant wishes to be represented at public expense before the Crown Court, he will need to submit a further application for a representation order to either the magistrates' court or the Crown Court (see Chapter 9, para. 9.10.3). If the defendant was granted a representation order to cover the proceedings in the magistrates' court, the original order will cover the provision of verbal and written advice on appeal as well as making an application for funding for representation in the Crown Court.

23.3.1 THE PROCEDURE FOR APPEALING TO THE CROWN COURT (CRIM PR, PART 63.2)

The notice of appeal must be made in writing within 21 days of the conviction and/or the sentence and be addressed to the chief executive to the justices of the magistrates' court that heard the case. The time for giving notice of appeal may be extended upon application in writing to the Crown Court.

The notice of appeal does not have to specify any detail other than indicating whether the appeal is against conviction and/or sentence. It is common to use a form of appeal which merely states that the 'defendant proposes to appeal on the ground that the magistrates erred in fact and in law in convicting him' or 'the defendant proposes to appeal against sentence on the ground that it was excessive in all the circumstances'.

There is no filter procedure and the court has no discretion not to accept the notice of appeal.

Where a custodial sentence was passed in the magistrates' court, the appellant may apply to be released on bail until the appeal hearing although the presumption to bail does not apply in this situation. If bail is refused, a further application may be made to the Crown Court (see Chapter 10).

23.3.2 HEARING THE APPEAL

The appeal in the Crown Court is a complete rehearing of the case before a judge sitting with two lay magistrates. New evidence may be heard if it has become available since the original trial. The decision of the Crown Court may be a majority decision; as the lay justices can out-vote the judge. The Crown Court can confirm, vary or reverse any part of the magistrates' court's original decision (i.e. quash a conviction or vary sentence) or remit the matter back to the convicting magistrates' court with its opinion (s. 48 Supreme Court Act 1981).

A convicted defendant should be warned that if his appeal fails, the Crown Court can impose any sentence that was available to the magistrates' court. This may result in a convicted defendant receiving a more severe penalty (although not one that would have been beyond the maximum sentence which the magistrates' court could have passed). An unsuccessful appeal may additionally result in the defendant paying some or all of the prosecution's costs.

23.4 APPEAL BY WAY OF CASE STATED—S. 111 MCA 1980 (CRIM PR, PART 64)

Section 111 MCA 1980 provides:

'(1) Any person who was a party to any proceeding before a magistrates' court or is aggrieved by the conviction, order, determination or other proceeding of the court may question the proceeding on the ground that it is wrong in law or is in excess of jurisdiction by applying to the justices composing the court to state a case for the opinion of the High Court on the question of law or jurisdiction involved;

(2) An application under subsection (1) above shall be made within 21 days after the day on which the decision of the magistrates' court was given.'

Appeal by way of case stated to the Divisional Court may be made by any party to the proceedings before the magistrates' court who seeks to challenge the conviction or any order or determination made by the court during the proceedings. If public funding is required, the appellant must submit an application for a representation order to the High Court. A representation order granted to cover the proceedings before the magistrates' court will also cover any verbal and written advice on appeal and assist the applicant to obtain funding for representation in the High Court.

The grounds for making an appeal by way of case stated are that the magistrates' court was:

- wrong in law; or
- in excess of its jurisdiction.

The issues that are commonly raised in a case stated application include whether:

- the justices had jurisdiction to try the case; or
- the justices were correct to find that there was a case to answer; or
- admissible evidence was excluded; or
- inadmissible evidence was admitted in evidence; or
- the justices' interpretation of the law was wrong.

23.4.1 THE PROCEDURE FOR STATING A CASE

- Within 21 days of the acquittal, conviction or sentence, the party must apply in writing (usually by letter), requiring the magistrates who heard the case to state a case for the Divisional Court's consideration. The party should identify the question of law on which the Divisional Court's opinion is sought.
- Within 21 days of receiving the application, a statement of case is prepared by the magistrates' legal adviser in consultation with the magistrates, which will:
  — outline the facts called into question;
  — state the facts as found by the magistrates;
  — state the magistrates' finding on the point of law being challenged, listing any authority cited; and
  — state the question for the Divisional Court to answer.
- Drafts of the case are then sent to the parties who may suggest amendments.
- The final form of the case stated is then sent to the appellant who must lodge it at the Crown Office of the Royal Courts of Justice in London. Notice and a copy of the case stated must be given to the respondent.
- The appeal is heard by the Divisional Court usually before three judges. Evidence is not called and the hearing takes the form of legal argument on the facts of the case as stated.
- The Divisional Court may reverse, amend or affirm the magistrates' decision or may remit the matter back to the magistrates with its opinion and a direction that the magistrates' court should, for example, convict the defendant or acquit him or the case should be tried again before a different Bench.
- Costs may be awarded to either party out of central funds.

Magistrates may grant bail to a defendant who has received a custodial sentence pending the hearing of his appeal (s. 113 MCA 1980). If bail is refused, application can be made to a High Court judge in chambers.

23.4.2 IS FURTHER APPEAL POSSIBLE?

No—unless the matter is appealed to the Supreme Court on a point of law of public importance and either the Divisional Court or the Supreme Court grants leave.

23.4.3 MAY THE SAME ISSUE BE APPEALED TO THE CROWN COURT AND BY WAY OF CASE STATED?

No—the right of appeal to the Crown Court is lost once an application is made to state the case. It is possible to appeal by way of case stated to challenge the conviction and to appeal to the Crown Court against the sentence in the same case. For this reason, the first avenue of appeal is usually the Crown Court (para. 23.3).

23.5 **JUDICIAL REVIEW**

Judicial review is available to a party in a criminal case where a magistrates' court as a 'public law' body has exercised its legal powers illegally or has failed to follow the correct procedure or has acted irrationally. Judicial review proceedings are governed by Part 54, Civil Procedure Rules. State funding for judicial review is through a civil funding certificate.

Judicial review will be appropriate to challenge a decision where the magistrates' court acted in excess of its jurisdiction by failing to follow the statute which confers jurisdiction, or by acting in breach of the rules of natural justice, by, for example failing to allow an adjournment requested by a defendant on proper grounds or failing to give proper time to prepare a defence, see *R v Thames Magistrates' Court, ex p Polemis* [1974] 1 WLR 1371. Judicial review will also be appropriate where there are grounds for suspecting bias on the part of the legal adviser or one or more of the magistrates.

23.5.1 **APPLYING FOR JUDICIAL REVIEW**

The Civil Procedure Rules Part 54 prescribes a two-stage procedure for applying for judicial review. The first stage is an application for leave to a High Court judge to obtain permission to proceed. A notice of application on the appropriate claim form setting out the grounds for review must be filed by the defendant. The claim form must:

- identify the applicant;
- identify the relief sought;
- identify the grounds on which the application is made; and
- include an affidavit (i.e. a sworn statement) that verifies those grounds and adds further argument.

A single judge usually determines the application for leave without a hearing and in the absence of the other side (the respondent).

If leave is granted, the judicial review hearing will be before the Divisional Court which hears arguments from the applicant, the respondent and any other body affected by the magistrates' decision. In a criminal case this will usually be the Crown Prosecution Service (CPS), the Ministry of Justice or the Home Office.

Bail pending the hearing of an application for judicial review may be granted by a judge in chambers.

At the end of the hearing, the court makes its decision, and if the applicant's case is proven, will grant relief by making a mandatory order; and/or a prohibiting order or a quashing order.

23.6 **APPEAL FROM THE CROWN COURT (CRIM PR, PART 68)**

A person convicted of an offence on indictment may appeal to the Court of Appeal against his conviction and/or sentence where he pleaded not guilty, or against sentence only where he pleaded guilty, s. 1 Criminal Appeal Act 1968 (CAA 1968). The advice of counsel or a solicitor-advocate should always be sought before commencing an appeal against conviction and/or sentence to the Court of Appeal.

23.6.1 **OBTAINING LEAVE TO APPEAL**

Leave to appeal against conviction and/or sentence to the Court of Appeal is always required. Leave may be given by the trial judge granting a certificate that the case is fit for appeal or the Court of Appeal can grant leave.

Where leave is required from the Court of Appeal, within 28 days of conviction or sentence, the appellant must serve on the Registrar of Criminal Appeals, a notice of application for leave to appeal, accompanied by draft grounds of appeal. The draft grounds will be settled by counsel or a solicitor-advocate.

23.6.2 FUNDING AN APPEAL TO THE COURT OF APPEAL

Where a defendant has been granted a representation order for trial on indictment, the order will cover advice in connection with a possible appeal, drafting the grounds of appeal and seeking leave. Once the notice and grounds of appeal have been lodged, the registrar will determine whether a representation order should be granted.

If the appeal is against conviction, a transcript should be provided of either of the judge's summing up or of some part of the evidence or where appropriate, the full transcript of the trial. The court's shorthand writer will then be asked by the registrar to transcribe the appropriate part of his notes. The papers are then put before a single judge.

This is a filtering stage at which a single judge considers whether leave ought to be given. If leave to appeal is given, public funding will be available for the hearing itself.

If the single judge refuses leave to appeal, the appellant has 14 further days in which to serve notice on the registrar that he wishes to renew the application before the full court. The papers are then put before the 'full' court, which considers the issue. If leave is refused, the application is lost and the appellant may be subject to a loss of time direction.

23.6.3 WHAT IS A DIRECTION FOR LOSS OF TIME?

Usually, any time spent in custody by an appellant between sentence being passed and his appeal hearing counts as part of any custodial sentence. A direction to the contrary called 'direction for loss of time' may be given by the court when refusing leave to appeal or dismissing an appeal purely on the grounds of law (s. 29 CAA 1968). This is a means of penalising an appellant for pursuing a frivolous appeal, although directions for loss of time are very rarely made if counsel has advised on an appeal. A direction for loss of time would normally be made against an appellant who proceeds with an appeal against counsel's advice.

23.6.4 GRANTING BAIL ON APPEAL

The Court of Appeal may grant bail to an appellant pending the determination of his appeal (s. 19 Criminal Appeal Act 1968). This may be exercised by the single judge when he considers the papers. Where the trial judge certifies that a case is fit for appeal, he may also grant bail pending determination of the appeal (s. 81 Senior Courts Act 1981).

23.6.5 APPEALS AGAINST CONVICTION

The Court of Appeal may only allow an appeal against conviction if it thinks that the conviction is 'unsafe' (s. 2(1)(a) CAA 1968, as amended by the Criminal Appeal Act 1995).

In deciding whether the conviction is 'unsafe', the Court of Appeal will hear legal argument from each side and may, exceptionally, hear fresh evidence under s. 23 CAA 1968. Fresh evidence will only be received under s. 23 CAA 1968 if it is:

- capable of belief;
- capable of founding a ground of appeal;
- it would have been admissible at the original trial; and
- there is a reasonable explanation for the failure to adduce the evidence.

The common practice is for an appellant to refer to specific legal or procedural errors that arose at trial, and then supplement these specific claims with the general ground that the conviction is unsafe.

The test to decide whether a conviction is 'unsafe' is subjective. Each member of the Court of Appeal must ask: 'Have I a reasonable doubt, or even a lurking doubt, that this conviction may be unsafe?' If the answer is affirmative, the appeal should be allowed (*Stafford v DPP* [1974] AC 878). In *Pendleton* [2002] 1 WLR 72, the House of Lords held that the correct test in a case where the Court of Appeal receives fresh evidence on appeal under s. 23 CAA 1968, is whether the conviction was safe, not whether the defendant was guilty. In such cases the Court of Appeal must consider what effect the fresh evidence would have had on the jurors if it had been received at the original trial. If it might reasonably have affected the jurors' decision to convict, the conviction should be regarded as 'unsafe'.

There was concern that the amendment to the single ground of appeal by the CAA 1995, that the conviction is 'unsafe', had restricted the Court of Appeal's powers to quash a conviction. In *R v Chalkley; Jeffries* [1998] 2 Cr App R 79, the Court of Appeal confirmed that, following the amendment of s. 2(1) CAA 1968, the Court had no power to allow an appeal if it did not consider the conviction to be unsafe but was in some other way dissatisfied with what had occurred at the trial, since the former tests of 'unsatisfactoriness' and 'material irregularity' were no longer available, except to determine the safety of a conviction.

In practice, however, the potentially restrictive interpretation of s. 2(1) CAA 1968 put forward in *Chalkley* has not been adopted and, in considering if a conviction is unsafe, the Court of Appeal is entitled to take into account:

- whether the conviction is unsatisfactory; or
- that the court made a wrong decision on a point of law; or
- there was a material irregularity in the course of the trial.

As a consequence, grounds for appeal against conviction can include:

- wrongful admission or exclusion of evidence;
- failure to properly exercise judicial discretion;
- errors on the part of counsel;
- defects in the indictment;
- conduct of the trial judge;
- errors in the trial judge's summing-up;
- problems associated with jurors.

23.6.6 DISPOSALS AVAILABLE TO THE COURT OF APPEAL

In deciding whether the appellant's conviction is unsafe, the Court of Appeal may:

- quash the conviction and order an acquittal;
- quash the conviction and order a retrial;
- find the appellant guilty of an alternative offence;
- allow part of the appeal; or
- dismiss the appeal.

23.7 APPEAL AGAINST SENTENCE FROM THE CROWN COURT

An appeal against sentence follows the same procedure as an appeal against conviction except that an appeal against sentence only will not attract a loss of time direction. An appeal can be made on the basis that the sentence imposed was:

- wrong in law (i.e. the sentence imposed could not legally be passed);
- wrong in principle or was manifestly excessive (the fact that the sentence was merely severe will not be sufficient, but if the sentence passed was outside the appropriate range

for the offence and the offender in question, it might be considered excessive. Further examples include where there has been a serious disparity in sentence between two or more co-accused which cannot in principle be justified, or if the defendant was given a legitimate expectation that he would receive a certain type of sentence giving him a justifiable sense of grievance, or there was a failure to obtain a pre-sentence report or to hold a Newton hearing when one was clearly required).

In considering an appeal against sentence, the Court of Appeal can:

- quash any sentence or order; or
- impose any sentence or order that could have been available to the Crown Court except the appellant should not be dealt with more severely than at the Crown Court (s. 11(3) CAA 1968).

23.8 APPEAL TO THE SUPREME COURT (CRIM PR, PART 74)

Appeal from the Court of Appeal to the Supreme Court may only be made where the Court of Appeal or the Supreme Court certifies the case involves a point of law of general public importance.

23.9 ATTORNEY-GENERAL'S REFERENCES (CRIM PR, PART 70)

Under s. 36 CJA 1988 (Crim PR, Part 70) the Attorney-General may, with leave of the Court of Appeal, refer to that court any sentence imposed by the Crown Court where he considers the sentence was unduly lenient. The Court of Appeal may then quash the original sentence and substitute such sentence (usually heavier) as it thinks appropriate for the case and which the court below had power to pass when dealing with the offender.

Under s. 36 Criminal Justice Act 1972 (Crim PR, Part 70) the Attorney-General has the power to refer a case to the Court of Appeal for its opinion on a point of law which arose in the case. The power relates to a case where the defendant was acquitted following trial on indictment. Whatever the outcome of the appeal, the defendant remains acquitted.

23.10 CRIMINAL CASES REVIEW COMMISSION

The Criminal Cases Review Commission, which was established by the Criminal Appeal Act 1995 is located in Birmingham and investigates and processes allegations of miscarriages of justice.

Under s. 9 CAA 1995, the Commission may refer to the Court of Appeal:

- a conviction for an offence on indictment;
- a sentence imposed for an offence on indictment;
- a finding of not guilty by insanity.

Under s. 11 CAA 1995, the Commission may refer to the Crown Court a conviction and/or sentence imposed by the magistrates' court.

23.10.1 WHAT TEST MUST BE SATISFIED BEFORE THE COMMISSION CAN REFER A CASE?

The Commission may only refer a case to the Court of Appeal or to the Crown Court where, under s. 13 CAA 1995, the Commission considers that there is a real possibility that the verdict or sentence would not be upheld if the reference was made.

Section 15 CAA 1995 enables the Court of Appeal to direct the Commission to investigate a particular matter 'in such manner as the Commission thinks fit'. Sections 17–21 CAA 1995 provide the Commission with the power to obtain documents and direct officers to investigate and report on a relevant matter.

23.11 **DOES THE PROSECUTION ENJOY A RIGHT TO APPEAL?**

Traditionally the prosecution enjoyed only limited rights to appeal and had no right to appeal against the acquittal of a defendant following a summary trial or trial on indictment. The only exception to this was the prosecutor's right to appeal a decision by a magistrates' court by way of case stated.

In relation to trials on indictment, the prosecution now enjoys a right of interlocutory appeal against binding rulings made by a trial judge at a preparatory hearing in accordance with ss. 35 and 36 Criminal Procedure and Investigations Act 1996 (Crim PR, Part 66).

The right of the prosecution to appeal against sentence is set out in para. 24.9. It requires a reference to be made by the Attorney-General.

The CJA 2003 has extended the prosecution's right of appeal in a number of important situations.

First, under s. 58 CJA 2003 the prosecution may appeal to the Court of Appeal against a terminating ruling made by the judge in relation to an issue at a trial on indictment and which cannot otherwise be the subject of an appeal to the Court of Appeal. The appeal can be against any judicial ruling made during the trial until the beginning of the summing-up to the jury. The procedure of appealing against a terminating ruling is detailed in Crim PR, Part 67. It includes a prosecution appeal against:

- a successful submission of no case to answer by the defence; or
- a ruling on a public interest immunity (PII) application in favour of the defence; or
- a decision to stay the proceedings for an abuse of process; or
- a successful defence application to sever the counts on the indictment.

In making the application the prosecution must agree that in the event of failing to obtain leave to appeal or if the appeal is abandoned, the defendant will be automatically acquitted.

Under the procedure, which is laid down in ss. 57–61 CJA 2003, the appeal can follow an expedited or non-expedited route. It is for the trial judge to decide which route is appropriate. In an expedited appeal, the trial may be adjourned to await the Court of Appeal's ruling. In a non-expedited appeal, the trial may be adjourned or the jury discharged.

Under s. 61 CJA 2003 the Court of Appeal may confirm or reverse or vary any ruling which the prosecution has appealed against. A ruling may only be reversed where the Court of Appeal is satisfied that:

- the ruling was wrong in law;
- the ruling involved an error in law or principle; or
- the ruling was not reasonable for the judge to make.

Where the court reverses or varies the terminating ruling, it must order either:

- the resumption of the Crown Court trial; or
- a fresh trial;
- or the defendant's acquittal (but only if he could not have a fair trial by resumption of the trial or ordering a new trial).

Second, the CJA 2003 has radically revised the traditional operation of *autrefois acquit*. Historically where a defendant has been found not guilty at trial and acquitted, the doctrine of *autrefois acquit* has prevented him from being retried for the same offence. Section 76 CJA 2003 allows the prosecutor to apply to the Court of Appeal for an order to quash the defendant's acquittal for a qualifying offence and to order a new trial. Generally a qualifying offence is any offence which carries a sentence of life imprisonment.

The Court of Appeal must order a retrial if there is new and compelling evidence in the case and it is in the interests of justice for the order to be made (see *Blackstone's Criminal Practice* for further information).

Looking Ahead

When in force, ss. 62 and 63 CJA 2003 give the prosecution the right of appeal on an evidential ruling made by the judge in relation to the admissibility of the prosecution evidence at trial. The appeal may be expedited or non-expedited and the Court of Appeal may confirm, reverse or vary the evidentiary ruling in question.

For a more detailed consideration of the process of appeal to the Court of Appeal, see 'A Guide to Commencing Proceedings in the Court of Appeal Criminal Division' published by Her Majesty's Courts Service. The document can be accessed at http://www.hmcourts-service.gov.uk/docs/proc_guide.pdf and via the Online Resource Centre.

KEY POINT SUMMARY

* Understand the avenues of appeal from the magistrates' court and which might be the most appropriate appeal mechanism from a defendant's viewpoint.
* Know the time limits and procedures that apply to a defendant who wishes to appeal against conviction/sentence.
* Be aware of the procedural steps in appealing from the Crown Court to the Court of Appeal.
* Understand what is meant by an 'unsafe' conviction under s. 2(1)(a) CAA 1968.

SELF-TEST QUESTIONS

1. When might it be appropriate to apply for the case to be reheard under s. 142 MCA 1980?
2. What is the potential danger to a defendant who appeals against sentence to the Crown Court?
3. Who may appeal by way of case stated?
4. Must leave be obtained to appeal from the Crown Court to the Court of Appeal?
5. On what ground may the Court of Appeal allow an appeal against conviction?

Analysis of all the above can be found on the Online Resource Centre.

FIGURE 23.1 APPEALS

APPEALS FROM THE MAGISTRATES' COURT

- **Rehearing the case,** s. 142 MCA 1980
  - on the defendant's application, the magistrates' court may set the conviction/sentence aside;
  - the application will be granted where 'it is in the interests of justice';
  - any retrial will be reheard by a different Bench of magistrates.

- **Appeal to the Crown Court,** s. 108 MCA 1980
  - against conviction and/or sentence;
  - within 21 days of conviction and/or sentence, defendant applies to magistrates' court which heard his case;
  - the appeal in the Crown Court takes the form of a rehearing;
  - the Crown Court can confirm, vary or reverse the magistrates' decision;
  - where the appeal fails, the Crown Court can impose any sentence which the magistrates might have imposed (which might include a harsher penalty).

- **Appeal by way of case stated,** s. 111 MCA 1980
  - to the Administrative Court;
  - where the magistrates' court was wrong in law; or
  - acted in excess of jurisdiction;
  - application from any interested party within 21 days;
  - appeal is heard by three judges in the Administrative Court;
  - the Administrative Court may reverse, amend or affirm the magistrates' court decision or may remit the case back to the magistrates.

- **Judicial review,** Part 54 CPR
  - application to the Administrative Court;
  - where a public law body acted irrationally or illegally or did not follow the correct procedure;
  - where applicant proves the case, the court may make a mandatory order, or a prohibiting order or a quashing order.

APPEAL FROM THE CROWN COURT

- Defendant may appeal to the Court of Appeal against conviction (where pleaded not guilty) and/or sentence;

- Leave must be obtained from the trial judge or the Court of Appeal;

- Appeal against conviction will be allowed where the conviction is 'unsafe', s. 2(1)(a) CAA 1968;

- Where conviction is 'unsafe', the court may:
  - quash the conviction and order an acquittal; or
  - quash the conviction and order a retrial;
  - find the appellant guilty on an alternative offence; or
  - allow part of the appeal; or
  - dismiss the appeal;

- In deciding an appeal against sentence, the Court of Appeal can:
  - quash any sentence or order; or
  - impose any sentence or order that was available to the Crown Court provided the appellant is not dealt with more severely than at his trial;

- Prosecution's right to appeal against:
  - rulings made by the trial judge at a preparatory hearing, ss. 35, 36 Criminal Procedure and Investigations Act 1996;
  - appeal against a terminating ruling during a trial on indictment, ss. 57–61 CJA 2003;
  - application to the Court of Appeal for an order to quash the defendant's acquittal for a qualifying offence and to order a new trial, s. 76 CJA 2003.

Part VI

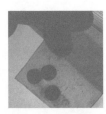

YOUTH JUSTICE

Part VI comprises three chapters, which examine the special considerations that apply to young offenders under the age of 18.

24.1 **INTRODUCTION**

The Audit Commission has estimated that approximately seven million crimes are committed each year by offenders under 18 years of age and that over £1 billon is spent annually dealing with offending by young people. In 2011/12, according to statistics published by the Ministry of Justice and the Youth Justice Board, the total number of proven offences by children and young people aged 10 to 17 years was 137,335. During this period 80 per cent of youth offenders in England and Wales were young men aged 15 to 17 years who were responsible for 78% of all the offences committed by young people; 80% of this group came from a white ethnic background.

The most common offences for disposal during 2011/12 were violent offences against the person including assault—21%; theft and handling—19%; and criminal damage—10%. During this period 58,839 young offenders were found guilty in court resulting in 59,335 sentences being passed; 3,925 offenders were sentenced to custody (primarily a Detention and Training Order, see Chapter 26, para 26.10), 39,118 offenders received a community sentence including 17,395 under a Youth Rehabilitation Order (see Chapter 26, para. 26.9) and 17,395 offenders received first-tier disposals including discharges and fines.

It is clear from these statistics that juvenile offending has important political, economic and social implications as well as making considerable demands on the criminal justice system and those who work in it. The final three chapters of this *Criminal Litigation Handbook* explain the practice and procedures that apply in this specialist area of criminal practice.

While many of the practices and procedures of youth justice will be familiar to you and are based on the adult model, there are also important differences in recognition of the special position and vulnerabilities of young people in the criminal justice system. These special considerations are reflected, for example, in the relative informality of proceedings in the youth court and the requirement that all participants in the youth justice system are under a statutory duty to prevent offending by children and young people. Youth justice also has a number of specialist organisations that formulate policy and deal with young offenders and their families on a daily basis. There are schemes which seek to divert young people from crime when they are in danger of offending for the first time and provision is also made for alternatives to prosecution where a young person admits an offence. Therefore prevention from offending and the opportunities for the early rehabilitation of those who have offended are pervasive to the aims and procedures of youth justice. Whether you are acting for a young person or prosecuting, you will need a good working knowledge of these issues.

Chapter 25 deals with the rules governing where the young person is to be tried and Chapter 26 covers the disposals available to each court including the new-style referral orders under ss. 16 to 17 Powers of Criminal Courts Act 2000 as amended by s. 79 Legal Aid, Sentencing and Punishment of Offenders Act 2012 (LASPO 2012). This chapter deals with the following issues:

* the terminology of youth justice;
* the youth justice organisations;
* the meaning of parental responsibility;
* the principal aims of the youth justice system;
* the early diversion procedures to prevent further offending;
* the juvenile at the police station;
* the alternatives to prosecution;
* the decision to charge.

24.2 THE TERMINOLOGY OF YOUTH JUSTICE

The terminology of youth justice uses a number of key words and phrases to categorise an offender who is not classed as an adult. Be aware of the meaning of each term and understand the context in which the term is used. A commonly used word is 'juvenile', which, while not defined in legislation, is generally applied to a person who is under 18 years of age. The Code for Crown Prosecutors para. 4.12(d) acknowledges that a child or young person is someone under the age of 18. However, in relation to his detention at the police station an arrested juvenile is a person who is under 17 years of age or appears to be under 17 years of age.

You will also come across the word 'child'. Some legislation, for example s. 107 Children and Young Persons Act 1933 (CYPA 1933), defines a child as a person under 14 years. However, in relation to a person in the care of the local authority, 'child' has an extended meaning to include a person aged under 18 years. The term 'young person' or 'young offender' or 'youth offender' is generally attributed to a person aged 14 to 17 years. This classification is relevant, for example, to sentencing where a distinction is drawn between the powers available over a child aged between 10 and 13 and a young person who is aged between 14 and 17.

In this chapter, as a matter of style, we adopt the generic terms of juvenile, youth, young person and young offender to mean a person under 18 years unless a different meaning is indicated.

24.2.1 PERSISTENT OFFENDERS (PO)

As a youth justice practitioner you will encounter a special category of young offender who has been assessed as a persistent offender. This classification is important for sentencing, because certain sentences are only available where the offender is classified as a persistent offender. These disposals include a youth rehabilitation order with intensive supervision and surveillance or fostering (see Chapter 26, para. 26.9.17) and a detention and training order in relation to an offender aged between 12 and 14 (see Chapter 26, para. 26.10). There is no statutory definition of the term 'persistent offender'. The Sentencing Guidelines Council (SGC) offers some guidance in its 2009 publication 'Overarching Principles— Sentencing Youths'. The guidance can be accessed through the Sentencing Council for England and Wales's website and via the web-links section of the Online Resource Centre. It provides that a young person is likely to be found to be persistent where they have been convicted or reprimanded, warned, cautioned or conditionally cautioned in respect of an imprisonable offence on at least three occasions in the last 12 months.

A young person may therefore be classified as a persistent offender even if he has not previously appeared in court but has a number of final warnings, reprimands, cautions or conditional cautions. It is for the court to decide whether a young person is a persistent offender by applying this guidance. In *R v L* [2012] EWCA Crim 1336, L, 14, appealed against a ten-month detention and training order imposed after his guilty plea to three offences of robbery and one attempted robbery. L had two reprimands for the theft of a bicycle and possession of an imitation firearm. L's appeal against sentence was allowed. A sentence of detention and training could only be passed on an offender aged 14 if he could be described as a 'persistent offender'. The two reprimands and three robberies committed on a single occasion did not justify the designation of 'persistent offender'.

24.3 THE YOUTH JUSTICE ORGANISATIONS

A number of specialist organisations operate in the youth justice system to develop and manage policies and resources or are involved in day-to-day contact with juveniles and their families. The Youth Justice Board for England and Wales (YJB) exercises a supervisory function over the youth justice system by working to prevent juvenile offending, to address the reasons for their offending and to ensure that when a juvenile is committed to custody, the accommodation is safe and secure. In fulfilling this role the YJB:

- advises the Home Secretary on the operation and standards of the youth justice system;
- monitors the performance of the youth justice system;
- provides accommodation for young persons who are remanded into custody;
- identifies and promotes good practice in the youth justice service; and
- commissions research and publishes information on the youth justice system.

The YJB's informative website can be accessed via the Justice website at http://www.justice.gov.uk/youth-justice.

At a local level in England and Wales the Criminal Justice Boards (CJBs) co-ordinate the work of the criminal justice agencies. There are 42 CJBs—one for each police force and Crown Prosecution Service area. Each CJB consists of the chief constable of the local constabulary, the area's chief crown prosecutor and chief probation officer and senior representatives from the local prison service and youth services. While CJBs play a strategic role in all aspects of local criminal justice matters, they play an especially important role in co-ordinating youth justice policies and practice.

The day-to-day administration of youth justice is undertaken by youth offending teams (YOTs), which are situated in every local authority in England and Wales. In 2011/12, 137,335 offences had been committed by young offenders on the YOT caseload. The multi-disciplinary membership of each YOT is drawn from the police, probation service, social services and education, the health authority, housing, and drug, alcohol and substance misuse agencies. An integral part of the YOT's role is to identify the needs of young offenders and to manage specific programmes to prevent them from offending or reoffending. The

YOT also exercises the statutory responsibility of supervising young people in custody and on community orders.

For the defence lawyer, establishing a good working relationship with the YOT to whom a client has been assigned is important, as often they are an invaluable source of information.

A good example of the collaborative project management undertaken by the youth justice agencies is provided by the Deter Young Offenders scheme (DYO). Since April 2009, the CJBs have been implementing a multi-agency approach to dealing with young offenders who are classified as DYOs. DYOs are a small number of juveniles who have been assessed as posing the highest risk of causing harm and/or of re-offending. The scheme requires the early identification by the YOT of high risk offenders at their first conviction where a pre-sentence report or a youth panel report has been requested. In assessing whether an offender comes within the DYO scheme, the YOT is required to produce a profile (known as the Asset Core Profile) of the offender's attitude to a range of factors including their attitude to offending, level of educational attainment and job prospects as well as the level and nature of their previous offending. Based on the offender's Asset Core Profile, the YOT is then required to recommend a 'standard', 'enhanced' or 'intensive' level of intervention under a Youth Rehabilitation Order or under a Referral Order to deal with the offender's specific needs. The greater the perceived risk of the young person causing harm to others or of him re-offending, the greater the intensity of the intervention. It is for this reason that the project has been named by the Youth Justice Board as Youth Justice: The Scaled Approach. The document, which provides guidance on the framework for assessment and interventions in the case of DYOs can be downloaded from the Justice website at http://www.justice.gov.uk/guidance/youth-justice/the-scaled-approach/index.htm.

24.4 THE STATUTORY AIMS OF THE YOUTH JUSTICE SYSTEM

Section 37(1) Crime and Disorder Act 1998 (CDA 1998) states the principal aim of the youth justice system is to prevent offending by children and young people. In support of the principal aim, s. 37(2) CDA 1998 requires that:

'In addition to any other duty to which they are subject, it shall be the duty of all persons and bodies carrying out functions in relation to the youth justice system to have regard to that aim.'

All participants in the youth justice system including the police, the CPS, defence lawyers, the local authority and the courts, must have regard to this overriding principle.

A further duty is the 'welfare principle' imposed by s. 44(1) CYPA 1933 which requires:

'Every court in dealing with a child or young person who is brought before it, either as an offender or otherwise, shall have regard to the welfare of the child or young person and shall in a proper case take steps for removing from undesirable surroundings, and securing that proper provision is made for his education and training.'

When making submissions to the court about the appropriate action to be taken against a young offender, the welfare principle should also be considered.

24.5 PARENTAL RESPONSIBILITY

Integral to youth justice is the concept of parental responsibility which was introduced by the Children Act 1989. Parental responsibility is defined by s. 3(1) of the 1989 Act as 'all the rights, duties, powers, responsibilities and authority which by law a parent of a child has in relation to the child and his property'. The principle applies to the person(s) who has (have) responsibility for looking after the young person on a daily basis and make(s) decisions about his life.

Married parents share parental responsibility for their child. If the parents are not married, parental responsibility is vested in the child's mother, although an unmarried father can acquire parental responsibility. Parental responsibility can be shared with or acquired by other legal bodies such as a local authority where, for example, the child is the subject of a care or supervision order.

Whilst liaising with the person with parental responsibility in the case is important to the police, it is especially important for the YOT and for the defence lawyer who will need to work closely with the person(s) having parental responsibility over the young person to ensure that the case has the best possible outcome. The person having parental responsibility may also be involved in other aspects of the case, such as acting as the young person's appropriate adult at the police station, or at the conclusion of the case, being made the subject of a parenting order or a parental bind over, or paying the fine imposed on the young person.

24.6 POLICE STATION DETENTION AND THE YOUNG PERSON

An explanation of the procedure for dealing with a suspect in police detention is covered in Part II of this book. Here we highlight the special rules that apply to juveniles who have been arrested and detained at the police station.

24.6.1 DETERMINING THE YOUNG PERSON'S AGE

Under s. 37(15) Police and Criminal Evidence Act 1984 (PACE 1984) and Code C, a juvenile is any person who is aged under 17 years or who appears to be under 17 years of age. This is likely to increase to 18 in the future as a result of the 'PACE review' highlighted in Chapter 3 at para. 3.1.1. Code C para. 1.5 stipulates that anyone who appears to be under the age of 17 shall be treated as a juvenile in the absence of clear evidence to the contrary. Therefore, if a person who may be a juvenile refuses to give his age to the custody officer or the officer believes the age the person has given is incorrect, the suspect must be treated as a juvenile. Remember that if the detained person is under ten years of age he has no criminal liability and therefore cannot be detained. In these circumstances, the custody officer will arrange for the child to be taken home or if there is concern for the child's physical or moral welfare, the local authority social services department will be contacted. A child safety order may be applied for.

While in police detention, a juvenile is classified as a 'vulnerable' suspect. Juveniles make up the largest number of suspects who fall into the category of a vulnerable suspect.

Where the person is identified as a juvenile, he will be entitled to a range of special protections which are dealt with here.

24.6.2 THE CUSTODY OFFICER'S DUTIES

Code C requires the custody officer to identify the juvenile's needs and vulnerabilities (Code C paras. 3.6–3.10). The custody officer must as soon as practicable identify the parent, guardian or local authority who has parental responsibility for the juvenile's welfare and inform that person of the juvenile's arrest, the reasons for the arrest and the place where the juvenile is being held. As the person who is responsible for the juvenile's welfare will usually act as the appropriate adult, that person will be asked to attend the police station immediately.

Code C 8.8. states that a juvenile shall not be placed in a police cell unless no other secure accommodation is available and the custody officer considers it is not practicable to supervise the juvenile if he is not placed in a cell or that a cell provides more comfortable accommodation than other secure accommodation in the station. A juvenile may not be placed in a cell with an adult detainee.

24.6.3 THE APPROPRIATE ADULT

The appropriate adult's role is to assist and advise the juvenile while he is in police detention. Code C, Guidance Note 1.7 requires that an appropriate adult for a juvenile should be:

- the juvenile's parent or guardian; or
- if the juvenile is in local authority care or in the care of a voluntary organisation, a person representing that organisation; or

- a social worker from a local authority social services department; or failing any of the above;
- a community volunteer aged 18 or over who is not a police officer or employed by the police.

The suitability of a person to be an appropriate adult is important because where the appropriate adult is considered incapable of effectively protecting the juvenile's interests, evidence obtained against the juvenile may be excluded at his trial. While it may appear that the juvenile's parent or carer will be the obvious choice, a parent may be incapable of acting through lack of experience or knowledge or through mental illness, or because the juvenile and parent are not on good terms. In these situations an alternative must be found. Depending on his age, the wishes of the juvenile as to who he wants to act as the appropriate adult should be taken into account. For example, in *R v Blake* [1989] 89 Cr App R 179, the police ignored the juvenile's request that her social worker act as the appropriate adult, asking the girl's father to attend the police station directly against the girl's wishes. In *R v Morse* [1991] Crim LR 195, the juvenile's father had an IQ of below 70 and was incapable of appreciating the importance of his role. In both cases the confession made by the juvenile in the presence of the appropriate adult was excluded at their trial.

A solicitor should not act as an appropriate adult as this leads to a conflict of interest between his role as a legal adviser and his role as an appropriate adult.

While Code C provides only a general indication about the appropriate adult's role, some assistance is provided by the Home Office Guidance for Appropriate Adults (http://www.homeoffice.gov.uk/publications/police/operational-policing/guidanceappadultscustody.pdf) which states that the appropriate adult is required to:

- support, advise and assist the detained person, particularly while they are being questioned;
- observe whether the police are acting fairly and with respect for the rights of the detained person;
- assist with communication between the detained person and the police;
- ensure that the detained person understands their rights and that the adult has a role in protecting those rights.

It is also important to make a juvenile client aware that, unlike his legal adviser, the appropriate adult is not bound by any duty of confidentiality or legal professional privilege. Best practice suggests that legal advisers at the police station should initially consult with their juvenile clients in the absence of the appropriate adult to warn them about the dangers of disclosing information that should remain confidential between lawyer and client.

24.6.4 THE JUVENILE'S OTHER RIGHTS

In addition to having an appropriate adult to support him, a juvenile is entitled to the full range of legal rights at the police station as other detainees. These include the right to inform someone of his arrest under s. 56 PACE 1984 and the right to legal advice under s. 58 PACE 1984.

While the grounds for suspending the right to legal advice under s. 58(8) PACE 1984 apply to a juvenile in the same way as for an adult detainee, once the appropriate adult has been requested to attend the police station, it is very difficult for the police to justify that one or more of the reasons for delaying legal advice under s. 58(8) PACE 1984 applies. While the time limits for detention without charge are the same for both a juvenile and an adult, in view of the juvenile's vulnerabilities every effort should be made to keep detention to a minimum, especially for a very young person. Generally a juvenile should not be held in a police cell unless there is no other way of guaranteeing his safety. Wherever the juvenile is detained, the custody officer must monitor his detention more closely than for an adult and undertake regular risk assessments.

With regard to the taking of an intimate sample from a juvenile, the consent of a parent or guardian must be given if the juvenile is under 14. If the juvenile is aged between 14 and 17, both his consent and that of his parent or guardian are required (s. 65 PACE 1984).

24.7 DEALING WITH A YOUNG CLIENT—A DEFENCE PERSPECTIVE

During an initial interview with a young person it is important for the defence practitioner to gain his trust and to encourage him to give a full and coherent response to the allegations that have been made against him. The defence practitioner should fully advise her client about the possible outcomes in the case, the consequences of admitting guilt and the possibility of being given a youth caution or youth conditional caution. Young offenders (and sometimes their parents or carers) can be the most challenging clients that a defence practitioner will encounter. Some young people have little respect for authority and are likely to test even the most patient defence lawyers. When acting for a young person, skilled interviewing techniques will be needed, to encourage the young person to recognise that you are there to help and are not part of the law enforcement machinery.

Leanne Black, aged 14, is an infamous example of a young offender. In March 2006, Black attacked the CPS lawyer and threw a jug of water at the magistrates as she was sentenced to four months' custody for her second offence of drink driving. These dramatic events occurred shortly after her lawyer had submitted in mitigation that Leanne was a reformed character. The family's disruptive behaviour was not, however, limited to inside the courtroom. As she arrived at court Leanne hurled eggs at the media, and Nora Black, Leanne's mother, flashed her bare bottom, inviting them to 'film this'.

Other infamous young offenders include twins Ben and Nathan Weeks, who became subject to ASBOs when they were just 10 after the court heard they had made life intolerable for their neighbours in Norfolk by shouting, swearing and even shooting at residents' cars and windows with a ball-bearing gun.

24.8 PREVENTING JUVENILE OFFENDING

A key part of youth justice policy is the hierarchy of diversion procedures to prevent a young person from becoming a convicted offender in the mainstream court system or to achieve their early rehabilitation where the young person has committed low-level crime or anti-social behaviour. Research commissioned by the YJB shows the peak age for juvenile offending is 14 years, so that if a juvenile can be diverted from offending before he reaches this age, the chances of him offending in the future will be much diminished. With this aim in mind, a number of intervention programmes and out-of-court disposals are available to divert a young person from offending or re-offending.

Since April 2013, the law has been governed by LASPO 2012, which has reformed the pre-court orders available for youth offenders by abolishing Penalty Notices for Disorder, reprimands, final warnings and the restricted use of youth conditional cautions. In their place, LASPO 2012 has established a simplified framework of out-of-court disposals provided by community resolution, youth cautions and the wider availability of youth conditional cautions.

The new disposals are intended to provide the youth justice agencies with greater flexibility to deal with cases based on a number of factors including the seriousness of the offence, the offender's offending history, the likelihood of the offender's compliance with the requirements of any out-of-court scheme and the views of the victim. The new disposals also increasingly focus on the public interest, public protection and welfare and, unlike the 'old' disposals of reprimands and final warnings, the new pre-court orders may be used in any sequence and are not limited to a strict incremental level of intervention to deal with the young person's offending. The effect of this incremental approach was that, having been given the most serious pre-court disposal of a final warning, it was not possible to give the young offender the less serious order of a reprimand for any later offence irrespective of the seriousness of the later offence.

24.8.1 COMMUNITY RESOLUTION

This is a non-statutory disposal which is based on local YOT practice and subject to implementation in accordance with the guidance of the Home Office and the Association of Chief

Police Officers (ACPO). The victim's interests must be taken into account when determining the type of resolution. The young person's agreement to participate and accept the conditions of the Community Resolution/Restorative Justice programme is also required. Community Resolution is aimed at very low-level offending or anti-social behavior and may, for example, require the young person to write a letter of apology or to make a personal apology to the shop owner against whom the young person committed theft or the householder whose property has been damaged.

24.8.2 YOUTH CAUTIONS

Youth Cautions (YC) and Youth Conditional Cautions (YCC) replace the previous system of reprimands and final warnings. Under s. 66ZA Crime and Disorder Act 1998 (as amended by s. 135 LASPO 2012) a child or young person may be given a Youth Caution (YC) as an alternative to prosecution where:

- there is sufficient evidence to charge the person with an offence (in accordance with the requirements of the Code for Crown Prosecutors);
- the child or young person admits the offence; and
- the police officer/prosecutor does not consider that the young person should be prosecuted or given a youth conditional caution.

A YC can be given to a child or young person as many times as it is considered appropriate, even where the child or young person had been convicted of an offence. When the caution is administered to an offender aged under 17, he must be accompanied by an appropriate adult. The offender will be automatically referred to the YOT which will assess the offender and determine the level of intervention—usually in partnership with the police. A failure by the young person to comply with the intervention requirements is citable in court and may inform any future disposal decisions.

If a second YC is given, the offender must be assessed by the YOT and be offered a voluntary rehabilitation programme unless it is considered inappropriate.

24.8.3 YOUTH CONDITIONAL CAUTION

Under s. 66B Crime and Disorder Act 1998 (as amended by ss. 136–138 LASPO 2012) a child or young person may be given a YCC as an alternative to prosecution where:

- the authorised person (police officer/prosecutor) must have evidence that the person has committed an offence (in accordance with the requirements of the Code for Crown Prosecutors);
- the authorised person must decide there is sufficient evidence to charge the young person with the offence and that a YCC should be given in respect of the offence;
- the young person must admit to the authorised person that he has committed the offence;
- the authorised person must explain the effect of the YCC and warn the young person that, although it is not a criminal conviction, it will be recorded and form part of the young person's criminal record and may be disclosed in certain circumstances and that a failure to comply with any conditions may result in prosecution for the original offence;
- the young person must sign a document containing details of the offence, the admission to the authorised person, consent to be given a YCC and details of the conditions attached.

The conditions attached to a YCC must have one or more of the following objectives:

- rehabilitation—to modify the young person's behaviour to reduce the possibility of reoffending and to be supervised by the YOT;

- reparation—to repair the damage done by the young person's offending to the community at large or directly to the victim of the offence or through a payment to a local charitable community fund; and

- punishment—to punish the young person for their offending by requiring unpaid work or attendance at a specified place to undertake an agreed activity, provided in either case the period does not exceed 20 hours. A financial penalty should only be made where rehabilitative and reparative conditions are not suitable.

The YOT advise the police on the appropriate conditions to prevent reoffending and the YOT is also responsible for monitoring the offender's compliance. Non-compliance may result in prosecution for the original offence.

Whilst a young person can be given a YCC where he has previously been convicted of an offence, the prosecution may refer in later criminal proceedings to any failure by the young offender to participate in any rehabilitation programme.

You will find a link to the Code of Practices for Youth Cautions and Youth Conditional Cautions on the Online Resource Centre (web-links—Youth Justice section).

online
resource
centre

24.9 **THE DECISION TO PROSECUTE**

Except in the most serious offences, the decision about how the case will proceed will not be taken immediately by the police or the CPS. A young person will usually be bailed until the decision is made. The case file will often be referred to a CPS youth offender specialist to decide whether to prosecute or take alternative action.

When making the decision, the prosecutor will apply the evidential and public interest tests under the Code for Crown Prosecutors in the same way as for an adult (see Chapter 8). If the prosecutor is satisfied there is sufficient evidence to provide a realistic prospect of conviction, the public interest stage is then considered. Particular guidance is found in Section 4.2(d) of the Code which identifies the specific public interest considerations when the offender is aged under 18 at the time the offence. The Code acknowledges that the criminal justice system treats children and young people differently from adults and that significant weight must be attached to the suspect's age. The best interests and welfare of the young person must be considered, including whether a prosecution could have an adverse impact on the young person's future prospects that is disproportionate to the seriousness of the offending. The prosecutor must also have regard to the principal aim of the youth justice system, which is to prevent offending by young people, and to the obligations under the United Nations 1989 Convention on the Rights of the Child.

Although the younger the suspect, the less likely a prosecution is required unless it is in the public interest to prosecute. The factors generally in favour of a prosecution include where:

- the offence is serious;

- the suspect's past record suggests there is no alternative to prosecution; or

- the suspect refuses to admit the offence, which precludes an out-of-court disposal.

24.10 **THE PROCEDURE UPON CHARGE**

The young person should be charged in the presence of the appropriate adult and his legal adviser. Having been charged, the custody officer must decide whether to release the young person on bail. As with an adult, the relevant criteria to be applied by the custody officer are set out under s. 38 PACE 1984 (see Chapter 4, para. 4.14.2) subject to an additional ground where it would not be in the young person's interests to be granted bail.

Where bail is refused, s. 38(6) PACE 1984 requires the custody officer to ensure that the young person is moved to local authority accommodation unless:

- it is impracticable to do so (in which case the officer must give reasons why this is so); or
- in the case of a child or young person aged between 12 and 17, no secure accommodation is available and it appears that local authority accommodation would not be adequate to protect the public from serious harm from that child or young person.

The principles of CJ-SSS/SDJ apply to the youth court in the same way as they apply in the adult court (see Chapter 9, para. 9.16).

24.11 **FUNDING THE YOUNG PERSON'S RIGHT TO LEGAL REPRESENTATION**

The cost of the young person attending the police station will be met under the Police Station Advice and Assistance scheme. The advice is free of charge. Post-charge, the defence practitioner will need to apply for a representation order as soon as possible using CRM14 (see Chapter 9). The young person will need to satisfy the interests of justice test unless he is charged with an indictable-only offence. However, the means test has no application to applicants under the age of 18. The young person should sign CRM14.

KEY POINT SUMMARY

- All those involved in the provision of youth justice services must work in accordance with the statutory duties of the youth justice system under s. 37 CDA 1998 and the welfare principle under s. 44 CYPA 1933.
- Be aware of who has parental responsibility over a young person.
- Be aware of the role of the YOT representative.
- Know the procedures the police have to follow under Code C when the juvenile is detained at the police station.
- Have a good working knowledge of the diversion procedures as alternatives to prosecution. The defence practitioner may well want to argue with the police and/or the CPS about the suitability of these alternatives for their juvenile client.

SELF-TEST QUESTIONS

1. Explain the role of the appropriate adult.
2. Is a young person entitled to a representation order?
3. Explain the role of the Youth Offending Team (YOT).
4. Remi, aged 14, is a first-time offender charged with a minor offence of criminal damage contrary to s. 1 CDA 1971. Explain the factors the police and/or the CPS will take into account in dealing with Remi.
5. Charlie, aged 12, is accused of assaulting a teacher. It is alleged that Charlie lost his temper and forcefully pushed the teacher against a door resulting in the teacher fracturing her nose. Charlie has since apologised. He admits he should not have lost his temper; however, he was incensed about being accused of something he did not do. Charlie has been in and out of care. He received a reprimand six months ago for an offence of common assault involving a pupil at his previous school. His mother is a drug addict and finds it difficult to cope with Charlie. Charlie's behaviour at school has been poor. He has poor concentration levels and is frequently in trouble for fighting. He has been excluded from school as a result of this incident. Explain the factors the police will take into account in dealing with Charlie.

An analysis of the above can be found on our Online Resource Centre.

25.1 INTRODUCTION

Where a prosecution is commenced against the young person the general rule is that he will be tried and sentenced in the youth court. The youth court adopts more informal and less adversarial procedures to deal with the needs and vulnerabilities of young defendants. The procedures must also comply with the young person's right to a fair trial under Article 6 European Convention on Human Rights 1950 (ECHR 1950).

While young persons are normally tried in the youth court, there are situations where they will be tried in the Crown Court or in the adult magistrates' court. This chapter explains:

* the rules for deciding where a young person is to be tried;

* the rules for trying a young person in the Crown Court;

* the rules for trying a young person in the adult magistrates' court;

* the young defendant's right to court bail;

* the procedure in the youth court.

For further information and to access some useful flowcharts summarising key areas of this chapter, see the revised *Youth Court Bench Book*, published by the Judicial Studies Board (http://www.estudo.co.uk/jsb/mod/resource/view.php?id=174). A link via the web-links section of our Online Resource Centre (Youth Justice section) will take you there.

25.2 THE YOUNG PERSON'S FIRST COURT APPEARANCE

In most cases the young person's first court appearance will be in the youth court. The principles of CJ-SSS (Simple, Speedy, Summary, Criminal Justice) and Stop Delaying Justice (SDJ) outlined in Chapter 9, para. 9.16.1 apply. If the case cannot be dealt with immediately, the court will either remand the young person in custody or release him on bail, as explained in para. 26.2.1.

If the young person pleads not guilty, the case is likely to be adjourned and a date set for trial in the youth court if jurisdiction to try the young person is accepted. If a guilty plea is entered, the court may sentence immediately following an outline of the facts and the plea in mitigation, or will adjourn sentence for the preparation of a pre-sentence report.

As exceptions to the general rule, the young person's first court appearance will be in the adult magistrates' court where the young person is:

- jointly charged with an adult (s. 46(1)(a) Children and Young Persons Act 1933 (CYPA 1933)); or

- charged with aiding and abetting an adult to commit an offence (s. 18(a) CYPA 1933, s. 46(1)(b) CYPA 1963); or

- charged with an offence which arises out of the same circumstances or is connected with the offence with which the adult is charged (s. 18(a) CYPA 1963).

25.2.1 COURT BAIL

As with adults, the young person's entitlement to bail will be dealt with at the first court appearance. All youths appearing before the youth court are entitled to unconditional bail unless the court considers that grounds exist for imposing bail conditions or refusing bail.

The law and procedure governing court bail under the Bail Act 1976 (as it applies to either-way/indictable-only offence/summary imprisonable offence and non-summary imprisonable offence) apply to a young person in much the same way as to an adult, except there is an additional ground on which bail can be refused where the young person should be kept in custody for their own protection or welfare (Bail Act 1976 Sch. 1, Part 1, para. 2). For an offender aged 17, the adult bail provisions apply. (For a more detailed consideration of the law and procedure governing court bail, see Chapter 10.)

In deciding to grant or refuse bail under Sch. 1 Part 1 para. 2 Bail Act 1976, the court will take into account the statutory factors identified in para. 9, Sch. 1 Bail Act 1976, including the nature and seriousness of the offence and the young person's bail record and community ties. The court must also have regard to the statutory aims of youth justice including the welfare principle under s. 44 CYPA 1933. In *R (B) v Brent Youth Court* [2010] EWHC 1893 (Admin) the Divisional Court ruled on the application of the welfare principle to repeated applications for bail by a young offender.

The provisions of ss. 14 and 15 CJA 2003 (see 10.6(2) and 6(6)) do not apply to offenders under the age of 18. Instead, for offences carrying life imprisonment, paras. 9AA and 9AB have been inserted into the Bail Act 1976 requiring a court to give particular weight to the fact that the defendant was on bail on the date of the offence or that the defendant has failed to surrender during the conduct of the case.

25.2.2 REMANDING A YOUNG PERSON

If bail is refused, the youth remand framework introduced by s. 91 Legal Aid, Sentencing and Punishment of Offenders Act 2012 (LASPO 2012) permits the court to remand a child in youth detention accommodation or in local authority accommodation (under s. 91(6) LASPO 2012 a child is classified as a person under the age of 18). In most cases the child will be remanded to designated local authority accommodation which will provide the child with appropriate community-led supervision, support, education and training. A child aged 10 to 11 years must be remanded in local authority accommodation.

Exceptionally, under ss. 98 to 101 LASPO 2012, a child aged 12 to 17 years may be remanded in youth detention accommodation where the child is either charged with a 'serious' offence or where the child has a history of offending whilst on bail.

The following conditions must apply before a child charged with a 'serious' offence can be remanded to youth detention accommodation:

- the child must be aged 12 to 17 years; and
- satisfy the legal representation conditions that the child is legally represented before the court or legal representation has been offered and refused on financial grounds or withdrawn because of the child's conduct; and
- the child is charged with a violent or sexual offence; or
- having been charged with an offence for which an adult may receive a custodial sentence of 14 years or more; and
- it is necessary to protect the public from death or serious personal injury; or
- it is necessary to prevent the commission by the child of further imprisonable offences.

The following conditions must apply before a child who has a history of offending whilst on bail or on remand can be remanded to youth detention accommodation:

- the child must be aged 12 to 17 years; and
- satisfy the legal representation conditions as above; and
- have a history of absconding whilst remanded to youth detention accommodation or local authority accommodation; or
- having been charged or convicted of an offence which, when taken with previous imprisonable offences for which they have been convicted, amounts to a recent history of committing imprisonable offences whilst on bail or on remand; and
- there is a real prospect of them receiving a custodial sentence for the present offence; and
- it is necessary to protect the public from death or serious injury; or
- it is necessary to prevent the commission by the child of further imprisonable offences.

These complicated remand provisions have been introduced following public concern that 17-year-olds were being remanded on the same basis as adults and not on the same principles as for younger children. The former practice and procedure had also attracted criticism from the UN Committee on the Rights of the Child.

25.2.3 CONDITIONAL BAIL

Where bail is granted, it may be unconditional or conditional. Conditions are imposed where the court considers it necessary to ensure the young person's attendance at the next court appearance or to prevent the young person from offending while on bail or interfering with witnesses or for the young person's welfare.

There are a wide range of conditions that can be attached to youth bail including bail supervision and support packages, electronic tagging and an ISSP. A member of the youth offending team (YOT) team will be present to assist the court to reach a decision.

Electronic tagging may be imposed as a bail condition in relation to a 12- to 17-year-old where:

- the young person is charged with or convicted of a violent or sexual offence or an offence which in the case of an adult carries a sentence of 14 years' imprisonment; or
- the young person has a recent history of repeatedly committing imprisonable offences while remanded on bail or to a local authority; and
- the court is considering conditional bail or a remand to local authority accommodation.

Electronic tagging can be imposed as a condition on its own or as part of a package and as a condition of remand to local authority accommodation. Given the availability of such a wide range of conditions, a remand to local authority accommodation should be viewed as a last resort.

For a child aged 10 and 11, there is no power to impose a tagging condition or to remand to secure accommodation.

25.3 WHERE WILL THE YOUNG PERSON BE TRIED?

There is a clear and well-established principle that a young person will be tried in the youth court where:

- the young person is charged alone; or
- the young person is charged with another young person.

Most young people are tried summarily in the youth court irrespective of the seriousness or the classification of the offence(s) with which they are charged. Section 24(1) Magistrates' Courts Act 1980 (MCA 1980) provides that this presumption applies even in the case of an indictable-only offence other than homicide.

Unlike an adult offender charged with an either-way offence, the young person has no right of election to the Crown Court. Therefore, if the youth court is considering declining jurisdiction by sending the case to the Crown Court, the only course of action available to the young person's advocate is to make representations against having the case tried before a judge and jury. In contrast to the adult magistrates' court, the youth court has a maximum sentencing power of 24 months in custody subject to the maximum term of imprisonment that the Crown Court could (in the case of an offender aged 21 or over) impose for that offence.

As exceptions to the general rule, the young person may be tried in the Crown Court in the situations explained here.

25.3.1 TRIAL OF A YOUNG PERSON IN THE CROWN COURT

There are a number of situations in which a defendant under 18 *may* and sometimes *must* be tried in the Crown Court.

- Where the young person is charged with homicide, s. 51A(2) and (3) Crime and Disorder Act 1998 (CDA 1998) requires the case *must* be sent forthwith for trial in the Crown Court—the term 'homicide' is widely defined to include murder, manslaughter and attempted murder.
- Where the young person is charged with a firearms offence under s. 51A Firearms Act 1968 or s. 29(3) Violent Crime Reduction Act 2006, s.51A (3)(a) CDA 1998 requires the case *must* be sent forthwith for trial in the Crown Court.
- Where the young person is charged with a specified offence under s. 224 CJA 2003 and it appears to the court that if found guilty he will be sentenced as a 'dangerous' offender under ss. 226 CJA 2003, s. 51A(3)(d) CDA 1998 requires the case *must* be sent forthwith for trial in the Crown Court.
- Where the young person is charged with a 'grave' crime *and* the youth court considers that the Crown Court should invoke its power under s. 91 Powers of Criminal Courts (Sentencing) Act 2000 (PCC(S)A 2000) to pass a lengthy custodial sentence, s. 51A(3)(b) CDA 1998 requires the case *must* be sent forthwith for trial in the Crown Court.
- Where the young person is jointly charged with an adult and it is in the interests of justice to send them both to the Crown Court for trial (s. 51(7) CDA 1998) he or she *may* be tried in the Crown Court.

If the power to send the young person to the Crown Court is exercised, the court will also send for trial any 'related' either-way or qualifying summary-only offence with which the young person is charged (ss. 51A (4)) and 51(8) CDA 1998). A jointly charged adult appearing at the same time as the young person or charged with a related either-way offence or qualifying summary-only offence will also be sent for trial in the Crown Court (s. 51A(6) CDA 1998).

25.3.2   PLEA BEFORE VENUE IN RELATION TO YOUNG PERSONS (CRIM PR, PART 9)

The plea before venue procedure (PBV), as it applies to defendants under the age of 18, is set out in s. 24A MCA 1980. The PBV applies where there is a possibility of the young person being tried in the Crown Court either because he is charged with an indictable offence to which s. 91 PCC(S)A 2000 applies, (see para. 25.3.3 below) or he is jointly charged with an adult and the magistrates' court needs to consider whether it is in the interests of justice to send the young person to the Crown Court alongside the adult (see para. 25.3.4 below).

In deciding where the young person's case will be heard in each of these situations, the court will conduct the PBV under s. 24(A)(6) MCA 1980 (see Chapter 11 for full details of the PBV procedure as it applies to adults charged with an either-way offence). The young person will be asked if the case proceeded to trial would he plead guilty or not guilty? If he indicates a guilty plea, the youth court will proceed to sentence. If the court considers that the offence is one to which s. 91 PCC(S)A 2000 applies (i.e. a custodial sentence in excess of 24 months is likely which can only be imposed by the Crown Court), the young person can be committed (in custody or on bail) to the Crown Court for sentence (s. 3B PCC(S)A 2000).

Alternatively, if at the PBV the young person indicates that he intends to plead not guilty (or gives no indication as to plea), the magistrates will hold a mode of trial enquiry/allocation hearing. (The allocation hearing as it applies to adult defendants is explained in Chapter 11.)

At the allocation hearing, the court will hear representations from the prosecution and the defence about the appropriate trial venue. The court will take into account the circumstances of the offence, the defendant's previous convictions, the allocation guideline and the youth court's sentencing powers. (Unlike for an adult defendant at the allocation hearing, the young person cannot request an indication of sentence from the court.)

The youth court will also be aware of the very strong presumption that a person under 18 years of age should be tried summarily and that there should be aggravating features in the offence which justify the youth court declining jurisdiction for a 'grave' crime.

25.3.3   'GRAVE' CRIMES

Where the young person is charged with a 'grave' crime, the case may be sent to the Crown Court for trial. A 'grave' crime is an offence which is punishable with at least 14 years' imprisonment in the case of an adult offender. Numerous offences carry a maximum custodial term in excess of 14 years including rape, robbery and causing death by dangerous driving. Also classified as a 'grave' crime are specified offences under the Sexual Offences Act 2003 including sexual assault under s. 3.

It is important to realise that the youth court's maximum custodial sentencing powers are restricted. The maximum custodial term that can be passed by the youth court on a young offender is a 24-month detention and training order (DTO). The youth court's power to impose a DTO is also restricted in the case of a young person under the age of 15 unless the young person is a persistent offender, s. 100 PCC(S)A 2000 (see Chapter 26, para. 26.10). These restrictions must be read in conjunction with s. 91(1) and (2) PCC(S)A 2000. Section 91 permits the Crown Court to sentence a young person who has been convicted of a 'serious' or 'grave' offence where the youth court is of the opinion that a longer sentence than it can impose is deserved. Only the Crown Court may impose a custodial term of more than 24 months on a young offender (s. 91 PCC(S)A 2000).

A highly relevant consideration for the youth court at the allocation hearing in connection with a grave crime will be whether its maximum sentencing powers on conviction will be sufficient if jurisdiction to deal with the matter is retained. There is no power to commit for sentence under s. 3B PCC(S)A 2000 if the youth court retains jurisdiction and the young person is convicted unless the 'dangerousness' provisions apply.

How then do the sentencing powers under s. 91 PCC(S)A 2000 inform the court's decision about trial venue? The short answer is if the youth court concludes that there is a real prospect, taking everything into account, that the young person will receive a custodial sentence of two years or more, the case should be tried in the Crown Court.

The basis upon which the youth court should decide to decline jurisdiction to try the young person and send (formerly to commit) to the Crown Court for trial has been judicially considered in several cases. In *R (D) v Manchester City Youth Court* [2002] 1 Cr App R (S) 573, it was stated that the youth court should not decline jurisdiction unless the offence and the circumstances surrounding it and the offender are such as to make it more than a theoretical possibility that a sentence of detention for a long period may be passed.

An overriding consideration for the youth court is that trial in the Crown Court for a defendant under the age of 18 is inherently less suitable than in the youth court. This is especially significant where the young person is under 15 years of age. The most authoritative guidance on the issue of venue is provided by *R (on application of H, A and O) v Southampton Youth Court* [2005] 2 Cr App R (S) 30, in which Leveson J in the Divisional Court stated as follows:

'In an effort to assist hard-pressed magistrates to determine this issue and thereby prevent the constant diet of cases of this nature before the court and, at the same time, seeking to avoid the need to trawl through the ever-growing list of authorities which touch on this point, with the approval of the Vice President of the Court of Appeal Criminal Division, I will attempt to summarise the matter in a way that can properly be put before the youth court whenever the situation arises.

1. The general policy of the legislature is that those who are under 18 years of age and in particular children of under 15 years of age should, wherever possible, be tried in the Youth Court. It is that court which is best designed to meet their specific needs. A trial in the Crown Court with the inevitably greater formality and greatly increased number of people involved (including a jury and the public) should be reserved for the most serious cases.

2. It is a further policy of the legislature that, generally speaking, first-time offenders aged 12 to 14 and all offenders under 12 should not be detained in custody and decisions as to jurisdiction should have regard to the fact that the exceptional power to detain for grave offences should not be used to water down the general principle. Those under 15 will rarely attract a period of detention and, even more rarely, those who are under 12.

3. In each case the court should ask itself whether there is a real prospect, having regard to his or her age, that this defendant whose case they are considering might require a sentence of, or in excess of, two years or, alternatively, whether although the sentence might be less than two years, there is some unusual feature of the case which justifies declining jurisdiction, bearing in mind that the absence of a power to impose a detention and training order because the defendant is under 15 is not an unusual feature.'

In the *Southampton Youth Court* case, the youth court declined jurisdiction to try a 14-year-old youth who was charged with indecent assault. The youth was not a persistent offender and for this reason and because he was under 15, he could not be sentenced to a DTO. The defendant successfully applied to the Divisional Court to judicially review the youth court's decision. The Divisional Court criticised the defence solicitor for not challenging the submissions made by the CPS and stressed the importance of ascertaining the seriousness of the offence and any relevant sentencing guidelines. The case was remitted to the youth court to continue hearing the matter.

In its definitive guideline on the *Overarching Principles for Sentencing Youths* (November 2009) (accessible through the Sentencing Council for England and Wales's website), the Sentencing Guidelines Council has emphasised that the general power to commit for trial under the 'grave' crime provisions should be used rarely. It advises that a young person aged

10 or 11 (or aged 12 to 14 but not a persistent offender—see Chapter 25, para. 25.2.1) should be committed to the Crown Court only where charged with an offence of *such gravity* that, despite the normal prohibition on a custodial sentence for a person of that age, a sentence exceeding two years is a *realistic possibility*. A young person aged 12 to 17 (for whom a detention and training order could be imposed) should only be committed to the Crown Court under the 'grave' crime provisions where charged with an offence of such gravity that a sentence *substantially beyond* the two-year maximum for a detention and training order is a realistic possibility. There is nothing to suggest that these principles have been superseded by the revised procedure for sending either-way offences for trial in the Crown Court and the effect of the guideline continues to raise the threshold for justifying the case being sent to the Crown Court for trial under the 'grave' crime provisions.

While the procedure for deciding whether the youth court should exercise its power under s. 24(A) MCA 1980 is not laid down, the general approach in a case where a young person is charged with a 'grave' crime is for the CPS to invite the magistrates to consider the issue of venue at an early stage in the proceedings, before a plea is taken.

In its legal guidance section, the Crown Prosecution Service instructs its prosecutors as follows:

'Prosecutors should assist the court to determine venue in grave crimes by:

- Drawing to the court's attention any relevant sentencing authorities;
- Informing the court of the aggravating and mitigating features of the offence;
- Providing the court with an accurate and agreed list of the youth's previous convictions, warnings and reprimands. This will assist the court to determine both the nature and length of sentence.'

If the defence opposes the application to decline jurisdiction, appropriate representations based on case law, applicable sentencing guidelines and possibly giving an informal indication of plea will need to be made.

If jurisdiction is declined the youth court may also send the young person for trial for any other indictable offence with which he is charged which can properly be joined in the same indictment (s. 51A(4) CDA 1998). A challenge by either the prosecution or the defence to the youth court's decision to either accept or decline jurisdiction to try a youth under the 'grave' crime provisions is by judicial review in the Divisional Court.

Where jurisdiction to try the young person is declined, the case will be sent forthwith to the Crown Court and a date will be set for a Plea and Case Management Hearing (PCMH)—see Chapter 13.

25.3.4 DECLINING JURISDICTION TO TRY A YOUNG PERSON UNDER THE DANGEROUS OFFENDER PROVISIONS (SS. 226 AND 228 CJA 2003)

Section 51A 3(d) CDA 1998 requires the youth court to send the young person for trial in the Crown Court where the conditions laid down by s. 226 are established, that is:

- the young person is charged with a specified offence as defined by s. 224 CJA 2003; and
- if convicted the young person would be classified as a dangerous offender within s. 226 in that:
  - it appears to the youth court that if the young person was found guilty of the offence, there is a significant risk to the public of serious harm occasioned by the commission of further specified offences by the young person; and
  - the young person satisfies the criteria for imposing detention for life or an extended custodial sentence under s. 226(b) CJA 2003 as amended by LASPO 2012.

A full list of the specified offences is found in Sch. 15 CJA 2003, and includes 'violent' offences such as manslaughter, kidnapping, offences under ss. 18 and 20 Offences Against the Person Act 1861 and 'sexual' offences, including rape, under s. 1 Sexual Offences Act 2003.

25.3.5   **DECIDING JURISDICTION AND THE ISSUE OF DANGEROUSNESS**

The dangerousness provisions as they apply to adult offenders are considered in Chapter 22, para. 22.8. A number of offences are 'specified' for this purpose. It follows that where a young person is charged with a 'specified' offence, the youth court has to consider whether the Crown Court would conclude that 'there is a significant risk to the public of serious harm occasioned by the commission by the offender of further specified offences'. Be aware that if a youth court tries a 'specified' offence, it retains the power to commit the young offender to the Crown Court for sentence if it concludes at that stage that the criteria for imposing a discretionary life sentence or an extended custodial sentence appear to be satisfied (s. 3C PCC(S)A 2000).

The main issue about whether to send the young person to the Crown Court for trial under s. 51A(3)(d) CDA 1998 is the assessment of whether the young person falls within the strict definition of a 'dangerous' offender (see Chapter 26, para. 26.18 and the guidance formulated in *R v Lang* [2006] 1 WLR 2509 covered in Chapter 22, para. 22.8). In deciding the issue of dangerousness, the court is required to take into account all the available information about the nature and circumstances of the offence and the offender. In many cases the court will not have sufficient details to make an informed decision at this early stage. A proper assessment of the dangerousness of the defendant is unlikely to be possible until a pre-sentence report has been prepared by the YOT, which can only occur once the young person is convicted.

It will be apparent that a 'specified' offence may also be classified as a 'grave' crime which may cause some practical difficulties. In considering whether to exercise its power under s. 51A(3)(d) CDA 1998 or under the 'grave' crime provisions, the Divisional Court observed in *CPS v South East Surrey Youth Court and MG* [2006] 1 WLR 2543 that the youth court should bear in mind:

(i)   the policy of the legislature identified in *R (on the application of H, O and A) v Southampton Youth Court* [2005] 2 Cr App R (S) 30 (which was discussed earlier) that those under 18 years of age should be tried in the youth court, which is best designed to meet their specific needs;

(ii)   the guidance of the Court of Appeal in *R v Lang and Others* [2006] 1 WLR 2509, particularly in relation to non-serious specified offences (see Chapter 22, para. 22.8);

(iii) the need, in relation to those under 18, to be particularly rigorous before concluding that there is a significant risk of serious harm by the commission of further offences (such a conclusion is unlikely to be appropriate in the absence of a pre-sentence report following assessment by the YOT); and

(iv)   in most cases where a non-serious specified offence is charged, an assessment of dangerousness will not be appropriate until after conviction, when, if the dangerousness criteria are met, the defendant can be committed to the Crown Court for sentence.

The Divisional Court tacitly approved the practice adopted by the Justice's Clerk for South East Surrey. In deciding whether the offence should be tried summarily or on indictment, the court should first consider whether the offence comes within the meaning of a 'grave' crime (see para. 25.3.3). If the offence is a 'grave' crime, the court is required to consider whether the defendant is 'dangerous'. If he is 'dangerous', the court can send him to the Crown Court for trial under s. 51A(3)(d) CDA 1998. If he is not 'dangerous' but is charged with a 'grave' crime, the court can consider sending him to the Crown Court for trial under s. 51A(3)(b) CDA 1998 where the criteria outlined in the *Southampton Youth Court* case are satisfied. If the defendant is not charged with a 'grave' offence, the issue of 'dangerousness' should only be considered following the defendant's conviction at a summary trial. It should always be borne in mind that wherever possible those under 18 should be tried in the youth court.

The CPS guidance on youth offenders suggests that there will be few cases in which it will be appropriate to exercise the power conferred by s. 51(3)(d) CDA 1998 and that the power should only be used where there is sufficient information for the court to determine whether the offender is dangerous and it is in the interests of justice for the youth to be tried on indictment.

25.3.6 **SENDING THE YOUNG PERSON FOR TRIAL UNDER S. 51(7) CDA 1998 WHEN JOINTLY CHARGED WITH AN ADULT**

Under s. 51(7) CDA 1998, a defendant under the age of 18 may be sent to the Crown Court for trial where:

• the young person is jointly charged with an adult; and

• the adult is going to be tried in the Crown Court (either because the offence is indictable-only or a mode of trial enquiry/allocation hearing has resulted in a decision to send an either-way offence for trial there); and

• the court considers that it is necessary in the 'interests of justice' for the young person to be jointly tried with the adult in the Crown Court.

The determination of where the case will be tried will follow the same allocation hearing procedure explained at para. 25.3.2 above. The determining issue about trial venue (where the young person indicates a not guilty plea or an equivocal plea) is whether the magistrates' court considers that it is in the interests of justice for the young person to be jointly tried at the Crown Court with an adult or to be tried in the youth court.

In applying the interests of justice test, the court will consider the representations made by each side and will have regard to the conflicting interests likely to be raised. On the one hand, it is desirable that there should be a joint trial as this avoids possible inconsistent verdicts and prosecution witnesses having to testify twice. On the other hand, the youth court is best equipped to deal with young defendants. The magistrates' court will apply the allocation guidelines issued by the Sentencing Council for England and Wales which state as follows:

'Where a youth and an adult are jointly charged, the youth must be tried summarily unless the court considers it to be in the interests of justice for both the youth and the adult to be committed to the Crown Court for trial. Examples of factors that should be considered when deciding whether to separate the youth and adult defendants include:

• whether separate trials can take place without causing undue inconvenience to witnesses or injustice to the case as a whole;

• the young age of the defendant, particularly where the age gap between the adult and youth offender is substantial;

• the immaturity of the youth;

• the relative culpability of the youth compared with the adult and whether or not the role played by the youth was minor; and

• the lack of previous convictions on the part of the youth.'

The power to send for trial applies under s. 51(7) CDA 1998 where the young person appears together with an adult in the magistrates' court or where the young person appears in the youth court and is jointly charged with an adult in connection with an indictable-only offence or an either-way offence and the adult has already been sent for trial in the Crown Court.

If the court considers that it is in the interests of justice for the young person to be jointly tried with an adult in the Crown Court, the case will be sent forthwith to the Crown Court and a date will be set for a Plea and Case Management Hearing (PCMH)—see Chapter 13. If the court considers that it is in the interests of justice to hold separate trials the matter will be adjourned to a trial date in the youth court.

It is generally accepted that to comply with the young person's right to a fair trial under Article 6 ECHR 1950, only rarely will it be in the interests of justice for the young person to be tried jointly with an adult and that the young person should not be exposed to the intimidating atmosphere in the Crown Court unless there are very strong and compelling reasons for overturning this presumption.

25.4 SAFEGUARDING THE YOUNG PERSON'S RIGHT TO A FAIR TRIAL IN THE CROWN COURT

If the court decides that trial in the Crown Court is appropriate for the young person, the Consolidated Criminal Practice Direction Part III requires that:

- the young defendant should visit the courtroom out of court hours to familiarise herself with the layout;
- where practicable, the trial should be held in a courtroom where all the participants are on the same level;
- a young defendant should normally be permitted to sit with her family and to engage in informal communication with her legal representative;
- the court should explain the course of proceedings to the young defendant in terms she understands and remind her legal representatives of their continuing responsibility to explain each stage of the proceedings to the young defendant;
- the trial should be conducted to a timetable which takes account of the young defendant's inability to concentrate for long periods;
- robes and gowns should not be worn unless the young defendant requests or the court considers there are good reasons for wearing robes and gowns;
- the court should be prepared to restrict attendance at court to those who have a direct interest in the outcome of the proceedings and to restrict the reporting of the proceedings by the media. As a trainee solicitor, it is likely that your principal will obtain the court's permission for you to attend the trial.

The Practice Direction was issued as a response to criticism from the European Court of Human Rights in *T and V v UK* [2000] 30 EHRR 121, which held that the boys accused of killing James Bulger had not had a fair trial in the highly formal proceedings of Preston Crown Court. The trial, which lasted for three weeks in November 1993, was accompanied by widespread media frenzy and great public hostility.

In appealing to the European Court of Human Rights (ECtHR), T and V submitted that their trial in the Crown Court constituted inhuman and degrading treatment within the meaning of Article 3 ECHR 1950 and that they had been denied a fair trial under Article 6.

Whilst the ECtHR rejected the submission that T and V's trial breached Article 3, it did accept that their right to a fair trial under Article 6 had been violated. The Court concluded that the formality and ritual of the Crown Court must have seemed incomprehensible to the young defendants, making it impossible for them to effectively participate in the proceedings.

Even with these requirements in mind, the procedure for trying a young person in the Crown Court is generally the same as for adult defendants. One important difference is the reporting restrictions that are imposed on the media. Section 39(1) CYPA 1933 permits the court to direct that no newspaper report shall reveal the name, address or school of the young defendant or publish a photograph. A further difference is that s. 34A(1) CYPA 1933 requires that where the young defendant is aged under 16 years, her parent or guardian must attend court. Where the young person is aged 16 or 17, her parent or guardian may attend court.

25.5 TRIAL OF A YOUNG PERSON IN THE ADULT MAGISTRATES' COURT

The circumstances in which a young person will be tried before an adult magistrates' court will be relatively rare. A youth must be tried before an adult magistrates' court where the youth is jointly charged with an adult in connection with a matter that is to be tried summarily (this would include an either-way offence which is to remain in the magistrates' court) and both the adult and the youth plead not guilty.

If the young person is later convicted at trial or chooses to plead guilty, the powers of the adult magistrates' court to sentence the youth are restricted (see Chapter 26). In these circumstances the adult court will normally remit the youth to the youth court for sentence if it considers its sentencing powers to be restrictive.

If the adult defendant pleads guilty but the youth pleads not guilty, the adult court may try the youth. However, it is much more likely to remit the youth to the youth court for trial (s. 29 MCA 1980).

Consider the following examples of the factors to be taken into account in deciding the place of trial of a defendant under the age of 18.

 Example

Josh, aged 14, is charged with theft. As he is charged alone and is a juvenile, he will be tried in the youth court.

Josh, aged 14, is charged jointly with Sharon, who is 16, with theft. As both defendants are under 18, both will be tried in the youth court.

Josh, aged 14, is jointly charged with Giancarlo, aged 33, with robbery. Assuming Josh appears at the same time as Giancarlo, the magistrates' court will be required to send Giancarlo to the Crown Court under s. 51 CDA 1998. Josh will also be sent for trial if the magistrates consider it is in the interests of justice that Josh be tried with Giancarlo (regard being had to s. 51(7) CDA 1998).

Josh, aged 14, is charged with rape and will indicate a not guilty plea. As rape is a 'grave' offence, the youth court may decline jurisdiction to try the case in favour of the Crown Court's more extensive powers of sentence under s. 91 PCC(S)A 2000. Consideration will also be given to the 'dangerousness' provisions as rape is a specified offence (ss. 226 CJA 2003).

Josh, aged 14, is jointly charged with Graham, aged 33, with common assault. If both Josh and Graham plead not guilty, the trial will be held in the adult magistrates' court. If Graham pleads guilty but Josh pleads not guilty, Josh will be tried in the youth court.

25.6 PROCEEDINGS IN THE YOUTH COURT

Most young defendants will be tried in the youth court where proceedings are more informal than in the adult court. The informality extends to the layout of the court, which enables the young person to fully participate in the proceedings (unless the defendant is remanded in custody). Magistrates are encouraged to sit on the same level as the other people present if the physical layout of the courtroom permits it. The witnesses usually remain seated during the proceedings, as do the advocates and other court officers. The defendant will be addressed by his first name and the language used should be appropriate to his age and maturity. The words 'conviction' and 'sentence' will be avoided as the phrases 'case proven' or 'not proven' are preferred. Sentences are described as 'disposals' and before disposing of the case, the court is required to inform the young person and her parent or guardian of the way it proposes to deal with the case. Magistrates who conduct cases before the youth court are specially trained. All youth court chairmen will have attended training on engaging with children and young people. You are reminded of the fact that the accused may be eligible for limited special measures (see Chapter 19, para. 19.3.1) and a wide range of special measures are available to vulnerable witnesses (defined to include a witness under the age of 18) to maximise the quality of the evidence provided (see Chapter 16, para. 16.4). The following may be present in court:

* court officers, including members of the YOT;
* the parties in the case including the young person, prosecution and defence lawyers and witnesses;

- the defendant's parents or guardians;
- the victim, unless it is not in the interests of justice for the victim to attend (this would be a rare occurrence);
- news reporters—although reports of the proceedings are generally restricted so as not to reveal the young person's identity, address, school, etc.

Even allowing for the greater informality, where the defendant denies the offence, the trial in the youth court will follow the same procedure as in the adult court:

- the prosecutor makes an opening speech;
- the first prosecution witness is examined in chief;
- the witness is cross-examined by the defence;
- the prosecutor may re-examine his witness;

(each prosecution witness gives evidence through this procedure);

- the prosecutor may also put before the court:
  - documentary evidence;
  - exhibits (known as real evidence); and
  - statements admissible under s. 9 CJA 1967, which permits the written statement of a witness who is not in court to be read to the Bench;
- at the close of the prosecution case, the defence may make a submission of no case to answer where the prosecution has failed to prove an essential element of the offence or the prosecution evidence has been so discredited that the court could not find the case proven against the defendant;
- the first defence witness, usually the accused, is examined in chief;
- the witness is cross-examined by the prosecution;
- the defence advocate may re-examine his witness;

(each defence witness gives evidence through this procedure);

- the defence advocate may also put before the court:
  - documentary evidence;
  - exhibits (known as real evidence); and
  - statements admissible under s. 9 CJA 1967, which permits the written statement of a witness who is not in court to be read to the Bench;
- the prosecutor and the defence advocate make a closing speech;
- the court decides whether the case is proven;
- if proven, the court will proceed to disposing of the case; or
- if the case is not proven the defendant is free to leave the court.

For further information on the conduct of cases before the youth court, see the Magistrates Association Youth Court Protocol contained in the *Revised Youth Court Bench Book* (2010)–Appendix A, available via the Judicial Studies Board website (http://www.estudo. co.uk/jsb/mod/resource/view.php?id=174).

For further information generally on youth justice, consult the Youth Justice Board's webpages at http://www.justice.gov.uk/youth-justice.

KEY POINT SUMMARY

- The rules governing the grant or refusal of bail in relation to a young defendant are governed by the Bail Act 1976 and, subject to one or two exceptions, are applied in much the same way as they are to an adult accused.

- A remand in custody in relation to a young person under the age of 17 is a remand into the care of a local authority with or without a security requirement.
- A young person under the age of 12 cannot be remanded into the care of the local authority.
- There is a strong presumption that a defendant under 18 should be tried in the youth court which is specifically designed for the special needs of younger offenders, even in a case where the young person is charged with a serious offence.
- A youth has no right of election to the Crown Court when charged with an either-way offence.
- Understand the circumstances in which a youth must be tried in the Crown Court and the circumstances where he might be tried in the Crown Court.
- Understand the concept of a 'grave' crime and why this is important in relation to mode of trial considerations for a youth.
- Understand when the 'dangerousness' provisions under s. 224 CJA 2003 bite and why they are important in relation to mode of trial considerations for youths.
- Be able to explain the differences in procedure between the adult court and the youth court.

SELF-TEST QUESTIONS

1. What is the general rule about where a young defendant should be tried?
2. Tracey is 15. She has been charged with an offence of arson contrary to s. 1(1) and (3) CDA 1971. It is alleged that she and a group of other girls set fire to a mobile classroom in the grounds of a high school, resulting in £20,000 worth of damage. The fire began at around 10.30 at night. The classroom was unoccupied. Tracey has no criminal record but comes from a family beset by social problems. She has recently been suspended from school. No one else has been charged in connection with the incident. Consider the following questions:
   - In which court will Tracey appear?
   - In which court is Tracey likely to be tried and dealt with?
3. Barry, aged 15, is charged with causing death by dangerous driving. He denies the offence. He has several previous convictions, including convictions for robbery, violence and aggravated vehicle-taking. What considerations will the youth court have regard to in deciding whether to accept jurisdiction to try Barry?

An analysis of the above can be found on our Online Resource Centre.

online
resource
centre

FIGURE 25.1 YOUTH PROCEEDINGS

WHERE WILL A YOUNG PERSON BE TRIED?

Youth court (the vast majority of young defendants are tried before the youth court).

This will be the case where:

- youth is charged alone; or

- youth is charged with another youth.

Crown Court where the youth is:

- charged with homicide, which includes both murder and manslaughter, s. 51A CDA 1998 or Firearms Act 1968 offence carrying mandatory minimum term; or

- charged with a 'grave' offence, s. 51A(3(b)) CDA 1998—'grave' offence includes an offence for which an adult could be punished with imprisonment for 14 years or more (there must be a realistic possibility that the young person will receive a custodial sentence substantially beyond 24 months); or

- charged with a specified offence and the young person would, if found guilty, be sentenced as a 'dangerous' offender under s. 226 CJA 2003 (s. 51A(3)(d) CDA 1988); or

- jointly charged with an adult and the adult is to be tried on indictment and the court considers that 'it is in the interests of justice' for them to be tried together, s. 51(7) CDA 1998.

Adult magistrates' court where:

- young person is charged jointly with an adult with a summary offence BUT

- the summary offence may be remitted to the youth court where:

  – the adult pleads guilty; and

  – the young person pleads not guilty; or

  – the adult is sent for trial or is discharged and the young person pleads not guilty.

When charged with an either-way offence, the young person has no right of election.

Youth court proceedings:

- are more informal in terms of procedure and terminology;

- have limited right of public access;

- have reporting restrictions; and

- are tried before specially trained 'mixed' Bench.

26 SENTENCING YOUNG OFFENDERS

26.1 INTRODUCTION

This chapter deals with the range of disposals available where a young offender admits the offence(s) or a finding of guilt is recorded against him. While most young offenders will be sentenced by the youth court, as you saw in Chapter 25, in specified situations an adult magistrates' court or the Crown Court may try a young person and/or sentence him.

The issues explained in this chapter include:

• the principles which guide the sentencing of youths;

• the youth court's sentencing powers;

• the adult magistrates' court sentencing powers;

• the Crown Court's sentencing powers;

• sentencing a 'dangerous' young offender.

To fully understand the principles of sentencing in relation to youths, you should be aware of sentencing practice and procedure in relation to adults explained in Chapters 21 and 22. As you will soon appreciate, in comparison, the sentencing of young offenders is more complex and much more directed at dealing with the young offender's specific needs.

26.1.1 WHAT ARE THE GENERAL PRINCIPLES THAT GUIDE YOUTH SENTENCING?

Significant reforms relating to the sentencing of young offenders came into force in November 2009 with the enactment of the Criminal Justice and Immigration Act 2008 (CJIA 2008). The reforms coincided with the publication of the Sentencing Guidelines Council's, *Overarching Principles—Sentencing Youths* (November 2009) referred to in this chapter as the guidelines. The guidelines set out the general approach to be applied by all courts when sentencing a young offender. The guidelines can be accessed at http://sentencingcouncil.judiciary.gov.uk/docs/web_overarching_principles_sentencing_youths.pdf and via our Online Resource

Centre. As with adult offenders, the starting point for deciding the appropriate sentence is the seriousness of the offence(s).

Section 142A CJA 2003 identifies the relevant considerations that apply when sentencing an offender under 18. A court must have regard to:

• the principal aim of the youth justice system which is to prevent offending and re-offending;

• the welfare of the offender; and

• the purposes of sentencing.

The statutory purposes of sentencing applicable to offenders under the age of 18 are listed under s. 142A CJA 2003 as being:

• punishment;

• reform and rehabilitation;

• protection of the public; and

• reparation to persons affected by the offence.

Whilst the same structured approach to sentencing that is applied to adults is adopted in relation to youths, the SGC's guideline highlights key differences in the approach to be taken when sentencing a young offender. A more individual, tailored approach is required based on an assessment of the risks posed by the young person and an assessment of his/her needs. Important to the sentencing process is the need to have regard to the principal aim of the youth justice system and the offender's welfare. The younger an offender, the more significant will the welfare principle be in sentencing. The guidelines state that emotional maturity is as important as the chronological age, and there is a general expectation that a youth will be dealt with less severely than an adult, although this diminishes as the offender approaches 18 (see guidelines, para. 3.1). Paragraph 2.4 of the guidelines states that whilst previous convictions aggravate the seriousness of an offence it does not mean that a more severe sentence must follow. Regard should be had to the fact that the sentence passed by the court is always likely to have a greater impact on a youth than an equivalent sentence would have on an adult offender. This is especially true of a custodial sentence and for this reason the guidelines emphasise that custody is the sentence of last resort. This principle is reflected by the custody threshold test being higher for youths than for adults (see para. 26.10). At para. 4.1 the Sentencing Guidelines Council summarises the considerations that should guide youth sentencing as follows:

'In determining the sentence, the key elements are:

- the offender's age (chronological and emotional);
- the seriousness of the offence;
- the likelihood of further offences being committed; and
- the extent of harm likely to result from those further offences.

The approach to sentence will be individualistic.'

For all of these reasons, it is important for the court to have access to the fullest possible information about the young person to enable it to determine the most appropriate sentence commensurate with the seriousness of the offence. Such information will invariably be supplied by a youth offending team (YOT) in a pre-sentence report.

26.1.2 THE SCALED APPROACH

As explained in Chapter 24, para. 24.3, an important development arising out of reforms to youth justice sentencing implemented by the CJIA 2008 has been the adoption of a framework under 'The Scaled Approach' which ensures that sentencing interventions recommended by the YOT are tailored to the individual defendant and based on an assessment of their risks and needs.

When a YOT prepares a pre-sentence report at the request of a court or a youth panel overseeing a referral order, it will assess the individual via the ASSET tool (which evaluates the likelihood of re-offending and the risk of serious harm) and will use the 'Scaled Approach'. Under the ASSET tool, the young offender's attitude to offending, level of educational attainment, employment prospects, lifestyle, living arrangements, habits relating to alcohol and substance abuse are assessed along with such factors as the level and nature of his or her previous offending. These factors are scored to produce a numerical assessment of the offender's risk of re-offending as well as providing guidance on the appropriate level of intervention required to deal with the offender's individual needs. The higher the score, the greater the level of intervention required by the YOT. The required intervention will be classified as either being at standard, enhanced or intensive. This classification will help determine the overall length of a referral order, the duration, and nature of any requirements imposed as part of any youth rehabilitation order and the nature of supervision following release on licence from custody under a detention and training order (DTO).

It should be noted that the *Magistrates' Court Sentencing Guidelines*, which provide offence-specific sentencing starting points when sentencing adult offenders, cannot easily be applied to young offenders, although they have some relevance where custody is the appropriate starting point for sentence in the case of an adult. Some definitive SGC sentencing guidelines exist for youths aged 17 in relation to sexual offences and robbery.

26.2 SENTENCING PROCEDURE IN THE YOUTH COURT

Where the case is proven against the young person or the offence is admitted, the youth court will proceed to sentence. As in the adult court, the CPS advocate will outline the full circumstances of the offence where a guilty plea is entered and will refer the court to any relevant previous convictions and any existing sentence of the court. Where appropriate, the CPS lawyer will seek ancillary orders, such as prosecution costs. The defence advocate will submit a plea in mitigation on the young person's behalf. Crim PR, Part 44 provides that the young person and/or his or her parent or guardian will be given the opportunity to make a statement to the court. Before determining the appropriate sentence, it is common practice in the youth court for the Bench chairman to directly engage with the young person in an effort to ascertain whether he/she has any insight into the reasons for and the effect of his/her offending behaviour. Also, when deciding sentence, the court will consider any relevant information about the young person's general behaviour, home environment and school record. If the information is not immediately available, the court must consider adjournment for enquiries. In most cases a written pre-sentence report will be provided by a member of the YOT (see para. 26.1.2).

When the youth court has all the necessary information, a range of disposals are available. Some disposals relate to the young offender only, while others can be imposed on his or her parent or guardian.

26.3 DEFERRING SENTENCE—S. 1 PCC(S)A 2000

The youth court can defer sentence for up to six months. Sentence may be deferred:

- because of an imminent and significant change in lifestyle; or
- to allow the young person to save up to pay compensation to the victim.

The court must give reasons for the deferment and explain what is required of the young person during the deferred period. If another offence is committed during the deferred period, the offender may be sentenced for the new offence in addition to the previous offence. A deferred sentence is very rare.

26.4 REFERRAL ORDER—SS. 16 AND 17 PCC(S)A 2000 (AS AMENDED BY S. 79 LEGAL AID, SENTENCING AND PUNISHMENT OF OFFENDERS ACT 2012 (LASPO 2012))

A referral order can be imposed by the youth court or a magistrates' court. Under a referral order, the young person is referred to a Youth Offender Panel (YOP). The YOP is composed of volunteers drawn from the local community and a member of the YOT. It will meet with the young person and his or her parent/guardian and agree a 'contract' with the offender. The contract should include a programme of interventions designed to address the causes of the young person's offending behaviour and to get the young person to take responsibility for the consequences of his or her actions. The victim of the offence may attend the YOP. The referral order is therefore capable of fulfilling two of the statutory aims of sentence: the prevention of offending and reparation.

Regular panel meetings are held to review the progress of a referral order. Importantly for the young person, the conviction is spent once the 'contract' is completed.

In some instances, a referral order is a mandatory sentence; in other situations a referral order is discretionary. Common to both the mandatory and discretionary referral order are the following requirements:

- the sentence for the offence must not be fixed by law; and

- neither a custodial sentence nor an absolute discharge are appropriate for the offence or any connected offence.

Circumstances in which a referral order is mandatory

Under ss. 16 and 17 PCC(S)A 2000 (as amended by LASPO 2012) a referral order must be imposed where the young offender:

- is sentenced for the first time in connection with an imprisonable offence; and

- has no previous convictions (a bind over and a conditional discharge are disregarded); and

- pleads guilty to an offence and any connected offence; and

- an absolute or conditional discharge, hospital order or custody is not appropriate.

A referral order must therefore be imposed on a 'first-time' offender, who pleads guilty to an offence which is not suitable for a custodial sentence or any of the other prescribed disposals even though the offence might be regarded as a serious offence.

 Example 1

Ali, aged 16, pleads guilty to possession of a small amount of a Class A drug with intent to supply. Ali has previously received a youth caution and a conditional discharge for other offences committed in the past. In these circumstances and assuming the offence is not so serious that a custodial sentence should be imposed, the youth court must sentence Ali to a referral order.

Circumstances in which a discretionary referral order can be imposed

A court may *choose* to impose a referral order under ss. 16 and 17 PCC(S)A 2000 (as amended by LASPO 2012) after considering the young person's age, plea, seriousness of the offence, previous convictions and disposals where the young offender pleads guilty to an offence (or where the offender is before the court for more than one offence, to at least one of those offences), even if it is not the offender's first offence. As a result of the amendment, the court is no longer prevented from offering referral orders to offenders who have previously received referral orders in the past. There is no limit to the number of referral orders that a repeat offender can receive.

 Example 2

Adam, aged 16, pleads guilty to possession of a small amount of a Class C drug with intent to supply. Adam has several previous convictions. Adam successfully completed a three-month referral order 24 months ago for an offence of criminal damage. He was made subject to a reparation order 18 months ago for an offence of theft which he also completed successfully. The pre-sentence report recommends a second referral order. The youth court can subject Adam to a referral order in these circumstances.

 Example 3

Joe, aged 16, pleads guilty to allowing himself to be carried in a stolen vehicle and is found guilty of being in possession of a small amount of a Class A drug after a trial. Joe has previously received a conditional discharge for other offences committed in the past. As Joe has been subject to a trial, he does not meet the criteria for a compulsory referral order. In these circumstances the youth court may sentence Joe to a referral order.

The length of a referral order is determined largely by the seriousness of the offence and can be between three and 12 months. In accordance with the 'Scaled Approach' previously outlined, the YOT is more likely to recommend an intensive contract in a case where the court indicated that custody is being considered, but because it is a first time guilty plea, a referral order is the only non-custodial alternative.

A referral order is a sentence in its own right although it can be combined with a compensation order. The YOP may refer the young person back to court if he or she fails to sign the contract or fails to agree or comply with its terms. The youth court can then revoke the referral order and re-sentence or allow the order to continue. The YOP may also refer an order back to the court with a request that it be extended. The youth court can extend the period of referral for up to three months (subject to the overall 12-month limit) if it is in the interests of justice. The youth court may revoke a referral order if it is in the interests of justice where a young person is making good progress.

26.5 FINE—PART VI PCC(S)A 2000

While imposing a fine on an offender is a common sentence passed by the adult magistrates' court (see Chapter 22, para. 22.15), fining a young person is relatively rare, for obvious reasons. When the court considers imposing a fine, the following considerations apply:

- The fine may be imposed as a disposal in its own right.
- The court must take into account the offender's financial circumstances and/or his or her parent/guardian.
- The parent/guardian must attend the court hearing if the court is considering making him or her pay.
- Where the offender is under 16, the parent/guardian will be ordered to pay, unless:
  - the parent/guardian cannot be found; or
  - it would be unreasonable to expect him or her to pay.
- The maximum fine that can be imposed where the young offender is aged between 10 and 13 is £250.
- The maximum fine that can be imposed where the young offender is aged between 14 and 17 is £1,000.

Priority is given to a compensation order over a fine.

26.6 CONDITIONAL DISCHARGE—S. 12 PCC(S)A 2000

A conditional discharge may be imposed on a young offender whatever the offence. In practice, they are reserved for the less serious offences and are relatively rare in the youth court given the availability of the referral order. The offender must not commit any further offences during the operational period of the conditional discharge, which can be up to a maximum of three years. If the young offender re-offends during the operational period, he or she may be punished for the later offence and for the original offence. A conditional discharge may be imposed where:

- the case is proven against the young offender;
- the court considers that it is not expedient to punish;
- the young offender has not received a final warning or been conditionally cautioned within the last two years.

26.7 ABSOLUTE DISCHARGE—S. 12 PCC(S)A 2000

As with a conditional discharge, an absolute discharge is appropriate for very trivial offences where the court considers that punishment is not required. An absolute discharge may be imposed where:

- the case is proven against the young offender; and
- the court considers that no punishment is required; and
- the court considers there is no risk of further offending by the young person.

26.8 REPARATION ORDER—SS. 73–75 PCC(S)A 2000

In deciding whether to make a reparation order, the court will obtain a report from the young person's YOT who will suggest a suitable form of reparation. The order is designed to confront the offender with the consequences of his or her offending behaviour and can only be imposed for an imprisonable offence. The reparation element shall be commensurate with the seriousness of the offence. A reparation order cannot be combined with any other order. The following considerations apply to a reparation order:

- the young person is required to give reparation to a specified person or to the community;
- the work to be carried out is under the supervision of a probation officer or social worker;
- no more than 24 hours work to be completed within three months of the order;
- the order is overseen by the YOT;
- in a case where a reparation order can be made, the court must give reasons for refusing to make one.

Failure to comply with a reparation order can lead the youth court to impose a fine not exceeding £1,000 or to re-sentence in some other way.

26.9 YOUTH REHABILITATION ORDER (YRO)

Section 1 of the CJIA 2008 completely overhauled youth community sentences by creating a single Youth Rehabilitation Order (YRO) which is a new generic community sentence for all offenders under the age of 18 within which a court must include one or more requirements designed to provide for punishment, protection of the public, reducing re-offending and reparation. A YRO can be imposed for any offence (whether imprisonable or not) which is 'serious enough' (s. 148 CJA 2003). The nature and number of requirements must be proportionate and suitable and any restrictions on the young person's liberty must be commensurate with the seriousness of the offence. A pre-sentence report will invariably be required. The pre-sentence report will be prepared in accordance with the 'Scaled Approach' outlined earlier. The maximum length of a YRO is three years. A YRO can, however, come to an end on the completion of all the requirements or can be extended for up to six months for the completion of all the requirements, s. 84 LASPO 2012.

A YRO is not available where the offender is before the court and the compulsory criteria for a referral order are present (see para. 26.4 above), or there is an existing reparation order or YRO in force. The requirements that may be attached to a YRO (which are similar to those for adults—see Chapter 22) are considered here.

26.9.1 ACTIVITY REQUIREMENT

This requires participation in activities for a specified number of days which must not exceed 90 days.

26.9.2 SUPERVISION REQUIREMENT

This is a requirement to attend appointments with a specified YOT officer. The period of supervision must be equal to the length of the order.

26.9.3 UNPAID WORK REQUIREMENT

This can only be imposed on an offender aged between 16 and 17. The number of hours must be between 40 and 240, to be completed over a 12-month period.

26.9.4 PROGRAMME REQUIREMENT

A requirement to participate in a systematic set of activities recommended by the YOT.

26.9.5 ATTENDANCE CENTRE REQUIREMENT

This requires a young person to attend a centre to engage in and to receive instruction. For those aged 16+ the minimum length is 12 hours and the maximum 36. For those aged 14 and 15, the minimum is 12 hours and the maximum is 24 and for those under 13, the maximum is 12 hours.

26.9.6 PROHIBITED ACTIVITY REQUIREMENT

A requirement to refrain from participating in specified activities.

26.9.7 CURFEW REQUIREMENT

The offender must stay at a specified location for a specified period of time of between two and 16 hours in any one day. The maximum length of a curfew is twelve months. The curfew will be supported by electronic monitoring unless the court considers this to be inappropriate or it is not available.

26.9.8 EXCLUSION REQUIREMENT

This requirement cannot exceed three months and prohibits a young person from entering a specified place during a specified time period. The court must also make an electronic monitoring requirement to ensure compliance.

26.9.9 RESIDENCE REQUIREMENT

This disposal applies only to those aged 16 and over and requires that the young person live with a specified person (who must consent) at a specified place.

26.9.10 LOCAL AUTHORITY RESIDENCE REQUIREMENT

This is a requirement to reside in accommodation provided by a local authority for a specified period which must not exceed six months and which ceases to apply when the offender reaches 18. There are a number of pre-requisites that apply before this requirement can be imposed.

26.9.11 ELECTRONIC MONITORING REQUIREMENT

This requirement will be imposed as part of a curfew, exclusion or attendance centre requirement.

26.9.12 MENTAL HEALTH TREATMENT REQUIREMENT

This requires the offender's willingness to comply and is a requirement for residential or non-residential treatment for a diagnosed mental condition that is susceptible to treatment.

26.9.13 **DRUG TREATMENT REQUIREMENT**

The court must be satisfied that the young person requires treatment, that suitable arrangements have been made or can be made to deal with the young person's needs and that the young person consents to comply with the conditions of the treatment.

26.9.14 **DRUG TESTING REQUIREMENT**

This disposal operates alongside the drug treatment requirement and requires the offender to voluntarily provide urine samples for drug testing.

26.9.15 **INTOXICATING SUBSTANCE TREATMENT REQUIREMENT**

The court must be satisfied that the young person is dependent on or has a tendency to misuse intoxicating substances and that the dependency is susceptible to treatment. It requires the offender's expressed willingness to comply.

26.9.16 **EDUCATION REQUIREMENT**

A requirement to comply with approved educational arrangements made by the parent or guardian and approved by the local education authority. The requirement must be necessary to secure the good conduct of the young person or to prevent further offending.

26.9.17 **INTENSIVE SUPERVISION AND SURVEILLANCE REQUIREMENT**

This requirement may only be included in an order where:

- the offence is imprisonable; and
- the custody threshold test is met (and in the case of an offender under the age of 15 at the time of conviction, the young person is a persistent offender).

It is important to note that a YRO combined with an intensive supervision and surveillance (ISS) requirement is a direct alternative to custody.

The order must include an 'extended activity requirement' of between 90 and 180 days, plus supervision, curfew and electronic monitoring. This is a highly intensive community order.

26.9.18 **FOSTERING REQUIREMENT**

This requirement (which is a direct alternative to the DTO) can only be imposed where the same circumstances exist as are required for the intensive supervision and surveillance requirement. In addition, the court must be satisfied that a significant factor in the commission of the offence was the circumstances in which the young person was living at the time and that this requirement would assist in rehabilitation. Extensive consultation with the young person's parent/guardian and the local authority are needed before this requirement can be imposed. The order must specify the period during which the young person must reside with the foster parent, which must not exceed 12 months. The order cannot operate after the young person has attained 18.

26.9.19 **DEALING WITH A BREACH OF A YRO**

In the event of the young person failing to comply with a YRO, a court can choose to do any of the following:

- take no action (there is no obligation on the court to make a more onerous order, in contrast to the adult offender);

- impose a fine subject to the young offender's means to a maximum of £2,500 for 14- to 17-year-olds and £250 for offenders under 14. The order may still continue in its original form in spite of the fine;

- amend the terms of the order by increasing or substituting requirements (in doing so the court can impose any requirement it could have imposed when making the original order save for an 'extended activity' or fostering requirement); or

- revoke the order and re-sentence the offender (this could involve the offender being made subject to an 'extended activity' or fostering requirement or custody if the court is satisfied that the YOT has taken all necessary steps necessary to ensure the young person has been given appropriate opportunity and support necessary for compliance). Revocation and re-sentence is unlikely for a first breach as the primary aim is to ensure compliance with the order.

Where an offender has 'wilfully and persistently' failed to comply with the order and the court proposes to sentence again for the original offence, additional powers are available. These additional powers include the power to sentence to a DTO for four months or a YRO with an ISS requirement even though the offence for which the original YRO was imposed did not carry a custodial term in the youth court or if it did, the original offence did not cross the custody threshold.

26.10 DETENTION AND TRAINING ORDER—SS. 100–107 PCC(S)A 2000

A DTO is the main custodial sentence for a young offender.

The custody threshold test must be met before a DTO can be passed in that the offence or combination of offence and any associated offence must be so 'serious' that neither a fine alone nor a community sentence can be justified (s. 152 CJA 2003). In fact, there is a further additional hurdle in the case of a youth in that not only must the custody threshold test be met but the court must also give reasons as to why a YRO with intensive supervision and surveillance or a YRO with a fostering requirement (see paras. 26.9.17 and 26.9.18) cannot be justified instead (s. 174(4B) CJA 2003).

The effect of the reforms to youth sentencing under the CJIA 2008 in conjunction with the Sentencing Guidelines Council's *Overarching Principles—Sentencing Youths* (November 2009) means that custody is very much the sentence of last resort for young offenders. For a first-time offender who has pleaded guilty to an imprisonable offence, in most cases a referral order will be the most appropriate sentence (see para. 26.4). Since any custodial term must be for the shortest term commensurate with the seriousness of the offence (s. 153 CJA 2003), and since the minimum length of a DTO is four months, unless the offence justifies a term of at least four months (taking into account any reduction for guilty plea), the sentence must be of a non-custodial nature. A pre-sentence report must be considered before a custodial sentence is imposed.

Apart from these important considerations, a court cannot pass a DTO on an offender under the age of 12, or on an offender under the age of 15 unless the court is of the opinion that he or she is a persistent offender (see Chapter 24, para. 24.2.1 for a definition of the term 'persistent offender').

The length of the DTO must be for one of the periods specified in the Act: 4, 6, 8, 10, 12, 18 or 24 months. (The term may not exceed the adult maximum term which a Crown Court could pass on an adult over 21, which in the case of a summary-only offence is currently six months or less if the statute so prescribes.) There is no power to suspend a DTO. The availability of a 24-month custodial term to the youth court means that its sentencing powers are considerably higher than those available to the magistrates' court sentencing an adult offender (see Chapter 21, para. 21.14.1). In its definitive guideline on youth sentencing, the Sentencing Guidelines Council suggests that the chronological age and maturity of the young person will be a relevant consideration in determining the length of any custodial sentence and that, as a general rule for offenders aged between 15 and 17, the court should consider a starting point from one-half to three-quarters of that which would have been identified for an adult offender. In establishing the length of the DTO, the young person will be entitled to a sentencing discount where he or she pleads guilty and will be given credit for periods spent on remand in custody or subject to a qualifying curfew (s. 144 CJA 2003/ s. 101(8) PCC(S)A 2000).

The young person will begin a period of supervision halfway through the sentence, which will cease when the full term expires, s. 103 PCC(S)A 2000. Where the supervision element is breached, the court may order the offender to be detained in youth detention accommodation for three months or the remainder of the term of the order (if shorter) or a further period of supervision not exceeding three months or a fine not exceeding level 3.

 Example

Jamal, aged 14, is convicted of serious assault in the youth court. He has 10 previous convictions and has previously been sentenced to a wide range of community-based disposals, many of which have not been successfully completed. As the court is satisfied that the offence is so serious that only a custodial sentence is appropriate and that Jamal is a persistent offender (PO), and that neither a YRO with an ISS requirement nor a YRO with a fostering requirement are justified, it imposes an eight-month DTO on him. Under the terms of the DTO, Jamal will serve four months in custody and four months in the community under supervision.

26.11 ENDORSEMENT OR DISQUALIFICATION OF THE JUVENILE'S DRIVING LICENCE/RECORD

For further information on driving penalties, see the chapter 'Sentencing in Road Traffic Cases' found in the Handbook's Online Resource Centre. Even though a young offender may not have a driving licence, his or her driving record can still be subject to endorsement and disqualification.

 online resource centre

26.12 COMPENSATION ORDER—SS. 130–135 PCC(S)A 2000

A convicted young offender may be ordered to pay compensation up to a maximum of £5,000 in either the youth court or the adult magistrates' court for any personal injury, loss or damage which resulted from his or her offence. The Magistrates' Court Sentencing Guidelines provide guidance as to the appropriate level of compensation. An important consideration will be the offender's ability to pay.

26.13 PARENTING ORDERS—SS. 8–10 CDA 1998

A parenting order is directed to improving the parenting skills of the young offender's parent or guardian. Where an offender under the age of 16 is convicted of an offence and the court considers that a parenting order would be desirable in the interests of preventing further offending by the young person, it *shall* make a parenting order. The pre-sentence report should provide information relevant to this decision. A parenting order requires the parent or guardian to attend parenting guidance sessions for up to 12 months. The sessions are supervised by a member of the youth offending team or a probation officer or a social worker.

26.14 PARENTAL BIND OVER—S. 150(1) PCC(S)A 2000

The young offender's parent or guardian must be bound over to prevent the juvenile under the age of 16 from committing further offences wherever the court is satisfied that it would be in the interests of justice to do so. If a court chooses not to make an order, it must give reasons in open court. A bind over may not be given where a court passes a referral order.

26.14.1 YOUTH COURT BENCH BOOK

For further information and a useful flowchart covering the various sentencing options available to the youth court, see the *Revised 2010 Youth Court Bench Book*, published by the Judicial Studies Board and accessible via http://www.estudo.co.uk/jsb/mod/resource/view.php?id=174 and via the web-link section (Youth Justice section) of our Online Resource Centre.

26.15 ANTI-SOCIAL BEHAVIOUR ORDER (ASBO)

The Crime and Disorder Act 1998 introduced a wide range of measures which seek to divert young people away from offending by imposing sanctions on their anti-social behaviour. They include ASBOs, child safety orders and local child curfew schemes. Breach of an ASBO is a criminal offence which carries imprisonment. An ASBO is an order which prohibits a young person from doing anything specified in the order. It can be imposed on application by the police or local authority and upon conviction (referred to as a CrASBO) where the court considers the offender has acted in a manner that caused or was likely to cause harassment, alarm or distress. A steady body of case law has started to emerge in relation to ASBOs (see *Blackstone's Criminal Practice*).

26.16 SENTENCING THE YOUNG OFFENDER IN THE ADULT MAGISTRATES' COURT

The adult magistrates' court has limited sentencing powers over a young offender. In the few situations where the young offender is sentenced in the adult magistrates' court, the following disposals are most commonly imposed:

- fine;
- referral order;
- conditional/absolute discharge;
- disqualification from driving;
- endorsement of the young person's driving licence/record.

The young offender will usually be remitted to the youth court for sentence. Relevant rules of court relating to the sentencing of a young person before an adult magistrates' court are contained in Crim PR, Part 44.

26.17 SENTENCING THE YOUNG OFFENDER IN THE CROWN COURT

While the Crown Court may pass any appropriate sentence on a young person, s. 8 PCC(S)A 2000 requires that where the young person has been convicted on indictment, it shall remit the offender to the youth court for sentencing unless it is 'undesirable' to do so. In applying the 'undesirable' test, the Crown Court judge may not remit to the youth court where doing so would cause:

- delay; or
- unnecessary expense; or
- unnecessary duplication of the proceedings.

As the judge will be familiar with the facts of the case, it is common for the young person to be sentenced in the Crown Court. With the exception of the referral order, the Crown Court has the full range of sentencing disposals available to it (reparation order, YRO and DTO), with the obvious addition that it can impose a much longer custodial sentence in accordance with s. 91 PCC(S)A 2000 for a 'grave' crime where the defendant has been *convicted on indictment* and, when it is in force, upon committal for sentence under s. 3B PCC(S)A 2000. In appropriate circumstances, it can also impose a sentence under the dangerousness provisions (see later). Where a custodial sentence is passed, the young offender will serve his or her time in a young offenders' institution or secure training centre.

Where the young person has been convicted of murder, s. 90 PCC(S)A 2000 prescribes the mandatory sentence of detention at Her Majesty's Pleasure. Guidance on setting the minimum term can be found in ss. 269–277 CJA 2003. The starting point for an offender under 18 is 12 years before taking into account any mitigating or aggravating factors.

26.18 SENTENCING A 'DANGEROUS' YOUNG OFFENDER

Sections 224–229 CJA 2003 introduced significant sentencing powers in the Crown Court to deal with 'dangerous' offenders. These provisions were extensively amended by the CJIA 2008. Further changes have now been introduced by LASPO 2012. The provisions apply to adults as well as youth offenders. The application of the dangerousness provisions in relation to adults is considered in Chapter 22, para. 22.8. We recommend you consider the provisions as they apply to adult offenders before reading further. The definition of dangerousness and other key terms can be found at Chapter 22, para. 22.8. Schedule 15A (which lists certain 'specified' offences relevant to sentencing dangerous adult offenders) has no application to youths.

Only the Crown Court can sentence a young offender under the dangerousness provisions. The powers of the Crown Court may be exercised following the young person's conviction in the Crown Court (see Chapter 25, paras. 25.3.1 and 25.3.2 for an account of the circumstances in which a young person can be committed for trial in the Crown Court) or where he has been remitted under s. 3C PCC(S)A 2000 to the Crown Court for sentence following summary conviction in the youth court.

Schedule 15 CJA 2003 lists the categories of violent or sexual offences which come within the definition of a specified offence. A specified offence is defined under s. 224 CJA 2003 as a violent or sexual offence which carries a sentence of between two years' and 10 years' imprisonment. A 'serious offence' is a violent or sexual offence specified in Sch. 15 which carries a sentence of at least 10 or more years in the case of an adult. The sentencing powers available to the Crown Court depend on whether the young person has been convicted of a serious, specified violent or sexual offence or a specified violent or sexual offence which carries a sentence of between two years' and 10 years' imprisonment. If the offender falls within the first category *and* is assessed as being dangerous, he must be detained for life. If the offender falls within the second category *and* is assessed as being dangerous, the court must pass an extended sentence of imprisonment.

26.18.1 DETENTION FOR LIFE

Under s. 226(1) CJA 2003, where a person under 18 has been convicted of a serious violent or sexual offence (carrying a maximum of 10 or more years' imprisonment) and the court is of the opinion that there is a significant risk to members of the public of serious harm occasioned by the commission by him of further specified offences, the court MUST impose a sentence of detention for life IF the offence he or she has been convicted of would be liable to a sentence of detention for life AND the court considers that the seriousness of the offence is such as to justify the imposition of a sentence for life (s. 226(2) CJA 2003).

If these precise circumstances apply BUT the sentence of detention for life is not available or not justified, the court MAY impose an extended sentence (see below).

26.18.2 IMPOSING AN EXTENDED CUSTODIAL SENTENCE

When can an extended custodial sentence be imposed on a youth? Section 226B CJA 2003 (as amended by ss. 123–125 LASPO 2012) provides that a court MAY impose an extended sentence on an offender aged under 18 where:

- the offender is convicted of a specified offence (this is not limited to a serious offence); and
- the court is of the opinion that he or she is a dangerous offender (i.e. there is a significant risk to members of the public of serious harm occasioned by the commission by him of further specified offences); and
- a sentence of detention for life is not available or not justified; and
- the appropriate custodial term for the offence would be at least four years.

Where the conditions for imposing an extended custodial sentence are met, the court will set the appropriate custodial term and a further extended period of supervision which the young offender is required to serve on licence. The extended period on licence should be for such period as the court considers necessary to protect the public from serious harm occasioned by the commission of further specified offences by the young offender. Two-thirds of the term is served in custody before the young person is released on extended licence of up to five years for violent offences (s. 226B (6) CJA 2003) and up to eight years for sexual offences (s. 226B(6) CJA 2003).

26.18.3 ASSESSING 'DANGEROUSNESS'

In deciding whether to detain an offender under 18 for life or for public protection or to impose an extended sentence, the court must consider the seriousness of the offence and/or other offences associated with it (s. 229 CJA 2003) to determine whether the young person will constitute a danger to the public. The court will take careful note of the facts of the offence, the pre-sentence report and any other relevant report. In these kinds of cases a psychiatric report is commonly obtained.

Guidance on these complicated provisions has been given by the Court of Appeal in *R v Lang and Others* [2005] EWCA Crim 2864 (see Chapter 22).

26.19 CROSSING A SIGNIFICANT AGE THRESHOLD BETWEEN COMMISSION OF AN OFFENCE AND SENTENCE

If the defendant is under the age of 18 at the time he or she enters a plea before the youth court he or she will be tried as a youth, notwithstanding the fact that the defendant reaches 18 during the currency of the proceedings.

Although the rules and the case law in relation to sentence on this point have never been absolutely clear, the position has been clarified by the 2009 *Overarching Principles—Sentencing Youths—Definitive Guideline*, published by the Sentencing Guidelines Council. The approach to be taken is set out in para. 5 as follows:

- where an offender crosses a relevant age threshold between the date on which the offence was committed and the date of conviction or sentence, a court should take as its starting point the sentence likely to have been imposed on the date on which the offence was committed;
- where an offender attains the age of 18 after committing the offence but before conviction, the adult purposes of sentencing under s. 142 of the Criminal Justice Act 2003 apply;

- it will be rare for a court to have to consider passing a sentence more severe than the maximum it would have had jurisdiction to pass at the time the offence was committed, even where an offender has subsequently attained the age of 18;

- a sentence at or close to that maximum may be appropriate, especially where a serious offence was committed by an offender close to the age threshold.

For further information on youth justice, consult the Youth Justice Board's website at http://www.yjb.gov.uk/.

KEY POINT SUMMARY

- Know the circumstances in which the youth court can impose a detention and training order (DTO) and be aware that a DTO cannot be imposed upon an offender under the age of 12, and in the case of an offender under the age of 15, he or she must be a persistent offender.

- Understand that only the Crown Court can impose a lengthy custodial term (in excess of 24 months) for a 'grave' crime or under the 'dangerousness' provisions. Consequently, the only court which can pass a custodial sentence on an offender under the age of 12 or under the age of 15 and who is not a persistent offender is the Crown Court.

- Know the circumstances in which a referral order must be made and the circumstances in which a referral order might be made.

- Know the range of requirements that are available to the youth court and Crown Court when sentencing a young offender to a youth rehabilitation order.

- Know the criteria that must be satisfied before a youth court or Crown Court can impose a youth rehabilitation order with intensive supervision and surveillance.

- Understand the dangerousness provisions as they apply to youths and their effect on sentencing.

SELF-TEST QUESTIONS

1. What is the main custodial sentence for a convicted young offender and when can it be passed?

2. Tracey is 15. She has been charged with an offence of arson contrary to s. 1(1) and (3) Criminal Damage Act 1971. It is alleged that she and a group of other girls set fire to a mobile classroom in the grounds of a high school, resulting in £20,000 worth of damage. The fire began at around 10.30 at night. The classroom was unoccupied. Tracey has no criminal record but comes from a family beset by social problems. She has recently been suspended from school. No one else has been charged in connection with the incident. If Tracey were to plead guilty to the offence, what sentencing options would be open to the youth court? Would your answer be different if Tracey had either (a) been found guilty of arson following a trial; or (b) having pleaded guilty, she had previous convictions for assault and criminal damage for which she has previously received a referral order and reparation order?

3. To which court would a young person appeal against conviction and/or sentence arising out of a decision taken by the youth court?

An analysis of these questions can be found on our Online Resource Centre.

online resource centre

APPENDIX 1

EXTRACTS FROM *R v LENNY WISE*

For reasons of space, we include only a selection of the documentation that forms the basis of the solicitor's file on this case study.

The complete documentation as listed overleaf, can be accessed on our Online Resource Centre in the case studies section. The documents selected for inclusion in this appendix are shown in **bold type.**

R v LENNY WISE: INDEX TO DOCUMENTATION ON SOLICITOR'S FILE

TIMESCALE OF EVENTS—*R v LENNY WISE*

- 20 March—charged with an either-way offence.

- 20 March—initial appearance before magistrates' court (short adjournment—defendant remanded in custody).

- 27 March—second appearance before magistrates' court. Plea before Venue. Not guilty plea entered followed by allocation hearing (mode of trial). Summary jurisdiction declined. Case adjourned and a date set for Plea and Case Management Hearing before the Crown Court. Bail refused. Remanded in to custody.

- 29 March—bail hearing before Crown Court—conditional bail granted.

- 30 June—first appearance before Crown Court at the PCMH—date set for trial.

- 22 August—trial.

DOCUMENT 1 ATTENDANCE UPON CLIENT AND RECORD OF FIRST APPEARANCE BEFORE MAGISTRATES' COURT
DATE 20/3/–

Attending Lenny Wise at Lyme Magistrates' Court in my capacity as Duty Solicitor. Lenny Wise is charged with a domestic dwelling house burglary. In the course of the interview, Lenny was less than coherent and kept asking me for a cigarette. He looked rough, dishevelled and appeared incapable of concentrating during the interview. It would appear that Lenny has bipolar depression for which he receives medication although he admitted to me that he had not been taking his medication properly. I tried to take him through the Advance Information that the CPS had provided me with but Lenny was unable to concentrate. Lenny was able to tell me that he was not represented at the police station and that he did not commit the burglary. At this point, Lenny said he felt sick and proceeded to vomit. I explained to Lenny that I would be seeking a short adjournment to enable me to properly take his instruction. He appears in custody as bail is opposed.

Based on my brief perusal of the Advance Information, the evidence linking Lenny to the burglary would appear to be based on admissions in interview and eye-witness evidence. A second person is suspected of being involved in the burglary but no charges have been brought against this individual. I informed the CPS lawyer that Lenny would be denying the offence and that I would be seeking a brief adjournment as my client was too unwell to provide me with firm instructions. The CPS lawyer indicated that he would not oppose my application for an adjournment but that bail would be opposed.

Attending before Lyme Magistrates and requesting a one-week adjournment as my client was appearing in custody; was unwell; had mental health problems and that I needed to take his full instructions before being in a position to advise on plea. The application was not opposed. The adjournment was granted. The CPS then opposed bail. An application for bail was made by me. Bail refused on the grounds of risk of absconding and commission of further offences. The case was adjourned for one week. Mr Wise was remanded to HMP Shawbury. **Date of next hearing is 27 March**.

I spoke to Lenny afterwards—he was clearly agitated and somewhat bewildered. I explained he could apply for bail to the Crown Court but that I would be able to reapply for bail before the Magistrates' Court in one week's time. If bail was refused on that occasion we could apply to the Crown Court. He agreed to this course of action. I explained that I or a member of my firm would be visiting him on remand in the next couple of days to take his full instructions. I also spoke to Lenny's sister who attended court and who is evidently concerned for her brother's welfare.

Time engaged:
Attending client 50 minutes
Advocacy 30 minutes

DOCUMENT 2 ADVANCE INFORMATION/STREAMLINED DISCLOSURE PLUS PREVIOUS CONVICTIONS RECORDED AGAINST LENNY WISE

POLICE REPORT (MG 5)

	URN	21	TL	4256	12

Defendant 1: Lenny Wise	Anticipated plea: Guilty
Defendant 2:	Anticipated plea: - select -

1. **Summary of the Key Evidence**—'Key evidence' establishes every element of the offence and that the defendant committed the offence with the necessary criminal intent.

   • Set out the facts in chronological order, telling the story and covering the 'points to prove'

   • The summary must be balanced and fair

   • Record address and contact details of civilian witnesses on MG9 (and *all dates to avoid on MG10*).

Key evidence: The offence alleged is domestic dwelling-house burglary at 19 Sunrise Road, Lyme on the 17th March between 11.15am-12.15pm.

Key witness(es) and their role (e.g. eye witness, person providing identity):

Lillian KENNEDY: (victim of the burglary). When returning home from collecting her pension she was approached by a black male who offered to help her carry her shopping. She declined help. She describes this male as being tall and thin with black, straggling hair and wearing a black top and white training shoes. Approximately 20 or 30 minutes later, KENNEDY answers her front door to another male individual who engages her in conversation and asks to use her telephone. During this time, a second male who KENNEDY does not see enters her bungalow via the back door and steals her handbag containing her purse and £75. KENNEDY only discovers the theft when she is alerted by her neighbour LEWIS. KENNEDY identified the defendant as being the black male who had approached her earlier whilst being taken on a tour of the immediate area by police. KENNEDY was unable to identify the defendant from a VIPER later that day.

Shirley LEWIS: (eye-witness). At midday approximately on the 17 March, LEWIS is pegging out some washing in her back garden when she observes a male in the back garden of KENNEDY'S bungalow. Witness describes the male as being Afro-Caribbean, 5 ft 8 inches tall, wearing a black hooded sweatshirt and white training shoes. LEWIS has previously seen this individual in the local area on other occasions. LEWIS identified the defendant at a VIPER later that day.

Harold FINNEY: (neighbour). Unable to identify the defendant. Will say that he observed a black car (registration number taken—car is registered to Lloyd Green) in Sunrise Road at around midday on the 17th March and witnessed a black male approach the car, wearing a black top and a pair of white trainers. The male is described as being in his twenties with long, dark hair.

Steven FARRINGTON: (arresting officer). Will say that he attended the scene of the burglary and took a statement from KENNEDY. Took KENNEDY on a tour of the immediate area whereupon KENNEDY identified an Afro-Caribbean black male (WISE) as being the male who had approached her near her property earlier that day. The male was identified by DC SHAW as being Lenny WISE. He was observed as being of Afro-Caribbean decent, 5' 10" with shoulder-length dreadlock hair and a slight beard, wearing brown training shoes and black hooded sweatshirt. WISE not arrested until the following day 18th March at 4a Lymewood Court. Will state that a s.32 PACE 1984 search of defendant's address was undertaken and a pair of white Nike training shoes and a black hooded sweatshirt were seized. A small quantity of cannabis resin was found in WISE's trouser pocket.

Officer also arrested and interviewed Lloyd GREEN (suspected accomplice) on the 18th March. GREEN was later released on police bail. He has not been charged.

State value of property stolen or damaged (or recovered). (See Sec 9 for recording compensation details): Theft of handbag and purse-pension money £75.

2. **Defendant Interview**

   • Set out the explanation given by defendant as to **how/why offence happened**: include any **mitigation/remorse** put forward.

   • Note any **Special Warnings** given.

- State if no comment made.
- Attach copy of CCTV if shown in the interview **(to file)**.

Defendant: **Lenny Wise**

Date of interview: 20/3

Interviewing officer(s): DS 4291 Farrington/ DC 2890 Sarah Shaw

Other person(s) present: None

Summary of defendant explanation: Questions put to WISE as to his whereabouts on the morning of the 17 March. Largely incoherent replies. Unable to offer alibi. Denied white training shoes seized from his flat belonged to him. Admits to knowing Lloyd GREEN.

Defendant's response/reaction to CCTV (if 'key evidence' and shown in I/V): N/A

Relevant admissions and their start/finish counter reference times:

Admission of involvement in the burglary at 44 minutes and 6 seconds. 'I stole it from the old lady, I needed the money . . .'. Refuses to identify accomplice.

3. **Non Key Evidence**—list witnesses present but not 'key'. State what evidence they contribute e.g. additional eye witness, arresting officer, charging officer; officer seizing CCTV. Record contact details of civilian witnesses on MG9 and dates to avoid on MG10.

Name of non-key witness(es) and their role:

Carol Jayne Lawton (SOCO)—processed crime scene and recovered several shoe marks. Confirms secure packaging and continuity of search/forensic samples.

DC 2890 Sarah Shaw—able to identify male pointed out by KENNEDY as being WISE based on previous dealings with this individual. Present during the interviews.

4. **Visually Recorded Evidence**—CCTV, photos, mobile phone(s). Attach a copy (*identify playback format*). Custody suite CCTV should be included as unused material unless 'key evidence'.

Is there VRE? No   If 'Yes', does it provide 'key evidence? - select -

Give details of what it shows (whether 'key' or not) and include tape counter reference times for relevant key sections (*i.e. defendant punching victim/kicking window*).

5. **Injuries**—a medical statement is **NOT** required unless needed to interpret x-rays or describe injuries not visible to the naked eye. Victim(s)/eye witness/police officer should **describe any visible injuries,** photos should be taken and attached (if not taken/attached, state why).

Description of injuries: Not applicable

6. **Forensic Evidence**—fingerprints, drugs evidence (weight, number of wraps, etc.). Include details such as street value and purity as this is essential for sentencing information. State if drugs field tested and by whom. State timescales for a full forensic statement (if required).

White training shoes recovered from WISE's flat have been sent for forensic comparison with shoe marks recovered from crime scene. Full report expected within 7 days.

7. **DIP testing**—attach DT2 for prosecutor.

Def. 1: Tested? ☐   Trigger off.: ☐   Result: (pos/neg) - select -   Drug: - select -

Def. 2: Tested? ☐   Trigger off.: ☐   Result: (pos/neg) - select -   Drug: - select -

8. **Application for Order(s) on Conviction**—consider applying for an order on conviction, e.g. compensation, forfeiture/destruction (see order list).

Defendant:

Order(s) applied for: - select -

9. **Application for Compensation**—state if an estimate. Attach quotes/receipts if available. An address for compensation must be provided on MG6. (*If more than one victim/defendant, list one after the other and give details in the description box*).

Defendant: Lenny Wise   Victim: Lillian Kennedy

Description of injury/loss and or damage:

Amount of compensation applied for: £120   Has an MG19 been sent to victim?: Yes

10. **Other: MG18 (TICs)?** ☐   **Pre-cons/cautions attached ? Y**☐   **MG6?** ☐

11. **Officer's certification:** I certify that to the best of my knowledge and belief, I have not withheld any material that might reasonably be expected to undermine the prosecution or might reasonably assist the defence in early preparation of their case, including the making of a bail application. I further certify that relevant material has been recorded and retained in accordance with the CPIA 1996, Code of Practice, as amended.

Name & rank/job title: DS 4291 Steven Farrington

Date:

12. **Supervisor's certification:** The information in parts 1–9 is an accurate summary of the available evidence and complies with the DPP's guidance for a Streamlined Process. The file has been built to the required standard.

Name & rank/job title: DI 4565 TAPP

Signature: *D. Tapp*   Date: 20/3/

DOCUMENT 2 WITNESS STATEMENT (LILLIAN KENNEDY)

Form MG11

RESTRICTED (when complete)

WITNESS STATEMENT

(CJ Act 1967, s. 9; MC Act 1980, s. 5A(3)(a) and s. 5B; Criminal Procedure Rules 2011, Rule 27.1)

URN					

Statement of: *Lillian Kennedy*

Age if under 18 (if over 18 insert 'over 18'): *Over 18* Occupation: *Retired*

Title: *Mrs* (Mr/Mrs etc...) Collar/ID Number:

This statement (consisting of....3.... page(s) signed each by me) is true to the best of my knowledge and belief and I make it knowing that if it is tendered in evidence I shall be liable to prosecution if I have wilfully stated in it anything which I know to be false or do not believe to be true.

Signature: *L Kennedy* Date: *18/3/—*

Tick if witness evidence is visually recorded ☐

I live at number 19 Sunrise Road, Lyme. I am 85 years old. On Tuesday 17th March, I went to fetch my pension from Lyme High Street. I drew £95. Once I had paid my weekly sums for gas and electricity I was left with around £75. I returned home at around 11am. As I was walking up the road, a man approached me and asked me if I wanted any help with my shopping. I told him, no thank you I would describe him as being quite tall and thin. He had a gaunt face, was black and had long, black straggling hair and a small beard on his chin. I think he was wearing a short, dark coloured top and a pair of white sports shoes. I saw

Signature: *L Kennedy* Signature Witnessed by: *S.*

RESTRICTED (when complete)

Form MG11 cont

Page No: 2 of 3

Continuation of Statement of: Lillian Kennedy

him walk of into the fields near the
back of my house
       I know I had my purse with me when
I went into my house, because a friend of
mine called in for ten minutes shortly after
I got back from the Post Office. She had
her grandchild with her and I gave her a
pound from my purse. A short time after
this I was putting some rubbish out
when I thought I heard the telephone
ringing. When I came in, I realised it
was my front door bell I answered the
door. There was a man standing there.
I have never seen this man before.
He was white but had a tanned
complexion. He was dressed smartly,
wearing a suit and tie. He was quite
bald. He was not very tall. I recall he
was wearing dark glasses. He told me
his car had broken down and asked

Signature: L Kennedy   Signature witnessed by: E L

RESTRICTED (when complete)

Form MG11 cont

Page No: 3 of 3

Continuation of Statement of: Lillian Kennedy

if he could use the telephone. I told him
he could not as I did not have a phone. Not
long after this, a friend of my neighbour came
round. She told me she had seen a man
in my back garden and that my back door was
open. I immediately checked my handbag
and saw that my purse was missing. She
telephoned the police. I realised that I had left
my back door open when I came to answer the
front door. It was silly of me. The only money
I get is my pension. The theft has left me
shaken and frightened. Later in the afternoon
of 14th March, the police took me around the local
area in one of their cars. They asked me if I could
see the man who had knocked on my front door.
I could not see the man who had called, but I
did see the man who had offered to help me
with my shopping earlier that morning. The
police car stopped outside the Co-op on the High Street.
I had a good look at the man and I am sure it was him

Signature: L Kennedy   Signature witnessed by:

DOCUMENT 2   WITNESS STATEMENT (SHIRLEY LEWIS)

Form MG11

RESTRICTED (when complete)

WITNESS STATEMENT

(CJ Act 1967, s. 9; MC Act 1980, s. 5A(3)(a) and s. 5B; Criminal Procedure Rules 2011, Rule 27.1)

| URN | | | | |

Statement of: Shirley Lewis

Age if under 18 (if over 18 insert 'over 18'): Over 18   Occupation: Retired Teacher

Title: MRS (Mr/Mrs etc...)   Collar/ID Number:

This statement (consisting of 3 page(s) signed each by me) is true to the best of my knowledge and belief and I make it knowing that if it is tendered in evidence I shall be liable to prosecution if I have wilfully stated in it anything which I know to be false or do not believe to be true.

Signature: Shirley Lewis   Date: 18/3

Tick if witness evidence is visually recorded ☐

On Tuesday the 17th March, I was visiting my elderly aunt at 19 Sunrise Road, Lyme. She lives next door to Lillian Kennedy at number 17. At around midday on 17th March, I went out the back of my aunt's property to bring some washing in that was pegged up on the washing line. The time was around midday.

I was facing Lillian's back garden. A low wall divides the gardens, it being largely open plan. I saw a man in her garden. I watched him for a good few seconds.

Signature: Shirley Lewis   Signature Witnessed by: [signature]

Form MG11 cont

Page No:..2..of.....3

Continuation of Statement of:...

In fact, I nearly called out to him, to ask what he thought he was doing, but something stopped me. He didn't see me because I was behind a large sheet pegged on the line. I do not know where he came from but I watched him wander out of Lillian's garden and off down the back lane. At this point, I noticed the back door to Mrs Kennedy's house was wide open.

I would describe the man as being of Afro-Caribbean origin. He was about 5" 8/9 inches tall. He was of slim build and was wearing a black hooded sweat shirt with the hood up, so I could not see his hair. The man I saw was wearing a pair

Signature:................................. Signature witnessed by:...............................

Form MG11 cont

Page No: 3 ...of... 3

Continuation of Statement of:...

of white training shoes. I
went round to see Lillian
almost straightaway and she
told me that her purse was
missing. I am certain I would be
able to recognise the man again.
I had the distinct feeling I had
seen the man before. In fact I
have seen him walking his dog,
a brown and white terrier, in the
grassy area nearby on more than
one occasion.

Signature: .... Signature witnessed by: ....

DOCUMENT 2   Print of PNC Record-PNCID: 005/6593V

Print For: WISE, LENNY

Date of Birth: 27/6/-

Date	Court	Offence/s	Sentence
10 years previous	Lyme Youth Court	Burglary (non-domestic dwelling)	Supervision Order (12 months)
7 years previous	Lyme Magistrates	Theft	Conditional Discharge (12 months)
5 years previous (February)	Blurton Magistrates	Theft Possession of amphetamine Driving without insurance	Community Order with supervision (15 months)/Licence endorsed
5 years previous (December)	Lyme Magistrates	Burglary (non-domestic dwelling) Possession of class B drug/Resisting constable/Failure to surrender/Breach community order 'Offences committed on bail'	Custody 5 months concurrent
4 years previous	Chorley Magistrates	Possession of class B drug/Theft Obtaining property by deception	Community Rehabilitation Order with supervision (12 months)
3 years previous (August)	Lyme Crown Court	Burglary (domestic dwelling) Possession of class A drug/Failure to surrender	Custody 12 months concurrent
2 years previous (April)	Blurton Magistrates	Theft/Possession of class B drug 'Offences committed on bail'	Custody 4 months concurrent + unexpired term 108 days
18 months previous	Lyme Magistrates	s. 4 Public Order Act 1986 Common Assault	Community Order with supervision (24 months)

DOCUMENT 4   ATTENDANCE NOTE

Date: 24th March

Attending Lenny in an interview room at Shawbury Remand Centre. I assisted Lenny to complete an application for a representation order. I took him through the Advance Information I had been served with. I took a detailed statement from him and obtained written authorisation to contact his consultant psychiatrist. I explained the prosecution's case against him and what would happen at his next appearance. I explained the credit available for a guilty plea. Based on his instructions, I advised Lenny to plead not guilty. I discussed mode of trial and his chances of securing bail at his second appearance and appeal thereto to a Crown Court judge in chambers. I explained that I would be seeking further disclosure of evidence from the CPS (including the taped interview and custody record plus a DVD copy of the parade) and that I would be sending him a client care letter and his proof of evidence which I needed him to read through and sign. I explained I would go through it all again with him at court on the 27th March.

Time engaged:
Travel: 70 minutes
Waiting: 15 minutes
Attendance: 1 hour

DOCUMENT 5   APPLICATION FOR REPRESENTATION ORDER—CRM14

Form © Legal Services Commission 2013. Reproduced with kind permission of the Legal Services Commission. Please note that this form is dated February 2012 and is current at the point of publication. The most recent versions of all such forms are held on the LSC's website.

Application for Legal Aid in Criminal Proceedings

Form
CRM14

Legal Aid
Agency

ⓘ Please use the Guidance
If you do not complete the form correctly, we will return it.
You will find Guidance to help you fill in the form correctly,
at: www.justice.gov.uk/legal-aid/assess-your-clients-
eligibility/criminal-means-assessment
If you need more help or advice, please contact a solicitor.

Protect - Personal
(see question 32)

MAAT Reference
(for official use)

For the Legal Representative's use

If the case is an **Appeal to the Crown Court** and there is no change in circumstances, answer **1** and then go to question **23**.

Case type
- [ ] Summary
- [x] Either way
- [ ] Indictable
- [ ] Appeal to Crown Court and no changes
- [ ] Committal for sentence
- [ ] Appeal to Crown Court
- [ ] Trial now in Crown Court

The court hearing the case
Lyme Magistrates Court

Priority case
- [x] Custody
- [ ] Vulnerable
- [ ] Youth
- [ ] Late application in the Crown Court for trial
Date of trial

About you: 1

1

ⓘ GUIDANCE

Mr Mrs Miss Ms Other title
- [x] Mr [ ] [ ] [ ]

Your forenames or other names (in BLOCK LETTERS)
LENNY

Your surname or family name (in BLOCK LETTERS)
WISE

Your date of birth
27 / 6 /

National Insurance Number and ARC Number: give one of these only.

National Insurance Number
F R 8 2 8 5 3 1 Y

Application Registration Card (ARC) Number

- [x] This is a new application.   [ ] This application relates to a change of financial circumstances.

Contacting you

2

Do you have a usual home address?
- [ ] No   [x] Yes ——→ Your usual home address

4A LYMEWOOD COURT, PARKDALE, LYME, LYMESHIRE, LY4 97Y

Postcode

3

✓ 'Your solicitor's address only, if you are of 'No Fixed Abode', or not at your usual address because you are on bail or remand.

To what address should we write to you?
- [ ] Your usual home address (the address in 2)
- [x] Your solicitor's address (see the side note)
- [ ] This address

HANNIBAL AND MOUNTFORD
20 HIGH STREET
LYME BANK LYME, LY4 82P

Postcode

4

Your email address

5

Your telephone number (landline)

Mobile phone number

050069734

Work phone number

About you: 2

6

✓one box and if it is 'someone else's home', give your relationship to that person

Your usual home address is:

☑ a Tenancy (rented) ☐ Temporary ☐ Your parent's home (you live with them)

☐ Someone else's home ⟶ Your relationship [   ]

Owned by: ☐ You ☐ Your partner ☐ You and your partner, jointly

7

Are you under 18 years old?

☑ No ☐ Yes ⟶ Are you charged with an adult?

☐ No: Go to **23** ☐ Yes: Go to **23**

8

①GUIDANCE

Do you have a partner?

☑ No: Go to **9** ☐ Yes: Go to **10**

9

✓ one box

①GUIDANCE

You are: ☑ Single: Go to **14** ☐ Widowed: Go to **14**

☐ Divorced or have dissolved a civil partnership: Go to **14**

☐ Separated ⟶ Date of separation?

[   ] Go to **14**

10

✓ one box

You and your partner are:

☐ Married or in a Civil Partnership ☐ Cohabiting or living together

About your partner

11

①GUIDANCE

National Insurance Number and ARC Number: give one of these only.

Your partner's details

Mr Mrs Miss Ms Other title Your forenames or other names (in BLOCK LETTERS)

☐ ☐ ☐ ☐ [   ] [   ] [   ]

Surname or family name (in BLOCK LETTERS) Date of birth

[   ] [   ]

National Insurance Number Application Registration Card (ARC) Number

[   ] [   ]

12

If you ✓ **Yes**, and your partner is a victim, prosecution witness, or co-defendant with a conflict of interest, do not give your partner's details for questions **13** to **22**.

Is your partner a victim, prosecution witness or a co-defendant in the case for which you require legal aid?

☐ No ☐ Yes ⟶ ☐ Victim: Go to **14**

☐ Prosecution witness: Go to **14**

☐ Co-defendant ⟶ Does your partner have a conflict of interest?

☐ No: Go to **13** ☐ Yes: Go to **14**

13 — Is your partner's usual home address different from yours (the address at question 2)?

☐ No ☐ Yes ⟶ Your partner's usual home address

Postcode

Your income and your partner's income

14 — Do you or your partner receive any of the benefits listed here?

☐ No ☑ Yes ⟶ You

	You	Your Partner
Income Support	☐ Go to **23**	☐ Go to **23**
Income-Related Employment and Support Allowance (ESA)	☐ Go to **23**	☐ Go to **23**
Income-Based Jobseeker's Allowance (JSA)	☑ When did you last sign on? 13 / 3 / Go to **23**	☐ When did you last sign on? Go to **23**
Guarantee State Pension Credit	☐ Go to **23**	☐ Go to **23**

GUIDANCE
In this form, if you answer Yes to any question which asks about you or your partner, and you can answer Yes for both of you, give details for you and your partner, not for one of you only.

15 — Do you or your partner, together, in a year have a total income from all sources before tax or any other deduction, of more than £12, 475 (£239.90 a week)?

GUIDANCE

☐ No: Go to **16** ☐ Yes ⟶ You will need to **complete form CRM15**: Go to **23**

16 — Sources of income for you and your partner. Please give details in the table:

EVIDENCE

GUIDANCE
about:
- Employment
- Total of other benefits
- Other source of income

For all parts of this question:
- If you do not receive income from a source, put **NIL** after the '£'.

- After '**every**' put either:
  week,
  2 weeks,
  4 weeks,
  month,
  or year.

	You	Your Partner
Employment (wage or salary)	£ every ☐ Before tax ☐ After tax	£ every ☐ Before tax ☐ After tax
Child Benefit	£ every	£ every
Working Tax Credits and Child Tax credits	£ every	£ every
Universal Credit	£ every	£ every
Total of other benefits	£ every	£ every
Maintenance income	£ every	£ every
Pensions	£ every	£ every
Any other source of income such as: - a student grant or loan - board or rent from a family member, lodger or tenant, or rent from a property - financial support from friends and family	£ every Source:	£ every Source:

17 _____ Are you or your partner self-employed, in a business partnership, or either a company director or a shareholder in a private company?

(!)GUIDANCE ☐ No   ☐ Yes ⟶ You will need to **complete form CRM15**: Go to **23**

18 _____ Do you or your partner have any income, savings or assets which are under a restraint order or a freezing order?

☐ No   ☐ Yes ⟶ You will need to **complete form CRM15**: Go to **23**

19 _____ Are you charged with a Summary offence, only?

(!)GUIDANCE ☐ No   ☐ Yes: Go to **22**

20 _____ Do you or your partner own or part-own any land or property of any kind, including **your own home,** in the United Kingdom or overseas?

☐ No   ☐ Yes ⟶ You will need to **complete form CRM15**: Go to **23**

21 _____ Do you or your partner have any savings or investments, in the United Kingdom or overseas?

(!)GUIDANCE ☐ No   ☐ Yes ⟶ You will need to **complete form CRM15**: Go to **23**

22 _____ Do your answers to the previous questions tell us that you have no income from any of the sources which we have asked about?

☐ No   ☐ Yes ⟶ How do you and your partner pay your bills and daily expenses?

```
┌─────────────────────────────────────────────┐
│                                               │
│                                               │
│                                               │
│                                               │
│                                               │
│                                               │
└─────────────────────────────────────────────┘
```

Information for the Interests of Justice test

23 _____ What charges have been brought against you?

(!)GUIDANCE

Describe the charge briefly: for instance, 'Assault on a neighbour'.

Charge	Date of offence
1 DOMESTIC DWELLING HOUSE BURGLARY	17 / 3 / ⌐ ⌐
2	
3	
4	

24 _____ The type of offence with which you are charged

(!)GUIDANCE
✓one box only.
If you are charged with two or more offences, ✓ the most serious.

☐ Class A: Homicide and related grave offences

☐ Class B: Offences involving serious violence or damage, and serious drugs offences

☐ Class C: Lesser offences involving violence or damage, and less serious drugs offences

☐ Class D: Sexual offences and offences against children ⟶

☑ Class E: Burglary etc

☐ Class F: Other offences of dishonesty (specified offences and offences where the value is £30,000 or less)

☐ Class G: Other offences of dishonesty (specified offences and offences where the value involved exceeds £30,000 but does not exceed £100,000)

☐ Class H: Miscellaneous other offences

☐ Class I: Offences against public justice and similar offences

☐ Class J: Serious sexual offences

☐ Class K: Other offences of dishonesty (high value: if the value involved exceeds £100,000)

25   **Do you have any co-defendants in this case?**

☑ No: Go to **27**   ☐ Yes ⟶ Their names

26   **Is there any reason why you and your co-defendants cannot be represented by the same solicitor?**

☐ No   ☐ Yes ⟶ The reason(s)

27   **Are there any other criminal cases or charges against you or your partner which are still in progress?**

☑ No   ☐ Yes ⟶ You   Your Partner

The charges

The Court hearing the case

Date of the next hearing

28   **Which Court is hearing the case for which you need legal aid?**

The Court hearing the case	Date of the hearing
LYME MAGISTRATES' COURT	20 / 3 /

29

Why do you want legal aid?

1 to **9** are possible reasons.

We suggest you choose one or more reasons with the help of a solicitor.

For each reason you choose, say why you have chosen it.

Mention any evidence that supports your choice of a reason.

If you need more space to answer, please use a separate sheet of paper and put your full name, date of birth and 'Question 29' at the top of the sheet. Please make sure you show which part of the question (**1** to **10**) your writing refers to.

1 It is likely that I will lose my liberty if any matter in the proceedings is decided against me.

SEE SEPARATE SHEET

2 I have been given a sentence that is suspended or non-custodial. If I break this, the court may be able to deal with me for the original offence.

SEE SEPARATE SHEET

3 It is likely that I will lose my livelihood.

4 It is likely that I will suffer serious damage to my reputation.

5 A substantial question of law may be involved (whether arising from legislation, judicial authority or other source of law).

SEE SEPARATE SHEET

6 I may not be able to understand the court proceedings or present my own case.

SEE SEPARATE SHEET

7 Witnesses may need to be traced or interviewed on my behalf.

SEE SEPARATE SHEET

8 The proceedings may involve expert cross-examination of a prosecution witness (whether an expert or not).

SEE SEPARATE SHEET

9 It is in the interests of another person (such as the person making a complaint or other witness) that I am represented.

SEE SEPARATE SHEET

10 Any other reason

SEE SEPARATE SHEET

Legal representation

30

ⓘ GUIDANCE

You must tell the solicitor that you have said in this form that you want them to act for you.

The solicitor who you want to act for you

Mr Mrs Miss Ms Other title

☐ ☐ ☐ ☑ ☐

Solicitor's initials, surname or family name (in BLOCK LETTERS)

RACHEL JAMES

Name and address of the solicitor's firm

HANNIBAL AND MOUNTFORD
20 HIGH STREET
LYME BANK
LYME
LY 82 P

Postcode

Telephone (land line)

01342220555

Mobile phone

0650097888

Document Exchange (DX)

DX 56499

Fax

email address

31

✓ **1** or **2**

If you choose **2**, ✓ one of the two other options to show whether you have been instructed by a firm with an LAA contract, or by a solicitor employed by the LAA. Examples of an LAA contract are the 2010 Standard Crime Contract or an Individual Case Contract.

Declaration by the legal representative

1 ☑ I represent the applicant. I confirm that I am authorised to provide representation under a contract issued by the Legal Aid Agency (LAA).

2 ☐ I represent the applicant. I confirm that I have been instructed to provide representation by:

☐ a firm which holds a contract issued by the Legal Aid Agency (LAA).

☐ a solicitor employed by the Legal Aid Agency (LAA) in the Public Defender Service who is authorised to provide representation.

Signed

Date

20 / 3 /

Provider's LAA Account Number

Y 5 6 8 8 D

Full name (in BLOCK LETTERS)

RACHEL JAMES

About the information which you have provided and its protection

32

ⓘ GUIDANCE

The guidance explains how we protect and use the information which you provide in our forms or in other ways.

■ The information which you give when you answer this question (which continues on page 8), will be treated in the strictest confidence and will not affect our decision on this application.

■ We, or HM Courts and Tribunals Service, may use the information on this form and on forms CRM15 and CRM15C, for statistical monitoring or research. The information we publish will not identify you or anyone else. We will process the information according to the Data Protection Act 1998 and other legal requirements.

1 Are you male or female?

☑ Male   ☐ Female   ☐ I prefer not to say

CRM 14 application: LENNY WISE: DOB: 27/6/-

Question 29-additional amplification

Reason 1
I am charged with domestic dwelling house burglary. Aggravating features of the offence include the fact that the victim is an 84 year old vulnerable woman who was tricked into giving access to her home. I have previous convictions of a similar nature. Based on the magistrates' court sentencing guidelines I am likely to be committed for sentence to the Crown Court where I am at risk of a custodial term in excess of twelve months.

Reason 2
I am subject to a community order for an offence of common assault. It was imposed eighteen months ago and has six months left to run for which I stand to be re-sentenced if convicted of the burglary charge.

Reason 5
I intend to challenge the admissibility of statements I made during interview at the police station under sections 76 and 78 PACE 1984. I was unrepresented at the police station and have a diagnosed mental illness. I felt unwell during my police interview and do not believe it was conducted in accordance with my rights.

Reason 6
I have diagnosed bipolar depression for which I take prescribed medication. I am subject to mood swings and cannot concentrate for long periods of time.

Reason 7
I believe I was at a betting shop when the offence occurred. My solicitors need to make enquiries of the staff in the shop to see if my presence at somewhere other than the crime scene at the relevant time can be established.

Reason 8
I intend to plead not guilty. There are several elderly eye-witnesses who identify me as being involved. They are all mistaken and need to be carefully cross-examined. The case against me also involves forensic expert evidence which I intend to challenge. The custody officers and investigating officers need to be cross-examined to enable me to challenge the admissibility of evidence obtained at the police station.

Reason 9
The eye-witnesses and the victim of the burglary are all elderly and therefore vulnerable. Each needs to be cross-examined.

Reason 10
The case is likely to be heard in the Crown Court due to the serious nature of the offence. I need to obtain an expert psychiatric report to assist my defence at trial.

② ✓ one box in the table to show the best definition of your disability.

The Equality Act 2010 defines disability as: 'A physical or mental impairment which has a substantial and long-term adverse effect on a person's ability to carry out normal day-to-day activities'.

③ ✓ one box in the table of ethnic groups.

② Do you consider that you have a disability?

☐ No   ✓ Yes ⟶ The best definition is:

✓ Mental health condition   ☐ Mobility impairment   ☐ Other

☐ Learning disability or difficulty   ☐ Long-standing physical illness or health condition   ☐ I prefer not to say

☐ Hearing impaired   ☐ Visually impaired

☐ Deaf   ☐ Blind

③ Which of the options in the table best describes you?

White	Mixed	Asian or Asian British	Black or Black British	
☐ British	☐ White and Black Caribbean	☐ Indian	✓ Black Caribbean	☐ Chinese
☐ Irish	☐ White and Black African	☐ Pakistani	☐ Black African	☐ Gypsy or Traveller
☐ White other	☐ White and Asian	☐ Bangladeshi	☐ Black other	☐ Other
	☐ Mixed other	☐ Asian other		☐ I prefer not to say

Evidence to support the information which you have given

33 _____ **Have you been directed to complete a form CRM15 (see questions 15, 17, 18, 20 and 21)?**

✓ No   ☐ Yes ⟶ If you have a partner, now go to **38**. If not, go to **39**.

34 _____ **Has a court remanded you in custody?**

☐ No: Go to **36**   ✓ Yes: Go to **35**

35 _____ **Will your case be heard in a magistrates' court?**

✓ No   ☐ Yes ⟶ If you have a partner, now go to **38**. If not, go to **39**.

36 _____ **Are you employed?**

ⓘ EVIDENCE

✓ No   ☐ Yes ⟶ ▪ **If your case will be heard in a magistrates' court, or it is a committal for sentence or appeal to the Crown Court** We need a copy of your wage slip or salary advice. You must provide it with this form: see the guidance about evidence.

ⓘ EVIDENCE

▪ **If your case will be heard in the Crown Court** We need a copy of your wage slip or salary advice. You must provide it with this form or within 14 days of the date of your application: see the guidance about evidence.

37 _____ If you have a partner, now go to **38**. If you do not have a partner, go to **39**.

Declaration by your partner

38

I declare that this form and any form CRM15 and CRM15C is a true statement of all my financial circumstances to the best of my knowledge and belief. I agree to the Legal Aid Agency and HM Courts & Tribunals Service, or my partner's solicitor, checking the information I have given, with the Department for Work and Pensions, HM Revenue and Customs or other people and organisations. I authorise those people and organisations to provide the information for which the Legal Aid Agency, HM Courts and Tribunals Service or my partner's solicitor may ask.

I have read the **Notice of Fraud** at the end of question **39**.

Signed

Date

Full name (in BLOCK LETTERS)

Declaration by you

39

When you read this declaration, keep in mind that some parts of it may not apply to you because the declaration is designed to cover several types of court case.

I apply for the right to representation for the purposes of criminal proceedings under the Legal Aid, Sentencing and Punishment of Offenders Act 2012.

I declare that this form and any form CRM15 and CRM15C is a true statement of my financial circumstances and those of my partner to the best of my knowledge and belief. I understand that this form must be fully completed before a Representation Order can be issued. I understand that if I tell you anything that is not true on this form or the documents I send with it, or leave anything out:

- I may be prosecuted for fraud. I understand that if I am convicted, I may be sent to prison or pay a fine.

- My legal aid may be stopped and I may be asked to pay back my costs in full to the Legal Aid Agency.

- If my case is in the Crown Court, the Legal Aid Agency may change the amount of the contribution which I must pay.

Crown Court I understand that in Crown Court proceedings the information I have given in this form will be used to determine whether I am liable to contribute to the costs of my defence under an Income Contribution Order during my case, or if I am convicted, under a Final Contribution Order at the end of my case, or both.

I understand that if I am ordered to pay towards my legal aid under an Income Contribution Order, or if I am convicted and ordered to pay under a Final Contribution Order, but fail to pay as an Order instructs me, interest may be charged or enforcement proceedings may be brought against me, or both.

I understand that I may have to pay the costs of the enforcement proceedings in addition to the payments required under the Contribution Order, and that the enforcement proceedings could result in a charge being placed on my home.

Evidence I agree to provide, when asked, further details and evidence of my finances and those of my partner, to the Legal Aid Agency, its agents, or HM Courts & Tribunals Service to help them decide whether an Order should be made and its terms.

Changes I agree to tell the Legal Aid Agency or HM Courts & Tribunals Service if my income or capital or those of my partner, change. These changes include the sale of property, change of address, change in employment and change in capital. →

It is important that you understand that by signing this declaration you agree to the Legal Aid Agency, the courts, or your solicitor, contacting your partner to check the information that you have given in this form, and in forms CRM15 and CRM15C, if you complete them.

Enquiries

I authorise such enquiries as are considered necessary to enable the Legal Aid Agency, its agents, HM Courts & Tribunals Service, or my solicitor to find out my income and capital, and those of my partner. This includes my consent for parties such as my bank, building society, the Department for Work and Pensions, the Driver and Vehicle Licensing Agency or HM Revenue and Customs to provide information to assist the Legal Aid Agency, it's agents or HM Courts & Tribunals Service with their enquiries.

I consent to the Legal Aid Agency or my solicitor contacting my partner for information and evidence about my partner's means. This includes circumstances where my partner is unable to sign or complete the form.

I understand that if the information which my partner provides is incorrect, or if my partner refuses to provide information, then: if my case is in the magistrates' court, my legal aid may be withdrawn or, if my case is in the Crown Court, I may be liable to sanctions. I understand that the sanctions may result in me paying towards the cost of my legal aid or, if I already pay, paying more towards the cost of my legal aid, or paying my legal aid costs in full.

Ending legal aid I understand that I must tell my solicitor and write to the court if I no longer want public representation. I understand that if I decline representation I may be liable for costs incurred to the date when my solicitor and the court receive my letter.

Data sharing I agree that, if I am convicted, the information in this form will be used by HMCTS or designated officer to determine the appropriate level of any financial penalty ordered against me, and for its collection and enforcement.

Notice on fraud If false or inaccurate information is provided and fraud is identified, details will be passed to fraud prevention agencies to prevent fraud and money laundering.

Further details explaining how the information held by fraud prevention agencies may be used can be found in the 'Fair Processing Notice', available on the Legal Aid Agency website at: www.justice.gov.uk/legal-aid/make-an-application

Signed	Date
Lenny Wise	20 3 —

Full name (in BLOCK LETTERS)

LENNY WISE

If your partner has not signed the declaration at **38**, please explain:

Official use

Interests of Justice test

Consider all the available details of all the charges, against the Interests of Justice criteria.

Mention issues here which you considered when you decided the application. Include information given orally.

I have performed the Interests of Justice test for case number: 42 9 5 1 0 0 L M 4 9 0 1 3 0

☑ The application is **passed**   ☐ The application is **refused.** My reason(s):

Signed _(signature)_

Name of the appropriate officer: JOHN GOODWIN

Date: 20 / 3 / —

Financial eligibility for

Magistrates' Court   ☑ Passed   ☐ Refused

Crown Court   ☑ No income contribution   ☐ Contribution of   £ _____

Signed _(signature)_

Name of the appropriate officer: JOHN GOODWIN

Date: 20 / 3 / —

DOCUMENT 6 PROOF OF EVIDENCE OF LENNY WISE

Lenny Wise of Flat 4a, Lymewood Court, Parkdale, Lyme, will state:

1. I am 27 years old and of mixed race origin. My father is from the Caribbean and my mother (who is deceased) was white. My date of birth is the 26/7/- I have been charged in connection with a burglary at the home of an 84-year-old woman in Sunrise Road, Lyme which occurred on the 17th March at around midday. I will plead not guilty and am innocent of the charge. I was not represented at the police station prior to being charged and have been refused police bail. I am also charged with possession of a small quantity of cannabis. I intend to plead guilty to this.

2. I was arrested at home on the 19th March as I was leaving my flat. I could not believe it. The next thing I knew they were searching my flat. They seized some of my clothing and a pair of training shoes. I was taken to a police car and shoved in the back and taken to the police station.

3. I was taken to Lyme Street Police Station, and had to stay there overnight. I cannot remember if my rights were explained. The police told me I would be detained overnight because they wanted me to participate in an identification procedure and it would take time to organise. I have been in this situation before. I recall asking for an identification parade but was told I would have a video parade. I was photographed not long after arriving at the police station. I watched the officer put together a video parade but I did not have a clue what was going on. I understand that several witnesses have been shown the video and one of them has picked me out.

4. It was a difficult night in detention. I did not get much sleep and I was really worried about my dog Butch. I live on my own and there is no one to see to him. The police did try to ring my sister but she could not be reached. I was also craving a cigarette as I am a chain smoker. Additionally, I am a diagnosed manic depressive. I am prone to erratic behaviour and mood swings. Sometimes I get very depressed. My medication helps but it has side effects and I do not take it as regularly as I should. I cannot recall whether I was asked about this when I arrived at the police station as it is all a bit of a blur. I told the police the following morning that I needed my medication and that I felt unwell. When I told the officer that I needed my medication for depression, a police doctor was called. Somebody must have gone to my flat to get my pills. I was checked over by the police doctor who gave me my tablets. He said I was fit to be interviewed which I was happy about. I thought that once I was interviewed I would be able to get out and see to things.

5. I believe it was explained to me that I could see a solicitor if I wanted to. To be honest I did not think there was much point as the police were going to charge me whatever I said. When the police said they were going to interview me at last, I did not want to delay matters further by requesting a solicitor. I regret the decision now. I kept telling the officers that I needed a smoke. I was told that it was up to me. In the circumstances, I just told the police what they wanted to hear. I wish to retract my confession. It is untrue.

6. I understand that another man is alleged to have been involved in the burglary. His name is Lloyd Green. I know of Lloyd Green. He is a drug dealer and has supplied drugs to me in the past. He is no longer my supplier. Green has got rough with me in the past when I owed him money.

7. I have been trying to recollect my whereabouts on Tuesday the 17th between 11.30am–12.30pm. My daily routine is to get up at about 10am. I usually leave my flat at around 10.30am and walk my dog. Pretty much every day, I go down the High Street to place a bet or visit my girlfriend who lives just off the High Street. I think I may have been in my bookmakers—Gladbrookes in the High Street at around 11.30am—and there might be someone there who could verify the fact. I place a small bet most days just before lunch time and I am fairly certain that that was where I was.

8. I do know the area around Sunrise Road. It is quite close to where I live. I often walk my dog on fields near to the back of Sunrise Road. I know one or two of the residents in the street. Most residents are friendly, but one or two of them are a little suspicious of me. The rear gardens of the houses in Sunrise Road which back onto the fields are not fenced off so it is possible for a person to wander onto the lawns at the back of the houses.

9. I do not understand how I have come to be identified as the man seen running away from the back of the burgled property. It was not me. I can only assume it must have been someone else who maybe looks similar in appearance to me. In actuality, I am 5'10". I am of slim build. I have medium length dreadlocked hair and a slight beard. The police mentioned something about the white training shoes being worn by the burglar. I do not own a pair of white trainers. The trainers recovered from my flat were left there by a friend. I have never worn them.

10. So far as my personal circumstances are concerned, I live on my own in a housing association flat. I have a girlfriend. Her name is Sonia. We have been seeing each other on and off for six months, although we have not been living together. Sonia is four months pregnant with my child. The pregnancy was not planned. Sonia already has a child of her own. She is hoping to move to better accommodation as her present flat only has one bedroom. I am anxious to see Sonia. I need to know if she and the baby are okay.

11. I do not work. I am in receipt of income support. With my criminal record and my medical condition, it is difficult for me to get work. Having said that, I have a job interview next week—something my probation officer has organised. It is with a floor laying company. The owner has taken on ex-offenders in the past and is prepared to give me an interview. This could offer me the first real prospect of a job leading to full-time employment.

12. I get on very well with my sister, Tessa. She is my half-sister. She is a single mother. I see my sister once or twice a week. She makes sure my flat is clean and that I have food in. My mother died when I was 14 and my father left us when I was three. I don't know where he lives. Tessa, who is six years my senior, looked after me when our mother died.

13. I have been smoking cannabis since the age of 15. I became addicted to hard drugs, including crack, in my early twenties. At this time I was mixing with a lot of low-life individuals and having to commit crimes in order to pay off debts and fund my drug habit. Prison was really hard. Drugs were available but I stayed off hard drugs. When I finished my prison sentence I got myself a girlfriend and some stability. However, it was at this time that I began suffering with mental problems which I assumed were due to my drug addiction. I wish to make it clear that I am no longer addicted to drugs and only smoke cannabis very occasionally when I am feeling really depressed and weird. I must get bail. I cannot face going back to prison. I had not smoked any cannabis in the 24 hours before my arrest.

14. My GP is Dr Shaw at the Havelock Medical Centre, Willow Lane, Lyme. I do see a consultant psychiatrist at the Royal Lyme Hospital but I cannot recall his name. I am happy for my medical notes to be released.

15. I am currently subject to supervision by the Probation Service as part of a community order I received for an offence of assault. As part of the order, I was ordered to undergo psychiatric treatment. It was as a consequence of this that doctors diagnosed my mental illness. I have a really supportive probation officer, Maxine, with whom I get on really well. She understands my problems and is the one who has secured me a job interview.

16. I do have previous convictions but I cannot recall them all. I have previous convictions for burglary, drug use and assault. My most recent offence of assault was committed 18 months ago. It was very much out of character for me. I am not a violent man. The assault stemmed from a breakdown of a relationship and was committed shortly before my illness was diagnosed and treatment for it began. Aggressive tendencies are not uncommon in sufferers of manic depression and this may have been a contributing factor in the commission of this offence.

17. I have convictions for possession of amphetamine and cocaine and convictions for theft. Most of the theft offences relate to shoplifting committed in order to obtain drugs. As far as I can remember the burglary offences were drug related. I have previous convictions for failing bail. I have no excuse. I simply did not turn up at court. I suspect I was so out of it while on drugs that I simply forgot. To the best of my recollection, I have always pleaded guilty.

Lenny Wise
27th March

DOCUMENT 7   CONSIDERATION OF ADVANCE INFORMATION

26th March

Engaged considering the Advance Information and drafting proof of evidence.

Having considered the evidence, I am of the view that Lenny should indicate a not guilty plea at the plea before venue. It is unlikely (given the seriousness of the offence and the likely sentence in the event of conviction) that the Magistrates' Court would accept jurisdiction to try this matter. In the unlikely event of Lenny being presented with a choice, my considered opinion is that he would, in any event, be best advised to elect a Crown Court trial for the following reasons:

- He stands a better chance of being acquitted.
- There are areas of disputed evidence which are best dealt with in the absence of the jury.
- A qualified judge would be more confident about excluding evidence.

Against is:

- The risk of a higher sentence (although I strongly suspect that the Magistrates' Court would commit for sentence in any event).
- It will take longer to come to trial and if remanded in custody throughout, this would be an important consideration for Lenny.
- Defence statement is mandatory—but if the case is sent to the Crown Court we stand a better chance of flushing out further disclosure.

The advantages of the Crown Court outweigh those in favour of the Magistrates' Court in Lenny's case. In any event the exercise is likely to be academic since the magistrates will almost certainly decline jurisdiction and send for trial in the Crown Court.

Time engaged: 20 minutes

DOCUMENT 11   LYMESHIRE POLICE CUSTODY RECORD

Station: **Lyme Street**

Reasons for Arrest
Burglary of dwelling house

Comments made by person, if present when facts of arrest were explained. Y/N [N]. If Yes, comments on log.

Video Tape Ref. No. LT/369

DETAINED PERSON'S RIGHTS
An extract from a notice setting out my rights has been read to me and I have been given a copy. I have also been provided with a written notice setting out my entitlements while in custody.

Signature: **Lenny Wise**
Date: 19/3/-   Time: 16.15

LEGAL ADVICE REQUESTED
DETAILS:
I want to speak to a solicitor as soon as practicable

Signature:
Time: Date:

LEGAL ADVICE DECLINED
I have been informed that I may speak to a solicitor
IN PERSON OR ON THE TELEPHONE:

I do not want to speak to a solicitor at this time.
Signature: **Lenny Wise**
Time: 19/3   Date: 15.45

Reasons given, for not wanting legal advice
None given

NOTIFICATION OF A NAMED PERSON
REQUESTED Y/N [Y]
Details of nominated person
Theresa Wise (Sister)

APPROPRIATE ADULT Y/N [N]

INTERPRETER Y/N [N]
Notices served & grounds for detention explained in the presence of Appropriate Adult/Interpreter

Signature of A/Adult

Time: Date:

Surname: **WISE**

Previous Name:

Forenames: **LENNY**

Address: **4A**
LYMEWOOD COURT
PARKDALE
LYME

Telephone

Occupation: **NONE**
Age: **27**   Date of Birth: **27/6/-**

Place of Birth: **LONDON**

Height: **5** Feet: **11** Inches: Sex: **M**

Arrested by:
Name: DS S Farrington
ID. No: 4291
Station: Lyme Street
Place of Arrest: 4a Lymewood Court, Lyme

	Time	Date
Arrested at:	15.30	19/3/-
Arrived at Station	16.10	19/3/-

Officer In Case:
Id. No: 4291
Name: DS Farrington

Officer Opening Custody Record

Signature: Mike Williams

Id No: 4231
Name: Sgt M Williams

CHARGES(S)

Surname **WISE**	Custody No. 2305/05
Forename (s) **LENNY**	Station: Lyme
	Sex M/F (M)
Address **4A Lymewood Court**	D.O.B 27/6/-
Parkdale	
Lyme	ID Code: 1
Postcode	Language: None

You are charged with the offence(s) shown below. You do not have to say anything. But it may harm your defence if you do not mention now something which you later rely on in court. Anything you do say may be given in evidence.

Consec. No.	Charge(s)
1.	That on the 17th March having entered as a trespasser a building, being a dwelling known as 19 Sunrise Road, Lyme you stole £75 in money property belonging to Lillian Kennedy contrary to s. 9(1)(a) Theft Act 1968
2.	That on the 19th March you unlawfully had in your possession a controlled drug of Class B namely cannabis, contrary to section 5(2) Misuse of Drugs Act 1971

Time and Date of Charge: 20th March   12.45hrs
Reply (if any): "you are racist pigs you lot are."

Signed (person charged)	Signed (appropriate adult)			
Officer charging Surname Farrington	Rank DS	No.4291	Station: Lyme St
Officer in case Surname	Rank	No.	Station
Charge accepted Surname	Rank	No.	Station

Appearing at LYME REMAND COURT at LYME SQUARE, LYME on the 20/3/   at 1400 hours

LYMESHIRE POLICE
DETAINED PERSONS MEDICAL FORM

Custody Ref: 2305/05

Name: Lenny Wise	DOB: 27/6/-	Time/Date: 20/3/-

Reason Doctor requested:
Detainee telling me he felt claustrophobic and needed to take medication for depression

VISUAL ASSESSMENT BY CUSTODY SERGEANT

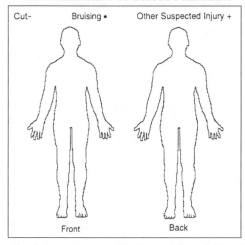

Cut-   Bruising •   Other Suspected Injury +

Front   Back

ADMINISTRATION AND MOVEMENT TIMES

	Time	Date
Doctor called	0700	20/3/-
Doctor replied		
Agreed Arrival Time		
Doctor Arrived	0745	20/3/-
Departure/Conclusion		
Ambulance Called		
Ambulance Arrived		
Detainee taken to Hospital		Time/Date

Police-Signs/symptoms & First Aid given:
Observed detainee seemed very fidgety

By whom:

DOCTORS OPINION OR TELEPHONE ADVICE (NON-CONFIDENTIAL)

Name of Doctor: Dr A Ghulam

Time/Date of Examination: 20/3/- 0800 hrs

Opinion: Anxious but lucid in thought. Orientated in time and space. Takes regular medication for manic depression

Medical Advice: Medicate per prescription

Examination/Observation: Completed/Refused   **Risk of Self Harm:** High/Medium/Standard

Location of Examination: Medical room/Cell/Other   **Station:** Lyme Street

RECOMMENDATIONS

	Yes	No		Yes	No
Recommended appropriate adult:		*	Medical review Required		*
Fit to be detained:	*		Time/Date required: Time/Date carried Out:		

	Yes	No
Fit for interview:	*	
Fit for transfer		
Fit for charge:		

Doctors Signature:
Ghulam

LYMESHIRE POLICE

| Station: **LYME STREET** | Detained Person Serial No: **2305/357** |

| Surname: **WISE** |
| Forenames: **LENNY** |

Last review of detention conducted at:

<u>Date</u>	<u>Time</u>	<u>Details of Action/Occurrence</u>	
19/3/-	1610	DP arrived.	MW
	1615	DP searched—property removed. Rights explained. Detention authorised to secure and preserve evidence and to obtain evidence by questioning. DP taken to cell by officers—Cell F4.	MW
	1630	Phone call to DP's sister 821249 (no contact made no answering machine). DP informed.	MW
	1700	DP accepted hot drink.	MW
	1730	DP taken meal—refused.	MW
	1800	DP seen in cell—in order.	MW
	1815	DP consents to taking saliva swab—non-intimate	MW
	1816	'I consent to providing a sample of my saliva.' Lenny Wise	
	1830	DP taken to Identification suite for photographing and parade compilation.	MW
	1930	DP returned to my custody—placed in Cell F4.	MW
	1935	DP given a cup of tea—asking for cigarette.	MW
	1955	DP uses toilet.	MW
	2015	In cell awake and pacing.	MW
	2030	In cell awake—muttering.	MW

LYMESHIRE POLICE

| Station: **LYME STREET** | Detained Person Serial No: **2305/357** |

Surname: **WISE**
Forenames: **LENNY**

Last review of detention conducted at: **2200 hours 19/3/**

Date	Time	Details of Action/Occurrence	
	2100	Banging on cell—uses toilet.	MW
	2130	In cell—pacing—requests cigarette—refused.	MW
	2200	In cell—in order. Custody transferred to Sgt Tom Slater. Detention reviewed. DP informed.	TS
	2230	In cell—sitting on bed wringing hands.	TS
	2300	In cell—in order.	TS
	2330	In cell—pacing.	TS
	2345	Given refreshment.	TS
	2359	DP—on bed awake.	TS
20/3/-	0015	DP in cell pacing. Requests cigarette.	TS
	0045	On bed—suspect rocking back and forwards. Asked if okay. Requested more blankets supplied. DP informed me he wanted to sleep.	TS
	0115	DP in cell—awake. In order.	TS
	0145	DP in cell—uses toilet.	TS
	0215	DP in cell—asleep.	TS
	0245	DP—awake lying on bed.	TS
	0315	DP seen pacing in cell.	TS

LYMESHIRE POLICE

Station: **LYME STREET**	Detained Person Serial No: **2305/357**

Surname: **WISE**
Forenames: **LENNY**

Last review of detention conducted at: **0700 hours 20/3/**

Date	Time	Details of Action/Occurrence	
20/3/	0345	DP awake—humming to himself.	TS
	0415	DP lying on bed—in order.	TS
	0445	DP awake—sitting on bed.	TS
	0515	DP taken to toilet.	TS
	0545	DP in cell pacing.	TS
	0603	DP complains of feeling unwell. Requests doctor.	TS
	0610	Transferred into custody of Sgt Brough.	DB
	0630	DP offered breakfast. Informed by DP that his regular medication for depression is at home. FME requested. Officer dispatched to DP's house to locate medication.	DB
	0645	DP uses toilet. Informed GP requested to attend.	DB
	0700	Review of detention. DP informed.	DB
	0740	DP taken to medical room for examination by Dr Ghulam.	DB
	0800	Dr Ghulam completes report—medication administered to DP who is fit to be interviewed. DP taken back to cell F4.	DB
	0815	DP in cell. In order.	DB
	0900	DP offered refreshment. Requests cigarette.	DB

LYMESHIRE POLICE

| Station: **LYME STREET** | Detained Person Serial No: **2305/357** |

| Surname: **WISE** |
| Forenames: **LENNY** |

Last review of detention conducted at: **0700 hours 20/3/**

Date	Time	Details of Action/Occurrence	
20/3/-	0915	DP informed of intention to interview—asked if requires solicitor—refuses one.	DB
	0930	DP in cell. In order.	DB
	1000	DP asking when interview will be.	DB
	1030	DP in cell—agitated—pacing.	DB
	1045	DP in cell—allowed to use toilet.	DB
	1100	DP in cell pacing.	DB
	1115	DP given to the custody of DS Farrington and taken to interview room 2.	DB
	1230	Returned to my custody.	DB
	1245	DP charged and documented. Bail refused on grounds of risk of absconding and commission of further offences. DP's sister contacted and informed. DP allowed to speak with sister.	DB
	1300	Into custody of Premier for transport to Lyme MC.	DB

DOCUMENT 15   RECORD OF ALLOCATION HEARING

27 March

Attending Lyme Magistrates' Court. I explained to Lenny and his sister that I did not feel that the magistrates would accept jurisdiction but that if they did he should elect trial by jury on the burglary charge in any event.

An indication of a guilty plea was entered in relation to the possession of cannabis charge and a not-guilty plea was entered in relation to the burglary matter. An allocation hearing was held with the CPS inviting the magistrates to decline jurisdiction. No representations from us in relation to allocation. Jurisdiction declined—case sent to the Crown Court and adjourned to 30th June for a PCMH (Plea and Case Management Hearing) before the Crown Court.

The magistrates indicated a willingness to sentence Lenny on the possession of cannabis matter. Consequently I briefly addressed the Bench in terms of sentence and a 12-month conditional discharge was imposed.

I made a second full application for bail on Lenny's behalf. Bail was once more refused on the grounds of the risk of absconding and commission of further offences.

Spoke to Lenny after the hearing and we agreed I would appeal the refusal of bail to the Crown Court.

Time engaged:
Advocacy 40 minutes
Waiting 10 minutes
Attending client 30 minutes
Travel to and from court 15 minutes
Preparing Notice of Appeal 15 minutes.

 online resource centre

You can see the plea before venue followed by the allocation (mode of trial enquiry) on the burglary charge in the Lenny Wise video section of our Online Resource Centre. It precedes Lenny's contested application for bail. A transcript, broadly based on the bail hearing, appears at Document 17. We would ask you to note that the prosecutor's reference to sentencing guidelines on burglary in the Magistrates' Court Sentencing Guidelines have now been superseded by revised burglary guidelines issued by the Sentencing Council for England and Wales in January 2012. Please note that this courtroom scene was filmed when the mode of trial (pre schedule 3 CJA 2003) procedure was in use. Under the new allocation procedure, the prosecutor would have disclosed Lenny's previous convictions as part of the allocation hearing further confirming the magistrates' court's decision in this case to decline summary jurisdiction to try Lenny.

DOCUMENT 16 STANDARD CASE SENT DIRECTIONS

MAGISTRATES' COURT

DIRECTIONS FOR CASE SENT TO THE CROWN COURT

..... *Lyme* .../.../..... ... . **Magistrates' Court**

Date sent: ...... 27 / 3 / — ......

The Plea and Case Management Hearing will take place

on...... 30th June ...... at .... Lyme ....**Crown Court**

Name of defendant	Case no	Remand status	Youth jointly charged with adult?	Represented by:
D1 Lenny Wise	T49521 9L	Bail/cust/*COM		Hannibal + Mountford
D2		Bail/cust/*COM		
D3		Bail/cust/*COM		
D4		Bail/cust/*COM		

* COM= in custody on other matters

Defence telephone numbers:
D1.01005 678 467(home)...........................(mobile)   D1 solicitor ....(office)
D2.............................(home)...........................(mobile)   D2 solicitor ....(office)
D3.............................(home)...........................(mobile)   D3 solicitor ....(office)
D4.............................(home)...........................(mobile)   D4 solicitor ....(office)

Prosecution telephone number...

CASE DETAILS

1. Has the defendant been advised that the case may proceed in his or her absence?

D1: Y ☑ N ☐   D2: Y ☐ N ☐

D3: Y ☐N ☐   D4: Y ☐ N ☐

2. Has the defendant been advised about credit for pleading guilty?

D1: Y ☑ N ☐   D2: Y ☐ N ☐

D3: Y ☐ N ☐   D4: Y ☐ N ☐

3. What pleas, if any, are indicated?
D1:..... Not guilty to charge of S 9(1)(b) Theft Act 1968.
D2:...
D3:...
D4:...

NOTE: If the defendant decides to plead guilty after sending, the Crown Court must be notified immediately. The Crown Court will then list the case for a hearing as soon as possible.

4. Does the defence intend to make an application under section 41 of the Youth Justice and Criminal Evidence Act 1999 to cross-examine the complainant about his or her sexual history? ....(to be served within 28 days of primary/initial disclosure)

5. Please give details of any other matters which should be dealt with at the same time as these proceedings (e.g. other offences, offences to be taken into consideration).
D1:...   D2:...
....
D3:...   D4:...
....

Insert date by which Action 1 to be completed in the blank box:

ACTION	TIME LIMITS	DIRECTIONS
1	**Cust:** 50 days after sent* **Bail:** 70 days after sent*	• Prosecution to serve draft indictment, case papers and primary or initial disclosure.
2	**14 days after Action 1**	• Defence to notify prosecution of witness requirements • Prosecution to serve any application for hearsay or defendant's bad character • Defence to serve: (i) Defence statement* (including any alibi details) OR notification of guilty plea (ii) Any application for hearsay/bad character (iii) Any notice of application to dismiss charges
3	**28 days after Action 1**	• Prosecution to serve final draft indictment and any special measures applications • Defence to serve any application under section 41 of the Youth Justice and Criminal Evidence Act 1999
4	**14 days after Action 2**	• Prosecution to serve responses to hearsay/bad character/dismissal of charges applications • Defence to serve response to hearsay/bad character application by prosecution
5	**14 days after Action 3**	• Defence to serve response to any prosecution application for special measures • Prosecution and defence to notify Crown Court of names of trial advocate and time estimate • Defence to notify Crown Court of non-availability of expert witnesses, with reasons • Witness Care Unit to notify Crown Court and prosecution of dates when witnesses required by defence are unavailable, with reasons

NOTE: if any party seeks a subsequent variation in the timetable or further direction, a written application must be made to the Crown Court within 14 days of date sent, and copies served on all other parties. A Crown Court judge may make directions as appropriate or fix a preliminary hearing. If at any time either party is unable to comply with any direction, it must notify the Case Progression Officer immediately and apply to the Crown Court for a variation.

* indicates those time limits which cannot be varied by a magistrates' court.

Please record any further directions here:

Received...................................(defence signature).........................(prosecution signature)

DOCUMENT 20   RECORD OF CROWN COURT BAIL HEARING

File Note—29th March

Attending Lyme Crown Court. Appearing before Mr Recorder Jay. Making a further application for bail on behalf of Lenny Wise. Bail was opposed by the CPS. Lenny was granted conditional bail as follows:

1. He resides at 4A Lymewood Court.

2. He reports to Lyme Street Police Station Mon/Wed/Friday 2–3pm.

3. He does not attempt to contact in any way Lillian Kennedy, Shirley Lewis or Harold Finney.

4. He does not go in to Sunrise Road or on the fields at the back of Sunrise Road.

Telephoning Lenny's sister to relay the good news. Explained he would be released and that I would be writing to him to stress the importance of abiding by bail conditions. Reminded her that Lenny was due to appear before Lyme Magistrates' on the 24th April.

Time engaged:
Advocacy 30 minutes
Waiting 5 minutes
Travel to and from court 15 minutes.

NB: Solicitor would need to write to Lenny advising him of his change in bail status and the importance of abiding by the conditions of his bail.

DOCUMENT 25 CPS LETTER REGARDING SERVICE OF CASE SENT BUNDLE

Important note: The letter below is the authors' interpretation of the type of letter that a solicitor might receive from the Crown Prosecution Service. The letter is not representative of any communication sent by the Crown Prosecution Service and should not be seen as representative of how the Crown Prosecution Service would respond in this scenario.

CROWN PROSECUTION SERVICE
Queen's Chambers
Blackburn Street
Lyme
LY3 2BE
Date: 15/5/-
Ref: AH/IW
Your ref: RJ/SAW

Hannibal and Mountford Solicitors
20 High Street
Lyme Bank
Lyme
LY10 34 T

Dear Sir
REGINA v LENNY WISE
PCMH: 30th JUNE
SECTION 51, CRIME AND DISORDER ACT 1998
NOTICE OF SERVICE OF CASE AND WITNESS REQUIREMENTS

Notice of Service of the case
The copy statements [and depositions] that accompany this notice constitute the copies of the documents containing the evidence on which the current charge or charges are based.

These documents are served in accordance with Paragraph 1 of Schedule 3 of the Crime and Disorder Act 1998 ("the 1998 Act") and the Crime and Disorder Act 1998 (Service of Prosecution Evidence) Regulations 2000.

You are reminded that by virtue of paragraph 5 of Schedule 8 of the 1998 Act, the bill of indictment in the Crown Court may include – either in substitution for or in addition to any count you are currently charged with any counts founded on the evidence hereby served on you (being counts which can be lawfully joined in the same indictment).

Request for information concerning defence witness requirements
The written statements [and depositions] referred to above have been made by the witnesses named below. Application may be made to the court by the prosecution for each of these statements [and depositions] to be read out at the trial without oral evidence being given by the witness who has made the statement or deposition, unless I hear from you to the contrary.

If you want a witness to attend and give oral evidence, and to be cross-examined if necessary, you should inform the Crown Court and me in writing as soon as possible, and in any case, at least two weeks before the date of the Plea and Case Management Hearing set by the Court. This will enable the police to check on a witness' availability to attend court and avoid the costs and delay associated with any further adjournments for this purpose.

Failure to let me know which witnesses you wish to be called may result in the court allowing a witness' statement [or deposition] to be read, and therefore in your being unable to cross-examine that witness.

You should however be aware that the prosecutor may, at his or her discretion, require the attendance of a witness to give oral evidence, even if you have indicated that you do not wish that witness to attend to give oral evidence at the trial.

Request for additional information: pleas and admissions

Additionally, you are requested to inform me as soon as possible:

- whether you intend to admit all or some of the current charges. If so, which ones?

- whether you are prepared to make any admissions under Section 10 Criminal Justice Act 1967, which may avoid the attendance of witnesses. If so, please give details.

If you have a solicitor acting for you in this case, you should take immediate steps to bring this notice and statements [and depositions] to his or her attention as soon as possible.

<u>Additional evidence</u>
Other evidence, if any and if relevant, may be served in response to any notice served by virtue of the Crime and Disorder Act 1998 (Dismissal of Charges Sent) Rules 1998, or under a notice of further evidence at a later stage.

<u>Name of witnesses whose statements (and depositions) are enclosed:</u>
See attached list

A copy of this Notice is being served on the court for their information.

Please send any reply quoting the case name and URN number to the address given above.

Yours faithfully,

For Chief Crown Prosecutor

For Graduated Fee Scheme purposes—the **updated** page count is now:		
Statements	**Exhibits**	**Photographs etc**

Yours faithfully,
Andrew Hurst
Principal Crown Prosecutor

DOCUMENT 26   EXTRACTS FROM THE CASE SENT BUNDLE

NOTE TO THE READER
We have included the front sheets of a typical case sent bundle. In addition to the extracts we have included here, you would also receive typed versions of the prosecution's witness statements (comprising used material) as well as a full transcript of interview.

The charge(s) set out on the Schedule(s) attached to the accompanying papers has/have been prepared in indictment form in consequence of the responsibility which the Crown Prosecution Service has in relation to the form and content of indictments.

Schedules also serve as draft indictments following a sending of a case to the Crown Court but may be subject to amendments, or replaced by a new draft settled by Counsel, before being preferred for signature by the appropriate officer of the Crown Court. A copy of the indictment as signed will be supplied in the usual way.

DRAFT INDICTMENT

INDICTMENT (No........)

CROWN COURT AT LYME

THE QUEEN -V- LENNY WISE

LENNY WISE is charged as follows:

Count 1: **STATEMENT OF OFFENCE**

BURGLARY, contrary to section 9(1)(b) of the Theft Act 1968.

PARTICULARS OF OFFENCE

LENNY WISE on the 17th day of March having entered as a trespasser a building, being a dwelling known as 19 Sunrise Road Lyme, stole therein £75 in money.

Lillian Kennedy

Officer of the Court

REGINA

-V-

LENNY WISE

Statements

No.	Name of Witness	Date of Statement	Page No (s)
1.	L Kennedy	18/3/-	
2.	L Kennedy	20/3/-	
3.	S Lewis	18/3/-	
4.	S Lewis	20/3/-	
5.	H Finney	18/3/-	
6.	H Finney	20/3/-	
7.	S Farrington	20/3/-	
8.	S Shaw	20/3/-	
9.	A Khan	20/3/-	
10.	E Mason	20/3/-	
11.	C Sutton	20/3/-	
12.	J Bradbury	20/3/-	
13.	P Reynolds (x2)	19/3/-	
14.	C Lawton	20/3/-	
15.	S Hardacker	25/3/-	

REGINA

-V-

LENNY WISE

Exhibit List

No	Reference	Item
1.	SF2	Left size 9 Nike training shoe
2.	SF3	Right size 9 Nike training shoe
3.	SF6/a	Tape recorded interview/Wise Tape Reference 21/SF/59217/03–*
4.	SF6/b	Transcript of interview/Wise*
5.	CJL1	Album of photographs of shoeprints in situ
6.	CJL2	Shoe print lift
7.	CJL3	Shoe print lift
8.	SF5	Black hooded sweatshirt
9.	PR1	DVD Compilation of Video Images Ref 05/01166/20A
10.	CS2	Video of Video Identification viewing process-film ref. no. 277/05

N.B. Exhibits marked * are served with the committal papers, other exhibits may be examined on suitable appointment.

DOCUMENT 26A   WITNESS STATEMENT: LILLIAN KENNEDY

WITNESS STATEMENT

(CJ Act 1967, s. 9; MC Act 1980, s. 5A(3)(a) and s. 5B; Crim PR, Part 27)

Name	Lillian Kennedy
Address	Supplied
Age/Date of Birth	Over 18
Occupation	Retired

....

Who states:

This statement, consisting of one page signed by me, is true to the best of my knowledge and belief and I make it knowing that if it is tendered in evidence I shall be liable to prosecution if I have wilfully stated in it anything which I know to be false or do not believe to be true.

Dated: 18th March   Signed: L Kennedy

....

I live at number 19 Sunrise Road, Lyme. I am 85 years old. On Tuesday the 17th March, I went to fetch my pension from Lyme High Street. I drew £95.00. Once I had paid my weekly sums for gas and electricity I was left with around £75. I got home at around 11 am. As I was walking up the road, a man approached me and asked me if I wanted any help with my shopping. I told him, no thank you. I would describe him as being quite tall and thin. He had a gaunt face, was black and had long, black, straggling hair and a small beard on his chin. I think he was wearing a short, dark coloured top and a pair of white sports shoes. I saw him walk off into the fields near the back of my house.

I know I had my purse with me when I went into my house, because a friend of mine called in for 10 minutes, shortly after I got back from the Post Office. She had her grandchild with her and I gave her a pound from my purse. A short time after this I was putting some rubbish out when I thought I heard the telephone ringing. When I came in, I realised it was my front door bell. I answered the door. There was a man standing there. I have never seen this man before. He was white but had a tanned complexion. He was dressed smartly, wearing a suit and tie. He was quite bald. He was not very tall. I recall he was wearing dark glasses. He told me his car had broken down and asked if he could use the telephone. I told him he could not as I did not have a phone. Not long after this, a friend of my neighbour came round. She told me she had seen a man in my back garden and that my back door was open. I immediately checked my handbag and saw that my purse was missing. She telephoned the police. I realised that I had left the back door open when I came to answer the front door. It was silly of me. The only money I get is my pension. The break in has left me shaken and frightened.

Later in the afternoon of the 17th March, the police took me around the local area in one of their cars. They asked me if I could see the man who had knocked on my front door. I could not see the man who had called but I did see the man who had offered to help me with my shopping earlier that morning. The police car stopped outside the Co-op on the High Street. I had a good look at the man and I am sure it was him.

Signed: Lillian Kennedy

DOCUMENT 26B WITNESS STATEMENT: SHIRLEY LEWIS

<u>WITNESS STATEMENT</u>

(CJ Act 1967, s. 9; MC Act 1980, s. 5A(3)(a) and s. 5B; Crim PR, Part 27)

Name	Shirley Lewis
Address	Supplied
Age/Date of Birth	Over 18
Occupation	Retired Teacher

....

Who states:

This statement, consisting of one page signed by me, is true to the best of my knowledge and belief, and I make it knowing that if it is tendered in evidence I shall be liable to prosecution if I have wilfully stated in it anything which I know to be false or do not believe to be true.

Dated: 18th March   Signed: S Lewis

....

On Tuesday the 17th March, I was visiting my elderly aunt at 19 Sunrise Road, Lyme. She lives next door to Lillian Kennedy at number 17. At around midday on Tuesday 17th March, I went out the back of my aunt's property to bring some washing in that was pegged up on the washing line. The time was around midday.

I was facing Lillian's back garden. A low wall divides the gardens, it being largely open plan. I saw a man in her garden. I watched him for a good few seconds. In fact I nearly called out to him, to ask what he thought he was doing, but something stopped me. He didn't see me because I was behind a large sheet pegged on the line. I don't know where he came from but I watched him wander out of Lillian's garden and off down the back lane. At this point I noticed the back door to Mrs Kennedy's house was wide open.

I would describe the man as being of Afro-Caribbean origin. He was about 5 ft 8/9 inches tall. He was of slim build and was wearing a black hooded sweatshirt with the hood up, so I could not see his hair. The man I saw was wearing a pair of white training shoes. I went round to see Lillian almost straight away and she told me that her purse was missing. I am certain I would be able to recognise the man again. I had the distinct feeling I had seen the man before. In fact I have seen him walking his dog, a brown and white terrier, in the grassy area nearby, on more than one occasion.

Signed: Shirley Lewis

DOCUMENT 26C   WITNESS STATEMENT: HAROLD FINNEY

<u>WITNESS STATEMENT</u>

(CJ Act 1967, s. 9; MC Act 1980, s. 5A(3)(a) and s. 5B; Crim PR, Part 27)

Name	Harold Finney
Address	Withheld
Age/Date of Birth	Over 18
Occupation	Retired Engineer

....

Who states:

This statement, consisting of one page signed by me, is true to the best of my knowledge, and belief and I make it knowing that if it is tendered in evidence I shall be liable to prosecution if I have wilfully stated in it anything which I know to be false or do not believe to be true.

Dated: 18th March   Signed: H Finney

....

I have lived in Sunrise Road for the past five years. I am a member of the local area neighbourhood watch scheme. On Tuesday the 17th March, at around 11.30am, I observed a black car drive into Sunrise Road, Lyme, and park. I could not see anyone in the car because the windows were dark. The car remained parked in the road for 15 minutes or so. I started to get suspicious and took a note of the registration number. It was DY 01 5JT. About five minutes after I first noticed the car I saw a man walking past my window. I watched him go over to the car and get in the passenger side. The telephone rang at this point and I did not see the man again. I was on the telephone for some time. When I went to look out of my window at around midday, I saw the black car been driven off.

I would describe the man I saw getting into the car as being black and in his twenties. He was tall and thin. He was black and had long, dark hair. He was wearing a short black top and a pair of white training shoes.

Signed: H Finney

DOCUMENT 26D   WITNESS STATEMENT SGT S FARRINGTON

WITNESS STATEMENT

(CJ Act 1967, s. 9; MC Act 1980, s. 5A(3)(a) and s. 5B; Crim PR, Part 27)

Name	Steven Farrington
Address	Lyme Street Police Station
Age/Date of Birth	Over 18
Occupation	Detective Sergeant

....

Who states:

This statement, consisting of two pages signed by me, is true to the best of my knowledge and belief, and I make it knowing that if it is tendered in evidence I shall be liable to prosecution if I have wilfully stated in it anything which I know to be false or do not believe to be true.

Dated: 20th March   Signed: S Farrington

....

On the 17th March I, in the company of Detective Constable 2890 Sarah Shaw attended the home of Lillian Kennedy at 19 Sunrise Road, Lyme. Mrs Kennedy is an 85-year-old widow. From our enquiries it was ascertained that Mrs Kennedy's purse had been stolen, containing her pension money of £75.00 in cash.

As a result of our enquires, during the afternoon of March 17th, we took Lillian Kennedy on a tour of the locality in an unmarked police car, to see if she could possibly spot the person or persons suspected of carrying out the burglary. In the course of the tour of the local area, Mrs Kennedy drew our attention to a man of Afro-Caribbean origin. The man was 5 ft 10 in and of slim build. He had shoulder-length, dreadlocked hair and a slight goatee beard. He was wearing a black hooded sweatshirt and black jogging bottoms. He was wearing a pair of brown training shoes. My colleague Detective Constable Shaw recognised the man as Lenny Wise. Mrs Kennedy was quite adamant that Lenny Wise was the man who had approached her in her street a short time before the burglary and who had offered to help her with her shopping before disappearing behind the back of Sunrise Road. Mrs Kennedy observed Lenny Wise in good light for a minute or two before confirming his identification.

A decision was taken not to arrest Lenny Wise at this time as further enquires were being pursued in connection with a possible accomplice.

At 09.30 hours on the 18th March, Lloyd Green was arrested in connection with the burglary. He was taken to Lyme Street Police Station where his detention was authorised. A video identification was convened but Mrs Kennedy failed to identify Lloyd Green. Mr Green was released on police bail at 15.30 hours on the 19th March.

At 15.15 hours on the 19th March, Lenny Wise was approached by me and Detective Constable Shaw just outside his flat at 4a Lymewood Court. Mr Wise was arrested and cautioned. A search of his flat was conducted pursuant to s. 32 PACE. In his presence, I seized a black hooded sweatshirt (Exhibit SF1) and a pair of size 9 white Nike training shoes were also seized (right shoe exhibit number SF2 and left shoe exhibit number SF3). In the course of searching Lenny Wise, a quantity of cannabis resin was found (exhibit SF4) in his trouser pocket. Also seized from Lenny Wise was his mobile phone.

Lenny Wise became obstructive at which point he was handcuffed and placed in the back of a police car. He was then taken to Lyme Police Station where his detention was authorised in accordance with the Police and Criminal Evidence Act 1984. A sample of saliva was taken from Mr Wise (Exhibit SF5).

Lenny Wise was detained overnight. On the 20th March, Lenny Wise was identified in the course of a video parade by a neighbour who lives near to the victim's burgled property, as the man she had seen in Lillian Kennedy's back garden around midday on the 17th March.

Wise was certified fit to be interviewed by a police doctor. Declining the services of the solicitor, Wise was interviewed the following day. The interview lasted 46 minutes. One tape was used during the interview and a copy of the sealed tape is available (Exhibit SF6).

In the course of the interview Wise admitted he had entered Mrs Kennedy's house and stole £75. At the conclusion of the interview Lenny Wise was charged with burglary and cautioned.

Mr Wise was denied police bail and was escorted to Lyme Magistrates' Court.

Signed: Sgt S Farrington 4291

DOCUMENT 26E

RECORD OF INTERVIEW

Policy Exhibit No:

No of pages: (3, as reproduced)

Signature of interviewing officer producing exhibit DS S Farrington

Person interviewed: LENNY WISE

Place of interview: LYME STREET

Date of interview: 20/3/-

Time commenced: 1130 HRS

Time concluded: 1216 HRS

Duration of interview: 46 MINUTES

Interviewing officer(s): DS 4291 FARRINGTON/DC 2890 SARAH SHAW

Other persons present: NONE

Tape reference number: 21/SF/59217/03/-

Exhibit Number: SF6

Tape counter Times(s)	Person speaking	Text
0000		Normal introductions were made and the interviewee was reminded of his legal rights and cautioned.
		The officer said WISE was under arrest in relation to a burglary at 19 Sunrise Road in Lyme.
0148	Sgt Farr.	Before we begin, Lenny, I just want to check you feel well enough to be interviewed. Do you feel OK?
0159	R	Just tired, okay okay.
0210	Sgt Farr.	Are you happy to be interviewed without a solicitor?
0218	R	Yeah.
0245	Sgt Farr.	I want to ask you about your whereabouts between 11 and 1pm on Tuesday the 17th March. Can you remember where you were and what you were doing?
0300	R	The usual routine. You know what I mean man?
	Sgt Farr.	What is your usual routine Lenny?
	R	(Suspect sits in silence)
0345	Sgt Farr.	I think lad, you'd better take the situation you're in a bit more seriously don't you?
0400	R	Yeah, yeah—you lot got it in for me.
0430	Sgt Farr.	You understand that you have been arrested in connection with a burglary at 19 Sunrise Road. The victim is an elderly woman and someone has stolen her pension.
0500	R	Yeah, yeah. (Suspect starts shaking his head.) Can I have a cigarette? I need a smoke. This needs sorting, right—got things that need sorting, right.
0525	Sgt Farr.	As soon as this interview is over and you start to answer my questions the sooner you can have a cigarette. Do you know the area around Sunrise Road?
0600	R	Yeah.
0624	Sgt Farr.	Did you go into Sunrise Road on the 17th March?
0635	R	No.

0702	Sgt Farr.	The old lady who was burgled has pointed you out as the man who approached her in Sunrise Road at around 11.30am and offered her help with her shopping. Was that you Lenny because she says it was?
0745	R	What day is it today?
0800	Sgt Farr.	It's Thursday—now just answer the question Lenny—the sooner we get your account the sooner this process will be over.
1100		Are we just going to sit here in silence Lenny?
1110		(Suspect stands up and starts pacing.) Sit down Lenny. The old lady describes the man who approached her in her street at around 11 or so as being a black youth, quite tall, with dreadlocks, wearing a short dark top and wearing white trainers. Would you accept that that description matches you?
1204	R	Don't know what you're getting at—don't know.
1227	Sgt Farr.	The old lady was taken on a tour of the High Street to see if she could see the man who had approached her earlier that morning. She pointed you out to us. You were seen wearing a dark hooded top. I will ask you again were you in Sunrise Road at anytime on the morning of 17th March? (Suspect starts pacing.) Sit down Lenny and answer the question. (Reply inaudible.)
1312		We have another eye-witness, Lenny, who has identified you near the back door of the old lady's house at just after midday on the 17th March. She has given us a clear description of the person she saw. She states she saw a man of Afro-Caribbean origin in the old lady's garden near the open back door. She describes the man has having pointy features, wearing a black hooded top with the hood up. Her description matches your appearance. She has subsequently identified you at a video identification parade. I am going to ask you again, can you tell me where you were between 11 and 1pm on Tuesday the 17th March?
1506	R	(Suspect makes no reply. Refuses to look at me.)
1724	Sgt Farr.	Are these your trainers Lenny? (Suspect shown a pair of white Nike training shoes.) Stop tapping the table Lenny.
1806	R	Not mine, no way.
1815	Sgt Farr.	Well they were found in your flat, amongst your other footwear. You see, all the eye-witnesses describe seeing a man matching your appearance, wearing a pair of white trainers. They are all very clear about this. It so happens that you have a pair of white trainers in your flat. Were you wearing these trainers on the morning of the 17th March?
1950	R	(Inaudible reply.)
2000	Sgt Farr.	You take a shoe size 9 don't you Lenny? These are a size 9. Are these your shoes?
2030	R	They ain't mine. Someone must have left them at my place.
2057	Sgt Farr.	Has anyone stayed at your flat recently?
2103	R	Come on, let's get this sorted. I've got big things to do.
2218	Sgt Farr.	When you were arrested you were found in possession of a quantity of cannabis. Are you using drugs at the moment Lenny?
2228	R	(No reply.) (Suspect rocking the table, asked to desist.)
2330	Sgt Farr.	Do you know a man by the name of Lloyd Green?
2400	R	I know who you are talking about right—he ain't no mate of mine.
2459	Sgt Farr.	Would it surprise you to learn that a car registered to him was seen in Sunrise Road at around 11.30am on Tuesday the 17th March?

2502	R	(No reply)
2613	Sgt Farr.	We have an eye-witness who describes a man just like you approaching Lloyd Green's car in Sunrise Road sometime before midday. I suggest that man was you. What do you have to say?
2640	R	Look—fuck you. I need a cigarette. I ain't into robbing no old woman right. I don't understand this. I don't understand all this.
2705	Sgt Farr.	Why did you need to speak with Lloyd Green, Lenny?
2804	R	(No reply.)
2905	Sgt Farr.	I will ask you again Lenny—was it you seen talking to Lloyd Green?
3000	R	(No reply.)
3104	Sgt Farr.	Is Lloyd Green putting pressure on you Lenny? Do you owe him money?
3219	R	(Suspect makes no reply.)
3315	Sgt Farr.	Look at me, Lenny. This is your chance to offer an explanation. Is there anything you wish to tell me?
3510	R	How much longer are you keeping me here? I've gotta go. I've got things to do—important things. You're fitting me up anyway like you always do.
3609	Sgt Farr.	I can't say how much longer you will be here Lenny. That's up to you.
3720	R	Don't know nothing right about Lloyd Green.
4010	Sgt Farr	Shall I tell you what I think? I think you owe Lloyd Green money. He wants it and wants it now. He tells you to get it or else. You don't have any so either you or he decides you should steal it. You know the area. You agree he will knock on the door of the old lady you saw earlier. When she is distracted, you will break in and see what you can get your hands on. Nice and easy. Is that how it happened?
4202	R	(No reply.)
4230	Sgt Farr.	Look Lenny—this is a serious matter. How do you explain the evidence against you? The eye-witness who has identified you, the white training shoes found in your flat which all the eye-witnesses make reference to and the fact that you have admitted knowing Lloyd Green. Is it all coincidence Lenny?
4406	R	Alright, I stole it from the old lady yeah. I needed the money right. Now fucking charge me and let me get out of here.
4440	Sgt Farr.	Calm down Lenny and sit down. There is no need to get uptight. Who was your accomplice Lenny? Who distracted the lady at her front door?
4500	R	I am not saying anything more. Charge me if you are going to and let me out of here. I ain't saying nothing more.
4530	Sgt Farr.	Did someone put you under pressure to commit this burglary? Was it Lloyd Green? Is he your supplier?
4600	R	(No reply.)

Suspect continues to be unco-operative and verbally abusive. Interview terminated at 46 minutes.

DOCUMENT 26F   FURTHER WITNESS STATEMENT OF SHIRLEY LEWIS

WITNESS STATEMENT

(CJ Act 1967, s. 9; MC Act 1980, s. 5A(3)(a) and s. 5B; Crim PR, Part 27)

Name	Shirley Lewis
Address	Supplied
Age/Date of Birth	Over 18
Occupation	Retired Teacher

Who states:

This statement (consisting of one page signed each by me) is true to the best of my knowledge and belief and I make it knowing that if it is tendered in evidence I shall be liable to prosecution if I have wilfully stated in it anything which I know to be false or do not believe to be true.

Dated: 20th March   Signature: S Lewis

I reside at the address shown overleaf.

I have been asked to view a video identification parade as a result of an incident that I witnessed on the 17th March, when at the home of my aunt at 19 Sunrise Road, Lyme. The incident occurred at around midday on the 17th March.

On the 20th March, I was at the Identification Suite at Lyme Police Station when I was shown a Video Identification Parade.

- After viewing the Video Parade, I identified the person at position No 2 on the Video

I can confirm that before viewing the Video Parade I was supervised by WPC Khan who informed me that I was not allowed to discuss the incident with any other person, including any other witness, and that no such conversation took place. I have not seen any broadcast or published films or photographs, or any descriptions relating to the offence for which I am a witness.

Signature: S Lewis

DOCUMENT 26G   FURTHER WITNESS STATEMENT OF HAROLD FINNEY

<u>WITNESS STATEMENT</u>

(CJ Act 1967, s. 9; MC Act 1980, s. 5A(3)(a) and s. 5B; Crim PR, Part 27)

Name	Harold Finney
Address	Withheld
Age/Date of Birth	Over 18
Occupation	Retired Engineer

Who states:

This statement, consisting of one page signed by me, is true to the best of my knowledge and belief, and I make it knowing that if it is tendered in evidence I shall be liable to prosecution if I have wilfully stated in it anything which I know to be false or do not believe to be true.

Dated: 20th March   Signature: H Finney

I reside at the address shown overleaf.

As a result of an incident that I witnessed on the 17th March when I saw a black man approach a car in Sunrise Road at around 11.50 am. On the 20th March I was at the Identification Suite at Lyme Police Station when I was shown a Video Identification Parade.

- After viewing the Video Parade, I identified the person at position No 4 on the Video

I can confirm that before viewing the Video Parade I was supervised by WPC Khan who informed me that I was not allowed to discuss the incident with any other person, including any other witness, and that no such conversation took place. I have not seen any broadcast or published films or photographs, or any descriptions relating to the offence for which I am a witness.

Signature: H Finney

DOCUMENT 26H FURTHER WITNESS STATEMENT OF LILLIAN KENNEDY

<u>WITNESS STATEMENT</u>

(CJ Act 1967, s. 9; MC Act 1980, s. 5A(3)(a) and s. 5B; Crim PR, Part 27)

Name	Lillian Kennedy
Address	Supplied
Age/Date of Birth	Over 18
Occupation	Retired

Who states:

This statement, consisting of one page signed by me, is true to the best of my knowledge and belief, and I make it knowing that if it is tendered in evidence I shall be liable to prosecution if I have wilfully stated in it anything which I know to be false or do not believe to be true.

Dated: 20th March   Signature: L Kennedy

I reside at the address shown overleaf.

As a result of an incident that I witnessed on the 17th March when I was approached by a black man in the street where I live in Sunrise Road, I was at the Identification Suite at Lyme Police Station when I was shown a Video Identification Parade.

- After viewing the Video Parade, I identified the person at position No .... on the Video

- I was unable to identify any person

I can confirm that before viewing the Video Parade I was supervised by WPC Khan who informed me that I was not allowed to discuss the incident with any other person, including any other witness, and that no such conversation took place. I have not seen any broadcast or published films or photographs, or any descriptions relating to the offence for which I am a witness.

Signature: L Kennedy

DOCUMENT 261 WITNESS STATEMENT OF SCIENTIFIC SUPPORT OFFICER

WITNESS STATEMENT

(CJ Act 1967, s. 9; MC Act 1980, s. 5A(3)(a) and s. 5B; Crim PR, Part 27)

Statement of: Carol Jayne Lawton   Title

Age if under 18: Over 18   Occupation: Scenes of Crime Officer

This statement (consisting of 2 pages signed each by me) is true to the best of my knowledge and belief and I make it knowing that if it is tendered in evidence I shall be liable to prosecution if I have wilfully stated in it anything which I know to be false or do not believe to be true.

Dated: 20th March

Signature: Carol Lawton

I am a Scientific Support Officer employed by Lymeshire Police based at Lyme Street Police Station. At 1430 hours on the 17th March, as a result of a message received, I attended 19 Sunrise Road, Lyme. The property is a house in a residential area and is occupied by an elderly female who lives alone. At the side of the house there is a concrete porch area which is covered from the elements by an enclosed carport. Access to the carport can be gained from the front of the property and from the rear. Access from the rear of the property involves walking through a garden which contains soil beds. The soil beds were wet from a heavy downpour of rain during the night and the preceding days. While I was in the garden area I noticed several footprints on soil beds. I conducted a visual examination of the concrete porch area leading up to the back door of the property and discovered several shoeprints bearing slight soil deposits.

While I was there I took certain photographs, some of which were duplicated, from which an album of prints has been produced marked CJL1, which I would describe as follows:

CJL1 (Shoe marks) Album of Prints (Exhibit No)

Photo 1 View of the back door of 19 Sunrise Road, Lyme

Photo 2 View of the car port from the garden gate of 19 Sunrise Road, Lyme

Photo 3 View of concrete porch

Photo 4 View of shoe mark on concrete

Photo 5 View of shoe mark on concrete

Photo 6 View of shoe mark on concrete

Photo 7 View of shoe mark on concrete

Photo 8 View of CJL2 and CJL3 (Exhibit No) in place before being lifted.

All negatives are filed at the Chief Constables office bearing reference number LP-200510965-0971.

During the course of my examination, I retained the following items, and packaged and labelled them as follows:
CJL 2 Shoe mark 16 cm from backdoor of property electrostatically lifted

CJL 3 Shoe mark 8 cm from backdoor of property electrostatically lifted

The above items were retained in my possession until I returned to the Scenes of Crime store. I placed items CJL2 and CJL3 into a laboratory sack and sealed it with a tag number B8760456. I placed the sack in the secure Scenes of Crime Store.

At 1700 hours on the 19th March, while on duty at Lyme Street police station, I attended the property store. There I took possession of the following items from reference number 256/789432:

SF2 Left white Nike training shoe (Exhibit No ....)

SF3 Right white Nike training shoe (Exhibit No ....)

I placed SF2 into a laboratory sack and sealed it with tag number B49304667. I placed the sack into the secure Scenes of Crime store. I placed SF3 into a laboratory sack and sealed it with tag number B49304668. I placed both sacks into the secure Scenes of Crime store.

At 1845 on the 19th March, I attended Lyme Street Custody Suite from where I collected the following item, labelled as:

SF5 (Exhibit no) DNA mouth swab (x2).

I placed this item into a transit sack which I then sealed with tag no B986740.

All the transit sacks collected in conjunction with this investigation were left in secure and appropriate storage within Lyme Street Scenes of Crime Department for collection and then onward delivery to the Forensic Science Laboratory.

Signature CJ Lawton SOCO 6512

DOCUMENT 26J   WITNESS STATEMENT OF FORENSIC SCIENTIST

Laboratory Reference: 500 679 4033
Order Reference: 400 593 1297
The Forensic Science Service

DS Steve Farrington
Lyme Street Policing Unit
Lymeshire Police

Client Reference: URN 05/2218

WITNESS STATEMENT

(CJ Act 1967, s. 9; MC Act 1980, s. 5A(3)(a) and s. 5B; Crim PR, Part 27)

Statement of: Sarah Hardacker BSc (Hons)

Age of Witness: Over 18

Occupation of Witness: Forensic Scientist for Forensic Science Service

Address of witness: Morley Laboratory, Forensic Science Service, Belfield House, Nile Street, Birmingham.

I declare that:

This statement (consisting of 4 pages signed each by me) is true to the best of my knowledge and belief and I make it knowing that if it is tendered in evidence I shall be liable to prosecution if I have wilfully stated in it anything which I know to be false or do not believe to be true.

Also that:

I am an expert in the field of forensic science. I hold the degree of Bachelor of Science with an Honours Degree in Applied Biochemistry and have worked as a Forensic Scientist since 1995. During this time I have dealt with many investigations involving footwear.

I have been asked to provide a statement. I confirm that I have read the guidance in a booklet known as *Disclosure Expert's evidence and unused material* which details my role and documents my responsibilities, in relation to revelation as an expert witness. I have the followed the guidance and recognise the continuing nature of my responsibilities of revelation. In accordance with my duties of revelation, as documented in the guidance booklet, I:

a. confirm that I have complied with my duties to record, retain and reveal material in accordance with the Criminal Procedure and Investigations Act-1996, as amended:

b. have compiled an Index of all material. I will ensure that the Index is updated in the event I am provided with or generate additional material;

c. understand that in the event my opinion changes on any material issue, I will inform the investigating officer, as soon as reasonably practicable and give reasons:

Date: 25th March   Signature: S Hardacker

FSS Reference: 203840/YTT34
DEFENDANT: LENNY WISE

RECEIPT OF ITEMS

Records show that on the 20th March amongst other items, the 4 items described below relating to an investigation of a burglary at domestic premises in Lyme were received at the Morely laboratory of the Forensic Science Service from Lymeshire Police.

From 19 Sunrise Road, Lyme

CJL2 Electrostatic shoeprint lift

CJL3 Electrostatic shoeprint lift

From Lenny Wise

SF2 Left white training shoe

SF3 Right white training shoe.

BACKGROUND INFORMATION

From the information provided by the Police, I understand the following:

On the 17th March a burglary occurred at 19 Sunrise Road, Lyme. Entry to the property was gained through an unlocked backdoor while the sole occupant of the property was distracted by a caller at the front door.

A subsequent Scene of Crime examination recovered footwear marks on a concrete surface near to the backdoor of the property. The shoeprints are believed to belong to the offender.

Lenny WISE was arrested on the 20th March and following a search of his home address 4A Lymewood Court, Lyme a pair of white size 9 white Nike trainers were recovered.

This is the information on which I have based my examination and have used in the interpretation of the findings.

PURPOSE OF EXAMINATION

To determine whether or not the recovered training shoes relating to Lenny WISE have made the footwear marks recovered from 19 Sunrise Road, Lyme.

LABORATORY EXAMINATION

With this aim in mind, the following items have been examined:-

Re: 4A Lymewood Court, Lyme (relating to Lenny WISE)

FS2 and FS3—Pair of Nike white training shoes

Re: 19 Sunrise Road, Lyme

CJL 2—Footwear lifts from concrete porch

CJL 3—Footwear lifts from concrete porch

These items have been examined with the help of scientific assistants, details of which are noted on the Forensic Examination Record, SH/FER/1 that accompanies this statement. Details of the examination are documented in the case notes which can be inspected at the laboratory under order number **400 593 1297**.

TECHNICAL ISSUES

When a person steps onto a surface, a mark may be left of the under-surface of their footwear. This footwear impression will persist for a long time if left undisturbed. It may be preserved, recovered and enhanced in order to facilitate a detailed comparison, at the Forensic Science Laboratory, between it and test impressions taken from the suspect's shoes. Details such as pattern, general size and degree of wear can be compared. Additionally, any marks in the scene impression that correspond to damage features on the under-sole of the shoe can provide conclusive evidence to connect that particular shoe to the scene. Any such footwear marks can be compared with any recovered items of footwear.

RESULTS OF EXAMINATION

Re: Lenny WISE

The training shoes (SF2 and SF3) are a pair of size 9 Nike with a sole pattern of zigzag fine bars and blocks. The soles of the training shoes are worn, with damage evident on both of the soles. The sole pattern of these boots is only one of a vast range of sole patterns available on sports/casual footwear and is one of the more frequently encountered patterns at the laboratory. On the right shoe there is a cut measuring 3 mm.

Re: CJL 2 and CJL 3

Items are two photographs of electrostatically dust print lifted footwear marks. The clearest mark, depicted on photograph CJL2 corresponds in pattern, size/configuration and wear to the submitted right training shoe (SF3). In addition there are features in the mark that correspond to features of random damage on the sole of the same right shoe. There was one mark in the impression taken from the right shoe and while not clearly defined nonetheless corresponded to the feature of damage on the right training shoe.

There is a poor quality and poorly defined footwear mark depicted on the lift CJL3 that corresponds in pattern and is appropriate in terms of size and configuration and wear to the submitted left training shoe SF2. However, given the quality of the mark and detail obtained from the footwear mark on the other lift (CJL2) this footwear mark has not been examined in any further detail.

INTERPRETATION

In my opinion, the degree of correspondence observed between the footwear mark on the concrete floor of the backdoor porch and the submitted right training shoe is of the utmost significance. Indeed, I consider the likelihood of the observed degree of correspondence occurring by sheer coincidence, if the training shoe did not make the respective mark on the concrete floor, to be so remote as to be discounted on a practical basis. There was one mark in one of the impressions that corresponds to damage features on the under-sole of Mr Wise's right training shoe. Damage features are acquired randomly on footwear and so

I therefore consider this finding enhances the significance of the pattern match and in my opinion the overall degree of correspondence is much more likely if this shoe made the impression rather than some other footwear taken from the random population.

CONCLUSION

In my opinion, the results of this examination provide very strong evidence that the right training shoe relating to Lenny WISE has made a mark on the concrete floor close to the backdoor of 19 Sunrise Road, Lyme.

(Scale of Evidential Support:—no, limited, moderate, moderately strong, strong, very strong, extremely strong, conclusive.)

Signed: S Hardacker

DOCUMENT 27 CPS LETTER REGARDING CPIA 1996 DISCLOSURE (SPECIMEN LETTER)

Important note: The letter below is the authors' interpretation of the type of letter that a solicitor might receive from the Crown Prosecution Service. The letter is not representative of any communication sent by the Crown Prosecution Service and should not be seen as representative of how the Crown Prosecution Service would respond in this scenario.

CROWN PROSECUTION SERVICE
Blackburn Street,
Lyme
LY3 2BE
15/5/-

Hannibal and Mountford Solicitors
20 High Street,
Lyme
LY10 34T

Dear Sirs,
Re: Lenny Wise
Date of Next Hearing: PCMH 30th June

Disclosure of Prosecution Material under section 3, Criminal Procedure and Investigations Act 1996 (CPIA).

Notice of intention to adduce evidence of your client's character under s 101 Criminal Justice Act 2003

I am required by section 3 of the above Act, to disclose to you any prosecution material, which has not previously been disclosed, which might reasonably be considered capable of undermining the case for the prosecution or of assisting the case for the accused.

Attached to this letter is a copy of a schedule of non-sensitive material prepared by the police in compliance with their duty under Part II CPIA and the provisions of the Code of Practice. The schedule has been prepared by the Police Disclosure Officer, who in this case is DS Hague.

Where the word 'evidence' appears alongside any item, all the items listed on the schedule are intended to be part of the prosecution case. You will receive a written notice should the position change.

Where indicated, copies of the items listed are attached. Material marked as available for inspection can be viewed by arrangement with myself.

This material is disclosed to you in accordance with the provisions of the CPIA, and you must not use or disclose it, or any information recorded in it, for any purpose other than in connection with these criminal proceedings. If you do so without the permission of the court, you may commit an offence.

If you supply a written defence statement to me and to the court within 28 days of the date of the receipt of this letter, material which has not been disclosed at this stage will be further reviewed in the light of that statement.

A defence statement is required in Crown Court cases. In magistrates' court cases, a defence statement is optional. In accordance with my continuing duty to consider disclosure, I will review the information you provide in the statement to identify any remaining material which has not already been disclosed. The statement will also be relied on by the court if you later make an application under section 8 CPIA. If you do not make a CPIA-compliant defence statement where one is required or provided, or do so late, the court may hear comment and/or draw an adverse inference.

It is essential that you preserve this schedule in its present form, as access to any material will only be granted upon its production to the disclosure officer.

I am also enclosing notice of my intention to adduce evidence of your client's bad character under s 101 Criminal Justice Act 2003.

If you have a query in connection with this letter, please contact myself.

Yours faithfully,
Lewis Rowe
Crown Prosecution Service

DOCUMENT 27A   POLICE SCHEDULE OF NON-SENSITIVE UNUSED MATERIAL

MG6C

RESTRICTED (when complete)

POLICE SCHEDULE OF RELEVANT NON-SENSITIVE UNUSED MATERIAL

R v LENNY WISE

The Disclosure Officer believes the following RELEVANT MATERIAL which does not form part of the prosecution case is NOT SENSITIVE. For further detailed guidance refer to the Disclosure Manual and Attorney General's Guidelines.

URN	74	95	21	7L

FOR CPS USE:
* Enter D = Disclose to defence
 I = Item disclosable and defence may inspect
 CND = Clearly not disclosable (by description)

Item No.	Record below MATERIAL of any kind, including information and objects, which is obtained in the course of a criminal investigation and which may be relevant to the investigation; and RELEVANCE is that it has some bearing on any offence under investigation or any person being investigated or on the surrounding circumstances of the case, unless it is incapable of having any impact on the case. **Do not speculate if it is not considered relevant do not record it on the schedule.** Give a sufficiently detailed DESCRIPTION of the relevant material for the prosecutor to make a decision on whether or not it should be examined.	LOCATION State precisely where the item can be found/located	*	REASON FOR DECISION
1	The relevant material is: Tape recording of 999 call 17/3/-from witness S Lewis-description of suspect	Lyme Street Police Station control room	D	Shoe colour different when seen later in street
2	The relevant material is: Incident (CAD) Log no. 3569/0/-(17/3/--details of witness S Lewis and description of suspects	Lyme Street Police Station control room	D	Shoe colour different when seen later in street
3	Pocket note-book entry-DC 2198 Shaw re details of crime report contains details of first description of suspects	With DC 2198 Shaw	D	Shoe colour different when seen later in street
4	Pocket note-book entry DS 4291 Farrington re: arrests and interview of GREEN and WISE	With DS 4201 Farrington	CND	
5	Pocket note-book details search of premises -DC 2198 Shaw, Flat 4a Lymewood Court, Parkdale, Lyme-home address of WISE	With DC 2198 Shaw	CND	
6	The relevant material is: Custody record no. 2346/12/-GREEN	Lyme PS	D	Disclosable under PACE 1984
7	The relevant material is: Custody record no: 2305/12/-WISE	Lyme PS	CND	
8	The relevant material is: PNC printout of previous convictions of GREEN	Lyme PS	CND	
9	The relevant material is: Record of interview with GREEN	Lyme PS	CND	
10	The relevant material is: Submission forms to FSS dated	Lyme PS	CND	

Signature:

Date: 28/4

Name: DC 2486 David Hague

Reviewing lawyer signature:

Print Name: Lewis Rowe

Date 14/5

Page 1 of 1

RESTRICTED (when complete)

2010/11

DOCUMENT 27B POLICE SCHEDULE OF NON-SENSITIVE UNUSED MATERIAL

RESTRICTED (when complete)

MG6C

POLICE SCHEDULE OF RELEVANT NON-SENSITIVE UNUSED MATERIAL

R v LENNY WISE

URN	T 4	95	21	9 L

The Disclosure Officer believes the following RELEVANT MATERIAL which does not form part of the prosecution case is NOT SENSITIVE. For further detailed guidance refer to the Disclosure Manual and Attorney General's Guidelines.

FOR CPS USE:
* Enter D = Disclose to defence
  I = Item disclosable and defence may inspect
  CND = Clearly not disclosable (by description)

Item No.	Record below MATERIAL of any kind, including information and objects, which is obtained in the course of a criminal investigation and which may be relevant to the investigation; and RELEVANCE is that it has some bearing on any offence under investigation or any person being investigated or on the surrounding circumstances of the case, unless it is incapable of having any impact on the case. **Do not speculate if it is not considered relevant do not record it on the schedule.** Give a sufficiently detailed DESCRIPTION of the relevant material for the prosecutor to make a decision on whether or not it should be examined.	LOCATION State precisely where the item can be found/located	*	REASON FOR DECISION
11	The relevant material is: Letter from FSS dated	On file	CND	
12	The relevant material is: DNA swab sample taken from WISE	On file	CND	
13	Inspector C Sutton –contemporaneous hand written notes of Video Identification procedure (Form 116/2)	On file	CND	
14	The relevant material is: Mobile phone records GREEN	On file	CND	
15	The relevant material is: Mobile phone records WISE	On file	CND	
	The relevant material is:			
	The relevant material is:			
	The relevant material is:			
	The relevant material is:			
	The relevant material is:			

Signature: .... Name: David Hague DC 2486

Date: 2·8·14

Reviewing lawyer signature: _____

Print Name: LEWIS ROWE

Date: 14/5

RESTRICTED (when complete)

Page 1 of 1

2010/11

DOCUMENT 30   ADDITIONAL STATEMENT OF LENNY WISE—COMMENTS ON EVIDENCE DISCLOSED BY THE CASE SENT BUNDLE

I have read the witness statements served by the prosecution and make the following observations.

Lillian Kennedy

I think I know this lady. I have seen her before when I have walked my dog Butch. If she says it was me who approached her on the day in question then she is mistaken. I do not recollect going into Sunrise Road on the 17th March.

Shirley Lewis

This witness is mistaken. There is no way she could have seen me at the back of the old lady's house. I was not there. She says the man she saw was wearing white training shoes. I do not wear white training shoes. She may have seen me in the area on one or two occasions. As I already said I walk my dog Butch (a terrier) in fields near to Sunrise Road. I am not the only black man who lives in the area. She is confusing me with someone else.

Harold Finney

I did not see or approach any black car in Sunrise Road.

DS Steve Farrington

I dislike this police officer. On the way back from the interview room he said that I deserved everything the court would throw at me. Nobody explained to me why I could not have an identification parade. The police let me make a phone call to my sister, but she wasn't in when I rang. I was offered a solicitor but I honestly didn't think there was much point in one being there. The police were going to fit me up whatever. I was really desperate to get out of the police station. I seemed to have been there forever. I wanted a cigarette and I was worried about Butch my dog and about Sonia. I didn't feel very well during the interview and cannot honestly remember what I said. Looking back I should have had a solicitor present. All I wanted was for the interview to be over and done with, so that I could be charged and released on bail. The police got me to say what they wanted to hear. What I said to them in interview about my involvement is untrue. I wish to retract my statement.

I told the custody sergeant the following morning that I was on medication. He asked me why I hadn't mentioned it before. I cannot remember whether I was asked at the outset whether I was on medication. I just felt totally out of it. He called the police doctor who examined me. I believe an officer went back to my flat to collect my medication.

I was examined by a GP. He didn't seem much interested in me. He gave me my medication and told me I was fine.

I swear I have never worn the white trainers. They were given to me by a friend. I cannot remember who because I often have friends come to see me and sometimes they stay over. I have not worn the shoes.

Lloyd Green

I believe Lloyd Green has not said anything against me. I do know Lloyd Green. He is a drug dealer and loan shark. I have owed him money in the past. He can get a bit rough with you when you don't 'come up with the goods'. I cannot say whether Lloyd Green was involved in this burglary or not as I wasn't there.

Dated ....22nd May

DOCUMENT 31 LETTER TO CPS DEALING WITH CPIA 1996 MATTERS AND BAD CHARACTER NOTICE UNDER S. 101 CRIMINAL JUSTICE ACT 2003

HANNIBAL AND MOUNTFORD SOLICITORS
20 High Street,
Lyme Bank, Lyme
LY10 34T
Telephone: 01576–455971
Fax: 01576–200345
Email: Hannibal@solicitors.co.uk

Crown Prosecution Service
Queen's Chambers
Blackburn Street
Lyme
LY3 2BE

Date: 30/5/-
Ref: LR/JW
Our ref: RJ/SW

Dear Sirs,
R v Lenny Wise
Date of Next Hearing—Plea and Case Management Hearing—Lyme Crown Court 30th June

We enclose our client's defence statement under s. 5, Criminal Procedure and Investigations Act 1996. With further reference to s. 6C CPIA 1996, our client does not propose to call any defence witnesses at this time. We shortly intend to take counsel's opinion in this matter and if we are in a position to agree prosecution witness evidence we will notify you accordingly.

We look forward to receiving further prosecution disclosure. In particular, we would like disclosure of Lloyd Green's interview. We note that you do not propose to disclose the telephone records pertaining to the mobile phones seized respectively from Lenny Wise and Lloyd Green. We assume this is on the basis that the records do not establish a connection between the phones? We would like to have this agreed as a formal admission under s. 10 CJA 1967 if this is the case.

We intend to dispute the admissibility of our client's interview with the police in connection with this matter. We have instructed our client's consultant psychiatrist, Dr Oliver A Mayhew to provide us with an expert opinion as to our client's state of mind at the time of his interview. Consequently we will want to cross-examine the custody officers who were responsible for compiling the custody record in relation to our client. We will also want to cross-examine the police doctor who examined our client and Inspector Rushton who reviewed our client's detention. Please confirm that you will ensure the attendance of these witnesses. We will of course require our client's custody record and the transcript of interview to be admitted into evidence. For these reasons we will require tape-playing facilities in court. We anticipate that the point of law which arises in connection with the interview in this case will form the basis of a pre-trial hearing in connection with this matter as we do not consider either side will be in a position to resolve the matter at the PCMH.

We also enclose notice of our intention to oppose the admission of our client's past bad character at his forthcoming trial.

We look forward to hearing from you accordingly.

Yours faithfully
R James
Hannibal and Mountford

Anthony Hannibal (BA Partner), Louise Mountford (LL.B Partner), Denis Davies
(LL.B Partner) Tim Howard (LL.B Associate Solicitor), David Temple (LL.B Associate Solicitor),
Rachel James (LL.B Associate Solicitor), Mike Tamworth (Fellow of the
Institute of Legal Executives), Lisa Hardy (Accredited Police Station Clerk),
Ali Khan (Accredited Police Station Clerk)
Regulated by the Solicitors Regulation Authority

Note: A copy of this letter and its enclosures will also be sent to the Crown Court.

DOCUMENT 32   DEFENCE STATEMENT

Sections 5 and 6, Criminal Procedure and Investigation Act 1996

REGINA v LENNY WISE

1. I, Lenny Wise deny that I was the person responsible for committing a burglary at 19 Sunrise Road, Lyme between 11.45am–12.30pm on the 17th March this year.

2. I take issue with those prosecution witnesses who suggest that I was one of the two men involved in the burglary.

I deny that I was in the vicinity of Sunrise Road at anytime between 11am and 12.30pm on the 17th March this year. I was not in the area at the relevant time. I cannot specifically recall my precise whereabouts during these times. My daily routine is to get up at around 10am and take my dog for a walk. I believe I was in Lyme High Street between 11am–12.30pm. Consequently, Lillian Kennedy is mistaken when she identified me on the street to the police on the afternoon of the 17th March as being the male who had offered to help her with her in Sunrise Road earlier that day. I take issue with Shirley Lewis's identification of me as the male she saw leaving the back garden of the burgled property. She is mistaken. Her identification of me is based on mistaken recognition. I accept that I have walked my dog on occasions in the area near Sunrise Road and that my appearance is somewhat distinctive. However, I was not in or near Sunrise Road on the 17th March. I do not take issue with Harold Finney's statement. He does not identify me as being the male he saw approaching a black car parked in Sunrise Road.

I do not take issue with the composition or conduct of the VIPER procedure. I contend however that Shirley Lewis and Lillian Kennedy are mistaken in their identification of me.

3. I wish to retract what I said in interview on the 20th March regarding the circumstances of this offence. What I said at the end of my interview is untrue. I intend to dispute the admissibility of my interview with the police. At the time of my interview I was and still am afflicted by bipolar depression. I did not have the services of a solicitor or an appropriate adult. I will contend, as a matter of law, that my interview should be excluded under ss. 76 (2)(b) and 78 PACE 1984 for breaches of the Police and Criminal Evidence Act 1984 and Code C of the PACE Codes of Practice.

4. I deny that the white training shoes recovered from my flat belong to me. I have never worn them.

5. I do not propose to call any witnesses in my defence other than a consultant psychiatrist who will tender an expert opinion as to the reliability of the statements I made during the interview process.

6. In compliance with my obligations under s. 6C CPIA 1996, I do not propose to call any defence witnesses at this time.

Signed: Lenny Wise   Date: 28th May

To: Crown Prosecution Service
    Lyme Crown Court

DOCUMENT 39 BRIEF TO COUNSEL TO ATTEND PCMH

<u>LYME CROWN COURT</u>   <u>LISTING NO.</u>

REGINA

-v-

LENNY WISE

BRIEF ON BEHALF OF THE DEFENDANT TO APPEAR AT THE PCMH—30th JUNE AT 10am AND AT THE SUBSEQUENT TRIAL ON A DATE TO BE FIXED

Counsel receives herewith copies of the following:

1. Proof of evidence of Lenny Wise dated 20th March

2. Draft Indictment

3. Case sent bundle including:

   a) Statement of Lillian Kennedy (x2)

   b) Statement of Shirley Lewis (x2)

   c) Statement of Harold Finney (x2)

   d) Statement of DS Farrington

   e) Statement of DC Shaw

   f) Statement of WPC Anjuna Khan

   g) Statement of WPC Emma Mason

   h) Statement of Inspector Christopher Sutton

   i) Statement of WPC Josie Bradbury

   j) Statement of PC Peter Reynolds

   k) Statement of Carol Lawton SOCO

   l) Statement of Sarah Hardacker

   m) Transcript of interview: Lenny Wise

   n) Previous convictions of Lenny Wise

   o) Exhibit List

4. Statement of Lenny Wise with comments on the prosecution evidence dated 22nd May

5. Defence Psychiatric Report

6. Custody Record

7. Tapes of interview

8. Initial Prosecution Disclosure (unused)

9. Defence Statement

10. Notice of intention to adduce evidence of Lenny Wise's previous convictions

11. Notice objecting to the admissibility of Mr Wise's previous criminal convictions

12. Further Prosecution Disclosure

    a) Record of interview with Lloyd Green

    b) Letter from Forensic Science Service

13. Copy letter to the CPS dated 30th May including witness requirements

14. Representation Order

15. Plea and Case Management Form

Introduction

Counsel's instructing solicitors act on behalf of Lenny Wise. As Counsel will see from the enclosed draft indictment, Mr Wise is charged with burglary. It is alleged he broke into 19 Sunrise Road on the 17th March this year and stole £75. Mr Wise intends to plead not guilty to the burglary allegation. Upon his arrest, Mr Wise was found to be in possession of a small quantity of cannabis. He pleaded guilty to simple possession and was sentenced to a conditional discharge for 12 months by Lyme Magistrates on the 27th March.

Chronology

Mr Wise was arrested on the 19th March. He appeared before Lyme Magistrates on the 20th March when bail was refused. He subsequently appeared again on the 27th March when bail was refused for a second time and jurisdiction to try the matter was refused and the case was sent to the Crown Court. On the 29th March our client appeared before a Crown Court Judge in chambers at Lyme Crown Court and was granted bail subject to a number of conditions.

The Plea and Case Management Hearing in this case has been listed for the 30th June. Counsel is instructed to attend. It is our intention to instruct counsel to represent Mr Wise at trial and would ask you to take note of this fact when considering listing arrangements.

Prosecution Case and Evidential Matters

On the 17th March a burglary occurred at 19 Sunrise Road, Lyme (the home of 84-year-old Lillian Kennedy) sometime between 11.45 hours and 12midday. The prosecution contend that this was a distraction burglary. It is alleged that a man knocked on the door of 19 Sunrise Road on the pretence of having to use the telephone and while the occupier was distracted, the burglar gained entry to the property via an unlocked back door and proceeded to steal £75 from the victim's purse. The prosecution contend that the person entering the property was Mr Wise. It is believed that the man responsible for distracting Mrs Kennedy at her front door is Lloyd Green. Although Green was arrested and interviewed he has not been charged with any offence arising out of this incident. In his interview with the police he denied any involvement in the burglary and did not implicate Lenny Wise. Instructing solicitors do not act for Lloyd Green and did not represent him at the police station.

The principal evidence against Mr Wise comprises eye-witness identification, confession evidence and forensic circumstantial evidence. We will deal with each in turn.

Counsel will see the statements of Lillian Kennedy contained in the case sent bundle that she did not see the man who entered her property. She states however that she was stopped by a man in her street who offered to help her with her shopping. This was approximately 30–40 minutes before the burglary. On a subsequent tour of the local area the afternoon of the burglary she identified Lenny Wise as being that person. The police did not immediately arrest Mr Wise. At a subsequent VIPER identification procedure, however, Mrs Kennedy failed to identify Mr Wise which rather casts her earlier street identification into doubt. Mrs Kennedy does however provide a description of the man who approached her which accords for the most part with the description of a man seen leaving the backdoor of the burgled property by another eye-witness. When Mrs Kennedy pointed Mr Wise out to the police he was wearing the same attire save in one significant respect—he was not observed to be wearing white training shoes. In the circumstances it is difficult to see what Mrs Kennedy's evidence contributes to the prosecution's case. Counsel is asked to advise on this point and consider whether her evidence may be challenged on the basis of its relevance. Counsel will note that Mrs Kennedy spoke with the man who knocked on her front door. She was however unable to identify Lloyd Green at a VIPER identification procedure.

Of central importance to the prosecution's case is the evidence of Shirley Lewis. Counsel will see from her statement that she was in the back garden of a neighbouring property at midday when she saw a man behaving suspiciously near the back door of 19 Sunrise Road. She was hanging out some sheets on the washing line. She observed the man for a few seconds and was able to provide the police with a description of the man and his clothing. Her description accords with Mr Wise's actual appearance. She observed the man was wearing white training shoes. At a subsequent VIPER identification procedure, Mrs Lewis identified Lenny Wise as being that man. Her identification is based in part on recognition. She states she has seen Mr Wise before in the area. Mr Wise does not dispute this possibility as he lives near the victim and has, on occasion, walked his dog in fields near the burgled property. Mr Wise is adamant, however, that this witness is mistaken and that it was not the man she saw.

A link in the chain of evidence is provided by the account of Harold Finney. Mr Finney lives in a property across the road from the burgled house. At 11.30am he observed a car drive along Sunrise Road and park. He was suspicious of the car and noted the registration number. The car is registered to Lloyd Green. Mr Finney states he observed a black man on foot approach the car. He describes a man whose appearance is similar to that of Lenny Wise. He also describes the clothing the individual was wearing which included a dark sweatshirt and white training shoes. At this point Mr Finney was diverted by a telephone call. He saw nothing more of any relevance. At a subsequent VIPER identification parade, he picked out someone other than Lenny Wise. He never saw the driver of the car.

Counsel is asked to note that Mr Wise was unrepresented at the police station. Consequently the identification procedure was conducted in the absence of legal advice. Having reviewed the DVD compilation and the video of the viewing process, instructing solicitors are satisfied that the procedure was conducted fairly in accordance with Code D. The DVD compilation is included should counsel wish to consider it.

Upon arrest and pursuant to a section 32 PACE 1984, a search of Mr Wise's flat was carried out. The police recovered a dark hooded sweatshirt and a pair of white size 9 Nike trainers. Counsel will note that in the course of the investigation shoeprint evidence was gathered from just outside the backdoor of the burgled property. Subsequent forensic comparison of the shoeprint lifts and the soles of the shoes recovered from Mr Wise's flat strongly suggest these training shoes were responsible for leaving the shoe prints. Mr Wise cannot offer an explanation for this other than to state the shoes were left at his flat by a friend, whose name he cannot recall. In interview he stated he had not worn the shoes. Document 12b disclosed by way of further disclosure is useful in this respect. Counsel is asked to see whether this statement can be agreed under s. 9 CJA 1967.

The prosecution will seek to rely on the account given by Mr Wise in his interview with the police. It amounts to a confession. Counsel is referred to the transcript of interview in this regard. Mr Wise wishes to retract his confession for reasons considered in detail below.

The prosecution have served notice of their intention to adduce evidence of Mr Wise's previous criminal convictions.

Defence Case and Evidential Matters

Counsel will see Mr Wise's comments on the prosecution evidence in document 4. Counsel will see that a defence statement has been filed in this case. Mr Wise intends to plead not guilty. He wishes to strongly challenge the admissibility of his confession. He maintains that he is not the man responsible for the burglary. Despite our best efforts, Mr Wise is unable to substantiate his precise whereabouts at the relevant time with an alibi.

Instructing solicitors feel there are strong grounds for seeking the exclusion of Mr Wise's confession under ss 76(2)(b) and 78 PACE 1984. Counsel is referred at this juncture to Mr Wise's statement and to the custody record. Mr Wise was unrepresented at the police station, although on the face of it, it would appear that the police acted within the law of s. 58 PACE, albeit not the spirit. An attempt was made by the custody sergeant to contact Mr Wise's sister once during our client's detention but no contact was in fact established. Counsel will note that Mr Wise suffers from a diagnosed psychiatric condition for which he receives psychiatric care and medication. It is not altogether clear why this fact was not ascertained by the custody sergeant who should have undertaken a risk assessment having authorised the continued detention of our client. Our client is not always inclined to help himself and upon his arrest he was not found to be in possession of any medication. Our client states that he cannot recall being asked whether he suffered from a medical condition requiring medication. Our client states he was not suffering drug withdrawal symptoms at the time but is chronically addicted to nicotine. Counsel will see that he was detained overnight. The custody record suggests that Mr Wise did not have much to eat and had little sleep.

It is evident from the custody record that some 14 or so hours after having first been detained, Mr Wise mentioned the fact that he felt unwell and needed his usual medication. A police surgeon was called. Dr Ghulam examined our client and having administered his medication pronounced him fit to be interviewed. Crucially, Mr Wise was not provided with an appropriate adult, contrary to Code C. As such he went into the interview completely unrepresented, craving a cigarette, desperate to relieve the pressure of the situation and suffering from a diagnosed psychiatric condition. In the circumstances, it is difficult to see how a court could regard Mr Wise's confession as being admissible. Counsel is referred to the decision in *R v Aspinall* [1999] 2 Cr App R 115 as being a decision of the Court of Appeal which supports our contention that the confession is both unreliable and unfair to admit. The admission of a confession obtained in these circumstances would in our view represent a violation of Article 6.

Counsel will see that we have obtained a report from Mr Wise's consultant psychiatrist. The report is extremely helpful and we intend to place reliance upon it. The report has been disclosed to the CPS in accordance with the requirements of s. 30 CJA 1988. Dr Mayhew would be prepared to attend court to give evidence if necessary.

Clearly if the confession can be excluded in this case, a major component of the prosecution's case is lost and counsel may wish to consider whether a submission of no case to answer might be mounted in these circumstances.

Instructing solicitors have notified the CPS of its intention to challenge the admissibility of the confession in this case. Unless the CPS decides to concede the point at the PCMH, we anticipate the issue will need to be listed for a judge's binding ruling on its admissibility. We would welcome Counsel's views on this point.

Instructing solicitors have served the appropriate notice on the prosecution objecting to the admissibility of Mr Wise's criminal convictions. Counsel is asked to use her best endeavours to ensure that this very prejudicial evidence is excluded at the Plea and Case Management Hearing.

Counsel is requested to advise on all issues likely to arise at the PCMH and generally on the evidence and on preparation for trial. A PCMH form is enclosed for counsel's consideration. At present we have asked the CPS for all the witnesses it tendered at the committal hearing to attend. We suspect a number of witnesses can be agreed in this case and would ask counsel to specifically consider this point so that we may write to the CPS. Should Counsel require a conference we would ask her clerk to contact us.

Counsel is instructed to appear on behalf of the defendant at the PCMH on the 30th June at 2.30pm.

Rachel James, Hannibal and Mountford Solicitors
Date: 15th June

DOCUMENT 41 FILE NOTE BASED ON PLEA AND CASE MANAGEMENT HEARING

30th June

Attending Crown Court for Plea and Case Management Hearing. Speaking with Ms Rhianna Stockley of counsel beforehand. There was considerable discussion between counsel on each side. Counsel for the CPS conceded breaches of Code C and indicated that the CPS would not be placing reliance upon Mr Wise's confession which is extremely good news.

Argument was heard in relation to the admissibility of Lenny's previous convictions under s 101(1)(d) of the Criminal Justice Act 2003. The judge His Honour J Baker ruled in favour of admitting them. The case has been listed for trial on the 22nd August. Certificate for solicitor to attend was granted. Counsel and I explained the proceedings to Mr Wise and his sister. Respective counsel agreed the following witness' evidence could be read at trial: WPC Khan/WPC Mason/Insp Sutton/Bradbury/PC Reynolds/WPC Lawton/ Dr Hardacker/Dr Leighton.

Time engaged:
Travel 20 minutes
Waiting 60 minutes
Conference 40 minutes
Hearing 30 minutes

BW

DOCUMENT 47   FILE NOTE BASED ON TRIAL

22nd August

Attending Lyme Crown Court for Lenny Wise's trial. Ms Stockley for Lenny Wise and Parminder Singh for the prosecution. His Honour Thomas Shand presiding. Before the trial began, Ms Stockley asked the judge to reconsider the ruling by His Honour Judge Baker to allow evidence of the defendant's previous convictions to be admitted on the basis that their prejudicial effect would outweigh their probative value. It was agreed that the prosecution in its opening would not refer to the defendant's previous convictions but that the matter would be kept under review during the course of the trial.

The prosecution called Shirley Lewis who was extensively cross-examined with Mrs Lewis conceding that she could have been mistaken. CPS called Lillian Kennedy and Harold Finney. Before the investigating officer was called, Ms Stockley asked for confirmation that the officer would not be asked questions regarding the defendant's previous convictions as she was minded to make a submission of no case to answer. The judge ruled in her favour, without prejudice to any decision he might make as regards a submission being made. DS Farrington also gave evidence and was cross-examined. Prosecution read out a number of s. 9 statements which included the forensic evidence. Ms Stockley then made a submission of no case to answer. She explained that the most important eye-witness linking Mr Wise to the crime scene was Shirley Lewis and her evidence had been discredited. There was no concrete forensic evidence to link the defendant to the crime scene. The only remaining 'evidence' was the fact of his previous convictions and that it was clearly contrary to the defendant's right to a fair trial that a conviction could be based on this fact alone. The submission of no case to answer was upheld by the judge. The jury were directed to acquit on the burglary charge. Mr Wise and his sister were immensely relieved and pleased.

Time engaged:
Travel 30 minutes
Waiting 40 minutes
Conference 30 minutes
Hearing 4 hours

BW

The case having now concluded, the defence solicitor can submit her final claim for costs from the Legal Services Commission via the Crown Court.

APPENDIX 2

EXTRACTS FROM MAGISTRATES' COURT SENTENCING GUIDELINES (EFFECTIVE 4 AUGUST)

At the point of publication, the extracted guidelines are current. The complete and most up-to-date version of the MCSGs is accessible via the Sentencing Council's (SC) website. A link to the MCSG is available via our Online Resource Centre.

The following 'offence-specific' guidelines taken from the MCSGs are reproduced in this appendix:

- Assault occasioning actual bodily harm*
- Burglary in a dwelling*
- Theft in breach of trust
- Theft from person

*[Note the appearance of these 'offence-specific' guideline are different from the others in the MCSGs because they have been revised by the Sentencing Council for England and Wales, which adopts a different format from its predecessor, the Sentencing Guidelines Council.]

Assault occasioning actual bodily harm
Offences against the Person Act 1861 (section 47)

Racially/religiously aggravated ABH
Crime and Disorder Act 1998 (section 29)

These are specified offences for the purposes of section 224 of the Criminal Justice Act 2003

Triable either way

Section 47
Maximum when tried summarily: Level 5 fine and/or 26 weeks' custody
Maximum when tried on indictment: 5 years' custody

Section 29
Maximum when tried summarily: Level 5 fine and/or 26 weeks' custody
Maximum when tried on indictment: 7 years' custody

Offence range: Fine – 3 years' custody

This guideline applies to all offenders aged 18 and older, who are sentenced on or after 13 June 2011. The definitions at page 145 of 'starting point' and 'first time offender' do not apply for this guideline. Starting point and category ranges apply to all offenders in all cases, irrespective of plea or previous convictions.

STEP ONE
Determining the offence category

The court should determine the offence category using the table below.

Category 1	Greater harm (serious injury must normally be present) **and** higher culpability
Category 2	Greater harm (serious injury must normally be present) **and** lower culpability; **or** lesser harm **and** higher culpability
Category 3	Lesser harm **and** lower culpability

The court should determine the offender's culpability and the harm caused, or intended, by reference **only** to the factors identified in the table below (as demonstrated by the presence of one or more). These factors comprise the principal factual elements of the offence and should determine the category.

Factors indicating greater harm	Use of weapon or weapon equivalent (for example, shod foot, headbutting, use of acid, use of animal)
Injury (which includes disease transmission and/or psychological harm) which is serious in the context of the offence (must normally be present)	Intention to commit more serious harm than actually resulted from the offence
Victim is particularly vulnerable because of personal circumstances	Deliberately causes more harm than is necessary for commission of offence
Sustained or repeated assault on the same victim	Deliberate targeting of vulnerable victim
Factors indicating lesser harm	Leading role in group or gang
Injury which is less serious in the context of the offence	Offence motivated by, or demonstrating, hostility based on the victim's age, sex, gender identity (or presumed gender identity)
Factors indicating higher culpability	**Factors indicating lower culpability**
Statutory aggravating factors:	Subordinate role in group or gang
Offence motivated by, or demonstrating, hostility to the victim based on his or her sexual orientation (or presumed sexual orientation)	A greater degree of provocation than normally expected
Offence motivated by, or demonstrating, hostility to the victim based on the victim's disability (or presumed disability)	Lack of premeditation
	Mental disorder or learning disability, where linked to commission of the offence
Other aggravating factors:	
A significant degree of premeditation	Excessive self defence

STEP TWO
Starting point and category range

Having determined the category, the court should use the corresponding starting points to reach a sentence within the category range below. The starting point applies to all offenders irrespective of plea or previous convictions. A case of particular gravity, reflected by multiple features of culpability in step one, could merit upward adjustment from the starting point before further adjustment for aggravating or mitigating features, set out below.

Offence Category	**Starting Point** (*Applicable to all offenders*)	**Category Range** (*Applicable to all offenders*)
Category 1	Crown Court	Crown Court
Category 2	26 weeks' custody	Low level community order – Crown Court (51 weeks' custody)
Category 3	Medium level community order	Band A fine – High level community order

The table below contains a **non-exhaustive** list of additional factual elements providing the context of the offence and factors relating to the offender. Identify whether any combination of these, or other relevant factors, should result in an upward or downward adjustment from the starting point. In some cases, having considered these factors, it may be appropriate to move outside the identified category range.

When sentencing **category 2** offences, the court should also consider the custody threshold as follows:
- has the custody threshold been passed?
- if so, is it unavoidable that a custodial sentence be imposed?
- if so, can that sentence be suspended?

When sentencing **category 3** offences, the court should also consider the community order threshold as follows:
- has the community order threshold been passed?

Factors increasing seriousness	
Statutory aggravating factors:	Exploiting contact arrangements with a child to commit an offence
Previous convictions, having regard to a) the nature of the offence to which the conviction relates and its relevance to the current offence; and b) the time that has elapsed since the conviction	Established evidence of community impact
	Any steps taken to prevent the victim reporting an incident, obtaining assistance and/or from assisting or supporting the prosecution
Offence committed whilst on bail	Offences taken into consideration (TICs)
Other aggravating factors include:	**Factors reducing seriousness or reflecting personal mitigation**
Location of the offence	No previous convictions **or** no relevant/recent convictions
Timing of the offence	Single blow
Ongoing effect upon the victim	Remorse
Offence committed against those working in the public sector or providing a service to the public	Good character and/or exemplary conduct
Presence of others including relatives, especially children or partner of the victim	Determination and/or demonstration of steps taken to address addiction or offending behaviour
Gratuitous degradation of victim	Serious medical conditions requiring urgent, intensive or long-term treatment
In domestic violence cases, victim forced to leave their home	Isolated incident
Failure to comply with current court orders	Age and/or lack of maturity where it affects the responsibility of the offender
Offence committed whilst on licence	Lapse of time since the offence where this is not the fault of the offender
An attempt to conceal or dispose of evidence	
Failure to respond to warnings or concerns expressed by others about the offender's behaviour	Mental disorder or learning disability, where **not** linked to the commission of the offence
Commission of offence whilst under the influence of alcohol or drugs	Sole or primary carer for dependent relatives
Abuse of power and/or position of trust	

Section 29 offences only: The court should determine the appropriate sentence for the offence without taking account of the element of aggravation and then make an addition to the sentence, considering the level of aggravation involved. It may be appropriate to move outside the identified category range, taking into account the increased statutory maximum.

STEP THREE
Consider any other factors which indicate a reduction, such as assistance to the prosecution
The court should take into account any rule of law by virtue of which an offender may receive a discounted sentence in consequence of assistance given (or offered) to the prosecutor or investigator.

STEP FOUR
Reduction for guilty pleas
The court should take account of any potential reduction for a guilty plea in accordance with section 144 of the Criminal Justice Act 2003 and the *Guilty Plea* guideline.

STEP FIVE
Dangerousness
Assault occasioning actual bodily harm and racially/religiously aggravated ABH are specified offences within the meaning of Chapter 5 of the Criminal Justice Act 2003 and at this stage the court should consider whether having regard to the criteria contained in that Chapter it would be appropriate to award an extended sentence.

STEP SIX
Totality principle
If sentencing an offender for more than one offence, or where the offender is already serving a sentence, consider whether the total sentence is just and proportionate to the offending behaviour.

STEP SEVEN
Compensation and ancillary orders
In all cases, the court should consider whether to make compensation and/or other ancillary orders.

STEP EIGHT
Reasons
Section 174 of the Criminal Justice Act 2003 imposes a duty to give reasons for, and explain the effect of, the sentence.

STEP NINE
Consideration for remand time
Sentencers should take into consideration any remand time served in relation to the final sentence. The court should consider whether to give credit for time spent on remand in custody or on bail in accordance with sections 240 and 240A of the Criminal Justice Act 2003.

Domestic burglary
Theft Act 1968 (section 9)

This is a serious specified offence for the purposes of section 224 Criminal Justice Act 2003 if it was committed with intent to:

(a) inflict grievous bodily harm on a person, or
(b) do unlawful damage to a building or anything in it.

Triable either way

Maximum when tried summarily: Level 5 fine and/or 26 weeks' custody

Maximum when tried on indictment: 14 years' custody

Offence range: Community order – 6 years' custody

Where sentencing an offender for a qualifying **third domestic burglary**, the Court must apply Section 111 of the Powers of the Criminal Courts (Sentencing) Act 2000 and impose a custodial term of at least three years, unless it is satisfied that there are particular circumstances which relate to any of the offences or to the offender which would make it unjust to do so.

STEP ONE
Determining the offence category

The court should determine the offence category using the table below.

Category 1	Greater harm **and** higher culpability
Category 2	Greater harm **and** lower culpability **or** lesser harm **and** higher culpability
Category 3	Lesser harm **and** lower culpability

The court should determine culpability and harm caused or intended, by reference **only** to the factors below, which comprise the principal factual elements of the offence. Where an offence does not fall squarely into a category, individual factors may require a degree of weighting before making an overall assessment and determining the appropriate offence category.

Factors indicating greater harm	**Factors indicating higher culpability**
Theft of/damage to property causing a significant degree of loss to the victim (whether economic, sentimental or personal value)	Victim or premises deliberately targeted (for example, due to vulnerability or hostility based on disability, race, sexual orientation)
Soiling, ransacking or vandalism of property	A significant degree of planning or organisation
Occupier at home (or returns home) while offender present	Knife or other weapon carried (where not charged separately)
Trauma to the victim, beyond the normal inevitable consequence of intrusion and theft	Equipped for burglary (for example, implements carried and/or use of vehicle)
Violence used or threatened against victim	Member of a group or gang
Context of general public disorder	**Factors indicating lower culpability**
Factors indicating lesser harm	Offence committed on impulse, with limited intrusion into property
Nothing stolen or only property of very low value to the victim (whether economic, sentimental or personal)	Offender exploited by others
Limited damage or disturbance to property	Mental disorder or learning disability, where linked to the commission of the offence

STEP TWO
Starting point and category range

Having determined the category, the court should use the corresponding starting points to reach a sentence within the category range below. The starting point applies to all offenders irrespective of plea or previous convictions.

Where the defendant is dependant on or has a propensity to misuse drugs and there is sufficient prospect of success, a community order with a drug rehabilitation requirement under section 209 of the Criminal Justice Act 2003 may be a proper alternative to a short or moderate custodial sentence.

A case of particular gravity, reflected by multiple features of culpability or harm in step 1, could merit upward adjustment from the starting point before further adjustment for aggravating or mitigating features, set out on the next page.

Offence Category	Starting Point *(Applicable to all offenders)*	Category Range *(Applicable to all offenders)*
Category 1	3 years' custody	2–6 years' custody
Category 2	1 year's custody	High level community order – 2 years' custody
Category 3	High Level Community Order	Low level community order – 26 weeks' custody

The table below contains a **non-exhaustive** list of additional factual elements providing the context of the offence and factors relating to the offender. Identify whether any combination of these, or other relevant factors, should result in an upward or downward adjustment from the starting point. **In particular, relevant recent convictions are likely to result in an upward adjustment.** In some cases, having considered these factors, it may be appropriate to move outside the identified category range.

When sentencing **category 2 or 3** offences, the court should also consider the custody threshold as follows:
- has the custody threshold been passed?
- if so, is it unavoidable that a custodial sentence be imposed?
- if so, can that sentence be suspended?

Factors increasing seriousness	Factors reducing seriousness or reflecting personal mitigation
Statutory aggravating factors:	Offender has made voluntary reparation to the victim
Previous convictions, having regard to a) the nature of the offence to which the conviction relates and its relevance to the current offence; and b) the time that has elapsed since the conviction*	Subordinate role in a group or gang
	No previous convictions **or** no relevant/recent convictions
Offence committed whilst on bail	Remorse
Other aggravating factors include:	Good character and/or exemplary conduct
Child at home (or returns home) when offence committed	Determination, and/or demonstration of steps taken to address addiction or offending behaviour
Offence committed at night	Serious medical conditions requiring urgent, intensive or long-term treatment
Gratuitous degradation of the victim	
Any steps taken to prevent the victim reporting the incident or obtaining assistance and/or from assisting or supporting the prosecution	Age and/or lack of maturity where it affects the responsibility of the offender
	Lapse of time since the offence where this is not the fault of the offender
Victim compelled to leave their home (in particular victims of domestic violence)	Mental disorder or learning disability, where not linked to the commission of the offence
Established evidence of community impact	Sole or primary carer for dependent relatives
Commission of offence whilst under the influence of alcohol or drugs	
Failure to comply with current court orders	
Offence committed whilst on licence	
Offences Taken Into Consideration (TICs)	

* Where sentencing an offender for a qualifying **third domestic burglary**, the Court must apply Section 111 of the Powers of the Criminal Courts (Sentencing) Act 2000 and impose a custodial term of at least three years, unless it is satisfied that there are particular circumstances which relate to any of the offences or to the offender which would make it unjust to do so.

STEP THREE
Consider any factors which indicate a reduction, such as assistance to the prosecution
The court should take into account sections 73 and 74 of the Serious Organised Crime and Police Act 2005 (assistance by defendants: reduction or review of sentence) and any other rule of law by virtue of which an offender may receive a discounted sentence in consequence of assistance given (or offered) to the prosecutor or investigator.

STEP FOUR
Reduction for guilty pleas
The court should take account of any potential reduction for a guilty plea in accordance with section 144 of the Criminal Justice Act 2003 and the *Guilty Plea* guideline.

Where a minimum mandatory sentence is imposed under section 111 Powers of Criminal Courts (Sentencing) Act, the discount for an early guilty plea must not exceed 20 per cent.

STEP FIVE
Dangerousness
A burglary offence under section 9 Theft Act 1986 is a serious specified offence within the meaning of chapter 5 of the Criminal Justice Act 2003 if it was committed with the intent to (a) inflict grievous bodily harm on a person, or (b) do unlawful damage to a building or anything in it. The court should consider whether having regard to the criteria contained in that chapter it would be appropriate to award imprisonment for public protection or an extended sentence. Where offenders meet the dangerousness criteria, the notional determinate sentence should be used as the basis for the setting of a minimum term.

STEP SIX
Totality principle
If sentencing an offender for more than one offence, or where the offender is already serving a sentence, consider whether the total sentence is just and proportionate to the offending behaviour.

STEP SEVEN
Compensation and ancillary orders
In all cases, courts should consider whether to make compensation and/or other ancillary orders.

STEP EIGHT
Reasons
Section 174 of the Criminal Justice Act 2003 imposes a duty to give reasons for, and explain the effect of, the sentence.

STEP NINE
Consideration for remand time
Sentencers should take into consideration any remand time served in relation to the final sentence at this final step. The court should consider whether to give credit for time spent on remand in custody or on bail in accordance with sections 240 and 240A of the Criminal Justice Act 2003.

Theft – breach of trust – factors to take into consideration

This guideline and accompanying notes are taken from the Sentencing Guidelines Council's definitive guideline *Theft and Burglary in a building other than a dwelling*, published 9 December 2008

Key factors

(a) When assessing the harm caused by this offence, the starting point should be the loss suffered by the victim. In general, the greater the loss, the more serious the offence. However, the monetary value of the loss may not reflect the full extent of the harm caused by the offence. The court should also take into account the impact of the offence on the victim (which may be significant and disproportionate to the value of the loss having regard to their financial circumstances), any harm to persons other than the direct victim, and any harm in the form of public concern or erosion of public confidence.

(b) In general terms, the seriousness of the offence will increase in line with the level of trust breached. The extent to which the nature and degree of trust placed in an offender should be regarded as increasing seriousness will depend on a careful assessment of the circumstances of each individual case, including the type and terms of the relationship between the offender and victim.

(c) The concept of breach of trust for the purposes of the offence of theft includes employer/employee relationships and those between a professional adviser and client. It also extends to relationships in which a person is in a position of authority in relation to the victim or would be expected to have a duty to protect the interests of the victim, such as medical, social or care workers. The targeting of a vulnerable victim by an offender through a relationship or position of trust will indicate a higher level of culpability.

(d) The Council has identified the following matters of offender mitigation which may be relevant to this offence:

(i) *Return of stolen property*
Whether and the degree to which the return of stolen property constitutes a matter of offender mitigation will depend on an assessment of the circumstances and, in particular, the voluntariness and timeliness of the return.

(ii) *Impact on sentence of offender's dependency*
Where an offence is motivated by an addiction (often to drugs, alcohol or gambling) this does not mitigate the seriousness of the offence, but a dependency may properly influence the type of sentence imposed. In particular, it may sometimes be appropriate to impose a drug rehabilitation requirement, an alcohol treatment requirement (for dependent drinkers) or an activity or supervision requirement including alcohol specific information, advice and support (for harmful and hazardous drinkers) as part of a community order or a suspended sentence order in an attempt to break the cycle of addiction and offending, even if an immediate custodial sentence would otherwise be warranted.

(iii) *Offender motivated by desperation or need*
The fact that an offence has been committed in desperation or need arising from particular hardship may count as offender mitigation in **exceptional circumstances**.

(iv) *Inappropriate degree of trust or responsibility*
The fact that an offender succumbed to temptation having been placed in a position of trust or given responsibility to an inappropriate degree may be regarded as offender mitigation.

(v) *Voluntary cessation of offending*
The fact that an offender voluntarily ceased offending before being discovered does not reduce the seriousness of the offence. However, if the claim to have stopped offending is genuine, it may constitute offender mitigation, particularly if it is evidence of remorse.

(vi) *Reporting an undiscovered offence*
Where an offender brings the offending to the attention of his or her employer or the authorities, this may be treated as offender mitigation.

(f) In many cases of theft in breach of trust, termination of an offender's employment will be a natural consequence of committing the offence. Other than in the most exceptional of circumstances, loss of employment and any consequential hardship should not constitute offender mitigation.

(g) Where a court is satisfied that a custodial sentence is appropriate for an offence of theft in breach of trust, consideration should be given to whether that sentence can be suspended in accordance with the criteria in the Council guideline *New Sentences: Criminal Justice Act 2003*. A suspended sentence may be particularly appropriate where this would allow for reparation to be made either to the victim or to the community at large.

Theft Act 1968, s.1

Theft – breach of trust

Triable either way:
Maximum when tried summarily: Level 5 fine and/or 6 months
Maximum when tried on indictment: 7 years

Offence seriousness (culpability and harm)
A. Identify the appropriate starting point
Starting points based on first time offender pleading not guilty

Examples of nature of activity	Starting point	Range
Theft of less than £2,000	Medium level community order	Band B fine to 26 weeks custody
Theft of £2,000 or more but less than £20,000 OR Theft of less than £2,000 in breach of a high degree of trust	18 weeks custody	High level community order to Crown Court
Theft of £20,000 or more OR Theft of £2,000 or more in breach of a high degree of trust	Crown Court	Crown Court

Offence seriousness (culpability and harm)
B. Consider the effect of aggravating and mitigating factors
(other than those within examples above)
Common aggravating and mitigating factors are identified in the pullout card –
the following may be particularly relevant but **these lists are not exhaustive**

Factors indicating higher culpability 1. Long course of offending 2. Suspicion deliberately thrown on others 3. Offender motivated by intention to cause harm or out of revenge	

Form a preliminary view of the appropriate sentence,
then consider offender mitigation
Common factors are identified in the pullout card – see also note (d) opposite

Consider a reduction for a guilty plea

Consider ancillary orders, including compensation
Refer to pages 168-174 for guidance on available ancillary orders

Decide sentence
Give reasons

Effective from 5 January 2009

Theft – person – factors to take into consideration

This guideline and accompanying notes are taken from the Sentencing Guidelines Council's definitive guideline *Theft and Burglary in a building other than a dwelling*, published 9 December 2008

Key factors

(a) Theft from the person may encompass conduct such as 'pick-pocketing', where the victim is unaware that the property is being stolen, as well as the snatching of handbags, wallets, jewellery and mobile telephones from the victim's possession or from the vicinity of the victim. The offence constitutes an invasion of the victim's privacy and may cause the victim to experience distress, fear and inconvenience either during or after the event. While in some cases the conduct may be similar, **this guideline does not apply where the offender has been convicted of robbery; sentencers should instead refer to the Council guideline on robbery**.

(b) The starting points and sentencing ranges in this guideline are based on the assumption that the offender was motivated by greed or a desire to live beyond his or her means. To avoid double counting, such a motivation should not be treated as a factor that increases culpability.

(c) For the purpose of this guideline, a 'vulnerable victim' is a person targeted by the offender because it is anticipated that he or she is unlikely or unable to resist the theft. Young or elderly persons, or those with disabilities may fall into this category. The exploitation of a vulnerable victim indicates a high level of culpability and will influence the category of seriousness into which the offence falls.

(d) Offences of this type will be aggravated where there is evidence of planning, such as where tourists are targeted because of their unfamiliarity with an area and a perception that they will not be available to give evidence.

(e) The guideline is based on the assumption that most thefts from the person do not involve property of high monetary value or of high value to the victim. Where the stolen property is of high monetary value or of high value (including sentimental value) to the victim, the appropriate sentence may be beyond the range into which the offence otherwise would fall. For the purposes of this form of theft, 'high monetary value' is defined as more than £2,000.

(f) A sentence beyond the range into which the offence otherwise would fall may also be appropriate where the effect on the victim is particularly severe or where substantial consequential loss results (such as where the theft of equipment causes serious disruption to the victim's life or business).

(g) The Council has identified the following matters of offender mitigation which may be relevant to this offence:

(i) *Return of stolen property*
Whether and the degree to which the return of stolen property constitutes a matter of offender mitigation will depend on an assessment of the circumstances and, in particular, the voluntariness and timeliness of the return.

(ii) *Impact on sentence of offender's dependency*
Where an offence is motivated by an addiction (often to drugs, alcohol or gambling) this does not mitigate the seriousness of the offence, but a dependency may properly influence the type of sentence imposed. In particular, it may sometimes be appropriate to impose a drug rehabilitation requirement, an alcohol treatment requirement (for dependent drinkers) or an activity or supervision requirement including alcohol specific information, advice and support (for harmful and hazardous drinkers) as part of a community order or a suspended sentence order in an attempt to break the cycle of addiction and offending, even if an immediate custodial sentence would otherwise be warranted.

(iii) *Offender motivated by desperation or need*
The fact that an offence has been committed in desperation or need arising from particular hardship may count as offender mitigation in **exceptional circumstances**.

Effective from 5 January 2009

Theft Act 1968, s.1

Theft – person

Triable either way:
Maximum when tried summarily: Level 5 fine and/or 6 months
Maximum when tried on indictment: 7 years

Offence seriousness (culpability and harm)
A. Identify the appropriate starting point
Starting points based on first time offender pleading not guilty

Examples of nature of activity	Starting point	Range
Where the effect on the victim is particularly severe, the stolen property is of high value (as defined in note (f) opposite), or substantial consequential loss results, a sentence higher than the range into which the offence otherwise would fall may be appropriate		
Theft from the person not involving vulnerable victim	Medium level community order	Band B fine to 18 weeks custody
Theft from a vulnerable victim (as defined in note (c) opposite)	18 weeks custody	High level community order to Crown Court
Theft involving the use or threat of force (falling short of robbery) against a vulnerable victim (as defined in note (c) opposite)	Crown Court	Crown Court

Offence seriousness (culpability and harm)
B. Consider the effect of aggravating and mitigating factors
(other than those within examples above)
Common aggravating and mitigating factors are identified in the pullout card –
the following may be particularly relevant but **these lists are not exhaustive**

Factors indicating higher culpability 1. Offender motivated by intention to cause harm or out of revenge **Factors indicating greater degree of harm** 1. Intimidation or face-to-face confrontation with victim [except where this raises the offence into a higher sentencing range] 2. Use of force, or threat of force, against victim (not amounting to robbery) [except where this raises the offence into a higher sentencing range] 3. High level of inconvenience caused to victim, e.g. replacing house keys, credit cards etc	

Form a preliminary view of the appropriate sentence,
then consider offender mitigation
Common factors are identified in the pullout card – see also note (g) opposite

Consider a reduction for a guilty plea

Consider ancillary orders, including compensation
Refer to pages 168-174 for guidance on available ancillary orders

Decide sentence
Give reasons

Effective from 5 January 2009

INDEX

Note – Figures are referenced in bold